This is a major, groundbreaking study by a leading scholar of continental witch-craft studies, now made available to an English-speaking audience for the first time.

Based on an intensive search through central and local legal records for south-eastern Germany, an area extending well beyond but including present-day Bavaria, the author has compiled a thorough overview of all known prosecutions for witchcraft in the period 1300–1800. He shows conclusively that witch-hunting was not a constant or uniform phenomenon, and that three-quarters of all known executions for witchcraft were concentrated in the years 1586–1630, years of particular dearth and famine. The book investigates the social and political impli-cations of witchcraft, and how the mechanisms of persecution served as a rallying cry for partisan factionalism at court. The author also explores the mentalities behind witch-hunting, emphasising the complex religious debates between be-lievers and sceptics, and Catholics and Protestants.

Past and Present Publications

Witchcraft Persecutions in Bavaria

Past and Present Publications

General Editor: JOANNA INNES, *Somerville College, Oxford*

Past and Present Publications comprise books similar in character to the articles in the journal *Past and Present*. Whether the volumes in the series are collections of essays – some previously published, others new studies – or monographs, they encompass a wide variety of scholarly and original works primarily concerned with social, economic and cultural changes, and their causes and consequences. They will appeal to both specialists and non-specialists and will endeavour to communicate the results of historical and allied research in readable and lively form.

For a list of titles in Past and Present Publications, see end of book.

Witchcraft Persecutions in Bavaria

Popular magic, religious zealotry and reason of state
in early modern Europe

WOLFGANG BEHRINGER

Historisches Seminar, Rheinische Friedrich-Wilhelms University, Bonn

Translated by
J.C. GRAYSON
and
DAVID LEDERER

 CAMBRIDGE
UNIVERSITY PRESS

BF
1583
.B4413
1997

PUBLISHED BY THE PRESS SYNDICATE OF THE UNIVERSITY OF CAMBRIDGE
The Pitt Building, Trumpington Street, Cambridge CB2 1RP, United Kingdom

CAMBRIDGE UNIVERSITY PRESS
The Edinburgh Building, Cambridge CB2 2RU, United Kingdom
40 West 20th Street, New York, NY 10011-4211, USA
10 Stamford Road, Oakleigh, Melbourne 3166, Australia

Originally published in German as *Hexenverfolgung in Bayern: Volksmagie, Glaubenseifer und Staatsräson in der Frühen Neuzeit* by R. Oldenbourg Verlag, Munich 1987 and © R Oldenbourg Verlag GmbH, Munich
First published in English by Cambridge University Press 1997 as *Witchcraft persecutions in Bavaria. Popular magic, religious zealotry and reason of state in early modern Europe*

English translation © Cambridge University Press 1997

First published 1997

Printed in the United Kingdom at the University Press, Cambridge

Typeset in Times 10/12 pt

A catalogue record for this book is available from the British Library

Library of Congress cataloguing in publication data

Behringer, Wolfgang.
[Hexenverfolgung in Bayern. English]
Witchcraft persecutions in Bavaria: popular magic, religious zealotry and reason of state in early modern Europe / Wolfgang Behringer: translated by J.C. Grayson and David Lederer.
p. cm. – (Past and present publications)
Includes bibliographical references and indexes.
ISBN 0 521 48258 5 (hardcover)
1. Trials (Witchcraft)–Germany–Bavaria–History.
2. Witchcraft–Germany–Bavaria–History. 3. Bavaria (Germany) – Social life and customs. I. Title.
F1583.B4413 1997
133.4'3'09433–dc20   96–43846
                                                                                     CIP

ISBN 0 521 48258 5 hardback

VN

Contents

List of illustrations	*page* ix
List of tables	xi
Preface and acknowledgements	xiii
List of abbreviations	xvii

1 Introduction   1
   Witch trials in historiographic context   1
   Investigating witch trials and learned discourse in southeastern
   Germany   17
   Methodology   29

2 Moving toward a social history of witchcraft   34
   Quantification in synchronic and diachronic juxtaposition   35
   Witch trials and popular magic   65
   A 'crisis of the late sixteenth century'?   89

3 The wave of persecutions around 1590   115
   Contemporary interpretations   115
   The course of the persecutions   121
   Triggering factors   158
   Mechanisms of persecution   183
   The breakdown of consensus   194
   Regulatory efforts at the end of the persecutions   206

4 The struggle for restraint, 1600–30   212
   The witch craze at its peak   212
   The Protestant solution   213
   The Catholic stance hardens   216
   Formation of an opposition party in Bavaria   230
   Learned debate, 1601–4   247

Conflict over the mandate against superstition and witchcraft of 1612   269
Predominance of the moderates in Bavaria   291
Triumph of the moderates in southern Germany   310

5   Perpetuation through domestication 1630–1775   322
Convergence of trial procedure   322
Novel polarities and structural changes of trials   331
The last executions for witchcraft 1749–75   344

6   The final Catholic debate   355
From Tanner to Spee   355
The onset of Catholic debate   357
Public debate and the victory of the Enlightenment, 1766–70   359
Combating superstition after the 'witchcraft war'   381

7   Conclusions   388
Witchcraft trials and learned discourse in southeastern Germany: a summary   388
Structures and regions in comparison   400
Witch trials and social crises   405

8   Sources and literature   416
Sources   416
Literature   425

Index   457

Illustrations

PLATES

1   Valentin, *End-Urthel [...]*, Augsburg 1760   *page* 40
2   Stealing milk by sorcery, from Hans Vintler, *Tugendspiegel*,
    Augsburg 1486   69
3   Deeds of the witches, from Ulrich Tengler, *Der neu
    Layenspiegel*, Augsburg 1511   75
4   White and black magic, from Cicero, *De Officiis*, Augsburg 1531   93
5   The *Erweytterte Unholden Zeyttung*, 1590   120
6   The witch in the Dance of Death at Füssen, Füssen 1602   127
7   Peter Binsfeld, *Tractat vom Bekanntnuss der Zauberer und
    Hexen*, Munich 1592   141
8   *Kurtze Erzöhlung und Fürbildung der übelthatten [...]*, Augsburg
    1600   231
9   Martin Delrio, *Disquisitionum Magicarum libri sex*, Cologne
    1657   264
10 *Landtgebott wider die Aberglauben, Zauberey, Hexerey und
    andere sträffliche Teufelskünste*, Munich 1611   284
11 The *Druten Zeitung Schmalkalden*, Nuremberg 1627   302
12 *Warhaffte Historische Abbild: und kurtze Beschreibung*,
    Augsburg 1654   329
13 *Warhaffte Beschreibung des Urthels [...]*, Augsburg 1666   332
14 *Relation oder Beschreibung [...]*, Augsburg 1669   335
15 Peasant magic: charms against bewitchment of the cattle   383
16 Gassner's *Weise wider den Teufel zu streiten*, Kempten 1774   383
17 Adam Tanner, *Theologia Scholastica*, Tomus 3, Ingolstadt 1627   396

FIGURES

1   Court proceedings against sorcery and/or witchcraft in Augsburg,
    in five-yearly periods, 1581–1653   45
2   Witch trials and executions of witches in the Duchy of Bavaria

every full decade, 1590–1750   51
3   Number of county courts in the provincial administration of
    Munich with trials for sorcery and witchcraft   52

MAPS

Map 1   Executions of witches around 1590: geographical distribution
        in southeastern Germany   xviii
Map 2   Executions of witches in southeast Germany   xx
Map 3   Comparison of witch hunts in three south German regions
        (southwestern Germany, Franconia, southeastern
        Germany)   xxii

Tables

1 Geographical distribution of witch trials, based on the material of the *H-Sonderkommando*   *page* 37

2 Court proceedings against sorcery and/or witchcraft in Augsburg, in five-yearly periods, 1581–1653   44

3 Court proceedings against sorcery and/or witchcraft in the Bishopric of Augsburg in five-yearly periods, 1573–1632   47

4 Decline in the importance of witchcraft after 1630 as reflected in the minutes of the Court Council at Munich   53

5 Statistical analysis of 103 witch trials held in Bavaria between 1608 and 1616   54

6 Witch hunts with more than twenty victims   61

7 Witch hunts with ten to nineteen victims   61

8 Witch hunts with four to nine victims   62

9 Chronological and quantitative distribution of minor and major witch hunts   63

10 Relationship between type of trial and number of victims   63

11 Trials and executions of witches in Bavarian county courts (1608–16), based on analysis of the minutes of the Court Council at Munich   291

12 Trials and executions of witches in Bavarian county courts (1629–31) based on analysis of the minutes of the Court Council at Munich   308

13 Intensity of witch hunting in four neighbouring regions of southeastern Germany and Austria   401

Preface

Witchcraft persecutions in Bavaria – isn't there already a monograph on the subject, and a noteworthy one at that? Even today, Sigmund Riezler's highly recommendable *History of Witch-Trials in Bavaria* (Munich, 1896) makes for good reading, and, like Burckhardt's *Culture of the Renaissance in Italy*, or Huizinga's *Waning of the Middle Ages*, is now a literary classic: its findings may be dated, but its powerful prose, scholarly facility and breadth of presentation never fail to stimulate. Nowadays, what established historian would dare to open their scholarly portrayal with anticlerical polemics and, after a radical critique of a colleague (Ranke!), culminate in a plea against his 'cold, earnest' narrative, arguing instead for one which 'allows emotions to have their say as well'? To act as if one held no opinions, Riezler added, was the mere affectation of modesty. Yet much of this sounds remarkably modern indeed, and reminds us of similar debates in recent years . . .

However, this study does not simply continue where Riezler left off. International research has made great strides and, above all, has refined its methods in the past two decades. Futhermore, our own historical situation and, consequently, our cognisant interests changed dramatically. Riezler and his contemporaries lived in the certainty that horrors like witchcraft persecutions could never recur on German soil. If we now know better, then hardly as a consequence of laudable achievements, but subsequent events have inextricably altered our perspectives. Together with Macfarlane and with ethnologists, we have learned to appreciate the social function of witchcraft accusations, and Midelfort has taught us to take contemporary discourse much more seriously. A lofty disdain for seemingly distant modes of thought is no longer tenable.

In my own considered opinion, it is only too comfortable for us to apply 'modern' criteria in judgement of witchcraft. After all, one has to consider the major differences between present social and mental structures and those of the distant past. At its core, the contingency of witchcraft remained a basic conviction during the later Middle Ages and the early modern period. If witchcraft was plausible, then it was logically consistent to threaten its misuse with punishment. Furthermore, evidence of witchcraft was always extremely difficult to obtain because, unlike other 'weapons', it was intangible and hidden. Beyond that, the source of witchcraft's power and its actual capabilities were hotly debated issues that forced human understanding to its limits. The demonological literature of the fifteenth to seventeenth centuries, so obscure to us now, found a wide audience. It is no coincidence that leading intellectuals of the time, including many we might hardly suspect, occupied themselves with it; even sceptical philosophers like Montaigne, Descartes, Althusius, Hobbes and Thomasius cogitated on the problem. For common people, jurists, theologians, town magistrates and local governments, witchcraft was an everyday, though hardly a routine matter. 'Human blood is not calves' blood', as one seventeenth-century jurist at the University of Dillingen put it. Because witch-hunting posed enormous theoretical problems and (owing to the apparently imminent danger) practical urgency, it is central to the history of early modern Europe. Witchcraft-beliefs evoked bitter debates, since three essential, early-modern 'world-views' collided on that very point; a traditional folk-culture of magical beliefs, a new, fanatical, religious zealotry stemming from the Reformation/Counter-Reformation, and an equally new secular rationalism, an early modern reason of state. Certainly, neither a conflict between ideological and pragmatic reasoning nor a confrontation with unfamiliar modes of thought is novel. Sometimes we might even recognise historical parallels.

The following regional comparison focuses on the former Duchy of Bavaria, its neighbours in eastern Swabia, southern portions of present-day Central Franconia and the Upper Palatinate, a region defined here as 'southeastern Germany'. Its witches did not fly to the Blocksberg (Franconia and central Germany) or the Heuberg (southwestern Germany). Neither were they called *Hexen*, *Zauberer* (sorcerers) nor, as in northern Franconia, *Trutten*, but rather *Unholden*. Their persecution began relatively late, but Bavaria eventually developed the most comprehensive witchcraft-legislation in Europe. And, as we will presently see, this region was peculiar in many other respects; but how could it be otherwise?

ACKNOWLEDGEMENTS

An engagement with the topic of witchcraft is an onerous endeavour requiring encouragement and discussion. In this regard, my primary appreciation goes to my advisor, Richard van Dülmen (Saarbrücken) and my friends and colleagues in Munich, Clemens Vollnhals, Helga Ettenhuber,

Andreas Mönnich and Otto Feldbauer, as well as Ulrike Schwarz-Behringer (Lindau), Norbert Schindler (Berlin), Rudlolf Schlögl (Konstanz) and Eva Labouvie (Saarbrüken), for their suggestions, corrections and the seemingly endless days and nights spent in discussions. I also wish to express my gratitude to the following archivists for their assistance: Dr Schenk (Frankfurt), Dr Richard Bauer, Dr Richard Heydenreuter and Dr Helmuth Stahleder (Munich) and Dr Hajo Hecker (Augsburg). Funding for this project was provided by a doctoral stipend from the *Stiftung des deutschen Volkes* and a fellowship at the *Historischer Kolleg* in Munich made possible by Prof. Winfried Schulze (at that time, in Bochum). The dissertation was reviewed by Profs. Friedrich Prinz and Eberhard Weis (Munich). It was accepted by the Faculty of Philosophy at the Ludwig-Maximilians University in 1987 and was published uncut that same year. The third edition will appear in 1997 simultaneously with the English translation.

I wish especially to commend my reviewers, among whom many scholarly associations and friendships later emerged: Ronnie Po-Chia Hsia (*Sixteenth Century Journal*), Bob Scribner (*EHR*), Donald Nugent (*AHR*), Robert Walinski-Kiehl (*Bulletin GHI London*), Louis Chatellier (*Francia*), Karl Vocelka (*MIÖG*), Marijke Gijswift-Hofstra (*Tijdschrift voor Geschiedenis*), Bernd Roeck (*VSWG*), Günter Jerouschek (*Zeitschrift für Neuere Rechtsgeschichte*) and Barbara Stollberg-Rilinger (*ZHF*). My appreciation also goes to the members of the Research Group for Interdisciplinary Witchcraft Studies (AKIH), including the editors of the series "Hexenforschung", Sönke Lorenz, Dieter R. Bauer, Heide Dienst and Wolfgang Schild. H. C. Erik Midelfort's seminal work *Witch-Hunting in South-Western Germany* served as a model for the present study. His present collaboration in conjunction with a translation of my *Chonrad Stoeckhlin und die Nachtschar* into American should ensure a degree of terminological untiy with this study. I have also benefited from the collegial support and friendship of Lyndal Roper and Nick Stargard. David Lederer's careful revisions, especially of the introductory and concluding remarks, as well as his help in having chapters five and six translated and included in the present volume added significantly to its quality. Finally, I wish to thank Cambridge University Press for patiently abiding so many corrections and revisions. Last but not least, I wish to excuse myself to Hizran, whose husband spent nights reading over the proofs in bed, and my son, Luis Alper, who could only be allowed to eat small portions of the manuscript.

Wolfgang Behringer
Munich, 1995

Abbreviations

ADB	*Allgemeine Deutsche Biographie*
Cgm.	Codex germanicus monacensis, Staatsbibliothek Munich
GR	Generalregistratur
HDA	*Handwörterbuch des deutschen Aberglaubens*
Hist. Ver.	Historischer Verein
HStAM	Hauptstaatsarchiv München
HZ	*Historische Zeitschrift*
KHR	Kurbayern Hofrat
NDB	*Neue Deutsche Biographie*
OA	Oberbayerisches Archiv
ÖNB	Österreichische Nationalbibliothek, Vienna
RP	Ratsprotokolle
SBM	Bayerische Staatsbiblothek, Munich
SHB	Soldan/Heppe/Bauer
StA	Staatsarchiv
StadtA	Stadtarchiv
UA	Urgichtenakten
UBM	Universitätsbibliothek, Munich
Urk.	Urkunde
ZA	Zulassungsarbeit
ZBLG	*Zeitschrift für bayrische Landesgeschichte*
Zs.	Zeitschrift
ZWLG	*Zeitschrift für württembergische Landesgeschichte*

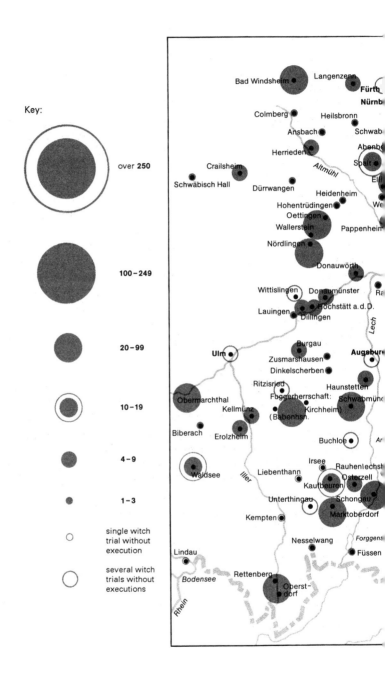

Key:

over **250**

100 – 249

20 – 99

10 – 19

4 – 9

1 – 3

○ single witch
trial without
execution

○ several witch
trials without
executions

Bad Windsheim   Langenzenn   **Fürth**
   Nürnb
Colmberg   Heilsbronn
   Ansbach   Schwab
   Abenb
Herrieden   Spalt
Crailsheim   Altmühl   Ell
Schwäbisch Hall   Dürrwangen   Heidenheim
   Hohentrüdingen   We
   Oettingen
   Wallerstein   Pappenheim
   Nördlingen
   Donauwörth
Wittislingen   Donaumünster   Ra
   Höchstätt a.d.D.
Lauingen   Dillingen   Lech
   Burgau
Ulm   Zusmarshausen   **Augsbur**
   Dinkelscherben
Ritzisried   Haunstetten
Obermarchthal   Fuggerherrschaft: Schwabmünd
Kellmünz   Kirchheim)
   (Babenhsn.
Biberach   Erolzheim   Buchloe   Ar
   Irsee   Rauhenlechsl
Waldsee   Iller   Liebenthann   Osterzell
   Kaufbeuren
   Unterthingau   Schongau
   Kempten   Marktoberdorf
   Nesselwang   Forggens
Lindau
   Füssen
   Rettenberg
Bodensee   Oberst-
   dorf
Rhein

1. Executions of witches around 1590

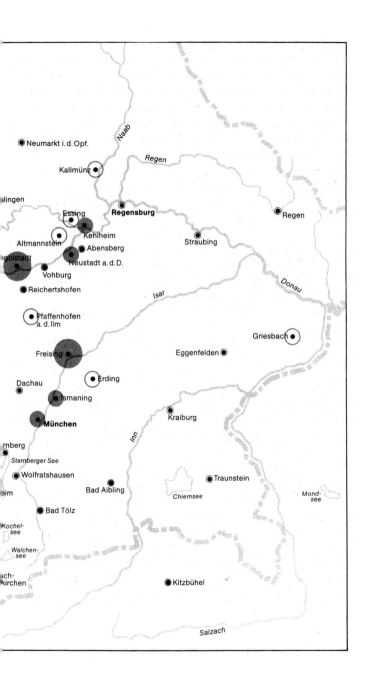

Neumarkt i. d. Opf.

Naab

Regen

Kallmünz

slingen

Essing   Regensburg   Regen

Kehlheim

Altmannstein   Abensberg   Straubing

golstadt   Neustadt a.d.D.

Vohburg

Reichertshofen   Donau

Isar

Pfaffenhofen
a.d.Ilm

Griesbach

Freising   Eggenfelden

Dachau   Erding

Ismaning

München   Kraiburg

rnberg   Inn

Starnberger See

Wolfratshausen

aim   Bad Aibling   Traunstein

Bad Tölz   Chiemsee   Mond-
see

Kochel-
see

Walchen-
see

ch-
kirchen   Kitzbühel

Salzach

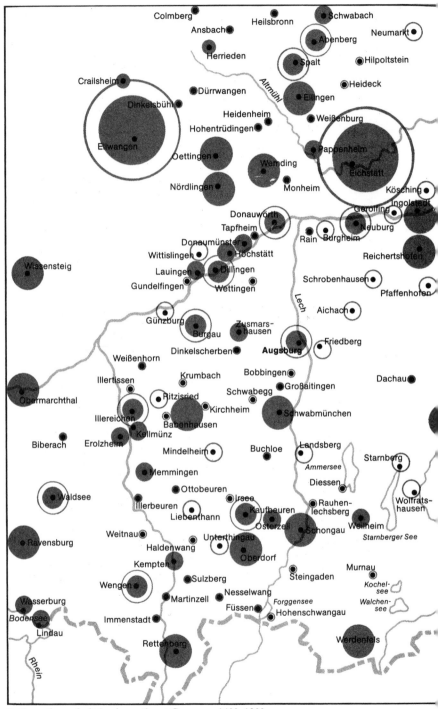

2. Executions of witches in southeast Germany, 1400–1800

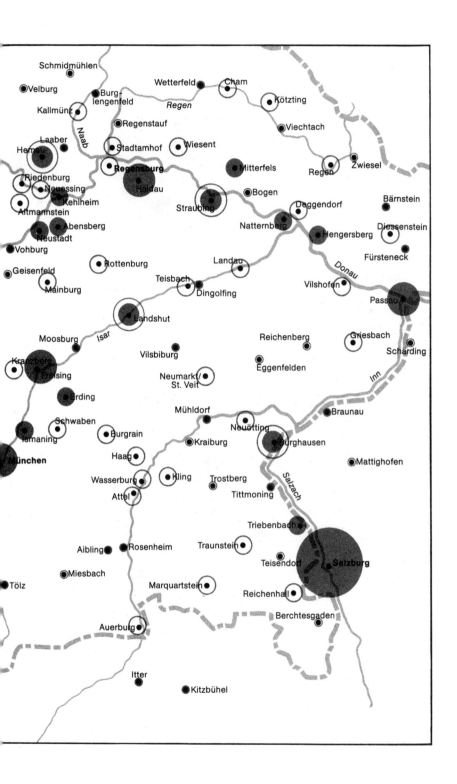

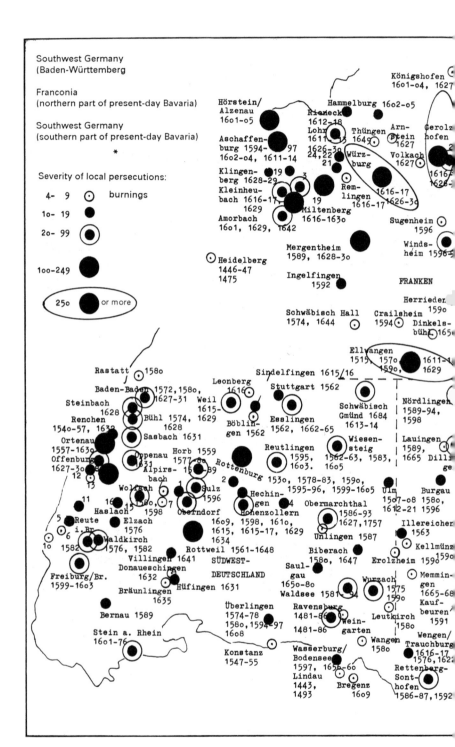

Southwest Germany
(Baden-Württemberg

Franconia
(northern part of present-day Bavaria)

Southwest Germany
(southern part of present-day Bavaria)

*

Severity of local persecutions:

4- 9   burnings

1o- 19

2o- 99

1oo-249

25o   or more

Königshofen
1601-04, 1627

Hörstein/   Hammelburg 1602-05
Alzenau   Rieneck
1601-05   1612-18   Arn-   Gerolz-
                 Lohr   Thüngen stein   hofen
Aschaffen-   1611   1649   1627
burg 1594-97   1626-3o   Volkach
1602-04, 1611-14 24,22   Würz-   1627   1616
                 21   burg
Klingen- 19   1626
berg 1628-29   Rem-
Kleinheu-   lingen 1616-17
bach 1616-17   19   1616-17 1626-3o
     1629   Miltenberg
Amorbach   1616-163o   Sugenheim
1601, 1629, 1642   1596

                 Mergentheim   Winds-
                 1589, 1628-3o   heim 1596
    Heidelberg
    1446-47   Ingelfingen
    1475   1592   FRANKEN

                                          Herrieden
                 Schwäbisch Hall Crailsheim 159o
                 1574, 1644   1594   Dinkels-
                                          bühl 165

                           Ellwangen
                           1515 157o 1611
Rastatt   158o Sindelfingen 1615/16   159o, 1629
Baden-Baden 1572,158o, Leonberg Stuttgart 1562
Steinbach   1627-31 Weil 1616   Nördlingen
     1628   1615-   Schwäbisch   1589-94,
Renchen   Bühl 1574, 1629 Böblin- Gmünd 1684   1598
154o-57, 163   1628   gen 1562 Esslingen 1613-14
Ortenau   Sasbach 1631   1562, 1662-65
1557-163o   Reutlingen Wiesen- Lauingen,
Offenburg Oppenau Horb 1559 1595, steig 1589,
1627-3o   1631 1577 Rottenburg 1603. 1605 1562-63, 1583, 1665 Dillin-
  12   Alpirs- 1530, 1578-83, 159o, 1605   ge
               bach   2   1595-96, 1599-16o5 Ulm Burgau
Wolfach   Sulz   Hechin-   Obermarchthal 15o7-o8 158o,
  16 158o, 7 1596 gen 4   1586-93   16 2-21 1596
Haslach 1598 Oberndorf Hohenzollern 1627,1757 Illereichen
5 Reute Elzach   1609, 1598, 161o, Unlingen 1587 1563
  i.Br. 1576   1615, 1615-17, 1629
1o 1582 1576, 1582 Rottweil 1561-1648 Biberach Kellmünz
     Villingen 1641 SÜDWEST-   158o, 1647 Erolzheim 159o 159o
Freiburg/Br. Donaueschingen DEUTSCHLAND Saul-   Memmin-
1599-16o3 1632   gau Wurzach   gen
     Bräunlingen Hüfingen 1631 165o-8o 1575 1665-68
          1635   Waldsee 158 - 159o   Kauf-
                 Überlingen Ravensburg   beuren
Bernau 1589   1574-78 1481-8 Leutkirch 1591
                 158o,1594-97 Wein- 158o   Wengen/
Stein a. Rhein   16o8   1481-86 garten   Trauchburg
16o1-76   Wangen 158o 1616-17
                 Konstanz Wasserburg/   1576, 162
                 1547-55 Bodensee   Rettenberg-
                          1597, 165 -6o   Sont-
                          Lindau   hofen
                          1443, Bregenz   1586-87, 1592
                          1493   16o9

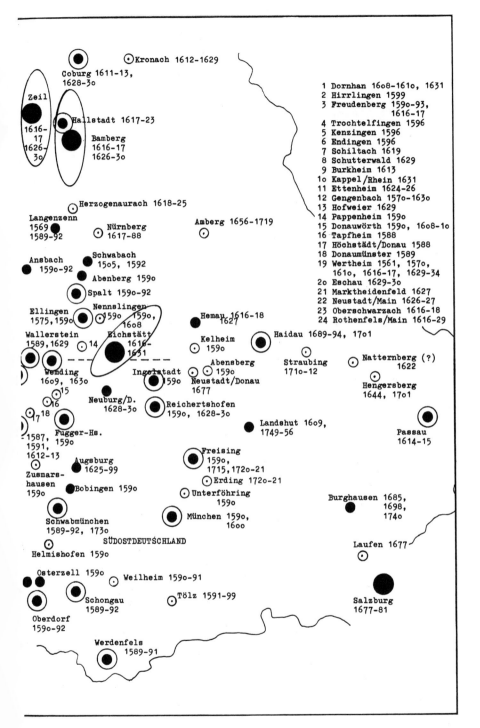

Kronach 1612-1629

Coburg 1611-13,
1628-30

Zeil
1616-
17
1626-
30

Hallstadt 1617-23

Bamberg
1616-17
1626-30

Herzogenaurach 1618-25

Langenzenn
1569
1589-92

Nürnberg
1617-88

Amberg 1656-1719

Ansbach
1590-92

Schwabach
1505, 1592

Abenberg 1590

Spalt 1590-92

Ellingen
1575, 1590

Nennslingen
1590,
1608

Wallerstein
1589, 1629

14

Eichstätt
1616-
1631

Hemau 1616-18
1627

Kelheim
1590

Haidau 1689-94, 1701

Natternberg (?)
1622

Wemding
1609, 1630

15

Ingolstadt
1590

Abensberg
1590

Straubing
1710-12

16

Neuburg/D.
1628-30

Neustadt/Donau
1677

Hengersberg
1644, 1701

7 18

Reichertshofen
1590, 1628-30

Landshut 1609,
1749-56

Passau
1614-15

-1587,
1591,
1612-13

Fugger-Hs.
1590

Augsburg
1625-99

Freising
1590,
1715, 1720-21

Zusmars-
hausen
1590

Bobingen 1590

Erding 1720-21

Burghausen 1685,
1698,
1740

Schwabmünchen
1589-92, 1730

Unterföhring
1590

München 1590,
1600

SÜDOSTDEUTSCHLAND

Laufen 1677

Helmishofen 1590

Osterzell 1590

Weilheim 1590-91

Schongau
1589-92

Tölz 1591-99

Salzburg
1677-81

Oberdorf
1590-92

Werdenfels
1589-91

1 Dornhan 1608-1610, 1631
2 Hirrlingen 1599
3 Freudenberg 1590-93,
1616-17
4 Trochtelfingen 1596
5 Kenzingen 1596
6 Endingen 1596
7 Schiltach 1619
8 Schutterwald 1629
9 Burkheim 1613
10 Kappel/Rhein 1631
11 Ettenheim 1624-26
12 Gengenbach 1570-1630
13 Hofweier 1629
14 Pappenheim 1590
15 Donauwörth 1590, 1608-10
16 Tapfheim 1588
17 Höchstädt/Donau 1588
18 Donaumünster 1589
19 Wertheim 1561, 1570,
1610, 1616-17, 1629-34
20 Eschau 1629-30
21 Marktheidenfeld 1627
22 Neustadt/Main 1626-27
23 Oberschwarzach 1616-18
24 Rothenfels/Main 1616-29

1 *Introduction*

WITCH TRIALS IN HISTORIOGRAPHIC CONTEXT

Since the 1970s, the researching of witch trials and their background has developed into an autonomous historical field – witchcraft studies.[1] However, historical interest in witchcraft has an even longer tradition: demonologists of the fifteenth to seventeenth centuries often substantiated their own opinions through references to historical accounts and preced-

---

[1] H. Lehmann, 'Hexenprozesse in Norddeutschland und in Skandinavien im 16., 17. und 18. Jahrhundert. Bemerkungen zum Forschungsstand', in C. Degn *et al.* (eds.), *Hexenprozesse. Deutsche und skandinavische Beiträge*, Neumünster 1983, 9–14, for example uses the term 'witch researcher', *ibid.*, 9. No bibliography has yet been produced. The resurgence of witchcraft research in the 1960s was marked by three essays: H.C.E. Midelfort, 'Recent Witch Hunting Research, or Where Do We Go from Here?', *Papers of the Bibliographical Society of America*, 62 (1968), 373–420; D. Nugent, 'Witchcraft Studies 1959–1971: A Bibliographical Survey', *Journal of Popular Culture*, 5 (1971), 711–25; and E.W. Monter, 'The Historiography of European Witchcraft: Progress and Prospects', *Journal of Interdisciplinary History*, 2 (1972), 435–51. At about the same time a series of essays began, which made access to the scattered specialist literature much easier: E.W. Monter (ed.), *European Witchcraft*, New York 1969; M. Douglas (ed.), *Witchcraft Confessions and Accusations*, London 1970; A. Kors and E. Peters (eds.), *Witchcraft in Europe 1100–1700. A Documentary History*, Philadelphia 1972; S. Anglo (ed.), *The Damned Art. Essays in the Literature of Witchcraft*, London 1977; G. Becker, S. Bovenschen, H. Brackert *et al.* (eds.), *Aus der Zeit der Verzweiflung. Zur Genese und Aktualität des Hexenbildes*, Frankfurt am Main, 1977; C. Honegger (ed.), *Die Hexen der Neuzeit. Studien zur Sozialgeschichte eines kulturellen Deutungsmusters*, Frankfurt am Main 1978. Some paradigmatic new researches have been discussed in collective reviews which are worth reading: L. Stone, 'The Disenchantment of the World', *New York Review of Books*, 2 December 1971, 17–25; H.C.E. Midelfort, 'The Renaissance of Witchcraft Research', *Journal of the History of Behavioral Sciences*, 13 (1977), 294–7. Information on the state of witchcraft research in Germany is given by G. Schormann, *Hexenprozesse in Deutschland*, Göttingen 1981. As witchcraft research has since become very popular in Germany too, Schormann's survey now has the character of an interim report.

ents, in addition to revelation, classical authors or scholastic authorities.[2] Opponents of trials also found it in their best interests to cite historical precedents or to stigmatise the outbreak of persecutions as a wrong turn on the path of history. To that extent, some historical awareness of 'witches' always existed in Western Europe.[3] Even Enlightenment thinkers were rooted in this tradition, although their examples had a different aim. Whereas precedent previously underscored the necessity of persecution, history served an apologetic function in the Enlightenment, unveiling the 'darkness' of a bygone era. Later, historical precedent provided them with a political weapon in the fight for enlightened reforms[4], only to regain an apologetic function shortly thereafter. Hardly any other theme lent itself so well to exalting the present at the expense of the past.

Historians initially treated the ostensibly exotic topic of witchcraft with negligence and, with few exceptions,[5] the field was tilled by outsiders. Theologians, jurists, archivists and journalists all took an early interest, followed by psychologists, physicians, sociologists, ethnologists and folklorists. While a journalistic approach often led, indeed still leads, to

---

[2] The basic works are J. Hansen, *Zauberwahn, Inquisition und Hexenprozess im Mittelalter und die Entstehung der grossen Hexenverfolgung*, Leipzig 1900; J. Hansen, *Quellen und Untersuchungen zur Geschichte des Hexenwahns und der Hexenverfolgung im Mittelalter*, Bonn 1901. In the early sixteenth century a north Italian Inquisitor investigated the archives of the Inquisition and fixed the beginning of this new heresy at around 1350, Hansen, *Quellen und Untersuchungen*, 454. Similar examples are quoted by H.C. Lea, *Materials Toward a History of Witchcraft*, 3 vols. New York/London 1957, I, 232. Not until the later sixteenth century do examples become plentiful: J.Bodin, *De Daemonomania Magorum*, Strasbourg 1581; *Theatrum de Veneficiis*, Frankfurt 1586. On the other demonological literature of the period: J. Janssen and L. Pastor, *Culturzustände des deutschen Volkes seit dem Ausgang des Mittelalters bis zum Beginn des Dreissigjährigen Krieges*, 8 vols., Freiburg im Breisgau 1885–94, VIII, 494–644.

[3] More radical opponents branded the executions of witches as an overt injustice, above all J. Weyer (Wierus), *De Praestigiis Daemonum*, Frankfurt am Main, 1586 (1st edn 1563). In our context the view of a Jesuit leader of opinion from Bavaria is interesting; he believed that the new witches had been known since 1475! A. Tanner, *Theologia scholastica*, 4 vols., Ingolstadt 1626–7, I, col. 1503f.

[4] B. Bekker, *Die bezauberte Welt*, 4 vols., Amsterdam 1693; C. Thomasius, *De crimine magiae*, Halle 1701. The 'historicising' approach to the alleged truths of the faith is clear from the title of G. Wahrlieb, *Deutliche Vorstellung der Nichtigkeit der vermeynten Hexereyen und des ungegründeten Hexenprocesses, Amsterdam, nach der Erfindung der Hexerey im dritten Seculo und nach der Einführung des Hexen-Processes ins Jahr 236*, Halle 1720. It is often overlooked that editions of sources began very early: E.D. Hauber, *Bibliotheca Acta et Scripta magica. Gründliche Nachrichten und Urtheile von solchen Büchern und Handlungen, welche die Macht des Teufels in leiblichen Dingen betreffen*, 3 vols., Lemgo 1736–45.

[5] One of the few exceptions was S. Riezler, *Geschichte der Hexenprozesse in Bayern. Im Lichte der allgemeinen Entwickelung dargestellt*, Stuttgart 1896. Riezler (1843–1927) had qualified as a lecturer in 1869, and the first volume of his monumental *Geschichte Baierns* (8 vols., Gotha 1878–1914) appeared in 1878. Riezler was appointed to the first chair of Bavarian history and became a co-editor of the *Historische Zeitschrift*.

eccentric interpretations,[6] most researchers (excluding special interest groups) accepted the explanations proposed in nineteenth-century German literature,[7] which could claim the detailed reconstruction of an elaborated concept of witchcraft pervasive in Western Europe from the fifteenth to the eighteenth centuries as its major accomplishment. Regional and chronological concentrations of trials and persecutions, though noted, never came to the foreground. One leading researcher, Joseph Hansen, identified the accumulated beliefs of sorcery and heresy subsumed in the fifteenth-century concept of witchcraft, and his findings are still valid today, but Hansen was over-generous when he conceded that early modern persecutions were

> only the natural echo of ideas fully developed around the end of the Middle Ages and the beginning of the modern era, influenced little by the Reformation, persisting far into the nineteenth century, and not effectively opposed until they came under the influence of a modern world-view based on science, and not theology.[8]

In Hansen's day, most researchers assumed that witch trials flowed into the continuous stream of persecutions from the end of the Middle Ages to

---

[6] Examples of eccentric interpretations of the witch theme from three leading modern German publications: *Der Spiegel*, 43 (1984), 117–28; *Stern*, 36 (1982), 58–65; *Süddeutsche Zeitung, Münchener Stadtanzeiger*, 65–70 (1984).

[7] Besides S. Riezler and J. Hansen the chief protagonists of the older German witchcraft research included G.W. Soldan, *Geschichte der Hexenprozesse*, Darmstadt 1843, whose work was repeatedly augmented and received its final form as G.W. Soldan, H. Heppe, H. Bauer, *Geschichte der Hexenprozesse*, Hanau 1912. It is still one of the basic standard works (reprinted 1972). Besides Janssen and Pastor the following must be mentioned: J. Diefenbach, *Der Hexenwahn vor und nach der Glaubensspaltung*, Mainz 1886; G. Längin, *Religion und Hexenprozess*, Leipzig 1888; O. Snell, *Hexenprozesse und Geistesstörungen. Psychiatrische Untersuchungen*, Munich 1891; L. Rapp, *Die Hexenprozesse und ihre Gegner im Tirol*, Innsbruck 1874 (enlarged edition, Brixen 1891); B. Duhr SJ, *Die Stellung der Jesuiten in den deutschen Hexenprozessen*, Cologne 1900; N. Paulus, *Hexenwahn und Hexenprozesse, vornehmlich im 16. Jahrhundert*, Freiburg im Breisgau 1910; also important are G. Roskoff, *Geschichte des Teufels*, II, Leipzig 1869; and H. Hayn and A.N. Gotendorf, *Bibliotheca Germanorum Erotica et Curiosa*, III, Munich 1913, s.v. 'Hexenwesen' 171–258. The older German research into witchcraft laid solid foundations for modern international research. Many an apparently new idea will be found in some detail in the authors named above. The view that gained currency among American psychiatric historians, under the influence of G. Zilboorg, *The Medical Man and the Witch During the Renaissance*, Baltimore 1935, and was for a time a received opinion, but is now again disputed, that witches were mainly psychiatric cases, is already found in Snell. The function of witch trials as an instrument of social discipline, over-emphasised by R. Muchembled, *Kultur des Volkes – Kultur der Eliten*, Stuttgart 1982, was as prominently defended in F. Stieve, 'Der Hexenwahn' in his, *Abhandlungen, Vorträge, Reden*, Leipzig 1900, 300–18. Also completely based on the old materials are Lea, *Materials*; H.R. Trevor-Roper, 'The European Witch Craze of the Sixteenth and Seventeenth Centuries', in his *Religion, the Reformation and Social Change*, London 1967, 90–192; K. Baschwitz, *Hexen und Hexenprozesse*, Munich 1963.

[8] Hansen, *Quellen und Untersuchungen*, Foreword.

the beginning of the Enlightenment. While occasional antiquarians might describe a single trial, they otherwise contented themselves with the prevailing paradigm. Individual cases served them only as examples and a systematic investigation was ignored, because this 'could accomplish little more than confirm the well-known pattern with grisly uniformity'.[9]

A few nineteenth-century researchers voiced concerns about the accuracy of this portrayal, but only recently has the challenge culminated in a true paradigm shift. New studies demonstrate major spatial and temporal fluctuations between trials conducted in a manner lacking any essential uniformity. They reveal how an event once scorned by 'enlightened' historians as a 'witch craze' actually displayed significant regional and individual anomalies, rightly pointing out pronounced variations in persecutions. In the 1960s, historical interest in early modern witch trials shifted from the ruling elites traditionally targeted for research – nobles, jurists and theologians – onto the 'lower' social strata of the population and their attendant actions and reactions; firm believers in witchcraft, they were more immediately affected than the highest echelons of society. Witchcraft studies broke new ground after several historians unearthed a mass of surprising information.[10]

In terms of chronology, international researchers now largely agree that witchcraft persecutions peaked between 1560 and 1630,[11] albeit with distinct conjunctures during this seventy-year period. If consensus seems unimportant, one should appreciate that the new chronology renders many former hypotheses obsolete and demolishes older explanatory models. Contrary to popular opinion, there was never any broad stream of witch trials running from the Middle Ages to the eighteenth century.

---

[9] Hansen, *Zauberwahn*, Foreword. Similarly also Riezler, *Geschichte der Hexenprozesse*, (1896) (henceforth *Geschichte*), 6.

[10] The chief paradigmatic works are J. Caro Baroja, *Die Hexen und ihre Welt*, Stuttgart 1967 (1st edn Madrid 1961, English translation, *The World of the Witches*, Chicago 1964); R. Mandrou, *Magistrats et sorciers en France au XVIIe siècle. Une analyse de psychologie historique*, Paris 1968; A. Macfarlane, *Witchcraft in Tudor and Stuart England*, London 1970; K. Thomas, *Religion and the Decline of Magic*, London 1971; H.C.E. Midelfort, *Witch Hunting in Southwestern Germany 1562–1684*, Stanford 1972.

[11] The period 1560–1630 is explicitly named by Muchembled, *Kultur*, 236; Trevor-Roper, 'European Witch Craze', 143f.; and Honegger, *Die Hexen*, 107; it can also be implicitly inferred from Janssen and Pastor, *Culturzustände*, VIII, 619–95; or Soldan *et al.*, *Geschichte der Hexenprozesse*, I, 481–563 and II, 1–130. H. Kamen, *The Iron Century, Social Change in Europe 1550–1660*, names 1550–1660; Midelfort, *Witch Hunting*, 201–19 refers to 1570–1630 as does P. Chaunu, *Europäische Kultur im Zeitalter des Barock*, Munich 1968, 651. Monter, *European Witchcraft*, xiii and following him Schormann, *Hexenprozesse* (1981), 55 consider 1580–1630 to be the decisive phase. C. Andresen and G. Denzler, *dtv-Wörterbuch der Kirchengeschichte* (Deutscher Taschenbuch Verlag), Munich 1982, 261, following F. Merzbacher, *Die Hexenprozesse in Franken*, 2nd edn Munich 1970, see an even shorter period, 1590–1630, as the core period of witch hunting. Cf. also Lehmann, 'Hexenprozesse', 11.

Following witch trials conducted by papal inquisitors around 1500, we now know that executions for witchcraft actually declined for decades, compelling contemporaries to remark that witches were hardly ever executed.[12] This decline coincided with the reign of Charles V, the age of the Reformation and its popular mass movements, and an epoch of benign capitalism (Braudel). One leading physician, Johann Weyer, launched a frontal assault on the dominant concept of witchcraft elaborated by later scholasticists in his epoch-making *De praestigiis Daemonum* of 1563. However, although he condemned persecutions as a 'slaughter of the innocents', Weyer's voluminous polemic was not intended as an attack on witch trials per se, but rather on the unexpected occasion of their resumption; by that time, he had hoped, they were long 'abolished and done away with'.[13] Obviously, we need no longer search the Middle Ages (perhaps not as 'dark' as they once seemed) for causes behind a rise in witch hunting after 1560, but instead in the 'iron century' (Henry Kamen) which now commands ever more attention from historians. Furthermore, the 'new' endpoint of the European witch craze has similarly unsettling implications. While Cartesianism and the early Enlightenment certainly played a decisive role in the marginalisation of witchcraft as a crime, they hardly explain the marked decline in persecutions as early as the first decade of the seventeenth century, even more pronounced after 1630.[14]

Recently, interest in the apex of witchcraft persecutions between 1560 and 1630 has mounted. Heightened public interest provided an external stimulus, but the scholarly bankruptcy of traditional explanations acted as a catalyst more endogenous to the historical community: repeated assertions of a connection with the Counter-Reformation or the tumultuous wars of religion are simply unfounded.[15] In Germany, the epicentre of witch hunting,[16] the first waves of persecution occurred during an extended period of peace between the Schmalkaldic War and the Thirty Years War.

[12] This view was defended by J. Trithemius, *Antipalus Maleficiorum*, Ingolstadt 1555 (MS of 1508), on which see Lea, *Materials*, 369f. and Baschwitz, *Hexen*, 15–18. The complaint of lack of persecuting zeal is found in many authors on witchcraft before 1580.
[13] Weyer, *De Praestigiis*, Foreword, i verso (cf. note 3); 'benign capitalism' is a phrase found in Braudel, 'Europäische Expansion und Kapitalismus 1450–1650', in E. Schulin, *Univeralgeschichte*, Cologne 1974, 255–94, 280.
[14] As does Trevor-Roper, 'European Witch Craze', 163–71; cf. the discussion in Honegger, *Die Hexen*, 126ff. A clearer perspective is that of Thomas, *Religion*, 681 and H. Lehmann, 'Hexenverfolgungen und Hexenprozesse im alten Reich zwischen Reformation und Aufklärung', *Jahrbuch des Instituts für Deutsche Geschichte (Tel Aviv)*, 7 (1978), 13–70, quotation from 54ff.
[15] G. Schormann, *Hexenprozesse in Nordwestdeutschland*, Hildesheim 1977, 7; idem, *Hexenprozesse* (1981), 110–16.
[16] Monter, *Witchcraft in France*, 191, assumes that 'probably more witches were killed within the confines of present-day Germany than in the rest of Europe put together'.

Interdisciplinary methods clearly provided new impulses for witchcraft studies. Apart from psychological and sociological theorems,[17] ethnographic methods long employed to study witchcraft in 'primitive societies' proved particularly fruitful.[18] Initially, research on witchcraft profited greatly from the general rapprochement between social history and social anthropology[19], most pronounced in an exchange between English and American anthropology and English witchcraft studies that resulted in several decisive encounters. Social anthropologists approached their subjects outfitted with different questions than historians, seeking the function of witchcraft in existing societies, rather than its origins or essence. Field research allowed them to test theories through direct interaction, never confined to the leading members of society – chieftains or shamans – as was customary in historical research. Instead, the 'popular magic' of a given society was considered within a cultural totality, neither as an isolated phenomenon, nor as some abtruse intellectual error. Unlike most historians, who viewed witchcraft beliefs as a virus infecting the intellectual body of European culture[20], ethnologists accepted the

[17] Stone, 'Disenchantment', 17, referred to the 'raids' of the historians of mentalities on Max Weber and E. Durkheim. References to older sociological and psychological attempts at interpretation in the English-speaking world are discussed in Midelfort, 'Recent Witch Hunting Research', 378f. and some more recent socio-psychologically oriented works are reviewed in Midelfort, 'Renaissance', 294ff. The necessity of sociological analysis is emphasised by R. Horsley, 'Who Were the Witches? The Social Roles of the Accused in the European Witch Trials', *Journal of Interdisciplinary History*, 9 (1979), 689–714, 692. Midelfort, *Witch Hunting*, 4ff. warned against oversimplifying sociological correlations and functionalist theories. T.J. Schoenemann, 'The Role of Mental Illness in the European Witch Hunts of the Sixteenth and Seventeenth Centuries: An Assessment', *Journal of the History of the Behavioral Sciences*, 13 (1977), 337–51, objected to overemphasis on the psychopathological aspect.

[18] E.E. Evans-Pritchard, *Witchcraft, Oracles and Magic among the Azande*, Oxford 1937 (German translation, *Hexerei, Orakel und Magie bei den Zande*, Frankfurt am Main 1978) had the most lasting influence. Explicit application of social-anthropological theories in Macfarlane, *Witchcraft*, 211–54, with discussion of ethnological theories and approaches.

[19] As such one should appreciate the special numbers of two journals: *The Journal of Interdisciplinary History*, 12 (1981–2), with a thematic block of articles on 'Anthropology and History in the 1980s'; *ibid.*, 227–78; and *Geschichte und Gesellschaft*, 10 (1984), Heft 3, 'Sozialgeschichte und Kulturanthropologie'. The theme of the 35th Historians' Conference in West Berlin of 1984 was 'Ways of life, mentalities, forms of action. Anthropological dimensions in history'.

[20] When Riezler, *Geschichte*, 197 places the members of the Bavarian princely house, because of their fear of witchcraft, 'auf jene Stufe, auf der wir viele heidnische Negerstämme treffen', this *bon mot* may have thrown light on an unknown side of Counter-Reformation piety, but it can no longer be appreciated as showing an understanding of the magical culture of the time in a social-anthropological sense. It is striking how little space is given to this central aspect of pre-industrial mentalities in historical standard works and textbooks. Only higher magic in its relationship to the emerging natural sciences is mentioned in the contributions to T. Schieder (ed.), *Handbuch der europäischen Geschichte*, III, Stuttgart 1971; T. Schieder (ed.), *Handbuch der Europäischen Geschichte*, IV, Stuttgart 1968, 126–36 *passim*, merely refers to 'superstition' which was repressed.

'otherness' of the mentalities they studied without ethnocentric arrogance.[21]

If functionalists sometimes regarded witchcraft as a stabilising factor in 'primitive' societies,[22] Malinowski was quick to notice that an exacerbated fear of bewitchment related to historical processes in a given society. The historisation of social anthropology by Evans-Pritchard[23] strengthened the perception that fear of bewitchment rises in times of social turmoil. The view of 'popular magic' as a self-regulating mechanism preserving social and moral equilibrium was thereby altered as accusations of bewitchment began to be regarded as symptoms of heightened internal tensions. Suspicions of witchcraft indicated a society that, as a whole, could no longer resolve problems by traditional means – a society in a state of crisis, so to speak.[24]

English witchcraft studies incorporated this paradigm, thereby achieving a novel interpretive quality for European history. Keith Thomas expressed this most clearly, stating:

> Witch-beliefs are therefore of interest to the social historian for the light they throw upon the weak points in the social structure of the time.[25]

From inauspicious beginnings as a trivial preoccupation with an apparently irrelevant cultural aberration, witchcraft studies forced their way into the heart of historical debate to stake a claim as a leading field of early modern research.[26]

The emancipation of witchcraft studies became clear when leading historians in England and France suddenly began to concern themselves with the topic, and continued to do so for many years.[27] As initial forays

E.W. Zeeden in H. Grundmann (ed.), *Gebhardt Handbuch der deutschen Geschichte*, IX, Deutscher Taschenbuch Verlag (3rd edition), Munich 1978, 175–80, at least addresses the problems. There are only scattered references in M. Spindler (ed.), *Handbuch der bayerischen Geschichte*, II, 2nd edn Munich 1977, and III, 2nd edn Munich 1979.

[21] E.E. Evans-Pritchard, *Theorien über primitive Religionen*, Frankfurt am Main 1981, 159f., refers to Mauss (note 17).

[22] So for example M. Douglas, 'Das Problem des Bösen', in her, *Ritual, Tabu und Körpersymbolik. Sozialanthropologische Studien in Industriegesellschaft und Stammeskultur*, Frankfurt 1981, 152–71; E. Gillies, 'Introduction' to the German translation of Evans-Pritchard (1978), 7–36, 26f.

[23] E.E. Evans-Pritchard, *Anthropology and History*, Manchester 1961; B. Malinowski, 'Gedanken zum Problem des Zauberwesens', in his, *Die Dynamik des Kulturwandels*, Vienna 1951, 185–96.

[24] Malinowski, 'Gedanken', 190ff.; Gillies, 'Introduction', 28–30; Macfarlane, *Witchcraft*, 249ff.   [25] Thomas, *Religion*, 669.

[26] This was heralded in Midelfort, 'Renaissance', 294.

[27] To name only a few: L. Febvre, 'Sorcellerie, sotise ou révolution mentale', *Annales, Economies, Sociétés, Civilisations*, 3 (1948), 9–15; P. Chaunu, 'Sur la fin des sorciers au XVIIᵉ siècle', *Annales, Economies, Sociétés, Civilisations*, 24 (1969), 895–911; Mandrou, *Magistrats*; Muchembled, *Kultur*; Stone, 'Disenchantment'; Kamen, *Iron Century*; Thomas, *Religion*.

passed into an experimental phase, attempts were made to link witchcraft with all sorts of social changes in the later Middle Ages and early modern period. Initially, historians rather naively sought to explain witchcraft persecutions by citing unique causes, such as the alleged self-enrichment of the judges, the sexual perversions of monks, the intended destruction of religious enemies, the eradication of ancient cults or secret medical lore, misogyny, or the fault of the Church, jurists or other social groups.[28] None of these explanations was entirely satisfying and more ambitious interpretations gradually made their appearance. They included the 'collapse' of the medieval 'cosmos' through 'rapid political, social and religious change in the fifteenth century',[29] a transformation of mentalities during the transition from feudalism to capitalism,[30] the potential for conflict in pre-industrial European village communities,[31] the birth of the absolutist state,[32] the disappearance of Catholic protective magic after the Reformation,[33] social disciplining and suppression of popular culture in the sixteenth and seventeenth centuries,[34] the 'price revolution' of the sixteenth century,[35] and changes in family structure, especially in the role of women in society.[36] A complete list of the factors linked to witchcraft persecutions in recent years would be redundant. Not all connections made equal sense, but it is no exaggeration to suggest that the socio-anthropological paradigm of 'fear caused by social change' has proven most fruitful indeed. It won general recognition among historians for the central role of witchcraft in the life and thought of early modern Europeans, at all social levels, albeit relative to a broad scale of social interpretations.[37]

A glimpse at the complex and burgeoning secondary literature indicates that little consensus remains about the connection of witchcraft to specific historical phenomena, leaving the impression that we lack fundamental information or an ability to differentiate adequately. The consequences are obvious, when some researchers suspect witch trials only in remote mountain regions, while others find them in highly developed centres of early capitalism. An interpretation of 'backwardness' dominates in the first

[28] Schormann, *Hexenprozesse* (1981), 80–9, 100–23.
[29] J.B. Russell, *Witchcraft in the Middle Ages*, Ithaca/London 1972; partially translated into German in Honegger, *Die Hexen* (1978) 159–87, cited from 165.
[30] Macfarlane, *Witchcraft*, 205f. Also Thomas, *Religion* (1980 edn), 669ff., 675f.
[31] Macfarlane, *Witchcraft*, 205f.   [32] Lehmann, 'Hexenverfolgung', 31f.
[33] Macfarlane, *Witchcraft*, 250f.; on this see Stone, 'Disenchantment', 19f., 24.
[34] Muchembled, *Kultur*, 232–77, explicitly 239, 241, 249; cf. note 7.
[35] Kamen, *Iron Century*, 249f.
[36] Midelfort, *Witch Hunting*, 184ff., makes this suggestion but does not draw the full conclusions from it.
[37] Further interpretative approaches in Schormann, *Hexenprozesse* (1981), 123f. A discussion of various approaches in Larner, *Enemies*, 15–28. The increasing acceptance of the theme is shown by its inclusion in important surveys, e.g. Kamen, *Iron Century*, 239–51; R. van Dülmen, *Entstehung des frühneuzeitlichen Europa 1550–1648* (= *Fischer Weltgeschichte*, vol. 24), Frankfurt am Main, 1982, 285–91.

example, 'fear caused by social change' in the second.[38] There are also a variety of opinions as to whether the witch craze was a rural or an urban phenomenon, or whether a greater proclivity to persecute witches existed among particular religious confessions, forms of government or economic structures. Marked regional and temporal variations make it difficult or even impossible to generalise at the present time and, as with other specialised historical fields such as the history of the family, the topic remains a minefield for non-specialists. For example, when the English historian H.R. Trevor-Roper published his brilliantly formulated essay 'The European Witch Craze of the Sixteenth and Seventeenth Centuries', he provoked reactions among historians of witchcraft ranging from ridi-cule, indignation, vigorous rejection or, at best, ambivalence.[39] In a lofty *tour d'horizon*, Trevor-Roper combined shrewd insights with absurd gener-alisations taken from the secondary literature unchecked or incapable of being checked against any sources.[40] The revival of Delrio's old 'mountain' theory was employed to suggest a belief in witches indigenous to Europe's mountainous regions: the Alps, the Pyrenees and elsewhere. Trevor-Roper's social psychology, limited to conjecture about 'thin mountain air' causing 'hallucinations' in the 'imaginations of the mountain peasants', served as the basis of proof for the witchcraft concept edified by the Church. Nor was that all: Trevor-Roper reduced the witch craze to a 'crusade against the Alpine peoples'.[41] Although this last quote is a crass example of disturbingly learned nonsense, one could, in principle, just as easily present other unfounded statements, confidently put forward as axioms, to assert the contrary.[42]

We can only arrive at more viable hypotheses through regional studies conducted on compact geographic areas, which explain where and when witch trials and witchcraft persecutions actually occurred, what triggered

---

[38] Here the interpretation of Russell, *Witchcraft*, 268, is opposed to that of Trevor-Roper, 'European Witch Craze', 107 (backwardness).

[39] Trevor-Roper, 'European Witch Craze' (cf. note 7).

[40] The verdict of the advanced witchcraft researchers was annihilating: Macfarlane (*Witchcraft*) wrote: 'the essay has nothing to say which is helpful ... The real defect of the essay is that its tone implies that we know a great deal about "witchcraft" and all that is needed is synthesis. In fact we know far too little.' Stone, 'Disenchantment', 22, even considered the essay an 'egregious error': 'almost all of Professor Trevor-Roper's over-confident asser-tions are either false or unproven'. Also critical is Thomas, *Religion*, 595, 684. Harsh criticism was also levelled at Russell: Midelfort, 'Renaissance', 294; and at Mandrou, who had to suffer the verdict of Soman: 'Mandrou's thesis simply bristles with fallacies': A. Soman, 'The Parlement of Paris and the Great Witch Hunt (1565–1640)', *Sixteenth Century Journal*, 9 (1978), 31–44, quotation from 33.

[41] Trevor-Roper, 'European Witch Craze', 106, 109, 133, 136, 160, 292; on this see Macfar-lane, *Witchcraft*, 9. The attempt to harmonise witch hunts and topography is obviously persistent: Schormann offers, instead of Trevor-Roper's exploded 'high mountain theory', a 'middle mountain theory', but on the same page he speaks of low-lying Westphalia and Mecklenburg as chief regions of witch hunting in the Empire.

[42] Macfarlane, *Witchcraft*, 9; Stone, 'Disenchantment', 22; see also note 40.

them, how they developed, what reactions they provoked, what expectations were coupled with them, which chronological, local and sociological differences accompanied them and why trials eventually came to an end. Only then can we establish a sensible international comparison and correlate the events with other historical processes on a broad basis.

Earlier regional studies in German-speaking countries (Bader for Switzerland and Byloff for Austria,[43] Riezler's research on the Duchy of Bavaria, the studies of Liebelt and Spielmann for Hesse[44] and the monographs of Merzbacher and Wittmann for Franconia,[45] to name only a few for southern Germany) have enhanced our knowledge of witch trials and have already presented a partial challenge to the earlier paradigm of German witchcraft studies. Nevertheless, their authors were caged by this paradigm insofar as their conclusions remained naive (blaming the Church, for example), the interpretation of trials unearthed as grisly examples of the age prior to the Enlightenment was retained (albeit with certain local and chronological concentrations), no new or illuminating queries were entered, and results were presented as curios of cultural history. As far as quantification is concerned, we remain in the dark as to their methods or the representative character of their sources. The authors usually examined trial records only, informing the reader, at best, that they were fragmentary. The heterogeneity and lack of intellectual rigour exhibited by many of these early regional studies make them inappropriate for any comparative survey on the 'national' level.[46]

Only with the 1960s did the onset of methodologically reflective witchcraft studies[47] lead to systematic, comparative, regional studies posing innovative questions.[48] Early in the 1970s, two extensive regional studies

---

[43] F. Byloff, *Hexenglaube und Hexenverfolgung in den österreichischen Alpenländern*, Berlin 1934; G. Bader, 'Die Hexenprozesse in der Schweiz', Dr. jur. thesis, Zürich 1945.

[44] K. Liebelt, 'Geschichte der Hexenprozesse in Hessen-Kassel', *Zs. der. Verf. f. hess. Gesch. u. Landeskunde*, 58 (1932), 1–144; H.K. Spielmann, *Die Hexenprozesse in Kurhessen. Nach den Quellen dargestellt*, 2nd edn Marburg 1932; for Hesse see also the work of C. Grebner, 'Hexenprozese im Freigericht Alzenau (1601–1605)', *Aschaffenburger Jahrbuch für Geschichte, Landeskunde und Kunst des Untermaingebietes*, 6 (1979), 141–240.

[45] F. Merzbacher, *Die Hexenprozesse* (cf. note 11); F. Merzbacher, 'Geschichte der Hexenprozesse im Hochstift Würzburg', *Mainfränkisches Jahrbuch für Geschichte und Kunst*, 2 (1950), 162–85; P. Wittmann, 'Die Bamberger Hexenjustiz 1595–1631', *Archiv für das katholische Kirchenrecht*, 50 (1883), 177–223.

[46] Schormann, *Hexenprozesse* (1981), 65–71, gives the first approximate quantitative geographical survey of the distribution of witch hunts in Germany, for which he was able to make use above all of the materials of the *H-Sonderkommando* (see chapter 2, pp. 35–64).

[47] Cf. notes 1 and 10.

[48] Midelfort, *Witch Hunting*, 232, note 28 was still able to cite only Macfarlane, *Witchcraft*. Soman, 'Parlement', could also refer to Midelfort, *Witch Hunting*, E.W. Monter, *Witchcraft in France and Switzerland; the Borderlands during the Reformation*, Ithaca/London 1976, and the work of Larner, then in progress. Larner, *Enemies*, for her part, cf. note 160, also knew G. Schormann (*Hexenprozesse*, 1977). The essays in Degn *et al.*, *Hexenprozesse*, should also have been added.

appeared, impressively confirming the paradigm shift: Macfarlane's on Essex (1970) and Midelfort's on Baden-Württemberg (1972).[49] However, they arrived at such disparate conclusions that, at times, one wonders whether they examined two unrelated topics. Despite this impression, reinforced by a choice of dissimilar methodologies, their results were doubtlessly informed by the substance of the material they examined.

The relatively wealthy county of Essex, east of London, was a citadel of Puritanism. By comparison with other English regions, Essex yielded the largest number of executions for witchcraft, eighty-two in all (notably less than some smaller German cities). Virtually all these trials were for malefi-cent magic. Since the typical components of witches' flight, witches' sab-baths or pacts with the Devil were conspicuously absent in England and Scotland, the danger of large-scale persecutions, always provoked by a fear of witches' sabbaths, was avoided.[50] Macfarlane modelled his study on the 'historical fieldwork' of social anthropologists like Evans-Pritchard. Using serial court protocols, he systematically investigated all sorcery and witch-craft trials, making a discovery that was nothing short of spectacular: the belief in sorcery and witchcraft was so pervasive among villagers that the associated activities (e.g. spells, counterspells, conversations and trials) dominated their imaginative world. Almost all trials arose within the context of village conflicts, but executions were rare in relation to the total number of trials.[51]

Midelfort investigated 'Southwestern Germany' (present-day Baden-Württemberg), a region fragmented into hundreds of small territories and Free-Imperial cities, each of which conducted its own witchcraft trials. Geographically nine times larger than the area considered by Macfarlane, witches were executed there fifty times more often than in Essex. Between 1561 and 1670 alone, Midelfort identified 3,229 witch burnings simply by adding verifiable cases and without any evaluation of serial documents, though we know that major persecutions already occurred in Upper Germany at the end of the fifteenth century.[52] Here, major witchcraft persecutions dominated a history of witch trials against which, at least in Midelfort's presentation, village magic faded into the background. As in Essex, witch trials in southwestern Germany increased after 1560, peaking in the 1580s. Unlike Essex, a general decline in trials after 1600 only occurred in territories under Protestant rule; Catholics went on to burn more witches than ever before. Socio-anthropological or socio-historical arguments took a back seat, as Midelfort breathed new life into a confes-sionalist interpretation of witch trials, analysing contemporary Protestant

[49] Cf. note 10. The contributions in Degn *et al.*, *Hexenprozesse*, revealed the great influence of the paradigmatic studies of Macfarlane, *Witchcraft* and Midelfort, *Witch Hunting*.
[50] Macfarlane, *Witchcraft*, 6.   [51] *Ibid.*, 6, 26–8, 57–61.
[52] *Ibid.*, 23, 62; Midelfort, *Witch Hunting*, 32.

treatises and sermons on witchcraft. Among Protestants, he argued, witch trials were always controversial. When they became dysfunctional, Protestants could fall back on theological arguments and bring persecutions to an abrupt end.[53]

The paradigmatic studies of Macfarlane and Midelfort illuminated yet other important historical aspects of witch trials, stimulating a series of less ambitiously framed investigations.[54] These works, and those of other participants in the growing witchcraft debate, forged beyond general historical theory[55] and they are considered at appropriate junctures in this study. However, we need to address several issues dealt with subsequently, in so far as our sources allow – always bearing in mind their regional limitations. For example, Midelfort might have asked whether the 'popular magic' discovered by Thomas and Macfarlane in England was just as prevalent in southwestern Germany – research in France, Switzerland, northern Italy, Denmark, northern Germany and Prussia suggests that it was[56] – and what relationship, if any, it shared with the 'dysfunctional' witch hunts. It is also unclear how circumstances might transform otherwise harmless accusations of superstition or a 'minor' trial for sorcery into a major persecution, or whether the myriad trials in the southwest were somehow all interrelated. Finally, we need more information on the relationship of Protestantism to the rejection of witchcraft persecutions since, at least in Austria and Transylvania, many Protestant preachers actually fuelled a new witch craze. In the Swiss Jura, Monter encountered Protestant authorities more inclined to hunt witches than their Catholic counterparts.[57] Was the rejection of witch hunting really a question of theological doctrine? If not, what factors motivated opponents of persecution to act and how did these differ from those motivating supporters?

---

[53] Midelfort, *Witch Hunting*, 6, 9, 86.

[54] To a certain extent these two studies created the context for the discussion, the absence of which was regretted by Monter, 'Historiography', 446.

[55] H.P. Duerr, *Traumzeit. Über die Grenze zwischen Wildnis und Zivilisation*, Frankfurt am Main, 1978, which uses the demonological literature of the early modern period to broach questions of the theory of knowledge. An extract from the ensuing discussion is offered by H.P. Duerr (ed.), *Der Wissenschaftler und das Irrationale*, I, *Beiträge aus Ethnologie und Anthropologie*, II, *Beiträge aus Philosophie und Psychologie*, Frankfurt am Main 1981.

[56] Muchembled, *Kultur*, 63–108, 232–77; Monter, *Witchcraft in France*, 142–91; Ginzburg, *Die Benandanti*; *idem*, 'Volksbrauch, Magie und Religion', in R. Romano *et al.* (eds.), *Die Gleichzeitigkeit des Ungleichzeitigen. Fünf Studien zur Geschichte Italiens*, 226–304, Frankfurt am Main 1980; K.S. Jensen, 'Zauberei in Dänemark 1500–1588', in Degn *et al.*, *Hexenprozesse*, 150–9; K.-S. Kramer, 'Schaden- und Gegenzauber im Alltagsleben des 16.–18. Jahrhunderts nach archivalischen Quellen aus Holstein', in *ibid.*, 222–40; H. Wunder, 'Hexenprozesse im Herzogtum Preussen während des 16. Jahrhunderts', *ibid.*, 179–204.

[57] Trevor-Roper, 'European Witch Craze', 135; Monter, *Witchcraft in France*, 196.

Midelfort, and especially Macfarlane, might also have considered why the witchcraft issue assumed central importance in the political decision-making process at particular times. Did each of the approximately 350 political units in southwestern Germany decide solely on the basis of their own experience, or was there some overriding regional or supraregional understanding? James I sat on the throne of England for a quarter-century; a vehement apologist for persecution, he authored, as King of Scotland, a work based on Jean Bodin.[58] Did any political struggles for moderation in England occur at that time? And, finally, the question of periodisation remains: in England, southwest Germany, and Bavaria too, the number of trials for witchcraft rose sharply after 1560, peaking around 1600, just as they peaked in other, geographically disparate regions around the mid-1580s. Can Macfarlane reasonably expect us to believe that the transition from feudalism to capitalism entered its decisive phase in all of these places simultaneously: England, Holland, Lorraine, the Basque Provinces, Rhineland, southwest Germany, Pomerania, Hanover, Hesse, the Bishopric of Paderborn, Brunswick-Wolfenbüttel, Electoral Mainz, Electoral Trier, the Spanish Netherlands, Alsace, Westphalia, the Counties of Waldburg, Oettingen-Wallerstein or Löwenstein-Wertheim, the Bishoprics of Augsburg, Freising and Eichstätt, the Duchy of Bavaria, and so on? Subsequent theories will stand or fall on their ability to explain the great wave of persecutions from 1585 to 1595,[59] an initial experience preceding a second major wave of persecutions in many areas, including Bavaria, during the 1620s.

The opposing positions of Macfarlane and Midelfort call for a moment of terminological reflection. Many historians have adopted terminology from the demonologists of the sixteenth and seventeenth centuries, above all from Bodin, Binsfeld and Delrio, who based their accounts on the *Malleus Maleficarum* (1487) of the Dominican Inquisitors Sprenger and Institoris and its confusing implications, whenever they met the needs of the later sixteenth century.[60] This elaborated concept of witchcraft combined perceptions of heresy and sorcery of late Antiquity and the Middle Ages into an exceptional crime, with these essential elements:

---

[58] Baschwitz, *Hexen*, 171–81; Larner, *Enemies*, 31.
[59] The special importance of this wave of witch hunting is already apparent in reading Soldan *et al., Geschichte der Hexenprozesse*, I, 481–532. Cf. also Schormann, *Hexenprozesse*, 55–61; Larner, *Enemies*, 204f.; W. Behringer, 'Hexenverfolgungen im Spiegel zeitgenössischer Publizistik. Die "Erweytterte Unholden Zeyttung" von 1590', *Oberbayerisches Archiv*, 109 (1984), 339–60.
[60] J. Sprenger and H. Institoris, *Der Hexenhammer*, Darmstadt 1974 (ed. J.W.R. Schmidt, Berlin 1906); J. Bodin, *De Daemonomagia*; P. Binsfeld, *Tractat von Bekanntnuss der Zauberer und Hexen ...*, Munich 1591; M. Delrio, *Disquisitionum magicarum libri sex*, Louvain 1599. On the last three works see Lea, *Materials*, 554–646.

1 the Devil's pact (and apostasy)
2 a sexual relationship with the Devil
3 the possibility of aerial flight to
4 the witches' sabbath to worship the Devil
5 maleficent magic

The early modern elaborated concept of witchcraft is essential to any attempt to fathom witch trials, because persecutions – those trials resulting in more than one execution – are only comprehensible in conjunction with the beliefs in witches' flight and witches' sabbaths. On the basis of the belief in a witches' sabbath (Bodin/Fischart: 'parliament of witches') visited by individual witches, torturers extracted the names of alleged accomplices from individual suspects, leading to further arrests and tortures. The elaborated concept of witchcraft, specific to the Western European witch craze of the fifteenth to eighteenth centuries,[61] is an integral historical concept with heuristic value. Schormann is the leading representative of a group of historians who only characterise persons executed for meeting all of these five aforementioned criteria as 'witches'. For that reason, he can maintain a view in keeping with traditional German witchcraft studies, that witchcraft trials were 'criminal proceedings without a crime',[62] an opinion recently coined as the 'classical rationalist paradigm' or the 'Soldan paradigm' by William Monter.[63] Thomasius, Simon and Sterzinger took the same position in the eighteenth century.[64]

If the concept remains disputed among historians and ethnologists, then this is because the term 'witchcraft' is applied differently in different societies, as well as by different social and religious groups. The socio-anthropological debate between Evans-Pritchard, Marwick and Turner[65] has been just as indecisive as one between Macfarlane and Schormann would be. Midelfort indicates that, within the same confession, very different opinions about the essence of witchcraft were held,[66] and Kieckhefer and Monter have demonstrated that peasant perceptions of witchcraft differed greatly from those of learned jurists and theologians.[67] Just like contemporaries, modern researchers are divided on such issues as whether

---

[61] Hansen, *Quellen und Untersuchungen*; Riezler, *Geschichte*, 50f.
[62] Schormann, *Hexenprozesse*, 22ff.   [63] Monter, 'Historiography', 437, 439.
[64] C. Thomasius, *Über die Hexenprozesse*, Weimar 1967 (ed. Rolf Lieberwirth, from C. Thomasius, *De crimine magiae*, Halle 1701). Ardoino Ubbediente Dell'Osa, *Das grosse weltbetrügende Nichts*, Würzburg 1761; F. Sterzinger, *Betrügende Zauberkunst und träumende Hexerei*, Munich 1767.   [65] Macfarlane, *Witchcraft*, 310–12.
[66] Midelfort, *Witch Hunting*, 30–66.
[67] R. Kieckhefer, *European Witch Trials. Their Foundations in Popular and Learned Culture 1300–1500*, London 1976; Monter, *Witchcraft in France*, 142–67; Horsley, 'Who Were the Witches?', criticised Kieckhefer's restriction of the distinction to a purely descriptive level. Muchembled, *Kultur*, on the other hand makes clear the sociological basis of the cultural dichotomy.

witchcraft was a personal quality, whether it worked through external means, whether it could be inherited, whether the witch's power was her own or was sanctioned by some higher authority (a demon), whether the witch engaged in an explicit pact with the Devil, and whether sorcery and a pact with the Devil were essential to the crime of witchcraft. Complete disagreement exists regarding the separate components of the elaborated crime of witchcraft and the characteristic attributes of witchcraft, such as flight, intercourse with the Devil, witches' sabbaths, transmutation into animal form (e.g. lycanthropy), milk theft, weather magic and causing insect plagues. Did all these things really happen, were they mere delusions or simply diabolically induced hallucinations? In the seventeen tracts by authors of four different confessions (Catholics, Lutherans, Calvinists and Zwinglians) contained in the comprehensive *Theatrum de Veneficiis* of 1586, each author held a different opinion.[68]

Practically speaking, it is impossible to work solely with the elaborated concept of witchcraft, since it excludes many types of magic not contained in the five-point list. A glance at trial records reveals that the boundaries between superstition, sorcery, bewitchment and witchcraft were exceedingly fluid. Depending on the location, superstitious activities or the practice of white magic could be regarded either as harmless or as evidence of the exceptional crime of witchcraft. Even in the same area, the juridical treatment of popular magic varied greatly from year to year, as will be shown for Munich. The decision to let a person off with a light penalty or to burn them as a witch was only reached during the trial itself, and the criteria for the use of torture played the decisive role. The sooner, more severe and more frequent the torture, the more likely it was for initially harmless accusations for superstition or even for common offences (such as theft, vagrancy or poaching) to be transformed suddenly into witchcraft trials.[69] However, if harsh torture was only applied reluctantly, an unequivocal trial for witchcraft could still end in acquittal. Even Otto Brunner's insistence on contemporary usage of terminology presents difficulties, when contemporaries call weather-conjurers 'witches', whether they copulated with the Devil and flew to witches' sabbaths or not, and described others who admitted all five points as 'sorcerers'. Supporters of persecutions tendentiously described anyone wearing an amulet as a 'witch', while opponents hesitated to apply the term even after the suspects referred to themselves as such, with or without torture.

[68] Cf. note 2.
[69] Example of a trial for theft which expanded into a trial for witchcraft: M. Kunze, *Der Prozess Pappenheimer*, Ebelsbach 1981; examples of trials for vagrancy in H. Nagl, 'Der Zauberer-Jackl Prozess. Hexenprozesse im Erzstift Salzburg (1675–1690)', *Mitteilungen der Gesellschaft für Salzburger Landeskunde*, 112/113 (1972–3), 385–541; 114 (1974), 79–243.

In order to ensure quantitatively compatible results, superstition, sorcery and witchcraft are handled comprehensively in this study. Today, just as before, the components of the witchcraft concept are controversial, because the concept itself is controversial. Since this problem cannot be manipulated away, it is only possible to contain misunderstandings through a precise definition of terminology. Therefore, the term 'witch' will be applied hereafter without quotation marks to refer to anyone appearing in the sources directly as a *Hexe, Unhold, Trud, lamia, striga, Bocks-* or *Gabelreiterin*, including male 'witches' (*Hexer* or *Hexenmänner*), or persons accussed of crimes indicating such activities. A 'witch trial' here – as opposed to in general usage – describes any court proceedings on charges of witchcraft, regardless of whether they ended in acquittal or execution. A 'trial for magic' describes proceedings against magical manipulations when the primary charge was neither witchcraft nor superstition, since trials for magic commonly ended in a light penalty for superstition, if the magic was considered as harmless.[70] Trials for witchcraft and magic often differed little from each other, especially if the accusation intoned a 'maleficium'; then the trial was conducted with the same severity as for a minor witchcraft offence. These two are most distinct from 'witchcraft persecutions' during which initial suspicion rapidly spread to encompass many persons. Midelfort defined persecutions with twenty or more executions within one year as 'large witch hunts'. In addition, Midelfort differentiated between these and small persecutions, 'small panic trials' as Monter calls them. These witchcraft trials resulted in several individual executions but fewer than twenty, although they included a wider circle of suspects. In this study, trials for witchcraft or magic with no more than three executions are distinguished from persecutions. The major witchcraft persecutions resulted in the execution of more than nineteen persons for witchcraft in one location; these are distinguished from two categories of lesser witch hunts which claimed four to nine, or ten to nineteen victims, respectively, within a short time span.[71] No persecution ever claimed more than 100 victims in our region, unlike neighbouring territories where up to 900 persons might be burned as witches in a single place, as a geographic overview would show.[72] Persons who actively campaigned for the systematic persecution of witches or, with this goal in mind, attempted to intervene in actual cases are termed 'supporters of persecutions'. Persons who took an active stance against persecutions or sought to implement moderation in trial proceed-

---

[70] The actual historical source material simply imposes limits on the conceptual clarity demanded by Horsley, 'Who Were the Witches?', 694, and others.

[71] Midelfort, *Witch Hunting*, 9; Monter, *Witchcraft in France*, 88. The adoption of this classification, which is justified by the facts, ought to make the results more easily comparable.   [72] Cf. Maps 1, 2 and 3.

ings are termed 'opponents of persecution', even if they never actually doubted the existence of witches in principle.

Were there really witches or not?[73] The answer to this question transcends the above definition, which is methodologically oriented from the standpoint of criminal investigators and therefore reflects the views of others. Certainly, there were no witches of the type defined by the elaborated concept of witchcraft, but there were persons who actually believed themselves to be witches.[74] In the early modern world, so alien to us, there were people who thought they could fly or contact angels, devils, benevolent spirits, God, Mary, the saints, wandering souls, and ghosts. Some of them were canonised or beatified (e.g. Theresa of Avila) while others were burned as witches, since many popular beliefs were subsumed under the new concept of witchcraft. And, not least of all, there really were those who attempted maleficent, 'black' magic within the bounds of 'popular magic'; Macfarlane calls them black witches. These malevolent dabblers in magic were not witches in the sense of the elaborated concept of witchcraft. It is questionable indeed, whether these magicians actually counted among the victims of witchcraft persecutions at all.[75]

INVESTIGATING WITCH TRIALS AND LEARNED DISCOURSE IN SOUTHEASTERN GERMANY

Finally Bavaria – what hasn't been said about this land in connection with witch trials!
                                                    (G. Schormann, 1981).[76]

The following regional study focuses on an area roughly corresponding to the modern state of Bavaria in southern Germany, specifically the districts of Upper and Lower Bavaria and Swabia – southeast Germany – bounded by the Alps to the south, the highlands to the east and north, and the river Iller to the west. The Austrian Alpine territories and Bohemia formed a large chunk of Habsburg territory to the south and east, alongside the independent bishoprics of Salzburg and Passau. Political fragmentation ruled to the west and north: in modern Baden-Württemberg (southwestern Germany) and Franconia there coexisted hundreds of princes, counts, abbots, free-imperial cities, free-imperial knights, and even free-imperial

---

[73] Monter, *Witchcraft in France* went into the relationship between interpretative approach and the answer to this question. On misunderstandings of the interpretation of Ginzburg's 'Benandanti', (*Die Benandanti*), 7f. (Foreword to the 1980 edn).   [74] Cf. chapter 3.
[75] The basic work on this is Mauss, *Soziologie*, I, 154–72. The witch trials of the early modern period cannot be understood unless we take into account the outlook of contemporaries, who in all layers of the population accepted the reality and permanent possibility of supernatural phenomena.   [76] Schormann *Hexenprozesse* (1981), 66.

villages. This region was heterogeneous, to say the least, in its political, confessional and economic composition.[77]

The boundaries of opposing political and confessional macrostructures cut clear across the region and the microscope of regional analysis magnifies supraregional structural contrasts. Three-fourths of the region belonged to the Duchy of Bavaria, a compact, well-organised, early absolutist state, where confessional and political opposition led by the estates (the so-called Bavarian Fronde) had already been crushed by the Catholic dukes in the mid-sixteenth century. Bavaria was primarily agricultural and, in its few large cities, merchant burghers lived alongside political, military, judicial and court administrators. The 'central state' (elevated from a Duchy to an Electorate in 1623) was governed from the dynastic residence in Munich. Provincial administrations (*Regierungen* or *Rentämter*) at Landshut, Straubing and Burghausen and, later, at Amberg comprised intermediary authorities directly subordinate to Munich, while the province of Upper Bavaria was administered directly from the capital, providing a laboratory of sorts for experiments in centralised absolutist rule. The latter province contained the only other large urban centre, Ingolstadt, with its fortifications, the territorial university and a Jesuit college. In addition to its own civic magistracy, a stadtholder and several military councillors administered the fortifications. The University of Ingolstadt was, apart from Freiburg, the only major Catholic university in southern Germany. The Wittelsbach dukes Albrecht V (1550–79), Wilhelm V (1579–97) and Maximilian I (1597–1651) transformed Bavaria into a political powerhouse and, despite minimal resources, intervened successfully in the European political arena on several occasions. They built Bavaria into the bulwark of the German Counter-Reformation, prevailing in the struggle for Cologne and ultimately founding the Catholic League. Wittelsbach power-politics included military interventions against Kaufbeuren and Salzburg, the temporary occupation of the Rhineland Palatinate and Upper Austria, the annexation of the Upper Palatinate and Donauwörth, and ecclesiastical secundogenitures in the north German bishoprics of Cologne, Münster, Paderborn, Hildesheim and Osnabrück (as well as Liège), all culminating in the acquisition of the electoral title in 1623. With Spanish, Papal and, to a lesser degree, Habsburg support, the Bavarian dukes/electors engaged in international affairs assisted by their Jesuit allies, who consequently relocated the headquarters of the Order's Upper German Province there, establishing a novitiate in Landsberg and

[77] M. Spindler (ed.), *Bayerischer Geschichtsatlas*, Munich 1969; W. Zorn (ed.), *Historischer Atlas von Bayerisch-Schwaben*, Augsburg 1955; M. Spindler (ed.), *Handbuch der bayerischen Geschichte*, II, *Das alte Bayern*, 20th edn Munich 1977; III, *Franken, Schwaben, Oberpfalz*, 2nd edn Munich 1979.

colleges in Munich, Ingolstadt and Altötting (until 1592). Bavaria 'naturally' represented the dominant power in the region examined.[78]

Apart from the bishoprics of Freising and Regensburg, episcopal principalities surrounded by Bavarian territory, the rest of the region under examination lay in eastern Swabia (the modern District of Swabia in Bavaria west of the Lech and northwest of the Danube).[79] Like neighbouring southwest Germany and the Franconian territories, this part of the Empire was politically, confessionally, socially and economically heterogeneous in the extreme. Concentrated in this small area were cosmopolitan Augsburg, home to early capitalist entrepreneurs (e.g. the Fuggers), and the Upper Swabian 'proto-industry' in textiles for export, not to mention more traditional handicrafts. Transshipment from Italy traversed routes studded with traditional peasant villages and more remote communities in the mountains and moorlands. In some political entities – such as the Habsburg Margraviate of Burgau – attempts at state formation failed, leaving behind an area described as a 'complicated conglomerate of possessions'.[80] A tangential location and political fragmentation allowed some subjects to enjoy greater political freedoms than they might have elsewhere. In some places there were 'free' peasants and in others subjects banded together against their rulers, as in the *Tigen* cooperative society of the Allgäu. Extreme heterogeneity also made Swabia an inviting refuge for persecuted groups, among them Anabaptists, Gypsies and Jews.

The largest territorial entity in eastern Swabia was the Bishopric of Augsburg. Ruled from Dillingen, it stretched along the river Lech from the Danube to the Alps. At the end of the sixteenth century, the episcopal government established effective supervision over all twelve districts (*Pflegämter*).[81] Other sizeable territorial complexes included the Prince-Abbacy of Kempten and the County of Rothenfels in the south, the Neuburg Palatinate on the Danube and the County of Oettingen in Ries to

---

[78] On the political development, Spindler, *Handbuch*, II, 297–346 (H. Lutz) and 351–405 (D. Albrecht). On the social development 559–90 (D. Albrecht). On the economic development 657–72 (A. Sandberger) and 673–720 (E. Schremmer). On the religious-ecclesiastical development 626–57 (D. Albrecht).

[79] Spindler, *Handbuch*, III/2, 1393–423 (H. Raab).

[80] *Ibid.*, 980–5 (A. Layer). On the economic and social structure, *ibid.*, 1067–121 (A. Layer and E. Schremmer); and W. Zorn, *Augsburg. Geschichte einer deutschen Stadt*, Augsburg 1972 ; and *idem, Handels- und Industriegeschichte Bayerisch-Schwabens 1648–1870*, Augsburg 1961.

[81] Spindler, *Handbuch*, III/2, 949–62 (A. Layer); A. von Steichele and A. Schröder, *Das Bistum Augsburg, historisch und statistisch beschrieben*, 10 vols., Augsburg 1861–1940; A. Wolff, *Gerichtsverfassung und Prozess im Hochstift Augsburg in der Rezeptionszeit*, Dillingen 1913; F. Zoepfl, *Das Bistum Augsburg und seine Bischöfe im Reformationsjahrhundert*, Munich/Augsburg 1969. The individual courts and guardianships are briefly described in Spindler, *Handbuch*, III/2, 952–5 (A. Layer).

the north.[82] Other significant holdings included those of the Fugger Counts, and the County of Rechberg, Habsburg possessions, the monasteries of Ottobeuren, Irsee, Roggenburg, Ursberg, Wettenhausen and Elchingen[83] and several important free-imperial cities: Augsburg, Donauwörth (annexed by Bavaria in 1608), Kaufbeuren, Lindau, Memmingen and Nördlingen.[84]

These seven cities embodied the extreme contrasts typical of the region at the end of the sixteenth century. Augsburg, with a population of roughly 50,000 before the Thirty Years War, was the largest city in southern Germany, a 'European trading and cultural centre of premier rank' (Layer) with nearly twice as many inhabitants as the other six cities combined. Augsburg prospered until the war, while Memmingen and Nördlingen, Lindau and Donauwörth had already passed their prime a century before, stagnating after the Peasants' War and the Schmalkaldic War. Kaufbeuren and Kempten suffered catastrophic collapses at the end of the sixteenth century, losing traditional markets for their exports.[85] Augsburg, Kaufbeuren and Donauwörth were bi-confessional cities, while Memmingen, Nördlingen, Lindau and Kempten were Protestant. Augsburg had a Catholic majority in its council, the other civic councils had a Protestant one. This kind of heterogeneity was replicated in the patchwork Swabian territories: the County of Oettingen was split into a Lutheran portion, Oettingen-Oettingen, and Catholic Oettingen-Wallerstein. The Bavarian branch of the Wittelsbachs were Catholics, the Pfalz-Neuburg branch Lutherans, and the Electoral Upper-Palatine branch Calvinists. Swabia was predominantly Catholic, a result of its proximity to Bavaria, the physical expanse of the Bishopric of Augsburg and the presence of many smaller ecclesiastical territories, but there were numerous Lutheran and some Calvinist territories. In the early seventeenth century there were

---

[82] Spindler, *Handbuch*, III/2, 963–8, Prince-Abbacy of Kempten (A. Layer); J. Rottenkolber, 'Geschichte des hochfürstlichen Stifts Kempten', *Allgäuer Geschichtsfreund*, new series, 34 (1932), 5–128; new series, 35 (1933), 129–283. On the County of Oettingen Spindler, *Handbuch*, III/2, 991–4 (A. Layer); on Pfalz-Neuburg, *ibid.*, 1335–53 (W. Volkert).

[83] On Fugger and other noble lordships *ibid.*, 994–1029 (A. Layer). On the imperial ecclesiastical territories *ibid.*, 968–77 (A. Layer).

[84] On the Free-Imperial Cities *ibid.*, 1030–43 (A. Layer) with references to further literature.

[85] *Ibid.* On Nördlingen see C. Friedrichs, *Urban Society in an Age of War: Nördlingen 1580–1720*, Princeton 1979. On the catastrophic situation of Kaufbeuren, whose population was already in decline in the 1580s, S. Alt, *Reformation und Gegenreformation in der freien Reichsstadt Kaufbeuren*, Munich 1932, 101–4; and F. Junginger, *Geschichte der Reichsstadt Kaufbeuren im 17. und 18. Jahrhundert*, Neustadt/Aisch 1965, 14. On the Free City of Kempten cf. the chronicle UBM 2 Cod. Ms. 500, fol. 42, 45. For the debate on the economic situation of Germany before the Thirty Years War, see most recently H. Haan, 'Prosperität und Dreissigjähriger Krieg', *Geschichte und Gesellschaft*, 7 (1981), 91–118.

still communities of Schwenkfeldians and Anabaptists; Gypsies, Paracelsians, alchemists and practitioners of 'black arts' roamed the countryside.[86] This region, with an area of just under 38,000 square kilometres – 10,000 in Swabia, the rest in Bavaria and its enclaves – is geographically equivalent to Midelfort's 'southwestern Germany'.[87] In 1600, the Duchy of Bavaria had some 900,000 inhabitants, slightly more than 20,000 of whom resided in Munich, the Duchy's capital and largest city. In Swabia, population density has to be regressively approximated. In 1800, the Bishopric of Augsburg had some 100,000 inhabitants, slightly more than it did just prior to the Thirty Years War, the County of Oettingen had about 60,000, and the Prince-Abbacy of Kempten about 40,000.[88] The Swabian metropolis Augsburg had regained its pre-war population of 50,000. Protestant Memmingen (6,000 inhabitants) was as large as Landshut and Ingolstadt.[89] Sixteenth-century Swabia, above all the Allgäu, was regarded as chronically overpopulated, a plausible assumption verified by reports of migration to Austria and southwestern Germany.[90] Even so, the total population of southeast Germany could hardly have been more than 1.4 million, and was probably less. It had risen steadily since the late fifteenth century, peaking prior to the Thirty Years War, sinking by about one-half by the mid-seventeenth century, only to regain its earlier level in the course of the eighteenth century.[91]

Recent studies examine the history of witch trials in three of the four neighbouring regions (excluding Bohemia), leaving out southeast Ger-

---

[86] On the confessional relationships in the Free Cities see P. Warmbrunn, *Zwei Konfessionen in einer Stadt. Das Zusammenleben von Katholiken und Protestanten in den paritätischen Reichsstädten Augsburg, Biberach, Ravensburg und Dinkelsbühl von 1548 bis 1648*, Wiesbaden 1983. For confessional relationships in the smaller territories see Spindler, *Handbuch*, III/2, 918–31, 949–1043, 1059–67 (A. Layer). Wandering black magicians were often arrested, e.g. in Memmingen 1566: StadtA Memmingen, Schubl. 344, no. 9. The case is also mentioned in C. Schorer, *Memminger Chronik*, Memmingen 1660, 96.

[87] K. Bosl, 'Die historisch-politische Entwicklung des bayerischen Staates', in *idem* (ed.), *Bayern, Handbuch der historischen Stätten Deutschlands*, VII, 3rd edn, Stuttgart 1981, XV.

[88] Spindler, *Handbuch*, II, 560 (D. Albrecht); Spindler, III/2, 961, 993 (A. Layer).

[89] *Ibid.*, III/2, 1105, 1043, 1038 (A. Layer). *Ibid.*, II, 569. Also the relevant articles in Bosl, Bayern and in E. Keyser and H. Stoob (eds.), *Bayerisches Städtebuch*, 2 vols., Stuttgart 1971. Historical demography has so far yielded few results for Bavaria in the sixteenth century. The field is dominated by older studies such as K. Kisskalt, 'Epidemiologisch-statistische Untersuchungen über die Sterblichkeit von 1600–1800', *Archiv für Hygiene und Bakteriologie*, 137 (1953), 26–42; and F. Schmölz and T. Schmölz, 'Die Sterblichkeit in Landsberg/Lech von 1585–1785', *Archiv für Hygiene und Bakteriologie.*, 136 (1952), 504–40; J. Scheidl, 'Die Bevölkerungsentwicklung des altbayerischen Landgerichts Dachau im Laufe früherer Jahrhunderte. Ein kritischer Versuch', *ZBLG*, 3 (1930), 357–86; J. Jahn, 'Augsburgs Einwohnerzahl im 16. Jahrhundert – ein statistischer Versuch', *ZBLG*, 39 (1976), 379–96. [90] Spindler, *Handbuch*, III/2, 1043–54 (A. Layer).

[91] *Ibid.*, II, 409 (D. Albrecht), 693 (E. Schremmer); *ibid.*, III/2, 933f. (A. Layer).

many.[92] Research on Franconian witch trials leaves much to be desired. Merzbacher's summaries[93] fail to consider territorial fragmentation or the peculiar historical development of Franconia, and only offer a generalised portrayal, unsuitable for comparative purposes. Therefore, manifold connections between southeast Germany (Bavaria/Swabia) and Franconia[94] have been dealt with here in periodic digressions.

The existing literature on the history of Swabian witchcraft trials offers little insight.[95] Of course, scattered essays and articles examine individual trials, a favourite theme of local antiquarians, but they cling to the paradigm of nineteenth-century German research. Trials are cited as examples of darker days and the reader is reassured that, at least in their own home town, the execution of a witch was exceptional. These interpretations only leave us guessing about their foundation in actual research as specific information on sources or methodology is usually absent. Local historians appear to have confronted witch trials with one rule of thumb: no local history without a witch trial. Still, this practice was advantageous for the present study and we do have some very valuable investigations of trials for the episcopal residence at Dillingen, the town of Lauingen in Pfalz-Neuburg, as well as the free-imperial city of Nördlingen.[96]

No one has, as yet, examined the situation in minor territories. This appears impossible for noble domains, counties, and even some imperial abbeys, owing to a lack of sources.[97] Documentation from neighbouring

[92] Midelfort, *Witch Hunting*; Merzbacher, *Die Hexenprozesse*; Byloff, *Hexenglaube*; Nagl 'Der Zauberer-Jackl Prozess'. For Bohemia the old work of J. Svátek, 'Hexenprozesse in Böhmen', in *idem, Culturhistorische Blätter aus Böhmen*, Vienna 1879, 3–40, has not yet been superseded.

[93] Merzbacher, *Die Hexenprozesse*, follows a legal-historical approach, which is hardly concerned with the territorial multiplicity of Franconia and not at all with historical development; he was chiefly interested in the problems of legal procedure. As the procedure was essentially the same in all the territories, Merzbacher came to the erroneous conclusion that this was also the case in the conduct of the trials, *ibid.*, 2. F. Merzbacher's essay on the witch trials in the Bishopric of Würzburg ('Geschichte der Hexenprozesse im Hochstift Würzburg', 1950) is less satisfying in this respect than the older work of Wittmann on the Bishopric of Bamberg ('Die Bamberger Hexenjustiz', 1883).

[94] The main interest here is in the interplay of the intransigent Catholic party, which culminated in the early seventeenth century in the formation of the Catholic League. But of course the Free Cities were in contact with one another also.

[95] Schormann, *Hexenprozesse*, 70.

[96] F. Zoepfl, 'Hexenwahn und Hexenverfolgungen in Dillingen', *ZBLG*, 27 (1964), 235–45; G. Ruluckert, 'Der Hexenwahn, ein Kulturbild aus Lauingens Vergangenheit', *Alt-Lauingen. Organ des Altertums-Vereins*, 2 (1907), 25–77 (in parts); G. Wulz, 'Nördlinger Hexenprozesse', *Rieser Heimatverein (Jahrbuch)*, 20 (1937), 42–72; 21 (1938), 95–121.

[97] According to information from the noble archives approached, they possess no records of witch trials (see Literature and Sources for a list of the archives written to). The class 'Mediatisierte Fürsten' in the HStAM contains only the witch records of the Fugger Lordship of Wasserburg/Bodensee, which were used by M. Wiedmann, 'Hexenprozesse' (1929). Witch trials in the noble territories (e.g. Kellmünz 1590, Erolzheim 1590, Osterzell 1590 etc.) are usually only recorded in sources from neighbouring Free Cities or territories.

cities or larger territories sometimes refers to trials in these areas, as we shall demonstrate. On the other hand, the situation in the imperial cities, the Allgäu and larger territories is much different. Here the superabundance of sources, rather than their absence has hindered research. Case files are often missing, but protocols of civic and court councils, and sometimes those of the judiciary,[98] lists of executions, chronicles, diaries, sermons all provide qualitative and quantitative information. The general absence of historical, socio-historical, biographical and prosopographical studies, indispensable to the reconstruction of trials in context, hinders research here far more than any lack of witchcraft studies.[99]

The condition of Bavarian witchcraft studies is decidedly better and the general historical literature operates on a qualitatively higher level.[100] Sigmund Riezler's *History of Witchtrials in Bavaria* has been available since 1896, a prototypical work in its time, indeed even until the aforementioned paradigm shift.[101] For that reason, the general literature has recognised the importance of witchcraft persecutions in Bavaria time and again, depicting Counter-Reformation Bavaria as a heartland of persecutions and its Dukes as 'the most tireless witch hunters of all the German princes' (Baschwitz). Trevor-Roper reduced this standard cliché to its lowest denominator:

[98] Minutes of the councils of the Free Cities are as a rule fairly continuously preserved from the sixteenth century. The relevant series of minutes begins for most of the territories at some time during the sixteenth century (e.g. Bishopric of Passau, Prince-Abbacy of Kempten, Bishopric of Augsburg, Duchy of Bavaria). In a few cases (e.g. Bishopric of Freising) there are no minutes of the Court Council, but in general these sources make it possible to reach more precise conclusions about criminality. This is very laborious and only sample soundings could be undertaken in this study.

[99] On these difficulties see also Spindler, *Handbuch*, III/2, 803 (A. Layer). The corresponding sections in III/2 on agriculture and trade, *ibid.*, 1067–120 (A. Layer, E. Schremmer), have many gaps. The *Lebensbilder aus dem bayerischen Schwaben* edited by G. von Pölnitz, and from vol. IX by W. Zorn, Munich 1952ff., only illuminate individual biographies. M. Henker, 'Zur Prosopographie der pfalz-neuburgischen Zentralbehörden im 17. Jahrhundert', PhD thesis, Munich 1984, on the other hand, sheds more light on political events, including the Neuburg witch hunts around 1629.

[100] Not only in quantity, but also in quality, because of the many years of concentration on the old state of Bavaria, research there is on a quite different level. We need mention only S. Riezler, *Geschichte Bayerns*, 8 vols., Gotha 1878–1914; such meticulous basic works as R. Heydenreuter, *Der landesherrliche Hofrat unter Maximilian I. (1598–1651)*, Munich 1981, have laid an excellent foundation for further research. K. Bosl (ed.), *Bosls bayerische Biographie; 8000 Persönlichkeiten aus 15 Jahrhunderten*, Regensburg 1983, is chiefly of use for the old Duchy/Electorate of Bavaria. For a general guide to the literature see Spindler, II.

[101] S. Riezler, *Geschichte der Hexenprozesse in Bayern. Im Lichte der allgemeinen Entwickelung dargestellt*, Stuttgart 1896. The edition of 1896 is definitely to be preferred, as the reprint of 1968 (Magnus-Verlag) contains numerous misprints which distort the sense (130, Herz for Herr; 178 n.2, Bader for Baader, indexed as Baden!, 239 Dettingen for Oettingen; 353, 1655 for 1665 etc.) as well as a very inaccurate map and an afterword by F. Merzbacher, *ibid.*, 341–57, which in no way represents the position of regional, much less international, witchcraft research.

It was the Catholic reconquest which brought the witch-craze in a terrible form to Bavaria, where dukes William V and Maximilian I, great patrons of the Jesuits, kept the witch-fires burning.[102]

The obvious implication of this passage, approvingly cited in a reader as late as 1977,[103] is that the pyres in Bavaria burned permanently for at least seventy years; in a territory as large as the Duchy of Bavaria, this should have resulted in thousands of executions. The connection to the Counter-Reformation had long been self-evident to most authors, even if no one ever actually demonstrated just what this connection was. Midelfort's research implied a special connection between Catholic confessionalisation and an intransigent stance toward witchcraft persecutions.[104] However, other recent studies suggest just the opposite; Monter demonstrated that Protestants in the French-Swiss Jura region persecuted witches more severely than their Catholic neighbours.[105]

In the case of the Duchy of Bavaria, one has to admit that Riezler went to great lengths to establish the confessional connection between Catholic reform and witchcraft persecutions. Leading Jesuits in the Duchy (e.g. Canisius, Gregor von Valentia, Jacob Gretser, Jeremias Drexel or Adam Contzen) were intransigent supporters of persecution. Furthermore, Bavarian Counter-Reformation policy favoured close contact with foreign Jesuits who wrote on the subject, including Binsfeld in Trier, Förner in Bamberg or Delrio in Graz,[106] as well as the Franconian 'witch bishops', whose persecutions in the bishoprics of Eichstätt, Würzburg and Bamberg were among the worst excesses of European history.[107] Riezler also

---

[102] Trevor-Roper, 'European Witch Craze', 136; Baschwitz, *Hexen*, 288. The summary of Riezler's findings in Lea, *Materials*, III, 1119–35, contains numerous errors. These errors are multiplied intolerably in the influential compilation of R.H. Robbins, *The Encyclopedia of Witchcraft and Demonology*, London 1959, 42–4. Many old errors have been perpetuated in H.-J. Wolf, *Hexenwahn und Exorzismus. Ein Beitrag zur Kulturgeschichte*, Kriftel/Taunus, 1980.

[103] H. Brackert, '"Unglückliche, was hast du gehofft?" Zu den Hexenbüchern des 15. bis 17. Jahrhunderts', in G. Becker, S. Bovenschen and H. Brackert, *Aus der Zeit der Verzweiflung. Zur Genese und Aktualität des Hexenbildes*, Frankfurt am Main, 1977, 131–88, quotation from 180. When prejudices are so firmly rooted, even literature with scholarly pretensions does not escape the adoption of false points of view, as shown, for example, by Larner, *Enemies*, 18.

[104] Cf. note 53.

[105] Cf. note 57.

[106] Riezler, *Geschichte*, 170, 213; L. Bauer, 'Die Bamberger Weihbischöfe Johann Schöner und Friedrich Förner. Beiträge zur Gegenreformation in Bamberg', *Berichte für die Pflege der Geschichte des ehemaligen Fürstbistums Bamberg*, 101 (1965), 305–530, esp. 397–416 *passim*, 457–9 *passim*.

[107] On the status of the Franconian 'witch bishops' Schormann *Hexenprozesse* (1981), 67. On the close political collaboration between Bavaria and the bishops, Spindler, *Handbuch*, II, 359f., 373–8 (D. Albrecht); III/1, 219–25, 427–36 (R. Endres).

correctly noted that Bavarian witchcraft legislation was unusually severe and extensive, with about one dozen legal briefs, mandates, general orders and procedural instructions composed in unhesitating verbal radicalism with a charm all its own.[108] He also pointed out that, at times, the dukes felt personally threatened by bewitchment.[109] Under these circumstances, one has to admit that Bavaria was a likely candidate for a leading role in the tragedy of witchcraft trials. After Riezler, no one bothered to approach the subject with different expectations.

And yet, one searches in vain for concrete confirmation of unusually virulent witchcraft persecutions in Bavaria, either in the general literature or in Riezler's own work. Those few executions he cites are more indicative of a minor territory, but, as Schormann correctly observed, they hardly evidence severe persecutions in a territory with four (five after 1623) provincial administrations, more than a hundred districts courts and a population of nearly a million.[110] As he himself conceded, more than 80 per cent of Riezler's examples, both chronological and individual, did not originate from the Duchy of Bavaria at all, but instead from neighbouring Swabia, Franconia, and even as far afield as southwestern Germany, Alsace, Switzerland, Italy, Austria and Bohemia. Riezler, an excellent scholar of German and Bavarian history,[111] blamed his lack of regional evidence on missing sources, although he never attempted to fill in the gaps by investigating serial records. At one point, he did comment on a fact overlooked by his critics: he suggested that the witchcraft persecutions in Schongau and Wemding were the most virulent in Bavarian history, because they were mentioned with such frequency in comparison to others.[112] Otherwise, Riezler only admitted an implicit contradiction between his expectations and his findings, sparing himself the effort of explaining those discrepancies.

Even though a number of individual studies have added pieces to the witchcraft puzzle since Riezler's time, these scattered articles, essays and

[108] Riezler, *Geschichte*, 187, 208–19, 272–5. Riezler's data are as a rule correct, but not always his interpretation (cf. chapter 4). Riezler overlooked the instruction on procedure in trials for witchcraft of 1590 (he knew only the copy of 1622) and the general mandates against witchcraft and superstition of 1629 and 1677. The mandate against superstition and witchcraft issued in 1612 was dated by Riezler to 1611, as the printed copy bears this date. Riezler was not clear about the context of the discussion from which the mass of opinions, mandates, general instructions and orders emerged.

[109] Riezler, *Geschichte*, 196. Also instructive are the biographical references to extreme fear of demons among the apologists for persecution Canisius, Gretser and Förner. G. Freiherr von Pölnitz, 'Petrus Canisius und das Bistum Augsburg', *ZBLG*, 18 (1955), 352–94; H. König, 'Jakob Gretser SJ (1562–1625). Ein Charakterbild,' *Freiburger Diözesanarchiv*, 77 (1957), 136–70; Bauer, 'Die Bamberger Weihbischöfe', 455.

[110] Schormann, *Hexenprozesse* (1981), 66.   [111] Cf. note 5.

[112] Riezler, *Geschichte*, 241f.

university dissertations have never been examined collectively.[113] Besides accounts of individual trials, there are studies of legal briefs from the University of Ingolstadt and the opinions of Jesuits toward trials in Bavaria that locate the theme of witchcraft in a broader perspective.[114] In addition to the studies of local historians and others by the so-called 'Munich school' of anthropology, one legal dissertation has also evaluated serial records: Leutenbauer systematically investigated the protocols of the administrator (*Rentmeister* or *Vize Dominus*) of the provincial government in Burghausen before 1550 in search of witchcraft and sorcery trials.[115] Others have worked with judicial receipts for the districts of Burghausen, Aibling, Auerberg, Wolfratshausen, Landsberg, Markt-Schwaben, Rosenheim, Friedberg, Traunstein and Reichenhall in Upper Bavaria and Straubing, Dingolfing, Bärnstein, Dissenstein, Hengersberg, Landshut, Griesbach, Regen and Kötzting in Lower Bavaria,[116] as well as trial

[113] The scattered references to the 'witch craze', witch trials and witch hunts in Spindler, *Handbuch*, II, 353 note 2, 616, 792 and 804f., Spindler, *Handbuch*, III/1, 360, 436, 630, 658; and *ibid.*, III/2, 1059 and 1134, do not do justice to the phenomenon. Cf. note 101. The titles of the numerous minor essays on the theme of witchcraft since Riezler's day cannot be listed here. They are documented in the bibliography and are included in their chronological context in the list of trials in the original German edition of this book: W. Behringer, *Hexenverfolgung in Bayern. Volksmagie, Glaubenseifer und Staatsräson in der frühen Neuzeit*, Munich 1987, 431–69.

[114] J. Schrittenloher, 'Aus der Gutachter- und Urteiltätigkeit der Ingolstadter Juristenfakultät im Zeitalter der Hexenverfolgungen', *Jahrbuch für fränkische Landesforschung*, 23 (1963), 315–53; B. Duhr, *Die Stellung der Jesuiten in den deutschen Hexenprozessen*, Cologne 1900; *idem*, 'Zur Geschichte des Jesuitenordens. Aus Münchner Archiven und Bibliotheken', *Historisches Jahrbuch der Görres-Gesellschaft*, 25 (1904), 126–67; 28 (1907), 61–83, 306–27; *idem*, *Geschichte der Jesuiten*.

[115] S. Leutenbauer, *Hexerei- und Zauberdelikt in der Literatur von 1450 bis 1550. Mit Hinweisen auf die Praxis im Herzogtum Bayern*, Berlin 1972.

[116] F. Markmiller, 'Verhandlungen über Hexen- und Zauberwesen im Pfleggericht Dingolfing. Nach Unterlagen des 15.-18. Jahrhunderts', *Der Storchenturm*, Heft 9 (1970), 67–71; U. Schmid, 'Von Zauberern und Hexen in Burghausen', *Heimatland. Blätter für Heimatfreunde in Schule und Familie*, 5 (1954), 42–4; A. Huber, *Hexenwahn und Hexenprozesse in Straubing und Umgebung*, Straubing 1975; H. Wagner, 'Aberglaube und Hexenprozesse im Bezirk Grafenau im 17. und 18. Jahrhundert', *Passauer Jahrbuch. Ostbaierische Grenzmarken*, 1 (1957), 91–5. Also interesting is the folkloristic study of F.S. Hartmann, 'Über schwarze und weisse Kunst in den Bezirken Dachau und Bruck', *Oberbayer. Archiv*, 41 (1881), 119–52. The Munich school of folklorists in the context of a study of customs, during the 1950s and 1960s court books and court accounts of Bavarian county courts were evaluated by H. Moser and K.-S. Kramer. The unpublished findings were entered in a card-index of customs, now kept in the Munich Institute of Ethnology (Bavarian Academy of Sciences). The data derived from this card-index are included in the chronological list of trials in the original German edition of this book under the reference IV-BK, since in some places the archive references were not given or have since been changed. Individual data can be verified in the court accounts of the relevant courts in StAM and StAL. (I am grateful to Prof. K.-S. Kramer, Kiel, for drawing my attention to the existence of this card-index.) H. Moser, *Chronik von Kiefersfeldern*, Rosenheim 1959; J. Brunnhuber, *Chronik des oberen Leizachtales*, Fischbachau 1928; R. Ettelt, *Geschichte der Stadt Kelheim*, Kelheim 1983; I.J. Hibler, *Geschichte des oberen Loisach-*

depositions (*Urgichten*), punitive oaths (*Urpheden*) and executioners' records.[117] Many of these efforts went unpublished, because the results did not appear spectacular: they often referred to trials which led neither to persecutions nor even to individual executions. Every analysis of serial documents disappointed those longing to believe that cherished legend of Bavaria as the heartland of witchcraft persecutions, as first depicted by Riezler and copied by subsequent authors – Baschwitz, Trevor-Roper, Brackert. Despite some recent essays on important trials that seemed to confirm their expectations,[118] the daunting gulf between these expectations and the absence of any firm evidence to support them still persists.[119]

By itself, the term 'regional study' tells us very little about the structure, historical significance and developments in a given region. The examples of Macfarlane and Midelfort demonstrate how very different approaches can be equally successful. From the outset of the present study, the choice of a region with varied political, social and confessional structures seemed to offer the best opportunity to discover which social characteristics were most closely connected with witchcraft trials and persecutions.[120] The heterogeneity of 'southeast Germany', consisting of the former Duchy of Bavaria, its enclaves and the neighbouring fragmented territories of Swabia, distinguished by a multiplicity of stress factors, seemed likely to guarantee a large number of trials and their associated conflicts. It lay between two larger regions, one (the southwest and Franconia) quite prone to persecutions, the other (Austria and Bohemia) lacking in such excesses, at least according to existing studies. Based on past research, it was unclear what direction this study would ultimately take.

It is the intention of this book to show where and when, and if possible why, regional and chronological concentrations of witch trials and persecutions occurred, and what their effects were. In that vein, the problem of witchcraft accusations, trials and persecutions is analysed from a variety of perspectives, while always attempting to fit the method to particular circumstances.

tales und der Grafschaft Werdenfels, Garmisch 1908; R. Hipper, *Sonthofen im Wandel der Geschichte*, Kempten 1978; G. Krahn, *Chronik von Reichertshofen*, Ingolstadt 1963; W. Krämer, *Geschichte der Gemeinde Gauting*, Gauting 1949; G. Westermayer, *Chronik der Burg und des Marktes Tölz*, 2nd edn Tölz 1893; M. Dömling, *Heimatbuch von Marktober-dorf*, Markt Oberdorf 1952; L. Dürrwanger, *Nesselwang in Kultur und Geschichte*, Marktoberdorf 1954; F. Eggmann, *Geschichte des Illertales*, Ulm 1862. (Further titles can be found in the Bibliography.)

[117] BundesA ASt Frankfurt, FSg.2/1–F, Film 3709–3710 (cited below as Film, without further details; on this secondary source see chapter 2, pp. 35–64, and the List of Sources).

[118] H. Hörger, 'Wirtschaftlich-soziale und gesellschaftlich-ideologische Aspekte des Hexen-wahns. Der Prozess gegen Simon Altseer aus Rottenbuch 1665', *ZBLG*, 38 (1975), 945–66. M. Kunze, *Der Prozess Pappenheimer*, Ebelsbach 1981.

[119] As in M. Kunze, *Die Strasse ins Feuer*, Munich 1982, a novel based on his dissertation.

[120] Schormann, *Hexenprozesse*, 4.

The choice of these goals had both practical and methodological consequences. It meant that a very wide variety of sources had to be 'tested'. Archival research targeted local authorities (records of the county courts, judicial receipts, trial transcripts, reports), as well as intermediary authorities and the central government (protocols of the Court Council, city councils, the Privy Council, the Ecclesiastical Council, Court Paymasters' accounts, legal briefs). The public stance of the universities and the internal reports of the clergy were evaluated, as were treatises, sermons, chronicles and diaries, so far as they were available. Each type of source has its own limitations and opens up its own possibilities. Therefore, a multiplicity of method is literally forced on any historian entering the investigation with an open mind; serial sources like the almost endless court protocols and account books facilitate a quantitative approach, while trial records offer concrete insights on microhistoric structures. Opinions, treatises, official reports and so on unveil contemporary interpretations and controversies. Ultimately, this book is based on the premise that only a combination of different methods, such as statistical, structural and textual analysis[121] and the reconstruction of mentalities, an armoury of quantitative and qualitative methods, allows for a sensible interpretation. The result is a pluralism of perspectives and methods that might appear eclectic, but endeavours to address contemporary views 'from below' as well as 'from above'. The attempt is to demonstrate how various groups with different world views looked at the same problem, employing a social-scientific or socio-anthropological approach whenever it appears possible to broaden the thematic horizon.[122]

As research on this study progressed, the learned debate on witchcraft assumed ever greater importance as a key to understanding witch trials in Bavaria (southeast Germany), while local and regional accounts gradually diminished in status, providing little more than a welcome introduction to a

---

[121] The concept seems to be becoming naturalised. Cf. for example C. Honegger (ed.), M. Bloch, F. Braudel, L. Febvre et al., Schrift und Materie der Geschichte. Vorschläge zur systematischen Aneignung historischer Prozesse, Frankfurt am Main 1977, which collects several essays by Mandrou, Febvre and Duby under the title 'Geschichte der Mentalitäten'.

[122] The debate begun in Heft 3/1984 of Geschichte und Gesellschaft can only bear fruit to the extent that historians display a greater consciousness of methodology in the search for the appropriate method for a particular subject; changes of perspective can only increase transparency in this. H. Medick, 'Missionare im Ruderboot? Ethnologische Erkenntniswesen als Herausforderung an die Sozialgeschichte', Geschichte und Gesellschaft, 10 (1984), 295–319; J. Kocka, 'Zurück zur Erzählung? Plädoyer für eine historische Argumentation', ibid., 395–408. Here we can only mention that witchcraft research has now come to be regarded as a showpiece of interdisciplinary cross-fertilisation. N.Z. Davis, 'Anthropology and History in the 1980s. The Possibilities of the Past', Journal of Interdisciplinary History, 12 (1981–2), 267–76, 269f.

very extensive body of source materials.[123] Additional questions arose as the massive and barely exploited source material was examined and the data compared with other witchcraft studies conducted during the past two decades, often compelling an unexpected reevaluation of the original problem.

This study attempts an integrative approach to the problem of witchcraft, seen as an essential component of European life and thought before the Enlightenment, among the 'lower classes' as well as the social and intellectual élite, and not as eccentric subject-matter for a history of ideas. This integrative approach further requires an examination of the 'conjunctures' of witchcraft – fluctuations in its significance – in the context of intellectual and social developments.

METHODOLOGY

In keeping with a systematic approach, all available 'witchcraft files' – trial records – in state, civic and ecclesiastical archives, as well as the collections of historical societies, were examined.[124] Case files form the core of any history of witchcraft, since these materials offer direct access to the trials themselves; they include, amongst other things, interrogations and correspondence between the local and superior courts. The interrogatory protocols are especially useful as they bring us into direct contact with individual suspects, the witches themselves, and depositions of witnesses often provide a glimpse into the complex circumstances leading to an accusation. The detail of these interrogatories and light shed from previous incidents allow the reconstruction of 'magical' assumptions made by judges, witnesses and defendants. Correspondence between judges and their superiors contains indications of how contemporaries conceived of individual trials, typically through references to precedents. Trial records generally offer qualitative information, but little indication of change over time or regional contexts.

Source material available for the quantitative study of trials is nearly inexhaustible. In southeast Germany, witchcraft trials were mentioned in serial sources at all administrative levels as events of primary concern. For

---

[123] The controversies, here called 'discussions on witchcraft', between hard-line apologists and opponents of witch hunting, only came to light during our research. They were either overlooked by earlier researchers (Riezler, *Geschichte*; Kunze, *Der Prozess Pappenheimer*) or their true significance was not appreciated. As a discussion that lasted for decades, especially in a Catholic area, is an exception in the field of witchcraft research we have made this one of the main themes of our research (chapter 4 below and chapter VI of the German edition, on the final Catholic discussions, 1630–1780).

[124] For an overview see the list of archives used and consulted in the List of Sources and Literature.

free-imperial cities, these sources include town-council protocols, registers of sentencing, lists of executions and chronicles.[125] Although urban sources are easier to survey, they are less interesting than serial sources for territories with more complex administrative systems. Suspected cases of witchcraft and records of witch trials allow for investigations at all levels of the judicial system: local courts, districts courts and town courts – the decentralised judicial districts – as well as intermediary provincial authorities (where the sources survive) and, finally, at the central level. Each level of government produced its own series of records, most of which exist from the sixteenth or seventeenth century onwards and are preserved in full or in part. These records include the account books of the more than a hundred Bavarian districts courts.[126] The Court Council protocols for the Duchy of Bavaria comprise over 900 volumes for the period 1590–1760, those of the Bishopric of Augsburg 381 volumes, those of the Prince-Abbacy of Kempten 130 volumes.[127] Each territory and city produced its own series of sources concerned with legal matters at every level of governance and all contain – at least potentially – information on trials for sorcery and witchcraft.

Domesticating the ocean of source materials is not as daunting a task as it might seem. Of course, definitive quantification is only possible if all the sources are systematically investigated, and even then, gaps in the individual series still leave some room for doubt. But there is a simpler way to estimate the distribution of cases reliably, both geographically and chro-

[125] The fullness of the notes differed from city to city. For example, the minutes of the council of Augsburg only include brief notes, and the Strafbücher give the final verdict, while all further information must be sought in the Urgichtenakten (records of depositions). In the minutes of the council of Memmingen, on the other hand, cases of witchcraft are treated in relative detail. In general one can assume that cases of witchcraft, because of their importance, are reflected in all the relevant serial sources, and also in the town chronicles, as has been demonstrated by a comparison of the chronicles and the lists of executions in Augsburg and Memmingen. The most unfavourable source situation was found in Kaufbeuren, Kempten and Lindau, where little material which could be used for this research has survived, apart from the council minute books. The individual sources used are listed in the Sources and Literature (Town Archives).

[126] On the administrative and judicial history of Bavaria see E. Rosenthal, *Geschichte des Gerichtswesens und der Verwaltungsorganisation Baierns*, 2 vols., Würzburg 1889/1906; W. Leiser, *Strafgerichtsbarkeit in Süddeutschland. Formen und Entwicklungen*, Cologne/Vienna 1971; G. Heyl, 'Die Protokolle der kurbayrischen Zentralbehörden', *Mitteilungen für die Archivpflege in Bayern*, 4 (1958), 54–6. On the sources used see Sources and Literature under StAM and StAL (Minutes of lower courts) and HStAM (Central minutes).

[127] HStAM, classes Kurbayern Hofrat (formerly Kurbayern Prot.); Hochstift Augsburg, Neuburger Abgabe, Akten; and Fürststift Kempten, Neuburger Abgabe, Literalien. According to Heyl, 'Die Protokolle', the Bavarian Court Council minutes comprise a total of 1,067 volumes (vol. 16 = Jan.–May 1589; vol. 915 = Dec. 1760); the references to the minutes of Dillingen and Kempten follow H. Schuhmann, *Der Scharfrichter. Seine Gestalt – Seine Funktion*, Kempten 1964, 281.

nologically. When the witch trials of the sixteenth century began, the legal system in these territories was already so centralised that cases of 'higher' justice precluded trials without decisive intervention from the central authorities. Witch trials, so exceptional from both a legal and a theological point of view, were of particular interest to rulers and governments, and were thus designated as 'a matter of direct interest to the ruler' (*causa domini*) in the court council protocols from the Duchy of Bavaria. Judges who acted on their own initiative and ordered torture without the approval of their superiors ran the risk of severe reprimands and fines. Only the central authorities were empowered to resolve the question of torture.[128] For that reason, court council protocols list trials for witchcraft and sorcery in all of the larger territorial units. As yet, no researcher has systematically examined these central sources to investigate witchcraft in the region.

Naturally, the present study could only access selected portions of these protocol series. Systematic analysis was conducted for the Duchy of Bavaria, the Bishopric of Augsburg and the free-imperial city of Augsburg, the dominant secular and the largest ecclesiastical territories and the outstanding city of the region.[129] The Bavarian court council protocols proved exceptionally rich, granting an unexpected insight into debates on the witch trials at the central level. The extreme bitterness of discussions concerning appropriate policies on witchcraft, as well as other relevant records of opinions and polemics, led to the inclusion of its own separate treatment in this book.

Despite the concentration of witchcraft trial records at the centre, random samples were also performed on the records of lower authorities. These records confirmed the theoretical expectation that, in practice, witch trials conducted by districts courts were also recorded by the central authorities.[130] The accounts of the districts courts were especially fruitful sources, for their account books allow the reconstruction of each criminal trial in minute detail (costs of imprisonment, messengers' wages, torturers'

---

[128] Heydenreuter, *Der landesherrliche Hofrat*, 228ff., for Bavaria. Also G. Christel, 'Die Malefizprozessordnung des Codex Maximilianeus von 1616, dargestellt in ihrem Verhältnis zur Carolina und den Rechtsquellen des 16. Jhs. in Bayern', Dr. jur. thesis, Regensburg 1975. Neither Leiser nor Spindler, *Handbuch*, III/2, provides any guide to the structure of the criminal justice system in the bishoprics or in the territories of eastern Swabia. Spindler explicitly refers to the centralised structure of the Bishopric of Augsburg (Spindler, *Handbuch*, III/2, 952) and the Prince-Abbacy of Kempten (*ibid.*, 966f.). In the other territories (Pfalz-Neuburg, Freising, Oettingen) this emerges from the trial records. The situation in the Margravate of Burgau and the noble lordships of Swabia, on the other hand, is not clear.

[129] See notes 78, 81, 84. On the methodology chap. 2, pp. 35–64. Three-quarters of the total population of the region lived in these three territories.

[130] This can be read from the chronological list of trials in the original German edition of this book, 431–69, e.g. Landsberg 1609, Dachau 1640, Munich 1640.

activities, doctors' and midwives' fees, as well as the costs of executions, if any). Therefore, the account books of the districts courts provide truly original insights into the problem of witchcraft away from the political centres, in addition to simple confirmation. Local court records also seem, at a glance, to have little to do with the elaborated concept of the exceptional crime of witchcraft, if only because they often reveal nothing more than initial suspicions. After all, not every suspicion led to a trial, much less to the burning of a witch, a fact far too often overlooked.

In addition to serial sources and case records, territorial depositions, punitive oaths, criminal proceedings and even executioners' records were searched for traces of witchcraft trials. These sources yielded many references and offered interesting perspectives, although they hardly seemed to alter the general picture, until they were considered as a whole along with other sources, including the forewords to treatises, the Fugger *Zeitungen*, diaries, chronicles[131] and so on, indicating connections that might have gone undetected had research been conducted on a narrower scale.

The initial task of this study was to survey geographical and temporal concentrations of witch trials in order to provide a firmer basis for future consideration (chapter 2, pp. 35–46). The results of quantification already

---

[131] The regional reconstruction showed that practically every printed work on the theme of witchcraft could be associated with a particular trial, to which it referred more or less directly. For example the foreword of the Munich printing of P. Binsfeld, *Tractat von Bekanntnuss der Zauberer und Hexen*, Munich 1591 (2nd edn 1592), unambiguously referred to the situation in Bavaria; the *Erweyterte Unholden Zeittung*, Ulm 1590, sought to incite the Catholic authorities to stage further witch hunts. The Ingolstadt *Disputatio juridica de maleficis et sagis*, held by Johann Christoph Fickler before the Italian jurist A. Fachineus in 1592, belongs in the same context. The Munich author and Secretary of the Court Council Aegidius Albertinus even had a Spanish treatise, which he had translated himself, printed during the debate on the principle of witchcraft in 1602: F. de Ossuna, *Flagellum diaboli oder des Teufels Gaissl*, Munich 1602. Several witch-burnings at Augsburg also found an echo in print. Besides the printed *Zeitungen* they also provoked three more extensive treatments: B. Albrecht, *Magia. Das ist: christlicher Bericht von der Zauberey und Hexerey (...)*, Leipzig 1628 (refers to the Augsburg witch-burning of 1625 on page 312. Albrecht was a Protestant preacher in Augsburg and his publication was supported by the other Protestant clergy in the city. See also Paulus, *Hexenwahn*, 90ff.); C. Ehinger, *Daemonologia, oder etwas Neues vom Teufel*, Augsburg 1681, which took the occasion of a case at Augsburg to inveigh against atheists, who in Ehinger's opinion were present throughout the region. (On this see L. Lenk, *Augsburger Bürgertum im Späthumanismus und Frühbarock (1580–1700)*, Augsburg 1968, 58f.) A particular ornament of his calling was the Protestant parson Spitzel, who justified the Augsburg witch executions of the 1680s: G. Spitzel, *Die gebrochene Macht der Finsternuss, oder zerstörte teuflische Bundes- und Buhl-Freundschaft mit den Menschen (...)*, Augsburg 1687. The scourge of atheists and believers in the Devil, Gottlieb (Theophil) Spitzel (Spicelius), who corresponded with Leibniz and Spener (cf. Lenk, *Augsburger Bürgertum*, 56; D. Blaufuss, 'Gottlieb Spitzel (1639–91)', Dr. Theol. thesis, Erlangen 1971), was opposed fifteen years later by C. Thomasius, *Kurtze Lehr-Sätze von dem Laster der Zauberey*, Halle 1703 (here cited from Lea, *Materials*, III, 1395–7). The list could be extended, but for reasons of space reference must be made to the Bibliography and to the chronological list of trials in the original German edition.

modified the line of inquiry. After it became clear that persecutions were concentrated in the years around 1590, new questions arose: how was the suspicion of witchcraft dealt with at other times (chapter 2, pp. 65–88) and what changes occurred in the years directly preceding 1590, that might have caused the same suspicions to end in persecutions (chapter 2, pp. 89–114). Finally, an attempt was made to analyse a distinctive regional event, the great witch hunt of 1590, in greater detail: the overall regional pattern, the triggering events, and the course of individual persecutions, the reason for their eventual ending, the consequences drawn from it, and how contemporaries interpreted the beginning and end of waves of persecution (chapter 3, pp. 115–211). Chapter 4 deals with the special position of southeast Germany following this great wave of witch hunting. While the neighbouring regions of Franconia and southwestern Germany witnessed a rise in the numbers of executions as persecutions became ever more virulent, the number of witches burned in southeast Germany declined sharply. Particularly in Munich and Ingolstadt, heated controversies followed between the supporters of persecution and their opponents, leading to the formation of a genuine faction of Catholics opposed to witchcraft persecutions, which influenced the discussion of the subject in the entire Empire during the 1620s. This raises the question of society's potential ability to defend itself against persecution; the traditional explanations for the end of persecutions in the 1620s – confessional opposition, the Swedes – are examined (chapter 4, pp. 212–321).

Two short chapters detail the conjuncture of the witchcraft thematic after 1630 and structural changes of witch trials until their cessation in the mid-eighteenth century (chapter 5, 322–354), as well as the final 'catholic' debate over witchcraft (chapter 6, 355–387). This history of witch trials and the discourse on witchcraft continued well into the second half of the eighteenth century. As is well known, a woman was executed for witchcraft in the Prince-Abbacy of Kempten as late as 1775, the last to pay with her life for the crime in the territories of the old Empire. The south-east German Luminaries capitalized on this demonstrated potential for further witch-burnings in the region from 1766 to 1770 during the so-called Bavarian 'witchcraft war', making their arguments in the debate all the more explosive. This demonstrates once again that the problem of witchcraft could not be considered in isolation, but was instead integral to a world-view which is so difficult for us to comprehend fully today.

In some concluding remarks (chapter 7, pp. 388–415), this new portrait of witchcraft persecutions in the region is recapitulated and characterised according to its socio-historical value and theoretical significance in the context of comparable studies and theoretical models.

2 Moving toward a social history of witchcraft

This chapter defines the object of study in order to bring out its specific regional contours. To begin with, quantitative synchronic and diachronic cross-sections establish when and where the crime of witchcraft is particularly evident in the legal sources, so that we know precisely where to point the microscope. This section also attempts to quantify the extent of witch hunting, and compares the results with the presumed intensity of persecution in southwestern Germany and Franconia (pp. 35–64). The second section examines the way in which the concept of witchcraft elaborated by the Inquisition was received in the region. This is less concerned with repeating the familiar story, found in almost any of the older legal dissertations, than with an 'individual' reconstruction of reception in the region. Nor is our interest confined to the reaction of the elites, the jurists and theologians, for we have also attempted to discover the attitudes of the mass of the population. Inspired by social-anthropological witchcraft research, we have tried to sketch the typical behaviour of the population when faced with suspicions of witchcraft, on the basis of generalisations from the early trial records (pp. 65–88). A third section outlines the rapid change in the attitudes of larger groups of intellectuals to the crime of witchcraft between 1560 and 1590, and asks how far this reflects social changes in the broadest sense, in particular a 'change of mentalities' that can be detected in other contexts (pp. 89–114).

All three sections are somewhat tentative, for thorough preparatory studies have not yet been undertaken. This is especially true of the social-historical data. Apart from M.J. Elsas' research into the history of prices, which dates from the 1930s, such data are difficult to collect. This may lead to gaps in the argument, but does not rule out the need for an attempt to place witchcraft in its social context.

QUANTIFICATION IN SYNCHRONIC AND DIACHRONIC JUXTAPOSITION

PRELIMINARY REMARKS

This work does not claim to have examined all the records of every trial for witchcraft in this region. Not even a team of historians could hope to examine all the eligible sources in a reasonable time. Moreover, the presence of gaps in the sources would still leave the validity of the results in doubt. Thus, it remains possible that a sounder basis for an evaluation of the quantitative aspects of the topic may be found if significant new serial sources come to light. The methodology has already been sketched in the introduction and will become clearer in the following sections. At the end of the present section, a cautious attempt will be made to extrapolate the data produced. The appendix to the original German edition of this book includes a full chronological list of trials, with references for individual proceedings. With a few minor variations,[1] this list covers the modern administrative districts of Upper and Lower Bavaria, Swabia and the Upper Palatinate. All the trials cited in the following pages, e.g. 'Munich 1666', can be found in this list and full references are therefore not given in this book.

The list comprises about a thousand trials for sorcery and witchcraft in the years 1300–1800, the great bulk of them concentrated in the years between 1560 and 1730 (about 900, or 90 per cent). During these thousand trials, about 3,000 persons were arrested. A very cautious calculation[2] suggests that rather more than 900 witches were executed, almost all of them in the shorter period mentioned (98 per cent). Three-quarters of all executions fell within an even shorter period, the 45 years between 1586 and 1631, and even here there were further concentrations: between 1628 and 1630 alone, 130 witches were burned (14 per cent), and between 1586 and 1595 at least 437 (48 per cent). The example of the wave of witch hunting of 1590 reveals some of the difficulties of quantification, which recur constantly: a poem in praise of the witch hunts conducted by Markus

---

[1] This refers to the administrative districts before the local government reforms of 1981, not only because all the guides (Spindler, *Handbuch*; Bosl, *Bayern*; Keyser and Stoob, *Städlebuch*) are still oriented to the former boundaries, but also because it makes no historical sense to include Eichstätt (Franconia) and Neuburg on the Danube (Swabia) in Upper Bavaria. The list of trials in the German edition, 431–69, also includes trials in the so-called 'Inn Quarter', which formed the eastern part of the provincial administration of Burghausen until 1779, when it was ceded to Austria. Trials are also included from county court seats which were then part of the Archbishopric of Salzburg but which later became part of Bavaria (e.g. Mühldorf on the Inn, Tittmoning).

[2] To avoid producing new imaginary figures, only unambiguously documented cases are counted. Midelfort, *Witch Hunting*, 199ff. was similarly cautious.

Fugger, written in 1590, says 'Marx Fugger the wellborn also has evil deeds rooted out, punished and judged in his courts far and wide, for which God be praised and thanks be given.'[3] The extensive possessions of the house of Fugger stretched throughout the whole of Swabia in 1590, from Oberndorf at the confluence of the Lech and the Danube to Wasserburg on Lake Constance. As no further sources for these witch hunts have survived, they do not appear in our quantification.

In any case an exact quantification of each individual trial is often impossible; it is more important to form a general picture of the course of a witch hunt, which was typically distinct from that in neighbouring regions, both in chronology and in intensity. In the southwest Midelfort's research revealed 843 witch trials between 1561 and 1670, with 3,229 documented executions. In the same period, in the region we have called 'southeast Germany', we found 671 witch trials, which between them yielded 'only' 717 executions. That means that four times as many witches were burned in the southwest.[4] If one compares the chronology of the two regions, it becomes clear that the intensity of persecution rose in the southwest after 1600, while it clearly declined in the southeast. As in Franconia, the high point of witch hunting was not reached in Baden-Württemberg until 1610–30, although witch hunts had been far more intensive there than in Bavaria as early as 1560. Quantitative research thus reveals that developments in the southeast, dominated by the former Duchy of Bavaria, were in some senses untypical. Here the number of witch trials and executions did not rise sharply until the 1580s, but declined again after a few years of harsh persecution. That means that if one wishes to use the number of executions as an index of the intensity of persecution, one must in the first place shed light on the witch trials of the years around 1590.

How was the chronological list of trials for southeast Germany compiled? First of all, the classical route was followed: all the eligible archives of the state, the cities, the dioceses and private families were investigated for references to witch trials.[5] This process showed that most of these procedural records had already been used and evaluated from a quantitative point of view in the 1930s by the so-called H-Sonderkommando. But, as always in research based on archival sources, it was still an open question how far the material collected was representative of the actual events. To discover this, we examined serial sources from the Duchy of Bavaria, the Bishopric of Augsburg and the Free Cities of Augsburg and Memmingen which had not previously been studied for this purpose. The H-Sonderkommando had not visited any of the archives of the Free Cities,

---

[3] Behringer, 'Hexenverfolgung', 357; from ÖNB, Vienna, Cod. 8963, fol. 751.
[4] Midelfort, Witch Hunting, 32, 73.
[5] Cf. the list of archives examined and consulted, below, pp. 416–25.

Table 1 *Geographical distribution of witch trials, based on the material of the 'H-Sonderkommando'*

	District	Cards	Percentage
SE Germany	Upper Palatinate	232	3.7
	Upper Bavaria	463	7.5
	Lower Bavaria	463	7.5
	Swabia	546	8.8
Franconia	Middle Franconia	747	12.1
	Upper Franconia	830	13.5
	Lower Franconia	2,897	46.9
	Federal State of		
	Bavaria	6,178	100.0

and had not evaluated any of the series of minutes of central bodies in Bavaria.

RESULTS OF THE *H-SONDERKOMMANDO* FOR THE PRESENT
FEDERAL STATE OF BAVARIA

During the preparation of this study, the possibility arose for the first time of making use of the findings of the extensive researches of the so-called *H-Sonderkommando*. The working methods of this team of about eight researchers, whose sole task it had been during the Nazi dictatorship to search German-language archives for records of witchcraft trials, on the instructions of Heinrich Himmler, have recently been described by Schormann,[6] so that a detailed account is not necessary here. The team took excerpts from the likely sources and entered them in a card index, classified by place, person and archive. The card index of places thus produced has been transferred to 3,621 numbered films which together comprise about 30,000 cards. Of these 6,178 cards, or rather more than 20 per cent, refer to the present Federal State of Bavaria.

If these 6,178 cards are classified into the seven present administrative districts, there are quite substantial imbalances: not much more than a quarter of the cards fall within the region studied here, with the Upper Palatinate; the rest refer to the three Franconian districts.

According to the material collected by the *H-Sonderkommando*, four times as many witches were put to death in Franconia as in our region of southeast Germany (Upper and Lower Bavaria, Swabia).[7] The relationship between southeast Germany and Franconia displays even more ana-

---

[6] Schormann, *Hexenprozesse*, 8–15.
[7] BundesA Ast Frankfurt, Bestand F 215–Zsg. 2/1–f (cited as Film).

logies to that between southeast Germany and the southwest: 95 per cent of the cards refer to the years 1585–1630. While the card index entries for places in Bavaria and Swabia are most frequent from the years around 1590, the absolute peak in Franconia lies between 1600 and 1630, especially around 1600, 1612, 1617, and between 1624 and 1630. As in southwestern Germany, the most intense persecution in Franconia was found in the Catholic territories, especially the five great ecclesiastical principalities: the upper part of the Archbishopric of Mainz around Aschaffenburg, the Bishoprics of Würzburg, Bamberg and Eichstätt, and the Prince-Abbacy of Fulda. In three of the four Franconian Bishoprics the number of victims of trials for witchcraft seems to have exceeded a thousand.[8] To a lesser extent the Commanderies of the Teutonic Order, a few of the Protestant Imperial Counts and the Duchy of Saxe-Coburg also appear to have taken part in the Franconian witch hunts.[9] Most of the victims perished in the great witch hunts, and this too appears to distinguish Franconia from the southeast: the five greatest witch hunts in Franconia claimed an average of 500 victims, the five greatest witch hunts in Swabia and Bavaria 'only' a little more than 50 each.

The researchers of the *H-Sonderkommando* were irritated by the imbalance in their results between Franconia on the one hand and Bavaria on the other, as they were familiar with the view repeated in the literature that the old Duchy of Bavaria had been a heartland of witch hunting. They therefore began to widen their search beyond the trial records in the archives. Several series of accounts in the state archives at Landshut were examined, and a large-scale search was made through the miscellaneous papers of the Bavarian courts in the Munich archives, as well as the miscellaneous papers of the Free Cities, the Bishoprics of Freising, Augsburg and Regensburg, the criminal and executioners' records, collections of depositions and recognisances and relevant documents from the miscellaneous accumulations in the 'State Administration' and 'General Registry' classes of the Central State Archives at Munich. This search revealed a whole series of interesting and hitherto unknown sources, but the results of quantitative value were few. Though one or two trials for sorcery or witchcraft could be found in almost all the archives investigated, the researchers came up against the same events in the various types of sources, especially when dealing with the more rigorously conducted trials that led to executions and even more with the larger and smaller witch

---

[8] Cf. the extent of the films: Film 173 (Aschaffenburg), Film 204–5 (Bamberg A–L, M–Z), Film 668–9 (Eichstätt A–K, L–Z), Film 847 (Fulda Bishopric), Film 901–2 (Gerolzhofen A–J, K–Z), Film 1096 (Hallstadt), Film 1222 (Hörstein), Film 1667 (Lohr), Film 1814–15 (Miltenberg A–G, H–Z), Film 3064–5 (Würzburg) and Film 3085–7 (Zeil A–K, L–Z).

[9] Film 693 (Ellingen); Film 494 (Coburg).

hunts. Their persistent irritation at their scanty results is evident from several marginal comments.[10]

Yet the researches of the *H-Sonderkommando* were of great use in the present work, and not only because they provided a key to all the trial records in the state archives of Bavaria, and in some of the city archives, which could be used for quantification by person and place. In their nationwide search for relevant material the team had indexed in their proper places references to documents which had strayed to other regions. Finally, a single researcher could not have examined so many archives with such thoroughness. In spite of their relatively high capacity for research the Nazi researchers omitted to form an overall impression of the intensity of persecution by consulting the central series of protocols in the cities and territories.

THE IMPERIAL CITIES (1300–1800) AS INDICATORS

The serial archives of the Free-Imperial Cities are not only fuller than those of the territories but reach further back in time. Of the fourteen former Free Cities in the present Federal State of Bavaria, seven are in Swabia (Augsburg, Memmingen, Kaufbeuren, Kempten, Lindau, Nördlingen, Donauwörth), six in Franconia (Nuremberg, Rothenburg, Schweinfurt, Windsheim, Weissenburg and Dinkelsbühl). The former Free City of Regensburg now forms part of the Upper Palatinate. As the position of the Franconian Free Cities was not significantly different from that of their Swabian counterparts, both groups of cities are dealt with together here.[11]

---

[10] Film 3709, 3710, 3711. Marginal notes of the researchers e.g. Film 3710, 31, 87.

[11] Augsburg: Film 181; S. Valentin, *End-Urthel und Verruf... Aller derjenigen... Persohnen, so von... Anno 1649 bis Anno 1759...justifiziert... worden*, Augsburg 1760; SBM, Cgm. 2026; SBA, 2 Cod. Aug. 284–7 ('Maleficanten, welche vom Leben zum Tode gebracht worden 1348–1760'); StadtA Augsburg, J. Bausch (MS), 'Verzeichnis derer Maleficanten, welche... von Anno 1353 bis zu diesen unsern Zeiten... vom Leben zum Tod gebracht worden sind', Augsburg 1755; *ibid.*, 'Verzeichnis derjenigen Personen welche allhier in Augsburg vom Leben zum Thod verurtheilt... (1513–1800)'; *ibid.*, Haid (MS), 'Hexenprozesse von dem Jahr 1525 bis zum Jahr 1728', Augsburg 1828 (unusable because of numerous errors); *ibid.*, Strafbücher 1563–71, 1581–1653 (8 vols.); *ibid.*, Register der Urgichtenakten (5 vols.); A. Buff, 'Verbrechen und Verbrecher zu Augsburg in der zweiten Hälfte des 14. Jahrhunderts', *Zs. des hist. Vereins für Schwaben und Neuburg*, 4 (1878), 160–231. Memmingen: StadtA Memmingen, Urgichtenbücher 1551–1683, 3 vols. Kaufbeuren: StadtA Kaufbeuren, W.L. Hörmann, 'Versuch einer General- und Special Registratur über die in... Kauffbeurer Cantzley-Archiv befindlichen Acta und Protocolla' (MS), 3 vols., Kaufbeuren 1739; *ibid.*, B 7; C.J. Wagenseil, 'Real Register über Sachen, welche im Rath alhier... verhandelt worden sind' (MS), Kaufbeuren 1782/3. Kempten: StadtA Kempten, 'Material-Index über Sämtliche... Raths Protocolla Von Anno 1477 biss Annum 1789 in 78 Tomis' (MS), n.d. Lindau: Film 1641; H. Wolfart, *Geschichte der Stadt Lindau i. B.*, I, Lindau 1909. Nördlingen: Wulz (1937/8); K.-S. Kramer, 'Volksglauben in Nördlinger Urfehdebüchern', *Bayer. Jahrbuch für Volkskunde*, (1957), 43–50;

1 Valentin Fnd Urlanl (..) Augsburg 1760. The list of executions at Augsburg shows the original ins. of the city of London, etched and pub...

The sources for the later Middle Ages are of course more fragmentary than those for later periods. Chronicles and lists of executions give the impression of completeness in the larger cities, but this cannot be tested. The same applies to the extant registers of sentences imposed (*Buss-, Acht-* or *Strafbücher*), which in any case only reflect a part of the spectrum of criminal penalties. Taken as a whole, it can be inferred that executions for sorcery must have been absolutely exceptional, that they were always directed against individuals, and that the cumulative offence of witchcraft only penetrated into the judicial system of the Free Cities at the end of the fifteenth century. Although sorcery was punishable, as a heresy, by burning at the stake, execution by drowning was a competing form of punishment. Not until the imperial legislation of 1532 was death by burning at the stake made compulsory. Executions of sorcerers by drowning are reported at Augsburg in 1469 (pardoned), and Nuremberg in 1520,[12] by hanging at Regensburg in 1467 and by burning at Lindau in 1443 and 1493. The numerous reports of punishment of sorcery in Augsburg, Nördlingen, Regensburg and Nuremberg make it clear, however, that the usual penalty was banishment from the city, with the addition of corporal punishment in the most serious cases.[13] Even more spectacular cases appear in the city chronicles, which makes it hard to accept that such banishments of sorcerers would have been recorded, but that burnings would not. Later it can be shown that virtually every case of execution by burning was recorded in the chronicles.[14] If the total number of executions mentioned in them is quite low, this means that very few witches were burned in each place. The later medieval system of penalties for sorcery retained its validity until the crest of the regional wave of persecution around 1590 and in some cities

---

Film 1992. Donauwörth: Film 596; M. Zelzer, *Geschichte der Stadt Donauwörth von den Anfängen bis 1618*, II, Donauwörth 1958; L. Grohsmann, *Geschichte der Stadt Donauwörth*, II, Donauwörth, 1978. Nuremberg: Film 2000; F. Bock, *Zur Volkskunde der Reichsstadt Nürnberg*, Nuremberg 1970; Rothenburg: K.-P. Herzog, 'Das Strafensystem der Stadt Rothenburg im Spätmittelalter', Dr. jur. thesis, Würzburg 1971; H. Schmidt, 'Vordringender Hexenwahn', *Fränkischer Feierabend*, 2 (1954), 77–95; *idem, Fränkischer Feierabend*, 7 (1959), 60–72; Film 2358. Schweinfurt: D. Hesse, 'Der Strafvollzug der freien Reichsstadt Schweinfurt', Dr. jur. thesis, Würzburg 1975; Film 2546. Windsheim: J. Bergdolt, *Hexenprozesse in Windsheim*, Bad Windsheim 1950; Film 2996. Weissenburg: Film 2920; Kunstmann, *Zauberwahn*, 25f. Dinkelsbühl: J. Greiner, 'Hexenprozesse in Dinkelsbühl', *Alt-Dinkelsbühl, Beilage zum Wörnitz-Boten*, 16. Jahrgang, no. 6, Dinkelsbühl 1929; Film 575. Regensburg: Film 2231.

12 Herzog's study, 'Das Strafensystem', is especially instructive for the medieval system of punishments; and for Nuremberg, Kunstmann, *Zauberwahn*, 27–44; the case of Augsburg in detail in StadtA Augsburg, 'Verzeichnis', Bausch, 78–83 and in several chronicles.

13 Herzog, 'Das Strafensystem', 115. For southeastern Germany cf. the list of trials in the original German edition, 431–69.

14 This is shown, for example, by a comparison of the data in Valentin, *End-urthel*, with MS Augsburg chronicles such as SBA, 2 Cod., 49–52; or C. Schorer, *Memminger Chronik*, Memmingen 1660, with StadtA Memmingen, Urgichtenbücher.

(Augsburg, Nuremberg, Memmingen) even beyond. It must be assumed that the deviation of the cities from the usual pattern of persecution was based on a policy of deliberate refusal.[15]

Investigations of alleged sorcery and witchcraft were not unknown in the Free Cities, however. During the witch hunt of 1590, one can detect a greater frequency.[16] In five Free Cities (Kaufbeuren, Nördlingen, Donauwörth, Weissenburg and Windsheim), the accumulation of suspicions turned into a witch hunt under the influence of persecutions in the surrounding territories. In these five cities at least eighty-one persons were burned as witches (seventy-seven women and four men) in the 1590s. In the whole of the seventeenth century, a period ten times as long, forty persons were burned (thirty-six women and four men) after twenty-eight trials.[17]

This gives the astonishing result for the cities of southeast Germany, that no witches were burned until 1590, except for the isolated case at Lindau in 1493 which fell in the period when the papal Inquisitor Heinrich Institoris was active in southern Germany. Even in 1590, only five of the fourteen Imperial Cities joined in the mania for witch burning, while the other town governments took a more cautious attitude toward those within their walls who were accused of witchcraft.[18] Not until the years 1610 to 1699, and especially from 1650, did almost all the Free Cities capitulate to the witch craze and carry out witch-burnings, though they no longer had the character of true witch hunts. In Augsburg, Memmingen and Dinkelsbühl, however, there were 'chains' of trials which were related to one another.[19]

It is remarkable that the fourteen Swabian and Franconian Imperial Cities and Regensburg only give a relatively weak reflection of the regional divide on the subject of witch hunting. The majority of the cities showed themselves apparently immune to the witch hunts in their hinterlands. In 1590, however, three of them, or four if we include Donauwörth, allowed themselves to be swept up in a genuine witch hunt, while that at Nördlingen was among the greatest witch hunts in the whole region. For the next half century, executions of witches in the Imperial Cities fell back sharply again. The thirteen executions in 1616–17 and 1625–8 were no more than pale shadows of the great persecution in Franconia, where witches went to

---

[15] Cf. Kunstmann, *Zauberwahn*, 186ff.

[16] Kramer, 'Volksglauben'; Kunstmann, *Zauberwahn*, 73–84.

[17] On the witch hunts in the two Franconian cities Bergdolt, 'Hexenprozesse'; and Kunstmann, *Zauberwahn*, 20f., 25f., also chapter 3, pp. 121–57.

[18] A certain scepticism remained here. On Regensburg H. Bayerl, 'Die letzte "Hexe" von Regensburg', *Die Oberpfalz*, 33 (1939), 160–83; Kunstmann, *Zauberwahn*, 74–8.

[19] For Dinkelsbühl, Greiner, 'Hexenprozesse'; also chapter V.1 of the German edition of this book.

the stake in their thousands. These trials took place, after all, in the very years when witch hunting was raging in the surrounding countryside, as in 1590. It is more difficult to correlate the executions in the later seventeenth century: while the figures for executions in the territories, especially the Catholic states, declined steeply, they rose in the Imperial Cities. In fact, it was at this date that the number of trials that ended in an execution, reached its peak in the cities. Around 1700 executions in the Imperial Cities ceased quite suddenly. During the trial at Lindau in 1730, other charges were more important at the end. Yet trials were still carried on; one may think of the case of an old woman who was arrested on suspicion of witchcraft in Nuremberg in 1766(!), and died in prison.[20]

Though it is relatively easy to form a general impression of executions for witchcraft,[21] it is only possible to see the total picture of trials for witchcraft and sorcery in a few of the cities. In this region, the researches of Wulz and K.-S. Kramer give us some insight into conditions in Nördlingen, while Gumpelzheimer, Knapp and the researches of the *H-Sonderkommando* have told us something of Regensburg. How far the local historical literature for Donauwörth and Lindau is representative must be doubted, as must the completeness of the subject indexes to the town council minutes of Memmingen, Kempten and Kaufbeuren. Only Augsburg offers an adequate source in this wider context.

FREQUENCY OF TRIALS IN THE FREE-IMPERIAL CITY OF
AUGSBURG 1581–1653

Of the total of seventeen executions of witches in the city of Augsburg, only two date from before 1650. Yet the assumption that there had not been any previous trials would be quite mistaken. The criminal punishment books of the city for the years 1581 to 1653 provide a source that allows us, uniquely, to analyse the whole development of trials for sorcery and witchcraft in the Swabian metropolis at its peak. In this period 101 trials were held before the city court, of which 64 ended in acquittal, 26 in banishment from the city, 8 in lighter penalties and 3 in the death sentence.[22]

The results of a quantitative investigation of the criminal punishment books for witchcraft and sorcery trials allow us to make some interesting correlations. Firstly, one can observe that the number of trials in the city tallied fairly closely with the trends of persecution in the surrounding countryside. It is true that there were no executions of witches in Augsburg

---

[20] StadtA Lindau, Akt 57,7; Bock, *Zur Volkskunde*, 64.   [21] Cf. note 11.
[22] StadtA Augsburg, Strafbücher 1581–1653, 8 vols.

Table 2 *Court proceedings against sorcery and/or witchcraft in Augsburg, in five-yearly periods, 1581–1653*[23]

	Five–year period	No. of trials	Quotient	Average	Executions
1	1581–4	1	4	0.25	–
2	1585–9	7	5	1.4	–
3	1590–4	21	5	4.2	–
4	1595–9	7	5	1.4	–
5	1600–4	8	5	1.6	–
6	1605–9	4	3	1.33	–
7	1610–14	12	5	2.4	–
8	1615–19	3	5	0.6	–
9	1620–4	7	5	1.4	–
10	1625–9	12	5	2.4	1
11	1630–4	4	5	0.8	–
12	1635–9	4	5	0.8	–
13	1640–4	6	5	1.2	1
14	1645–9	3	5	0.6	–
15	1650–3	2	4	0.5	1
		101	70	1.44	

before 1625, a marked contrast with the Bishopric, which surrounded the city on three sides, and with the adjacent Duchy of Bavaria, but the number of trials kept pace with the witch hunts in the neighbourhood. While the frequency of trials in the city over the seventy-year period averaged 1.44 per annum, the average rose from 0.25 in 1580–4 to 1.4 in 1585–9 and 4.2 in the persecuting years 1590–4. The absolute maximum was reached in 1590 with eight trials, and there were six more in 1591.

The number of trials per year in 1600–4 (1.6), 1610–14 (2.4) and 1625–9 (2.4) was also above average; 1625 with five and 1628 with eight trials, were the years of harshest persecution after 1590. Finally, in 1625 the first witch was burned in the city. In later years, although the number of trials declined, the number of executions rose.

Secondly, the almost unbroken data on the frequency of trials in the Free City of Augsburg, leaving aside witch hunts in the neighbouring districts, allow us to make other quantitative correlations. One need not have much hesitation in asking what these correlations must be in an early modern society: the question of daily bread, of actual survival, must come first. That means harvests, grain prices, disease, mortality.[24]

---

[23] *Ibid.*, the annual volumes for 1606 and 1607 are missing.
[24] W. Abel, *Massenarmut und Hungerkrisen im vorindustriellen Europa*, Hamburg/Berlin 1974. Cf. chapter 2, pp. 89–114. Now also W. Behringer, 'Sozialgeschichte und Hexenver- folgung', in S. Lorenz (ed.), *Hexenverfolgung*, Würzburg 1987.

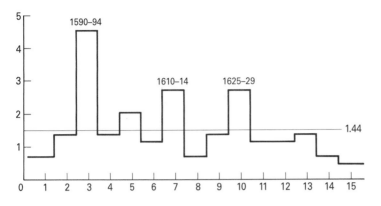

1. Court proceedings against sorcery and/or witchcraft in Augsburg, in five-yearly periods, 1581–1653

FREQUENCY OF TRIALS AND EXECUTIONS IN THE PRINCE-BISHOPRIC OF AUGSBURG

In principle the same rule seems to apply to the bishoprics as to the secular territories and the Free Cities. For the later Middle Ages we have very few reports of executions of sorcerers, except for one case of a woman being drowned in the Main at Würzburg for sorcery in 1470.[25] It is known that witches were burned during the campaign of Sprenger and Institoris in the diocese of Constance. It is unlikely that the Inquisitors were active in the bishoprics of Augsburg, Freising and Salzburg, but it is worth investigating whether their influence may have led to executions of witches in the diocese of Regensburg, for which a *vicarius* was appointed.[26] The earliest post-Reformation burnings of witches in our region took place within the jurisdiction of the Prince-Bishops of Eichstätt. The circumstances of the trial reflect the extraordinary character of the proceedings. Like the Syndic of Metz Agrippa von Nettesheim, in the roughly contemporary trials in Alsace, here too an attorney defended the suspected woman against the Bishop's prosecutor.[27] Although persecution had not yet settled into a

[25] Merzbacher, *Die Hexenprozesse*, 42.
[26] Hansen, *Quellen und Untersuchungen*, 393, 506–10.
[27] On the role of Agrippa, see Baschwitz, *Hexen*, 100f. On the early executions of witches in the Bishopric of Eichstätt, Leutenbauer, *Hexerei- und Zaubereidelikt*, 172f.; Merzbacher, 'Das 'alte Halsgerichtsbuch' des Hochstifts Eichstätt. Eine archivalische Quelle zur Geschichte des Strafvollzuges im 15. und 16. Jahrhundert und zur rechtlichen Volkskunde', *Zeitschrift der Savigny Stiftung für Rechtsgeschichte. Germanistische Abteilung*, 73 (1956), 375–96; Film 3662. There were executions in 1494, then in 1532, 1535 and 1562. The trial of 1532 appeared so important that it was often inserted by hand in copies of the *Malleus*.

routine, this suggests that the ecclesiastical princes were already more inclined to put witches on trial. It can hardly be regarded as a coincidence that the great wave of witch hunting in 1590 began in the Bishopric of Augsburg.[28]

The protocols of the Court Council of the Prince-Bishopric of Augsburg, which sat at Dillingen, begin in the early 1570s, twenty years before their Bavarian counterparts, and allow us to investigate the way in which the Prince-Bishopric of Augsburg took the lead in witch hunting in this region. As there was until recently complete uncertainty about the trials of witches in the Bishopric,[29] the research technique chosen has differed from that applied to the protocols in Munich. All the volumes preserved from 1573 to 1632 were examined to gain a clearer picture of the extent of witch hunting during the core phase 1590–1630 and its immediate prehistory. There are four gaps in the protocols, for twenty of the sixty volumes are missing. Those still extant cover the years 1573–97, 1607–13, 1621–4, 1627–9 and 1632.[30]

While the protocols of town councils naturally reflect events in a single place, those of the Court Councils of the territories allow a survey of a wider area, as witchcraft trials could not proceed without the cooperation of the higher authorities in the relatively strongly centralised states of southeast Germany.[31] From 1543 to 1690 the Prince-Bishopric of Augsburg was administered from Dillingen, because of recurrent conflicts with the authorities of the city of Augsburg. The minutes of the Court Council at Dillingen allow us to follow the trend of persecution from 1590 at the level of the twelve county courts. Whereas only one of the twelve held an investigation into witchcraft in 1577 and in 1585, more and more of them began to follow up suspicions of witchcraft from 1586. A witch hunt began in one court in 1586, and in 1587 there were proceedings in two courts, in 1588 in three, in 1589 in four. In 1590 the wave of trials reached its crest with investigations in ten of the twelve courts, before falling back gradually: in 1591 there were still proceedings in eight courts, in 1592 in four and thereafter only in one. It is characteristic that witches were not put to death

One of these copies was in the possession of the Landgrave of Hesse (Hansen, *Quellen und Untersuchungen*, 612), the other in that of Prior Kilian Leib of Rebdorf (Film 3662, 1–11). The court was presided over by suffragan Bishop Antonius of Eichstätt. The Bishop at the time was Gabriel von Eyb (1496–1535). Demonological literature (the 1517 edition of the *Malleus*, Nider's *Formicarius* of 1519) was also found in the estate of the suffragan Bishop of Eichstätt, Leonhard Haller. Cf. L. Ott, 'Leben und Schrifttum des Eichstätter Weihbischofs Leonhard Haller (gest. 1570)', *Sammelblatt des. Hist. Ver. Eichstätt*, 67 (1974), 83–133. On Haller's role in the Council of Trent R. Bauerreiss, *Kirchengeschichte Bayerns*, VI, Augsburg 1965, 208, 230–4, *passim*.   [28]   Cf. chapter 3, pp. 121–57.

[29]   Schormann *Hexenprozesse* (1981), 70.
[30]   HStAM, Hochstift Augsburg, NA, Akten No. 1183–1225
[31]   See above chapter 1, pp. 29–33.

Table 3 *Court proceedings against sorcery and/or witchcraft in the*
Bishopric of Augsburg in five-yearly periods, 1573–1632[33]

Five–yearly period	No. of trials	Quotient (no. of years)	Average	Executions
1573–4	1	2	0.5	–
1575–9	5	5	1.0	3
1580–4	1	5	0.2	–
1585–9	10	5	2.0	36
1590–4	24	5	4.8	112
1595–7	4	3	1.3	1
1598–1606	Gap in the source	–	–	
1607–9	2	3	0.7	–
1610–13	6	4	1.5	18
1614–20	Gap in the source	–	–	
1621–4	10	4	2.5	6
1627–9	11	3	3.7	–
1632	1	1	1	–
	75	40	1.88	176

by all of the courts in which they were brought to trial. Even in the courts
that did order executions, the witch hunts differed widely in their extent.

Comparable concentrations of trials during the sixty-year period
studied only occurred around 1590. This concentration of trials represented the peak intensity of persecution in the Prince-Bishopric, with trials in
ten of the twelve courts, and a total of 150 executions by burning in only six
years. The individual witch hunts of the years around 1590 in the Prince-
Bishopric of Augsburg have left traces in several other sources. Further
smaller concentrations of trials can be found in 1575, 1597, 1613 and in the
1620s, but in each case they led to fewer executions than in 1590.[32]

The synchronicity of witch hunts in the Prince-Bishopric of Augsburg
with those in Bavaria and the Free City can be regarded as an important
finding. Independently of the size, population, political system, administrative, economic and social structure or type of settlement (urban or
rural) of the territories examined, a relatively uniform trend can be detected for both frequency of trials and numbers of executions.

While a large part of the executions took place in the years around 1590,
clusters of witchcraft trials can be observed in all three territories in the
years 1590–4, 1610–14 and 1625–9. The minutes of the Court Council of
the Prince-Bishopric in particular reveal a smaller wave of trials in the
1570s, which preceded the greater wave that began in the mid-1580s. The
synchronicity observed elsewhere suggests that the neighbouring terri-

---

[32] Cf. the list of trials in the German edition, 431–69.

tories must have been affected by this as well. An explanation of this synchronous development will be offered in another context (pp. 89–114).

FREQUENCY OF TRIALS AND EXECUTIONS IN THE DUCHY OF BAVARIA

Bavaria, until 1623 a Duchy and thereafter an Electorate, had possessed a relatively tightly centralised system of county courts since the later Middle Ages. The judges of these courts were forbidden to decide independently on matters of 'higher justice'. In theory capital crimes could only be judged by the Duke, but in practice they were the affair of his Court Council or of the central authorities, and of the so-called *Viztumämter*, usually called *Rentämter* or (provincial administrations) *Regierungen* in the sixteenth century. Each case of higher justice had to be passed on by the district court to the local *Regierung* for decision. Before torture could be applied, with a few exceptions which did not include witchcraft, the approval of the higher authorities had to be obtained, while the verdict in cases of higher justice was pronounced on the instructions of the higher authorities acting as a college.[34] Before the annexation of the Upper Palatinate in 1623 the Duchy was divided into four *Regierungen*, which between them comprised the districts of about a hundred courts (more or less, depending on whether one includes courts administered in personal union with Bavaria). After 1623 the *Regierung* at Amberg was added, and brought a further twenty-two county courts into the system. According to Ferchl, the county courts were divided between the *Regierungen* as follows:

Munich	35	(Upper Bavaria)
Burghausen	16	(Upper Bavaria)
Landshut	22	(Lower Bavaria)
Straubing	25	(Lower Bavaria)[35]

The provincial administration of Munich occupied a special position in several respects, for it comprised more than a third of all the county courts in Bavaria. Even more important, this part of the Duchy was administered directly by the central authorities, and not through an intermediate tier of government. The Court Council responsible for justice in Munich was also the central authority for the *Regierungen* in Burghausen, Straubing and Landshut, but for the thirty-five county courts in the provincial administration of Munich it acted as central and intermediate authority in one.

---

[33] Cf. note 30.

[34] Heydenreuter, *Der landesherrliche Hofrat*, 185, 218; Christel, 'Die Malefizprozessordnung', 47–52.

[35] G. Ferchl, 'Bayerische Behörden und Beamte (1550–1804)', I–IIII, *Oberbayerisches Archiv*, 53 (1908/12); 64 (1925) (each article comprises a whole volume).

The two most important cities of the Duchy, Munich and Ingolstadt, despite their recognised privileges in cases of higher justice, were also *de facto* subject to the Court Council in Munich. They were denied any autonomy in matters of witchcraft trials, which led to repeated conflicts of competence.[36] In questions of witchcraft, if we are to believe contemporaries, the Court Council at Munich was more zealous than the other three *Regierungen* during the period of most intense persecution, 1585 to 1630, and often reproached them with lack of interest in investigating the problem. The intellectual apologists of witch hunting were also concentrated in Munich and Ingolstadt.[37]

The protocols of the Court Council in Munich, parts of which were examined and evaluated for this work, give us a synchronic cross-section of the cases of higher justice in the thirty-five county courts of the provincial administration and the capital, that is of more than a third of the country. In theory, witch trials from the other *Regierungen* could be brought before the central authorities, but in practice they only crop up in the Munich records when other *Regierungen* consulted the Court Council on their own initiative. That seems to have been the practice in the more important cases, for example at Landshut in 1609, Haidau/Straubing in 1689–94, Burghausen in 1690 and Landshut in 1752. This consultation was not obligatory, however. Each case of witchcraft was assigned to a *Commissarius* from the Scholars' Bench in the Court Council, who had to submit the case to the full Council before any important decision was taken, for example on the application of torture, the appraisal of the circumstantial evidence and statements, and the verdict. Decisions were taken by simple majority, but dissenting opinions were minuted. Difficult cases were taken out of the hands of the county courts altogether. The *Regierungen* thus developed into centres where witches were imprisoned, if the authorities were unwilling to release or to sentence them. The so-called 'witch-towers' in some cities still testify to the fate of these prisoners, some of whom were held for years.[38] The Falkenturm in Munich, the central criminal gaol of the Duchy,[39] became a true laboratory of early modern criminal justice: the councillors from the Scholars' Bench of the Court Council attended in person the tortures they had ordered, which they would then discuss. When witch hunting in Bavaria was at its height there

[36] M. Kunze, 'Zum Kompetenzkonflikt zwischen städtischer und herzoglicher Strafgerichtsbarkeit in Münchner Hexenprozessen', *Zeitschrift der Savigny Stiftung für Rechtsgeschichte. Germanistische Abteilung*, (1970), 305–14. On a wider basis, W. Behringer, 'Scheiternde Hexenprozesse. Volksglaube und Hexenverfolgung um 1600 in München', in R. van Dülmen (ed.), *Kultur der einfachen Leute*, Munich 1983, 42–79, 218–225, esp. 61–78.   [37] Cf. chapter 4, pp. 216–29.

[38] Riezler *Geschichte*, 197; M. Schattenhofer, 'Henker, Hexen und Huren im alten München', *Oberbayerisches Archiv*, 109 (1984), 113–43, 129; Merzbacher, *Die Hexenprozesse*, 117ff.; Film 3866–78 (witch towers in Rain, Kaufbeuren, Memmingen, Munich etc.).

[39] Heydenreuther, *Der landesherrliche Hofrat*, 53, 229f.

cannot have been any jurists in the *Regierungen* who did not regularly attend the torture and interrogation of suspects. Each interrogation of witches in the Falkenturm was attended by at least three Court Councillors, one of whom had to be the *Hofoberrichter* or superior judge. Not infrequently others were also present, among them the Chancellor of the Court Council or high-ranking nobles.[40]

As the protocols of the Court Council record all the witchcraft trials carried on in the provincial administration of Munich, they form a valuable source for the history of witch trials in Bavaria. They begin in 1580 and continue until 1760, in 915 volumes, including indexes and separate volumes. Shortly after 1590 one forms the impression that the minutes cease to be as fragmentary as they were to begin with. In the present study, they have been evaluated in five ways.

Firstly a diachronic cross-section was taken by sampling every tenth year between 1580 and 1760. The whole-decade year was chosen as the sample year in each case, as by chance all the great witch hunts were grouped around these years (1590, 1600, 1608–11, 1628–31, 1689–94, 1720). Secondly, all further years were investigated in which more than average legislative activity gave reason to expect that witch trials would be especially prominent (1590, 1601, 1608, 1612, 1616, 1622, 1625, 1629, 1665, 1677, 1746). Thirdly, a nine-year period was examined (1608–16) in which the internal disputes on the policy to be adopted on witchcraft raged most fiercely in the government at Munich. Nine years correspond to a fifth of the forty-five-year core period of persecution, 1586–1631. Fourthly, several selected years were studied in an attempt to relate the complex of witchcraft and sorcery to other crimes described as *causa domini* in the protocols. Here too, years were chosen in which the problem of witchcraft was particularly urgent (1629, 1630, 1665, 1677, 1680, 1690). Fifthly, of course, the protocols were not examined merely from a quantitative point of view, but from that of their content as well. In total 20 per cent of the protocols for the period 1580–1760 were studied, or 190 of the 915 volumes, or forty years out of 180.[41]

The diachronic cross-section through a period of more than 150 years shows that both the number of county courts holding trials for witchcraft and the number of witches executed were subject to wide fluctuations. If one analyses the number of county courts at which trials for witchcraft were held each year, the years 1590, 1610, 1670 and 1700 stand out. On

---

[40] *Ibid.*

[41] HStAM, Kurbayern Hofrat, Nos. 1, 4–7, 16–19, 41–5, 59–64, 65–72, 73–80, 81–6, 87–92, 97–102, 107–13, 114–18, 119–25, 126–31, 155–63, 172–9, 225–30, 231–4, 266–9, 305–10, 345–9 (346 missing), 365–8, 385–8 (385 missing), 412–15, 424–8 (427 missing), 464–8 (465 missing), 469–76, 503–7 (503 missing), 508–11, 543–7 (545 missing), 583–8 (586, 587 missing), 623–6, 663–6, 687–90, 703–6, 743–6, 880, 884, 886, 893–4, 913–15.

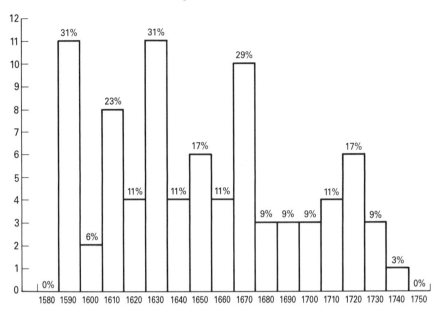

2. Witch trials and executions of witches in the Duchy of Bavaria every full decade, 1590–1750[42]

average, for these five peak years, witchcraft trials were held in sixteen county courts. As the sources for 1590 in Bavaria were still fragmentary, the number for that year may have been even higher. Only thirty-eight of the seventy-eight witch trials for that year fell within the provincial administration of Munich, where an average of eight county courts, or about one fifth of the total, staged trials in these years when witch hunting was at its height. In the worst year, 1630, suspicions of witchcraft were investigated in eleven, or almost one-third of county courts in the provincial administration.

Of course such a large number of trials cannot have been the norm. For our analysis, we deliberately chose years which could be expected to yield a greater frequency of trials. In the other twelve sample years, the average number of county courts holding trials was five, in the provincial administration of Munich three to four. That means that the percentage of county courts that tried suspected witches fluctuated between 10 and 30 per cent,

[42] As the minutes of the Court Council for 1589–91 appear fragmentary (nos. 16–19), they have been supplemented by other available sources for the year 1590, especially from StAM, Gerichtsrechnungen (cf. List of Sources); other additional sources (see list of trials in the German edition) have been consulted.

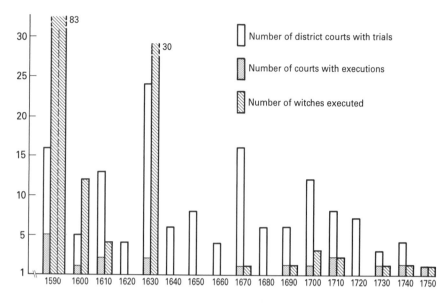

3. Number of county courts in the provincial administration of Munich with trials for sorcery and witchcraft

but as a rule was at the lower end of this band, until the middle of the eighteenth century.[43]

It is clear that the number of courts where trials for witchcraft were held is not a key to the number where witches were executed, which was much lower. The number of courts with executions, in turn, is not a key to the number of executions, since the numerous minor witch trials, in which one person was burned at the stake, count for less in the statistics than a single great witch hunt that claimed fifty victims. If we look at the number of witches and sorcerers executed, we are struck by the dramatic decline after 1590. This can be demonstrated by taking the three years with the greatest number of trials. Nearly a hundred were executed in the wave of persecution around 1590, though the sources are not complete enough to establish an accurate figure, whereas in 1630 there were only thirty executions and in 1670 only one. Three executions in one year also represented the maximum found in our samples of the protocols of the Court Council after 1630, including the years 1665 and 1677, when the mandate against witchcraft was renewed. It is clear from other sources that several witches were condemned to death in Lower Bavaria in some years at the end of the

[43] This table only includes the district courts in the provincial administration of Munich, in order to make it possible to calculate the percentage share.

Table 4 *Decline in the importance of witchcraft after 1630, as reflected in the minutes of the Munich Court Council*[44]

Type of offence	1629 (%)	1630 (%)	1665 (%)	1677 (%)	1680 (%)	1690 (%)
Against property	32	30	30	40	35	35
Against morality	30	33	19	16	14	17
Crimes of violence	6	6	27	17	15	14
Begging and similar	9	5	1	4	2	10
Poaching	3	5	8	10	18	17
Other	10	7	10	7	11	6
Sorcery	2	5	4	5	4	–
Witchcraft	6	9	1	1	1	1
Sorcery and Witchcraft	8	14	5	6	5	1

seventeenth century (1685 Burghausen; 1692, 1694, 1702 Haidau), but the numbers were no longer comparable to those of the period 1590–1630.

The decline in the importance of witchcraft as a problem, at least so far as it is expressed in the number of trials and executions, can be correlated with the relative importance of 'magical' offences and other types of 'serious crime', as reflected in the protocols of the Court Council; this is shown in Table 4.

The years 1629, 1665 and 1677 were the years when the mandate against witchcraft was renewed. While trials for harmless sorcery remained relatively constant in the second half of the seventeenth century, witchcraft no longer played any great part, even in 1665 and 1677.

By examining every tenth year and some years in between, we have cast a wide-meshed net around our subject, and much could have slipped through the mesh. To correct this we have taken a shorter period and examined it in full for the provincial administration of Munich. For the nine years 1608–16, a fifth of the core period of witch hunting, all the protocols of the Court Council, or sixty eight volumes, have been evaluated. They yielded a total of 103 trials; there were no fewer than eleven investigations in Munich in these nine years, five each in Aichach and Dachau, while persecutions in Wemding and Donauwörth lasted five years. Four trials were held in Landsberg on the Lech, three in Ingolstadt, Mainburg, Pfaffenhofen, Reichenhall, Rosenheim, (Markt-) Schwaben, Tölz, Traunstein, Vohburg and Weilheim, two in the courts of Abensberg-Altmannstein, Aibling, Burghausen, Friedberg, Kling, Kranzberg, Landshut, Marquartstein, Rain, Wasserburg on the Inn and Wolfratshausen, and one each in Deggendorf, Dingolfing, Gerolfing, Griesbach, Hohenschwangau, Kösching, Kötzting, Murnau, Regen, Riedenburg, Stadtam-

[44] The data are based on an evaluation of the protocols: HStAM, Kurbayern Hofrat, nos. 225–9 (1629), 231–2 (1630), 365–6 (1665), 412–13 (1677), 424–5 (1680) and 464–5 (1690).

Table 5 *Statistical analysis of 103 witch trials held in Bavaria between 1608 and 1616*[45]

Year	1608	1609	1610	1611	1612	1613	1614	1615	1616	Total
Trials	17	12	12	8	10	5	12	16	11	103
Imprisoned	37	37	26	14	21	10	15	20	23	203
Women	25	34	22	8	18	6	10	12	15	150
Men	12	3	4	5	3	4	5	6	8	50
Children	–	–	–	1	–	–	–	2	–	3
Executed	2	10	4	1	–	–	–	1	–	18
Banished	7	–	4	4	1	4	4	–	1	25
Minor punishments	4	4	1	4	–	–	1	6	4	24
Released	16	3	12	2	18	4	9	8	16	88
Outcome uncertain	7	20	5	3	2	2	1	4	2	46
Died in prison	1	–	–	–	–	–	–	1	–	2

hof, Starnberg, Straubing and Zwiesel. Fourteen of the forty-two county courts involved were outside the provincial administration of Munich, in which 80 per cent of the courts were affected.

The results of statistical analysis of the 103 trials are given in Table 5.

These results show a statistical average of eleven to twelve trials a year, affecting twenty-two to twenty-three persons. Almost three quarters of those arrested were women, and an average of two persons a year were executed as witches. Three were banished from the country, three sentenced to lighter penalties (fines, pilgrimages etc.), ten more were released, and in five cases the outcome is uncertain, but a minor penalty or release is most likely in these cases too. If we compare the average for this nine-year period with the sample year 1610, that year happens to coincide with the statistical average, with eleven trials, but exceeds it in executions, with four. This finding is not surprising, to the extent that the whole-decade was deliberately chosen for the diachronic section because the harshest trials were clustered in those years. The numbers of executions for 1600, 1630 and above all for 1590, are well above the statistical average for the period of witch hunting.

The unexpectedly high number of trials for sorcery and witchcraft is striking in each case. If we deduct from the 103 trials the 20 held outside the provincial administration of Munich, this still leaves an annual average of 9. That means that trials for witchcraft were held in 25 per cent of the county courts each year.

These are purely statistical averages, which tell us little about the actual

[45] The data are based on an evaluation of the minute books nos. 65 (first quarter of 1608) to 131 (fourth quarter of 1616); in each case the minutes of the plenary Council were consulted, as all decisions were taken in the plenum.

frequency of trials in individual district courts. Our analysis of the 103 trials held from 1608 to 1616 has shown that some individual courts are overrepresented. If we take only the eighty-three trials in the provincial administration of Munich, there is a probability of rather more than two trials a year per county court in these nine years. Apart from Munich, where the 'state' prisoners in the Falkenturm find their way into our statistics alongside the victims of 'civic' justice, we find an above-average frequency of trials especially in the courts of Aichach, Dachau and Landsberg, as well as in ten other county courts in Upper Bavaria.

If we compare this topography of witchcraft trials with that of crime in general, certain parallels become apparent. The courts of Landsberg, Aichach and Dachau are prominent in the provincial administration circuit reports of the years 1591–2 and 1601, followed at some distance by Weilheim, Pfaffenhofen and Vohburg.[46] It is an easy inference that the two phenomena have a common cause, but the lack of suitable preliminary studies of the population density, economic and social structure of individual court districts means that this must remain speculative at present. Here it can only be pointed out that the crime of witchcraft must be seen in the context of criminality in general, if we are not to draw erroneous conclusions. Like the protocols of the Court Council, the circuit reports of the provincial administration (*Rentmeister*), although unfortunately preserved for only a few years, allow a statistical insight into the cases of higher justice in the county courts. The most useful additional information they offer is on the number of those who had fled the country or had been banished from it. Murder and manslaughter seem to have been the main reasons for flight from the country. Sentences of banishment, when analysed, reveal a pattern of crime which resembles that reconstructed from the Court Council minutes: offences against property and morality each account for a third, crimes of violence for around 10 per cent, sorcery and witchcraft for about 5 per cent each in the years examined. The remaining offences cover a wide spectrum: malfeasance in office, infanticide, refusal to perform labour services, blasphemy, incest, eating meat on fast days, slander, nocturnal trespass, poaching, threatening language, as well as offences whose character is not made clear. There was no case of flight from the country because of a charge of witchcraft in the years investigated.[47]

In spite of the concentration of reports of witch trials in the central protocols, other serial sources were also examined, using samples, at the lower administrative levels. As a rule about 10 per cent of the former account books of the individual county courts have been preserved. Some of them begin at the end of the fifteenth century, a hundred years before the

---

[46] StAM, RL, Fasc. 24, nos. 99–101.   [47] *Ibid.*

central protocols, but normally they do not begin until the first decade of the sixteenth century. From about 1550, up to nine-tenths of the account books have fallen victim to the 'weeding' of archives in the nineteenth century. For the district courts of Erding in Lower Bavaria and of Schongau in Upper Bavaria, twenty-two books have been preserved between 1550 and 1750, in each case. For the court of Dachau, every third year has been kept for the years 1560–1603.[48] The twenty-two court account books from Erding yielded three witchcraft trials, with a total of nine suspects, all of whom were released, in some cases after torture (in 1590, 1720 and 1740). There were also two trials for sorcery (1630 and 1670), which ended in a penance in Church and in exile, respectively. In 1565 a 'wicked old crone' was banished for unspecified reasons, possibly a case of witchcraft. Six trials with twelve suspects in twenty two-years represent a very high quota, comparable to the frequency of trials in the Court Council protocols at the height of the witch hunting mania.

The degree to which the finds in the 10 per cent of surviving court account books depend on chance is illustrated by the following results: in the twenty-two accounts of the court of Schongau, only one trial was found, and this ended in the punishment of the accuser (1710). For the period 1589–92, when the witch hunt at Schongau took place, the court accounts are missing.[49]

The fifteen court account books that survive for Dachau in the period named did not yield a single case of sorcery or witchcraft, although between ten and fifty prisoners are listed each year, a very high figure compared to other courts. In 1589 a woman was tortured 'because she was suspected of wickedness', and finally banished from the country after swearing an oath to keep the peace.[50] This may have been, though it was not necessarily, a case of witchcraft. What the imprecise description conceals remains the secret of the court clerk. In six account books of the court of Moosburg for the years 1550–1600, no case of sorcery or witchcraft was found.[51]

Though one may doubt the statistical relevance of these investigations of fragmentary sources, one must remember, in the first place, that evaluation of the court accounts gives important pointers to the practice of criminal justice in the countryside, and clarifies the 'qualitative' side at the

---

[48] StAM Hofkammer, Ämterrechnungen, GR Schongau; *ibid.*, GR Dachau; StAL, Rechnungsarchiv, Rentmeisteramt Landshut, GR Erding.

[49] B. Her, 'Grosser Hexenprozess zu Schongau von 1589 bis 1592. Aus den Originalacten geschichtlich dargestellt', *Oberbayr. Archiv*, 11 (1850), 356–80; StAM, Hofkammer Ämterrechnungen, GR Schongau 1710, fol. 8v. No annual account has been preserved between 1576 and 1599.   [50] *Ibid.*, GR Dachau, 1589, fol. 55.

[51] StAL, Rechnungsarchiv, Rentmeisteramt Landshut, GR Moosburg. For further researches in court accounts cf. note 115 to chapter 1 and List of Sources under StAL and StAM.

local level. Quantitatively, the composition of crime as a whole, as reflected in the court accounts, resembles that shown in the central protocols, even though the problems of beggary and vagabondage appear much more often. These prisoners, who in some places account for more than half of all captives, rarely came to the notice of the central authorities, as it was not obligatory to report them. Otherwise the accounts of the district courts also reflect chiefly crimes against property and morality, and crimes of violence. Executions were mainly resorted to in order to punish crimes against property, followed at a distance by crimes of violence, while crimes against morality were only punished by death in the extreme cases of sodomy, incest or rape. Without wishing to anticipate future research it can be stated here that from one to three persons were executed each year in a relatively large number of the years investigated (in the county court of Erding). Executions for offences outside the three groups named above appear to have been rare. In the accounts we have used, only one execution (Erding 1730 for sacrilege) does not fall into these categories. Torture was by no means confined to suspected sorcery or witchcraft, but was used in all other types of offence. It is worth noting that all twelve suspects in the district court of Erding were ultimately released. This fits the current cliche as little as the fact that the use of torture was not distinguished from other 'painful' procedures: 'minor' torture was inflicted for 'minor' suspicions, harsh torture was applied when the suspicion was much more serious. The procedure during witch hunts, in the strict sense, formed the only exception to this rule in many respects. But there are no grounds at all for the view, common in the literature, that a person accused of witchcraft, especially if tortured, was inescapably doomed to die at the stake.

Another favourite theme of the secondary literature must be drastically qualified: the idea that there were long-lasting and wide-ranging persecutions of witches, is shown by analysis of the serial sources to be a mere fantasy, especially if it is coupled with the assumption of massive executions. This conclusion would be reinforced if further series of court accounts were examined. Even though a series is fragmentary in itself, in combination they radically alter the view of the treatment of witchcraft by the judicial authorities of early modern Germany. This can be established from the accounts already investigated, in full or in part.[52] These refer to the courts of Schongau, Dachau (see above), Wolfratshausen, Landsberg, (Markt-)Schwaben, Rosenheim, Friedberg, Auerburg, Starnberg, Aibling and Munich in the provincial administration of Munich; the courts of Traunstein, Reichenhall, Kraiburg and Burghausen in the provincial administration of Burghausen; Erding (see above), Moosburg, Dingolfing

---

[52] *Ibid.*

and Griesbach in the provincial administration of Landshut; and Keil-heim, Regen, Kötzting, Hengersberg, Bärnstein, Dissenstein and Straub-ing in the provincial administration of Straubing.[53] Further accounts were studied for the year of the most intense witch hunts, 1590.[54] In total, these serial sources were investigated for more than twenty county courts. Even though these researches rarely provide the key to the principles on which these cases were dealt with, their object as a rule must have been to discover possibly spectacular cases of sorcery and witchcraft. Time and again it proved, as the *H-Sonderkommando* had already found, that such events were quite out of the everyday judicial routine and far less common, in a local perspective, than had been generally assumed.[55]

At a lower administrative level than the princely county courts stood the local courts of the nobles, the ecclesiastical territories and the towns, as well as those of the prince. At first sight they seem to have had little to do with the supercrime of witchcraft. Yet the records of these local courts form an extraordinarily important supplement to the sources drawn from the higher levels, the county court accounts, protocols of the provincial administrators and protocols of the Court Council. One has to remember that the crime of sorcery, and even more the crime of witchcraft, were practically unpro-vable. At the same time, an accusation of witchcraft was so serious that it could not simply be brought before the county court. An unprovable accusation traditionally rebounded on the accuser, in cases of witchcraft as in other offences.[56] The result was that suspicions circulated outside the courts. When they assumed more massive proportions, it was worthwhile for the suspect to bring proceedings for slander or to seek an injunction to

---

[53] On this the already mentioned studies of Schmid; Brunnhuber; Moser; Markmiller 'Verhandlungen'; Wagner; Huber; the *Heimatbücher* of Ettelt (1981); Kramer. The essay of J. Paulus, 'Mittelalterliche Justiz in Rötz (1589–1700)', *Die Oberpfalz*, 60 (1972), 22–4. On Hengersberg Film 1165. The card-index of customs in the Munich Institute of Ethnology (IV–BK) contains data from the court accounts of Wolfratshausen, Lands-berg, (Markt-)Schwaben, Rosenheim, Friedberg, Traunstein, Reichenhall, Griesbach, Regen, Kötzting, Rottenburg, Kraiburg and Deggendorf. On Straubing also Film 2677.

[54] For the year 1590, to make up for the minutes of the Court Council, which had not yet begun to function as a source, the following were consulted: StAM, Hofkammer Ämter-rechnungen, Gerichtsrechnungen Abensberg-Altmannstein, Auerberg, Dachau, Diessen, Gerolfing, Kösching, Kranzberg, Marquardtstein, Landsberg, Pfaffenhofen, Rain, Reichenhall, Riedburg, Rosenheim, Schrobenhausen, Schwaben, Starnberg, Traunstein, Vohburg, Wasserberg on the Inn, Wemding and Wolfratshausen. Where the sample year 1590 was missing (Dachau, Landsberg), the year 1589 was substituted. All the available annual volumes for the years 1580–1630 were worked through for the courts of Abenberg-Altmannstein, Dachau, Reichenhall, Schongau, Wasserberg on the Inn, Wemding and Wolfratshausen, as well as StAL, Rechnungsarchiv, Rentmeisteramt Landshut, GR Erding. For the period 1550–1600 we also consulted *ibid.*, GR Moosburg, and StAM, Hofkammer Ämterrechnungen, GR Traunstein, GR Schongau, GR Dachau and GR Wolfratshausen.   [55] Film 3709, 3710,

[56] Leutenbauer, *Hexerei- und Zaubereidelikt*, 171f.

desist, against the slanderer. Such private complaints were dealt with by the local courts. Usually they ended in the official lifting of the accusation by the court and the formal withdrawal of the unprovable slander. Frequently the slanderer was punished as well, mostly by a fine of two to three gulden, quite a heavy penalty. In some cases a heavier punishment was imposed. The frequency of such complaints cannot be generally estimated until more extensive studies are made, but a single example may suffice: in the monastic estate of Attel near Wasserburg on the Inn, in the second half of the seventeenth century (1648-1700), six such complaints were made in a population of about 200 adults. In three cases the complaint resulted in the court lifting the slander *ex officio* (in 1649 and 1663), and in three other cases the slanderer was punished: in 1677 and 1684 by fines of 2 to $2\frac{1}{2}$ *pfennige*, and in 1685 by a period in the stocks. Nothing is known of any of the inhabitants of the estate being tried for witchcraft during this period.[57] As to the quantification of these complaints of slander as a witch, we can only say that they are found far less often in the records of the local courts than the more common slanders (thief, rogue, whore). Yet it should be borne in mind that the number of those slandered as witches who went to court and left a record of their complaint must have greatly exceeded the number actually tried as witches. The fact that the cases usually ended in the punishment of the slanderer should alter our perspective substantially.[58] Finally, it is interesting that slanderous accusations of witchcraft, like criminal proceedings on the same charge, were concentrated at certain times. Investigations at Nördlingen, Munich and the Lower Bavarian county court seat of Griesbach reveal that the frequency of actual trials for witchcraft between 1587 and 1594 coincided with an increase in complaints of slander, and that the complaints of slander had increased before the criminal proceedings began.[59]

[57] StAM, Briefprotokolle Wasserberg nos. 697–700 (Klosterhofmark Attel). I owe these data to my colleague R. Schlögl, Erlangen/Münster, who consulted these minutes in another context: R. Schlögl, 'Bauern, Krieg und Staat. Oberbayerische Bauernwirtschaft und Territorialstaat im 17. Jahrhundert', PhD thesis, Erlangen-Nuremberg 1985.

[58] There are data in many local historical articles on the frequency of slanders, e.g. W. Kramer, *Geschichte*; Moser, *Chronik*, 220; Ettelt, *Geschichte*, 247; where it is said that as a general rule these and similar insults (milk-stealer, fork-rider, witch etc.) were quite rare. A different view is taken by K.-S. Kramer, *Volksleben im Fürstentum Ansbach und seinen Nachbargebieten (1500–1800). Eine Volkskunde auf Grund archivalischer Quellen*, Würzburg 1961, 300: 'Trud und Hexe gehören zu den Bezeichnungen zu denen man am ehesten greift.' But it seems open to question whether his few archival references to three different series of sources (Titting, Raitenbuch, Ansbach) justify such a conclusion. Perhaps the insult was more common in areas where witch hunting was more intensive. The data in K.-S. Kramer, *Volksleben im Hochstift Bamberg und im Fürstenthum Coburg (1500–1800)*, Würzburg 1967, 231–41, do not suggest this. The insult 'witch' belonged to the standard repertoire of the people, but when the matter came before the authorities, in most cases the slanderers claimed not to have meant it.

[59] Kramer, 'Volksglauben'; IV–BK (cf. list of trials in the German edition).

The number of witch trials in Bavaria can be estimated approximately from the protocols of the Court Council in Munich. Between 1608 and 1616 103 trials were found, of which 83 took place in the provincial administration of Munich. Extrapolating this figure, one would arrive at a total of 515 trials in this part of the country between 1586 and 1630, or 1,545 in the whole of Bavaria. A similar total is given by extrapolating the results for the five sample years 1590, 1600, 1610, 1620 and 1630. For the hundred years following that date, the ten sample years give an average of rather more than five trials per annum. Extrapolating these figures and making certain corrections, one reaches a further total of a little over 1,500 trials, and a grand total of more than 3,000 trials for sorcery or witchcraft in Bavaria (excluding the Upper Palatinate) between 1586 and 1730. Extrapolation of the number of executions from this assumed number of trials is only possible with some difficulty, as the next section will show.

THE WITCH HUNTS IN SOUTHEAST GERMANY

Adding up the figures for the larger witch hunts brings out once again the outstanding importance of the wave of persecution around the year 1590. Of the fourteen larger witch hunts found during the research for this book, no fewer than ten took place in these years.

The greater witch hunts were concentrated in the core period of persecution between 1586 and 1631. Apart from the witch hunt at Passau in 1614–15, all of them can be grouped either at the beginning or at the end of this period. The 446 victims of these 13 witch hunts who can be counted account for 50 per cent of all those executed!

The minor witch hunts, which claimed ten to nineteen victims, were more spread out over time than the greater ones.

Between these minor witch hunts and purely individual trials, or witch hunts in which the majority of the accused were ultimately released (e.g. Augsburg 1724–8), lay a wider group of small witch hunts or larger trials, in which between four and nine persons were burned for witchcraft. In most cases these were larger witch hunts abandoned prematurely (e.g. Donauwörth 1609) or a 'reduced' form of witch hunt (chains of trials, trials of whole families of witches, etc.) in which an attempt was made to avoid excesses and to adhere strictly to the usual model of procedure.[60] A whole series of these minor witch hunts can be grouped around the great wave of persecution in 1590.

A survey of the chronological and quantitative distribution of witch hunts gives us a graphic representation of the intensity of persecuting zeal

[60] Cf. on this chapters 4 and 5.

Table 6 *Witch hunts with more than twenty victims (Upper Bavaria, Lower Bavaria, Swabia)*

1586–1588	Rettenberg (Bishopric of Augsburg)	25 victims
1589–1591	Schwabmünchen (Bishopric Augsburg)	27 (M)*
1590–1592	Oberdorf (Bishopric Augsburg)	68
1589–1591	Schongau (Duchy of Bavaria)	63
1589–1591	Ingolstadt (Duchy of Bavaria)	22
1589–1591	Werdenfels (Bishopric of Freising)	52
1590–1591	Freising (Bishopric of Freising)	22
1589–1591	Fugger Lordships	–
1589–1594	County of Oettingen–Wallerstein	25 (M)
1589–1594	Free City of Nördlingen	34
Sub-total 1586–1594		338 (M)
1614–1615	Bishopric of Passau	20 (M)
1628–1630	Reichertshofen (Principality of Pfalz–Neuburg)	51
1628–1630	County of Oettingen–Wallerstein	20 (M)
1629–1631	Wemding (Electorate of Bavaria)	40
Sub-total 1614–1631		131 (M)
1586–1631	Total minima (M) of victims of the great witch hunts	469

*M, minimum number.

Table 7 *Witch hunts with ten to nineteen victims (Upper Bavaria, Lower Bavaria, Swabia)*

1563–5	Illereichen (County of Rechberg)	8 (M)*
1575–8	'Allgäu' (?)	10 (M)
1591	Free City of Kaufbeuren	17
1600	Munich (Duchy of Bavaria)	12
1609	Wemding (Duchy of Bavaria)	10
1612–13	Dillingen (Bishopric of Augsburg)	14
1630	Neuburg (Principality of Pfalz–Neuburg)	16 (M)
1656–60	Wasserburg (County of Fugger)	10 (M)
1689–92	Haidau (Electorate of Bavaria)	14
1701–2	Haidau (Electorate of Bavaria)	18
1721–2	Freising (Bishopric of Freising)	11
		140 (M)

*M, minimum number.

in the region over a longer period (see Table 9). It should be said once again that this tabulation does not include trials with fewer than four executions or for which there are only imprecise statements of the numbers involved. As always, our figures are minima.

Summary

If one looks at the quantitative distribution of executions of witches across the various types of trial, one finds that a small number of large witch

Table 8 *Witch hunts with four to nine victims (Upper Bavaria, Lower Bavaria, Swabia, Upper Palatinate)*

1580	Burgau (Margravate of Burgau)	6
1587	Dillingen (Bishopric of Augsburg)	7
1588	Höchstädt (Principality of Pfalz–Neuburg)	5
1589	Donaumünster (Abbey of Holy Cross, Donauwörth)	4
1590	Free City of Donauwörth	2 (M)*
1590	County of Ismaning (Bishopric of Freising)	4
1590	Lordship of Kellmünz (von Rechberg)	5 (M)
1590	Lordship of Osterzell (von Kaltenthal)	9 (M)
1590	Munich (Duchy of Bavaria)	5 (M)
1591	Dillingen (Bishopric of Augsburg)	9
1592	Rettenberg (Bishopric of Augsburg)	9
1595	Burgau (Margravate of Burgau)	4
Sub total 1580–95		69
1608–10	Free City of Donauwörth	4 (M)
1616–17	Wengen (Lordship of Trauchburg in Allgäu/Truchsessen von Waldburg)	9
1616–18	Hemau (Principality of Pfalz–Neuburg)	6
1622	Natternburg (Duchy of Bavaria)	6 (?)
1621–4	Dillingen (Bishopric of Augsburg)	6 (M)
1627	Hemau (Principality of Pfalz–Neuburg/Upper Pal.)	5
Sub total 1608–27		36
1655–8	Free City of Memmingen	5
1677	Neustadt a.d. Donau (Electorate of Bavaria)	5
1677	Laufen (Bishopric of Salzburg)	6
1679	Freising (Bishopric of Freising)	7 (?)
1685	Burghausen (Electorate of Bavaria)	5
1685–6	Free City of Augsburg	5
Sub total 1665–86		33
1715–17	Freising (Bishopric of Freising)	5
1720–1	Erding (Electorate of Bavaria)	5
1730–1	Schwabmünchen (Bishopric of Augsburg)	4
Sub total 1715–31		14
1580–1731	Total minima (M) of victims of small witch hunts (4–9 persons)	152

hunts were responsible for a large share of the total executed (Table 10). It should be noted that the figures in this table are provisional; the absolute figures could be increased by further research in sources not used here. Yet one can form an idea of the way in which the percentage shares of the various groups of trials might be changed. The finding of further major witch hunts is relatively unlikely in view of the surviving sources used in this study. Almost all of them are documented more than once in a variety of independent sources (exception: Illereichen 1563). One may assume that the more important the witch hunt, either quantitatively or qualitatively, the more likely it was to leave traces in the sources. To a lesser extent this applies to smaller witch hunts as well.

Table 9 *Chronological and quantitative distribution of minor and major witch hunts*

Quarter century	Size of witch hunt 4–9	10–19	Over 20	Total	No. of victims
1551–75	–	1	–	1	8
1576–1600	12	3	10	25	446
1607–25	5	2	1	8	75
1626–50	1	1	3	5	132
1657–75	1	1	–	2	15
1676–1700	5	1	–	6	42
1707–25	2	2	–	4	39
1726–50	1	–	–	1	4
200 years	27	11	14	52	761

Table 10 *Relationship between type of trial and number of victims executed (†)*

%	Type of trial	Total	Number of victims
1.4	Major witch hunt (more than 20)	14	469 (= 51%)
1.1	Minor witch hunt (10–19†)	11	140 (= 15%)
2.5	Minor witch hunt (4–9†)	27	152 (= 16%)
13.5	Witch trial (1–3†)	136	168 (= 18%)
81.5	Witch trial (no †)	815	0 (= 0%)
100.00		c.1,000	929

The converse also holds: the less important a witch hunt, the less likely it is to be mentioned in the sources. Town chronicles record executions of witches but hardly ever mention trials that ended in lesser penalties or acquittal (exception: Augsburg 1469). More thorough investigations of town council minutes and official accounts in the future will probably greatly increase the number of known trials which ended in a sentence other than death, and so raise the percentage share of this category. The same may be true to a lesser degree of witch trials with one to three executions and perhaps also of smaller witch hunts, but the percentage share of these groups in the total number of victims will not rise much, since individual executions count for less in the statistics.

The very rough extrapolation above yielded a total of rather more than 3,000 trials in Bavaria (Duchy and Electorate) between 1586 and 1730, a figure which would have to be increased by about a quarter to a third for southeast Germany as a whole. There may therefore have been about 4,000 trials in the region. The number of executions cannot be extrapolated in this way, since one must bear in mind the distribution of executions between the various types of trial. Large witch hunts, which have the greatest statistical weight in quantification, took place in this region only between 1586 and 1630, and are more likely to have been identified in this study, but can therefore be omitted from our extrapolation. Likewise, in the case of lesser witch hunts, it seems, unless the sources used have misled us, that these were singular phenomena, to which one can hardly apply a coefficient in order to extrapolate them. The share of the small witch hunts recorded can scarcely be estimated. If we take the diachronic cross section based on the Munich Court Council minutes from 1580 to 1760, and exclude three years of intense persecution (1590, 1600, 1610), we arrive at a total of six executions, which include two minor witch hunts in 1610. A coefficient of 40 would give 240 additional executions of witches in the region,[61] to be included in our total. One can therefore say, very cautiously, that the total number of witches executed in southeast Germany lay between 1,000 and 1,500.

The extrapolated figures are perhaps less interesting than the direct results of the quantitative research, since these are important in defining the concepts to be applied in this study. First of all, we must again stress the concentration of the problem of witchcraft in the period 1586–1631, distinguished from later years not only by a greater frequency of trials for sorcery and witchcraft but also by the number of executions. The great witch hunts of these years are particularly important in the statistics, especially those at the beginning and end of the period.

The witch hunt of 1590 was crucial for the region. It had already been given prominence in earlier works (Riezler, the *H-Sonderkommando*) and its preeminence has now been confirmed by investigation of serial sources in the Duchy of Bavaria, the Bishopric of Augsburg and the Free City of Augsburg. At the same time, the whole western part of the region was shaken by the force of this wave of persecution. *In less than five years more people were put to death as witches than in all the previous centuries.* Immediately afterwards the number of trials and executions for witchcraft fell back again sharply. This great witch hunting mania therefore deserves particular attention.

The approach to witchcraft after 1590 in this region took a different course from that adopted among its neighbours. In southwestern Germany and in Franconia witch hunting continued to increase in intensity after 1590, the Catholic territories being particularly inclined to stage the greatest witch hunts. In our region, on the other hand, although it was largely Catholic to begin with, and became almost exclusively so as the

---

[61] Coefficient of 40, since every tenth year was examined, and the district investigated makes up a quarter of the region. This rather schematic method serves merely to obtain an idea of the order of magnitude of the figures to be expected.

Counter-Reformation gained ground (Donauwörth 1608, Pfalz-Neuburg 1614, Upper Palatinate 1623), the number of executions declined. The search for an explanation of this untypical development has to form a further main theme of our study.

Other important questions include: what happened when someone was suspected of witchcraft, but was not brought to trial; and how is the rapid rise in executions in 1590 to be explained? The following two sections attempt to answer these questions.

WITCH TRIALS AND POPULAR MAGIC

> What a witch might be?
> That I never heard tell,
> what a witch might be,
> that a woman could ride on a calf,
> that would be a wonderful sight,
> but I would never claim
> that I had seen it with my own eyes
> (Der Stricker, before 1250)[62]

THE RECEPTION OF THE IDEA OF WITCHCRAFT IN THE REGION

Contemporary penitential manuals bear witness to the manifold magical beliefs of the populace in the early and high Middle Ages, and to the attitude of the Church to them, which was one of almost total rejection and arbitrary punishment.[63] Secular legislation fell between two stools: in part it punished harmful sorcery, which implied an admission of its effectiveness, and in part it punished those who punished sorcery, because in the teaching of the Church, the actions of sorcerers were of no effect.[64] That witches could fly through the air was one of the popular beliefs which the Church struggled to eradicate. The most important document for this struggle is the so-called *canon Episcopi* of the tenth or possibly the ninth century, which stigmatised belief in this flight as a heathen error and a

---

[62] J. Franck, 'Geschichte des Wortes "Hexe"', in Hansen, *Quellen und Untersuchungen*, 614–70, 638.

[63] On this in general Hansen, *Zauberwahn*; H.J. Schmitz, *Die Bussbücher und die Bussdisziplin der Kirche, Nach handschriftlichen Quellen dargestellt*, Mainz, 1883; idem, *Die Bussbücher und das kanonische Bussverfahren. Nach handschriftlichen Quellen dargestellt*, Düsseldorf 1898. The material brought to light by Schmitz is exhaustively studied in A. Gurjewitsch, 'Probleme der Volkskultur und der Volksreligiosität im Mittelalter', in *idem, Das Weltbild des mittelalterlichen Menschen*, Munich 1982, 352–401.

[64] Merzbacher, *Die Hexenprozesse*, 13–15; D. Harmening, *Superstitio. Überlieferungs- und theoriegeschichtliche Untersuchungen zur kirchlich- theologischen Aberglaubensliteratur des Mittelalters*, Berlin 1979, 247.

snare of the Devil.[65] The 'Stricker', a south German poet of the first half of the thirteenth century, tried to refute these popular beliefs with arguments that were to be repeated three hundred years later by Montaigne. The attitude of both men was defensive but unequivocal.

The *Lex Baiuvariorum* punished a few special forms of sorcery with money fines, e.g. *aranscarti*, a kind of damage to crops.[66] But popular fury at supposed sorcerers was not always appeased by such mild punishments. A few recorded cases from Saxony, Swabia and Bavaria show that occasionally the people resorted to lynch law, against the will of the Church, and burned sorcerers. At the end of the eleventh century three women were tortured and burned by an enraged mob below the cathedral mount at Freising; monks from the monastery of Weihenstephan secretly gathered their remains and gave them proper burial. The monastery chronicler believed that the women had died a martyr's death.[67]

The Freising example has become quite well known, and is cited in the literature as the prize example of the 'enlightened' attitude of the Church before the later Middle Ages, together with the famous statements of Agobard of Lyons from the ninth century. Agobard was provoked by a similar case of lynch law to deplore the 'abysmal stupidity' of many people, who had been deluded by the Devil into believing in the power of sorcerers and those who tried to control the weather.[68] But one should be careful to observe that the attitude of the Church to sorcery in the early Middle Ages was ambiguous, and not all her representatives could differentiate as clearly as Agobard or the Benedictine chronicler of Weihenstephan. Another story from Freising makes the attitude of the churchmen to popular sorcerers clearer: around 720 the Frankish itinerant Bishop Corbinian was on his way to visit Duke Grimoald of Bavaria in Freising, when he met

a peasant woman, whom he had long suspected of sorcery. She was accompanied by men who were laden with meat and one who was leading a live animal. Corbinian asked her what had brought her here, and she replied: the Duke's son had been harmed by secret glances of demons; she had healed him with her shameful spells and forbidden arts. Then such a rage overcame the Bishop that he sprang from his horse, struck the aged woman with his own hands and distributed all the gifts

---

[65] Hansen, *Quellen und Untersuchungen*, 38f.

[66] Soldan *et al.*, *Geschichte der Hexenprozesse*, I, 305.

[67] *Ibid.*, 118. This case has often been commented on since, most recently by Schormann, *Hexenprozesse*, 26 f., who pointed out that the *veneficae* and those who harmed people and crops were sorcerers in the old sense. He takes a position opposed to that of L. Weiland, 'Ein Hexenprozess im elften Jahrhundert', *Zeitschrift für Kirchengeschichte*, 9 (1888), 592ff.; cf. also Riezler, *Geschichte*, 27–9.

[68] A. Borst, *Lebensformen im Mittelalter*, Frankfurt am Main, 1979, 372–4.

that she had with her to the poor, in front of the town gates. And from that time he avoided the city . . . and lamented the faithlessness of the Duchess.[69]

Gurjewitsch's subtle analysis of medieval sources has collected examples of 'popular magic', which illustrate the depth of magical beliefs among the populace. These glimpses of a world of ritual actions and customs and the invocation of spirits reveal the direct forerunners of that magical world of early modern Europe whose importance has lately been emphasised by Thomas and Muchembled, in particular. Gurjewitsch pointed out the 'extraordinary tenacity of that potential of ideas, assumptions and forms of behaviour, which were alien to Christian teachings, and which the Church was never able to bring under its control throughout the whole of the Middle Ages'.[70] The priests of the Christian Church could not be indifferent to the magical lore that was so widespread among the people, since it was by definition an invasion of that metaphysical territory, the interpretation of which the clergy sought to monopolise for itself. The mere existence of adepts of this competing 'learning' must have been an irritant to the priesthood, and even more so their acceptance by the people or the great ones of secular society. Christian doctrine was endangered if the 'shameful spells and forbidden arts' of the magicians proved successful, as in the case of the peasant woman at the court of Duke Grimoald. Their success could only be explained by invoking 'diabolical hallucinations'. From an early date this theory of devilish illusion was in competition with an alternative, the idea of the pact with the Devil: only demonic assistance could make it possible for 'unauthorised' persons to achieve these unusual successes. The writings of the early and high Middle Ages, which were still unfamiliar with the cumulative offence of witchcraft and explicitly denied that witches could fly, are characterised by this ambivalence toward popular magic.[71]

In the twelfth and thirteenth centuries, as it strove to suppress heretical movements, the Church, led by the Dominican Inquisitors, began to acknowledge the effectiveness of certain forms of popular magical belief. Through Thomas Aquinas and other influential theologians, the findings of the Inquisition made their way into scholastic discussion, but they did not become the received opinion on all points. Many of the components of the emerging cumulative crime of witchcraft, such as flight through the air, influencing the weather, changing into animals and intercourse with the Devil, always remained matters of dispute, a fact which is often overlooked in the secondary literature. Even so, it is unmistakable that the thirteenth century, with the authority of papal bulls, saw a drastic revaluation of

[69] Riezler, *Geschichte*, 28.   [70] Gurjewitsch, 'Probleme' 394.
[71] Harmening, *Superstitio*, 250.

sorcery as a whole (and not merely of harmful sorcery), which was no longer treated as a heathen error or deception, but as a heretical mortal sin. The first mass persecutions of sorcerers were directly associated in both time and place with the great persecutions of heretics in the fourteenth century. The connection of ideas allows the continuity of persecution to be recognised, though it does not explain the shift of emphasis from heresy to witchcraft. The *Secta Gazariorum* and the *Secta Vaudensium* were names applied in treatises of the early fifteenth century to those groups who had been put to death, chiefly in Savoy and France, as *lamiae, strigae* and *maleficae*.[72] Shortly afterwards, similar persecutions of sorcerers began in northern Italy. Contemporaries were of course aware that there was something qualitatively new about these persecutions. The north Italian Inquisitor Bernhard of Como dated the beginning of the new heresy of sorcery to around 1360, and used the fact of the historical novelty as an argument against the *canon Episcopi*, which could not be applied to the flying ability of these new consorts of the Devil.[73]

The ecclesiastical revaluation of all sorcery was also reflected in German legislation. The legal treatises or *Rechtsspiegel* ('Mirrors of Justice') of the thirteenth century, the *Sachsenspiegel, Deutschenspiegel* and *Schwabenspiegel*, sought to have sorcery punished like any other heresy, by burning at the stake.[74] As we know from town chronicles and lists of executions, this legal penalty was rarely, if ever, applied in this region. Heretics, sodomites, counterfeiters and arsonists were burned. In the few known cases of execution of sorcerers, death was by drowning, the usual punishment for poisoners. These were cases where a love philtre had been administered (Würzburg 1470, Nuremberg 1520, perhaps also Straubing 1435, the famous case of Agnes Bernauerin). At Regensburg in 1467 a man was executed by hanging, like a thief, for encouraging the peasants to dig for buried treasure and to steal milk by magic. The Augsburg city law code of 1276 laid down that sorcery was to be punishable only when harm had been caused to life or limb, and then the penalty was to be breaking on the wheel, as for murder. As in the cases cited from Regensburg and Würzburg, it was not the means (sorcery) but the deed itself that was punished here.[75]

The tendency to confuse sorcery and heresy was much less widespread in

[72] Hansen, *Quellen und Untersuchungen*, 118, 149, 183, 408–15, 455, 533–7.

[73] *Ibid.*, 279ff.

[74] Merzbacher, *Die Hexenprozesse*, 15f.; Huber, *Hexenwahn*, on Berthold of Regensburg; S. Lorenz, *Aktenversendung und Hexenprozess. Dargestellt am Beispiel der Juristenfakultäten Rostock und Greifswald*, Frankfurt am Main, 1982, 68–96 (describes the situation for all of Germany).

[75] Huber, *Hexenwahn* 4–8; Merzbacher *Die Hexenprozesse* (1970), 42; Kunstmann, *Zauberwahn*, 39–44. H. Knapp, *Alt-Regensburgs Gerichtsverfassung, Strafverfahren und Strafrecht bis zur Carolina. Nach urkundlichen Quellen dargestellt*, Berlin 1914, 256. On the Augsburg law book, Lorenz, *Aktenversendung*, 91.

Des nachtes auff die schlauffende leüt
Das es in hepmliche ding bedeüt
Vnd vil zauberp vndapn
Die sehent an dem schulter papn
Was dem menschen sol beschehen
Vnd etlich die pehen
Es sep nit güt das man
Den lincken schüch leg an
Voz dē gerechten des morgens frü
Und vil die iehen man stoß der kü
Die milch auß der wammen
So sepnd etlich der ammen

2. Stealing milk by sorcery, from Hans Vintler, *Tugendspiegel*, Augsburg 1486.

southern Germany than in the classical homes of heresy, northern Italy and southern France. In fact, tendencies to the contrary can be observed from time to time: the Freising law book of 1328 classed sorcery with the crimes that were to be brought first before the ecclesiastical judge, as heresy, but all the later editions of this law book followed the *Schwaben-spiegel* in taking the view that sorcery, unlike heresy, was a matter for the lay courts and not those of the Church.[76] Paradoxically the postulates of the *Schwabenspiegel* had no parallels in secular legislation. Augsburg law only punished sorcery with death if it involved murder, and the Bavarian law of Emperor Ludwig of Bavaria of 1346, the most important codification of law in the region, did not contain any provisions on sorcery at all.[77]

It is hard to say what legal basis underlay the sorcery trials that can nevertheless be identified in the region in the fourteenth and fifteenth

[76] *Ibid.*, 96f.
[77] Riezler, *Geschichte*, 62; on the importance of the *Schwabenspiegel* for Bavaria see Spindler, *Handbuch*, II, 529f. (Volkert).

centuries. The penalty demanded in the 'Mirrors of Justice' was not imposed, but it is clear that certain forms of sorcery were punished as harmful, including soothsaying. Numerous cases prove that the death penalty was not usually inflicted in such cases, but that, apart from church penances and humiliations, in the worst cases the penalty was corporal punishment or exile. In 1417, for example, at Landshut, a woman was punished by a public humiliation for practising sorcery, and threatened with banishment if she offended again. At Munich in 1427 a woman who had bewitched a chaplain with a love charm was banished from the city.[78] This way of dealing with cases of sorcery persisted well into the sixteenth century. Among the numerous sorcerers and soothsayers banished from the towns of Bavaria we find the name of Dr Jörg Faustus, whose presence had alarmed the magistrates of Ingolstadt.[79]

The reception of the new concept of witchcraft seems to have got under way in Germany at about the time of the Council of Basel. At that time great persecutions of witches were being staged in southern France, Savoy and parts of northern Italy, Joan of Arc was accused of witchcraft, and even in Rome some women were burned as witches. In the German-speaking countries, the new idea seems to have taken particularly firm root in Switzerland: *hexerye* is a Swiss German word first found in 1419 in a legal document of the city of Lucerne, at that time in the southern part of the diocese of Constance, which in turn was part of the province of Mainz.[80] The first detailed description in German of an extensive witch hunt, in the Canton Valais in 1428, is also from Lucerne; indeed this is the first German text on the crime of witchcraft as such.[81] Like numerous other theologians who attended the Councils, the Dominican Johannes Nider, who came from the Free City of Isny in the Allgäu, concerned himself with the new offence of witchcraft.[82] This widely travelled preacher and author had not seen a witch burned in the regions where he himself was active: Vienna, Cologne, Lindau, Nuremberg or Regensburg. He gathered his proofs of the existence of the crime from the reports of witch hunts in France (diocese of Autun, the case of Joan of Arc) and southwestern Switzerland (Valais and Bern) that were collected at the Council.[83]

---

[78] Riezler, *Geschichte*, 77f.; F. Solleder, *München im Mittelalter*, Munich 1938, 403; further examples in Schattenhofer, Henker, 128.

[79] G. Mahal, *Faust. Die Spuren eines geheimnisvollen Lebens*, Zürich 1982, 135f. Faust was also found undesirable in Nuremberg, *ibid.*, 142.

[80] Franck, 'Geschichte', 528; Monter, *Witchcraft in France*, 17–23.

[81] Hansen, *Quellen und Untersuchungen*, 533–7; on this Bader, 'Die Hexenprozesse, 190.

[82] Soldan *et al.*, *Geschichte der Hexenprozesse*, I, 216; the texts in Hansen, *Quellen und Untersuchungen*, 109–18, 133–45.

[83] Janssen and Pastor, *Culturzustände*, VIII, 504ff.; Riezler, *Geschichte* (1896), 58f.; Soldan *et al.*, *Geschichte de Hexenprozesse*, I, 216f.

The next two south German authors, after Nider, to justify the burning of witches could hardly cite examples from their own experience either. Johann Hartlieb, from Neuburg on the Danube, a political adviser of several Dukes of Bavaria, could only instance two executions of witches in his *Puch aller verpotten kunst, unglaubens und der zauberey* of 1458: one he had seen at Rome in 1423, the other at Heidelberg in 1447.[84] This Heidelberg trial was also discussed by the third eye-witness, the humanist Mathias Widmann from Kemnath in the Upper Palatinate, who also referred to a more recent witch burning at Heidelberg in 1475. These witch burnings were becoming more frequent, but Widmann still described the witches as '*sect Gazariorum*, that is the witches and those who fly by night on brooms, oven forks, cats, goats or other things that serve the purpose'. The author drew his theoretical knowledge from an anonymous treatise written in Savoy around 1440, entitled *Errores Gazariorum*.[85] Nider, Hartlieb and Widmann gave schematic accounts of witchcraft, with the intention of making the offence known in their home countries. Indeed, witches exerted a sort of exotic fascination for Hartlieb, a physician. As an official guest of the Elector Palatine in Heidelberg he had been allowed to speak to a witch who was under arrest. He would have been glad to learn the secret of controlling the weather, but renounced this intention when he learned that he would have to abjure God.[86]

The new concept of witchcraft became established in Germany in the last quarter of the fifteenth century, through the activities of the two papal Inquisitors Sprenger and Institoris, the authors of the *Malleus Maleficarum*.[87] The Heidelberg case of 1475 must have been within the competence of the Dominican Institoris, who had been equipped with extraordinary powers for the whole German-speaking region of Europe in 1474, and since then had been systematically engaged in bringing witches to trial. As the importance of the two Dominicans for the history of witch trials is well known,[88] we shall only mention a few points here, of special importance for southeast Germany. In the first place, it is worth remembering that in spite of their great authority the papal Inquisitors encountered widespread scepticism among both lay and ecclesiastical authorities. To overcome this opposition, in 1484 they procured the notorious papal bull *Summis desiderantes affectibus*. This stated that in the

[84] Hansen, *Quellen und Untersuchungen*, 130–3.   [85] *Ibid.*, 118–21, 231–5.

[86] *Ibid.*, 133. Hartlieb was himself interested in magical arts and wrote works on astrology and chiromancy. Riezler, *Geschichte*, 64ff.

[87] J. Sprenger and H. Institoris, *Der Hexenhammer*, Darmstadt 1974 (reprint of the first German edition, translated and introduced by J.W.R. Schmidt, 1906). On the activity of the Inquisitors, Hansen, *Quellen und Untersuchungen*, 360–408.

[88] Hansen, *Quellen und Untersuchungen*, 360–407; Riezler, *Geschichte*, 71, 81, 102ff; Monter, *Witchcraft in France*, 24ff.

archbishoprics of Mainz, Cologne, Trier, Salzburg and Bremen – that is in practically all the German provinces of the Church except the Archbishopric of Magdeburg – 'very many persons of both sexes' had given themselves over to the heretical practice of sorcery, and that the Inquisitors were authorised to use the machinery of the Inquisition against 'all and every person, of whatsoever estate and dignity they might be'.[89] Secondly, it is important to recall that resistance continued even after this bull. It is well known that the Bishop of Brixen rejected Institoris' attempt to launch a great witch hunt in Innsbruck. Like the bishoprics of Freising, Chiemsee, Passau and Regensburg, Brixen belonged to the Archdiocese of Salzburg. But, thirdly, the secular Estates also protested at the Diet of the Tyrol at Hall in 1487, against excesses committed during torture.[90] The infamous *Hammer of Witches* of 1487, which was partly provoked by the continued resistance to the Inquisitors, tells us that these excesses had been debated in the Estates 'because of the novelty of the work'.[91] Fourthly, Sprenger and Institoris trusted chiefly to the power of example to convince these doubters, as the question of the existence or nonexistence of witches could not be resolved by scholastic disputation. The Inquisitors had a shrewd sense of the power of suggestion associated with the ritual of witch burning:

> furthermore . . . who could be so stupid as to call all their deeds of witchcraft and harmful sorcery delusions and imaginary, when the exact opposite is quite clearly evident to the senses?[92]

Fifthly, it is clear that the activities of the Inquisitors were concentrated at first in the dioceses of Constance and Strasbourg, which were to play a special role in persecuting witches in later years. The prototypical witch hunt was carried out at Ravensburg in 1481–5, where forty-eight witches were burned in five years.[93] In the next three decades before the Reformation, witch hunting on the pattern established by the Inquisitors expanded down the Rhine to the North Sea, as the new idea of witchcraft spread throughout the Empire.[94] The exact geography of this first great wave of witch hunting has not yet been studied, nor has its extent been quantified, so that we have to fall back on the estimate of a Bavarian jurist of 1590,

---

[89] Schmidt, Introduction to *Der Hexenhammer*, xxxvii. Text of the bulls, *ibid.*, xxxii–xli.

[90] L. Rapp, *Die Hexenprozesse und ihre Gegner aus Tirol*, Innsbruck, 1874, 12f.; Byloff, *Hexenglaube*, 31–3. Cf. notes 99 and 100.

[91] Schmidt, Introduction to *Der Hexenhammer*, 'Apologia' of the author Sprenger, *ibid.*, xlii–xlvi.

[92] Sprenger and Institoris, *Der Hexenhammer*, Zweiter Teil, 52.

[93] *Ibid.*, Zweiter Teil, 61; Midelfort, *Witch Hunting*, 201.

[94] Hansen, *Quellen und Untersuchungen*, 586ff.; on the lack of resistance to the new paradigm, Monter, *Witchcraft in France*, 26–32.

who said, without quoting any sources, that 3,000 people had been burned as witches in Upper Germany at that time.[95]

The influence of the Inquisitors in the region studied in this book seems to have been slight to begin with, perhaps because the mendicant orders did not have a firm base in largely agricultural Bavaria. The examples that the authors of the *Malleus* drew from the dioceses of Augsburg, Freising and Regensburg are risibly trivial and not taken from direct experience.[96] On the other hand, the great Imperial Cities offered Institoris and Sprenger, who was also leader for a time of the German province of the Dominicans, demonstrable possibilities of exerting influence.

In Nuremberg, where Sprenger himself had led the provincial chapter of the Dominicans since 1486, the theologians of the order were asked to give their opinions on a difficult case of witchcraft in 1489. A little later the city council of Nuremberg asked Institoris for a copy of the *Malleus Maleficarum*, which he presented to them with an accompanying letter. An edition of the *Malleus* was printed by Koberger at Nuremberg in 1494.[97] In 1497 Institoris appointed the Provost of the Augustinian chapter at Rohr in the district of Rottenburg, as his vicar for the diocese of Regensburg, which included large parts of northern Lower Bavaria as well as the Upper Palatinate. The vicar was empowered to punish witches by burning, under the law of the later Roman Empire. In 1499 this vicar attempted to bring witches to trial in the Lower Bavarian town of Abensberg, by inciting the local priest to preach a series of sermons against witchcraft. The tone of the letter suggests that the Inquisitor's vicar met with little sympathy in the exercise of his office.[98]

Anti-witchcraft sermons of this time have been preserved in a collection of sermons by the Upper Bavarian Benedictine Holzapfler, Prior of Tegernsee, but he did not approach the question in the spirit of the papal Inquisitors. Holzapfler preferred to impose pilgrimages as a penance for witchcraft and suspected that pacts with the Devil were found largely in Styria.[99] Other Bavarian clerics, among them Wann, a canon of Passau

[95] Statement of the Ingolstadt jurist and Bavarian Court Councillor Dr Caspar Lagus (1533–1606), occasioned by the discussions on the witch hunt at Schongau in 1590: 'Sagt diese Handel, wie dann vor 80 Jarn bei 3000 verprennt worden in ober Teutschland . . .', StadtA Munich, Hist. Ver. Urk. 2050, fol. 3.

[96] Sprenger and Institoris, *Der Hexenhammer*, Zweiter Teil, 20; *ibid.*, 44, a story in which a priest from a village near Landshut was sent to fetch beer at a drinking bout, and was said to have been carried through the air by a demon. The champions of the Enlightenment amused themselves greatly at this proof of the danger of the Devil in their homeland.

[97] Kunstmann, *Zauberwahn*, 11, 34; Riezler, *Geschichte*, 104.

[98] Riezler, *Geschichte*, 99; text in Hansen, *Quellen und Untersuchungen*, 509f.

[99] J. Staber, 'Die Predigt des Tegernseer Priors Augustin Holzapfler als Quelle für das spätmittelalterliche Volksleben Altbayerns', *Bayrisches Jahrbuch für Volkskunde* (1960), 125–35. On this see Byloff, *Hexenglaube*, 33f. The monastery of Tegernsee was at the centre of Bavarian intellectual life in the fifteenth century and had close connections with

and one of the leading men in the Church, rejected the new belief in witchcraft propagated by the Inquisitors.[100] Outside Bavaria too, direct theoretical support for Sprenger and Institoris was rarely voiced. In most cases the new doctrine was only accepted in a modified form, as by Geiler von Keisersberg or the Tübingen theologian Martin Plantsch. Nevertheless, the inquisitorial picture of witchcraft spread to the whole Empire within three decades, between 1480 and 1510, and witch hunts were especially frequent in the Rhineland. In the first decade of the sixteenth century the Benedictine Abbot Trithemius was asked to give his opinion in principle on the reality of witches by both Elector Joachim of Brandenburg and Emperor Maximilian I. Trithemius, who was then at the head of an abbey in Würzburg, gave a reply that echoed the *Malleus*: the whole country was full of witches, and even in the smallest village a witch could be found; many people had been bewitched without knowing it, but hardly anywhere was there an Inquisitor or a judge who 'would avenge these public insults to God and nature'.[101]

The clearest example of the reception of the new doctrine in this period comes from the University of Ingolstadt. Christoph Tengler, professor of canon law, was irritated that the scandalous deeds of the witches, revealed in the trials staged by Sprenger and Institoris in Upper Germany, were held to be of so little account by most contemporaries, and that

among the learned in the law there has been much doubt and disputation, as if there were no reason to believe in this heretical custom of the witches, that they do or cause harm to anyone through it . . .[102]

the University of Vienna, as well as with Munich and Brixen (Cusanus), and with the Council of Basel. Spindler, *Handbuch*, II, 744–9 (H. Glaser). V. Redlich OSB, *Tegernsee und die deutsche Geistesgeschichte im 15. Jahrhundert*, Munich 1951. The preacher at Passau cathedral P. Wann, who, at the request of Archduke Sigmund, defended the women arrested at the Innsbruck witch trials of 1485 against the papal Inquisitor Institoris, wrote a letter about the case to Abbot Konrad Airimschmalz of Tegernsee on 21 October 1485; Redlich, *Tegernsee*, 68–71, from HStAM, KL Tegernsee, 234½. In confessional manuals of the fifteenth century witchcraft still played only a limited role. J. Staber, 'Ein altbayerischer Beichtspiegel des 15. Jahrhunderts (Cgm 632)', *Bayr. Jb. f. Volkskunde* (1963), 7–24.

[100] Redlich, *Tegernsee*, 68–71. Wann opposed Institoris' suspicions in Innsbruck and promised to give a sermon in which he would restore the reputation of the Holy See, damaged by the Inquisition (!). The statements of Wann reveal the vigorous opposition to the Inquisitors among the population of Innsbruck. He himself spoke of 'ungerecht verdächtigten Frauen'.

[101] Baschwitz, *Hexen*, 13–19. Hansen, *Quellen und Untersuchungen*, 291–6; Soldan *et al.*, *Geschichte der Hexenprozesse*, I, 408–12.; J. Trithemius, *Antwort Herrn Abts zu Spanheim auff acht fragstuck ime von weylandt Maximilian Roem. Kayser hochlöblichster gedachtnuss, fürgehalten*, Ingolstadt 1556.

[102] U. Tengler, *Der neu Layenspiegel*, Augsburg 1511; cited here from the Strasbourg edition of 1544, fol. cv.

3. Deeds of the witches: pact with the Devil, intercourse with the Devil, flight to the witches' sabbath, weather 'cooking', the 'witches' shot', milk stealing. From Ulrich Tengler, *Der neu Layenspiegel*, Augsburg 1511.

Even well-meaning contemporaries, such as the professor's father, Ulrich Tengler, Governor of Höchstädt for Pfalz-Neuburg and author of a legal handbook (the *Layenspiegel*, Augsburg 1509), had difficulties in classifying the crime of witchcraft. The *Layenspiegel* dealt with witchcraft but placed it in the section on 'murder and other homicides', and under 'Jews and other unbelievers', in which heresy was also discussed. When Christoph Tengler revised the fourth edition of the *Layenspiegel* (*Der neu Layenspiegel*, Augsburg 1511), these uncertainties were swept aside. Nine pages were inserted 'On heresy, soothsaying, black arts, sorcery, witches etc.' with an explanatory woodcut. This was the first German legal handbook to inform the interested reader of the way in which the Inquisition thought witchcraft was to be dealt with. Tengler prescribed the harshest procedure and 'the most cruel torture of all' for witches.[103] Because it went into so many editions the *Layenspiegel* has been credited with great influence on the legal practice of the sixteenth century, but, at least in the region studied here and with reference to cases of witchcraft, this is a view that we cannot confirm. In Pfalz-Neuburg and other Lutheran territories disinclination to accept the emphasis placed on the papal Inquisitors' findings may have played some part. In 1587–8, when the first serious witch trials were held in Höchstädt, Tengler's home town, the allegedly influential *Layenspiegel* was not cited as an authority even in the most detailed legal opinions. Rather, the courts proceeded as if there had never been any previous trials for witchcraft in the district, or even theories about how to conduct them.[104] Nor has the influence of the *Layenspiegel* yet been demonstrated in the Catholic territories either.

Although there were no new editions of the *Malleus* anywhere in Europe between 1520 and 1580, it remained the standard work and was available in libraries in the region.[105] The reception of the Inquisitorial concept of witchcraft took place against the background of overt popular magical activities, and the boundaries of what was considered 'sorcery' in a given case were always fluid. For committed Lutherans certain Catholic rituals and practices were stigmatised as sorcery (e.g. the blessing of livestock, veneration of relics etc.). The practice of magic, sorcery and so on was, however, not the same as the new crime of witchcraft, the reception of which was decisively completed in the last quarter of the fifteenth century. Some examples may illustrate the direction that this reception followed

[103] Hansen, *Quellen und Untersuchungen*, 296–306, quotation from 306.
[104] HStAM, Hexenakten 16, fol. 141v, opinion of the highly regarded jurist Dr Christoph Mumprecht (1560–1620) for the Count Palatine Philipp Ludwig von Neuburg. On Mumprecht Henker, 'Zur Prosopographie', 231. Tengler's influence is generally overrated, e.g. by Riezler, *Geschichte*, 131f., 137; R. von Stintzing, *Geschichte der deutschen Rechtswissenschaft*, I, Munich 1880 (reprint 1957), 640–9.
[105] Ott, *Das Bürgertum*, 83–133; Film 3662, 1–11; Kunstmann, *Zauberwahn*, 12.

and how far it can be traced in the sources which have been made available to date.

In principle the reception of the new doctrine seems to have spread from west to east. The early theoreticians Nider, Hartlieb and Widmann disseminated their knowledge from Switzerland or the Palatinate to southeast Germany. The Inquisitors Sprenger and Institoris conducted their paradigmatic witch trials in the southwest, in the diocese of Constance. From here they exercised a manifold influence on the regions to the east. This was quite direct in the first documented witch trial in southeast Germany (Nördlingen 1478), which was provoked by a denunciation from Sélestat in distant Alsace, where the papal Inquisitors had taken a decisive part in the Inquisition.[106] But the Inquisitors were called in for local reasons as well. The *Malleus* itself relates one such case. In a town between Ravensburg and Salzburg, but still in the diocese of Constance and so presumably in the Allgäu, all the crops and orchards were devastated by a frightful hailstorm, so that the people demanded punishment of the evildoers, using the procedure of the Inquisition:

> when this event became known through the notary of the Inquisition and because of the clamour of the people, an inquisition became necessary, in as much as some, yes almost all the townsfolk held that such a thing had come about through bewitchment, with the consent of the councillors an inquisition was held by us in legal form for fourteen days into heresy, namely witchcraft, and proceedings were brought against at least two persons, who were in evil repute with the others, who were present in no small numbers. The name of one, a bath-house keeper, was Agnes, and that of the other Anna of Mindelheim.[107]

Besides these two witch burnings, we have proof of two others, one at Immenstadt, the chief town of the County of Rothenfels in the Allgäu, and another in the Free City of Lindau in 1493. There was a serious accusation of witchcraft in 1484 in Unterthingau, a district of the Prince-Abbacy of Kempten in the Allgäu, but in this case the accuser was forbidden to make further charges against the supposed witch.

East of the river Lech, that is chiefly in the territories of the Duchy of Bavaria, cases of comparable seriousness have not yet been documented. The trials in the Free City of Regensburg between 1470 and 1500 show the procedures becoming harsher, but even so these trials remained within the normal bounds, measured by the severity of punishment imposed. The Bavarian trials of this period which have been found to date – in Burg-

---

[106] Wulz, 'Der Prozess', 42–5.
[107] Sprenger and Institoris, *Der Hexenhammer*, Zweiter Teil, 157–60.

hausen, (Markt-)Schwaben, Dingolfing, Braunau, Landsberg, Munich and Rottenburg – do not indicate that the procedure desired by the Inquisitors was followed. In a remarkable number of cases the accused was acquitted or the accuser punished for making unfounded accusations.[108]

The best-documented pre-Reformation trials for witchcraft in the region were two in the Free Cities, both of which show the relative openness of the town magistracies in dealing with complaints of witchcraft. In the Nördlingen case of 1478, the accused, the town midwife, was imprisoned but the authorities could not make up their minds to torture her. Ultimately they were less willing to believe the accusations of some peasant women from Alsace, even if confirmed by the magistrates of Sélestat, than the statements of the midwife, who was a person in their confidence and under oath to them.[109] A peasant woman from the noble territory of Pless near Memmingen was not so fortunate; she and her family were regarded as witches by the villagers, but no legal proceedings had ever been taken against them. In 1518 the holder of the rights of lower justice in Pless, a patrician from Memmingen, applied to the town council of Memmingen to have an inquiry held. As the Memmingen executioner felt that the matter was more than he could manage, the city turned to the towns of Saulgau and Waldsee, both under the jurisdiction of the Habsburgs, and in the old sphere of influence of the Papal Inquisitors, where there was experience with trials for witchcraft.[110] The executioner of Saulgau was famous, in fact, for his skill in interrogation. When he arrived in Memmingen he had new implements of torture made, and it is clear that the course of the proceedings was largely influenced by the executioner, who was familiar with every refinement of witchcraft trials: he used holy water, incense, consecrated salt, shaving, the weeping test, repeated torture in cases of *maleficium taciturnitatis*, and so on. The town council of Memmingen was unwilling, however, to let this continue for long with no prospect of an outcome. The executioner of Saulgau was dismissed and the accused woman released after a few weeks in gaol.[111] The sources for the years 1470–1518 are too scanty to be able to exclude further executions of witches entirely, all the more so as there are some documented cases in neighbouring regions.[112] But it is unlikely that there was any regional wave of witch hunting at this time.

[108] Cf. list of trials in the German edition, 431–69.   [109] Wulz, 'Der Prozess', 45.

[110] StadtA Memmingen, Schubl. 344, no. 9/1. The patrician Jörg Besserer held the rights of lower justice at Pless. Midelfort, *Witch Hunting*, 201 cites only the witch trial at Waldsee, and omits that at Saulgau.

[111] StadtA Memmingen, Schubl. 344,. no. 9/1; *ibid.*, Ratsprotokoll, vol. 1517–19, s.f., entries of 8, 12, 24, 26, 29 November and 13 December 1518.

[112] Riezler, *Geschichte*, 141f.; Hansen, *Quellen und Untersuchungen*, 598; Kunstmann, *Zauberwahn*, 19; G. Heckel, 'Hexenverfolgung in Schwabach', *Die Heimat. Beilage zum Schwabacher Tagblatt* (1932), nos. 6, 7, 8; Leutenbauer, *Hexerei- und Zaubereidelikt*, 173.

REJECTION OF THE PARADIGM OF WITCH HUNTING

Although we find a few decided apologists of witch hunting in southern Germany in the decades before the Reformation (Kramer, Institoris, Trithemius, Tengler), such zealots seem to have disappeared after the Reformation, like the anti-witchcraft tracts, production of which suddenly declined after 1520. Even so, we can find a few nuclei where the developing belief in witches continued to crystallise after 1520,[113] but for the time being its official acceptance had been halted. The best illustration of this is the rejection of popular accusations of sorcery and witchcraft by the authorities. Of course, they had to yield to the 'clamour of the people', which still branded a few individuals as witches, but the treatment of these accusations, slanders and rumours reveals that there was no real willingness to persecute on the part of the authorities.

A few executions of sorcerers are recorded between 1520 and 1560 (Weissenhorn 1542, Regensburg 1552), but the victims were not witches, or else the trials did not display the distinctive trait of a witch hunt, the tendency to expand to numerous other suspects. Spectacular complaints of witchcraft, such as that at Günzburg (Margravate of Burgau) in 1530, at Gundelfingen (Pfalz-Neuburg) in 1538 or in the Prince-Abbacy of Kempten in 1549, were repressed. Not uncommonly, at the end of the trial it was not the alleged witch but the overzealous accuser who was punished. A plaintiff who could not prove the charge adequately – which was practically impossible in cases of sorcery or witchcraft[114] – had to expect a heavy fine. Examples can be found in the accounts of the district courts of Dingolfing, Markt-Schwaben, Landsberg, Rosenheim and Traunstein. But making such charges could entail even more serious consequences. In the Nördlingen trial of 1534 it seemed as if the suspect woman was about to be found guilty of witchcraft, and the executioner of the Free City of Ravensburg had been called in as an expert, when the town council had the accusers, both women, arrested. They feared that they would be put on trial themselves, and withdrew their charges. The suspect and her alleged accomplice were then released. The two plaintiffs were exiled from the town for life, and one of them had to sell her house and lost her income from a civic office.[115] The trial was held under the strict supervision of the three councillors who took part, so that the executioner was unable to act on his own initiative. The magical practices of the accused were not held against

---

[113] See note 27; cf. also Midelfort, *Witch Hunting*, 202.

[114] HStAM, Hexenakten 4, Prod. 15, fol. 7.

[115] Wulz, 'Der Prozess', 45–50; Kramer, 'Volksglauben', 44. As in the Memmingen trial of 1518 or the trials in the Bishopric of Augsburg of 1586–7, an executioner was called in from the southwest.

them, since they could not be shown to have any connection with harmful sorcery, as required by article 109 of the *Constitutio Criminalis Carolina*, enacted in 1532.

The *Carolina* was enacted at a time of relative scepticism toward the papal Inquisitors' theory of witchcraft, and not merely from the Lutherans. Article 109 of this criminal ordinance for the Empire, which distinguished harmless from harmful sorcery, and left its punishment to the judge's discretion, represented a minimum consensus between apologists of witch hunting and sceptics. Yet witches could be burned on the basis of this article, even though it made no mention of witchcraft. As is well known, the *Carolina* was only of subsidiary importance in the territories. When we look at the legislation of the territories in the years 1470–1570, we find that witchcraft as such was not punishable under any of the laws of the region studied in this book, or its neighbours. The terms of the criminal ordinance of Bamberg of 1507, adopted in the Margravates of Ansbach and Baden in 1516, followed the *Schwabenspiegel* in equating harmful sorcery with heresy, and reserved death at the stake for this offence alone. The corresponding passage served as the example, but without the religious reference, for article 109 of the *Carolina*.[116] The Tyrolean criminal ordinance of 1499 contained no provisions against sorcery, nor did the ordinances of 1526 and 1532. The first reference in a mandate to sorcery and soothsaying as 'fraud' and 'deceit' is in 1544, and the first explicit references to the suppression of sorcery, though without any mention of the death penalty, are in ordinances of 1552, 1568 and 1573.[117]

The Duchy of Bavaria lay between Franconia and Tyrol, and not just in a geographical sense, but in this case in its legislative development as well, as far as the crime of sorcery was concerned. It was first included among the *Viztumhändel*, or crimes reserved to the Duke's courts, in 1506, but it was not until the next Diets of 1507 and 1516 that agreement was reached on the exact place of this offence in a catalogue of such crimes. The Estates would have preferred to combine robbery and sorcery in a single article, but the Duke's spokesmen criticised this view, and maintained that robbery belonged with theft, while considering sorcery as a separate crime. Finally, the following sequence of offences was agreed: coinage offences, rape, unnatural vice, false oaths and false witness, 'whoever practises sorcery that causes harm', theft, robbery, crimes in the churchyard. In serious cases the death penalty was reserved for these crimes, but in lesser

---

[116] G. Radbruch (ed.), *Die Peinliche Gerichtsordnung Kaiser Karls V von 1532 (Carolina)*, 4th edn Stuttgart 1975, for the relevant articles 21, 44, 52 and 109. Radbruch was right to emphasise in his introduction the moderating character of the *Carolina*, which is often overlooked in the literature (*ibid.*, 10). The text of the *Bambergensis* of 1507 in Hansen, *Quellen und Untersuchungen*, 279.   [117] Rapp, *Die Hexenprozesse*, 13.

cases the sentence was commuted to a fine. As Leutenbauer has convincingly shown, the treatment of sorcery under Bavarian criminal law before 1550 corresponded to this scheme.[118] This catalogue of offences of 1516 was taken over without alteration in the Ordinance of 1553.

Not only the legislation, but the commentators on criminal law as well, ignored the inquisitorial concept of witchcraft and its uncritical adoption in Tengler's *Layenspiegel*. In Bavaria, the *Halsgerichtsordnung* of the Munich jurist Andreas Perneder (d. 1543) was influential, and it explicitly excluded harmless sorcery (Macfarlane's 'white magic') from punishment:

> Whoever by black arts, invocation of evil spirits or other sorcery causes harm to people or purports to prophesy the same to them, shall be burned.
> But if someone has helped a sick person through his art, or has protected orchards and fields from damage, shower or hail, this is not punishable under the secular law.[119]

Perneder's work enjoyed the highest reputation in the whole region. In 1544 it was revised by the Ingolstadt jurist Wolfgang Hunger, and went into several more editions. In a new edition of 1573, prepared by the Munich patrician Octavian Schrenck, the article on sorcery was left unchanged. The mere fact that Hunger later became Chancellor of the Prince-Bishopric of Freising, and Schrenck Chancellor of the Prince-Bishopric of Regensburg, is enough to show that Perneder's commentary and his interpretation of the crime of sorcery were important beyond the frontiers of the Duchy of Bavaria.[120]

Rejection of Sprenger and Institoris' paradigm of witch hunting was not confined to the magistrates and jurists, but was shared by the clergy of the region. When he examined the metropolitan and diocesan synods of the region Riezler found that women soothsayers and sorceresses (*incantatrices*) were not placed on the long list of those who were to be excluded from communion until 1490. A Regensburg synod of 1512 laid down a similar rule, which seems to include a reference to the new concept of 'witches' (*artesque maleficas Phitonissarum*), but it was not until the provincial synod of Salzburg in 1569 that pacts and intercourse with the Devil and witches' sabbaths were mentioned, and the need for punishment by the secular arm pointed out. Yet the same source adds that priests should only

---

[118] Leutenbauer, *Hexerei- und Zaubereidelikt*, 97–9.
[119] A. Perneder, *Vom Straff und Peen aller und yeder Malefitzhandlungen (. . .)* Ingolstadt 1551, fol. 7, Lit. B. On Perneder see Bosl, *Biographie*, 579; or *Allgemeine Deutsche Biographie*, 25, 385f. On Perneder's importance for legal history see also Stintzing, *Geschichte*, I, 645.
[120] On Hunger see Bosl, *Biographie*, 380; on Schrenck *ibid.*, 701; Riezler, *Geschichte*, 139f.

report soothsayers to the bishop if they could not be led back on to the right path, and were already in evil repute with others. Otherwise they were to be taught that 'these are only delusions of the Devil'.[121]

For the period 1520–60 internal debates about the seriousness with which witchcraft was to be taken have only been preserved from Nuremberg; thanks to the legal opinions eagerly sought from it by others (e.g. Passau in 1527, Weissenburg in 1533, Ulm in 1538), these were of more than regional importance. To outsiders the Free City acted as if it were unanimously of the opinion

> that my lords do not believe in witches and the work of the Devil, nor that such cases have occurred, but they have found from their learned men and theologians and jurists that there are no grounds for it, but that it is pure fantasy, and therefore they have not imposed any punishment except to banish them from the country.[122]

Yet there were acrimonious debates inside the council. It seems to have been divided between a party willing to stage witch hunts, led by the famous Dr Christoph Scheurl, and a larger moderate faction, whose spokesman, Dr Johann Hepstein, declared that he did not believe in the existence of witches at all. In Hepstein's opinion sorcery and witchcraft were mere 'fantasies and delusions' based on 'unbelief, unreason and the fevered imagination of the people'.[123] This moderation, which may be seen, if wished, as an expression of civic rationalism, forms the ideological background to the treatment of the theme of witchcraft in the culture of the time. In the woodcuts of Albrecht Dürer or Baldung Grien, the young witch, with all her wonderful attributes, was shown purely as an exercise in the representation of the female figure, a kind of contemporary Susannah in the bath.[124] These witches have little of the demonic about them, as little as the witch in Hans Sachs' 'Wonderful Talk of Five Witches'. This poem ends with the author waking from a dream: 'it was just a dream and fantasy, as it is with these women who practise such black arts'. The lengthy dream is followed by a lengthy moralising conclusion: love charms, fortune telling, invocation of the Devil, crystal gazing, weather spells, intercourse with the Devil, witches' flight, changing into animals, all

---

[121] *Ibid.*, 32–5. Leutenbauer, *Hexerei- und Zaubereidelikt*, 174, quotes the corresponding texts verbatim.

[122] Kunstmann, *Zauberwahn*, 177. Nuremberg undoubtedly surpassed all other places in southern Germany in its importance as a centre of secular thought in the early sixteenth century. The high point of the development is formed by the Nuremberg *Mandat des Trautenwercks, Zaubereien und Wahrsagereien Halben* of 1536, which declared in print that all these crimes were 'ein offentlichen greyfflichen yrrthumb falschen Betrug'. The death penalty was not provided for them. Kunstmann, *Zauberwahn*, 69–71, gives the text.

[123] *Ibid.*, 62; in general *ibid.*, 58–65 and 186–8.

[124] Merzbacher, *Die Hexenprozesse*, 10.

are 'mere lies and deceit'. No true Christian can believe such nonsense: 'this is heathen mockery, of those who do not believe in God'.[125] Who can be surprised, therefore, when the Ingolstadt humanist Johannes Turmair of Abensberg (Aventinus) includes witches among the creatures of mythology? For him, a witch was a kind of female healer from the tribe of the Amazons.[126]

In the introduction we have already mentioned that publicists did not begin to debate the inquisitorial paradigm of witch hunting in Germany until the early 1560s, as a reaction to a revival of witch hunting which contemporaries had not expected.[127] The size of the shift in opinion among the authorities in the region only becomes clear when set against this background of a phase in which belief in witchcraft had been latent. This makes it all the more astonishing that the reception of the idea of witchcraft should have gathered pace again and led to a climax of witch hunting between 1560 and 1630.

DEALING WITH HARMFUL SORCERY IN 'POPULAR MAGIC'

It may at first seem trite to conclude that the behaviour of 'subjects' was in an interdependent relationship to that of the authorities. Turning to particular cases one often sees that soon after the arrest of the first suspects, accusers appeared and named others as witches, but without wishing to act directly as plaintiffs. Accusations of suspected witchcraft were normally far too hazardous, since secret crime could never be proved. Hence, unless they admitted their guilt, witches could usually only be convicted when the authorities had resolved to apply harsh torture. Bringing a charge of witchcraft then lost its risk for the accuser, because the accused would probably confess and be executed. The beginning of witchcraft persecutions on the inquisitorial pattern therefore provoked a veritable flood of such denunciations, pent up for years or even decades.[128]

Yet our quantification has led to the conclusion that in individual places, witch hunts were very exceptional events, so that such an opportunity was rare. Finally, there were long periods when accusations or denunciations for suspected witchcraft had very little prospect of success. This had been the case in Germany in the last quarter of the fifteenth century before

---

[125] Kunstmann, 212–14, gives the full text.

[126] J. Turmair (Aventinus), *Bayerische Chronik*, Ingolstadt 1534, here cited from Franck, 'Geschichte', 644.   [127] See above, chapter 1, pp. 1–16.

[128] The Kaufbeuren *Verruf von wegen Beschreiung des Hexenwerckhs* of 1591 says that all the slanders since the beginning of the witch hunt had been uttered in 'unzeitig gefasten neyd und zorn oder sunsten frevelem und frechem muetwillen unbedächtlich'. The Council forbade further charges 'Höchsten Ernsts und bey straff Leibs und guets'. StadtA Kaufbeuren, B 106, fol. 164f.

the activity of the papal Inquisitors, and was again the rule in the long period of latency between 1520 and 1560. What happened to the many suspicions of witchcraft in the region during these years when the authorities could not be induced to put witches to death?

Obviously the people managed to cope with this serious problem without the intervention of their rulers, though it must be said at once that cases of lynch law are hardly ever found.[129] As the authorities were always relatively interested in finding out new information about the secret arts of their subjects, the records of such hearings allow us to say something about these coping mechanisms. The following paragraphs attempt to use regional sources to reconstruct the popular mechanism for dealing with sorcery, especially suspected cases of harmful sorcery. This analysis reveals a relatively unknown side of 'our' past: as in Macfarlane's Essex and, as several other studies have shown, probably in the whole of pre-industrial Europe, we find traces of an intensive 'popular magic', a world of spells and counterspells, of belief in magical relationships in nature, demonic apparitions, benign spirits, angels and so on, without which the phenomenon of witch trials cannot be properly understood. The most important lesson we must learn from these sources is that reason and belief in magical relationships or supernatural phenomena were not opposed to each other,[130] and that sorcery was not regarded as morally reprehensible or 'wicked' by the people, but as neutral.[131] It was evidently seen as a kind of instrument, which could be used for good purposes – to heal the sick, to recover lost or stolen objects, to predict the future – or for evil – to make others fall ill, to steal milk, to control the weather etc. Many practices could be seen as either good or evil depending on the point of view, and their position was therefore ambivalent. In theory the Church condemned every form of sorcery, since in the view of theologians, it required at least a

---

[129] Byloff, *Hexenglaube*, 39, 141, gives several examples of the suppression of witch trials by the central government. The same author, however, also documents several cases of popular resistance to witch trials staged by the authorities, *ibid.*, 60, 136, 150.

[130] Basic for the understanding of this complex are the accounts in Mauss, *Sociologie*, I, 154–76; Evans-Pritchard, *Hexerei*, 60–76; Thomas *Religion* (1980 edn), 3–26 and 209–334; Gurjewitsch, 'Probleme', 352–401.

[131] Muchembled, *Kultur*, 85. Also impressive is the example in F. Markmiller, 'Die Beschwörungen des Martinsbucher Pfarrers Johann Weiss gegen Ende des 16. Jahrhunderts', *Der Storchenturm* (1970), Heft 9, 55–66. The Catholic parish priest, who held his living for nearly forty years as successor to his father (!) did not possess a catechism, but he owned a book of sorcery, which made him famous far and wide. With incredible tenacity he defended his activities against Duke Albrecht V; and neither the famous Petrus Canisius nor the assembled clergy of Straubing were able to persuade him to give them up. Such men as Weiss, who was widely popular with his concubine, his children and his flock because of his magic arts, must have been the despair of the strict religious activists.

tacit understanding with a demon.[132] The people, the regional authorities and probably many priests as well, were far removed from this theological-rationalist view. At any rate the people were faced with the problem of dealing with supposedly harmful sorcery, especially when it could not be unequivocally proven, and the chances of a successful complaint to the official courts appeared slim. What usually happened when such suspicions were aroused? Either the victim (and there was no sexual preference here) already knew the person who had caused the harm, usually a case of sickness of human or animal, or damage to crops, or he did not. In the first case the existing suspicion had to be substantiated, and in the second the perpetrator had to be found. Frequently, the victim went to a competent outsider, perhaps a doctor, a midwife or an executioner, to confirm that it was a genuine case of sorcery. If their cures did not work, they often diagnosed sorcery ('unnatural illness'). Another form of diagnosis involved the use of oracular and soothsaying techniques.[133] These skills were widely known among the population, and there were 'experts' who had specialised in them and won fame for their skill. These so-called 'soothsayers' can be regarded as the axis around which the world of popular magic revolved. As a rule they confirmed their clients' suspicions of witchcraft and, as the following case from Nördlingen in 1534 will show, they were not without psychological skill in playing on their clients' needs: a man approached a soothsayer, believing that his wife had been bewitched, after all the doctors' attempts to cure her had failed:

First of all I went to a soothsayer. First she said to me, I had had many doctors. And before I spoke to her, she had known half my business beforehand. After that she put a crystal on the table. Then I asked her 'I would like to know, good woman, whether my wife's illness was caused by someone or not?' Then she began and said, how it had come about.[134]

---

[132] On this complex, in exhaustive detail, Harmening (*Superstitio*), who traces the way in which the Christian theory of signs became more specific, *ibid.*, 81–117, 303–8.

[133] On this the parallels in Evans-Pritchard, *Hexerei*, 181–245. Examples of this function of the soothsayer are found in all records of trials for sorcery and witchcraft. The Nuremberg mandate of 1536 (cf. note 122) explicitly aimed to suppress soothsayers, because they had more authority among the populace than had the clergy. The Bavarian *Landtgebott wider die Aberglauben, Hexerey und andere sträffliche Teufelskünste* of 1612, fol. 9–11, also denounced soothsayers for the same reasons. In the literature there is already an example in the Malleus Maleficarum of nobles consulting 'a certain peasant' when they felt themselves bewitched. The peasant then pronounced his oracle, in this case by melting drops of lead. Sprenger and Institoris, *Der Hexenhammer*, Zweiter Teil, 190f. Examples from folklore literature in Kramer, *Volksleben* (1961), 189. *Idem, Volksleben* (1967), 178; R. Beitl, *Wörterbuch der deutschen Volkskunde*, 3rd edn Stuttgart 1974, 614f.; other impressive examples in F. Kuisl, *Die Hexen von Werdenfels*, Garmisch-Partenkirchen, n.d., 9.   [134] Wulz, 'Der Prozess', 46.

The soothsayer did honour to her profession and discovered her client's request, presented him with the usual story and produced her crystal as a tangible pledge of her magical skills. The proverbial and now rather comical accessory was then a tool of the trade. Unknown to the client, she guided his suspicion where he himself expected to find it:

> And I said, 'good woman, as to whom I suspect, I am not yet sure' . . . when I said this she turned the crystal to me and said 'you wished her ill and because of a children's quarrel you did this to her'.

When the suspicion of a certain person had been confirmed, the next step was by no means to go directly to the authorities; in fact this was probably very rare, and not only because of the frequently observed unwillingness of the authorities to entertain such accusations, but also because of the position of the suspects. Sorcerers and witches were powerful, and taking action against them might well bring down even greater afflictions on the accuser's head. Moreover, a sentence in the courts would not remove the existing harm done. For this reason the victim did not go to the court, but to the witch or sorcerer presumed to have caused the harm, who could 'turn' it and render it harmless again. We also find that sorcery or witchcraft was regarded by the people as a personal skill, and not as an emanation of demonic power, for that would hardly have permitted healing and other benign sorcery. When we return to the 'practice' of the Swabian soothsayer, we are told that she ended her 'consultation' as follows:

> After this I said 'good woman, how then can she be helped? Do you know anything?' And she said, 'the one who did this to her, must and can help her. For if she can make the weather, she can and may turn this too . . .'[135]

The sources show us that a visit to the witch or sorcerer often followed a ritualised form, no doubt because witch and victim were often enemies, and a ritual made it easier for them to communicate. But it should not be forgotten that the ritual contained a magical component as well. There are several cases in the region which reveal that the conjuration took the following form. In 1586 a soothsayer in Oberstdorf (Bishopric of Augsburg) gave an allegedly bewitched woman this advice:

> 'You shall therefore go to her Anna [the alleged witch] and ask her three times for God's sake and the sake of the Last Judgement, to help you, and so she must help you.' Which is what happened.[136]

---

[135] *Ibid.*

[136] HStAM, Hochstift Augsburg, NA, Akten 6737, fol. 3v. Very similar examples are often found, e.g. StadtA Augsburg, Urgichtenakten 1589 (Maria Blumenscheinin), or *ibid.*, 1590 (Sabina Wagnerin); HStAM, Hochstift Augsburg, NA, Akten 1204, fol. 411–411v (Nesselwang). Cf. also Stadelmann, 'Hexenprozesse', 52 ff.

This example tells us that the conjuration of the evildoer, in which the magical ritual was mingled with Christian elements, could also be successful. Twentieth-century readers will of course think of psychosomatic effects caused by otherwise pointless actions, but in popular magic they were far from pointless: ultimately everyone, or at least the great majority, who took part in the ceremonies, believed in their effectiveness. If the spell disappeared after such a ritual invocation, the whole matter could be regarded as closed. If the spell was not 'turned' further steps had to be taken.

Even then, against our expectations, the next step was rarely to approach the authorities. Even if this happened, the bringing of criminal proceedings was still far from certain. Often the plaintiff was punished.[137] In 1549, when an accusation was made in the Prince-Abbacy of Kempten, the nobleman who held the rights of justice said that he had never had to deal with a similar complaint before. Before passing on the accusation to the government of the Prince-Abbacy in Kempten, the Imperial Knight Veit Werdenstein of Ebersbach himself visited the suspected woman in her village, and implored her to withdraw her spells. The 'witch' refused to cooperate: 'she merely laughed and mocked me'. In the end the case escalated so far that the whole village accused the woman of witchcraft. The government of the Prince-Abbacy dismissed the charges after hearing both sides and forbade the villagers to spread further slanders.[138]

The usual way of dealing with a spell that could not be 'turned' was to use a counterspell. In criminal law, this was of course open to objection, since a counterspell, in principle, was an attempt to cause harm by sorcery. The presumed emergency situation lent it a legitimacy, however, in the eyes of those who resorted to it. The methods of counterspells were generally known, in part, among the populace: amulets, talismans, crossings, 'characters' (especially the pentagram, or *Trudenfuss*), customs and rites which today are chiefly of interest to folklorists,[139] were all connected with it.

---

[137] Wulz, 'Der Prozess', 46f.

[138] HStAM, Fürststift Kempten, NA, Akten 1605, fol. 206–14. The witch was alleged to have harmed the crops in the village on several occasions by weather spells.

[139] K.-S. Kramer, 'Schaden- und Gegenzauber im Alltagsleben des 16.-18. Jahrhunderts nach archivalischen Quellen aus Holstein', in Degn *et al., Hexenprozesse*, 222–40; but also the chapter on 'Countering witchcraft' in Macfarlane, *Witchcraft*, 103–46; and the corresponding section in Monter, *Witchcraft in France*, 167–90. Stone described the state of affairs very well ('Disenchantment', 20): 'The prosecutions were only the tip of the iceberg, and below the surface there was a constant warfare between white and black magic. Only if black magic seemed to be unstoppable by other means was there recourse to the courts.' The latter was less problematical in England than, for example, in southeastern Germany, where accusations of witchcraft could rebound on the accuser. This problem was known to contemporaries, and was repeatedly addressed, e.g. in Tengler, *Der neu Layenspiegel* (1511), here cited from Hansen, *Quellen und Untersuchungen*, 302.

There were also 'specialists' who gave advice to the bewitched and the victims of sorcery. Many supposed victims visited numerous soothsayers and other wise women and men in their search for an effective counterspell. In a witch trial in a village near the Free City of Memmingen, in 1518, a peasant witness told the court of his numerous fruitless attempts to find a counterspell against a woman who had been known for stealing milk for more than thirty years:

> and so he had been told many kinds of arts, and he had tried them, but they had been no help. For a woman had told him of an art with [the witch] Ursula Strewbin, fire from her oven. When he does this, then it helps him for a while, but as soon as Strewbin pokes her head in his house, or walks round his house, it is as it was before . . .[140]

Sometimes the counterspell served the function of an ordeal; a man or woman admitted guilt, if the counterspell had an effect on him or her. That the counterspell was usually a very drastic remedy for harmful sorcery is shown by the following statement of a peasant from a village near Schongau in 1589. He had visited several soothsayers because of the unnatural sickness of his cattle, and at last one of them knew the appropriate counterspell:

> And so someone told him, he should hack off the head of a cow and hang it above the fire by the mouth, and then he would know who had done this to him. And so when he had done this, the wife of Hans Leuter, carpenter of Soyen went blind. [She had] sat for weeks behind the oven and howled like a cow, and so it was obvious that she was such [a witch] . . .[141]

If a counterspell was so obviously effective, it could be dangerous for the person affected. At a village near Hindelang (in the district of Rettenburg, in the Bishopric of Augsburg), in 1583, an extremely dramatic case is recorded, in which a woman who had been publicly accused defended herself against the charge: before the assembled congregation she challenged the slanderer, a woman neighbour whose son had been lamed, before God's judgement in the valley of Josaphat.[142] Such public ritual curses and successful counterspell ordeals are rarely related in the sources, so that it must be assumed that they were rather exceptional.

The conclusion has to be that everyday dealings with sorcery took place

---

[140] StadtA Memmingen, Schubl. 344 No. 9/1, d.
[141] StadtA Munich, Hist. Ver. Urk. 2018.
[142] HStAM, Hochstift Augsburg, NA, Akten 6737, fol. 125–6v. In popular belief, in this example, the person challenged had to follow the challenger by dying within a certain time, if he or she bore any guilt toward the challenger; Beitl, *Wörterbuch*, explains it rather differently, and characterises it as a curse, but it seems to be a challenge or kind of excommunication. Parallel in Buck, 'Hexenprozesse', 111–13.

within the world of popular magic, of spells and counterspells, and did not lead to court proceedings. This informal method of self-regulation of suspicions of witchcraft has been largely overlooked in the secondary literature, though it must be pointed out that the phenomenon has been known for some time in German folkloristic literature, and there are quite astonishing and extensive parallels in English ethnological literature.[143] We must assume that in a culture permeated almost everywhere by a belief in the reality of sorcery, it was nothing out of the ordinary. Only when essentials were endangered – destruction of the crops, or the illness of a son – were the victims forced to take tough countermeasures, and ultimately to bring an accusation before the authorities.

Several historians have defended the view, on various grounds, that an increase in popular magical belief in the sixteenth century was ultimately responsible for the great witch hunts of the second half of the century. Keith Thomas believes that the decline of 'ecclesiastical' magic as the Reformation progressed created a kind of 'mental vacuum', which was filled by popular magic. Janssen and Pastor, and Chaunu, blame the collapse of the Church's authority for the 'reversion' of the people to 'heathenism with its simple magical ideas and practices'.[144] As Lawrence Stone remarked in a critique of Thomas, this is a very attractive idea but unfortunately incapable of proof, since pre-Reformation popular magic cannot be quantified.[145] The regional sources for the pre-Reformation period lead us to suspect that there was a fairly unbroken popular magic throughout the whole pre-industrial era.[146]

A 'CRISIS OF THE LATE SIXTEENTH CENTURY'?

Recently, and particularly since the paradigm shift in witchcraft research, several historians have tried to connect the phenomenon of witch hunting with another current theme of research in early modern Europe: the

---

[143] Cf. note 139 esp. the citation from Stone.

[144] Thomas, *Religion* (1980 edn), 763; Janssen and Pastor, *Culturzustände*, VIII, 359–441, the beautiful chapter on 'General religious and moral degeneration'; Chaunu, *Kultur*, 651. [145] Stone, 'Disenchantment', 25.

[146] Gurjewitsch and Muchembled, 'Witches', 46, unlike Thomas and Macfarlane, seem to assume a relatively constant popular magical potential. The reason for this is that the latter interpret popular magic as a consequence of the elimination of official ecclesiastical magic after the Reformation, Chaunu and Janssen and Pastor, even seeing it as a result of the general loss of the Church's authority at the time while Gurjewitsch and Muchembled place magic in its structural relationship in a pre-industrial agrarian society. Yet the regional sources reveal the huge importance of popular magic as early as the decades before the Reformation, for instance in the mandates of the bishops and the cities against soothsayers, sorcerers and those who sold charms, Hansen, *Quellen und Untersuchungen*, 506; Riezler, *Geschichte*, 97f.; Knapp, *Alt-Regensburgs Gerichtsverfassung*, 256, and also from the few trial records preserved from this period, e.g Wulz, 'Der Prozess', 46f. etc. Cf. List of trials in the German edition, 432–3, for the trials before 1520.

so-called 'crisis of the seventeenth century'. Although few arguments have yet been exchanged, a connection has been asserted on the one hand and dismissed in lapidary terms on the other.[147] In most of the literature the high point of the European witch craze has been placed in the 1620s, not too far removed from the 1640s, which are almost unanimously accepted as the culminating years of the long term social crisis.[148] But this attempt to harmonise the secular crisis and the peak of witch hunting was always vulnerable on two fronts: the idea of a crisis of the seventeenth century as a new interpretative focus for the period between the Reformation and the French Revolution has not gone unchallenged.[149] Moreover, it overlooks the fact that the witch hunts were at their fiercest at different times in different regions – in southeast Germany, for example, around 1590. Now southeast Germany is not a particularly exotic example, and this wave of persecution in the 1590s can be demonstrated in several other parts of Europe, for example in Macfarlane's Essex, or in northwestern Germany, investigated by Schormann. If recent witchcraft research has generally placed the peak of witch hunting between 1560 and 1630, this can be made more precise by dating the second peak between 1615 and 1630, the first between 1570 and 1590.[150] The only logical consequence that can be

---

[147] On the crisis of the seventeenth century see in general T. Aston (ed.), *Crisis in Europe 1560–1660*, New York 1965; the essays of E.J. Hobsbawm, 'The Crisis of the Seventeenth Century', 5–58; and H.R. Trevor-Roper, 'The General Crisis of the Seventeenth Century', 59–96. Also G. Parker and L.M. Smith (eds.), *The General Crisis of the Seventeenth Century*, London 1976; and T.K. Rabb, *The Struggle for Stability in Early Modern Europe*, New York 1975. It is characteristic that the theme of witchcraft came under discussion as soon as cultural aspects began to be included as well as political and economic ones. Mandrou spoke of a 'great crisis of ideas and feeling, a revolution in the manner of thinking and understanding the universe', and then passed directly to 'the growth of witchcraft' (untitled contribution to the discussion in Aston, *Crisis*, 103f.). Trevor-Roper took up these ideas of Mandrou but only to warn against oversimplification, while agreeing in principle. *Ibid.*, 115. Rabb, *Struggle*, 25, 116, 149, also assumes a connection but without explaining what it must have consisted of. The chapter on witchcraft in Kamen, *Iron Century*, 239–51, is very instructive, although he rejects the extended concept of crisis, because to speak of a crisis that lasted almost a hundred years seems a misuse of terminology, *ibid.*, 307–9. In connection with the high point of the European witch hunts, 1560–1660, however, Kamen speaks of an 'equation of crisis and witchcraft', *ibid.*, 249. In Germany Schormann, *Hexenprozesse* (1981), 89–95, rejected a connection between the theme of witchcraft and any concept of crisis, however formulated, on the rather unconvincing grounds that the whole history of Europe could be written as the history of crises. H. Lehmann, on the other hand, has tried to reinstate the connection, 'Hexenprozesse in Norddeutschland und Skandinavien im 16., 17. und 18. Jahrhundert. Bemerkungen zum Forschungsstand', in Degn *et al., Hexenprozesse*, 9–13, and some of his arguments are worth pondering; *idem*, 'Hexenglaube und Hexenprozesse in Europa um 1600', in Degn *et al.*, 14–27.

[148] To this extent one must admit that Schormann, Hexenprozesse (1981), 90, was right to argue that this rigid model of crisis, oriented toward the English Revolution, cannot be applied to the Continental witchcraft problem.

[149] On this the survey in Rabb, *Struggle*, 17–28.

[150] Schormann, *Hexenprozesse* (1981), 55; Muchembled, *Kultur*, 234f.

drawn from this is that the beginning of the crisis, or another, 'first' or earlier crisis, has to be looked for in this period. A 'crisis of the later sixteenth century'?

WITCH TRIALS AND AGRARIAN CRISES

In his *Essays* of 1588 Michel de Montaigne recalled that a prince of the Empire had once tried to refute his scepticism about witchcraft by showing him ten or twelve arrested witches; they had repeated their confessions before him and bore the witches' mark. This must have been during Montaigne's tour of the spas in 1580, which took him from the neighbourhood of Paris through Lorraine, Alsace, the Rhine between Basel and Constance, Lindau and the Allgäu, to Augsburg, Munich and over the Mittenwald and the Brenner to Italy. Montaigne admired the wealth of upper Germany, but his secretary-servant found it expensive compared to France.[151] In fact, though the travellers could not have known this, they were experiencing the fifth great price rise of the second half of the sixteenth century. In southwestern Germany one of the first great witch hunts was raging at the time of Montaigne's journey, and even became the subject of a *Neue Zeitung*, which was intended to spread the news of this sensation throughout the German-speaking lands.[152] The connection of witch hunting and inflation was not coincidental, as a glance at the dates of other witch hunts in southern Germany will show. Because of the absence of social-historical monographs in this field, the reconstruction of these connections is laborious, but the results are worth the effort in spite of the fragmentary sources.[153]

---

[151] M. de Montaigne, *Tagebuch einer Badereise*, Gütersloh (n.d.), 81. The famous passage in Montaigne on his attitude to the problem of witches is in *Essais*, Book 3, xi, 'Des Boyteux'.

[152] Midelfort, *Witch Hunting*, 205.

[153] M.J. Elsas, *Umriss einer Geschichte der Preise und Löhne in Deutschland*, I (Munich, Augsburg, Würzburg), Leiden 1936; Elsas took as his basis the best-preserved series of grain (rye) prices: Munich, *ibid.*, 560–5; for Augsburg, *ibid.*, 593–8; for Würzburg, *ibid.*, 634–40. Further data on climatic, agrarian, demographic and epidemiological events were added to this solid basis. Besides the already mentioned demographic studies of Kisskalt, Schmölz and Jahn, the data for individual cities are evaluated in Keyser and Stoob, and are shown to be very fragmentary for the period from the Schmalkaldic War to the Thirty Years War; also G. Lammert, *Geschichte der Seuchen-, Hungers- und Kriegsnoth zur Zeit des Dreissigjährigen Krieges*, Berlin 1890 (reprint Niederwalluf 1971). The picture thus revealed was not very different from the old caricature which A.E. Imhof, *Die verlorenen Welten*, Munich 1984, presented in his survey map of epidemics from 1576 to 1600, and the following maps, *ibid.*, 97–9. To be able to show more than 'blank spaces on a map', besides the literature a systematic search was also made of chronicles from Memmingen, Augsburg, Kempten, Freising and Passau, as well as some diaries of the period: M. Gertrudis (ed.), 'Aus dem Tagebuch der Äbtissin Magdalena Haidenbucher (Frauenchiemsee)', *Studien und Mitteilungen aus dem Benediktiner- und*

The first wave of persecution in the southwest occurred in 1562–3, and can be related to the widespread epidemics of these years. With sixty-three witches burned at Wiesensteig and further witch hunts at Stuttgart and Esslingen, as well as at other towns in Württemberg, this was, as far as we know at the moment, the greatest witch hunt since the Reformation. Only the western fringes of southeast Germany and Franconia were affected by this wave (Illereichen 1563, Spalt 1562). The background to the epidemics was, as usual, harvest failure, which made humans and livestock more susceptible to disease because of malnutrition. These harvest failures can be identified in the price series compiled by Elsas for Augsburg, Munich and Würzburg, where an above-average increase can be found in each case between 1559 and 1563. In Augsburg the epidemic of these years, where more than 5,000 people died, was the greatest for forty years. Only a crisis of mortality in the aftermath of the Schmalkaldic War had claimed anything like as many lives in that time. We have similar reports from other towns, Spalt among them.[154]

After the inflationary year 1566, which is especially pronounced in the Munich price series,[155] and four 'cheap' years, the whole region was hit by catastrophic inflation in 1569–75. In all the price series agrarian prices, especially vital rye, reached nearly four times the levels of the previous decades. Contemporary poems describe in minute detail the mechanism of the crisis, from the failure of the harvest to the rise in food prices, a fall in demand for the crafts, the dismissal of servants and day labourers, hunger, unusual diseases in humans and animals, and the plague. At Augsburg more died in 1571–2 than in 1563–4, a pattern repeated at Memmingen and the Allgäu, Munich and Dillingen. The extent of this hunger throughout Europe has been emphasised by the exemplary research of Wilhelm

Cistercienserorden, 28 (1907), 122–42, 379–92, 559–76; P.M. Sattler, *Chronik von Andechs*, Donauwörth 1877, 405–503, for the diary of Abbot Maurus Friesenegger; P.H. Dussler, *Magister Hieronymus Tauler*, Kempten 1961; O. Fina (ed.), *Klara Staigers Tagebuch* (Eichstätt), Regensburg 1931; H. Leuchtmann, 'Zeitgeschichtliche Aufzeichnungen des bayerischen Hofkapellaltisten Johannes Hellgemayr aus den Jahren 1595–1633', *Oberbayr. Archiv*, 100 (1975), 142–229. Also scattered references in archive sources and local historical literature. In general, of course, H. Aubin and W. Zorn, *Handbuch der deutschen Wirtschafts- und Sozialgeschichte*, Stuttgart 1971; and W. Abel, *Massenarmut und Hungerkrisen im vorindustriellen Europa*, Hamburg/Berlin 1974; he rightly refers to M. Radlkofer, 'Die Teuerung zu Augsburg in den Jahren 1570 und 1571 (. . .)', *Zeitschrift des Historischen Vereins für Schwaben und Neuburg*, 19 (1892), 45–87. All these sources combine to give a sufficiently usable picture.
[154] The epidemic was clearly evident everywhere; Jahn, 'Augsburgs Einwohnerzahl', 390 ; J.F. Unold, *Geschichte der Stadt Memmingen*, Memmingen 1826, 176; Elsas, *Umriss*, I, 188; SBM, Cgm. 2811, fol. 455 (Regensburg); F.L. Baumann, *Geschichte des Allgäus*, Kempten 1894, 652; Keyser and Stoob refer to plague around 1563 in Augsburg, Aibling, Freilassing, Kempten, Lindau, Memmingen, Neumarkt, Oberviechtach, Plattling, Regensburg, Schrobenhausen, Sonthofen, Velburg and Spalt.
[155] Elsas, *Umriss*, I, 561.

4. White and black magic as a function of the pact with the Devil: spells, 'weather cooking', harmful sorcery. From Cicero, *De Officiis*, Augsburg 1531.

Abel.[156] In these years witch hunts became a permanent feature in the southwest, while there is only evidence for sporadic executions of witches in the southeast (Dillingen 1575, Allgäu 1575) and in Franconia (e.g. Ellingen 1575). Here too, after passing through the hunger catastrophe people were ready to blame witches after any hail shower, as at Weilheim

[156] W. Abel, *Massenarmut und Hungerkrisen im vorindustriellen Deutschland*, 2nd edn Göttingen 1977, 37–46; Radlkofer, 'Der Teuerung'; Keyser and Stoob refer to plagues in 1570–5 in Mindelheim, Neustadt/Donau, Augsburg, Freilassing, Freising, Memmingen, Munich, Rosenheim, Traunstein, Vilsbiburg, Neumarkt, Velburg, Neustadt/Aisch; for Augsburg cf. also Elsas, *Umriss*, I, 188; Jahn, 'Augsburgs Einwohnerzahl', 390; for Memmingen, Schorer, *Chronik*, 69; for Garmisch, Kuisl, *Die Hexen*, 6; for Dillingen, HStAM Hochstift Augsburg, NA Akten, 1187.

in 1577–8 (which led to the first execution of a witch at Munich in 1578).[157]

After four 'cheap' years the next inflation, that experienced by Montaigne in 1579–80, provoked similar phenomena; in many parts of the Allgäu the plague broke out again, and witches were burned at many places in southwest Germany, while some women were also executed in the Allgäu towns of Wangen, Isny and Leutkirch, at Constance and Überlingen on Lake Constance, at Wurzach, Waldsee, Biberach, Obermarchthal and Burgau, on the borders of the southwest.[158] The Bishop of Freising's district judge (*Pflegrichter*) in Garmisch was implored by his subjects to hunt down the witches after a heavy shower of hail in the County of Werdenfels in 1581, but the episcopal government forbade the trial.[159]

Once again, after four years of low prices a bout of inflation began in 1585, and lasted, with two cheaper years, in the Munich and Augsburg price series, until 1594 – ten long years. The basic foodstuffs were dearest in 1586, 1587, 1588, 1589 and 1590, and again in 1592, 1593 and 1594. From September 1585 the plague raged at Augsburg, reaching the Allgäu a little later and Freising, Lindau, Kempten, Kaufbeuren, Landsberg, Burghausen Amberg, Beilngries, Abensberg and Windsheim in 1586, to name only a few of the more important places where evidence has been found. The year 1592 saw a second wave of plague in many towns during this period of persistent inflation.[160] During these years of flood, drought, hail, harvest failure, frost, plagues of mice, epidemics and disease among their livestock, many contemporaries must have thought of the return of the biblical plagues or feared the imminent end of the world. As before the Peasants' War, there was no lack of astrological predictions; as early as 1580 and 1582 octavo booklets were published in Augsburg, foretelling dire consequences from the conjunctions of Saturn and Jupiter in 1583 and Saturn and Mars in 1588.[161] Le Roy Ladurie has recently spoken of 'the return of the accursed time before the Black Death of 1348', in connection with the plague of 1586.[162] Even if this is an exaggeration, contemporaries were struck by the extraordinary character of these years, not least because

---

[157] Midelfort, *Witch Hunting*, 203ff.; Film 693. Cf. list of trials in the German edition.
[158] Midelfort, *Witch Hunting*, 205.   [159] Kuisl, *Die Hexen*, 7.
[160] For 1585 the chronicles offer a chorus of laments of harvest failure, inflation, plague from autumn/winter. UBM 2° Cod. Ms. 500 (Kempten), fol. 42; P. von Stetten, *Geschichte der Heyl. Rom. Reichs Freyen Stadt Augsburg (. . .)*, I, Frankfurt 1743, 692; Jahn, 'Augsburgs Einwohnerzahl', 390; Schorer, *Chronik*, 109; Junginger, *Geschichte*, 14; J. Mayr, *Epitome Cronicorum seculi moderni (. . .)*, Munich 1604, fol. 176; the other places from Keyser and Stoob, *Städtebuch*; reports of catastrophes are also scattered through all possible types of source. Cf. Schormann, *Hexenprozesse* (1981), 58.
[161] G. Ursinus, *Zwo Practicken. Vom 1580. Jar, biss man schreiben wird 1600. Jar*, Augsburg 1580, fol. E. i. N. Winkler, *Bedenken von künfftiger verenderung Weltlicher Policey und Ende der Welt*, Augsburg 1582.
[162] E. Le Roy Ladurie, *Karneval in Romans*, Stuttgart 1982, 9.

of the coincidence of an exceptionally harsh agrarian crisis with a crisis in commerce.[163] It was in these years of double crisis that the witch craze, until then largely confined to the southwest, spread into southeast Germany and Franconia. The great witch hunts of 1589–91 in southeast Germany took place between the two plague epidemics of 1585–8 and 1592–3.

The link between agrarian crisis and witch trials persisted. During the next inflationary period of 1598–1602 the great persecutions began in the Prince-Bishopric of Fulda, in Franconia, as well as in the upper Archbishopric of Mainz and the *Freigericht* of Alzenau. Extensive witch hunts were also begun at Abensberg and Munich in Bavaria, though they were soon effectively stopped, after the first executions, by the emerging opposition party. Naturally, these years too were marked by plagues.[164]

In Franconia the first six years of the seventeenth century were years of normal prices; in Augsburg the next phase of inflation began in 1606, and in Munich in 1607; with only one 'cheap' year in between (1613), it continued until 1615 in Augsburg, 1616 in Munich and 1617 in Würzburg. The price level of these nine years was about the same as those of the previous long agrarian crises. The plague raged above all in 1607–8, 1611–12 and 1614. The most expensive years in the Munich price series correspond in time to the witch hunts at Donauwörth, Wemding and Passau, and to the general rise in witch trials in the records of the Court Council at Munich, while the dearest years at Augsburg correspond with witch hunts at Dillingen in 1612–13, and those at Würzburg, 1610–12 and 1614–16, with the beginning of the huge witch hunts at Ellwangen, Würz-

---

[163] For example the chronicle of Kempten, UBM 2 Cod. Ms. 500, fol. 42f., blames the civil wars in France and Holland as well as the crop failure for the misery, because of the harm caused to the craft industries. Several trading houses went bankrupt in Augsburg, Stetten, *Geschichte*, I, 700; J.D. Gould, 'The Crisis in the Export Trade', *English Historical Review*, 71 (1965), 212–22, deals more with the internal political problems in England caused by the closure of the ports, but points out that the climatically caused harvest failure also led to great complications in England, *ibid.*, 216. Now also Clark, *European Crisis*.

[164] The cycle of agrarian crises between 1597 and 1601 is variously reflected in the sources. The Regensburg chronicle, SBM Cgm. 2811, refers to a 'grossen Sterb' in Germany as early as 1597, the Munich chronicler Hellgemayr noted harvest failure and dearth in 1598 (Leuchtmann, 'Hellgemayr', 156); also Schorer, *Chronik*, 114f., who records the rising of the weavers in Isny at the same time. SBM Cgm. 2811, fol. 460, records 800 deaths from the plague in Regensburg in 1599; the first epidemic recorded by Keyser and Stoob is in 1600 at Amberg, Augsburg, Burglengenfeld, Dillingen, Friedberg, Neustadt on the Danube, Regensburg, Lauf on the Pegnitz, Wassertrudingen and Windsbach; and plague in 1602 in Schwandorf and Oettingen. On the witch hunts in Franconia Grebner, 'Hexenpozesse'; Film 127; Film 135; Film 173; Film 668–9; Film 847; Film 901; Film 1222; Film 1667; Jäger, 'Geschichte des Hexenbrennens in Franken im siebzehnten Jahrhundert aus den Original Process-Acten', *Archiv des historischen Vereins Unterfranken*, 2 (1834), 1–72, 4f., 66f. On the situation in the Duchy of Bavaria cf. below, and the List of trials in the German edition, 454f.; Kunze, *Der Prozess*; on this chapter 4.

burg, Bamberg and Eichstätt, which put all previous witch hunts in southern Germany in the shade.[165]

During the few 'cheap' years that followed, and amazingly also during the currency inflation of the years around 1622, we hear nothing of great witch hunts, apart from the Bishopric of Eichstätt, where witch hunting became a permanent feature from 1617. The harvest failures of the year 1624 marked the beginning of a long crisis that lasted until 1629; with only three 'cheap' years in between, this culminated in the catastrophe of 1632–6. In 1626 and 1634 rye prices at Augsburg, Munich and Würzburg were more than 100 per cent above those of the crisis years after 1570 or 1585, and 1,000 per cent above the 'normal' years between 1560 and 1590. These were years of war, extreme hunger and plagues of unprecedented virulence. Between 1624 and 1636 probably every place in southern Germany suffered an outbreak of plague, so that to cite particular cases would be pointless. The plague of 1628, which claimed 9,000 dead in Augsburg alone, began the demographic collapse in southern Germany, famous in the literature, which reduced the population by around a half by the end of the Thirty Years War.[166] In Franconia, 1624 saw the start of the indescribable excesses in the

---

[165] Elsas, *Umriss*, I (as note 153). The agrarian crisis cycle of 1607–8 in Leuchtmann, 'Hellgemayr', 162f.; Elsas, *Umriss*, I, 190, who records more than 2,000 deaths from plague in Augsburg. Keyser and Stoob found plagues in Augsburg, Munich, Rosenheim, Abensberg, Langenzenn and Rothenburg ob der Tauber, but these were undoubtedly only a small sample. The Würzburg cloth shearer Röder wrote in his diary: 'Tribulare pestilenciam, o deus!' Kerler, 'Unter Fürstbischof Julius. Kalendereinträge des Tuchscherers Jacob Röder', *Archiv. d. Hist. Ver. Unterfranken*, 41 (1899), 1–69. The plague of 1610–12, according to HStAM, SV, 2243, s.f., extended to Swabia, Franconia, the Tyrol, Nuremberg, Mühldorf, Altötting and Straubing; Schorer, *Chronik*, 120f. mentions plague and livestock mortality in Memmingen; Keyser and Stoob found plagues in 1612 at Amberg, Diessen, Lindau, Memmingen, Mühldorf and Neumarkt (Upper Palatinate), Neuötting, Straubing, Iphofen and Ornbau. The next plague was already raging in 1614–16, after the livestock diseases of 1614. HStAM, SV 2243 mentions a shortage of seed corn in Bavaria and plague at Regensburg and Reichertshofen; Gertrudis, 'Aus dem Tagebuch', 137, illustrates crop failures, dearth and hunger in the Chiemsee region; Elsas, *Umriss*, I, 190 for Augsburg in 1615; Sattler, *Chronik*, 358; Leuchtmann, 'Hellgemayr', 170. The witches were sent out by the Devil to spoil the crops in the fields and – in Franconia – the wine. Jäger, 'Geschichte', 48f. Hunger often provided the motive for a pact with the Devil, *ibid.*, 34f.

[166] The begining of the 1620s seems to have been only relatively better, as the Munich chronicler saw 'in diesen Jaren überall . . . grosse Noth, Teuerung und Jamer . . .', Leuchtmann, 'Hellgemayr', 172f. The actual misery began, however, from 1624 when thunderstorms battered the crops in autumn and plague began soon afterwards. Schorer, *Chronik*, 130; Leuchtmann, 'Hellgemayr', 174f.; Elsas, *Umriss*, I, 192; next year the plague was raging at Munich, Freising, Augsburg, Freyung, Rötz, Vohburg, Waldmünchen, Neustadt on the Danube and Spalt. Keyser and Stoob, *Städtebuch*; Lammert, *Volksmedizin*, 79f., 83f. A family chronicle from Zeil describes the connection of harvest failure and witch hunting: 'Anno 1626 den 27. Mai ist der Weinwachs im Frankenland im Stift Bamberg und Würzburg aller erfroren, wie auch das liebe Korn, das allbereit verblüett (. . . alles erfroren . . . grosse Teuerung). Hierauf ein grosses Flehen und bitten unter den gemeinen Pöffel, warumb man solang zusehe, das allbereit die Zauberer unt

Prince-Bishoprics of Würzburg and Bamberg, Eichstätt and Upper Mainz, around Aschaffenburg, which culminated in 1628–9 in the absolute high point of witch hunting in south Germany. There were further minor persecutions in the southeast and southwest from 1627.[167]

If we draw up a balance sheet of these data for price developments, crises of mortality and witch hunting, we can say that practically every great witch hunt had its roots in a time of agrarian crisis, while only minor witch trials can be found in the cheap years between 1560 and 1630. The greatest waves of persecution corresponded with the four greatest agrarian crises of the region, and this relationship is not surprising when one realises that this modern and abstract concept meant, in concrete historical reality, hunger, disease and death. The danger of an immediate threat to life itself, to which the population was exposed in times of crisis, seems to have been an essential factor in the witchcraft equation. A search for examples shows that this rule also holds good outside the core period of witch hunting. If we go back to the first great witch hunt known in Germany, Ravensburg in 1481–5, we find that 1481 and 1482 had been years of harvest failure and very high prices.[168] We may presume that other pre-Reformation witch hunts between 1470 and 1520 can be similarly related to the agrarian crises that can be clearly detected in this period. If we take the severity of agrarian and mortality crises as our yardstick, the latent phase of the witch mania between 1520 and 1560 appears in a different light; although farm prices naturally fluctuated in this period, the great crises of mortality that were typical of the second half of the century are not found.[169] The regional sources also show a connection between agrarian crises and witch trials for the period after 1630, until about 1730.[170]

While we can formulate a rule that witch hunts mostly began in years of agrarian crisis, we cannot infer the converse, that they were the inevitable consequence of them. During the severe agrarian crisis of 1632–6, and even in districts not immediately affected by the war, there were no witch hunts.

Unholden die Früchten sogar verderben, wie dann ihre Fürstliche Gnaden nichts weniger verursacht, solches übel abzustrafen, hat also den Anfang [of the witch hunts] bis Jars erreicht.' J. Denzinger (ed.), 'Auszüge einer Chronik der Familie Langhans in Zeil', *Archiv d. Hist. Ver. Unterfranken*, 10 (1850), 144f. Finally the harvest failure of 1627 led to catastrophic plagues in 1628: Lammert, *Volksmedizin*, 97–107, esp. 100f. In Augsburg alone 9,000 people died, or 20 per cent of the population, *ibid.*, 100; Elsas, *Umriss*, I, 192. In the minutes of the Bavarian Court Council a whole folio volume is concerned exclusively with the plague, HStAM, KHR 216. According to Leuchtmann, 'Hellgemayr', 193, however, there were also 'vil erfroren und verhungert'. Documents on the places hit by the plague are too numerous to be listed here; see Keyser and Stoob, *Städtebuch*; Lammert, *Volksmedizin*; HStAM, KHR 216.

[167] On the connection of agrarian crisis and witch trials see chapter 4, pp. 291–309 and 216–29. Cf. quotation in note 266. Midelfort, *Witch Hunting*, 216f.

[168] Unold, *Geschichte*, 107; Elsas, *Umriss*, I, 593, 643.   [169] Jahn, 'Augsburg', 390f.

[170] Chapter 5, pp. 331–43.

In principle, in each individual agrarian crisis, although they mostly affected the whole region, witch hunts were always confined to some of the courts. The Free Cities of Kempten or Memmingen, both of which were badly hit by the double crises of 1586, saw no reason to execute witches or even to stage witch hunts. Even the Free City of Augsburg, where eight witch trials were held in 1590 alone, in the end did not find any of the women guilty, though the charges were serious and several of the accused had evidently dabbled in sorcery.

The relationship of witchcraft and sorcery trials to the cycle of agrarian crises is also clear at a level below that of executions and witch hunts. Sometimes one can observe an increase in complaints of witchcraft just before the witch hunts themselves, as for example before those at Nördlingen, Munich and Schongau in 1590. As the records of the local court of Griesbach reveal, the same trend can be seen in courts where there were no executions.[171] The criminal sentence books of the Free City of Augsburg offer a good source for the analysis of this trend; they record 101 trials for witchcraft and sorcery in the eighty annual volumes examined between 1581 and 1653. Striking correlations emerge between the number of criminal proceedings and the prices of basic foodstuffs as indicators of agrarian crisis: from 1585 prices and the number of trials rose until 1587, both fell back in 1588, both reached their highest level in 1589–90 during the agrarian crisis, and then declined sharply. Both lines rose again until 1595, fell in 1596 and so on. The curves are not exactly parallel every year, but as the number of trials is not a large sample in statistical terms, the general parallelism is more surprising than the occasional deviations.[172]

Not all the accusations of bewitchment have a recognisable connection with the agrarian crisis. In many cases, of course, the link is obvious, especially when whole village communities whose crops had been devastated by hail banded together to demand that their rulers and judges should hunt down the guilty witches (e.g. Garmisch 1581). A direct causal relationship can often be inferred after cases of cattle disease or 'unusual sicknesses' (e.g. Illereichen 1563). Frequently one finds that interfering with the weather was only one of many charges (e.g. Garmisch 1589, Schongau 1589, Reichertshofen 1628). In many cases the consequences of the agrarian crisis were more individualised. A Freising chronicle speaks of the great number of monstrous births in 1588, immediately after the first peak of the ten-year crisis.[173] Deformed babies, general disease among children, or their premature death were important in many accusations against witches, for contemporaries were unable to see the connection

---

[171] Cf. list of trials in the German edition.
[172] StadtA Augsburg, Strafbücher 1581–1653, 8 vols. The price of rye from Elsas, *Umriss*, I, 594f.   [173] Mayr, *Epitome*, 174v.

between malnutrition and greater susceptibility to disease. Witches were held to be directly responsible for affecting the weather,[174] and thus causing harvest failures, an evil which contemporaries wanted to 'root out', to use their own phrase, but the more individual 'unnatural' consequences of the crisis were also blamed on witchcraft.

We also find countless accusations of witchcraft, which cannot be seen as either direct or indirect consequences of a crisis in agriculture. Although such accusations were made more frequently in times of crisis, this is to be seen as one of the socio-psychological side-effects, the result of a general increase in the anxiety level or a greater willingness to notice 'unnatural' phenomena; in 1614, for example, 'little forest men' were seen in Lower Bavaria, and wolves were believed to be werewolves.[175] The general hysteria can also explain why children and other psychologically unstable persons were ready to incriminate themselves (e.g. Bobingen 1590, Augsburg 1625).

SOCIAL CHANGE

It is obvious that in an agrarian society the short-term cycles of the climate were of vital importance, because of the far-reaching effects of harvest failures, well beyond particular localities. One can also admit that a deterioration of the climate, as assumed by Le Roy Ladurie, who calls the period after 1560 the 'Little Ice Age',[176] played an important part in the witch mania; one might even consider it at first sight a very elegant explanation of the recrudescence of the subject and the increased clamour for witch hunting: a harsher climate, more crop failures, a greater desire to root out those who had caused the damage, the witches. But such an explanation would be too facile, for even a climatic deterioration would operate as an exogenous factor on an existing system and would act as an additional source of stress, accentuating existing tendencies. The assumption of a climatic deterioration after 1560, with especially cold winters, severe, or, as contemporaries called them, 'unnatural' storms, cannot be a substitute for an explanation based on relationships within a society, but can only supplement it. We shall briefly discuss several sectors in which decisive changes took place in this region, at least as far as our current knowledge goes. Several of these phenomena were not confined to southeast Germany.

In the first place is the secular social-historical development of the early

---

[174] E.g. Kuisl, *Die Hexen*, 7, 10, for the mood in the County of Werdenfels in the years 1581 and 1589. Cf. note 166.   [175] HStAM, KHR 115, fol. 74v.

[176] E. Le Roy Ladurie, 'Die Geschichte von Sonnenschein und Regenwetter', in Honegger, *Schrift*, 220–46; *ibid.*, 232, 236, 241.

modern period which used to be known as the price revolution, but which had far deeper implications. The cause of the long-term inflationary trend in the sixteenth century is seen as the great increase in population observable everywhere between 1500 and 1628. The chief characteristic of the trend was that in the second half of the century the prices of basic foodstuffs, for which demand was inelastic, soared, while the incomes of the rural and urban lower clases lagged well behind. The fall in the purchasing power of wages is usually demonstrated, in both international and German literature (Braudel and Spooner), from the excellent source material for the Free City of Augsburg. Saalfeld's revised calculations for a basket of consumer goods were based on changes in the structure of demand as purchasing power fell and diet was adapted to meet the need for calories. In concrete terms this meant a shift to lower-value foods, from meat or butter to rye. The result of these calculations is that in the decade 1566–75 the wages of a fully employed qualified journeyman bricklayer fell for the first time below the level needed to feed a family of four, so that it was necessary for his wife or children to work as well. This remained the case after 1585, as the purchasing power of money wages continued to fall until the Thirty Years War.[177] In fact, these calculations based on a family of four may be too optimistic, as families were often larger, full employment was not always guaranteed and in many cases part of the labour force was unemployed or underemployed. The situation therefore was even less tolerable, above all in the years of acute crisis. The result of this long-term trend, punctuated by the short-term agrarian crises, was the 'pauperisation of wide strata of society' and the growth of beggary to previously unheard-of levels; it is a constant complaint in the sources. The number of beggars and vagrants is astonishing to an observer used to settled populations, and the multiplicity of distinctions made by contemporaries between the different sorts of beggar speaks for itself.[178] Yet it would be wrong to assume that the secular inflation had no effect on the countryside. Here the growth in population led in part to greater fragmentation of holdings, and in part to the growth – especially in eastern Swabia – of groups of sub-peasant proto-industrial workers who had to buy their food. As an Augsburg poem on the dearth of 1570–1 reminds us, in times of crisis farming families often dismissed the servants who boarded with them, and so exposed them to the threat of hunger.[179]

[177] D. Saalfeld, 'Die Wandlungen der Preis- und Lohnstruktur während des 16. Jahrhunderts in Deutschland', in W. Fischer (ed.), *Beiträge zu Wirtschaftswachstum und Wirtschaftsstruktur im 16. und 19. Jahrhundert*, Berlin 1971, 9–28, esp. the calculations on 16–25. *Ibid.*, 14, briefly summarises the development of the discussion of the basket of consumables in international literature on the basis of the Augsburg price data of Elsas.
[178] *Ibid.*, 23.
[179] Radlkofer, 'Die Teuerung'; Abel, *Massenarmut*, 37–45, sketches the phases of the hunger crisis of 1570–1 on this basis.

The secular trend meant that particular agrarian crises became more and more desperate; exogenous factors reinforced this tendency, which was already present. It was also important from a socio-psychological point of view that the other face of this trend to the pauperisation of the masses was the accumulation of huge profits by those who could exploit the crises: the richer peasants, the monastic houses, some of the nobility, merchants and speculators, moneylenders (5 per cent was proverbially a source of strife), and the state, which siphoned off money in taxes. We can describe the result as an increase in social polarisation and differentiation; on the one hand, the life of the courtiers, the wealthy nobles and patricians reached new heights of magnificence, while on the other there was a growing proletariat for whom every crisis threatened the total loss of their income, hunger or forced emigration to assure their survival. In a culture permeated by magical beliefs, the curses and imprecations of such people, whose very existence was threatened, possessed, or were thought to possess, magical powers, as a poem by the Augsburg painter Holzmann on the inflation of 1570–1 makes clear:

> and thus it happened
> that there was much unchristian speech;
> often many wished that a thousand devils
> should carry off the usurers
> and wring their necks
> so that they would give up the ghost,
> and that the corn would pour out of them
> and that the hail would strike them . . .[180]

The 'two faces of the century' (Wilhelm Abel) can be seen in many sectors of society. Riezler pointed out that in the Duchy of Bavaria the 'most outstanding feature of social legislation was a genuine fear of people without property'.[181] Between 1550 and 1599 there were no fewer than thirty-four mandates against beggars, 'rabble', 'wandering young men' and vagrants; in the first half of the sixteenth century there had been only one, while the first half of the seventeenth century saw ten more, and the second half a further five.[182] The targets of these mandates were treated with dramatic severity, at least in theory: people of no fixed abode could be arrested and tortured without reason and without the prior approval of the central authorities, an exception to the usual procedural rules which was

[180] M. Radlkofer, 'Die Theuerung zu Augsburg in den Jahren 1570 und 71', in *Zeitschrift des Historischen Vereins für Schwaben und Neuburg* 19 (1892), 45–87, quotation here from 83, Vers 204–11. On the general development Aubin and Zorn, *Handbuch*, I, 405–13 (W. Abel).　　[181] Riezler, *Geschichte Baierns*, VI, 64.
[182] Research project 'Police legislation in the Duchy of Bavaria', under Prof. H. Schlosser, University of Augsburg (typewritten list of mandates). I am grateful to Dr R. Heydenreuter of the HStAM for the opportunity to inspect this list.

not made even for cases of witchcraft.[183] The last quarter of the sixteenth century also saw that indescribable brutalisation of criminal justice which was expressed not only in an increase in the number of executions – as at Augsburg[184] – but also in the extreme cruelty with which they were carried out, often before huge crowds. The death penalty was extended from the classical capital crimes to vagrancy, minor theft and qualified adultery. Executions were 'celebrated' in such theatrical style that the literature speaks of a 'liturgy of punishment' and a 'theatre of death'. Tens of thousands gathered to witness these demonstrations of the power of the state and the law, especially in spectacular cases. An execution of several witches in Munich in 1600 became so famous that it was not only re-counted in numerous contemporary broadsheets and poems, but was still being cited as an example in a 'Handbook for Townsfolk and Countryfolk' printed at Leipzig in 1744.[185]

If the century had two faces in the social sense, the trend in politics and culture throughout the region was unequivocally towards political central-isation, ideological uniformity and the formation of social hierarchies. The power of the turbulent nobility had been broken in the Duchy of Bavaria in the 1560s, and in the 1570s the Protestant part of the population was forced to emigrate, as the rigid structure of the absolutist state was put in place. The trend is indicated by the differentiation of the central authori-ties, the mania for legislation in the latter half of the century, and the tightening of central control over the lower organs of state power.[186] By the end of the century it can be assumed that the princes in almost all the territories were absolute rulers, though the cathedral chapters and the Estates had managed to retain certain residual functions. The increasing power of the princes over their subordinates must probably be related to the greater structural advantages, both material and intellectual, that the central authorities came to enjoy in the sixteenth century: consent to permanent indirect taxes and the princes' right to determine the confession to be followed (*cuius regio, eius religio*).

The growth in the power of the rulers also greatly altered the position of

---

[183] Christel, 'Die Malefizprozessordnung', 13, 81f.

[184] Schuhmann, *Der Scharfrichter*, 142.

[185] The 'Liturgy' in M. Foucault, *Überwachen und Strafen. Die Geburt des Gefängnisses*, 3rd edn Frankfurt am Main, 1979; R. van Dülmen, 'Das Schauspiel des Todes. Hinrich-tungsrituale in der frühen Neuzeit', in Dülmen and Schindler, *Volkskultur*, 203–46. The famous Munich execution of 1600: J.G. Gregorius (Melissantes), *Gemüths vergnügendes Historisches Hand-Buch für Bürger und Bauern (...)*, Frankfurt/Leipzig 1744, 512–14. Cf. chapter VI.4 of the German edition.

[186] Spindler, *Handbuch*, II, 562–84 (D. Albrecht) and 644ff. (*idem*). Absolutist policies with similar tendencies can also be observed in the smaller ecclesiastical and secular territories of Swabia and Franconia. Spindler, *Handbuch*, III/1, 353–9, 369–80 (Endres); III/2, 961f. (Layer).

the highest classes of society. No longer was the place of the nobility in the country, as Aventinus had written, but – if it wanted to exert power – at court or in the service of the prince. The same applied to the urban patricians. If they did not wish to sacrifice their chances of social advancement, they had to cut themselves off from their bourgeois past, make the transition into the nobility, and then secure their position by tactical marriages and service to the prince. Of course this also had an effect on the cities: around 1570 the patricians of Munich were a class of rentiers, who no longer engaged in any bourgeois activities that would derogate from their status. Yet they still formed the governments of their towns. In 1586 the patricians of Munich requested a ducal confirmation that their seats in the city council did not impair their freedom as nobles.[187] Both the rural nobles and the higher civic patriciate lost some of their independence as a result of this adaptation to their new role in the service of the prince and the court. High officials and professors, understandably, had had to swear an oath to accept the decrees of the Council of Trent since 1569, but serving the state and the court also required a greater measure of self-discipline in general. Norbert Elias has referred to this a new modelling of the affective personality as 'social constraint through self-constraint', and has shown how it was required of the social elite who flocked to serve the prince at his court. It is significant that the first German translation of Castiglione's *Cortegiano* appeared in 1565, at Munich.[188]

   If one sought to reduce the social tendencies of the sixteenth century to a common denominator, one could speak of a 'hardening' in all fields. By this we mean not only the increasingly desperate crises of subsistence for the lowest classes, the possible deterioration of the climate or the brutalisation of justice, but also the increasing rationalisation of confessional ideologies and the state, as well as the ossification of legal and social structures. As a growing population made more demands on static resources, all the privileged institutions tried to protect themselves against an unwelcome decline in their standing: access to the cities for new citizens was made more difficult, entry to the guilds became harder, it was less easy for guild craftsmen to take part in the government of their cities or for new men to join the civic patriciate, while the old nobility closed ranks against the newly ennobled. The prince, to whom the chief personages of the country, including ennobled patricians, had had almost free access in the first half of the century, now surrounded himself with new institutions

---

[187] Spindler, *Handbuch*, II 566f, 570ff.; M. Schattenhofer, 'Das Münchner Patriziat', *ZBLG*, 38 (1975), 877–900.

[188] N. Elias, *Über den Prozess der Zivilisation. Soziogenetische und psychogenetische Untersuchungen*, II, *Wandlungen der Gesellschaft. Entwurf zu einer Theorie der Zivilisation*, 5th edn Frankfurt am Main 1978; 242–50, 272, 312 (passage quoted). The interesting ideas on the psychological and mental consequences of changes in social structure: *ibid.*, 372ff.

which bureaucratised the business of government. The Jesuit advisers, Roman influence and the Spanish example of the self-discipline required of a ruler also helped to alienate the prince from his subjects. As the prince became more distant from the nobles, and regulated their affairs in an ever-growing body of legislation, the courtly nobility became remote from its vassals and the patricians of the cities were alienated from the other citizens. The gulf between the people and the authorities was further widened by humanistic education, Roman law training at the universities and confessional ideologies. As social relationships changed, mentalities changed with them.[189]

HARDENING AND THE REVOLUTION IN MENTALITIES 1560–90

And to begin with it is unfortunately obvious that the wrath and plagues of God, in this time of recurrent privations of war, pestilence and all kinds of dangerous diseases and sicknesses, not only do not decrease but, the longer they go on, the more they increase frightfully in more places and partly also in our principalities, which comes about most of all because in this godless and accursed world all kinds of sins and vices are gaining the upper hand from day to day . . .[190]

(Bavarian General Mandate, 1598)

The hardening in various spheres of society corresponds to a radical shift in mentalities in the second half of the sixteenth century, which apparently ran its course independently of confessions and allowed similar reactions to be recognised in territories with varied forms of society or government.[191] Broadly speaking, we can observe a shift away from the life-loving, open, sensual mentality of the Renaissance, with its orientation to this world and its points of contact with a widespread popular culture of pleasure, and a flight towards dogmatic, confessional-religious, ascetic modes of thought and behaviour, their sights fixed on the next world, which appeared to offer a refuge in a situation that was growing more and more precarious.

Clear signs of this shift of mentalities were evident in the 1560s, when the powerful Jesuit preacher Petrus Canisius aroused excitement among the population of Augsburg by hard-hitting sermons and sensational exor-

---

[189] Briefly characterised for the social structural field by R. van Dülmen, 'Formierung der europäischen Gesellschaft in der Frühen Neuzeit', *Geschichte und Gesellschaft*, 7 (1981), 5–41, esp. 20–5. On the change in mentalities J. Engel, 'Von der spätmittelalterlichen respublica christiana zum Mächte-Europa der Neuzeit', in T. Schieder (ed.), *Handbuch der europäischen Geschichte*, III, Stuttgart 1971, 1–448, esp. 12–23, is instructive.
[190] *Ernewerte Mandata und Landtgebott*, Munich 1598, 2.
[191] Engel, 'Von der . . . respublica', 16–18.

cisms. Götz von Pölnitz has described the reactions of the upper classes in the city to Canisius' missionary activity in 1569 as follows:

The increasingly frequent reports of the sudden penitential mood of an ecstatically excited, mystically overwrought patriciate are remarkably moving witnesses to the atmosphere of transition. It lies between that fading aristocratic joy in life of the almost decadent late Renaissance and an ascetic rigorism of certain Counter-Reformation saints.[192]

The radical nature of the shift in mentality is occasionally revealed in individual biographical fragments, stimulated by conversion experiences. Wilhelm V of Bavaria, for example, who had spent years as heir apparent in the secondary residence at Landshut, enjoying the pleasures of a lively Renaissance court, suffered a dangerous illness in 1575, after which he became a convert to the deeply ascetic and anxious piety that was to characterise the whole of his reign from 1579 to 1597.[193] Duke Wilhelm V (the Pious) of Bavaria became, in fact, the embodiment of 'the princely type of the Counter-Reformation' (D. Albrecht), whose sombre severity was not confined to his princely role but penetrated his whole being.[194] While Albrecht V had had his portrait painted in 1555, like his predecessors, as a worldly ruler in a flat beret and coloured slashed doublet, his hand on his sword and a lion at his feet, Wilhelm V's famous portrait by Hans von Aachen of 1590 shows him dressed in black from head to foot, with no ornament, lean and ascetic. Whereas his predecessors had stood as if rooted to the spot, Wilhelm V appears almost to float in the air. His portrait is matched by one of his Duchess, Renata of Lorraine; she too is entirely in black, with no jewellery except for a crucifix, her right hand resting demonstratively on a prayer book.[195] These portraits depict more than their subjects: they reflect a programme which had revived and reinvigorated divine services, processions, pilgrimages, the cult of relics

---

[192] G. von Pölnitz, 'Petrus Canisius und das Bistum Augsburg', *ZBLG*, 18 (1955), 352–94, quotation 382f. Similar in a more general form, Engel, 'Von der . . . respublica', 17.

[193] B. Hubensteiner, *Vom Geist des Barock*, Munich 1978, 112f. On anxiety-ridden piety see also K. Schellhass, *Der Dominikaner Felician Ninguardia und die Gegenreformation in Süddeutschland und Österreich 1560–1583*, 2 vols., Rome 1930–9; *ibid.*, II, 232ff.

[194] Spindler, *Handbuch*, II, 352 (D. Albrecht). This was felt above all in the capital, Munich. M. Schattenhofer, 'Die Wittelsbacher als Stadtherren von München', *Oberbayer. Archiv*, 109 (1984), 39–52, esp. 45–51. Wilhelm V of Bavaria is merely taken as an example for the other protagonists of the religious renewal.

[195] The illustrations in H. Glaser (ed.), *Wittelsbach und Bayern. Katalog der Ausstellung in der Residenz in München, 12. Juni–5. Oktober 1980*, II/1, Munich 1980,; *ibid.*, II/2, 12f., 38f., 50f. Suggestions for the interpretation of these paintings in Engel, 'Von der . . . respublica', 15–17; Rabb, *Struggle*, 41–8. Rabb writes of the changes in artistic styles as an indicator of the change in mentalities at the time: 'Mannerists emanated discomfort, imbalance and restlessness. Nothing seems solid or dependable. The distortion . . . casts doubt on reality . . .' *Ibid.*, 41. Also instructive on this is Evans, *Rudolf II*, 166–72.

and the veneration of Mary, and had created many new cult sites. In Munich fifty citizens' houses were torn down to make way for the church of St Michael and the Jesuit college; in Augsburg the Fuggers built a college for the Jesuits. The programme is expressed again in the bronze figure of the Archangel Michael overthrowing the Devil, erected in the centre of the façade of the church of St Michael at Munich in 1588. If Wilhelm V revived the cult of Mary and the veneration of saints, his successor Maximilian raised it to new heights in Bavaria. In 1620 he led the army of the League into battle at the White Mountain to the cry of 'Maria', and named the Virgin *Patrona Baiariae*. Besides the numerous old sites of Marian pilgrimage, including Altötting, which were regularly visited by the Dukes, many new ones were founded, eleven in Munich alone. Countless chapels of Mary, including two court chapels in the princely residence, were built, and this was also the period when the so-called 'house madonnas' began to be displayed, the largest of course being that which adorned the façade of the princely residence at Munich. Later, columns were erected to Mary in town squares, medals and coins were struck in her honour, banners flown and fraternities founded to organise the pilgrimages, the Marian Congregation among them. The daughters of the Dukes were normally named Maria, and even the heir apparent of Elector Maximilian was named Ferdinand Maria. Not without reason, the literature speaks of the 'Marian programme of the state'.[196]

Mary the consoler and comforter certainly represented a point of light in the gathering cultural darkness of the last third of the sixteenth century. 'We fly to your protection, where we live safely and happily', read the words on the statue of Mary on the residence in Munich.[197] Mary was the projection of all the positive qualities that could not be found in the God of the Old Testament with his plagues and scourges. But beyond this divine schizophrenia, the exuberant veneration of Mary contained another element of interest for the theme of witchcraft: as one learns from the *Malleus* and other sources, Mary was seen in hagiographical literature as the antitype of Eve. While Eve had brought evil into the world through her sin, Mary had borne the Redeemer. 'All the evil that the curse of Eve brought, the blessings of Mary have removed.'[198] Eve had been the first sinner, who had yielded to the Devil's blandishments; the witches were continuing and completing his struggle for power. But in many points Mary was more the female antitype of the witches than of Eve; she symbolised the divine covenant, grace, forgiveness, purity and virginity,

---

[196] P.B. Steiner, 'Der gottselige Fürst und die Konfessionalisierung Altbayerns', in Glaser, *Um Glauben*, II/1, 252–63, esp. 259; Hubensteiner, 'Vom Geist', 118.
[197] Steiner, 'Der gottselige Fürst', 255.
[198] Sprenger and Institoris, *Der Hexenhammer*, Erster Teil, 98.

while the witches stood for pacts with the Devil, eternal damnation, the most extreme contamination (intercourse with the Devil) and unbridled licentiousness. If Mary was the protectress of humanity, especially of the sick, of travellers, women in labour and children, of growth and crops, of the vintage and of good weather for agriculture,[199] the witches sought to harm people's lives and faith, damaged the crops, conjured up hail, frost and storms, brought hunger, disease and death. The author of the Malleus Maleficarum had invoked the blessing of Mary as a charm against witchcraft, and even attributed great power to the mere mention of her name:

As the most effective preservative for places, people and animals, the words of the title of our Saviour may be used, when they are written in the form of a cross in four parts of the place : Jesus + Nazarenus + Rex + Judaeorum +; or with the addition of the name of the Virgin Mary.[200]

It must be more than a mere coincidence that the first spectacular witch burnings in southeast Germany, at Dillingen and Munich, occurred at the same time as the renewal of the cult of Mary, illustrated by the foundation of the Marian Congregation between 1575 and 1578.[201] The exemplary piety of the new generation of princes in the region had, as we have seen, both its public and its private side. Besides devotions and prayers at intervals throughout the day, this included ascetic exercises and self-mortifications. Perhaps the deepest and most intimate acts of devotion were the secret 'blood pacts' of Dukes Maximilian and Ferdinand Maria with the Virgin of Altötting.[202] They were the direct antitype of the witches' pact with the Devil, which contemporaries also believed to be written in blood on a scrap of paper; their symbolic value must be regarded as all the greater because such acts were far from common.

Harvest failures, hunger, disease and war were experienced by contemporaries as God's punishment of human sins. If the princes spent their days free from sin and in deep devotion, these punishments could only be blamed on the misconduct of their subjects. In the following decades the people were bombarded with laws and decrees on their morals: blasphemy and cursing were of course prohibited, but so were adultery, fornication and licentiousness, priestly concubinage, indecent clothing, short skirts, tight hose, 'naked' bosoms, over-rich ornament, mixed bathing, mixed servants' quarters, climbing through windows to meet one's lover, poach-

---

[199] Beitl, *Wörterbuch*, 536–9.
[200] Sprenger and Institoris, *Der Hexenhammer*, Zweiter Teil, 9.
[201] On the date of the foundation of the Congregation in the region see R. Bauerreiss, *Kirchengeschichte Bayerns*, VI, 335. On the specifically aggressive attitude of the members at the beginning, Hubensteiner, 'Vom Geist', 73ff.
[202] Steiner, 'Der gottselige Fürst', 259; Hubensteiner, 'Vom Geist', 117, who also regards the blood signature as a counterpart to the pact with the Devil.

ing, begging and idleness, dancing, drinking, cardplaying, midsummer bonfires, rowdiness in taverns, carol singing at Epiphany, excessive expense on weddings and christenings, conjurors, singers and rope-dancers, religious controversies between craftsmen, drinking healths, 'free nights' (on which the young men were traditionally allowed to sow their wild oats), masquerades (especially dressing as the Devil), shouting and singing in beer houses as well as the use of superstitious signs and charms. In their stead the law demanded the keeping of fast days, kneeling at the Ave Maria and the prayer against the Turks three times a day when the bell rang to summon the faithful, both at home and on the road – horsemen, for example, had to dismount. The list of the prohibitions and requirements is even longer, and the tendency is perhaps best shown by the title of a mandate of 1593, which was brief and to the point: 'Mandate against all worldly pleasure'.[203] The cultural revolution that the authorities sought to enforce affected almost all areas of life and every social stratum or group.

There is no longer any connection between the coarse behaviour which knew no secrecy and performed even the most intimate actions in all innocence in the bath-house, in the alleys of the city, the cottages of the lowly and the palaces of the great, as numerous sources well into the sixteenth century document, and the dismal, sour and gloomy life that was enforced on contemporaries – in a spirit of the purest religious morality – with rigorous strictness and fanatical zeal by those puritans who can be found in all confessions.[204]

But the worst of all sins were those committed by the witches, who in fact represented the very essence of sinfulness, and thus gave God the greatest provocation to punish his people. For this reason the first great persecutions in the southwest and southeast were carefully noted. In 1563 Petrus Canisius, then Provincial of the upper German province of his order, wrote to Laynez, the General of the Jesuits:

---

[203] Many prohibitions are collected in the *Ernewerte Mandata* of 1598 (cf. note 190); numerous examples are given in Schattenhofer (as n. 194) and in F. Merzbacher, 'Gesetzgebung und Kodifikation unter Kurfürst Maximilian I', in Glaser, *Um Glauben*, II/1, 225–36, esp. 226–9. The *Landtgebott wider die Aberglauben, Zauberey, Hexerey und andere sträffliche Teufelskünste*, Munich 1611, is of course a veritable quarry of popular magical customs. Cf. below; the *Mandat wider alle weltliche Freud* is mentioned in M. Kunze, 'Der Prozess Pappenheimer', Dr. jur. thesis, Munich 1980, 368. That an effective enforcement of the mandates was intended was convincingly shown by F. Stieve, *Das kirchliche Polizeiregiment in Baiern unter Maximilian I, 1595–1651*, Munich 1876. For similar tendencies all over Europe, P. Burke, *Popular Cuture in Early Modern Europe*, London 1979, esp. 207–34; Muchembled, 'Witches', 181–231.
[204] Engel, 'Von der . . . respublica', 17.

Everywhere witches are being punished, but they increase remarkably. Their outrages are horrifying . . . formerly in Germany one never saw people yield themselves up to the Devil and sign pacts with him so often. It is unbelievable how much godlessness, sexual immorality and cruelty these outcast women have committed openly and in secret under Satan's guidance. The authorities do not dare to publish the scandalous crimes which they confess in captivity. In many places these pernicious creatures in human form and special enemies of the Christian faith, are being burned. They bring many to their deaths through their devilish arts and raise up storms and bring frightful harm on the countryfolk and other Christians. Nothing seems to be secure against their terrible arts and powers. The righteous God allows it because of the grievous error of his people, which is not atoned for through any penance.[205]

Canisius' words should be read not as those of a leading spokesman of the Counter-Reformation but as those of a member of an intelligentsia whose world-view appears to have changed or 'darkened' dramatically since the middle of the century – irrespective of confessional allegiance. Canisius was not the only one to be firmly convinced that he was engaged in a constant struggle with the Devil or with demons: his sensational exorcisms of members of the Fugger family and their servants in Augsburg were still serving as examples hundreds of years later.[206] It was in the Lutheran territories of the Empire that the first great persecutions after the Reformation took place, and it was Calvinist Scotland that first equated 'white magic' with harmful sorcery in 1563, and branded it as witchcraft.[207] The Lutheran Electorate of Saxony followed this example in 1572 and dismissed the arguments of Weyer and other Protestant opponents of perse-

---

[205] Janssen and Pastor, *Culturzustände*, VIII, 652f.
[206] Duhr, *Geschichte der Jesuiten*, I, 731ff.; *ibid.*, II, 499ff.; III, 751–66. Witch trials frequently originated in exorcisms, C. Ernst, *Teufelsaustreibungen. Die Praxis der katholischen Kirche im 16. und 17. Jahrhundert*, Bern 1972. Ernst shows that exorcisms could be therapeutic in character (*ibid.*, 130ff.). The possessed were rarely regarded as witches themselves but often denounced as witches those who had allegedly caused the demon to take possession of them. The 'great exorcism' also included the question of whether the demon had possessed a victim because of sorcery practised by a witch. The corresponding terms are still in force today, *ibid.*, 19f. Canisius' exorcisms did not lead to any trials for witchcraft, unlike those of the hardly less famous Georg Scherer SJ in Vienna in 1583; Duhr, *Die Stellung*, 25–8.
[207] Trevor-Roper, 'European Witch Craze', 139. Such leading Calvinist theologians of the time as Lambert Daneau in France or John Knox in Scotland also preached sermons against witchcraft in the 1570s, as did their Jesuit opponents, *ibid.*, 296; Larner, *Enemies*, 66f. It seems like a new version of Manichaean doctrine when Knox describes the Devil as the 'God of this world'; Thomas, *Religion*, 561. Yet it was typical of the position of the purists in all the great confessions, and is based on St Paul's Second Epistle to the Corinthians (2 Cor. 4:4). Cf. also O. Pfister, *Das Christentum und die Angst*, Frankfurt am Main, 1985, 206.

cution, appealing instead to the findings of the inquisitorial doctrine of witchcraft, and thus acknowledging its validity beyond the Catholic confession. Professor Wesenbeck of Wittenberg wrote that Weyer had been a physician, and his arguments therefore carried little weight.[208] Calvinists, Lutherans and Catholics were agreed in the 1560s on the existence of the crime of witchcraft and the necessity to root it out; their agreement derived from the same reasoning: harvest failure, hunger and plague were punishments from God, caused by the sins of humanity. If the punishments were harsher than before, this was because people were more sinful. The greatest sin of all was assumed to be committed by the witches, who were also the cause and the agents of the plagues,[209] although of course God's freedom of decision as the supreme and omnipotent judge was not questioned.

In principle, then, the agrarian crises of the later sixteenth century, whose close connection with outbreaks of persecution has been demonstrated, were still seen in all confessions as signs of God's wrath, as were other marvels and prodigies that excited contemporaries: comets,[210] the almost constant news of strange events, now disseminated more rapidly, rains of blood, monstrous births, signs seen in the heavens, the bloody civil wars in France, the revolt of the Netherlands, peasants' risings, the murder of abbots, bishops and kings, the ever-present pressure of the Turks on the Christian west. Soothsayers, alchemists, astrologers and other obscure figures who could profit from the atmosphere of crisis carried on a thriving trade.[211] And finally – not only as a symbol, though he was that too – in

---

[208] Paulus, *Hexewahn*, 55–7; the problem of white magic is not discussed in Merzbacher, *Die Hexenprozesse*, who gives the dates of the earliest legislation on witchcraft in the German territories (Saxony, 1572; Electoral Palatinate 1587; Baden-Baden 1588), *ibid.*, 31. The text of the Saxon Constitution is in H. Brackert, 'Daten und Materialien zur Hexenverfolgung', Becker *et al., Aus der Zeit*, 313–441, 374.

[209] On this see chapter 3, pp. 115–20.

[210] Thus for example in Mayr, *Epitome*, fol. 118, 145v, 167v. As early as the year 1560 the Freising chronicler remarked on 'vil wunderliche Sachen in Europa, als Cometstern, Blut regnen, stillstehende Feuer, Straalen in Luft etc. . . .' In 1577 he says of the comet of that year: 'was diser schröckhliche Lufftstern mit sich bracht, bezeugt der Curs folgender Zeiten'. At the beginning of the great persecutions, that is in the Wonder Year 1588, predicted as long ago as 1580 (cf. note 161 and p. 94), he says that there had been in that year 'viel Missgeburt und seltsame Wunder in Luft und Wasser abgeben und ist dergleichen in vil hundert Jaren nit gewest . . .' Schorer's Memmingen chronicle refers to comets in 1572, 1577, 1582, 1596 and 1618, and other portents in blood and in the heavens in 1575, 1581 and 1582. In 1625 a 'feurigen Drachen' was seen in the firmament (Schorer, *Chronik*, 102–31). Of course a comet was also seen in the witch hunting year 1590. L. Westenrieder, *Beyträge zur vaterländischen Historie, Geographie, Statistik und Landwirtschaft, samt einer Übersicht der schönen Literatur*, 10 vols., Munich 1788/1817; *ibid.*, V, 104. For the reaction to these comets, Janssen and Pastor, *Culturzustände*, VI, 440ff. In 1591 a priest wrote: 'Nirgends nichts denn Furcht und Schrecken, Teufel und Gespenster, Unholde, Hexen, Missgeburten, Erdbeben, Feuerzeichen am Himmel, dreiköpfige Gesichter in den Wolken und so viele andere Zeichen göttlichen Zorns. . .', *ibid.*, VI, 456.

[211] 'Daneben treiben Höllenzwinger, Geisterklopfer und dergleichen Gelichters mehr ungescheut ihr Werk und verunehren und schänden das göttliche, geoffenbarte Wort. Wun-

the person of Rudolf II the imperial throne was occupied by a man who was on familiar terms with these wonder-working representatives of the higher magic. As the Emperor withdrew from the affairs of the world, many came to believe him mad, others thought him bewitched or under a spell, and some even believed him to be a sorcerer himself.[212]

It is far from adequate merely to explain the growth of persecution by pointing to the progress of the Counter-Reformation or the increased tensions between the confessions after 1560, as has been common in the secondary literature. Rather, these tensions themselves can be seen as further signs of the general trend, of which the persecution of witches was another expression: the growth of stresses within European societies, the social catastrophes that became more frequent after 1560 in the wake of devastating agrarian crises and their aftermath, and the view upheld in all confessions that these hardships were signs of God's wrath with sinful humanity. The reaction was a tightening of morality which assumed the proportions of a cultural revolution. This does not mean that the so-called 'revolution of mentalities' of the later sixteenth century is to be exclusively correlated with these events. There had, after all, always been periodic attempts to purify Christianity. The process of centralising absolutism, the formation of hierarchies and the trend to rationalisation, the 'process of civilisation', had roots that were far older,[213] as did the development of the

derdoctoren schreiben Bücher und Scharteken für Gelehrte und gemeines Volk. Andere ziehen umher als Goldmacher, betrügen hoch und niedrig, andere verbreiten den seltsamen Missglauben, als könnten sie . . . Geister bezwingen . . . und solcher geheimen teufflischen Künste gibt es viele. . .', *ibid.*, VI, 457. (And besides the conjurors of devils, spirit rappers, and more of this crew carry on their work without shame, and bring dishonour and scandal on the divine revealed word. Wonder doctors write books and pamphlets for the learned and the common people. Others go about pretending to make gold, deceiving high and low, others spread the strangest beliefs, as if they could compel spirits . . . and there are many of these secret diabolical arts . . .')

[212] G. von Schwarzenfeld, *Rudolf II, Der saturnische Kaiser*, Munich 1961. Rudolf's star sign was Saturn, according to the astrologers. Saturn was regarded as the sign of sorcerers. Even in the *Malleus* Saturn had had a malign influence, and brought about melancholy (Sprenger and Institoris, *Malleus*, I, 71). For the sorcerers at Rudolf's court, and on the fear of bewitchment and the suspicion of the Jesuits for the Emperor, see R.J.W. Evans, *Rudolf II. Ohnmacht und Einsamkeit*, Graz/Vienna/Cologne 1980, 134–61. (First published as *Rudolf II and His World: A Study in Intellectual History*, Oxford 1973.)

[213] Here it must suffice to mention again the general investigations of Elias (cf. note 188), also in general M. Weber, *Wirtschaft und Gesellschaft*, Tübingen 1976. A discussion of long-term tendencies is important for the evaluation of the phenomenon of witch trials, but caution is required. Cf. the criticism in Schormann, *Hexenprozesse* (1981), 89–95, of over-hasty conclusions in the wider field. With reference to the theme of witchcraft a linkage with long-term developments only becomes interesting when definite leaps in development coincided with times of extreme concern about bewitchment. This is obviously the case in both social history (cf. Kamen, *Iron Century*, 249f.) and the history of mentalities. What traditional historians, looking at it from the religious point of view, have labelled, for example, the 'Zeitgraben des 16. Jahrhunderts' (Hubensteiner, 'Vom Geist', 58), or the 'völligen Grabenbruch' or 'Krise des 16. Jahrhunderts' (*ibid.*, 63, 134), is understood by Mandrou as an 'ökonomische und soziale Krise' in the period 1590–

money economy and early capitalism. The increasing disequilibrium between population growth and agricultural output heralded the end of a
secular phase of social and economic growth which had begun after the
great demographic collapse of the 1340s, the so-called crisis of the fourteenth century, when the persecutions of Jews had been at their most
savage. That crisis too had marked the end of several hundred years of
growth.[214]

Most historians place the high point of the so-called crisis of the seventeenth century in the 1640s. Yet social tremors can be detected long before,
and the darkening of the world-view in all confessions had begun much
earlier. In terms contemporaries would have understood, Henry Kamen
has called the years 1550–1660 the 'iron century', and has reminded us that
in this age of hunger, disease and war the victims were more willing than
ever to see the hand of the Devil behind their sufferings.[215] The flood of
Protestant 'devils books' literature began in the 1560s, at the same time as
the first persecutions. Though such treatises on the works of the Devil were
forbidden in the Catholic Duchy of Bavaria, it was not because the rulers
did not share their views, but only because they were written by Protestants
and were therefore works of the Devil themselves.[216] It is clear that from
the middle of the century there was a greater willingness among the
educated classes to attribute every conceivable misfortune, not to natural
causes, but to the machinations of the Devil. As catastrophes struck ever
more frequently, Christ the Redeemer took second place to Almighty God,
who had nothing better to do than inflict cruel punishments on his sinful
followers, or put them to the test like the pious Job.

There was a constant clamour for witch-burning from the populace,
hard hit by 'unnatural' disease, sickness of livestock or harvests destroyed
by hail. When the authorities in the Rechbergs' Lordship of Illereichen

1640, part of the crisis of the seventeenth century; Mandrou is precise in fixing the dates
of the breach: 'Ist die Verbindung zwischen der mentalen, fast physiologischen Gleichgewichtsstörung und der unterschwelligen sozialen Krise nicht offensichtlich? . . . in den
Jahren nach 1580 – Scharnierjahre wenn es je solche gegeben hat . . .' ('is the connection
between the mental, almost physiological, disequilibrium and the underlying social crisis
not obvious? . . . in the years after 1580 – hinges of fate if ever there were'). R. Mandrou,
'Der europäische Barock: Pathetische Mentalitäten und soziale Umwalzung', in Honegger, *Schrift*, 368–92 (= *idem*, 'Le baroque européen, mentalité pathétique et révolution
sociale', *Annales E.S.C.*, 15 (1960), 898–914). The years of the first European wave of
witch hunting after 1580 would indeed qualify as 'hinges of fate'.

[214]   The parallel between the persecutions of Jews and of witches has been remarked relatively often. e.g. Trevor-Roper, 'European Witch Craze', 113; R. Romano and A. Tenenti,
Die Grundlegung der modernen Welt. Spätmittelalter, Renaissance, Reformation, Frankfurt am Main, 1967, 16. A more differentiated approach is offered by R. van Dülmen,
Entstehung des frühneuzeitlichen Europa, 1550–1648, Frankfurt am Main, 1982, 282–8.

[215]   Kamen, *Iron Century*, 249f.; Janssen and Pastor, *Culturzustände*, VI, 458–527.

[216]   Quantification of books on the Devil in Midelfort, *Witch Hunting* (1972), 70.

yielded to this clamour in 1563 their response was still exceptional; similar communal demands for a persecution were rejected in the Prince-Abbacy of Kempten in 1549, in the Bishopric of Freising in 1581 and the Duchy of Bavaria in 1587. In 1586–9 the apologists of persecution gained the upper hand. In a decree of Duke Wilhelm V of Bavaria, we read:

Since through God's doom, because of our sins, the foul and frightful vice of sorcery and witchcraft is spreading from day to day and, through the work of the evil one, who always lies in wait and seeks to ruin mankind, is becoming more and more common in Germany . . . and also threatens this country . . . our gracious prince . . . to save the honour of God and to avert all temporary misfortune and harm that threatens mankind because of this accursed vice which is most offensive to God, has finally considered, resolved and decided to cause everything that is proper to root out the same and which a worldly authority ought to do, to be maturely and thoroughly deliberated, and then executed to the best of his ability . . . so that the honour of the Almighty may be saved, the spiritual welfare of the poor misguided people promoted, and the common harm with which such a terrible vice threatens the people, may be averted.[217]

The contradictions which we see in this reasoning were not evident to contemporaries, who did not puzzle over problems of theodicy. Almost unnoticed, the good tidings of the redemption were pushed into the background, and the world became a battlefield between the followers of God and those of the Devil. Many contemporaries saw this surprising development, which almost resulted in a Manichaean dualism, from an eschatological perspective. The return of the Devil was a sign that the 'latter days' had arrived, in which, according to the Book of Revelation, the struggle was to be renewed: 'and when the thousand years are completed Satan will be released from his prison and he will go out to lead the peoples astray. . .'[218] Without the eschatological connection, which was not universally made, the picture of a wrathful, punitive God itself had demonic traits, almost unredeemed by any trace of the fundamental Christian virtues of love, goodness or forgiveness; it may be seen as an extreme symbol of growing pessimism in the latter half of the sixteenth century.

Of course not all contemporaries shared this sombre vision. Many

[217] Riezler, *Geschichte*, 59f. HStAM, Hexenakten 1, Decree of 2 April 1590.
[218] StA Bamberg, Bamberger Verordnungen, no. 44. *General Instruction von den Truten*, Ansbach 1591, fol. 1 (based on Revelations 12:12 and 20:7–8). On dualism cf. Muchembled, 'Witches', 32, who claims that the dualism of popular culture was different from that of the culture of the elite: 'below', both God and the Devil were ambivalent figures; 'above', on the other hand, they were adversaries with unequivocal moral bases.

remained uninterested in religion, despite the greater purity and intensity with which it was practised. Others were horrified by the falsification of the Christian gospel. Forty years later Friedrich Spee wrote:

> We must show that our God is not like the idols of the heathen, who cannot leave off their wrath.[219]

[219] F. Spee, *Cautio Criminalis*, Munich 1982, 138.

3 The wave of persecutions around 1590

CONTEMPORARY INTERPRETATIONS

Sorcery must be rooted out everywhere . . . in Christendom, everywhere,
far and wide . . . all the authorities must use the same vengeance, so that
for once we can have peace and quiet without any harm.[1]

(Swabian chaplain, 1590)

In all the territories the persecutions began without reflection; nowhere
was there a concerted plan for the systematic expansion of individual
trials. Nor was there any special agreement between the territories to
collaborate in hunting down witches, or a special body of legislation on
witchcraft or even the theoretical foundations for such a law. The basis for
the trial of witches in all the towns and territories was the paragraph
(article 109) on harmful sorcery in the *Constitutio Criminalis Carolina*. The
'outbreak' of the wave of persecution in the years around 1590 found the
region unprepared. People did not begin to reflect on the events until after
their extraordinary character had become apparent.

It was clear to contemporaries that such persecutions in the region were
quite out of the ordinary. A professor at the University of Ingolstadt and
councillor of the Duke of Bavaria referred to the precedent of the persecutions in upper Germany of more than eighty years earlier.[2] The Munich
printer Adam Berg wrote in the foreword to his first edition of Binsfeld's
Tractatus von Bekhanntnuss der Zauberer und Hexen of 1591 that he had

understood from old people that a hundred years ago this vice had been
fought with utmost earnestness and this appetite rooted out.[3]

---

[1] ÖNB Vienna, Cod. 8963, fol. 751/8v (Fugger Zeitunben).
[2] StadtA Munich, Hist. Ver. Urk. 2050, fol. 3, opinion of Dr Kaspar Lagus (1533–1606); on
him see Bosl, *Biographie*, 459.
[3] Binsfeld, *Tractatus*, a ii verso; (dedication to Duke Ferdinand of Bavaria, 1550–1608,
younger brother of the reigning Duke Wilhelm V and ruler of the Lordship of Schongau,
scene of the controversial witch hunt of 1589–91).

Others could not remember anything at all comparable. The adviser of the Lutheran Count Palatine Philipp Ludwig von Neuburg, loftily dismissing the 'papist' *Malleus*, explained that witchcraft must be a completely new crime, because it was not mentioned in the Bible, in ancient literature or in the secular codes of law, which only spoke of the much less serious offence of sorcery. In his view, witchcraft was a new kind of crime, or accumulation of crimes, which was characteristic of the 'latter days':

> when one speaks of witchcraft, one understands by it all kinds of vice that can be imagined, against all the commandments of God, which come together and combine in the same, as idolatry, the most vicious blasphemy, wanton rejection and despising of the word of God, of the holy sacraments, the most wilful denial of God's grace, of the Holy Ghost, *crimen laesae majestatis utriusque*, the cruellest murder, theft, unspeakable immorality, which far exceeds the sin of Sodom . . . in conclusion, it is the most frightful sin that man can commit . . .

At another point, in giving his opinion, he says: 'in these unhappy latter days, when it is unfortunately becoming very common, it is called witch-craft'.[4]

Eschatological features are even more marked in the opinion submitted to the authorities in the Lutheran Margravate of Ansbach, to the north of Pfalz-Neuburg. The Margrave Georg Friedrich (1556–1603) caused a *General Instruction von den Truten* (General Instruction on Witches) to be drawn up, which begins:

> what the dear God in Heaven proclaimed with deep sorrow to the dwellers on the earth in the 12th chapter of the Revelation of John, that the Devil would come to them and his anger would be great, because he knew that he had little time, that is being powerfully fulfilled in these our latter days, when we see and experience how the wicked Devil rages and roars most cruelly with witchcraft, sorcery and outrageous knavishness, which is part of the scandalous work of the witches, as if he wished . . . to ruin man and beast for ever, and even cast down God himself from Heaven . . . [5]

---

[4] HStAM, Hexenakten 16, fol. 140v, 141v (opinion of Dr Christoph Mumprecht, 1560–1620; on him see Henker, 'Zur Prosopographie', 231f.).

[5] StA Bamberg, Bamberger Verordnungen, no. 44, 'General Instruction von den Truten', fol. 1 (the author was Adam Francisci, titular Abbot of Heilsbronn, and a Court Councillor of the Margrave). Cf. G. Muck, *Geschichte von Kloster Heilsbronn*, Nördlingen 1879, 3 vols., I , 501–3; II, 55–9. On the apocalyptic mood at the court of the Margrave cf. K.H. Lang, *Neuere Geschichte des Fürstenthums Baireuth*, vol. III (1557–1603), Nuremberg 1811, 40, 373, 379. Acute attacks of expectation of the end of the world followed the cycles of agrarian crisis: 1570, 1581, 1585, 1591; *ibid.*

Even those who did not fear the imminent end of the world were impressed with a sense of acute danger. Even in Nuremberg, where the very existence of witchcraft had been doubted in the first half of the century, opinions began to change. The Lutheran theologians of the Free City now came to the conclusion

> that such vice has spread so wide that it will be feared that if once we begin [to hunt witches; WB] we shall not be able to stop soon. For the more common this vice becomes, and gains the upper hand, the more it will be necessary to think of ways to root it out totally, and to cleanse the land of such grisly vermin.[6]

A contemporary opinion from the Catholic Duchy of Bavaria adopted almost the same tone. There, the writer felt that

> the detestable and frightful vice of sorcery and witchcraft spreads wider from day to day and through the instigation of the evil one, who lies in wait to ruin mankind, becomes more and more common in Germany, and not just according to the common rumour, but as experience unfortunately tells us, will soon attack this country . . .[7]

In the whole region, without any distinction between Lutherans and Catholics or territories and Free Cities, the idea had taken root by 1590 that the Devil's power was on the increase, and that his followers, the witches, with God's permission, were bringing misfortune on the country.

Amazingly, many of these contemporary considerations pushed the traditional harmful sorcery of the witches into the background. In all confessions we find a pronounced spiritualisation of the crime of witchcraft, in which the heretical or diabolical components (rejection of God, pacts with the Devil, witches' sabbaths, prayer to the Devil) were regarded as central. In this spiritualised view, the witches no longer caused harm through their own powers, or even with the aid of the Devil; rather, they were simply the indirect agents of evil, through their wickedness. As God was omnipotent, then all plagues and suffering came from God. In this orthodox view, the Devil acted, not as a free agent but with the permission of God, on whose orders he punished sinners or led the steadfast into temptation. As Midelfort rightly observed, the Book of Job was at the heart of this spiritualised interpretation, for it was here that the Devil's freedom of action was circumscribed.[8] Witches did not really bewitch people, but merely indicated their will by certain signs (spells, magical practices and so on) to the omnipresent demon, who then, with God's

---

[6] Kunstmann, *Zauberwahn*, 189.
[7] HStAM, Hexenakten 1, Prod. 2, fol. 2 (decree of Duke Wilhelm V of Bavaria to his Councillors in Munich, 2 April 1590).   [8] Midelfort, *Witch Hunting*, 12f.

leave, performed the desired sorcery or held out the illusion of its performance.

This spiritualised interpretation had certain remarkable consequences: in the first place it led to a change in attitudes to 'harmless' or white magic, which was now seen in principle as an invocation of, or even as a tacit pact, with the Devil. All sorcery was thus, in principle, brought closer to the crime of witchcraft.[9] Secondly, witches could no longer be dealt with under the paragraph (Art. 109) of the *Carolina* which covered sorcery, if they were not even in a position to practise harmful sorcery. The consequence was a tendency for the territories to pass laws on witchcraft in which the pact with the Devil was central. Typically, confessional formers of opinion prepared the ground: Calvinist Electoral Saxony in 1572, the Lutheran Palatinate in 1587, Catholic Baden-Baden in 1588, Bavaria *de facto* in 1590, *de jure* in 1612.[10] The spiritualised view also recognised an undeniable link between the crime of witchcraft and the general worsening of the situation in the decades before 1590, the appalling series of storms, harvest failures, famines, diseases or other catastrophes. In the opinion of the Nuremberg theologians witchcraft was

> the highest and most gruesome vice, by which God's wrath is most roused, and from which common plagues to the whole country must necessarily ensue if it is not punished.[11]

God would punish people with his rod for their sins, and witchcraft was the wickedest of all imaginable sins, which therefore would deserve the severest punishment. Exactly the same view was taken in Ansbach, Pfalz-Neuburg, the Catholic Bishoprics and the Duchy of Bavaria.[12]

If we examine the argument of these opinions more closely, however, we find that the traditional belief in sorcery continued to exist alongside the new view, although, at least in these opinions, it survived in a rather altered form. We might say that witchcraft played a double role in the interpretations of the theologians and jurists who wrote these opinions. It was both a sin and a punishment! God punished people because of their great sins, and the greatest sin was witchcraft. As punishment the Devil was given freedom of action; he in turn incited people to practise witchcraft and joined with the witches to inflict the punishments – through sorcery. The flaw in the reasoning is not resolved until we leave the 'higher' level of

---

[9] Binsfeld, *Tractatus*, 4v, who appeals to Augustine and Thomas Aquinas. For the Christian theory of signs and the pact with the Devil in patristic and scholastic literature see Harmening, *Superstitio*, 114–16, 303–17; Midelfort, *Witch Hunting*, 60.
[10] Merzbacher, *Die Hexenprozesse*, 31.   [11] Kunstmann, *Zauberwahn*, 207.
[12] 'Bedenken, die Unhulden betreffend' (9 Aug. 1591)', *Ansbachische Monatsschrift*, 2 (1794), Heft 6, 534–48 ('Ein merkwürdiges Aktenstück aus dem 16. Jahrhundert'); StA Bamberg, Bamberger Verordnungen, no. 44; 'General Instruction'; HStAM, Hexenakten 1 Prod. 2; *ibid.*, Hexenakten 16, fol. 139–43.

theological and legal opinions – in which both views are found alongside each other[13] – and turn to other sources. We soon realise that beneath the thin veneer of the spiritualised view of the nature of witchcraft lay a widespread and deep-rooted belief in the possibility of the direct magical power of the witches. In any case, the spiritual view was of no use in criminal proceedings, which had to deal with concrete cases of sorcery. In everyday dealings with sorcery and witchcraft the possibility of harmful sorcery was taken as axiomatic by theologians, jurists and the common people, in Nuremberg as in Augsburg, in Pfalz-Neuburg as in Bavaria.[14]

The central importance of sorcery for the wave of persecution of 1590 is clear from the *Erweytterte Unholden Zeyttung* of that year, which describes the events in Swabia and Bavaria as follows:

As in our times all sorceries and devilish tricks gain the upper hand to such a degree that almost every town, market and village in the whole of Germany is full of such vermin and servants of the Devil, who not only venture to ruin the crops in the field . . . by unusual thunders, lightning, showers, hail, storm winds, frosts, droughts, mice, worms and other things, that God has sent as his doom on them, through the Devil's aid and support . . . but they also try with all their might to take the food from the people, by harming the livestock, cattle, calves, horses, sheep, and the like, and not only the beasts and fruits of the earth alone, but also they do not spare the young and unbaptised children . . . and do their utmost to lame and cripple the old, to cause them painful illnesses and in the end to bring them to their deaths, so that manifold pain and sorrow grow among the people.[15]

The lip service to God's omnipotence is pushed into the background by the apparently overt power of the witches, which was now to be rooted out by every available means. In reality witchcraft was regarded not just as a symptom of human sinfulness and God's wrath, but as a direct root of the evils by which people were being oppressed. The judge in the district court of Schongau pleaded in 1594 for the erection of a memorial to his persecution of witches, because the grain harvests had been better in the last three years than for twenty years before.[16] In 1601, after the next hunger crisis, a

---

[13] *Ibid.*
[14] The spiritualised view was obviously no more than a thin varnish which could scarcely cover a rather rustic superstition even among the intellectual elite. Cf. the *Erweytterte Unholden Zeyttung* of 1590 (edited in Behringer, 'Hexenverfolgung', 346–54), or the poem in honour of the regional witch hunters written by the Swabian chaplain (cf. note 1): 'Ain kurzes Tractätlen unnd Anmahnung, wie sich etliche Christliche Fürsten unnd Herren . . . gegen den bösen Weyberen und Hexin erzaigt unnd verhalten'. For Nuremberg, Kunstmann, *Zauberwahn*, 190.
[15] *Erweytterte Unholden Zeyttung*, a i v–a ii; Behringer, 'Hexenverfolgung' (1984), 346f.
[16] StadtA Munich, Hist. Ver. Urk. 2005, fol. 1v.

**Erweytterte Vnholden
Zeyttung.**

Kurtze Erzelung wie viel

der Vnholden hin vnd wider / sonderlich
inn dem Obern Teutschland / gefängklich eingezo-
gen: was für grossen schaden sie den Menschen /
vermög jhrer vrgicht/zügefüget/ vnd wieviel vn=
gefehrlich deren / inn disem 1590. Jar / biß auff
den 21. Julij / von dem Leben zum Todt hin=
gericht vnd verbrandt worden
seyen.

5. *Erweytterte Unholden Zeyttung,* Ulm 1590. The woodcut on the title page seems to depict a strange proceeding which probably refers to an execution of witches at Ellingen: 'how ... first ... of some of those there, two were bound to a pillar, cauldrons of gunpowder were placed under them, lit and so they were put to death'.

Court Councillor in Munich proposed a persecution because 'it is to be presumed that if there were no such *mancipia and instrumenta diaboli,* there would be hope of greater fruitfulness in the country'.[17]

[17] HStAM, Hexenakten 4, Prod. 25, s.f.

In 1590 almost all the authorities argued for a ruthless persecution of witches. Their eradication appeared to offer a quick means of escape from the 'plagues' from which people in the largely agrarian society of the time were suffering. Persecution had not been tried in the region before 1590. The hope it seemed to offer generated a high degree of consensus in all confessions and social groups.

THE COURSE OF THE PERSECUTIONS

The theme of the way in which the wave of persecution grew is as old as the comparison with another evil of the time, epidemics. It goes back to the time of the persecutions themselves and has only been confirmed by historical research.[18] The cause of the expansion has been identified as 'incitement' by witchcraft trials in neighbouring places, which allowed the 'infection' to spread by denunciations or by their example. The analogy between persecution and epidemics involves a remarkable consequence, which resembles the anthropological or social-historical argument of Keith Thomas: greater susceptibility to disease indicates physically or mentally weakened 'bodies' which are less able to resist infection than those whose health is unimpaired.[19]

In spite of the insight it would provide into the importance of the waves of persecution in the overall history of the problem, it is astonishing to find that no attempt has ever been made to reconstruct such a wave systematically, perhaps because it would be such a laborious task. Putting it a little more precisely we could say that the lack of such a reconstruction has prevented an accurate qualitative and quantitative evaluation of persecution in the region. As Schormann rightly pointed out, the virulence of a persecution cannot be measured by referring to the paradigm, it has to be demonstrated by detailed chronological and geographical reconstruction,[20] particularly when several political units in a region were involved. Even in making typological generalisations, caution is required; for example, we find that the smaller Free Cities reacted quite differently to the wave of persecution in 1590. In spite of the lack of monographs of all kinds on the places affected, which makes it very difficult to establish correlations, we can at least recognise that we cannot draw a direct connection between crisis and persecution. Obviously, we are dealing with several 'waves', depending on the level at which we examine them. Looking at Europe as a whole, one could identify a wave of persecution by which large parts of Western Europe were more or less strongly affected. Taking the

---

[18] Schormann *Hexenprozesse* (1981), 52–62; Riezler, *Geschichte*, 155.
[19] Cf. chapter 1, pp. 1–16.
[20] Schormann, *Hexenprozesse*, 4 and the discussion on 47f.

Empire, one would detect a wave-like expansion from the southwest to the north and east, down the Rhine and the Danube and along the Alps, which penetrated into large parts of the Empire by 1590.[21] The unusual expansion of persecution was noticed in southeast Germany. A chronicler of Freising wrote in 1589 that

> around Trier, in Swabia and Denmark many sorcerers and witches have been seized and burned. The same thing happened soon afterwards in Bavaria, Saxony, Moravia and other places.[22]

Nevertheless the region offers us another perspective. In the three surrounding regions of Austria, Bohemia and northern Franconia, only individual witch trials took place, in southwestern Germany they were already in decline. The region, seen from within, occupied a rather insular position among its persecution neighbours, and within it there were several centres of power, from which smaller waves spread in all directions, apparently in a confused and unconnected way. Only the systematic analysis of numerous individual sources to establish their chronological and geographical connection, has made a reconstruction of these events possible.

THE INCREASE IN ACCUSATIONS OF WITCHCRAFT, 1586–9

It seems to be a characteristic of the beginning of the wave of persecution that accusations of witchcraft had been growing more numerous in the preceding years. Since the beginning of the agrarian crisis in 1586–7 the number of accusations in places as far apart as Griesbach in Lower Bavaria, Schongau in Upper Bavaria, Oberdorf, Augsburg and Nördlingen in Swabia, had been on the increase.[23] The serial source offered by the minutes of the Court Council of the Bishopric of Augsburg shows that the total number of courts in the Bishopric which received serious accusations of witchcraft was growing.[24] Finally, in some places these accusations were transformed into persecutions.

THE BEGINNING IN THE BISHOPRIC OF AUGSBURG

> The very reverend prince and lord
> Marquard von Berg, I honour him greatly,
> an illustrious Bishop is he
> in Augsburg, may God long preserve him,
> he began these affairs.

---

[21] Behringer, 'Hexenverfolgung', 346ff.   [22] Mayr, *Epitome*, 176.
[23] Cf. list of trials in the German edition, 448ff.   [24] *Ibid.*

Countless witches has he sent to the stake,
because of the evil they have committed in broad daylight . . .
(Swabian chaplain, 1590)[25]

The wave of persecution of the year 1590 began under Prince-Bishop Marquard vom Berg (1575–91). The Bishopric of Augsburg was the second largest Catholic territory in southeast Germany after the Duchy of Bavaria. Even before the close of the Council of Trent Bishop Otto Truchsess von Waldburg (1543–73), in collaboration with Petrus Canisius, had begun to enforce the Counter-Reformation in the Bishopric. The foundation of the University of Dillingen, which was placed under Jesuit control in 1563, made the Bishopric a 'citadel of German Catholicism', with an enormous influence in the region.[26] This influence was felt in the persecution of witches as well; the persecutions in the Bishopric between 1587 and 1617 were taken as models by the persecution party in the Duchy, at the court in Munich and at the University of Ingolstadt, until they were overshadowed by the mass trials in the four Franconian bishoprics.[27] We may assume that the trials in Dillingen also had a lasting influence on the smaller territories, and not only the Catholic ones. As late as the 1620s, the Dillingen trials of 1587 were being cited as precedents in disputed cases.[28]

Dillingen was quick to offer a platform for prominent supporters of

[25] ÖNB Vienna, Cod. 8963, fol. 751/3v (Fugger Zeitungen).
[26] Spindler, *Handbuch*, III/2, 928f. (A. Layer).
[27] The opinion of principle of the University of Ingolstadt of April 1590 refers explicitly to the exemplary character of the witch trials in the Bishopric of Augsburg. HStAM, Hexenakten 1, Prod. 1, fol. 1v. Even in 1615 the witch hunts at Dillingen, this time those of 1612–13, were still regarded as models in Munich, HStAM, Hexenakten 1, Prod. 3, 'Capita Deliberationis', fol. 1v. The Chancellor of the Bavarian Court Council conferred, at the command of the ex-Duke Wilhelm V, with the leader of the persecution party in Dillingen, Dr Paulus zum Ackher, about emulating the example of Dillingen in the Duchy of Bavaria. The Dillingen witch hunt of 1587–8 was noted in the whole region. Dillingen depositions and recognisances were found in the following archives: ÖNB Vienna, Cod. 8960, fol. 360–7 (Fugger); HStAM, Hexenakten 16, fol. 3, 14ff., 20 (Pfalz-Neuburg); StadtA Lauingen, Acta Scharfrichter, 1470–90 (Pfalz-Neuburg); StadtA Weissenburg No. 5471 (Free City of Weissenburg); Waldburg-WolfeggA, Akt 160 (Waldburg-Zeil); StadtA Munich, Stadtgericht 866/1, fol. 210 (Duchy of Bavaria). Through its publication in von Klarwill (ed.), *Fugger Zeitungen. Ungedruckte Briefe aus das Haus Fugger aus den Jahren 1568–1605*, Vienna 1923, 103–10, the verdict on the midwife Walburga Hausmännin of Dillingen found its way into international literature: e.g. Monter, *European Witchcraft*, 75–81; E.W. Zeeden, *Deutsche Kultur in der frühen Neuzeit*, Frankfurt 1968, 260–4; Becker *et al., Aus der Zeit*, 380–5. For the contemporary conflict about the publication of the verdict cf. Behringer, 'Hexenverfolgung', 348.
[28] HStAM, Hochstift Augsburg, NA, Akten no. 1222 (1624), fol. 427–9v. The trial of Margarethe Kellnerin had an importance in the region which was compared to that of the Burgomaster of Trier, Dr Flade. She was a patrician and the wife of the Secretary of the Court Council Barthelme Kellner, who had died in 1584. Her close relatives included canons of Augsburg cathedral, one of them a syndic of the chapter. On the case of Dr Flade, see E. Zenz, 'Dietrich Flade, ein Opfer des Hexenwahns', *Kurtrierisches Jahrbuch*, 2 (1962), 41–69.

persecution, who included Petrus Canisius and Gregor von Valentia. Valentia taught at the University of Dillingen during the brief episcopate of Johann Egolf von Knöringen (1573–5), before being called to Ingolstadt. It was in these years that a sensational witch trial was held at Dillingen, one of the first in the region that can be proved to have ended in an execution.[29] The old legend that the Bishop believed his fatal illness to have been caused by bewitchment,[30] receives some support from the discovery of this trial. Yet the Dillingen witch trial of 1574–5 did not grow into a persecution, nor did the charges that were to be brought in the next decade.

The beginning of the witch trial in the episcopal court of Rettenberg-Sonthofen in July 1586 was not different from many similar events. A horse herdsman who had been active as a soothsayer and 'witchfinder', and who believed he had clairvoyant powers, was arrested because a woman in Oberstdorf had accused him. The district judge of the episcopal court of Rettenberg himself believed Conrad Stöckhlin, the herdsman, to be a warlock, after hearing his statement.[31] The government of the Bishopric took the case very seriously and had the Bishop's provincial administrator in Augsburg make enquiries of the city executioner, Däubler, who had taken part in the trials in 1574–5, about a suitable 'master'. Such a man was found in the executioner of the Free City of Biberach, who had recently carried out the great persecutions in the territory of the Imperial Abbey of Obermarchthal. Later a headsman was fetched from the County of Tettnang, while the Bishop's own 'masters' of Schwabmünchen and Oberdorf were apparently only allowed to assist.[32]

---

[29] HStAM, Hochstift Augsburg, NA, Akten nos. 1187 and 1188, with numerous entries. Gregor von Valentia (1551–1603) was the most important and influential (*doctor doctorum*) Catholic theologian in the region. From 1575 to 1592 he taught at the University of Ingolstadt, and according to Duhr, *Die Stellung*, I, 746, played a decisive part in the framing of the opinion on witchcraft. According to a Jesuit source he was its author. *Ibid.* Probably this is because of his keen participation in the early witch trials at Dillingen during his time there. Later he sided with Binsfeld; Gregor von Valentia, SJ, *Commentariorum Theologicorum Tomi IV*, Ingolstadt 1591–7, Tomus III, col. 2002–10; see Duhr, *Die Stellung*, 36–9. On Gregor von Valentia see also Wilhelm Hentrich SJ, *Gregor von Valentia und der Molinismus. Ein Beitrag zur Geschichte des Prämolinismus*, Innsbruck 1928 (apologetic tendency in the question of witchcraft, but interesting to the extent that the question of free will was not without importance for the appreciation of the pact with the Devil).

[30] On the bewitchment of the Bishop, Zoepfl, 'Hexenwahn', 240. Bishop Johann Egolf von Knöringen (1537–75) died in the same year.

[31] HStAM, Hochstift Augsburg, NA, Akten no. 6737 (trial record). *Ibid.*, Akten no. 1199, fol. 413ff.; no. 1200 (numerous entries from the beginning of the trial). Literature on this witch hunt: K. Hofmann, *Oberstdorfer Hexen auf dem Scheiterhaufen*, Oberstdorf 1931; R. Hipper, *Sonthofen im Wandel der Geschichte*, Kempten 1978; H.B. Zirkel, *Geschichte des Marktes Oberstdorf*, Parts 1–4, Oberstdorf 1974f., vol. II, 87–96; and an anonymous essay in *Deutsche Gäue*, 39 (1938), 135–6.

[32] HStAM, Hochstift Augsburg, NA, Akten no. 6737. On the notorious executioner of Biberach, whose sphere of activity during the witch hunt of 1590 reached from the

The government of the Bishopric under the Chancellor Dr Seld (1584–91) was evidently contemplating a systematic persecution, as its instructions make clear. The trial was kept under tight control from Dillingen from the beginning, and the *interrogatoria* betray a familiarity with the *Malleus* and with current literature on witchcraft. The question asked about witches' meetings, and the use of the phrase 'diet of witches' reveal the influence of Fischart's translation of Bodin's *Daemonomania*, the most bitterly anti-witch in tone of all the literature available at the time.[33] The tortures were carried out with unbelievable brutality by the two southwest German executioners, with the blessing of the episcopal government. The alleged warlock confessed that he had regularly attended meetings of witches on the Heuberg (in the Swabian Alb), which had often figured as a resort of witches in trials in the southwest, but had otherwise played no part in the beliefs about witches held east of the river Iller.[34] After Stöckhlin had been convicted, his denunciations of others were also believed, and the persecution began to spread. It can only be partially reconstructed from the records of trials, the minutes of the Court Council, and the accounts, but it is clear that at least twenty-three persons were executed. This persecution of 1586–7 was the first time that the elaborated concept of witchcraft was radically applied in the region.

The persecution at Dillingen in 1587–91 was even more important. It was provoked by the outbreak of 'unnatural' diseases. The proceedings at Oberstdorf had taken place in a remote valley, but this time the witches were burned in the episcopal residence, and their fate aroused wide attention. Copies of depositions of the women burned at the stake in Dillingen in 1587 can still be found in the archives of the city of Munich, the Free City of Weissenburg, the Counts of Waldburg-Wolfegg and in the Fugger

Vorarlberg through southwestern Germany and Bavaria into Middle Franconia, cf. K. Seifritz, 'Ein Hexenprozess und der Scharfrichter Meister Christoph Hiert von Biberach', *Anzeiger vom Oberland*, no. 160 (6 July 1933); R. Dengler, 'Das Hexenwesen im Stifte Obermarchthal von 1581–1755', PhD thesis, Erlangen 1953, 139, who refers to a Master Hans of Biberach, who was active in Obermarchthal from 1586–90 and executed fifty-nine witches. Kuisl, *Die Hexen*, 18, names, besides Master Christoph, a young executioner's mate Jacob as the third 'Master of Biberach'. Master Christoph Hiert took part in the witch hunt at Werdenfels (Riezler, *Geschichte*, 177) and in the Vorarlberg (Byloff, *Hexenglaube*, 60) from 1597; Master Hans Volmair/Vollmann of Biberach took part in the witch hunt at Schwabmünchen (HStAM, Hochstift Augsburg, NA, Akten no. 2816) and Ellingen (Film 693, 38, 82). The headsman of Biberach was also active in the witch hunts in the Free City of Esslingen and Freising.

[33] HStAM, Hochstift Augsburg, NA, Akten no. 6737, fol. 11f.

[34] This was the work of the headsmen of Biberach. The witches of Bludenz in the Vorarlberg, according to their evidence under interrogation, also flew to the Heuberg, Byloff, *Hexenglaube*, 60. The Heuberg had been the witches' central dancing place since the early fifteenth century. Hansen, *Quellen und Untersuchungen*, 260, 437, 609. There was no comparable central dancing place in the imaginations of the people of southeastern Germany. (The famous Blocksberg never played a role throughout south Germany and Austria. It was a north German obsession.)

Zeitungen.[35] The case of the Dillingen patrician Margarethe Kellerin was still being used as an immediate precedent in Munich three years later, and was cited thirty years later as a precedent for the execution of a member of the upper classes, together with the case of Dr Flade of Trier.[36] The confessions of another witch make it clear that several members of the government of the Bishopric felt that they had suffered from the witches, who were said to have caused the deaths of the wife and four children of the former Chancellor Dr Peuter and a child of the Bishop's Governor Count von Stauffenberg, whose wife had survived thanks to a counter-spell.[37]

The persecutions in Dillingen had a direct influence on the Principality of Pfalz-Neuburg; as Dillingen lay near the border, the witches accused Pfalz-Neuburg subjects in Wittislingen and Höchstädt, perhaps also in Lauingen. These accusations began the witch trials in the Principality.[38]

A third great persecution began in 1589 in the so-called *Strassvogtei* (in the judicial district of Schwabmünchen) south of Augsburg. It was provoked by the fantasies of a child. Although the child was described in the report of the judge as 'both simple minded and of an evil countenance', the Court Council in Dillingen ordered a systematic inquisition and removed the trial from the district court at Bobingen to Schwabmünchen, where there was an executioner. Court officers and executioners from the neighbouring district court of Oberdorf were also to be called in, as they had been during the persecution at Rettenberg-Sonthofen. In May 1589, after accusations of maleficient magic had also been made against the women accused by the child, the authorities ordered that a persecution should be launched. The experience of the last two years provided the 'infrastructure' that was required. The procedurel and spiritual care were dictated by Dillingen, a standard set of questions was drawn up, the prison made ready and additional executioners brought in.[39]

Once again the decisive role was played by the now notorious Master Hans of Biberach, but whole companies of executioners now gathered at Schwabmünchen, which was well situated as a rendezvous. Master Hans Vollmair brought his wife and daughter, and also his stepson Master Christoph of Biberach. From Bavaria came the executioner of Landsberg

[35] Cf. note 27. The sources for the trials at Dillingen include, besides ÖNB Vienna, Cod. 8960–8963 (numerous entries), the minutes of the Court Council of Dillingen, HStAM, Hochstift Augsburg, NA, Akten no. 1200–4 (numerous entries). Zoepfl, 'Hexenwahn', 241f.   [36] Cf. notes 27 and 28.   [37] ÖNB Vienna, Cod. 8960, fol. 360–7.
[38] HStAM, Hexenakten 16.
[39] HStAM, Hochstift Augsburg, NA, Akten no. 1202, fol. 216ff (numerous entries), no. 1203, fol. 65, 219, 286, 289, 365, 510; also 454 and 527; no. 1204 fol. 214, 234, 280, 339, 353, 400; *ibid.*, no. 2816; ÖNB Vienna, Cod. 8962, fol. 507–8v, 540–5v, 578–9v, 654–5v; Cod. 8963, fol. 255–6v, 284, 305–v, 588–9, 593, 851–4. *Ibid.*, 788–9v, a mandate of Count Octavian Fugger, which forbids all worldly pleasures in connection with the plague of 1592, and alludes to the danger of witches.

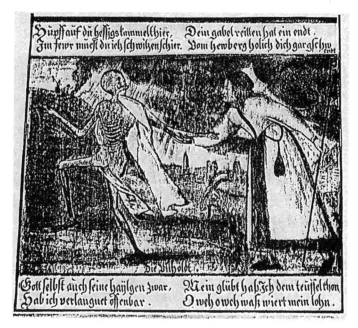

6. The witch in the dance of death at Füssen, Füssen, 1602. Panel painting showing pact with the Devil, 'weather cooking' on the mountain. Text: 'Jump, you hateful beast, now you must sweat in the fire. Your riding on forks is at an end, I will soon be coming to fetch you away from the Heuberg.' 'God himself and his saints I have openly denied, I have put my faith in the Devil, alas, alas, what will be my reward?'

and Master Jörg Abriel of Schongau, and from the Free City of Kaufbeuren Master Barthlemess Aberhöll, probably a relation of the Schongau executioner. From the Bishopric of Augsburg Master Veit of Schwabmünchen was joined by the executioners of Oberdorf, Grossaitingen and Oberstdorf, while the Master from the Imperial Abbey of Ochsenhausen travelled from the west. The importance of these executioners for the wave of persecution in 1590 cannot be overestimated. The 'sphere of influence' of Hans and Christoph of Biberach was to extend, a little later, as far south as Garmisch and as far north as Langenzenn (northwest of Nuremberg). Jörg Abriel travelled all over Bavaria and served the Princt-Bishop of Freising. Only the executioners of Eichstätt, Oettingen-Wallerstein and Lauingen approached Vollmair and Abriel in importance.[40] The remarkable feature of the persecution at Schwabmünchen is that the local authori-

[40] Cf. note 32. On Abriel see Riezler, *Geschichte*, 172f. On the Master of Eichstätt, Kunstmann, *Zauberwahn*, 74–7, and the 'Bedenken, Die Unhulden betreffend' (cf. note 12); on the headsman of Lauingen cf. G. Rückert, 'Der Hexenwahn, ein Kulturbild aus Lauingens Vergangenheit', *Alt-Lauingen, Organ des Altertums-Vereins*, 2 (1907), 25–77 (a series). On the executioner of Schwabmünchen and the rendezvous of executioners, see HStAM, Hochstift Augsburg, NA, Akten no. 2816 (executioners' records, Schwabmünchen).

ties showed no interest in the proceedings. Even before the first execution the *Landamman* had asked the government for a transfer while the judge complained bitterly that he, a nobleman, was often forced to spend hours in stinking prison cells because of the trials.[41] The impetus continued to come from the government at Dillingen. Of course, the companies of executioners also had an interest, for besides their fixed wages they also received free board and lodging. A executioner and his retinue (wife, assistant, messengers, horse) earned 291 gulden in two months, or about as much as it cost to keep a person sentenced to 'perpetual imprisonment' for three years. Moreover, the executioners enjoyed a lavish meal at each execution – at one such meal, seven persons drank more than a hundred pints of wine.[42] It is obvious that the executioners would have little interest in bringing a persecution to an end, at least until the next had already begun. Yet it was not they but their employers who determined the extent of a persecution. Bishop Marquard and his government had already

> appointed or contracted with [the Master of Biberach] for a whole year . . . for his Princely Grace is resolved to proceed with the utmost earnestness against this accursed sin in his territory . . .[43]

From its origin at Bobingen the persecution spread to the neighbouring episcopal courts of Wehringen, Göggingen and Schwabmünchen, to Kleinaitingen (in the lands of the chapter of Augsburg cathedral) and to the Free City of Augsburg. Women were even brought from Augsburg to Schwabmünchen to be confronted with their accusers.[44]

The fourth great persecution in the Bishopric of Augsburg began in 1590, after several women from the district of the episcopal court at Helmishofen were accused of witchcraft in the Lordship of Osterzell. The government transferred the trial to Oberdorf, the headquarters of the executioner. Before the accused women were arrested, the ceilings of the prison were repaired and five blockhouses were erected in Oberdorf and Helmishofen as additional prisons. Another witch trial began at the same time at Nesselwang, for local reasons, but it too was transferred to Oberdorf.[45]

After the fourth great persecution had begun, further trials sprang up

---

[41] HStAM, Hochstift Augsburg, NA, Akten no. 1202, fol. 458, fol. 495–6; *ibid.*, fol. 581v.
[42] Cf. notes 32 and 40.   [43] ÖNB Vienna, Cod. 8963, fol. 255f.
[44] *Ibid.*, fol. 513, 613r–v; StadtA Augsburg, Reichsstadt no. 45 (minutes of the Council, 1587–90), fol. 340–7 *passim; ibid.*, Strafbuch 1588–96, fol. 75; *ibid.*, Urgichtenakten 1590 c, VII, 2, 23; *ibid.*, Strafbücher 1587–90, fol. 78v., Urgichtenakten 1590 c, VII, 4; *ibid.*, Strafbücher 1587–90, fol. 79; Urgichtenakten 1590, c, VII, 4; Reichsstadt no. 46, fol. 2–5 *passim*; HStAM, Hochstift Augsburg, NA, Akten no. 1203, fol. 433.
[45] HStAM, Hochstift Augsburg, NA, Akten no. 1203, fol. 366, 385, fol. 467; fol. 431, 451, 467, 571.

throughout practically the whole territory of the Prince-Bishop. Trials were begun in the courts of Rettenberg, the district of Füssen, at Dinkel-scherben (chapter lands), in Zusmarshausen, in Grossaitingen (chapter lands) and again in the capital, Dillingen. Local reasons were always at the bottom of the trials, which in the atmosphere of persecution of 1590 soon led to torture and executions.[46]

The great persecutions were planned more and more thoroughly and their conduct became a matter of routine. If accusations of witchcraft were made anywhere, the machinery of persecution was set in motion: enquiries were made into the life of the accused, reports of 'unnatural' harm were collected and checked for their possible connection with the accused. If such a connection was found, the prison was put into repair or a new prison was built, contracts were signed with suitable executioners and reliable court officers and priests were chosen to carry out the persecution. Superficially, this 'routine' might seem to explain the increase in the number of executions (Rettenberg twenty-three, Schwabmünchen twenty-seven, Oberdorf sixty-eight). From 1590, however, witch trials that led to individual witches being burned, again became more common. All trials were officially suspended in 1592 because of the plague. After the end of the plague, none of the persecutions was resumed.[47]

PRINCIPALITY OF PFALZ-NEUBURG

The highborn Prince and Lord Philip Ludwig also follows a very similar line [on witches] and causes many to be executed. . .[48]

(Swabian chaplain, 1590).

Under Duke Philipp Ludwig (1569–1614) the Principality, in which the Reformation had been enforced in 1542, was under a strict Lutheran regime, comparable to that of its western neighbour, the Duchy of Würt-

[46] *Ibid.* (a total of entries on sixty-two days in the year 1590).
[47] *Ibid.*, no. 1206. In Nesselwang a woman was still under arrest, and died in the year 1593. *Ibid.*, 168–168v, 316r–v, 375–6. Otherwise it usually concerned the settlement of costs and estate questions. The Prince-Bishop always confiscated the share of executed persons, but never that of the husbands or children. The deficit which was almost always incurred was borne by the state treasury. The witch trials in the Bishopric of Augsburg were led by Bishop Marquardt vom Berg (1528–91, Bishop 1575–91), and then by Bishop Johann Otto von Gemmingen (1561–98), the Chancellor Dr Thomas Seld (1584–91), the Chancellor Dr Albrecht Faber (1591–1604), the Councillors Dr J. Saur, Dr T. Vogel, Dr C. Schilling, Dr J. Ram, Wilhelm Schenck von Stauffenberg, E. von Westernach, H.J. von Rietheim, G.W. von Stadion and W.H. von Werdenstein. The names have been taken from the minutes of the Court Council at Dillingen 1587–92 (HStAM, Hochstift Augsburg, NA, Akten no. 1200–5). Biographical details from Zoepfl, *Das Bistum Augsburg und seine Bischöfe im Reformationsjahrhundert*, Munich/Augsburg 1969; and Bosl, *Biographie*. Cf. R. Böhm, *Der Füssener Totentanz*, Füssen 1978.
[48] ÖNB Vienna, Cod. 8963, fol. 751–4v.

temberg. Unlike Württemberg, however, no executions are yet known to have taken place in Pfalz-Neuburg before 1587.[49]

The persecution at Dillingen in 1587 was watched with interest in Pfalz-Neuburg from the beginning, quite understandably in view of the fact that Dillingen formed a bridgehead in the territory of the Principality. The execution of a witch at Dillingen in 1575 had already led to a dispute between the two princes of the Empire, since Philipp Ludwig maintained that the witch had been burned on his territory.[50] In 1590 the Palatine Governorship at Höchstädt was once again involved from the start, since women from Dillingen fled to Pfalz-Neuburg and 'witches' from Dillingen had accused alleged accomplices from several villages within the jurisdiction of the Princes of Neuburg. Philipp Ludwig showed himself willing to cooperate with the Bishopric, without any recognisable confessional misgivings, though his Court Councillors stressed that the Governor of Höchstädt, Hieronymus von Diemantstein, was to be extremely thorough in investigating alleged cases of sorcery.[51] Diemantstein was the right man in the right place: he was completely uncritical in his attitude to the persecutions at Dillingen, and soon after the witch trial at Höchstädt had begun in 1587, he felt that he himself had been bewitched. He urged the government at Neuburg to launch a persecution on the model of that in the Bishopric of Augsburg.[52]

Although the authorities in Neuburg agreed in principle that witches were to be hunted down, they went about it in a different way. At first they instructed Dr Christoph Mumprecht, a councillor of Höchstädt, to draw up a legal opinion on the nature of witchcraft and how it was to be dealt with,[53] and then they brought in reliable theologians from the Principality to Höchstädt to care for the spiritual needs of the three arrested women. The theologians included the Superintendent of Lauingen and Dr Philipp Heilbrunner, the brother of the more famous Lutheran court theologian in Neuburg. They not only tried to convert the old women to Protestantism, but also admonished them 'not to wrong anyone by false accusations'.[54] This helped to prevent the trial spreading to become a persecution. In the end only seven of twenty suspected women were arrested, and most of

---

[49] Film 1354; Film 1530; Film 1574; Film 1839; Film 2234; Film 2711; Film 3716; the only known execution of a male sorcerer is that at Höchstädt on the Danube in 1570. Film 1218.   [50] HStAM, Hochstift Augsburg, NA, Akten no. 1188, fol. 12v.
[51] HStAM, Hexenakten 16, fol. 34f.   [52] *Ibid.*, fol. 124f.   [53] *Ibid.*, fol. 139–43.
[54] *Ibid.*, fol. 100–5; the court theologian was, according to Henker, 'Zur Prosopographie', 172f., Dr Jacob Heilbrunner (1548–1618), a not unimportant Lutheran controversialist theologian. His elder brother Dr Philipp Heilbrunner (1546–1616) had been professor of theology at the Gymnasium Illustre in Lauingen since 1573. Both men had studied at Tübingen in the 1570s and took their doctorates together in 1577. *Ibid.*, 173f. The Superintendent of Lauingen in 1587 was one M. Abraham Manns. The Dean of Höchstadt Marcus Wegmann was also concerned for the spiritual welfare of the witches, HStAM, Hexenakten 16, fol. 144–5v, 151.

them had been handed over to the Palatine Governor by the officers of the Prince-Bishop of Augsburg. Ultimately five women were burned at the stake in Höchstädt.[55] The executioner of Lauingen was assisted by the headsmen of Donauwörth, Wertingen (Pappenheim) and Holzheim.[56]

Witch trials spread to many parts of the fragmented Principality of Pfalz-Neuburg in 1589–90. We know of further executions at Lauingen and Tapfheim, but the result of a persecution in Reichertshofen, in which the executioner of Lauingen was again involved, is not known. Other trials in Lauingen and Kallmünz ended in acquittals.[57]

Some of the clergy, the high officials and the citizenry of Höchstädt took a recognisably critical view of the witch trials. As in the Bishopric of Augsburg, general enquiries were made in the home villages of the alleged witches about cases of harmful sorcery; the litany of complaints was always the same: thunderstorms and crop damage, sickness of people and animals, especially among children, were blamed on 'unnatural' causes, that is on witchcraft. The accused women had often been under suspicion for years, or else their parents had had a reputation for witchcraft. A precise analysis of thirty-eight alleged cases of harm caused by sorcery, however, shows that in seven cases the suspects were cleared and in twenty-nine there was no possibility of proof. In two cases the accusation had been corroborated by soothsayers.[58]

COUNTIES, NOBLE LORDSHIPS, MINOR ECCLESIASTICAL
TERRITORIES

Count Wilhelm of Oettingen, Prince of Wallerstein . . . as is only right, leaves them no peace. . . until they are all bound to the stake . . .
Marx Fugger the well-born also has evil deeds rooted out, punished and avenged far and wide in his Lordships . . .
The venerable Lord of the Holy Cross does not act differently either . . .
(Swabian chaplain, 1590)

Politically the southeast of Germany, apart from the regional great power

[55] All decisions were taken by the government in Neuburg. Those taking part were the Count Palatine Philipp Ludwig (1569–1614), the Chancellor Dr Drechsel, his successor Dr G.L. Frolich (1562–1612), and the Councillors Dr Zorer, Dr Maroldt, Dr Heininger (Heynung) and von Wildenstein. *Ibid.* In the witch trials in the Palatinate there is no question of the enrichment of the state treasury either. In the first place all those condemned were poor ('allein arme, schlechte Leuth, so keine ehehalten nicht haben', HStAM, Hexenakten 16, fol. 124), and secondly, the claims of the husband and children to the property were always given priority.   [56] Rückert, 'Der Hexenwahn', 26.
[57] *Ibid.*, 26f. B. Mayer, *Geschichte der Stadt Lauingen*, Dillingen 1886, 93.
[58] HStAM, Hexenakten 16, fol. 133–7v. The relatively distant attitude of some Councillors and clerics may have been connected with their education at the Universities of Tübingen and Heidelberg. For these universities cf. Midelfort, *Witch Hunting*, 34, 39–42, 58, 88, 92, 94; 58, 65, 241.

Bavaria, was characterised by its territorial fragmentation. Swabia and Franconia above all were exceptionally heterogeneous in their political, confessional and economic structure. Besides the Catholic Bishoprics, the Lutheran Principalities of Pfalz-Neuburg and Ansbach-Bayreuth and the Free Cities, there were countless small and very small secular and ecclesiastical Lordships, many of which had the right to their own criminal courts.

Although the sources for these minor states are poor by comparison with the larger territories or the Free Cities, the fragmentary sources available and information from their neighbours show that their role in the wave of persecutions of 1590 was disproportionately great given their unimportance in other fields. In many cases persecutions in the small states provoked trials in adjoining larger territories or Free Cities. The first persecution in the region took place in 1563 in a small noble lordship, and the greatest individual persecution during the wave of persecution of 1590 began in a very small state.[59]

Taking all the small states of Swabia and Franconia together, the wave of persecution followed the same course as in the larger territories: individual persecutions began in 1586–7, the bulk of the trials were held between autumn 1589 and the plague of 1592, with the crest of the wave in the summer of 1590. In middle Franconia the persecution continued after 1592.

The most zealous persecutors were the Counts of Oettingen, though it is not clear whether the Protestant line of Oettingen-Oettingen also took part, or only the Catholic Counts of Oettingen-Wallerstein. The trials were held at Wallerstein, but two women were put to death in 1592 in the northern, Protestant part of the County. The persecutions in the County had begun in 1587 and lasted until 1594. The literature does not give usable figures for the number of victims.[60] A source from Bamberg says that the 'old Master of Oettingen' had executed thirty-two witches,[61] but it is not clear if this includes all the executions in the County. On 4 June 1589 alone ten witches were burned at a sensational mass execution which drew thirty thousand spectators from all quarters.[62] The proceedings at Wallerstein

---

[59] Film 693 (Commandery of the Teutonic Order, Ellingen, Middle Franconia). The opening reference is again ÖNB Vienna, Cod. 8963, fol. 751/5–6v. The source for the first witch hunt in the region under study (Illereichen, 1563), is HStAM, RKG 10688.

[60] Kunstmann, *Zauberwahn*, 20; Riezler, *Geschichte*, 146. According to information from the archives of the house of Oettingen in Spielberg and Wallerstein, no records of witchcraft trials have been preserved there. On the other hand the documents in UBM, Cod. Ms. 214 contain fragments of trial records from Wallerstein in a collection of the Jesuit college at Ingolstadt, one of them a trial from 1593. *Ibid.*, fol. 192–208.

[61] Film 2869, 7.

[62] A. Gabler, *Altfränkisches Dorf- und Pfarrhausleben 1559–1601. Ein Kulturbild aus der Zeit vor dem Dreissigjährigen Krieg. Dargestellt nach den Tagebüchern des Pfarrherrn Thomas Wirsing von Sinbronn*, Nuremberg 1952, 23.

were regarded as so harsh that at the height of the persecution in Nördlingen, women from the city begged not to be extradited to Oettingen.[63] On several occasions subjects of the Free Cities were forcibly abducted by officials from Oettingen.[64] The trials were conducted by Dr Paulus zum Ackher, who later led the persecution party in the Bishopric of Augsburg for twenty years as Court Councillor at Dillingen.[65] The Free City of Nördlingen was especially vulnerable, for it formed an enclave surrounded by the territory of the Counts of Oettingen.

Once again, it is only from external sources that we know anything of the persecutions of 1590 in the noble Lordships of Kellmünz (von Rechberg) and Erolzheim,[66] Osterzell (von Kaltenthal) and Randeckh,[67] and the Fugger Lordships of the line of Fugger-Kirchberg-Weissenhorn and Fugger-Oberndorf-Nordendorf[68] in Swabia. Women were also executed as witches in the Habsburg Margravate of Burgau.[69]

From Franconia we have evidence of persecutions in the Lordship of Pappenheim,[70] the County of Limpurg,[71] the County of Löwenstein-Wertheim,[72] the Lordship of Geyern[73] and the County of Seinsheim,[74] but the number of executions in each case cannot be accurately determined.

Among the minor ecclesiastical territories executions of witches are known to have taken place in the lands of the chapter of Augsburg cathedral[75] and in the village of Donaumünster, where criminal justice was

---

[63] Film 3718, 101.

[64] Women from Nördlingen were repeatedly accused from the surrounding territory of Oettingen-Wallerstein. Film 1992, 23; Film 2869, 22, 24. Between 1591 and 1596 the city of Nördlingen brought three actions before the Imperial Chamber Court against Oettingen-Wallerstein, for unauthorised abduction of persons to Wallerstein, unauthorised intervention in witch trials at Nördlingen and excesses of confiscation. Film 3667. The trial records are now in HStA Stuttgart. (The old RKG shelfmarks were N/1522, N/1523 and N/2514.)

[65] UBM, Cod. Ms. 214, fol. 192. In 1593 Dr Paulus zum Ackher conducted the trials as commissioner for the Count. According to Zoepfl, *Das Bistum*, 717, 'Dr Paul Zumacker' was appointed a Court Councillor at Dillingen in 1598, at the time of the accession of Bishop Heinrich V von Knöringen (1598–1646). During his time at Dillingen (1598–1628) Dr P. zum Ackher led the witch hunting party there in all the internal controversies and in 1615 he conferred with the Chancellor of the Bavarian Court Council Wagnereckh on the carrying out of a systematic witch hunt.   [66] Unold, *Geschichte*, 197.

[67] StadtA Kaufbeuren, Hörmann-Registratur, vol. 2, fol. 206,; *ibid.*, B 112, fol. 50f. HStAM, Hochstift Augsburg, NA, Akten no. 1203, fol. 431v–2, 451, 467, 474; fol. 366. On the Lordship of Randeckh HStAM, SV 2243, s.f.; Film 3709, 54–60; the holder of the Lordship before 1596, according to Bosl, *Bayern*, 601f., was Count Alexius Fugger.

[68] ÖNB Vienna, Cod. 8963, fol. 751–5v. The holder was Markus Fugger (1529–97), a leading promoter of the Counter-Reformation.   [69] Schuhmann, *Der Scharfrichter*, 81, 246.

[70] Wulz, 'Nördlinger Hexenprozesse' (1937–8), 115.   [71] Film 1156.

[72] Midelfort, *Witch Hunting*, 207f.   [73] Film 1914 (Nennslingen, Middle Franconia).

[74] Film 1751 (Marktbreit, Upper Franconia).

[75] HStAM, Hochstift Augsburg, NA, Akten no. 1203, fol. 541v; *ibid.*, no. 1204, fol. 412 (Dinkelscherben, Grossaitingen).

in the hands of the Abbot of the Abbey of the Holy Cross in Donauwörth.[76] The greatest persecution of 1590 was held in the Commandery of the Teutonic Order in Ellingen, where at least seventy-two and possibly even more witches were burned at the stake.[77] It was said of the Commandery of Ellingen:

> I must mention the strict and very dear hero
> Walbrecht von Schwalbach,
> who boldly attacks the witches,
> he has already had many burned,
> he spares neither poor nor rich,
> he keeps true justice,
> and scarcely has his equal.[78]

Their limited geographical expansion means that the example of the miniature states illustrates more clearly the effectiveness of denunciations in trials for witchcraft; the trials in the Protestant Lordship of Osterzell, for example, triggered the persecutions in the episcopal district court of Oberdorf and the Free City of Kaufbeuren.[79] The persecutions at Nennslingen (Lordship of Geyern) and Ellingen provoked the trials in the Free City of Weissenburg.[80]

The persecutions in the smaller territories were led by the same executioners as in the larger states. The persecution at Ellingen was carried out by Master Hans Vollmair of Biberach.[81]

THE DUCHY OF BAVARIA

True persecutions in the Duchy of Bavaria did not begin until 1589. Accusations of witchcraft were voiced in many of the district courts, and there were repeated arrests of suspected women and ultimately numerous executions, especially in 1590–1. Unfortunately the best source, the protocols of the Court Council in Munich, does not survive for this year, so that

[76] *Ibid.*, no. 1202, fol. 661, 674, 681. The witches in the Catholic town of Donaumünster had been denounced from the Lutheran town of Tapfheim. Some of the accused women fled to Kaisheim, but were rearrested. The Lutheran Count Palatine had as little objection to the death sentence passed by the Abbot as did the Prince-Bishop; both of them were evidently consulted. On the politico-legal situation cf. Spindler, *Handbuch*, III/2, 959 (Layer).
[77] Film 693. Fragments of trial records in P.P. Beck, 'Zwei Hexenprozesse aus dem Fränkischen', *Jahresberichte des Hist. Vereins Mittelfranken*, 43 (1889), 7–25. Cf. also *Erweytterte Unholden Zeyttung*, in Behringer, 'Hexenverfolgung', 348.
[78] ÖNB Vienna, Cod. 8963, fol. 751–6.   [79] Cf. note 67.
[80] Film 693; Film 1914; Kunstmann, *Zauberwahn*, 25. The witches of Ellingen danced in the Weissenburg Forest. Beck, 'Zwei Hexenprozesse', 9. StadtA Weissenburg, Akt 1055, 1056, 1057; records of the witch trials at Ellingen are also found in StA Ludwigsburg in Württemberg, Hexenprozesse Mergentheim nos. 3, 11, 13, 62 (from Film 693).
[81] Film 693, 38, 62, 82, 95. The highest-ranking victim of the witch hunt at Ellingen was Barbara Strauss, the wife of the Chancellor Hans Strauss of Ellingen; she was burned on 7 February 1590.

the overall picture remains patchy. Nevertheless, one can recognise where persecution raged most fiercely: along the Danube between Ingolstadt and Kelheim, in the neighbourhood of the Bishopric of Augsburg, in the district of the court of Schongau, and of course in the capital Munich, where a centralising government kept tight control of the most important criminal proceedings, and where the city itself also saw executions of witches in 1590.

The greatest persecution in Bavaria began in 1589 in the judicial district of Schongau. Nominally this was under the rule of Ferdinand, the younger brother of the reigning Duke Wilhelm V, but in practice, as in all other trials for witchcraft, the proceedings were directed from Munich by the Court Council. The models for the persecution at Schongau, as one can see from the sources, were the trials at Dillingen in 1587 and in the Margravate of Baden in 1586; in 1591 depositions made by witches executed at Kaufbeuren were entered in the court files.[82] Witches were also executed in the more easterly districts of Weilheim and Tölz in 1590 and 1591, but these trials remained smaller in scale. Several years after the end of the persecutions, it was proposed that a memorial be erected to the greatest witch trial in Bavaria:

> since 63 of the women who had committed the horrid crime of sorcery were brought to justice in about two years . . . and for such a work of solemn justice . . . it could be ordered that an eternal memorial column be built and erected in a place here in the street, not only in memory of the trial itself, and to celebrate the fame of the authorities, but also to serve as a reminder, warning and sign to passing strangers and the multitude . . . [83]

The persecution at Schongau was directly related to the preceding harvest failures, which had been caused by thunderstorms. Whole villages around Schongau sent deputations to the judge, demanding relief by the burning of the witches, whom they held responsible for the disaster. They may have been stimulated by the example of the trials in the Bishopric of Augsburg, or those in the district court of Rettenberg in 1586–7 and at Schwabmünchen, which had begun a few months before the persecution at Schongau. In particular the catastrophic hailstorm of 26 June 1588, which destroyed the grain harvest in several places, so that even seed corn had to be bought in,[84] was blamed on witches. There had also been a thunderstorm on 20 May 1589, 'a frightful thunderstorm, so bad that it was feared everything

---

[82] StadtA Munich, Hist. Ver. Urk. 1996–8.   [83] *Ibid.*, 2005.
[84] HStAM, Hochstift Augsburg, NA, Akten no. 2629 (dispute between the Bishopric of Augsburg and the Duchy of Bavaria because of an armed attack by the judge of Schongau on the village of Schwabsoyen in the Bishopric, to arrest witches); *ibid.*, no. 1201, fol. 106–7v (hailstorm); StadtA Munich, Hist. Ver. Urk. 2051.

would be ruined'.[85] The villagers even offered to have the executioner of Biberach brought in at their expense, if that would speed up the persecution.[86] One of the first witches to confess admitted that she had caused the storm which had destroyed the crops.[87] But the villagers were not satisfied with one witch, they wished to tackle the evil at the root and burn them all. The method of finding the other witches was the normal one: to demand the names of the witch's accomplices at the witches' sabbaths, under torture. The tortures were applied by Master Jörg Abriel of Schongau, who, unlike the Master of Biberach, discovered that the witches' sabbaths were held not in Württemberg (on the Heuberg) but almost on the spot (the Peissenberg and the Auerberg, on the heath and on the Lechfeld).

The second Bavarian persecution area, along the Danube between Ingolstadt and Kelheim, also emerged in 1589. In Ingolstadt alone twenty-two women were put to death as witches in 1589–91.[88] This persecution was especially important, for it was at this time that both the later Bavarian Elector Maximilian I (1597–1651) and the later Emperor Ferdinand II (1619–37) were studying at the University of Ingolstadt under the tutorship of the Jesuit Gregor von Valentia. Valentia was one of the most outspoken apologists of persecution; we know from the correspondence of Maximilian that he often attended trials of witches, including those where torture was applied.[89] Although the city of Ingolstadt had its own criminal

---

[85] Schorer, *Chronicle*, 111.

[86] HStAM, Hochstift Augsburg, NA, Akten no. 2629, s.f.; StadtA Munich, Hist. Ver. Urk. 2051.

[87] StadtA Munich, Hist. Ver. Urk. 2043, 2044; statement of Els Kerblin, wife of the judge of Soyen: 'Sie habe ein Schauer gemacht, das alles Getreide um Soyen, Altenstadt und Prugg erschlagen habe.' A relatively large amount of material has been preserved on the witch hunt at Schongau: StadtA Munich, Hist. Ver. Urk. nos. 1996–2098; StA Innsbruck, Sammelakten, Reihe B, Abteilung XVI, Lage 4, no. 4; HStAM, Hexenakten 9a (*passim*); *ibid.*, Hofzahlamtsrechnungen no. 36, fol. 429; *ibid.*, Hochstift Augsburg, NA, Akten no. 2629; *ibid.*, no. 1203, fol. 138v; B. Her, 'Ein Hexenprozess zu Schongau vom Jahr 1587. Nach den Originalacten geschichtlich dargestellt', *Oberbayr. Archiv*, 11 (1850), 128–44. *Idem*, 'Grosser Hexenprozess zu Schongau von 1589 bis 1592. Aus den Originalacten geschichtlich dargestellt', *ibid.* 356–80; *Erweyterte Unholden Zeyttung*, in Behringer, 'Hexenverfolgung', 352; Riezler, *Geschichte*, 165–8. Opinions on the trials at Schongau have been preserved for the Chancellor of the Court Council Dr Gailkircher (1543–1621), the Court Councillor Dr Kaspar Lagus (1533–1606), the Court Councillor and Chancellor of the League of Landsberg Dr Hieronymus Nadler (1535–92), the Court Councillor Dr Johann Gabler (1606) and the Court Councillor Dr Joachim Donnersberger (1561–1650), the later Supreme Chancellor; StadtA Munich, Hist. Ver. Urk. 2049–53. Biographical details from Bosl, *Biographie*.

[88] Sources on the witch hunt at Ingolstadt: HStAM, SV 2243, fol. 127v–34; *ibid.*, GR, 323/16, Prod. 10, 12; *ibid.*, KHR 19, fol. 28v; *ibid.*, Kurb. Äusseres Archiv 4826, fol. 71, 182; *ibid.*, Geh. Hausarchiv, no. 618; StadtA Ingolstadt A IV a; Film 1304; Film 3709, 45ff.; Riezler, *Geschichte*, 169, 192f., 195f.; H. Geyer, 'Hexen und ihre Verurteilung in den Beschlüssen des Ingolstädter Rates zu Ende des 16. und Anfang des 17. Jahrhunderts', unpublished dissertation, Munich 1964; *idem*, 'Die Ingolstädter Hexenprozesse um 1600', *Ingolstädter Heimatblätter*, 28 (1965), nos. 5–8 (series).

justice, the government in Munich exercised its absolutist authority, took over the proceedings and sent ducal commissioners to conduct the trials. The university professors, if they had not already been among those consulted about the trials at Schongau, could convince themselves that the practice of the trials confirmed the theories of the *Malleus*, Bodin and Binsfeld.

East of Ingolstadt, witch trials can be documented in the Bavarian county courts of Vohburg, Neustadt on the Danube, Abensberg, Altmann-stein, Kelheim, Neuessing/Randeckh, Straubing, Eggenfelden and Griesbach, but their extent is unclear. The ruler of the noble Lordship of Randeckh in the lower Altmühl valley complained that several women had been accused in his market town of Essing, 'as in our neighbourhood [witches have been] zealously hunted down at Abensberg, Neustadt, Kelheim and other nearby places'.[90] One of the usual lists of questions put to the accused has survived in the town archives of Kelheim, and has become known in the secondary literature under the erroneous title of the 'Kelheim Hammer of Witches, 1487'.[91] Besides Ingolstadt and Abenberg, Kelheim may well have been particularly hard hit by persecution. According to Riezler there were formerly voluminous trial records still in existence at

[89] Riezler, *Geschichte*, 188, 194ff.; H. Dotterweich *Jugend und Erziehung des bayrischen Herzogs und späteren Kurfürsten Maximilian I. (1573–1593)*, Munich 1962, 123ff. Gregor von Valentia (cf. note 29) was the Prince's confessor from 1587 to 1591 and also his mentor and constant travelling companion. Dotterweich, *Maximilian*, 111ff.

[90] HStAM, SV 2243, s.f. For Abensberg see Riezler, *Geschichte*, 193, 197. For the other places where trials were held, cf. the list of trials in the German edition.

[91] *Der Kelheimer Hexenhammer. Facsimile-Ausgabe der Original-Handschrift aus dem Kelheimer Stadtarchiv*, Grünwald, n.d. The dates given in this volume (1487 or c. 1550) are without foundation, as is the title *Hexenhammer*. A useful comparison of three lists of questions (*interrogatoria*) is found in S. Hofmann, 'Protokoll eines Verhörs eines Hexenprozesses von 1629 aus Reichertshofen', *Sammelblatt des Hist. Ver. Ingolstadt*, 89 (1980), 153–229; *ibid.*, 188–9 (Kelheim, n.d. – Bavaria 1622 – Pfalz-Neuburg). A list of questions from Eichstätt was published by F. Merzbacher, in C. Hinckeldey (ed.), *Strafjustiz in alter Zeit. Band 3 der Schriftenreihe des mittelalterlichen Kriminalmuseums Rothenburg ob der Tauber*, Rothenburg o.T. 1980, 213–15. The dating of the Bavarian questions is also to be corrected. Hofmann, 'Protokoll', 188 and Riezler, *Geschichte*, 338–40, date it from a later copy to 1622 (HStAM, Hexenakten 1½). In reality the Bavarian instruction on procedure in trials for witchcraft was – one might almost say naturally – issued in 1590. The instruction was demanded by the Court Councillors in early April 1590 and composed after the receipt of the opinion on witchcraft from Ingolstadt at the end of April, that is probably in May 1590. Undated copies are found in HStAM, Hexenakten 1, Prod. 5 (not the final text); StadtA Munich, Bürgermeister und Rat, no. 60 B 2, fol. 707–17. A dated copy from the archive of the *Rentamt* of Landshut (1590) which was taken as the basis for the Ansbach opinion on witchcraft of 1591, has been preserved in StA Bamberg, Bamberger Verordnungen no. 44, 'General Instruction von den Truten', fol. 14–23. The questions in it are identical with those edited by Riezler and Hofmann. *Ibid.*, fol. 15v–17. The instruction was issued around 31 July 1590. HStAM, SV 2243, fol. 129. The Governor in Ingolstadt was sent his copy on this date. The instruction appears to have been issued to the district court judges only on request, e.g. to the district judge of Aibling in March 1591, HStAM, KHR 18, fol. 129v.

Kelheim. Schmeller's *Bayerisches Wörterbuch* even cites the expression *Kelheimer Basel* as a synonym for witch, and it is not surprising that this phrase can be dated to the persecution years around 1590.[92]

Even after consulting a wide range of sources on the witch trials in the capital, Munich, we are little the wiser about them. It is only clear that at least four women were put to death as witches, possibly nine, ten or more. The trials caused considerable concern to the magistracy, both because their judicial privileges had been flouted by the ducal commissioners, and because of the unusual tortures inflicted by the executioner Jörg Abriel of Schongau.[93] We also have reports of witch trials from the district courts of Rauhenlechsberg, Aibling, Kraiburg and Rain in Upper Bavaria, and Griesbach, Erding, Straubing and Regen in Lower Bavaria.[94] When one recalls that the Duchy comprised more than a hundred judicial districts, the number of those in which one or more witches were executed during the persecution of 1590 is relatively small. The Prince-Bishoprics of Augsburg, Freising and Eichstätt, the Protestant Principalities of Pfalz-Neuburg and Ansbach-Bayreuth were hit equally hard by the trials, that is at least as much or more of their territory was affected, judging by the available reports of trials for witchcraft in Bavaria. Of course, the sources are fragmentary and do not permit exact quantification in each case. Nevertheless, the picture sketched here can be regarded as exact enough for corrections to concern matters of detail only. This is the impression given not only by the trial records, protocols of the Court Council and town councils that have been evaluated, but also by court account books and correspondence. In 1594 Hans Friedrich Herwarth, judge at Schon-

[92] J.A. Schmeller and G.K. Fromann, *Bayerisches Wörterbuch*, 2 vols., Munich 1872/1877 (reprint, Aalen 1973), I, col. 1234. Riezler, *Geschichte*, 197.
[93] On the witch trials in Munich: StadtA Munich, Stadtgericht 886/1; fol. 180–4; *ibid.*, fol. 213v–215v for the precedents; *ibid.*, Bürgermeister und Rat, no. 54 A 17 (minutes of the City Council, 1565–98), fol. 163r–v; *ibid.*, no. 54 A 19 (minutes of City Council, 1586–96), fol. 33v–9 *passim*; fol. 45v, 46v, 53–5v *passim*; StadtA Munich, Kammerei no. 1/199 (Chamber minutes, 1590), fol. 123f.; *ibid.*, no. 200, fol. 106, 113; HStAM, HZR 36, fol. 410, 426v–9 *passim*; *ibid.*, HZR, 37 fol. 508; HStAM, SV 2243 fol. 127v; HStAM, GR 323/16, fol. 45–8; HStAM, Hexenakten 4, Prod. 46, fol. 1ff.; *ibid.*, Hexenakten 9a, fol. 314, 374, 396; ÖNB Vienna, Cod. 8963, fol. 312r–v. The sources allow a quantification only to the extent that they show the significant size of the witch hunt at Munich. More than fifteen women were arrested, several of them wealthy innkeepers. The trials were conducted by city and ducal councillors (cf. Behringer, 'Hexenverfolgung', 352f.), and both the city and ducal prisons were full of 'witches'. The costs of custody alone in the Falkenturm rose continuously from 1588, until in July 1590 they were ten times what they had been in 1588 or 1589. In July 1590 at least five or as many as ten women were executed as witches. The costs of custody (the only serial source) then fell steeply to half of what they had been and continued to fall in stages until 1595 (HStAM, HZR 34–41). The trial conducted by the ducal councillors, which involved torture applied by Abriel, ran into the sharpest protests from the city, which sent an ultimatum demanding an end to it. StadtA Munich, Bürgermeister und Rat, no. 54 A 19, fol. 45v.
[94] Cf. the list of trials in the German edition.

gau and a brother of the Bavarian Court and Estates Chancellor Hans Georg Herwarth,[95] wrote to Duke Ferdinand that the persecution at Schongau had been the greatest in the whole country, while the trials under the responsibility of Duke Wilhelm in Munich, Abensberg, Weilheim and Tölz, on the other hand, had 'soon come to an end', and therefore 'looked unequal', and were not be compared with the example of Schongau in scale.[96]

The persecution party in the government was on the whole dissatisfied with the results of the persecutions. In April 1590 an opinion of the Court Council discussed the paucity of persecutions in Bavaria compared with the Bishopric of Augsburg, and listed three reasons: the secrecy of the offence, which made any proof very difficult; the risk for the accusers, who endangered themselves, as they had to produce proof; and the lack of interest of the county courts, which simply cast such accusations 'to the wind' when they were brought before them.[97] In principle the Council seems to have assumed that many county court judges, and of course others, doubted the reality of the crime of witchcraft, or some of its components. Otherwise it is hardly comprehensible that an argument for the very existence of witchcraft or a discussion of its nature should have run like a red thread through all the treatises, memoranda, learned opinions and instructions on the subject.

In 1590 Duke Wilhelm V was interested in a solution which would go to the heart of the matter – a 'final solution', we might say. On 2 April 1590 he instructed his competent central ruling body, the Court Council, to prepare a written opinion on the right way to suppress witchcraft.[98] After an exhaustive discussion the Council concluded on 6 April that witchcraft was undeniable, that it was the worst of crimes and that it was therefore to be eradicated. Orders to this effect were to be given to the subordinate authorities (the *Regierungen* and the county courts). General rules for the trial of witches could not be drawn up, but an opinion on this point was to be obtained from prominent theologians and jurists.[99] The Duke ordered the University of Ingolstadt to produce an opinion in principle on the possible errors committed in the hunting of witches. The answer of the faculties of theology and law was signed on 28 April 1590.[100] It formed the basis for further discussion in Bavaria.

[95] *ADB*, 13 (1881), 169–73 (Eisenhart).
[96] StadtA Munich, Hist. Ver. Urk. 2005, fol. 5r–v.
[97] HStAM, Hexenakten 1, Prod. 4, fol. 5r–v.
[98] HStAM, Hexenakten 1, Prod. 4, fol. 1r–v (Decretum Ducis).
[99] *Ibid.*, Prod. 4, fol. 106v (opinions of the Court Council).
[100] *Ibid.*, Prod. 1, fol. 1–14 (University opinion). Copies of the Ingolstadt opinion (cf. note 29 for its authorship) are to be found in numerous Bavarian archives, mostly in Latin. It formed the basis of the discussion of witchcraft in the region (cf. chapter 4). As the

The Ingolstadt opinion of 1590 called for a 'public edict to all and sundry'.[101] The discussion of this demand continued until 1611–12, when the Bavarian mandate against witches was issued. The demand also formed the basis of a set of procedural instructions for judges of the county courts, which was sent to individual courts later, for example in 1600 and 1622.[102]

The contents of the University's opinion reveal the lines of the internal conflict that was to continue through the following decades. On the one hand the harshest persecution of witches was demanded, even at the cost of neglecting elementary precautions of safety, for example the ability to prove the denunciations; it was suggested, on the basis of Binsfeld's argument, that God would not suffer the innocent to be put to death. Even a minor suspicion (a denunciation) was to be grounds for arrest; torture was to be more readily applied for this 'secret' crime than for other offences; and confessions obtained under torture were to be believed, as they represented the surest evidence in these cases.

On the other hand the same document calls for extreme caution in trials for witchcraft, and for care to be taken to see that 'the innocent are not sentenced or condemned from time to time'.[103]

Yet these vague rules of caution were devalued by the references to the literature and to precedents for witch trials in Bavaria, which were exclusively to the harshest variants of procedure:

It will be very useful for the judges who wish to take in hand the proceedings in Bavaria, to bear in mind and consult several trials of witches held in the neighbourhood, as in the Bishopric of Augsburg, and Eichstätt. For as it is to be believed that the vices and misdeeds of witches are the same in Bavaria and other neighbouring regions, so they may lawfully be dealt with in the same way.

And it will also be very useful that several books which are freely, agreeably and concisely written on this subject, should be read, especial-

opinion appealed to the precedents of Dillingen and Eichstätt, it also had a reverse influence on these territories, which was due not only to the special position of the University of Ingolstadt but also to the prestige of the author among the Jesuits and more generally to the prominence of Bavaria in the region. Even the Lutheran Margravate of Ansbach oriented itself after 1590 to the example of the dominant Catholic power Bavaria. StA Bamberg, Bamberger Verordnungen no. 44, 'General Instruction von den Truten', fol. 1–23. After the death of the Bishop of Eichstätt, Martin von Schaumburg (1560–90), Eichstätt too oriented itself to the Bavarian example. In a 'Gemain Bedencken der F. Ey[ch]stättisch[en] Rathe de Captura et Tortura Sagarum' of 1592, it is explicitly recommended that future proceedings should follow the instruction for witchcraft trial procedure of Duke Wilhelm V. HStAM, GR 323/16, fol. 11v–13, esp. fol. 12v.
[101] HStAM, Hexenakten, Prod. 1, fol. 3v (3, 'Wie ein Inquisition soll angestellt werden').
[102] StadtA Munich, Bürgermeister und Rat no. 60 B 2, fol. 707–17; HStAM, Hexenakten 1½ (cf. note 91).   [103] HStAM, Hexenakten 1, Prod. 1, fol. 11v.

TRACTAT

Von Bekanntnuß der Zau-
berer vnd Hexen. Ob vnd wie viel
denselben zu glauben.

Anfängklich durch den Hochwürdigen Herrn
Petrum Binsfeldium, Trierischen Suffraganten/ vnd
der H. Schrifft Doctorn/ kurtz vnd summarischer
Weiß in Latein beschrieben.

Jetzt aber der Warheit zu stewr in vnser Teutsche Sprach
vertiert/durch den Wolgelerten M. Bernhart Vogel/deß löblichen
Stattgerichts in München/Assessorn.

EXOD XXII. CAP.

Die Zauberer solt du nicht leben lassen.

Gedruckt zu München bey Adam Berg.

ANNO DOMINI M. D. XCI.

Mit Röm:Bay:Mayt.Freyheit/ nit nachzudrucken.

7. Peter Binsfeld, *Tractat von Bekanntnuss der Zauberer und Hexen*, Munich 1592. Title page with woodcut showing pact with the Devil, flight to the witches' sabbath, intercourse with the Devil and [kellerfahren], harmful sorcery and 'weather cooking'.

ly the *Malleus Maleficarum*, or Hammer of Witches, in the 2nd and 3rd part, and Binsfeld, suffragan Bishop of Trier, published last year.[104]

It would take us too far from our subject to go into all the remarkable

[104] *Ibid.*, fol. 1v.

aspects of this opinion here. Some points will be discussed elsewhere. The opinion may have had a stimulating effect on some judges or commissioners in the spring of 1590, for in the summer the persecutions reached their peak. As early as the following year, however, most of them had been brought to an end, and only in the area along the Danube did they continue until 1594–5. A systematic expansion of the persecutions to the whole of the Duchy failed to materialise.

PRINCE-BISHOPRIC OF FREISING

For Prince-Bishop Ernst of Freising (1566–1612), the brother of Duke Wilhelm V of Bavaria, his Bishopric of Freising was merely an uninteresting minor territory. The Bishop resided at Liège and Cologne, and was represented in Freising by a Governor. The territory of the Bishopric consisted of three portions, separated by larger areas under Bavarian rule: the capital, Freising, with the neighbouring County of Ismaning, the County of Werdenfels, including county courts at Garmisch, Partenkirchen and Mittenwald, and the small Lordship of Burgrain. The Bishop's Governor in Freising was exposed to constant pressure from Bavaria, which claimed a kind of suzerainty over the interests of the little Bishopric, since the diocese under the spiritual authority of the Bishops of Freising comprised largely Bavarian territory.[105]

Yet we can rule out any Bavarian influence on the beginning of the persecutions in the Bishopric, and in fact not even the Governor in Freising was to blame. The trials began in the County of Werdenfels in September 1589, when the local county court judge acted on his own initiative and began to make arrests without consulting his superiors. The judge had long been under pressure to begin a persecution from the population in Garmisch and Partenkirchen; they had even offered to meet the cost of employing the notorious executioner of Schongau, Jörg Abriel. After the persecutions began in Garmisch a deputation from Mittenwald went to the village and demanded that the judge should begin a persecution in their court as well.[106]

The pressure for persecution had been caused by sicknesses and harvest failures, the result of storm damage in 1589, which revived old suspicions of witchcraft. As in many other trials for witchcraft, the suspicion was corroborated by soothsayers, and thus came to be seen as indisputable. The judge was more or less forced to persecute, but was apparently not

---

[105] Spindler, *Handbuch*, III/2, 1389–99; L. Weber SDB, *Veit Adam von Gepeckh. Fürstbischof von Freising, 1618 bis 1651*, Munich 1972, 518f.

[106] Kuisl, *Die Hexen*, 11f.; the trial records of the witch hunt at Werdenfels are in StadtA Munich, Hist. Ver. Ms. 183/1–8.

unwilling, as his enthusiastic letters to the government in Freising indicate: he mentions the necessities of his subjects, brought on them by the witches through storms, harvest failure, hunger and disease.[107] The fact, mentioned in the same letter, that the persons accused had been under suspicion for forty years, shows that a long pent-up demand for persecution had existed in the County of Werdenfels, as elsewhere.

After the government in Freising had approved the torture of the suspected women, a veritable company of executioners gathered at Garmisch. Master Jörg Abriel of Schongau brought his wife, son and brother-in-law, the executioners Jacob and Christoph of Biberach joined the band, as well as two excutioners from Hall in the Tyrol. The executioner Veit Vischer of Schwabmünchen asked his superiors in Dillingen for leave to travel to Garmisch.[108] The role of the executioners was clearly illustrated in Werdenfels. A master from Biberach, for example, travelled around the lower courts of the County for three days, and examined twenty-seven suspected women, of whom he found ten 'sorcerous'. They were arrested and the others released.[109]

A remarkable degree of clerical interest was aroused by the persecutions. Besides the judge and his three assistants, a priest also attended at the tortures. The burnings resembled an *auto da fé*, and were attended by the parish priests of Garmisch, Partenkirchen and Mittenwald, as well as the priests of Eschenlohe (the Abbey of Ettal), Lermoos and Seefeld (Tyrol) and other unspecified clerics, with the Abbot of Schlehdorf and the Provost of Rottenbuch.[110]

The persecution at Werdenfels claimed the lives of fifty-one victims, burned at seven executions. Thirty-three of them came from the court of Garmisch, eleven from Partenkirchen, seven from Mittenwald. At least 127 others were under suspicion of witchcraft, but the persecution was broken off in 1591.[111]

The second persecution in the Bishopric affected the episcopal residence itself and its neighbouring County of Ismaning. It did not begin until April 1590, and was the result of local causes. The immediate cause was several severe hail showers, which had badly damaged the whole town, including the Bishop's palace. The damage to the castle hill was so great that it was

[107] Kuisl, *Die Hexen*, 10f.
[108] HStAm, Hochstift Augsburg, NA, Akten no. 1202, fol. 322.
[109] Kuisl, *Die Hexen*, 25,   [110] *Ibid.*, 13, 17, 21f., 24, 27, 29, 35f.
[111] *Ibid.*, 43–60 (list of executions). Little more can be learned of this. The record of a Freising trial in HStAM, Hexenakten 9a, offers only a few additional indications of the proceedings in the County of Werdenfels. There are no minutes of the Court Council of Freising for this period. The minutes of the episcopal Ecclesiastical Council only mention the witch hunts in connection with a case of desecration of the host, EOAM, GR Prot., no. 003–012 (1587–93); *ibid.*, no. 008, fol. 20v; no. 012, fol. 2v, 61v.

feared that the castle and cathedral would 'come crashing down the hill'.[112] Another severe thunderstorm on 4 June 1590 exacerbated the anti-witch hysteria in the town, and strengthened the Governor in his resolve to root out 'the detestable, frightful, very widespread, damnable and pernicious work of the witches as far as possible'.[113]

The conduct of the trials was entrusted to the skill of the executioner Abriel of Schongau, until towards the end of 1590, at about the same time as in the County of Werdenfels, doubts began to be felt about the rightness of the persecution. In both cases the rapid expansion of the persecution – in Freising and Unterföhring at least twenty-one witches were burned, and twice as many or more were under suspicion – was fed by the combination of belief in the fully developed doctrine of witchcraft and brutal torture.

The Bishop, far away in Cologne, had little interest in events in Freising. Symptomatic of his attitude is an order of October 1590, when doubts of the value of the trials had already begun to emerge, in which he commanded his officers to act 'earnestly' against witches, but to take care that no one suffered wrong as a result.[114]

FREE IMPERIAL CITIES WHERE WITCHES WERE EXECUTED

In general one can say that the golden age of the Free Cities of upper Germany was over in the second half of the sixteenth century. Some of the greater cities, for example Nuremberg, Augsburg or Ulm, managed to retain their prosperity until the Thirty Years War, but many of the smaller cities were suffering serious decline for a variety of apparent reasons.[115] Death reaped a rich harvest in the four agrarian crises between 1562 and 1592, and it is characteristic that in many cities there was an absolute fall in population in this period. At Kaufbeuren, for example, the number of inhabitants fell from 3,130 in 1565 (after the plague of 1563) to 2,600 in 1588,[116] and even in the prosperous metropolis of Augsburg the losses in crises of mortality were no longer made up as quickly as they had been before the middle of the century.[117]

---

[112] *Erweytterte Unholden Zeyttung*, in Behringer, 'Hexenverfolgung', 353; HStAM, Hexenakten 9a, fol. 287v. As well as this record see also HStAM, HL Freising, III, 320/39 (belongs chronologically with the trial record).

[113] *Ibid.*, Hexenakten 9a, fol. 293, 318.   [114] Kuisl, *Die Hexen*, 30f.

[115] H. Schilling, 'The European Crisis of the 1590s: the Situation in German Towns', in P. Clark (ed.), *The European Crisis in the 1590s*, London 1985, 135–56. In southern Germany, however, we should think rather of the 1580s. S. Alt, *Reformation und Gegenreformation in der freien Reichsstadt Kaufbeuren*, Munich 1932, 99, 101–4; C. Friedrichs, *Urban Society in an Age of War: Nördlingen 1580–1720*, Princeton 1979. Further literature on this subject in Schilling, 'European Crisis', 152ff.

[116] Junginger, *Geschichte*, 14.

[117] Jahn, 'Augsburgs' Einwohnerzahl, 386f. Cf. Schilling, 'European Crisis', 136ff.

Respected firms 'failed' because of the ever more frequent state bank-
ruptcies, while the wars in France and the Netherlands closed important
markets to the Swabian textile industry. A chronicle of the Free City of
Kempten speaks of 'great poverty among the common folk' during the
cycle of crises around 1585–7, and blames it not only on the harvest failure
of the previous year, but on the wars in the export markets. A secondary
cause also seems to have been at work in the inflation of 1589–90.[118] At
Kaufbeuren the weavers' trade was 'at a standstill for a time' in 1587, while
simultaneously storms, floods and harvest failures added to the city's
economic misery.[119] In many cities there were social or religious disturbances, and Bavaria used military force to intervene in favour of the
Catholic party in Kaufbeuren.[120]

In the case of Kaufbeuren the equation of crisis and persecution seems
to be demonstrated, at least by the coincidence in time, but the city is an
exception. Kempten was just as hard hit but managed to avoid persecuting
witches, while the greatest persecution took place at Nördlingen, a city
with no apparent symptoms of a local crisis.[121] It is a natural conclusion
that persecution was a function of a specific crisis mentality rather than of
a crisis itself. The effects of the great crisis were supraregional, and were
seen in a general rise in accusations of witchcraft, at Augsburg, Nuremberg, Regensburg and Ulm as at Nördlingen. Local difficulties could
exacerbate the crisis, but they cannot be held directly responsible for
persecutions.

Two Franconian and three Swabian Free Cities allowed themselves to
be dragged into executing witches in 1590: Weissenburg and Windsheim;
Nördlingen, Donauwörth and Kaufbeuren. At Windsheim[122] and Nördlingen there were outright persecutions. At Donauwörth too, several
women appear to have been executed, as an outside source speaks of
witches being burned over two days.[123] The trials at Weissenburg and
Kaufbeuren were the result of other influences, and they were soon
brought to an end. The council of Weissenburg was simply put under
intolerable pressure by the Teutonic Order of Ellingen, and saw no option
but to stage a witch trial, which ended in the execution of two women.
After seeking reassurance and advice from the council of Nuremberg,

[118] UBM, 2° Cod. Ms. 500, fol. 42, 45.   [119] Alt, *Reformation*, 104.
[120] Spindler, *Handbuch*, III/2, 1086 (Schremmer); Alt, *Reformation*, 101ff.; P. Warmbrunn,
   *Zwei Konfessionen in einer Stadt. Das Zusammenleben von Katholiken und Protestanten in
   den paritätischen Reichsstädten Augsburg, Biberach, Ravensburg und Dinkelsbühl von 1548
   bis 1648*, Wiesbaden 1983, 30–40, 45, and the chapter on the conflicts over the calendar,
   359–86.
[121] Friedrichs, *Urban Society*, 206–14, does not believe that the witch hunt at Nördlingen can
   be ascribed to social tensions. For this see the criticism of R.W. Scribner, *Social History*,
   7 (1982), 94–6.   [122] Cf. above, chapter 2, pp. 35–64.
[123] ÖNB Vienna, Cod. 8963, fol. 751/7v–8.

Weissenburg broke off the trial before it could develop into a persecution.[124] The trial at Kaufbeuren had already taken on the character of a persecution when the council courageously resolved to break it off, and issued a public edict forbidding further complaints of witchcraft. The impetus for persecution had been given by denunciations from the neighbouring Lordship of the Protestant family of von Kaltenthal, possibly reinforced by the example of the persecutions in the Bishopric of Augsburg, by which the city was surrounded on three sides. Kaufbeuren too had asked the nearest large Free City for advice, but the opinion of the famous Augsburg consul Dr Georg Tradel has not survived.[125]

Tradel was also asked to advise the city of Nördlingen on several occasions, but his opinions do not seem to have had a moderating influence at first.[126]

The persecution at Nördlingen allows us to observe the way in which a great persecution developed without denunciations from outside. Although the Free City was not short of denunciations from the County of Oettingen, within which it formed an enclave, the persecution ultimately emerged from local causes. A woman who thought herself possessed by the Devil was employed as a children's nurse; three children in her care died within a few days, and she was accused of witchcraft because of her suspicious behaviour: a combination of rare chances, but one which would not automatically have provoked a persecution. The harshness of the proceedings can only be explained by the specific mentality of the new city government, which had just come into office at the time. In previous years, other suspicions of witchcraft had been allayed and moderately handled.[127]

The persecutions in the Protestant cities of Donauwörth and Nördlingen were marked by their extreme radicalism. In Nördlingen, four patrician women and a sister-in-law of Count Friedrich of Oettingen were put to death, as well as at least five other women whose education and property place them in the upper classes of the town.[128] In Donauwörth the

[124] Kunstmann, *Zauberwahn*, 25f.
[125] StadtA Kaufbeuren, Hörmann-Registratur, II, fol. 205ff; *ibid.*, B 106, fol. 164–7v.
[126] Wulz, 'Nördlinger Hexenprozesse' (1937–38), 112; G. Eschbaumer, *Bescheidenliche Tortur. Der ehrbare Rat der Stadt Nördlingen im Hexenprozess 1593/94 gegen die Kronenwirtin Maria Holl*, Nördlingen 1983, 48f.
[127] Friedrichs, *Urban Society*, 206–14; Wulz 'Nördlinger Hexenprozesse' (1937–8); Kramer, 'Volksglauben'; further literature on the witch hunts at Nördlingen: G. Wulz, 'Der Prozess der Hexe Rebecca Lemp', *Der Rieser Heimatbote*, no. 131 (1937); *idem*, 'Nördlinger Hexenprozesse vor 1589', *ibid.*, no. 140 (1938); *idem*, 'Die Nördlinger Hexen und ihre Richter. Eine familiengeschichtliche Studie', *ibid.*, nos. 142–7 (1939); the best information on the available sources is given by Wulz, 'Nördlinger Hexenprozesse' (1937–8) (cf. chapter 1, note 96, 494f.). The researches of the *H-Sonderkommando* were independent of this: Film 1992; Film 3716.   [128] Wulz, 'Die Nördlinger Hexen', nos. 142–7.

daughter of the burgomaster who had introduced the Reformation into the city, fell victim to the trials.[129]

The persecutions in the Free-Imperial Cities also had an influence outside their walls. Because of the marriage relationships between the cities, the danger of suspicions 'jumping' from city to city was involved. Women from Nördlingen denounced women in Dinkelsbühl and Weissenburg. The executioner of Nördlingen, Caspar Vollmair, who may have been a relation of the headsman of Biberach, gained influence in 1590 and was called in to assist at trials for witchcraft in Weissenburg and in the Lordship of Pappenheim. Citizens of Rothenburg and Speyer who were travelling through the region had the implements of torture from Nördlingen shown to them.[130]

PLACES WITHOUT EXECUTIONS OF WITCHES

Places where no witches were executed are not places for which we simply have no reports of such events. In such an intense wave of persecution as that of 1590, a place can only be said to have been free of executions if sources without gaps allow us to prove this. Surprisingly, these sources also reveal that more witch trials were held in these places also – an index of the enormous size of the wave of persecution – but that they all ended in light sentences, acquittal or even the punishment of the slanderer.

This can be illustrated from the examples of the great Free Cities of southeast Germany. Augsburg and Nuremberg, as leaders of opinion, held back and exerted a restraining influence on the smaller cities; Ulm and Memmingen with their territories and the important city of Regensburg did not burn any witches; Augsburg resisted the desire of its Bishop for persecution; Nuremberg criticised the proceedings in the neighbouring Margravates, though it was keen to protect its good reputation: after all, the Council did not wish to be seen as a protector of witches! (The same concerns were felt in Munich, where the city believed itself to be under pressure to justify its conduct to the more zealous persecutors in the Bishoprics of Eichstätt and Augsburg.)[131]

---

[129] Zelzer, *Geschichte*, 208, 256, 395; Stetten, *Geschichte*, I, 718; Behringer, 'Hexenverfolgung', 349; Film 596; ÖNB Vienna, Cod. 8963, fol. 751/7v-8.

[130] Wulz, 'Nördlinger Hexenprozesse' (1937–8), 115f., note 12.

[131] Kunstmann, *Zauberwahn*, 183, 194 for the attitude of Nuremberg. Ulm: Film, 2778; the last witch burning in Ulm had been in 1507–8, the next burnings took place during the agrarian crisis of 1612, then in 1616 and finally in 1621. But there were numerous trials for sorcery and witchcraft between them, mostly in years of agrarian crisis. The trials in 1562–3 were connected with those in the Lordship of Wiesensteig. After further trials in 1570 and 1577, six trials in the years 1591–5 deserve particular mention, though they did not end in executions. On Memmingen: StadtA Memmingen, Urgichtenbücher II (1574– 1614), which show that no sorcerers or witches were executed in the jurisidiction of the

Everywhere in 1590 soothsayers appeared and offered to find witches. 'Witchfinders' had an immense following among the people, and posed a threat to the policy of the city governments, which showed little inclination to hunt witches. In 1591 Augsburg banished a witchfinder from the city; he ad tried to extort money from a member of the house of Fugger by exploiting the general fear of witches.[132] At Nuremberg one of these troublemakers was executed. Friedrich Stigler, a native of Nuremberg, had been a mate of the executioner of Eichstätt. After he returned to Nuremberg he rose in his profession as fear of witches increased, sold 'consecrated little bags against the spells of the witches', and accused eleven women of witchcraft. The council had him arrested and interrogated under severe torture. On 28 July 1590, at the height of the persecution frenzy in the region, Stigler was beheaded by the sword. The grounds for the judgement say that he had dared

> from mere bold insolence . . . falsely to accuse several citizens' wives here as witches, without any grounds or truth, and thus had tried to sow and arouse unrest, evil suspicion and ill feeling among the citizenry . . . [133]

This does not mean that the authorities in the cities denied the existence of witches or opposed trials for witchcraft on principle. If that was the case, it has left no trace, at least in the internal written records of the city governments, but remained private. Every accusation of witchcraft was carefully checked, and if the grounds for suspicion appeared adequate the cities did not shrink from torture. In Augsburg torture was even applied until the executioner himself refused to carry out the instructions of the Council, as he feared that the accused woman was in such poor health that permanent physical injury would be caused.[134]

In the Swabian metropolis of Augsburg, where the sources allow a full survey, no fewer than twenty-eight cases of witchcraft or sorcery were heard between 1586 and 1595, of which thirteen were for witchcraft. Ten of the thirteen cases fell within the shorter period 1589–91. Three of the thirteen alleged witches were exiled from the city, a very old woman died in prison two weeks after her arrest,[135] and nine women were acquitted or

city. Schorer, *Chronicle*, 111, and the other chronicles only report executions of witches in the surrounding noble lordships. Unold, *Geschichte*, 197. Augsburg: cf. above. pp. 43–4, 102; Regensburg: H. Bayerl, 'Die letzte Hexe von Regensburg', *Die Oberpfalz*, 33 (1939), 180–3; C.G. Gumpelzheimer, *Regensburgs Geschichte, Sagen und Merkwürdigkeiten*, 4 vols., Regensburg 1830–8, II, 1010ff.

[132] StadtA Augsburg, Strafbuch 1591, fol. 101v.   [133] Kunstmann, *Zauberwahn*, 77f.
[134] StadtA Augsburg, Urgichtenakten 1591, Magdalena Hofherrin.
[135] Cf. above. StadtA Augsburg, Strafbuch 1588–96, fol. 108v. The city council ordered a report after the death of the aged inhabitant of the hospital (cf. note 134). The woman might have been executed as a witch, as she had admitted her guilt.

released; five of the remaining fifteen sorcerers and sorceresses were exiled, ten released. Two thirds of the persons arrested under grave suspicion were able to resume their business in the city.

This means that the seeds of a persecution existed at least twenty-eight times in Augsburg in ten years, for the increase in charges of witchcraft in the city corresponded exactly with the rhythm of the persecution in the surrounding countryside.[136] Twenty-six of the accusations came from within the city itself, and only two women were suspected of witchcraft because of denunciations made in the persecutions in the district courts of Zusmarshausen and Schwabmünchen.

These two cases are particularly interesting, for the accused women in fact knew a great many spells and played an active role in the popular magical 'subculture', even performing rites that could be described as 'black magic'. The council of Augsburg regarded their activities as sorcery but did not take them for a sign of a pact with the Devil, and instead investigated the individual cases of sorcery for the harm they had caused; this was, after all, the only grounds for punishment under the criminal law of the Empire. Torture was applied, but not so harshly that the will of the women was deliberately broken. The executioner Däubler was closely supervised by the council, two members of which always attended at the tortures, so that he was unable to act on his own initiative. As early as 1587 the 'evil custom' of leaving the headsman alone to torture the victims was abolished.[137] As the two accused women denied all charges of witchcraft, they were released in spite of the grave charges against them and their real activity as sorceresses. Exile from the city was not a harsh punishment; one woman bought a new house directly in front of the city gates, the other was allowed to return to the city after only five months, and was pardoned three months later.[138]

---

[136] Cf. chapter 2, pp. 35–64.   [137] Stetten, *Geschichte*, I, 701f.

[138] The observers from the surrounding Bishopric were indignant: ÖNB Vienna, Cod. 8963, fol. 613v. On the confrontation in Schwabmünchen: StadtA Augsburg, Stadtrats-protokoll 1590 (= Ratsbuch no. 45), fol. 340–7 *passim*; Ratsbuch no. 46, fol. 11, 37, 65; *ibid.*, Strafbücher 1588–96, fol. 75; *ibid.*, Urgichtenakten 1590 c VII, 2, 23, Anna Stauderin (Widenmännin). HStAM, Hochstift Augsburg, NA, Akten no. 1203, fol. 433, illuminates the whole affair from the perspective of Dillingen. Stauderin was obviously involved in white magic. She was released, but banished from Augsburg. A little later she gave birth to a child and was allowed to return. Not more than three months later she was completely pardoned. StadtA Augsburg, Strafbuch 1588–96, fol. 75. Two other cases aroused the indignation of the Bishop's officials: those of Catharina Pretzellerin (Pausin-gerin) (Strafbuch 1588–96, fol. 78v; *ibid.*, Urgichtenakten 1590c; Ratsbuch no. 45, fol. 2–6 *passim*, 49, 96f., 107) and Anna Modestin (Gsellin) (Strafbuch 1588–96, fol. 79; *ibid.*, Urgichtenakten 1590c; Ratsbuch no. 45, fol. 2–5 *passim*). A correspondent of the Fuggers wrote from Augsburg: 'Die bösen Weyber betreffend, deren Zwee allhier mit namen Modestin, so brändtwein feil gehabt, die andere Pretzelerin genendt, so im Zwinger gewesen, Seindt selbige unlanngs über scharpf Examen wider menigelichs verhoffen umb Mittags zeit auss der Statt gefürt und der Statt verwiesen, wölche

The authorities in Schwabmünchen and Dillingen looked on aghast at the outcome of the witch trials in the Free Cities, which they had initially welcomed warmly. The Councillors of the Prince-Bishop did not conceal their criticism, and wrote that the many witches executed in the Bishopric would have denied everything, if they had not been tortured properly.[139] A correspondent of the Fuggers from Augsburg wrote that the outcome of the trials 'seemed a mild way of proceeding', and had caused great surprise;[140] another correspondent from Schwabmünchen in the Bishopric wrote to Augsburg:

> Among you though, when you get hold of some people you do not want to tackle them and you do not act without deliberation but, be that as it may, the authorities should look to it, as they will have to answer for it before God . . .[141]

A Free City the size of Augsburg could not be intimidated by neighbouring territories quite so easily before the Thirty Years War. The council was independent enough not to deviate from the normal procedure in all cases of witchcraft and sorcery, and to take into account any mitigating circumstantial evidence. In the case of a woman who was the subject of accusations from the city and from Zusmarshausen in the Bishopric, the consul of the city, Dr Tradel, claimed that the statements of a witch executed at Zusmarhausen had been contradictory, and the accuser from Augsburg had long been known as an eccentric. The sickness of a woman who was alleged to have been bewitched was due to natural causes (opinions of the doctors), and the accused had sufficiently purged herself by standing up to torture, so that there was no objection to her release.[142]

The council of Regensburg took a similarly pragmatic line, for although it shared the general belief in witchcraft it hesitated to execute witches. At

Pretzelerin anjetzt fürhabens, zue Kriegshabern ein hauss zu kauffen, und allda einzunüsten', ÖNB Vienna, Cod. 8963, fol. 613r–v. ('As for the wicked women, of whom there are two here, one called Modestin, who sold brandy, and the other Pretzelerin, who was in the dungeon, the same were recently, against the hope of many, and after severe examination, led out of the city and banished from the city; the said Pretzelerin now intends to buy a house at Kriegshaber and settle there.')

[139] StadtA Augsburg, Urgichtenakten 1591a (Maria Köchin).
[140] ÖNB Vienna, Cod. 8963, fol. 513.   [141] *Ibid.*, fol. 593.
[142] StadtA Augsburg, Urgichtenakten 1591a (Maria Köchin); *ibid.*, Strafbücher 1588–96, fol. 97: 'Maria Köchin, Kaspar Ruprechts Beckhens und burgers alhie nachgelasne witib, ist Hexerey verdachts halben auf ein Dillingisch schreiben In fronvest kommen: weil sie aber nichts bekennen wöllen: und nit indicia [for torture, WB] vorhanden gewesen, hat ein Ersamer Rhat . . . erkant, das sie auf widerstellen erlassen werden soll'. (Maria Köchin, the widow of Kaspar Ruprecht, baker, a citizen here, was imprisoned on suspicion of witchcraft, following a letter from Dillingen, but because she was unwilling to confess anything and there was no circumstantial evidence [for torture] the Honourable Council agreed that she should be released').

the end of 1591 a woman exiled from the city was readmitted after half a year. In 1594–5 a girl accused herself of witchcraft and was generally believed to be a witch. The Councillors of Regensburg came to the conclusion that the girl was 'behaving foolishly', and had their doubts about her mental condition.[143]

It was not just the greater Free Cities that showed themselves resistant to the witchcraft hysteria of the years around 1590. As we have already mentioned, many of the county courts in the Duchy of Bavaria were extremely cautious about trying witches. Apart from the fact that simultaneous trials of witches in more than a hundred county courts would have been technically impossible, most of the nobles who served as judges displayed a reluctance to become involved in persecution that was the partly the result of simple ignorance (witch trials meant a great deal of disagreeable work), and partly of their adherence to the old theory of sorcery and suspicion of the new, fully developed and spiritualised idea of witchcraft; to some extent, also, they were unwilling to shoulder the responsibility that conducting a witch trial entailed. A noble judge wrote:

There is the further inconvenience with persons suspected of sorcery, that where one of them is examined in prison, they soon incriminate one or two others by their confessions, and they in turn accuse three or four others or more until in the end the number is so great that . . . those of standing, birth and wealth are spared for friendship's sake, and so an end is put to the burning; or one must go on so long with the everlasting continuance of the burning and torturing until at last the judge, the headsman's mate and the headsman himself are weary of it, and the costs grow too great . . .

Nor could one rule out the possibility that there were innocent victims among those executed.

On the other hand that one should not torture a prisoner out of untimely zeal, tear his limbs, or make him a cripple and a poor man . . .
execute him in revenge and fury but ultimately find him innocent, so that he or his friends in his stead may cite the judge or lower authority before the Prince or the Emperor's Chamber Court, for amends for the martyr and for the honour of friendship, with lengthy proceedings and expenses; and besides his troubled conscience hangs an everlasting burden round his neck.[144]

Witch trials brought nothing but trouble with subjects and authorities

---

[143] Film 2231; Gumpelzheimer, *Regensburg's Geschichte*, II, 1010ff.; Bayerl, 'Die letzte Hexe'.   [144] HStAM, SV 2243, s.f.

alike, and if it did not appear urgently necessary to act, the judges tended to take a moderate line, or even to prevent witch trials from being held. A tried and tested means of preventing unnecessary and abusive accusations of witchcraft was to impose heavy fines on the accusers (usually about two gulden), or even to imprison them or threaten them with banishment from the country. Such penalties can be documented, in spite of the fragmentary sources for 1589–93, in the county courts of Griesbach (twice), Eggenfelden, Traunstein (two persons), Munich and Starnberg.[145]

The ecclesiastical territories apparently did not generally take part in the persecutions either, though further studies are needed to clarify the picture here. It is remarkable, for example, that we have no reports of trials in the Bishopric of Regensburg and the great Swabian monastic Lordships of Roggenburg, Ursberg, Irsee, Wettenhausen, Ottobeuren and the Prince-Abbacy of Kempten. A sample test in the protocols of the Court Council of the Prince-Abbacy of Kempten shows that accusations of witchcraft were voiced there in 1590. The Prince-Abbot was in contact with the Abbey of Irsee and two noblemen about the treatment of several charges of witchcraft, but there is no reference to any executions. At the same time military preparations were ordered, in case the District Judge of Oberdorf should attempt to use force to arrest five suspects at Unterthingau in the territory of the Prince-Abbot of Kempten.[146] Neither chronicles from the Prince-Abbacy nor the (incomplete) lists of depositions, recognisances and sentences suggest that any witches were executed during the persecution of 1590, nor are executions reported from the district of the Bavarian monasteries of Ettal and Benediktbeuren, but this may reflect the absence of serial sources.[147]

It is fairly probable, on the other hand, that the Calvinist Electoral Upper Palatinate abstained from persecution during this wave of persecution. In the hunger crisis after 1570 the government at Amberg – no doubt after agreeing with its superiors at Heidelberg – had refused to hold a witchcraft trial in an exemplary case, dismissing witchcraft as a 'fantasy'.[148]

---

[145] Cf. list of trials in the German edition.
[146] HStAM, Fürststift Kempten, NA, Lit. 2661, fol. 163v, 168, 179, 190v, 207–v.
[147] HStAM, Fürststift Kempten, NA, Akten no. 1605; *ibid.*, Fürststift Kempten, NA, Lit. 2052; *ibid.*, NA, Lit. 1422. HStAM, KL Ettal (Rep.); HStAM, KL Benediktbeuren no. 16 (Urfehdbriefe 1378–1521; Vizdomwändel 1530–1615).
[148] See B. Thieser, 'Die Oberpfalz im Zusammenhang des Hexenprozessgeschehens im süddeutschen Raum während des 16. und 17. Jahrhunderts', PhD thesis, Bayreuth 1987. It is evident that the middle-tier authorities in Amberg, influenced by the cautious attitude of the government in Heidelberg and perhaps also by that of Nuremberg, opposed executions of witches, although they kept a close watch on possible attempts at sorcery (Visitation 1579–80). A key role was played by a trial for witchcraft in 1572 in the county court of Schneeberg-Treffelstein (in the *Landkreis* Waldmünchen), in which the judge was informed that the women accused themselves 'aus geschöpfter fantasei und aberglauben'. The judge had wished to order the execution of the woman who had made

EXCURSUS: EFFECTS ON MIDDLE, UPPER AND LOWER
FRANCONIA

Prince-Bishopric of Eichstätt

The history of persecution in the Bishopric of Eichstätt has not yet been written. Only individual sources have been examined, and interest has understandably concentrated on the great persecutions of the 1620s.[149] This emphasis has overlooked the fact that the Bishops of Eichstätt had had individual witches executed from time to time since the end of the fifteenth century; this must be seen as a peculiarity, as long as similar executions cannot be documented for other territories in the region.

The persecutions at Eichstätt in 1590–3 have received hardly any attention, perhaps because almost no source material survives. We have reports of executions in the episcopal jurisdictions of Abenberg, Spalt and Herrieden, at which between four and twelve women were burned as witches. The burning of twelve witches at Spalt on 12 April 1590 seems to have set a new record for the region. There is definite evidence for the burning of sixteen witches over two days at Abenberg.[150]

Though the persecutions began later than those in the Bishopric of Augsburg, Pfalz-Neuburg, Nördlingen, Ellingen, Oettingen and Bavaria, they soon came to be regarded as exemplary by the apologists of persecution, because of their radicalism. They found supporters in both Catholic Bavaria and Protestant Ansbach-Bayreuth. The University of Ingolstadt referred in an opinion to the examples set by the Bishoprics of Augsburg and Eichstätt, while the Margrave of Ansbach brought in the executioner of Eichstätt to conduct the trials in his territory.[151]

Under the reforming Bishops Martin von Schaumburg (1560–90) and Caspar von Seckendorf (1590–5), there were already signs of the special

a full confession. StA Amberg, Oberster Lehnhof no. 1456 (Halsgericht Treffelstein Anno 1572). By all appearances the executions of witches in the Upper Palatinate before 1630 were confined to the Pfalz-Neuburg district around Hemau and Laaber, which once again makes clear the share of the authorities in trials for witchcraft. As in Bavaria, witch trials in the Upper Palatinate not infrequently ended in the punishment of the accuser. I am grateful to Dr Bernd Thieser, Oberölbühl/Brand, for these references. There are also references in K. Ried, *Neumarkt in der Oberpfalz*, Neumarkt 1960; A. Reger, *Aus der Geschichte der Stadt Kemnath*, Kallmünz 1981.

[149] Merzbacher, *Die Hexenprozesse*, largely spares Eichstätt. His 'Das "alte Halsgerichtsbuch"' does not deal with the period of the witch hunts. On these see R. Gänstaller, 'Zur Geschichte des Hexenwahns: Der Fall Barbara Reuterin in Eichstätt', unpublished dissertation, Nuremberg 1974, 4; Riezler, *Geschichte*, 221–7.

[150] The following remarks are based entirely on the researches of the *H-Sonderkommando*, which combed the Eichstätt witchcraft archives thoroughly. Film 68, Film 668–9, Film 1183, Film 2589, Film 3662, Film 3709, 572–686 (Eichstätt witchcraft records in the StA Nuremberg), Film 3840–4. On the witch burnings at Abenberg see also Behringer, 'Hexenverfolgung', 349.

[151] HStAM, Hexenakten 1, Prod. 1 (Ingolstadt opinion on witchcraft of 1590). 'Bedenken, die Unhulden betreffend', 540–7.

role that Eichstätt was to play in the region under the persecution Bishop Johann Christoph von Westerstetten (1612–36), when it became the chief engine of persecution in the region.

Margravates of Ansbach and Bayreuth, Saxe-Coburg.

The Protestant Principality of Coburg and the upper Margravate of Bayreuth, east of the Bishopric of Bamberg, were outside the region gripped by the persecution mania in 1590, and the affinities of both lay elsewhere. In the Principality of Coburg two persons had been executed for witchcraft in 1586, while the chief concentration of persecution in the Saxon Principalities may have been as early as the 1560s and 1570s.[152] There was an important witch trial at Creussen in Bayreuth in 1569, in which Margrave Georg Friedrich ultimately decided on a mild sentence (a penance in church).[153] In the upper Margravate of Bayreuth there do not appear to have been any executions for witchcraft in 1590.[154]

At the time of the wave of persecution in 1590 the Margravates of Ansbach and Bayreuth were ruled in personal union by the Margrave Georg Friedrich (1556–1603), but retained their separate administrations. Their example shows that the persecution of 1590 was a regional affair, which is hard to relate to political and structural characteristics: while the infertile 'highlands' of the agrarian Margravate of Bayreuth remained free from persecution, the comparatively wealthy 'lowlands' west of the territory of the Free City of Nuremberg were within the sphere of the persecutions, as was the Margravate of Ansbach further south.

The Protestant Margravate of Ansbach was covered by witch trials as almost no other territory. The first safely datable trials were held in 1589, when the executioner of the Count of Oettingen was called in to assist at a trial in Langenzenn.[155] An opinion of 1591 looks back to the execution of several women in the county courts of Hohentrüdingen, Heidenheim, Colmberg and Emskirchen, and refers to a current trial at Mainbernheim.[156] We know of great burnings of witches at Langenzenn and Heilsbronn in 1590,[157] and at Schwabach, Langenzenn, Heilsbronn and Ansbach in 1591. Trials were still continuing in 1592. At least seven

---

[152] Janssen and Pastor, *Culturzustände*, VIII, 680–6; H.-J. Kretz, 'Der Schöppenstuhl zu Coburg', Dr. jur. thesis, Würzburg 1972, 64–80; Film 494, Film 1955.

[153] K. Lory, 'Hexenprozesse im Gebiet des ehemaligen Markgrafenlandes', in *Festgabe für K. Th. von Heigel*, Munich 1904, 290–304; *ibid.*, 291–6.

[154] The only execution of a witch yet known to have taken place in Bayreuth occurred in 1563, during the wave of witch hunting of that year. W. Kneule, *Kirchengeschichte der Stadt Bayreuth*, I, Neustadt/Aisch 1971, 37f.; Film 226.

[155] For the Margravates in general see Spindler, *Handbuch*, III/1, 396–405 (Endres). Film 1557.   [156] 'Bedenken, die Unholden betreffend', 537, 540.

[157] Kunstmann, *Zauberwahn*, 78.

witches were burned at Schwabach, and trials were also held at Hohen-trüdingen and Furth (in the district of Cadolzburg). In Ansbach an accusation brought by a shepherd led to the arrest of a seventy-year-old member of the Imperial nobility, *Erbmarschallin* Cäcilie von Pappenheim, one of the family that provided the hereditary Marshals of the Empire. The shepherd accused her of having been seen at witches' sabbaths by witches under arrest at Ellingen, Abenberg and Schwabach. The noble lady was not released until 1595, after an opinion had been obtained from the University of Altdorf.[158] Trials were still under way in 1593 at Heilsbronn and Windsbach, and four witches were burned at Crailsheim in 1594.[159]

The territory of Ansbach formed a patchwork with numerous other lordships (the Bishopric of Eichstätt, the Teutonic Order, the Imperial Knights, the Free Cities). While there were only conflicts with the Free City of Nuremberg, which was reluctant to persecute, the Margrave's officials joined in a productive collaboration with the officers of the Bishop of Eichstätt, the Teutonic Order in Ellingen and the Counts of Oettingen-Wallerstein. They were particularly eager to employ the executioner of Eichstätt to interrogate the witches, although the stricter Lutherans regarded his magical ceremonies as popish works of the Devil.[160] In 1591 the Chancellor of Oettingen had to explain the value of the witches' mark as evidence to the Chancellor of Ansbach, Stadtmann, who was unwilling to sign an opinion on witches in Swabia.[161]

The 'General Instruction on Witches' of 1591 refers explicitly to the examples followed by the persecution party in the Margravate: the authorities of the Lutheran Free City of Nördlingen and the 'high authorities' in Bavaria, the dominant large state of the neighbouring region. The immediate precedent for the 'General Instruction' was the Bavarian instruction on procedure in witch trials issued for the provincial administration of Land-shut in 1590.[162] Although a faction opposed to persecution began to take shape in Ansbach in 1591, the executions lasted at least until 1594.

Ecclesiastical territories of Upper and Lower Franconia.

The wave of persecution reached as far as Upper and Lower Franconia. The ecclesiastical territories of Franconia, where persecution was to become almost unending in the first decades of the seventeenth century, were on the margins of the persecution region in 1590. In many of the later

---

[158] Lang, *Geschichte*, III, 340.   [159] Film 1183; Midelfort, *Witch Hunting*, 308.
[160] Kunstmann, *Zauberwahn*, 191–5; 'Bedenken, die Unhulden betreffend', 540ff.
[161] Lang, *Geschichte*, III, 340,.
[162] StA Bamberg, Bamberger Verordnungen no.44, 'General Instruction von den Truten', fol. 11, fol. 14–23.

centres of persecution – Bamberg, Gerolzhofen, Würzburg, Aschaffenburg
– the first executions are not recorded until 1590. In the Upper Archbishopric of Mainz, around Aschaffenburg, large trials were held as early
as 1594, after which more than ten persons were executed.[163]

Upper Franconia was largely spared before 1600. Apart from the executions in the territory of Coburg, mentioned above, the only reports are
from Bamberg, where a trial was already under way in 1590 and a witch
was burned in 1595.[164]

In southern Lower Franconia, which was in closer contact with the
persecution region, there was a smaller zone that followed the rhythm of
the great wave of persecution. At Hellmitzheim, the seat of a court of the
Lordship of Limpurg, five women were burned as witches over two days in
1587.[165] The example was followed in the neighbouring town of Mainbernheim in the Margravate, while the Bishopric of Würzburg saw its first
executions at Würzburg and Gerolzhofen in 1590.[166] The Prince-Bishop at
this time was Julius Echter von Mespelbrunn (1573–1616), whose rigorous
Counter-Reformation domestic policy and 'Catholic' foreign policy were
very much in tune with those of contemporary Bavaria. The Counter-
Reformation 'axis' from Würzburg to Munich naturally operated in questions of witchcraft as well. There were also persecutions in the Protestant
County of Löwenstein-Wertheim in 1590.[167]

We know of trials at Mellrichstadt in Würzburg in 1594, at Iphofen in
1596 and in nearby Marktbreit (County of Seinsheim).[168] When persecutions were held in the Free City of Windsheim in 1596–7, an executioner
was no longer summoned from the south but from the Upper Archbishopric of Mainz.[169] The centre of gravity of persecution was shifting to Lower
Franconia.

SUMMARY

The wave of persecution in the years around 1590 covered almost the
whole region between the Alps in the south and the river Main in the north.
Almost all the political units in the region conducted trials for witchcraft;
witches were burned in most territories, in many the trials grew into
extensive persecutions; and in many states the majority of the county
courts were involved in witch trials, so that we can speak of a 'comprehen-

---

[163] For the ecclesiastical territories of Franconia in general: Spindler, *Handbuch*, III/1, 353–9, 219–22 (Endres).
[164] Längin, *Religion*, 137; Wittmann, 'Die Bamberger Hexenjustiz', 178f.; Merzbacher, *Die Hexenprozesse*, 53.   [165] Film 1156.
[166] Merzbacher, *Die Hexenprozesse*, 42; Film 901.
[167] Janssen and Pastor, *Culturzustände*, VIII, 669.
[168] Film 1779, Film 1308, Film 1751.   [169] Kunstmann, *Zauberwahn*, 31.

sive' coverage. Even in the few places where no witches were burned, numerous trials were held, as the example of the Free City of Augsburg shows.

The centre of gravity of persecution within the region at first moved from west to east, then from south to north. In 1587 it lay in Swabia, in 1589–91 in Swabia, Bavaria and southern Middle Franconia, in 1592–4 along the Danube and in Middle Franconia, in 1594–7 in northern Middle Franconia and southern Lower Franconia. The regional wave of persecution thus had a connection with the persecutions in the southwest in 1586–7, for it was from the southwest that the 'experts' were first called in. The executioner of Biberach played a key role in this initial phase, but as early as 1589 the region could provide its own competent headsmen, the executioners of Schongau, Lauingen, Oettingen and Eichstätt, who served all the territories as far as the Margravate of Bayreuth. In a broad semicircle the wave of persecution reached the Upper Archbishopric of Mainz (Amorbach, Aschaffenburg) by 1594, from where the tide of persecution began to flow back in 1596; during the persecution at Windsheim an executioner from Odenwald in Electoral Mainz was brought in. Between 1600 and 1630 Franconia along the Main was the persecution district *par excellence*, while the Protestant territories of Middle Franconia and the Catholic lands to the south of the Danube grew increasingly reluctant to become involved.

Important though they always were, it was not chiefly the denunciations that caused the wave of persecution to spread; in most cases local causes were decisive in beginning the persecution, while denunciations helped it to expand within a town or territory. The wave of persecution could only expand if the authorities accepted the persecution paradigm and kept witch trials under close supervision whenever they heard of them. It was impossible for a persecution to develop unless the authorities were involved, but the lower courts could avoid trials if they resolved complaints at their level. The example of persecution in adjoining territories influenced both subjects and their rulers. Villagers demanded that their superiors should follow the example of their neighbours and burn witches, governments followed the procedure adopted by their neighbouring territories, and often called in their executioners to conduct their trials. In many cases this allows the wave-like expansion of the persecution to be reconstructed in detail.

Often the beginning of the persecutions revealed a pent-up demand for persecution, which shows that no steps had been taken in the previous decades against those who had long been under suspicion as witches or sorcerers. In many cases earlier witch trials were raked up again, and often it is clear from the attached files of old cases that the suspects had been acquitted or released for lack of evidence (examples of this can be found in Rettenberg, Schongau and Garmisch). Even in those places where individuals had been put to death as witches in the previous two decades (Dillingen, Munich, Spalt, Rettenberg, Ellingen, Langenzenn) the old cases were less influential than the example of the adjoining territories, which seemed to be quite different in quantity and quality from the earlier domestic cases.

Contrary to a widespread expectation[170] the expansion of witch trials – at least during the wave of persecution in southeast Germany around 1590 – did not coincide geographically with any political, economic or confessional structures. Witch trials were held in both Catholic and Protestant territories, in secular and ecclesiastical lordships, in absolutist states and in those where the cathedral chapter or the Estates had retained some say, in the Free Cities and in the territorial states, in rich and poor districts, in places that suffered local catastrophes and in those that did not, in towns and in the countryside. The smaller noble territories, where decisions were in the hands of the ruler, were as willing to persecute witches as the Free Cities or the larger territories, where several colleges of councillors, jurists and theologians were consulted on the measures taken. This relative uniformity of persecution is one of the most astonishing findings of research into this wave of persecution.

Also surprising are the intense savagery of the persecutions, from which hardly any authority between the Alps and the Main managed to stand aloof, and the possibilities for differentiation which some of the authorities were able to exploit, in spite of pressure for persecution from their subjects. While the smaller Free City of Weissenburg was only able to avoid a massive persecution by enlisting the support of Nuremberg, the Prince-Abbot of Kempten was even willing to use military force to resist the pressure for persecution exerted by the Bishop of Augsburg.

Persecutions made heavy demands on the time of the authorities. The government of the Prince-Bishopric of Augsburg spent thirty-two days discussing persecution in 1589, forty-two days in 1591 and sixty-two days in 1592; the minutes of these discussions only reflect the deliberations and decisions of the full Court Council, and not the activity of individual members of the government, such as participation in hearings, study of documents, preparation of opinions and service on committees.

TRIGGERING FACTORS

GREATER SUSCEPTIBILITY AS A RESULT OF MISFORTUNE

In normal times people were not too ready to believe in the power of witches. Great natural catastrophes, earthquakes and wars were seen as

[170] Schormann, *Hexenprozesse*, (1977), 5.

direct divine punishments, and were no more blamed on witches than were the numerous minor mishaps in the home. Viewed over a period of many years, the literature of witchcraft concerned itself with the question of how far witches could influence the course of nature; could they, for example, cause severe storms? Normally their influence was regarded as limited in both time and space, and confined to a definite object.[171] This was still essentially the prevailing opinion around 1590. The greater part of the damage alleged to be caused by witches took the form of the bewitchment of individual children, cattle or horses, 'stolen' crops, milk, wine, corn and so on. Endless lists of such minor damage exist, which show that in most cases witches were accused of bringing misfortune on individuals, although the scarcely credible frequency of the accusations indicates a belief that witches had been growing more numerous in the previous decades. Normally, too, it seems to have been believed that witches kept to the rules of a society divided into estates, for otherwise many princes, counts, knights and dignitaries of the Church might have felt less secure.

In the decades before 1600 these limits to the power of witches became less clear-cut. Members of the ducal family in Bavaria blamed their illnesses on witchcraft, as did many bishops, and – how symbolic! – the Emperor Rudolf II (1576–1612) was widely regarded as either a sorcerer himself or the victim of sorcery. Persecutors constantly reiterated that the power of witches did not extend to persons in high office, but subjectively many of the noble judges felt that they had been bewitched: the judge of Griesbach had lost his cattle, the wife of the judge of Werdenfels had died, the Palatine Governor von Diemantstein believed that he had been bewitched.[172] Around 1590 witches were crossing both social and natural boundaries. They flew through the air, made themselves invisible or changed into animals, had the potential to be everywhere, except when they were kept at bay by relics, consecrated objects or counterspells. They caused harm not only by salves and poisons (*veneficae*) but by the mere exercise of their will, or their 'evil eye'. Finally, they were held to be capable of 'cooking' bad weather, and the damage caused by this 'witches' weather' could be very extensive: the harvest was destroyed in whole districts, hunger and dearth were blamed on them and even imposing buildings were not safe from them: in Freising the cathedral was so badly damaged that it was feared that the Bishop's palace and the cathedral would collapse into the Isar, all the windows in the palace were broken,[173] and in Munich the newly built tower of the church of St Michael, the triumphant symbol of the Counter-Reformation, collapsed. Such events

---

[171] Lehmann, *Hexenprozesse*, 21.
[172] Evans, *Rudolf II*, 135; Riezler, *Geschichte*, 196; Kuisl, *Die Hexen*, 37; HStAM, Hexenakten 16, fol. 124v; IV–BK (cf. List of trials in the German edition).
[173] Behringer, 'Hexenverfolgung', 352f.

directly affected the virulence of the persecutions of 1590. A correspondent of the Fuggers in Munich wrote:

> There has been such dreadful weather in the last few days that it has done not a little to further [the collapse of] the tower and building, for many are of the opinion that such unusual weather is caused by the accursed wicked women, and it would be very good to suppress them, and to spare nobody, rich or poor.[174]

There was no lack of events that could be blamed on witchcraft. In times of inflation, when diet deteriorated and the risk of disease increased, suspicions of witchcraft accumulated. Often they were directly associated with damage to crops, as at the beginning of the persecutions in Schongau and Garmisch; often 'unnatural' sickness or other events that are hard to attribute to inflation provided the impetus, so that one has to speak in terms of a general increase in susceptibility to the influence of witches in times of misfortune.

As contemporaries constantly lamented, witchcraft was not only the worst (*atrocissime*) but also the most secret (*occultissime*) of all crimes. Pacts or intercourse with the Devil, flight through the air and witches' sabbaths, even harmful sorcery itself, were all performed without witnesses. The only visible effects were God's punishments and the damage that was said to be caused by the witches, but could not be directly linked to them. The main question, therefore, was how the witches were to be recognised at all.

Our investigation of individual persecutions has shown that there was no difference in principle between the situations that triggered the greatest persecutions and those that led to lesser trials ending in only a few executions or in acquittals. Every persecution began with individual accusations of witchcraft and drew further accusations in its wake – apart from the denunciations made during the trials themselves. This section will discuss the problem of the 'first witches'. It will examine how they were recognised as witches, not on the basis of a theory but by analysing the trial records and the protocols of the Court Councils.

THE PHENOMENON OF THE WITCH

> It is a proverbial saying: as hateful and ugly as a witch
> (J. Bodin and J. Fischart, 1581)[175]

The theological, social-psychological and social-historical reasons why women in particular came to be identified as witches will not be discussed

---

[174] ÖNB Vienna, Cod. 8963, fol. 312r–v (11 May 1590).
[175] Bodin, *Daemonomania*, 163.

here.[176] We shall simply show from contemporary sources that there were quite specific expectations of what a witch was supposed to look like, and that these expectations significantly narrowed the field of potential witches. As a rule, though not absolutely without exceptions, at the beginning of a persecution the witch was expected to be an old and ugly woman.

In 1590, when the Bishop's Governor in Freising made enquiries about witches of the judge of the neighbouring Bavarian county court in Kranzberg, the Bavarian judge replied that the persons wanted were not known to him, but that an old cowherd with a red beard lived in the village of Garching, whose wife was often 'rather misshapen and scabby' in the face, and was suspected of stealing milk, because she sold more butterfat at the market in Munich than her own cows could produce.[177]

The population and the executioners tried to recognise witches from visible outward marks, as the *stigma diaboli* was hidden under clothing, and could not be seen until the trial had begun. One man, for example, swore that he recognised witches by their eyes, another claimed to identify them from their gestures, a third from their figure.[178]

In many cases the aged suspects themselves are recorded as complaining

[176] Cf. on this Schormann, *Hexenprozesse* (1981), 116–22; Paulus, *Hexenwahn*, 195–247; Wunder, *Hexenprozesse*, 187–9 puts forward the interesting thesis that the increase in accusations of witchcraft against women was connected with their role in production and reproduction, as sorcery was often connected with specifically female activities, e.g. food preparation. There were connections in this field in southeast Germany as well. The preponderance of women in trials for witchcraft obviously did not present a problem for contemporaries, either men or women. To that extent it would be a gross oversimplification to speak, as does Monter, *Witchcraft in France*, 122–4, of 'patriarchal social fears' which were supposedly projected onto old women. It should not be forgotten, in all these socio-historical and psychological interpretations, that many of these ideas went back to the pre-Christian Indo-European period, as early and high medieval glossaries from the region show. For example a tenth-century manuscript from Tegernsee translates *lamia* as *holzmuoia vel wildaz wip* (Franck, 'Geschichte', 618), and a twelfth century manuscript from Schaftlarn as *uneholdi* (*ibid.*, 619); the term *incubus* (masculine) is glossed as *waltschrato, holtdiuval, trut* and *alp* (*ibid.*, 624). In the pre-Christian period it seems that the idea of influencing the weather, damaging the crops, sorcery and nocturnal flight was at least associated with a picture that resembled that of the early modern witch as an old woman. Riezler, *Geschichte*, 11–29; Schmitz, *Bussbücher*, 25, 29, 44; Schmeller and Fromann, *Wörterbuch*, I, col. 1047, 1090 (from SBM, Clm. 14138: 'unholdin alias weiczenfarerin'; or Clm. 17736 of the eleventh century: 'Cum daemonum turba in similitudinem mulierum transformata, quam vulgaris stultitia hominum unholdam vocat certis noctibus equitare debere super quasdam bestias', with numerous parallels), 1497; *ibid.*, II, 1072–4. This does not, of course, mean that clerical antifeminism, as expressed in Sprenger and Institoris, *Der Hexenhammer*, I, 92–109, played no role. But in particular cases of witchcraft one can often establish that antifeminism must have been less important in everyday reality than in the literary tradition.

[177] HStAM, Hexenakten 9a, fol. 299.

[178] Eyes: Kunstmann, *Zauberwahn*, 76; gestures: StadtA Augsburg, Urgichtenakten 1590c (Anna Gsellin); figure: Riezler, *Geschichte*, 172.

that every old woman was now under suspicion.[179] At Nördlingen in 1593, a woman who was to be executed said that 'the same was being said of almost every woman'.[180] Age, sex and appearance alone, however, were not as a rule enough to brand a woman as a witch. Further characteristics had to be present, for example suspect actions or knowledge of magical things. A soothsayer admitted on record at Augsburg in 1590 that 'she no longer gave advice, as people rarely came to her now'. General mistrust focused on age and skill in soothsaying: 'if an old woman has some knowledge, right away she must be a witch'.[181]

Suspicious behaviour could also lead to accusations, as could chance events that pointed the finger of suspicion at an old woman. But at the beginning of the persecutions it seems to have been a general rule that suspicion did not fall on men or younger women, though there were exceptions (Oberstdorf, Nördlingen). Even during the persecutions old women were the chief targets of denunciations and may have made up about 80 per cent of the victims in 1590.[182] Yet appearance and individual abilities were not enough to trigger witch trials; special constellations of events had to be found first.

PUBLIC ACT, PUBLIC OUTCRY

Though witchcraft was the most secret of all crimes, often the cause and effect seemed to be so closely linked that the act of sorcery or witchcraft resembled a 'public and undoubted misdeed' (Article 16 of the *Carolina*) and attracted an immediate public suspicion of witchcraft.

The witchcraft trials in the court of Zusmarshausen (Bishopric of Augsburg) began with an apparently overt case of sorcery, which occurred at the meat market in Augsburg. A mother had put her eight-year-old daughter down for a moment while buying meat, and an old woman from Oberhausen, near Augsburg, gave the child a piece of bread. Soon afterwards the child went pale, began to gasp and breathe heavily, and her face swelled up before the eyes of the horrified crowd. The mob accused the old woman of witchcraft, the Bishop's administrator in Augsburg had her arrested and transferred to the district court of Zusmarshausen, to which she was subject. The incident took place on 6 June 1590. The very next day the Court Council in Dillingen ordered an inquisition for witchcraft against the woman, and ten days after her arrest the executioner Christoph

179 The seventy-year-old Anna Widmann from Hemau said at her trial in 1618, 'dass die Kinder allen alten Leute Unholden haissen'. Film 1160, 79.
180 Wulz, 'Nördlinger Hexenprozesse' (1937–8), 58.
181 StadtA Augsburg, Urgichtenakten 1590 c (Cath. Pretzelerin).
182 The women's share in this first wave of witch hunting was probably even greater but cannot be precisely established because of the gaps in the sources.

of Biberach, who was still carrying on a persecution at Schwabmünchen, was ordered to travel to Zusmarshausen to torture the old woman. On 12 September she was condemned to be burned, but by then she had denounced numerous other women of Oberhausen.[183] Three months later the first of the women she had denounced was burned, and the persecution at Zusmarshausen continued into 1591. Some of the denunciations spread to nearby Burgau, Göggingen and Augsburg.[184]

The persecution at Nördlingen also began with events that seemed to eye-witnesses to be obvious cases of witchcraft. A children's nurse, under whose care all three children of a family had died, was suspected of witchcraft. Her refusal to approach the deathbed of one of the children had already aroused suspicion. When she was finally compelled to approach the bier, the 'sign' occurred: the body of the child began to bleed again, an event which had been taken as proof of the presence of the murderer as long ago as the *Nibelungenlied*. This 'bier test' transformed the popular suspicion into a certainty, and the nursemaid was accused as a witch.[185]

One may regard such events as chance coincidences, but there is undoubtedly a certain statistical probability that they were repeated. Amazingly, even in 1590, trials that began with such events did not necessarily end in executions. In the Free City of Augsburg a butcher's wife visited a bath-house with her child in 1589. The child urinated unintentionally on a woman employed in the bath-house, who asked the name of the child. Soon afterwards the child's chest began to swell, and the butcher's wife publicly accused the bath-house attendant, a widow, of witchcraft 'not only in the public bath, but in the neighbourhood, at the butcher's and elsewhere', and this caused grave difficulties for the attendant and for the master of the bath-house. The council of Augsburg, unlike the Bishop's administrator, critically examined the credibility of the accuser and concluded that she behaved 'as if she were not right in the head'. The bath-house attendant, who had been the subject of such serious charges, was released without being threatened with torture, and her accuser was forbidden to make further accusations against her, on pain of punishment.[186]

---

[183] HStAM, Hochstift Augsburg, NA, Akten no. 1203, fol. 374f., fol. 387v, fol. 410v, fol. 544, fol. 575v, fol. 706.
[184] ÖNB Vienna, Cod. 8963, fol. 851–4; StadtA Augsburg, Urgichtenakten 1591 a (Maria Köchin).
[185] Wulz, 'Nördlinger Hexenprozesse' (1937–8), 50ff. A similar beginning can be found in a trial at Hemau in Pfalz-Neuburg: an old woman who had been harassed by children in front of her house, threw water at them to drive them away. One of the children died a few days later, Film 1160, 49.
[186] StadtA Augsburg, Urgichtenakten 1589 (Sabina Wagnerin/Catharina Burkartin). *Ibid.*, Strafbuch 1588–96, fol. 49v. We often find in cases of secret sorcery that gestures, verbal threats, even merely suspected feelings of hatred or envy were taken as circumstantial evidence of or as motives for witchcraft. Cf. on the beginning of the witch hunt at Ellingen in 1590, Behringer, 'Hexenverfolgung', 348.

A similar case in Dillingen might have had a more dangerous outcome. A student accused a woman of 'doing something to him in the bath', after which he had developed a 'strong gripe'. The doctor diagnosed an 'unnatural' sickness, and the woman probably only escaped with her life because the student withdrew his charge and convinced the court that the gripe was the fault of his unreasonable diet. The woman was again denounced as a witch during the persecution of 1591.[187]

CHILDREN AND FOOLS

Children and fools tell the truth
(proverb)

As a rule it was dangerous to utter suspicions of witchcraft, for every unprovable accusation rebounded on the accuser. Unless it was a case of an overt act, therefore, victims were reluctant to bring charges before the authorities, but tried instead to counter the sorcery by using traditional means. Two groups could not exercise this self- control, and it was no coincidence that they often provoked trials and persecutions, either by incriminating themselves or by accusing others, mostly old women. The statements of children and 'fools' give an undistorted reflection of contemporary points of view on witchcraft, by which they felt threatened or even bewitched. These genuine self-accusations, which were not obtained by torture or by psychological pressure during an interrogation, posed the most difficult problems for opponents of persecution until well into the eighteenth century; as early as the time of Johann Weyer, the voluntary confessions of such people formed the central problem for his argument.[188] For apologists of persecution voluntary confessions were always the surest proof of the correctnes of the fully developed theory of witchraft, for the fantasies of children and 'fools' did not stop at sorcery, but included the more spectacular components of the crime: flight, pacts and intercourse with the Devil and witches' sabbaths.

The great persecution in the episcopal courts 'along the road' (the districts of Bobingen, Schwabmünchen and Buchloe) began in 1589 with the fantasies of a fourteen year old boy from Bobingen. The boy claimed that he had regularly flown with his cousin to witches' sabbaths, and knew the women who were always bewitching the cattle. As the boy accused several women by name, he was arrested and interrogated by the Guardian of Bobingen. On 20 March 1589 the official reported to the government of the Bishopric at Dillingen,

---

[187] HStAM, Hochstift Augsburg, NA, Akten no. 1204, fol. 538v.
[188] Weyer, *De praestigiis Daemonum*, foreword.

as strange claims are made by Hansen Vischer's young 14 year old son Bernhard, that he has a cousin Hansen, who led him wildly to strange places, that he knew many of the women whom he had seen there especially from Bobingen, who do not dance but only pluck fowl, item that the boy . . . claimed to know and say where the cattle were harmed, where and through whom such a thing happened.[189]

The judge of Bobingen clearly had little inclination to hold a witch trial, for he added that the child was 'both simple minded and of an evil countenance'. The government of the Bishopric was not put off by this, but ordered an inquisition against two of the accused women. The investigation proved that the two were in fact generally suspected, and that several cases of harmful sorcery had been noticed in the villages. The boy, who had meanwhile been 'beaten with the rod' several times, stuck to his charges. In May the government ordered the arrest of the two suspects, both old women, one of them the widow of a mason, the other a wealthy peasant.[190] The trial was removed from Bobingen to Schwabmünchen, and the executioner Hans of Biberach, who had proved his skill in the persecutions at Sonthofen-Rettenberg and Dillingen, was entrusted with the tortures. When the first woman confessed that she was a witch and denounced others, the executioner was engaged for a whole year. The persecution spread to include at least forty five persons, of whom at least twenty seven were burned as witches.

The role of children in triggering witch trials has hardly been given its due in the secondary literature, yet it can be seen that their fantasies were important in many spectacular persecutions. We may mention the beginning of the trials in the Electorate of Trier in 1585, at Ellwangen in 1611, Würzburg in 1628, the first execution in the Free City of Augsburg in 1625, the last mass trials in southwest Germany and in Sweden, Massachusetts and Bavaria.[191] Statements made by a child also played

---

[189] HStAM, Hochstift Augsburg, NA, Akten no. 1202, fol. 216f.

[190] *Ibid.*, fol. 409, 458, 511v.

[191] Duhr, *Geschichte der Jesuiten*, II/2, 501–5; *ibid.*, I, 742; Baschwitz, *Hexen*, 318, 329, 388f.; Riezler, *Geschichte*, 195; Wittmann, 'Die Bamberger Hexenjustiz', 214. Particularly from the second half of the seventeenth century the number of children in the trials increased so greatly that an observer wrote: 'Bedenklich ist, dass wenn man der Hexen Gesellschaft betrachtet, dass man nichts anderes darinnen findet als lauter Canaillen-Volk, Bettler, oder armer Leute Kinder von zehen, zwölf und fünfzehn Jahren.' J.F. Rübel, *Systematische Abhandlung von denen fast allgemeinen eingerissenenen Irrthümern betreffend die Besizung des Menschen vom Teufel, Hexerey (. . .)*, n.p., 1758, 131. Once denunciations were no longer believed, fools and children remained. Cf. chapter V. E. Caulfield, 'Pediatric Aspects of the Salem Witchcraft Tragedy', *American Journal for the Diseases of Children*, 65 (1943), 788–802; M. Tramer, 'Kinder im Hexenglauben und Hexenprozess des Mittelalters', *Acta Paedopsychiatrica. Zeitschrift für Kinderpsychiatrie*, 11 (1945), 140–9, 180–7. Other references in Kamen, *Iron Century*, 244. The contemporary *Tractat von der verführten Kinder Zauberey*, Aschaffenburg 1629, could only see it as a sign of 'Göttlichen Providenz', *ibid.*, fol. 4.

an important part in the persecution at Ingolstadt in 1590.[192]

The effects of mental disturbances or psychological illnesses in the origin of witch trials are better known. As early as 1563 Johann Weyer had expressed the view that those who believed themselves to be witches 'have been led by the nose by Satan in their crazed imagination and fantasy'.[193] The more exact psychological classification of the various forms of 'folly', the subject of a whole branch of witchcraft research,[194] will not detain us here.

In general three groups of 'fools' tended to provoke witchcraft trials: those who thought they were witches, those who believed they had supernatural gifts that enabled them to recognise witches, and the 'possessed'. The third group was dangerous because of the widespread view that possession was caused by witches, who induced a demon to enter the body of their enemy. In the Catholic rite of exorcism the victim of possession was explicitly asked if the demon had entered his or her body on the instructions of a witch. As exorcists commonly also asked the name of the witch, exorcism repeatedly led to trials for witchcraft.[195]

The persecution at Nördlingen in 1589 was triggered by a woman who thought that she was possessed, and on the other hand also had traits of a witch herself. The affair of Ursula Haiderin of Nördlingen is almost a test case for the tolerance of the Free City towards social and mental deviants. Like most of the 'possessed', Haiderin was a relatively young woman. She was one of the poorest of the poor in the city, and had neither property nor relatives; she also suffered from physical and mental fits and seizures. Her mother and her father, who had been a local carrier, were long dead. For years the woman had had the impression of a 'tumbling and rumbling' in her head. At times she was unable to speak or hear. Ursula Haiderin thought she was possessed, but suffered from struggles with the Devil that went beyond the normal bounds of diabolical possession; in her imagination the Devil often visited her at night in the form of a peasant lad called 'Papperlin'. She had sexual relations with him in this shape.

Ursula Haiderin had already told other women of her lover before the witch trials began, but they had only laughed at her. They made fun of her by asking about her lover, and it was generally agreed that the woman was mad; she was called 'Papperlin's fool',[196] but no more significance was attached to her foolish words. Not until after the events connected with the 'bier test',[197] mentioned above, did Ursula Haiderin's confes-

[192] Riezler, *Geschichte*, 192.   [193] Weyer, *De praestigiis Daemonum*, foreword.
[194] Snell, *Hexenprozesse*; Schoenemann, 'Witch-Hunt' (for further specialised literature). Wolfgang Behringer, 'Kinderhexenprozesse. Zur Rolle von Kindern in der Geschichte der Hexenverfolgungen', in *Zeitschrift für historische Forschung*, 16 (1989), 31–47.
[195] Ernst, *Teufelsaustreibungen*, 20, 24; Duhr, *Geschichte der Jesuiten*, I, 738.
[196] Wulz, 'Nördlinger Hexenprozesse', 52.   [197] *Ibid.*, 52f.

sions gain plausibility. She had an attack of possession at the home of a relation of one of the dead children, and admitted in the presence of witnesses that she had killed the children by 'smearing on' a salve – the usual method chosen by witches. Only then was she reported to the authorities as a witch.

After the hearings of witnesses had confirmed the statements of the plaintiff, Ursula Haiderin's trial began. In her mental confusion, she now withdrew her previous confessions but at the same time told the court of her flights through the air and her relations with the Devil. The council decided to put her to torture. Under torture she was repeatedly asked about her 'accomplices' at the witches' sabbaths. All the women she named were arrested in the following months and burned as witches.[198] Ursula Haiderin herself was burned to death on 15 May 1590, the first victim at Nördlingen, six months after the trial had begun, with two of the women she had first denounced.

Women accused themselves of witchcraft in other persecutions elsewhere in the region. In 1590 a woman confessed voluntarily at Schongau, without being asked. Her village had not been previously affected by denunciations, so far as one can judge from the trial records.[199] Under the impression of the persecutions in the neighbouring court of Schwabmünchen, a young woman subject of the chapter of Augsburg, an unemployed servant girl, accused herself of witchcraft. Her trial in the capitular court at Dinkelscherben brought further denunciations in its wake. At Grossaitingen, another of the chapter's courts, a woman was burned as a witch as a result. The further course of this case cannot be reconstructed.[200]

A special role in the history of witchcraft trials was played by those institutions where children, 'fools' and old people were concentrated: orphanages, educational institutions of all kinds (e.g. Jesuit schools and seminaries), hospitals and nunneries. Duhr has collected examples of diabolical possession and accusations of witchcraft in Jesuit schools and orphanages at Bamberg, Würzburg, Aschaffenburg, Eichstätt, Munich, Ingolstadt and Neuburg in the early seventeenth century.[201] Like possessed nuns[202] they do not seem to have played any recognisable role in the persecution of 1590, when the typical witch was still expected to be an older woman.

The case was very different in the town hospitals. As early as 1590 they were a constant source of suspicions of witchcraft in many towns. We have

---

[198] *Ibid.*, 59.   [199] StadtA Munich, Hist, Ver. Urk. 2048.
[200] HStAM, Hochstift Augsburg, NA, Akten no. 1203, fol. 511; *ibid.*, no. 1204, fol. 412, 450v.   [201] Duhr, *Geschichte der Jesuiten*, II/2, 500–5.
[202] A. Memminger, *Das verhexte Kloster. Nach den Akten dargestellt*, Würzburg 1904; Baschwitz, *Hexen*, 222–34.

evidence of this from Dillingen, Ingolstadt, Freising and Munich, in each of which hospital inmates were executed for witchcraft.

Leaving aside self-accusations, we can say that as a rule denunciations by children and 'fools' affected older women who had long been under suspicion. In 1587 a seventy-year-old woman fled from the hospital at Dillingen, after 'unnatural' disease had broken out there, because she had already been accused of witchcraft in her home village.[203] The peculiarity of such incidents seems to have been that they articulated and reinforced existing suspicions to such a degree that witch trials could be provoked.

THREATS FULFILLED

Sufficient indication of sorcery 44. Item if someone . . . threatens to use sorcery on another and works the like on the person threatened . . .

(*Constitutio Criminalis Carolina*)

One of the few possibilities of proving a connection between witches and harmful sorcery was given by threats that were actually followed by misfortune. Numerous examples can be found in contemporary texts. The *Carolina* of 1532 referred to this connection as adequate grounds for the use of torture, as did the Ingolstadt opinion on witchcraft of 1590.[204] Taken as a whole threats were one of the two most important triggers of witch trials (popular magical practices being the other), for unlike vague suspicions they lent a complaint of witchcraft plausibility in the eyes of the populace and the authorities alike.[205]

Threats were important in the persecutions of 1590. As so often, the threats actually uttered in practice were distinguished from those that the theory of the persecutioners seems to expect. For direct threats of sorcery were rare, in most cases they remained vague or simply warnings that God's justice would not suffer a wrong to go unpunished. Occasionally a simple prediction was interpreted as a threat. During the persecutions in the Bishopric of Freising, where weather spells were important, the remarks of an old woman after a violent thunderstorm led to the expansion of the inquisition into witchcraft. The city judge reported to the Bishop's Governor:

On the next Sunday evening there was a very violent shower, and all kinds of talk, and some people let themselves be heard saying that we

---

[203] HStAM, Hexenakten 16, fol. 11. In the case of children it was often simply women relatives, as shown by the trial of a child for witchcraft, which led to the first execution of a witch at Augsburg in 1625. StadtA Augsburg, Urgichtenakten 1625 (Maria Braunin).

[204] HStAM, Hexenakten 1, Prod. 1, fol. 6 (§4 on how witchcraft is to be recognised).

[205] Radbruch, *Kaiser*, 50.

could expect a greater and more violent storm this week . . . and so there was some suspicion of these women, so that it is suspected that they caused this weather . . . [206]

The summer of 1590 was unusually hot. The chronicles record that the corn harvest began on 10 July. The thunderstorm at Freising on 4 June was soon followed by another, so that the 'threats' of the old woman appeared to be fulfilled. She was arrested and handed over to the executioner, who was to torture her and look for the *stigma diaboli*.

A woman's predictions about storms and the prospects for the harvest also helped to start the persecutions at Schongau, at least, here too there were predictions that there would no more good weather that year.[207] The villagers concluded that she could influence the weather, and in the course of the persecution the woman, the wife of the judge of Schwabsoien, was considered to be one of the chief culprits behind the damage to crops caused by the thunderstorms of the past year.

Actual or alleged threats were often made to the health of man or beast. In a village near Hindelang (in the district of the court of Sonthofen-Rettenberg), a woman was suspected of witchcraft following a quarrel between neighbours. A seven-year-old child stole pears from a neighbour's garden, and the owner of the pear tree threatened that she would soon 'salve the pears so that he must not steal many more of them'. Not long afterwards the child was struck suddenly lame, and was confined to his bed for ten years. The desperate parents increasingly suspected witchcraft on the part of their neighbour, and tried to force her to withdraw the spell.[208]

The great persecution at Ellingen began with a vague threat of witchcraft.

This execution or rooting out began in such a way. A poor serving maid who was not willing to stay any longer in the service of her mistress at Ellingen, offered to serve another, and had agreed with her for the coming term. When she came home again, and told her of this, her mistress was rather unwilling, and a neighbour who happened to be present scolded the woman, saying: you should not have done it, and you will not have any more good luck. The next night the same neighbour came to the maid in bed, gave her a pinch in the arm, from which she soon began to suffer inhumanly great pain in the arm, and because she says that this woman said such words, and that she came to her by night and gave her a pinch, she could only think that she had caused her such pain. When this became known, the said Lord [Walbrecht von

[206] HStAM, Hexenakten 9a, fol. 918.
[207] Schorer, *Chronik*, 111, on the harvest date; the positive prognosis: StadtA Munich, Hist. Ver. Urk, 2018.   [208] HStAM, Hochstift Augsburg, NA, Akten no. 6737, fol. 126vff.

Schwalbach of the Teutonic Order's Commandery of Ellingen: WB] had her taken into custody, and she not only admitted the devilish sorcery herself, but also revealed others in the same place . . .[209]

Remarkably, the threats cannot be classified in a particular social context, as some anthropologically oriented historians have appeared to accept. Even if we are unwilling to dismiss as implausible Stone's suspicion that 'witchcraft was the weapon of the weak against the strong',[210] we must conclude from the sources we have investigated, that a difference in social level between the person uttering the threat and its intended victim was by no means a precondition.

At least in 1590 all threats which appeared to have been fulfilled, without a direct cause and effect being demonstrable, seem to have been regarded as potential grounds for an accusation of witchcraft.

SOOTHSAYERS

Of the reporting of those who engage in sorcery and soothsaying.
21. Item no one shall be imprisoned or put to the torture on the report of those who presume to practise soothsaying through sorcery or other arts
. . .   (*Constitutio Criminalis Carolina*)

Corroboration by a soothsayer was an important traditional method of dealing with suspicions of sorcery in popular magic. It was not applied in judicial proceedings for witchcraft, since the oracular pronouncements of soothsayers were themselves regarded as sorcery by the authorities. Nevertheless, in the persecutions of 1590 there are repeated signs that soothsayers were present in the background of accusations of witchcraft, and had given the plaintiffs the first subjective certainty about their suspicions.

This is clear in the persecutions in the County of Werdenfels (Bishopric of Freising), which began in 1589. The suspicion of the 'first witch', Ursula Klöck of Obergrainau, arose from the activities of the soothsayer Mang Resenberger, who had almost provoked a trial for witchcraft eight years previously, though the government in Freising had stepped in to forbid it. A fisherman who lived in a remote spot visited the soothsayer because he felt that he was being persecuted by a witch. Resenberger sold the fisherman the advice to boil water in a pot until the pot burst. He was to throw the potsherds in the Eibsee (below the Zugspitze), and then the guilty witch would make herself known to him. Soon after he had performed the ritual, the fisherman was visited by Ursula Klöck, whom he had already suspec-

[209] Behringer, 'Hexenverfolgung', 348.
[210] Stone, 'Disenchantment', 21.

ted of causing the sickness of his cattle. Presumably the fisherman had spoken of his suspicion before, since the woman came to complain to him about it. The fisherman's suspicions became certainties and the judge of Werdenfels also thought these were sufficient grounds to begin a trial for witchcraft.[211]

The arrest of the 'first witch', as so often, gave the signal to the populace for further accusations. Two women were arrested at Garmisch even before torture had begun. Once again the suspicion can be traced back to two soothsayers, who had already corroborated it as long ago as 1581 to such an extent that there had been continual quarrels about it during the 1580s, until the beginning of the persecution in 1589 provided the opportunity for a renewal of the accusation. Then 'unnatural' diseases had been the reason to consult the famous soothsayer Els of Ettringen, in the Bavarian Lordship of Schwabeck.[212] She had confirmed the suspicion of witchcraft that the Garmisch soothsayer Resenberger, a peasant and trader, had pointed at a seventy-year-old woman from Garmisch, 'a strange looking person'.[213] An alliance of victims kept the suspicions alive, until the woman, by now eighty, was arrested as a witch in 1589 and burned six months later.

Soothsayers were also in the background of the persecution at Schongau. Women had been identified as witches by soothsayers as early as 1575 and 1587, the first by the executioner of Kaufbeuren, who was knowledgeable in the matter, and the second by Els of Ettringen. Twice the Abbot of Steingaden attempted to save the life of the accused, and his first intercession at least was successful.[214] Both the accused had already been under suspicion, and the soothsayers had been so persuasive that accusations had been made. We can also find soothsayers behind the great persecution of 1589–91,[215] but their precise share in triggering it is impossible to determine.

The first persecution in the region, in the district court of Sonthofen-Rettenberg, was provoked by the soothsayer Conrad Stöckhlin. This unusual case will be discussed elsewhere.[216] The records of hearings in the Free City of Augsburg make the central function of soothsayers in popular magic very clear. Besides selling love charms and finding lost or stolen objects, one of their chief roles was to confirm suspicions of witchcraft and to identify the witches. An old woman soothsayer who was often examined by the city court, had corroborated several suspicions of witchcraft through crystal gazing and oracles, and was then reported to the authori-

[211] Kuisl, *Die Hexen*, 7–10; *Carolina* §21: Radbruch, *Kaiser*, 38.
[212] Kuisl, *Die Hexen*, 7f.   [213] Riezler, *Geschichte*, 175.
[214] Her, 'Ein Hexenprozess', 128ff., from StadtA Munich, Hist. Ver. Urk. 2029–42.
[215] StadtA Munich, Hist. Ver. Urk. 2108.   [216] Cf. chapter 3, pp. 158–82.

ties. She confessed that she had learned her art thirty years before from Els of Ettringen.[217]

Soothsayers were at the height of their prestige in town and country at the end of the sixteenth century, as we see from a comparison of numerous individual statements in the records of hearings. The witchfinder Stigler, who was executed at Nuremberg, was obviously hard pressed to cope with demand. He deposed that 'many people had come to him, and one had asked here and the other there, whether she had bewitched someone'. The council was forced to admit that the 'the people had flocked' to the witchfinder because of his fame.[218] In 1591 a soothsayer of Augsburg confessed that he had cured about a hundred persons of 'the witches' shot' (lumbago) in one year, and this figure gives only a vague indication of his total clientele. The consultation of soothsayers, crystal gazers, palmists, gypsies and so on was by no means confined to the lower classes. The soothsayers questioned in Augsburg numbered Count Friedrich of Oettingen, the Margrave of Burgau, several members of the house of Fugger and patricians from the Free City (von Stetten, Rehlinger) among their clients, and these names are no more than a random sample, since most of the consultations would not have been recorded on paper. The possibility of 'soothsaying' was widely admitted, and the services of soothsayers were in demand. Naturally, people were equally willing to accept the truth of the facts prophesied or revealed, including the identification of witchcraft.[219]

As a rule the soothsayers confirmed the suspicions of their clients in sibylline form, and avoided naming names. They thereby lent existing suspicions greater credibility. Yet many of the oracles employed were liable to arouse new suspicions, for example if it was predicted that the first person who wanted to borrow something or who would be met on a given day, was a witch.

POPULAR MAGIC AS AN INDICATOR (SUSPECT SKILLS, SUSPECT BEHAVIOUR, SUSPECT POSSESSIONS)

Sufficient indication of sorcery 44. Item if anyone presumes to teach others sorcery . . . or goes about with such suspect things, gestures, words and manners which are signs of sorcery. . .

(Constitutio Criminalis Carolina)

---

[217] StadtA Augsburg, Urgichtenakten 1589 (Maria Marquartin).
[218] Kunstmann, Zauberwahn, 74, 77. Representing numerous other examples, Muck, Geschichte, I, 501–3; ibid., II, 55–9. Cf. also chapter 2, pp. 65–88, in which reference is made to the central role of the soothsayers in the popular magical culture of the region. In general Thomas, Religion (1980 edn), 252–300.
[219] StadtA Augsburg, Urgichtenakten 1591 (Maria Köchin). On the participation of the upper classes in 'popular magic', ibid., Urgichtenakten 1589 (Maria Marquartin); ibid., Urgichtenakten 1590 (Maria Schönauerin).

Since the Enlightenment, writers on witchcraft have been eager to assume that the great majority of those burned as witches were 'innocent'. If one applies the fully developed theory of witchcraft as the yardstick, this is certainly true. That individuals could subjectively have believed they had made a pact with the Devil, has always been admitted.[220] Yet such phenomena were irrelevant in triggering witch trials or persecutions, since they could not be proved. The case was quite different with the very real expressions of popular magic which theologians at the end of the sixteenth century were increasingly ready to stigmatise as 'sorcery', whether they had a veneer of Christianity or not. As the possibilities of administrative and pastoral control became more effective, educated contemporaries paid more attention to these heterodox or downright unchristian practices. Sorcery was practised, and on a massive scale.[221] We have already referred to the way in which sorcery was criminalised in the second half of the century.[222] For contemporaries real attempts at sorcery were circumstantial evidence of the much more serious crime of witchcraft, and around 1590 there was even a tendency to equate sorcery with witchcraft.

Suspect skills and behaviour or the possession of suspect objects did not directly provoke any of the great persecutions, but were present in the background of most trials as circumstantial evidence. They represented the substratum of many accusations of witchcraft, and their role in arousing suspicion was almost as important as their significance in the trials, where they formed the most important evidence after confessions.

Paragraph 4 of the Ingolstadt opinion on witchcraft of 1590, following Binsfeld, deals with the question, 'How witchcraft is to be recognised?' A very broad definition states that:

> *maleficium* or witchcraft, however, is a work which exceeds the usual powers and strength of man, and so it is performed by the aid of the Devil and the free collaboration of human will.

The explanation of this definition shows that the witches' skills were by no means restricted to *maleficium*, but included all the other possible skills that exceeded the 'normal' capacities of a human being, even if they did not cause any harm. The following five 'types' of diabolical work were distinguished, all of them being taken as indicators of witchcraft:

---

[220] E.g. Riezler, *Geschichte*, 158. *Carolina*, §44: Radbruch, *Kaiser*, 50.

[221] The city physician of Hall, Guarinoni, a pupil of the Jesuits and a strict Catholic, upheld the view that superstition was stronger among the people than belief. J. Bücking, *Kultur und Gesellschaft in Tirol um 1600. Des Hippolytus Guarinonius' 'Grewel der Verwüstung Menschlichen Geschlechts' als kulturgeschichtliche Quelle des frühen 17. Jahrhunderts*, Lübeck/Hamburg 1968, 181. A parish priest from a village near Munich speaks of his 'Bauern mit ihrem gleichsam heidnischen Leben und Aberglauben'. K. Hobmair, *Hachinger Heimatbuch*, Oberhaching 1979, 181. See note 218.

[222] Cf chapter 2, pp. 65–114.

Either . . . that they wish to learn to know hidden or strange things (if they are beyond human mental and physical powers),
how to inflict sickness or disease miraculously,
or on the other hand bring good health,
or false and deceitful phenomena and appearances of sorcery,
or movements and changes of things and miraculous effects which are impossible to ordinary human reason.
Therefore witches can be recognised by several similar arguments or signs . . . if anything similar is done which belongs to one of the types, *genera* or kinds of the five works of the Devil named above . . .[223]

All the normal forms of popular magic – soothsaying, predictions, health and love charms etc. – were included in this wide definition as circumstantial evidence for witchcraft and the existence of a pact with the Devil.

This definition was diametrically opposed to the way in which popular 'sorcerers' themselves understood their activities. All the soothsayers and sorcerers who appeared before the courts continued to maintain[224] that harmless magic was a permissible exercise of natural skills, and felt no sense of wrongdoing whatever. The magical knowledge of many of the lower levels of the population was very extensive. Without the aid of writing, the accused women could remember long rhymed formulae, which reveal a rich repertoire of skills.[225] Naturally only the harmless spells were entered in the court records, to prove the harmlessness of magical activities. But the transition to black magic was easy, and the use of skulls, bones, black hens etc., reveals that the 'natural arts' of the popular sorcerers were not quite as harmless as they would have had the authorities believe.

It was therefore not so far fetched for the Bavarian instruction on procedure in witchcraft trials of 1590 to require the homes of the sorcerers to be searched for suspect objects, such as 'poison, hosts, toads, human limbs, wax images stuck with pins and needles',[226] for these objects and many more were repeatedly found when houses were searched. Hosts were found in the homes of the witches of Werdenfels,[227] and one of the witches of Schongau was found to have no fewer than forty-eight suspect objects, dozens of amulets, magic bags, salves, roots, oddly shaped stones, hosts, a small wooden horse whose legs were bound with twine, wax dolls, cryptic

[223] HStAM, Hexenakten 1, Prod. 1, fol. 5–7.
[224] Cf. Ammann, 'Die Hexenprozesse'; Markmiller, 'Die Beschwörungen'. Perneder, *Von Straff*, fol. 7.
[225] StadtA Augsburg, Urgichtenakten 1589 (Maria Marquartin); *ibid.*, 1590 (Anna Stauderin); they reveal a considerable repertoire.
[226] StadtA Munich, Stadtgericht 952 A 2, fol. 15.
[227] Kuisl, *Die Hexen*, 14. EOAM, Hochstift Freising, GR-Prot. no. 8, fol. 20.

characters on slips of paper, papers of powders, bundles of herbs, magical plants, feathers, human skin, animal bones, coal, pitch, old iron, axle grease, roots knotted in leather, rotten wood sewn into bags, pots, pans and buckets full of objects whose purpose was not recognisable, and which therefore could only be of magical significance.[228] Such mysterious objects repeatedly aroused the fear and suspicion of neighbours who had suffered any kind of apparently 'unnatural' ill luck.

Suspect behaviour could also arouse mistrust in a climate of tension, especially if its repetition seemed to suggest a magical rite. A woman of Freising was observed to walk around a church several times for no apparent reason. The city judge reported to the Governor that

> item we have found that the witch early yesterday morning, Monday, walked four times around the church of St George, and behaved as if she had lost something and were looking for it. Why it happened is not yet known at this time . . .[229]

The same woman was also under suspicion because she had left the city several times on the same day and visited a certain cornfield. Particular suspicion fell on those who were seen in the open field during a violent thunderstorm, as sources from Freising, Nördlingen and Schongau illustrate. A woman of Schongau who was seen in the vicinity of a witches' dancing place (the Peissenberg) during a severe hail shower aggravated the suspicion by apologising for it without being asked; her excuse later proved to be false.[230]

Often suspect behaviour was only recognised as such after the event. If bad luck or harm befell someone, the victim would ponder who could have been responsible. After a child died, for example, a man from the neighbourhood of Höchstädt recalled an old woman who, whenever she begged for alms, 'always came near the child in the cradle in the room, and he and his wife had not liked to see her and it had frightened them every time'.[231] A peasant of Peiting whose crops had been destroyed by hail, while his neighbour's fields had been spared, remembered that he had sent a beggar woman away empty-handed, while his neighbour had given her alms.[232] Although there were no threats to suggest cause and effect, witchcraft seemed plausible in this case.

In 1590 those at risk were persons who were known to have certain magical skills, and who had a specialised function within popular magic: soothsayers, healers etc. Astonishigly, no systematic steps were taken against this group of people, and they were only investigated when specific

---

[228] StadtA Munich, Hist. Ver. Urk. 2069.   [229] HStAM, Hexenakten 9 a, fol. 320.
[230] StadtA Munich, Hist. Ver. Urk. 2067.   [231] HStAM, Hexenakten 16, fol. 57f.
[232] StadtA Munich, Hist. Ver. Urk. 2067.

accusations were made. As far as we can judge from trial records, popular magic survived the great persecutions of 1590 intact, and no feeling of guilt seems to have been found among the soothsayers and sorcerers. Accusations against them seem to have been made only if they were held responsible for particular misfortunes, or if their accusers felt threatened by them.

In Augsburg, for example, a seventy-five-year-old woman, who supported herself by practising soothsaying, was reported because she had told several people, without being asked, that they would be threatened by 'wicked people', that is, witches; of course, there was speculation about the source of her knowledge. A godmother of the old woman had been burned as a witch in Württemberg, and many witnesses claimed to have heard her describe herself as riding on a fork. Her ambiguous utterances caused alarm among the people. She had said before several witnesses that 'nine maidens went to the horsefair and only two of them were women', which her audience took to mean that she accused the other seven of being witches. Several witnesses' statements added to the suspicion against the old woman, so that in the end she was tortured several times, before being released[233] 'against the hope of many', as a correspondent of the Fuggers wrote from Augsburg. The old woman had made such a good living from soothsaying that she planned to buy a house near Augsburg after her release.[234]

Popular magic with its ceremonies and trappings was the background for many suspicions of witchcraft, but like all the other circumstantial evidence it was not an unequivocal proof.

POPULAR BELIEFS

Quite apart from popular magical practices with a 'practical' object, certain magical assumptions firmly believed by the people were bound to come into conflict with the new and more rationalist-deductive religious thinking of the later sixteenth century. Many of the traditional assumptions were very hard to reconcile with schematic confessional doctrines, and quite at odds with official religion. In general this meant world-views that peopled the world with beings other than man, angels and demons, as well as all the 'natural magic' that permeated peasant culture with its rites and customs, and formed the background to the luxuriant growth of popular magic in the later sixteenth century.[235] But there were also par-

---

233 StadtA Augsburg, Urgichtenakten 1590 (Cath. Pretzelerin).
234 ÖNB Vienna, Cod. 8963, fol. 613r–v.
235 Muchembled, 'Witches', 63–93, 101–7. C. Ginzburg, 'Volksbrauch, Magie und Religion', in R. Romano (ed.), *Die Gleichzeitigkeit des Ungleichzeitigen. Fünf Studien zur Geschichte Italiens*, Frankfurt am Main 1980, 226–304, esp. 265–88. Janssen and Pastor, *Culturzustände*, VIII, 527–37.

ticular popular beliefs that theologians could not understand, and there-fore could only dismiss as diabolically inspired. A well-known example is the case of the *Benandanti* in Friuli, the 'good-walkers', a popular cult which the Venetian Inquisition so successfully reinterpreted as a form of witchcraft that its own practitioners came to believe the charge.[236] The development of the elaborated concept of witchcraft made it dangerous to believe in the possibility of flight or contact with non-human entities. When even a Johannes Kepler could be involved in a brush with persecutors because of his utopian literary fantasy about a flight to the moon,[237] this applied even more to ordinary members of the public and their naive ideas about the 'wild hunt' or the 'raging army' or wandering 'lost souls'. Local cults or contacts with alleged angels, spirits, ghosts and so on were also liable to be branded as works of the Devil by theologians at the end of the century.

The first great persecution in the region examined here – in the district court of Rettenberg-Sonthofen, in the Bishopric of Augsburg, in 1586–8 – began as a frontal collision between modern demonology and such popular beliefs. Only three years earlier a woman accused of witchcraft in the same court had been punished by a short term of imprisonment. She had claimed that 'God and his holy angels' had given her commands in a dream.[238] In 1586 the soothsayer Conrad Stöckhlin was dealt with less tenderly. After his arrest he was tortured so brutally that he confessed to everything he was accused of, and incriminated twenty others, who were all burned as witches on the grounds of his denunciations.

Conrad Stöckhlin was thirty-seven, and had been village horse herds-man of Oberstdorf for nineteen years; he had had seven children by his wife, of whom two were still alive. His mother had been dead for fifteen years; his aged father, who had held the post of horse herdsman for twenty-eight years, was an inmate of the hospital at Sonthofen. Stöckh-lin's position as herdsman meant that he spent a great deal of time outside the village in the mountain pastures, where his only companion was another marginalised character, the cattle herdsman Jacob Walch. Stöck-hlin's mother had been regarded as a witch in Oberstdorf – at least, that was asserted after the trial had begun – and he himself was considered to be not only expert in magic,[239] but a soothsayer of quite exceptional quality. In the village it was said that he 'rode with the raging horde', that is, he was one of the 'wild huntsmen' whose loud cries filled the night air.[240] As a soothsayer Stöckhlin asserted that he knew the witches in the

---

[236] C. Ginzburg, *Die Benandanti. Feldkulte und Hexenwesen im 16. und 17. Jahrhundert,* Frankfurt am Main 1980 (1st edn Turin 1966).

[237] B. Easlea, *Witch Hunting, Magic and the New Philosophy. An Introduction to the Debates of the Scientific Revolution 1450–1750,* Brighton 1980, 74f.

[238] HStAM, Hochstift Augsburg, NA, Akten no. 6737, fol. 126 (Guardian's court of Rettenburg 1583). [239] *Ibid.,* fol. 44–54.

village. A tavern keeper of Oberstdorf who suffered from an unnatural illness had asked him to help her. Stöckhlin denounced a sixty-year-old woman in Oberstdorf as a witch, and advised the bewitched tavern keeper that she

> should go to her, Anna, and ask her three times for the sake of God and the Last Judgement, to help her; then she must help her.[241]

The tavern keeper followed these instructions and her sickness improved. The accused witch, Anna Enzensbergerin, fell under deeper suspicion, for one who could 'turn' a sickness had presumably caused it. She added to the suspicion against her by running away. Several villagers approached the *Landamman* Alexander von Schwendi, claiming that witches had harmed their cattle and their own health. When Enzensbergerin returned, several of the 'leaders and court men of Oberstdorf'[242] demanded that the Bishop's officer should arrest her. Schwendi sent a report to Dillingen and received orders to arrest both Enzensbergerin and the denouncer, Stöckhlin, the usual procedure when a grave charge was made.[243] Many of these proceedings for defamation ended in the punishment of the plaintiff, or, if the accused shared in the guilt, both parties were forbidden to slander each other again. The further course of the trial in Rettenberg-Sonthofen can only be understood from Stöckhlin's statements.

The court wanted to hear from Stöckhlin how he had been able to recognise Anna Enzensbergerin as a witch. He replied that he had been told by his 'angel', whom God Almighty had 'created' for him. Questioned further on this point, which had aroused the mistrust of the Court Council in Dillingen, he gave this answer:

> On his rides, he asked his guide, whom he presumed to be an angel, about it, and he answered that Enzensbergerin had done it to her.[244]

When the court asked him whether he himself was a warlock and his 'rides' were witch's flights, Stöckhlin made a distinction:

> He also says that there are three kinds of rides, and that on which he went was called the *Nachtschar*, the other the 'right journey'. That was

[240] *Ibid.*, fol. 9–34, question 95; Enzensbergerin and Luzin said 'Er Stöckhl fare mit dem Wuettens hör.' On this complex Beitl, *Wörterbuch*, 970–2.
[241] HStAM, Hochstift Augsburg, NA, Akten no. 6737, fol. 3v.
[242] Remnants of the communal *Tigen* organisation. Cf. Spindler, *Handbuch*, III/2, 952, 954, 961 (Layer). H.B. Zirkel, *Geschichte des Marktes Oberstdorf*, 4 vols., Oberstdorf 1974f., II, 52, 58–62; R. Hipper, *Sonthofen im Wandel der Geschichte*, Kempten 1978.
[243] HStAM, Hochstift Augsburg, NA, Akten no. 1199, fol. 413v.
[244] *Ibid.*, Akten no. 6737, fol. 3v.

the one in which the dead are led to their abode. The third was the witches' ride. They fly through the air, and he knows nothing of this ride, for he was never in it nor present at it.[245]

Like the *Benandanti*, the members of the *Nachtschar* were not believed to go on their travels physically; their souls left their bodies while they slept or were in a kind of trance, and travelled under the guidance of a white-robed angel with a red cross on his brow to secret places, 'where there was pain and pleasure, he believed it was purgatory and paradise, where he saw many people but knew none of them'.

He also says that he had to go on the *Nachtschar* every Embertide, Friday and Saturday after Ember Wednesday, and often by night. But when he had to go on it, a tiredness like a swoon came over him a short time before. Then he supposed his soul left his body and remained outside it for about 2 or 3 hours, sometimes with pain and sometimes without. But his body remained where the fit had seized him.[246]

Stöckhlin had other fantastic tales to tell, of a pact with the cattle herdsman Walch that whoever died first must report to the other from the beyond, of Walch's death and reappearance, and about a nocturnal vision in a forest above Oberstdorf.

Although Stöckhlin claimed that his angel urged him to pray and to attend services, was dressed in white and bore a red cross on his brow, and that he had not had to give any undertaking or pray to anyone, the court at Rettenberg, guided by the government at Dillingen and the executioners of Biberach and Tettnang, twisted the herdsman's statements against him. The Court Councillors deduced from the writings of 'the learned' that there were not three kinds of flight through the air, but only two: by God's permission, with the aid either of angels or of the Devil. As it was not to be thought that an angel would have appeared to the herdsman at God's command, it must have been the Devil. His guide could therefore not have borne a cross on his brow, as the Devil feared this sign.[247] After several interrogations under torture Stöckhlin, fearing further tortures, altered his statements to conform to what the court expected, and the white angel with a cross became a black devil paramour with cloven feet.[248] Now it was

---

[245] *Ibid.*, fol. 1–4. The *Nachtschar* or *Nachtvolk* was regarded as identical with the 'wild hunt'. In the Vorarlberg and around Lake Constance the phenomenon was also called *Wuotahee* or *Wuetas*. Cf. Beitl, *Wörterbuch*, 586f. While the Bishop's judges classed Stöckhlin with those who went to the witches' sabbath, the women of the village (note 240) were convinced that he rode with the 'wild hunt'. Stöckhlin's tales differed somewhat from this, in his account of the '*Nachtschar*'. Cf. Beitl, *Wörterbuch*, 970–2.

[246] HStAM, Hochstift Augsburg, NA, Akten no. 6737, fol. 1–4.

[247] *Ibid.*, fol. 9–34 (*Interrogatoria* of 15.11.1586).

[248] *Ibid.*, fol. 44–54 (questioning under torture of 23.12.1586, question 65).

clear why Stöckhlin knew the witches: he had seen them dancing at their witches' sabbaths on the Heuberg!

ACCUMULATION OF FACTORS

The sources for individual persecutions vary greatly in fullness. In some cases, chiefly those in the noble lordships, we know only that they occurred, and cannot even estimate their duration and extent, much less their causes. In others, we know only the immediate cause of the trials, as in the persecution in the episcopal *Strassvogtei* (Schwabmünchen), which was triggered by the fantasies of a child, as the minutes of the Court Council at Dillingen confirm more than once.

It is safe to assume that the limitations of the sources are responsible whenever we find only a single cause, as in the case of Ellingen. Better-documented persecutions, such as those at Rettenberg, Werdenfels and Nördlingen, and to a lesser extent Freising and Schongau, as well as the trials in the Free City of Augsburg, reveal that it took many more contributing factors, besides the immediate complaints against the 'first witch', to trigger a persecution. Oversimplifying, we could say that while complaints are always to be understood in their individual context, the triggering events often followed an accumulation of circumstantial evidence, which in the end made an accusation of witchcraft acceptable.

For example, it is clear from the 'first witches' at Rettenberg and Werdenfels that the parents of the accused had already been suspected, and in Garmisch and Schongau the same persons had already been tried years before, but had been acquitted for lack of proof. In Garmisch in 1589 we find a specific combination of external misfortune (thunder, harvest failure, inflation, hunger), individual misfortune, conflict between neighbours, the intervention of soothsayers, accidents and a tendency to persecution on the part of the villagers and the authorities.[249] In Oberstdorf (court of Rettenberg-Sonthofen) soothsaying, the social isolation of the herdsman, his suspect family background, the frightened reaction of the suspect, strange popular beliefs in the returning dead, personal angels and membership of the 'raging horde', as well as the persecuting inclinations of the members of the *Tigen* or communal peasant organisations, and the authorities at Dillingen, all played a part. In the Schongau complaints of 1587 we find a conflict between neighbours, the work of soothsayers, personal 'faults' of the accused (quarrelsomeness, threats), and the raking up of old accusations.[250] In the persecution at Nördlingen, a general

---

[249] Kuisl, *Die Hexen*, 9ff.
[250] B. Her, 'Ein Hexenprozess zu Schongau vom Jahr 1587. Nach den Originalacten dargestellt', *Oberbayr. Archiv*, 11 (1850), 128–44.

increase in accusations of witchcraft since 1586 was followed by unusual infant mortality in one family, the conviction of the same family's nurse-maid that she was possessed, her social marginalisation, the coincidence at the 'bier test' and the extreme persecution zeal of the newly elected town magistracy and newly appointed town consul.[251]

It may be that such an accumulation of factors was typical of the beginning of large persecutions, as it can be recognised wherever the sources allow a more detailed reconstruction of the events. Yet to assume a typical process behind the beginning of the trials, on the basis of this hypothesis, takes us little further, for the accumulation of specific factors still means that the events were no less individual. It seems that there were in fact certain typical constellations of events that made trials for witch-craft more likely, but that no constellation led automatically or necessarily to a persecution. All the individual main factors are found in trials which did not lead to executions, and even when several of them were present, they did not necessarily lead to persecutions, as the example of Augsburg shows.

This finding suggests that we should turn our attention to the attitude of the local 'powers', the communal representative bodies where they still existed, and the authorities.

PEOPLE AND AUTHORITIES

In principle persecutions seem to be found when the interests of the people and their authorities coincided. Where they did not, conflicts soon occur-red, as a persecution was normally only demanded when apparently vital interests were at stake. In 1581, for example, the judge of Werdenfels, Hans Paul Herwarth von Hohenburg,[252] was reproached to his face by the

---

[251] Cf. note 127.
[252] H.P. Herwarth von Hohenburg (1519–83), patrician of Augsburg and Privy Councillor, gave up his citizenship in 1576 and transferred to the Bavarian nobility. From 1580–3 he held the office of judge of Werdenfels and held out against the massive demand for witch hunting from his subjects in 1581. See J.B. Prechtl, *Chronik des ehemals bischöflich freisingischen Grafschaft Werdenfels*, Augsburg 1850, 45–50; Kuisl, *Die Hexen*, 7f. Two of his sons also played a role in the history of witchcraft trials in the region: Hans Friedrich Herwarth von Hohenburg (?–1598), known as the author of a book on the art of riding, led the witch hunts at Schongau in 1589–91, shortly after he had been appointed county judge there in 1588. His predecessor had shown greater caution in 1587. Johann Georg Herwarth von Hohenburg (1553–1626), who served in the Imperial Chamber Court at Speyer from 1583–5, and then became a Court Councillor in Munich, was appointed Supreme Chancellor by Wilhelm V in the critical witch hunting year 1590; this does not at first suggest that he was opposed to witch hunting. Soon after Herwarth's appointment, however, a persistent tendency to restrain and legalise the persecution of witches in Bavaria began. During his term as Chancellor of the Estates, 1598–1626, Herwarth was always to be found in the background of the anti-witch hunting party;

village representatives of Garmisch and Partenkirchen, because he took no steps against sorcery. Even at that date there was a pronounced persecuting mood among some of the population, though there were still voices openly opposed to it. Herwarth reported the details of the complaints to the government at Freising, which forbade him to make any arrests, as the evidence was inadequate. The villagers of Werdenfels would not believe Herwarth had received such an order until he read it out to them word for word, but even this did not allay their suspicions. The judge was accused of doing nothing against the witches because they were too poor for him to get anything out of them. In 1581 he wrote to the Governor in Freising for help, saying that 'if your grace and favour makes no other provision, great unrest will follow'.[253]

The persecutions of 1590, especially those in the southern districts of the Bishoprics of Augsburg and Freising and in the Duchy of Bavaria, reveal that there was massive pressure for persecutions from the representatives of the communities. Only in formal expression did the communities with a tradition of popular participation differ from those that were under the firmer control of the authorities. While subjects of the Bavarian county court of Schongau appealed to the judge 'humbly imploring and desiring'[254] him to 'help them and wholly root out the prevailing sorcery', in 1596 in the court of Rettenberg-Sonthofen, the 'leaders and court men of Oberstdorf' appeared in person and demanded that trials be held.[255] The Guardian of Werdenfels, Poissl, began to make the first arrests in 1589, after pressure from the communal representatives of his three subordinate courts, and before he had obtained permission to do so from the government at Freising. Possibly the districts at the edge of the Alps were especially hard hit by the harvest failure of the years before 1590, since such a determined popular campaign for persecutions cannot be found elsewhere in the region.[256]

Yet there were many other places where persecutions were held, where the increasing accusations of witchcraft from the populace (Nördlingen, Griesbach, Munich, Augsburg, Dillingen) and the lack of any sign of resistance, suggest that at least the majority of the people approved the conduct of the authorities. Conversely, in the persecutions of 1590, one finds that the trials soon came to an end once signs of greater resistance

because of his interest in science and his attitude in the question of witchcraft his opponents mocked him as a sorcerer. Yet his social, political and scholarly reputation raised him above such insults. For Herwarth's attitude to the witchcraft question cf. chapter 4. The biographical data are from *ADB*, 13 (1881), 169–75; *NDB* 8 (1969), 720–3; Bosl, *Biographie*, 341.   [253] Kuisl, *Die Hexen*, 6–9.
[254] HStAM, Hochstift Augsburg, NA, Akten no. 2629.
[255] HStAM, Hochstift Augsburg, NA, Akten no. 1199, fol. 413v.
[256] Cf. chapter 3, pp. 121–57.

began to be seen among the people (cf. chapter 3, pp. 194–205). In principle every trial was provoked by accusations from the people, or by specific denunciations from neighbouring courts. A purely official inquisition into witchcraft, such as is often assumed in the literature,[257] was never behind the beginning of a persecution. Although this was contrary to the intention of the apologists of persecution, as a rule, therefore, the beginning of the trials involved all the difficulties of accusatorial procedure, in which the plaintiff had to bear the onus of proof and the risk.

This explains why the first stages of many persecutions were quite exceptional in character, so far as the triggering events were concerned: it also explains why 'overt acts', children and 'fools', the fulfilment of threats and the activities of soothsayers all played such a prominent part. The collective popular demand for persecutions was also part of this exceptional constellation, for it must have been a very unusual phenomenon in criminal justice as a whole over a longer period. Both the behaviour of the people and that of the authorities helped to bring about persecutions, but ultimately it was the attitude of the latter that was the decisive variable in this region. Before 1586 the scepticism of the authorities had hampered persecutions; after that year their increasing willingness to persecute led to an escalation of persecutions – initially with the consent of society.

MECHANISMS OF PERSECUTION

TORTURE

Even when people were convinced that they had found a witch for the reasons discussed in the previous section, these were not enough, on their own, for complete certainty. For that, a confession was needed. Even cases of harmful sorcery were impossible to verify. Of course there were always 'victims' whose crops had been damaged by thunderstorms, or whose child or horse had mysteriously fallen ill or died; but how was one to know who was responsible? If sorcery was practised in secret, this was even truer of the 'spiritual' elements of the crime of witchcraft, pacts or sexual intercourse with the Devil, flight through the air, the witches' sabbath. But hardly a single suspect would confess voluntarily – apart from the 'possessed'. Even the Ingolstadt opinion on witchcraft of 1590 could find only one solution to this:

[257] For criticisms of this antiquated legal-historical position see D. Unverhau, 'Akkusationsprozess – Inquisitionsprozess. Indikatoren für die Intensität der Hexenverfolgungen in Schleswig-Holstein? Überlegungen und Untersuchungen zu einer Typologie der Hexenprozesse', in Degn *et al., Hexenprozesse*, 59–143, who practically deprives the old antithesis of all validity.

Since witchcraft is committed in secret, the guilty will be much more easily recognised either from their own confession, through the inquisition by torture or being put to the question, or by another witness, for example the statements of their accomplices and partners in vice.[258]

Confession obtained by torture was thus the only way to learn anything about this crime. Only after the 'first witch' had been interrogated could further witches be discovered from her statements. Two things were necessary before a trial for witchcraft could be held. In the first place, the requirements of proof had to be less stringent than in normal criminal trials. In trials for witchcraft certainty about the actual culprit could not be obtained before torture, but only through torture. The conditions on which torture was permissible had to be relaxed. Secondly, the proceedings ended after the execution of the first witch, if her statements about her partners in witchcraft were not given unconditional or partial credence, since otherwise the same problem, the admissibility of torture, was faced as before. Trials for witchcraft stood or fell on the readiness to allow torture, and this ultimately depended on the nature and duration of the torture applied. The law of the Empire prescribed that both should be 'at the discretion of a good and reasonable judge' (*Carolina*, article 58), and the territorial codes were not much more precise.[259] There were certain regional customs which governed the duration of torture (e.g. a quarter of an hour, half an hour),[260] and the ways in which it could be applied, but the vital point was that in witchcraft trials these customary limits were often exceeded. In many cases harsher torture was deliberately applied because of the seriousness of the offence.

EXECUTIONERS

In most places where trials for witchcraft were held in the years around 1590 it was the executioner who determined the way in which suspects were tortured and for how long. Not every executioner was competent to conduct a witch trial. Although the extraordinary brutalisation of criminal justice at the end of the sixteenth century meant that many smaller places had their own executioners, in essence five men determined the course of the proceedings in the region: the executioners of Biberach (all of Swabia, the Bishopric of Freising and minor territories in southern Middle Franconia), of Schongau (all of Bavaria and the Bishopric of Freising), of Lauingen (Pfalz-Neuburg, all parts of the district), Oettingen (County of

[258] HStAM, Hexenakten 1, Prod. 1, fol. 6v.
[259] Christel, 'Die Malefizprozessordnung', 81–110.
[260] Merzbacher, *Die Hexenprozesse*, 147.

Oettingen and Margravate of Ansbach) and Eichstätt (northern Bavaria, parts of the Upper Palatinate and the whole of Middle Franconia). They were reputed to be exceptionally experienced in dealing with witches, and were called in to conduct trials in distant places, where they set an example to the local executioners. Only a few authorities made no use of their services during the persecution of 1590. As a rule the Free Cities relied on their own executioners, while Bavaria and Pfalz-Neuburg as well as Oettingen and Eichstätt depended almost exclusively on the executioners named, so far as the sources allow us to judge, except when there were too many simultaneous trials for them to cope with.[261] Skill in 'recognising' witches and in performing the proper rites and procedures to extract a confession from them was regarded as a kind of arcane knowledge, in which they excelled over the other executioners and the officers of the courts. The notorious executioners purported to be able to tell a witch by her appearance, her figure, her gestures, her eyes and from the witches' mark (*stigma diaboli*) that was tested by the needle test. Often the woman's fate was decided at her first meeting with the executioner; if he found no stigma and saw no other grounds to suspect her, she was released. During the persecution at Werdenfels the executioner Hans Volmair of Biberach inspected twenty-seven women during a tour of the lower courts at Garmisch, Partenkirchen and Mittenwald, and found ten of them to be 'sorceresses'. The other suspects were released.[262] Even after the suspects had been removed to prison the executioner still determined the course of the proceedings in 1590. The executioner's 'art' began long before the actual torture. On his instructions special meals were prepared for the prisoners, who were given holy water and baptismal water as well as consecrated salt. The mate of the executioner of Eichstätt said:

> For when a witch comes into the prison, she must strip naked, and then his master puts consecrated salt in her mouth, as much as he can hold between two fingers, and a drink of holy water and a drink of baptismal water. After this he inspects her for the sign, which is a little mark, as if it was scratched, and when he has found this he sticks a needle in it, and if she is a witch it does not bleed, and she does not flinch.[263]

The so-called 'needle test' was regarded even by the executioners themselves as such a delicate matter that the executioner of Schwabmünchen

[261] The Bishopric of Freising obviously had no executioner of its own, and had to correspond continually with outside sources for executioners for its witch hunts in Freising and the Counties of Ismaning and Werdenfels. These headsmen were employed everywhere. This correspondence and the dates of executions could be used to establish executioners' itineraries. Kuisl, *Die Hexen*; HStAM, Hexenakten 9a; HStAM, HL, Freising III, Fasc. 320, no. 39.   [262] Riezler, *Geschichte*, 172; Kuisl, *Die Hexen*, 25.
[263] Kunstmann, *Zauberwahn*, 75.

asked the government in Dillingen to bring in the Master of Biberach to perform it, a whole year after the persecution had begun. The witches' mark was considered to be important circumstantial evidence for the application of torture by the persecution courts during the wave of persecution in 1590.[264]

The torture itself had to be ordered by the government, but in the territorial district courts the way in which it was carried out was decided, as we can see from the trial records, by the executioners. Examples of torture have been described time and again in the literature; here we shall merely cite the procedure of the Master of Biberach in the first persecution of the wave of 1590:

> When we reminded him of this point only, and he did not wish to admit it, as always, he was handed over to the Master for hard torture, orders having been given, and at 2 in the afternoon he was racked and until 4 he was strewn with fire, pitch and brandy, mixed with gunpowder. And also harshly tormented with two red hot irons which were placed under his arms, so that his skin was burned from the genitals to the head, but he would not confess or say the least thing . . .[265]

After several such tortures the Oberstdorf herdsman Stöchlin had confessed everything that the trial judge wanted to know, following the questions sent down from Dillingen. The brutality of the tortures led to many deaths in prison. During the persecution in Rettenberg-Sonthofen, six of twenty-three named prisoners died before they could be brought to trial, or more than a quarter of all the accused. Naturally many women whose 'guilt' had been 'proven' by the finding of the witches' mark, confessed during the 'amicable' hearings that preceded the 'territion' (the showing of the implements of torture) and the torture itself. Women also committed suicide because of suspicions of witchcraft or tried to escape trial by flight.

PLAUSIBILITY OF SUSPICIONS

When the 'first witches' were taken away for interrogation the trials began to develop their own momentum, which led critical contemporaries to conclude that the persecutions would never end once they had begun.[266] If the courts believed the confessions extracted through torture and treated those denounced in them with an equal disregard for the consequences, the

---

[264] Riezler, *Geschichte*, 172; 'Bedenken, die Unhulden betreffend'; HStAM, Hochstift Augsburg, NA, Akten no. 1204, fol. 581.

[265] HStAM, Hochstift Augsburg, NA, Akten no. 6737, fol. 5v.

[266] HStAM, SV 2243, s.f.

trials were bound to expand. The systems of denunciations, which were the result of questioning designed to make suspects divulge the names of their fellow witches, have some characteristics which have been rather neglected, but which appear to be typical of the diachronic development of persecutions.

The witches' accomplices were usually discovered by questions put to the suspect by an interrogator; the executioner, who was often not a local man, was not involved at this stage. The suspect was under pressure to name as her accomplices persons who would appear plausible to her interrogator, otherwise she could only expect further severe torture. The interrogators belonged to the local social elite,[267] their victims to the lower classes or the margins of society.

At first the plausibility of these denunciations was measured by criteria similar to those applied in identifying the 'first witch'. The age, sex and appearance of the persons denounced were important, and in most cases they were old women. When the persecution began to spread, it can be seen that not all those accused were arrested at once, but only those on whom most suspicion fell. The courts selected from the wider circle of the denounced, those who had been the targets of other popular accusations, those most closely associated with the 'first witch' or her relations. If we assume that as a rule suspects would not willingly denounce their close relations, we must see this as a sign that the interrogators applied heavy pressure on them to make such statements. In the trials at Werdenfels five of the twelve arrested were related to the first three women to be executed.[268] There was also a social selection. Even when the 'first witches' denounced the wealthy or patricians, the first arrests were always of those whose social status was closest to the 'first witch' – that is, humble. The 'possessed' Ursula Haiderin in Nördlingen, for example, claimed to have seen several patricians and burgomasters' wives at the witches' sabbath. But only women whose guilt appeared more plausible to the city court were arrested at first: a sixty-year-old herdswoman, a possibly even older pedlar woman who lived in a hospital and a former midwife who was so old that she had lived through the Peasants' War of 1525.[269]

Even during the persecutions of 1590, as far as we can observe, court proceedings were never entirely arbitrary. The courts tested denunciations for their plausibility, paying particular attention to the reputation and social relationships of the denouncer. Further grounds for suspicion were needed before the persecution could spread. In the district court of Bobingen in the Bishopric of Augsburg, for example, the women accused

---

[267] Spindler, *Handbuch*, II/1, 549 (Volkert).   [268] Kuisl, *Die Hexen*, 43–60.
[269] Wulz, 'Nördlinger Hexenprozesse' (1937–8), 55–7; *idem*, 'Die Nördlinger Hexen', no. 142. A similar scheme can also be seen in Freising. HStAM, Hexenakten 9a, fol. 328.

by the fourteen-year-old boy were regarded as 'merely simply suspect'.[270] During the general persecution hysteria of 1589 and 1590, however, the minimum requirements for further circumstantial evidence were widely disregarded and replaced by the search for the witches' mark. For a time this was believed to be safer evidence than the reputations of those concerned, which were often the product of spite, or of the oracles of soothsayers.

GEOGRAPHICAL AND SOCIAL EXPANSION OF THE PERSECUTION

Once the first witches had been interrogated – for example, Stöckhlin in Oberstdorf, Haiderin in Nördlingen, the witch-boy at Bobingen, the aged Els Schlampin at Garmisch – a wave of arrests began in those places where persecutions were held. In most cases the arrests were guided by the plausibility of the denunciations. The first batch of suspects arrested was tortured with unbelievable frequency and cruelty. Of two women of Nördlingen one was interrogated fourteen times and tortured four times, the other sixteen and six times.[271] The confessions of the second wave of victims confirmed the statements of the 'first witches' and added to their credibility. This programmed an expansion of the persecution in advance: the court believed the confessions and used every means to obtain more. Yet, to begin with, the expansion of the persecutions was not precipitate. The reason for this was very simple: the capacity of the prisons was too small. The dungeons of the castle of Werdenfels held twelve prisoners, the witches' prison at Schwabmünchen only six. The persecutions therefore went ahead in stages, for only when the previous prisoners had been executed or released could new suspects be imprisoned. Often the scanty prison accommodation had to be repaired or new cells provided.[272]

At first the persecution expanded geographically. As the arrests were made on the basis of plausibility, the judges selecting the most suspect from the larger number of those denounced, the persecutions expanded within the local vicinity. The persecution at Schwabmünchen of 1589–91 was at first confined to the village of Bobingen, spread first to nearby Wehringen, and then to the neighbouring villages of Oberottmarshausen and Kleinaitingen, before jumping to the more distant towns of Schwab-

[270] HStAM, Hochstift Augsburg, NA, Akten no. 1202, fol. 216–17.
[271] Wulz, 'Die Nördlinger Hexen', no. 142.
[272] Kuisl, *Die Hexen*, 15, 18. Prisons had to be repaired or additional blockhouses built in the district court seats in the Bishopric of Augsburg before the trials could begin. HStAM, Hochstift Augsburg, NA, Akten, no. 1203, fol. 595, 652, 700 (Helmishofen); *ibid.*, 436, 470 (Sonthofen); no. 1205, fol. 140 (Schwabmünchen).

münchen and Augsburg after the denunciation of persons who can be shown to have had close personal ties or relationships with prisoners who had been interrogated. The geographical expansion, therefore, was not systematic but casual. It originated in the circle of the 'first witches' and depended on the plausibility of their statements.[273] No persecution in southeast Germany was conducted by the courts using abstract or systematic criteria.

The 'social expansion' of the persecution began at the latest in the third stage of arrests, that is after two collective executions. As the credibility of denunciations increased, the social standing of those arrested changed. Persecutions were no longer confined to outsiders and those at the bottom of the social scale, but affected the urban and rural middle classes. The plausibility of accusations was borne in mind during this 'social expansion' as well. Otherwise it would be hard to explain why denunciations hit particularly hard at those trades and professions which had dealings with magical practices because of their occupation (e.g. midwives, cowherds, apothecaries) or were in contact with foodstuffs (tavern keepers, butchers, bakers). The latter were seen as particularly capable of causing 'unnatural' sicknesses by poisoning or bewitchment.[274] As the persecutions progressed, the witches became freer in the choice of their alleged accomplices. Consequently, suspects facing death tended not to name friends and relations any longer, but to choose their enemies and members of the local elites, persons of wealth or standing, or both. In Schwabmünchen, for example, several wealthy farmers' wives and tavern keepers were burned,

---

[273] Trial records for the witch hunt at Schwabmünchen have not been preserved, but it was possible to reconstruct the sequence and the mechanism of expansion from three parallel sources: the reports of the Fugger correspondents (ÖNB Vienna, Cod. 8962–4); the minutes of the Court Council at Dillingen (HStAM, Hochstift Augsburg, NA, Akten nos. 1202–4) and the accounts of the executioner of Schwabmünchen (HStAM, Hochstift Augsburg, NA, Akten 2816). The witch hunts at Schongau, Werdenfels, Rettenberg and Oberdorf, for which the geographical distribution of the victims can be determined exactly, confirm these inferences on the geographical expansion of the witch hunt. StadtA Munich, Hist. Ver. Urk. nos. 1996–2088; Kuisl, *Die Hexen*, 43–60; HStAM, Hochstift Augsburg, NA, Akten no. 6737; StA Neuburg, Gerichtsbuch Oberdorf 1576–96 (contains names, place of origin and date of execution of all witches burned in Oberdorf from the judicial districts of Oberdorf, Helmishofen and Nesselwang). ÖNB Vienna, Cod. 8963, fol. 593.

[274] This finding tallies with the observation of Wunder, *Hexenprozesse*, 187–9, albeit with some change of emphasis: while the question of plausibility arose in the individual witch trials in Prussia, as it did in Macfarlane's Essex, in southeast Germany it helped the mechanism of social and geographical expansion. This observation can probably be generalised to all regions with expansive witch hunts. Wunder's recourse to the interpretative model of a 'peasant society' with the idea of 'limited good' is not convincing in the context of early modern society (*ibid.*, 189 and 201, note 65), but her reference to the risk of occupations specific to women is valuable (cf. note 174).

in Oberstdorf several women bore the names of families with coats of arms, and in Garmisch too the gentry families were hit.[275] In the Free Cities the persecutions spread to the patrician families during this stage. In Nördlingen a tavern keeper and the widow of a councillor had been executed as early as the second burning of witches, and in the fourth the keeper of the town hall, the city paymistress and the widow of a burgomaster were executed. Among the thirty-three women burned in the city between 1590 and 1594 there were two former burgomasters' wives, two wives of town councillors, two close relations (mother and daughter) of councillors and the wife of a high official who was eligible to sit on the council. Besides seven women from families with the right to serve on the council, several wealthy tavern keepers and a sister-in-law of Count Friedrich of Oettingen were burned. The wife of the former town clerk, the daughter of a high Württemberg official, had to flee to Stuttgart. Because of the duration of the persecution, the higher ranks of the citizenry were disproportionately overrepresented.[276] When the persecutions were broken off, the wives and daughters of several councillors in office and local noblemen were on the list of the denounced.[277]

It was the same wherever persecutions were held. In Munich the persecution spread to the rich brewing trade in July 1590, in Dillingen a patrician woman who was related to members of the cathedral chapter was burned, in Donauwörth the daughter of the burgomaster who had introduced the Reformation to the city committed suicide in prison. In Freising the wives of the Court Purveyor and the Court Brewer were under suspicion, and wealthy tavern keepers were also denounced at Ingolstadt. If matters were allowed to go so far, denunciations crossed from the wealthy burgesses to the highest classes. Women from Garmisch denounced nobles from Innsbruck, Bozen, Tramin and Kaltern, ultimately accusing Benigna von Gumppenberg, the wife of the Guardian, and in the end the Guardian Poissl von Atzenzell himself.[278] In Oettingen-Wallerstein the denunciations were concentrated in the end on the Countess, in Ansbach the

---

[275] On Schwabmünchen ÖNB Vienna, Cod. 8962, fol. 578v.; Cod. 8963, fol. 255–6v. Oberstdorf: Straub, Kappeller and Frey were families with coats of arms: Zirkel, *Geschichte*, II, 273. Garmisch: Kätzler, Feuerer, Arnold and Rösch were among the families entitled to a seal. Kuisl, *Die Hexen*, 43–60.

[276] Nördlingen: Wulz, 'Die Nördlinger Hexen', no. 147.

[277] *Ibid.*, no. 142 (von Gundelsheim, von Absperg, von Welwart).

[278] *Erweytterte Unholden Zeyttung*, in Behringer, 'Hexenverfolgung', 353 and *ibid.*, note 78. For Dillingen see notes 35–7. Donauwörth: Zelzer, *Geschichte*, 395. Freising: HStAM, Hexenakten 9a, fol. 321, fol. 323f., fol. 394–5. Garmisch; Kuisl, *Die Hexen*, 31, 34. Brigitta Kätzler, a member of a family with the right to a seal, denounced the noble B. von Gumppenberg. At her execution Kätzler publicly accused the Guardian Poissl: 'sie wisse keinen anderen Puhl-Teufel als den Pfleger, der auf dem Ross vor ihr sitzt [in the witches' flight; WB]'.

Erbmarschallin Cäcilie von Pappenheim was arrested.[279] The tendency to equalisation of the social 'estates' could not be overlooked. The Fuggers' correspondent in Munich demanded that 'no one should be spared in this, rich or poor', and popular criticism of the proceedings, the effect of which should not be underestimated, pointed in the same direction.[280]

MOTIVES OF THE WITCHES IN NAMING THEIR ACCOMPLICES

The denunciation of socially more exalted persons – in 1590, contrary to later persecutions, the denunciations maintained the cliche of the witch as an aged woman – was the result of three main motives, when personal revenge was not involved. We must look for the first motive in the effects of social resentment. In persecutions, and only in persecutions, there was a possibility of involving members of the upper classes in the trials, whereas they were usually able to escape criminal proceedings. A vagabond executed as a witch in Munich said 'let it hit the rich for once, otherwise only the poor would be executed'.[281] Perhaps an even stronger motive was the wish to be revenged on those who bore the guilt for the persecutions themselves, either because they were responsible for conducting the trials, or because they had incited popular demand for persecution. In the persecution at Schongau the wife of the judge of Schwabsoien, whose husband had publicly called for a persecution, was unanimously de-

[279] Riezler, *Geschichte*, 239; Janssen and Pastor, *Culturzustände*, VIII, 666. It should be remembered that in the Commandery of Ellingen Barbara Strauss, the wife of the Chancellor Hans Strauss, had already been burned as a witch in February 1590. Film 693, 114. The *Erbmarschallin* Cäcilie von Pappenheim, nee von Hornstein, was not released until 1595, after four years under arrest, following an opinion from the University of Altdorf. Lang, *Geschichte*, III, 338ff.

[280] ÖNB Vienna, Cod. 8963, fol. 312–v. The standard reproach from the populace, which embarrassed the authorities not a little, was that they only punished the simple folk. A letter to the Governor of Freising says of the mood in the city: '... bey der gemain, dabey vil gesagt und aussgeben wurdet, Man straff nur die armen, aber die ansehnlichen lass man aus'. HStAM, Hexenakten 9a, fol. 350. This charge of 'class justice', which of course was repeatedly confirmed in principle, was very effective in the precarious question of witchcraft, in which the authorities were unwilling and unable to do without the consent of the people, at least in the region studied here. Muchembled's thesis of the witch hunts as an instrument of acculturation, for the 'cultural conquest of the rural areas' ('Witches', 232ff.) and the connection he suggests between peasant revolts and witch hunts (*ibid.*, 238f.) find no confirmation. The peasants of the Bishopric of Augsburg, for example, were just as rebellious after the witch hunt as they had been before, and the husbands of women burned as witches were among the leaders of the rising at Rettenberg in 1605–8; their demands included a change in the allocation of the costs of witchcraft trials, to shift more of the burden on to the state treasury. Zirkel, *Geschichte*, II, 273. The Bishop of Freising's Guardian at Werdenfels also began to go in fear of his subjects after the breakdown of consensus. Kuisl, *Die Hexen*, 34.

[281] Kunze, *Der Prozess*, 148. Similarly HStAM, Hexenakten 9a, fol. 328.

nounced as the 'mistress' of all witches by the other accused.[282] In Rettenberg-Sonthofen, Werdenfels and Oberdorf, the instigators of the trials were drawn into the persecution and there were even attempts to hit back at the authorities. In Nördlingen in 1594 Dorothea Gundelfingerin, whose husband had played a leading role in carrying out the persecutions as burgomaster, was herself burned as a witch.[283] It can be said that it was quite normal for those responsible for the trials, sooner or later – and more and more frequently – to be accused of witchcraft themselves.[284]

A third motive was, by denouncing as many persons as possible, especially those of higher rank, to involve as many families and interest groups as possible in the persecution in order to bring about an end of the persecution. In Freising in 1590, for example, denunciations were aimed at the wives of Court Purveyors and Court Brewers whose husbands were able to exert great pressure to secure their release. It was not long before it was realised at Freising that

> the guilty witches and sorceresses, when they are condemned to death, often wish that all women should be sentenced to death likewise, and this trait they have from their father the Devil, whom they follow . . . [285]

In principle three options were open to the authorities as the denunciations expanded: they could continue to conduct trials as before, and extend the

[282] HStAM, Hochstift Augsburg, NA, Akten no. 2629, s.f.

[283] *Ibid.* Kuisl, *Die Hexen*, 23, 29; Dömling, *Heimatbuch*, 91; Wulz, 'Die Nördlinger Hexen', no. 144.

[284] The most impressive evidence for the deliberate involvement in the trials of those who had promoted them comes from Franconia. In 1627 in Bamberg, Anna Maria Müllerin, daughter of a physician from Nuremberg said that '...das blutbadt möchte zuletzt über denen zusammenschlagen, welche die Leuth examinierten, dann als sie noch zu Würtzburg in Verhafft gelegen, hätte sie von anderen gefangenen einen Ratschlag gehört, uff alle Examinatores auch zu bekhennen'. ('The bloodbath should at last hit those who examined the people, for when she was under arrest at Würzburg she heard a suggestion from the other prisoners, to denounce all the interrogators in their confessions.') Film 3634, 196. These targeted accusations were so successful that as early as 1628 the Prince-Bishop was obliged to write to Vienna and Munich, pleading for the evil genius of the witch hunts, suffragan Bishop Förner, to be taken into protection, L. Bauer, 'Die Bamberger Weihbischöfe', 457f.; Duhr, *Geschichte der Jesuiten*, II/2, 483f. In the witch hunts at Eichstätt in the early 1620s the denunciations of those under sentence of death concentrated on the preacher of the cathedral Joachim Meggelin SJ, who had been inciting witch hunts for years. This is the origin of the well-known episode in which a prince asked his spiritual adviser at table how many denunciations he should regard as adequate for a condemnation, and the adviser replied with such a small number that they would have sufficed for his own condemnation. Duhr, *Geschichte der Jesuiten*, II/2, 488. This episode was first taken up in the literature by F. Spee and related in detail. Of course Spee did not give the names of the Prince-Bishop and his fellow Jesuit from Eichstätt, but spoke of 'einem wohlbekannten Orte Deutschlands ... wo schon fast alles zu Asche zerfallen ist', an allusion to the witch hunts at Eichstätt, which had already lasted fifteen years in 1630. Spee, *Cautio*, 253 f.

[285] HStAM, Hexenakten 9a, fol. 413.

persecution to the upper classes, and even the nobles; they could ignore the accusations against persons from the higher estates, which would not have been so easy given the prevailing mood among the people; or they could question the general credibility of the denunciations, but this did not shake the foundations of the way in which the trials were conducted.

REFLECTIONS ON THE MECHANISMS OF PERSECUTION

Contemporaries reflected on the expansion of persecutions and commented on it, either to agree with it or to deplore it. An enthusiastic apologist for persecution, the Fuggers' correspondent in Schwabmünchen, wrote in 1590:

It is also said that when they have got rid of the idle and ugly they want to start on the fair. And among these four [the most recently arrested, WB] there is supposed to be a well-to-do tavernkeeper. If the Bishop wishes to eradicate all the vermin in his territory (in so far as it should raise its head again at Dillingen), he would have enough to do and to burn for a while, and at last perhaps many of the nobles would also end up in golden chains. But if things are to go so far, usually they call a halt.[286]

In principle in 1590 even members of the higher nobility were suspected of witchcraft, as the arrest of the *Erbmarschällin* Cäcilie von Pappenheim in Ansbach proves. But ultimately there were considerations that could not be so easily dismissed. The inner momentum of their quantitative, geographical and social expansion ended by leading persecutions into absurdity. A nobleman from Lower Bavaria summed it up at the end of the persecution:

There is the further inconvenience with persons suspected of sorcery, that when one of them is examined in prison, they soon incriminate one or two others by their confessions and these in turn 3 or 4 others or more, until at last the number grows so great that, if not the many, at least those of standing, birth and wealth are spared for friendship's sake and an end is made of the burning; or else one must go on so long with the everlasting continuance of the burning and torturing that at last the judges, the headsman's mate and the headsman themselves are weary. And the costs grow too great, but the persons executed before and the thoroughgoing equality of justice are not served.[287]

---

[286] ÖNB Vienna, Cod. 8962, fol. 507r–v.   [287] HStAM, SV 2243, s.f.

THE BREAKDOWN OF CONSENSUS

The statement that persecutions were ultimately led into absurdity by their inner expansionist mechanism is not quite correct, to the extent that it is an abstraction from the deeds and thoughts of those who took part, which anticipates and simplifies the results of a very laborious learning process – a learning process characterised by many reverses and which by no means described a straight line.

Though influences from the past and from outside should not be denied, it is nevertheless clear that the persecutions of 1590 in the region created a constellation of conflicts of a new type, which formed the starting point of discussions of witchcraft in the following decades – when the 'witch craze' in Germany and other parts of western Europe reached its peak. From 1590–1 a 'party' existed in most towns and territories which spoke up for further persecutions on the model of 1590. Likewise, from this time there was an opposition party in most towns and territories, which was not willing to become involved in such excesses again. These opponents of persecution, as we shall show, represented a powerful force. Their formative experience had been the persecution of 1590, and the ensuing breakdown of consensus on the purpose and possibility of persecution.

RESISTANCE OF THE ACCUSED

The resistance of the accused operated on four levels: against the judges at the hearings; through confessors; through illegal contacts in prison, and through public protests at executions. The tactic of expanding the denunciations, and its effectiveness, has already been mentioned.[288]

Very few people confessed their alleged witchcraft 'amicably', that is without torture. In trials for sorcery and witchcraft numerous magical practices were revealed, but the accused did not regard them as illegal, and in their opinion they had nothing to do with the crime of witchcraft. In most cases it needed the harshest torture and all the 'art' of the executioner to compel them to confess, as one can see from most of the trial records and numerous statements by executioners.[289] In the hearings, which were often very tedious, the accused repeatedly insisted on their innocence, pleaded for their release and complained that all their confessions had been or would be extracted by torture. Although it was normal to deny guilt in criminal trials, the hearings of witches must have shocked many judges. The executioner may have been used to brutal tortures, but the interrogators were always members of a higher bourgeois, patrician or noble social group. It must have dawned on many of them that almost everyone would

[288] Cf. note 284.   [289] Cf. chapter 3, pp. 183–93.

confess almost anything under such tortures,[290] even if torture was customary in contemporary criminal proceedings. Women were most vocal in their complaints against torture, which left them no chance of survival. Lucia Dieterin of Schongau was recorded as saying in 1590: 'Our Lord God will repay Master Jerg well, for wanting to make witches of women . . .'[291] The executioner, however, was only *pars pro toto*, as the judges must have understood. The constant struggle that led many women to their deaths and their appeal to God's justice and vengeance may have given many judges food for thought, all the more so since in the cities it was the burgomasters and town councillors, or Court Councillors, who conducted the hearings. It is in this connection that we should see the proposal of the University of Ingolstadt, that a judge must accept a verdict against a woman 'although the judge has his own private knowledge that she is innocent and has been falsely accused'.[292]

The persecution also led many confessors to change their minds on the unconditional guilt of the witches or the infallibility of religiously motivated justice. Trials were continually hindered by priests who urged the person under interrogation, on their conscience, not to denounce the innocent. Time and again, those who confessed revoked all their statements, which meant that torture had to be begun again. While at first confessors were only suspected because of keeping concubines – rightly for the most part[293] – from 1590 the suspicion that many priests would favour the revocation of confessions came to the fore. The Bavarian Instruction on procedure in trials for witchcraft of 1590 explicitly prescribed that priests should 'not give the witches cause to revoke or accept the same from them without good cause'.[294] The effectiveness of immediate resistance of the suspects in the hearings is also clear from the relevant passages in the works of Adam Tanner.[295]

Perhaps the most effective protest was the public revocation of condemned witches at executions. The presence of large crowds allowed their words to reach a public that was otherwise hardly attainable at that time.

[290] See an example from Munich in chapter 4, pp. 230–46.
[291] StadtA Munich, Hist. Ver. Urk. no. 2067; Wulz, 'Nördlinger Hexenprozesse', 102.
[292] HStAM, Hexenakten 1, Prod. 1, fol. 11v (opinion of 1590).
[293] For the comical efforts of the Prince-Bishop of Augsburg at least to procure a confessor without a concubine or children for the witches arrested in the witch hunt at Rettenberg, see HStAM, Hochstift Augsburg, NA, Akten no. 6737, *passim*. All the priests in the neighbourhood proved unacceptable in this respect. Finally a suitable spiritual guide was found in Füssen, many miles away.
[294] StadtA Munich, Stadtgericht 952 A 2, fol. 30.
[295] A. Tanner, *Theologia Scholastica*, III, col. 993. See also Duhr, *Geschichte der Jesuiten*, II/2, 519. Spee, *Cautio*, 150f., appealed to the corresponding passage in Tanner: 'Man könnte fragen was der Beichtvater zu tun hat, wenn er (was nicht ausgeschlossen ist; man lese nur bei Tanner nach) aus der Beichte oder sonst irgendwie erkennt, dass ein Angeklagter unschuldig ist?'

Here too we find that the consensus did not begin to break down until the persecution was under way. The first witch burnings appear to have had the character of *auto da fés*, great solemn ceremonies at which the repentant 'witches', who had been well coached in their roles by priests, were burned to death. As the report of a deacon from Höchstädt shows, the practice in Protestant areas was much the same.[296] Later this harmony was broken by dramatic incidents. Women screamed their innocence to the crowd from the stake itself. At the fourth great burning of witches in Werdenfels, in July 1590, the condemned cried to the women onlookers:

You pious women, fly across all the mountains; for whoever of you falls into the hands of the torturer and is severely tortured, must die![297]

RESISTANCE OF RELATIONS

While at the beginning of the persecutions even close relations believed in the guilt of the women, when they were presented with their written confessions by the authorities, this acceptance declined as soon as the persecution expanded, undoubtedly because circles were now being affected in which family cohesion and the possibilities of influence were greater. Cowherds, orphan children and solitary inmates of hospitals did not have the support that the wives of artisans, tavern keepers or patricians could mobilise for themselves.

The records of trials contain numerous petitions from family members, above all from husbands, who gave a positive character witness for their wives and demanded their release.[298] Yet there were also more 'discreet' means of exerting influence, which have only been recorded in exceptional cases. At Vohburg in 1592, for example, a tavern keeper stabbed a district court judge because his wife had been suspected of witchcraft.[299] A tavern keeper from Abensberg obtained an opinion from the University of Ingolstadt in favour of his wife.[300] Numerous town magistrates also seem to have been accessible to requests for a milder procedure.

The influence of relations was especially successful when their request was supported by external authorities. In Nördlingen the relations of a woman who originated from Ulm interceded with the Nördlingen authorities through the delegation from Ulm at the Imperial Diet of Regensburg in 1594. A consul of Nördlingen advised the council that there was a risk of proceedings in the Imperial Chamber Court or that the relations would

---

[296] HStAM, Hexenakten 16, fol. 186ff., fol. 278–80.
[297] Kuisl, *Die Hexen*, 27. It is typical that the reporter substitutes 'fly' for 'flee'.
[298] Cf. note 278.   [299] StAM, RL, Fasc. 24. no 99, Vizdombuch 1591–2, fol. 106.
[300] HStAM, RKG 6519.

take the case to the Emperor, and proposed that the woman be released on tactical grounds. Count Friedrich of Oettingen-Oettingen and a high official and councillor of the Duke of Württemberg also interceded on behalf of relations in Nördlingen.[301] The council of Nuremberg intervened several times to oppose proceedings against its subjects who faced accusations in the Margravate of Ansbach.[302]

The persecutions at Garmisch in 1591 were subjected to particularly intensive criticism. The husbands of two women declared in their petition that

> whoever falls into the hands of the torturer and is put to harsh torture, they must all die, as has happened and will happen. [In the event that; WB] the poor women say they are innocent of the act, they must be put to the strict torture again at once, and this is done for so long, until they must all be witches.[303]

This is criticism in principle, and no longer merely an attempt to save the lives of individual women. The district court judge of Werdenfels felt himself directly threatened by the husbands of the alleged witches, and feared that they would stir up a riot.[304] The criticism of the men unmistakably reflects the public protests of the 'witches' during their executions. The breakdown of consensus far from the residences of the rulers was not expressed in a difference of opinions, but threatened to take a more robust form.

PUBLIC PROTEST

Public protest at the persecutions can relatively seldom be documented, since discussion of persecution normally took place behind closed doors. Only a few individuals or corporations, not even the council of Nuremberg,[305] were willing to attract the reputation of protecting witches from the punishment they deserved. Moreover, there was no institutionalised public opinion in the modern sense. Nevertheless we can detect forms of opposition to persecutions that can be described as public, since they were not addressed to a special group of persons, but tried to influence the

---

[301] Wulz, 'Nördlinger Hexenprozesse' (1937–8), 110–12. Count Friedrich of Oettingen used his influence on behalf of his sister-in-law Margarethe Stachelin, wife of the Guardian in the House of Heilsbronn and daughter of a rich innkeeper. She was burned as a witch in 1594. Wulz, 'Die Nördlinger Hexen', no. 144. The wife of the Town Clerk, Anna Zweifel, who was related to the patriciate of Nördlingen, only escaped burning by fleeing to Stuttgart. Her case was defended by her father Balthasar Moseck von Filseck, a Councillor of the *Rentkammer* of Württemberg, but it proved impossible for her to return to Nördlingen, *ibid.*, no. 147.   [302] Kunstmann, *Zauberwahn*, 78–84.
[303] Kuisl, *Die Hexen*, 33.   [304] *Ibid.*, 32.   [305] Kunstmann, *Zauberwahn*, 194.

opinion of the whole population. Although the spoken word at gatherings, in taverns and in church has not usually been recorded, there are a few scattered reports. We have already mentioned the public and very effective protests of the women at their execution, and the stirring up of the population in Garmisch by relations of the executed women.

That account had to be taken of public protest by the clergy against the persecutions is shown by the case of a confessor and a hospital chaplain in Schongau, who incurred the particular wrath of the government because they not only accepted the revocation of confessions, but allowed themselves to form their own opinion, that the women were innocent, and openly proclaimed it.[306] The crassest case of disobedience and public protest took place in Nördlingen, where the Superintendent and city pastor Dr Wilhelm Friedrich Lutz took a stand against the persecutions from the very beginning, in biting sermons. Lutz must have been one of the most interesting personalities of the time in the region. A relation of the Württemberg Reformer Johann Brenz,[307] he had studied at the University of Tübingen in 1566–70, where he adopted the outlook of the local school of critics of the witchcraft trials.[308] He won his spurs as a confessional polemicist in Vienna and its neighbourhood, travelled in western Europe and took his doctorate at Tübingen, before being appointed Superintendent at Nördlingen. Lutz did not shrink from any conflict with the city government, and preached against social oppression (*pauper ubique iacet*) and also against the trial of witches. As early as December 1589 he voiced biting criticism of the Council in two sermons, for arresting 'some poor little dogs' who had certainly not committed the crime of which they were accused. Lutz thought little of alleged weather 'cooking' and witches' flight, and consequently of the witches' sabbath. He frankly criticised the procedure of the council, and preached sermons on torture and on the powerlessness of the witches (*de potestate lamiarum et de praestigiis*).

---

[306] StadtA Munich, Hist. Ver. Urk. no. 2058 (24.11.1590): Cf. note 295. The confessor referred to was probably a Jesuit from the Jesuit college at Landsberg, which was not far away. Adam Tanner was a novice at Landsberg at this time, and must have known of the case.

[307] G. Wulz, 'Wilhelm Friedrich Lutz (1531–1597)' *Lebensbilder aus dem Bayerischen Schwaben*, 5 (1956), 198–220. On the position of Brenz, especially as distinguished from that of Weyer, see H.C.E. Midelfort, 'Witchcraft and Religion in Sixteenth Century Germany. The Formation and Consequences of an Orthodoxy', *Archiv für Reformationsgeschichte*, 62 (1971), 266–78. On the reception of Weyer and Brenz by Catholics and Protestants in southeast Germany, see below, chapter 4, pp. 212–15.

[308] Wulz, 'Nördlinger Hexenprozesse' (1937–8), 108; Lutz appealed above all to the Tübingen theologians and Reformers Erhard Schnepf, Jacob Andreae and Jacob Heerbrand. When Lutz took his master's degree at Tübingen in 1570, Heerbrand had defended a disputation on witchcraft, arguing that witches could neither influence the weather nor commit sorcery. Heerbrand defended the effectiveness of *magia naturalis*, and merely condemned the witches' pact with the Devil. Midelfort, *Witch Hunting*, 40f.

The city council, following the Lutheran doctrine of the two kingdoms, forbade the Superintendent to interfere in criminal justice, to which he replied that 'he would not let himself be bound in his preaching on witchcraft'. When the Council made a direct appeal to him to keep silent on the matter at least during Easter 1590, he replied 'where he had no cause to do otherwise'.[309] In fact, by his sermons Lutz managed to put off the burnings for more than half a year, before the council of Nördlingen overrode the pastor's objections and had the first witches executed in July 1590. The Superintendent continued to form the centre of resistance to persecution in the Free City and defended his views in sermons, and on other occasions, for example at wedding feasts. The council kept trying to prevent him 'vilifying the Honourable Council because of the punishment of the work of the witches', but Lutz would not yield an inch:

For his person, he wished to preach God's word as before, and to have warned the Honourable Council to moderate the punishments.[310]

The open conflict between secular and spiritual authority found in Nördlingen between 1589 and 1594 was an exceptional phenomenon, the result of the direct clash of two opposing views. But one must bear in mind that the views of many Protestant clergy in Nuremberg, Ulm, Augsburg and Memmingen must have differed little from those of the Superintendent of Nördlingen, and that confrontation was only averted because of the moderate attitude of the local magistrates, including the largely Catholic city council of Augsburg. On the Catholic side too, one may assume that many priests exerted a moderating influence, and were satisfied to avoid persecutions in their towns and district courts.

Even if there was no public protest against the persecutions conducted by the authorities, it was clear to contemporaries that there were people at all levels of the population who could not agree with the persecutions. The pressure on the apologists of persecution to legitimise their activity can be proved from every single publication and many trial records.[311] They may

---

[309] Wulz, 'Lutz', 211f.   [310] *Ibid.*, 215.

[311] As an example we may mention the witchcraft tract of Binsfeld, translated into German and published at Munich in 1591, in which not only Binsfeld himself but also the foreword of the Munich printer Adam Berg, speak of doubts and attacks on the attitude of the authorities. *Ibid.*, dedication to Duke Ferdinand, a ii verso ff.: '... Dises alles ... hab ich darumben erzellen sollen, auff das die jenigen so irgent hierinn zweifelen, ein bericht haben, und nit also freventlich die hohe Obrigkeit in straffung solcher Laster urtheilen und nachreden, als ob sie die gemelten Hexen hierinn unrecht theten, darumben, das sie vermeinen, der Hexen Aussfahren und Verderben sey ein lauter Phantasey und Traumwerck (...) Datum München den 7. Aprilis, Im 1591. Jar.' ('I have been obliged to relate all this so that those who have any doubts on this matter may have an account of it, and not frivolously condemn the high authorities for the punishment of such vice, and talk as if they did the said witches an injustice, because they think that the witches' rides and the

have thought they were fighting God's battle: but they were often seen for what they really were.

CRITICAL VIEWS AMONG THE PEOPLE

Nor was the populace quite so firmly in the grip of the witch craze as the literature appears to assume. Accusations of witchcraft from the people represent only a small part of the spectrum of views, though it must be admitted that the opposition tendencies are more difficult to prove, as no records of hearings were kept if someone did not believe in witchcraft or did not bring an accusation. For all that, the belief in witchcraft was mentioned in a general way in trials for sorcery. It is evident that some of those questioned did not believe in the effectiveness of witchcraft, and others did not even believe in the existence of witches. A woman from Augsburg, whose husband was a mason by trade, told her interrogators she had 'never believed before that there were such people' (i.e. witches).[312] People who felt that they had been bewitched were a constant target of mockery. In 1590 an acquaintance complained to the wife of a 'man of war' that the wine in her cellar was growing less and less: to which she answered laughingly, 'since there was so much outcry now about witches, perhaps the witches had drunk the wine'.[313]

Critical voices were raised against the trials soon after they began. The chief complaint was that any old woman was now seen as a witch, and that, as always, it was only the poor who were being executed, while the rich went free. Such objections could even come from apologists for the trials. We can see a clear rejection of the trials in the statement of a woman from Nördlingen:

> she had often told her neighbour, how much they did the people wrong, when they accuse one of being a witch.[314]

From a gradual rejection of the persecutions, these views tended more and more to turn into a desire for them to be brought to an end, as soon as their catastrophic extent began to be clear. The methods of torture applied by

harm they do are fantasy and dreams.') The preface by the author, Binsfeld, also speaks of those who wish to prevent the witch burnings, because 'sie mit irer Vernunfft nit begreiffen mögen, für unmöglich halten' the deeds attributed to the witches. In general one can say that the appearance of tracts on witchcraft points to the theme being topical in a given locality. A tract was also written against the Superintendent of Nördlingen, Lutz (Melchior Fabricius, 'Tractetlin von dem Hexenwerk', Ms. Nördlingen 1593) but the City Council forbade its publication, Wulz, 'Lutz', 216.

[312] StadtA Augsburg, Urgichtenakten 1590 (Anna Gsellin), hearing of 5.7.1590.
[313] StadtA Augsburg, Urgichtenakten 1590 (Cath. Pretzelerin), hearing of 16.8.1590.
[314] Film 3718, 131.

the executioners were at the centre of the criticism, for one critic thought they made 'many more witches than we have in the country with their unbearable tortures', while others were already thinking about more drastic remedies:

> Why do the torturers have the freedom that they are not stretched on the outrageous rack? That would soon find out whether their art comes from the holy spirit or from the evil one.[315]

This suggestion reveals a dialectic in the background, since it connects the problem of torture with the question of principle posed by the persecutions. If the work of the notorious executioners of Biberach and Schongau could be described rhetorically as a work of the Devil, what was one to think of those who gave them their orders, the county court judges, the bishops and the princes? The clearest sign of the shift in the mood of the population comes from the County of Werdenfels (Bishopric of Freising), where in the summer of 1591 the Bishop's judge no longer dared to go among the people, believing his life was in danger, because of open resistance and the threatening attitude of his 'subjects'.[316]

During the persecutions the population became increasingly aware that if not all, at least some of those burned as witches were innocent, a view that contradicted the doctrine of the apologists of persecution. This conviction weakened popular support for the trials and helped resistance to grow. Relations were increasingly confident in coming forward with their criticism. We even have a record of a case in Höchstädt in which a prisoner was urged to revoke her confession, by people standing outside the prison at night.[317] Revocation and criticism even raised doubts in the government itself.

To counter such criticism a German translation of Binsfeld's treatise on witchcraft was prepared and printed at Munich in 1590–1. In the foreword, which was written in Munich, we read:

> And though one might find certain persons at this time who dare to say that people [who are burned as witches; WB] are wronged . . . many should be warned and protect themselves against such wicked evil talk . . . and conclude that the authorities do not wrong anyone . . .[318]

RESISTANCE OF TOWN MAGISTRATES

If, with the exception of Nördlingen, the governments of the Free Cities can be seen to have taken a rather moderate line, this also applies to the

[315] Kuisl, *Die Hexen*, 27.   [316] *Ibid.*, 34.   [317] HStAM, Hexenakten 16, fol. 261v.
[318] Binsfeld, *Tractatus*, Foreword, a ii.

larger territorial cities. Of course they were in a much more difficult position, since they were forced to hold trials for witchcraft by the central governments, while the Free Cities, or at least the larger ones, could stand up to the pressure of their territorial neighbours. This situation led to repeated conflicts between the territorial cities and their superiors. There are records of such conflicts in Dillingen (Bishopric of Augsburg), Günzburg, the chief town of the Habsburg Margravate of Burgau, and from Höchstädt in Pfalz-Neuburg under the jurisdiction of the Count Palatine.[319]

In the Duchy of Bavaria the government regarded the cities of Ingolstadt and Munich as notoriously recalcitrant. As early as 1589 the later Duke Maximilian wrote to the reigning Duke Wilhelm V in Munich that the Council of Ingolstadt was not showing 'much enthusiasm' for the arrest and torture of witches. This attitude did not change later. Time and again authors of reports from Ingolstadt complained that the citizenry showed no signs of holding trials for witchcraft even when accusations arose among the people. A close confidant of the Duke wrote from Ingolstadt that

although there are very shrewd suspicions against several persons who at any rate have a bad reputation for witchcraft, no questions are asked about it, and people here are blind and deaf.[320]

It was no different in the capital, Munich, itself, where trials for witchcraft, which in themselves fell within the competence of the city court, had been withdrawn from it in advance, because the city magistrates were not trusted to conduct a trial.[321] Remarks in the minutes of the city council for 1590 allow us to infer that the citizenry made vigorous protests to the government. The question of homage to the future Duke was to be made dependent on a restriction of arrests and of the practice of torture![322]

[319] HStAM, Hochstift Augsburg, NA, Akten no. 1188, fol. 52, 58, fol. 115v. J. Völk, 'Ein Günzburger Hexenprozess', *Schwäbische Heimat. Beilage zum Günz-und Mindelboten* (1928), no. 809; HStAM, Hexenakten 16, fol. 185f. StA Neuburg, Grassegger-Sammlung no. 15377.   [320] SBM, Cgm. 2210, fol. 119v, 'nit vil ...' Riezler, *Geschichte*, 192.
[321] M. Kunze, 'Zum Kompetenzkonflikt zwischen städtischer und herzoglicher Strafgerichtsbarkeit in Münchner Hexenprozessen', *Zeitschrift der Savigny Stiftung für Rechtsgeschichte. Germanistische Abteilung*, 87 (170), 305–14. More on this in Behringer, 'Scheiternde Hexenprozesse', 61–8, 75–8.
[322] StadtA Munich, Bürgermeister und Rat no. 54 A 19 (Stadtratsprotokoll 1586–96), fol. 45v. Three points are raised, to be considered as preconditions before the city would pay homage to Duke Maximilian ('erbhuldigung ea conditione ...'). The points were fixed at the end of May or in early June 1590. All three refer to the witch hunts of that time. The first two are concerned with the interventions of the state government in the city's criminal justice ('1. erclärung der landsfreyheiten ... nit zu schmelern. 2. modo non sit in praeiudicium privilegiorum'), the third directly with the unlawful procedure of the ducal commissioners in the trials ('3. non facile ad capturam et torturam procedendum'). These

CHANGING OPINION IN THE GOVERNMENTS

At the very beginning of the persecutions, individual voices in the territorial governments had already been raised against persecution. In Ansbach a councillor was unwilling to sign a verdict against some witches,[323] in Pfalz-Neuburg the weeping test was found unacceptable and doubt was expressed about the possibility of witches' flight.[324] In Bavaria the Ingolstadt professor and Court Councillor Dr Caspar Lagus had from the start supported a 'general pardon' for witches who confessed, because he wished to avoid the persecutions bursting their bounds.[325] Presumably there were other sceptical voices, but like those of the critics who have come down to us, they were outvoted.

In one territory after the other, however, the critical voices grew louder from the summer of 1590, as the damage caused by the persecutions became apparent. Councillors of the Duke of Bavaria, who were in charge of the persecution at Ingolstadt, came to the conclusion:

It is difficult to deal with these persons. They are fickle. They soon go back on their word. They say they have confessed because of the pain and torture. But they persist in saying that they have yielded themselves to the Devil . . . but they insist they did not know who their accomplices were. They only confess to those who are all under suspicion, so that they should not be tortured and tormented any more [and it is evident; WB] that at times they only name them out of spite.[326]

Members of the governments too now began to come round to the view that too much trust had perhaps been placed in denunciations, and that it was hardly possible to decide the guilt or innocence of those denounced on the basis of the statements.

In Freising, where massive resistance from the subjects of Werdenfels

demands were put forward in the capital before the first witch burning (2 July 1590), but had little effect initially. The Estates paid homage, in the end, at the Diet of 1593–4 (11.1.1594). In return Duke Maximilian confirmed the existing law and the right of the Estates to object to and to oppose unjust interventions. P.P. Wolf and C.W.F. Breyer *Geschichte Maximilians I. und seine Zeit*, 4 vols., Munich 1807–11, I, 135–9.

[323] Lang, *Geschichte*, III, 340. Chancellor Stadtmann refused to sign a sentence of death on witches from Schwabach because such crimes could not be proven and the learned were not in agreement. The Chancellor of the County of Oettingen-Wallerstein was then asked to convince the Chancellor of the Margravate.

[324] StAM, Hexenakten 16, fol. 97v: '... dass aber auch diss angezogen und gleichssam vor ein sonderlich merckzeichen einer hexen will fürgeben werden, dass die Turnerin [Appollonia Galgenmüllerin of Wittislingen, burned as a witch on 20.1.1588; WB] in ihrem Weinen keine Zecher [tears; WB] von sich geben, das halte ich meinestheils ... für lächerlich'. ('But that this is cited too, and supposed to be a special mark of a witch, that Turnerin shed no tears even when crying, for my part I find it ridiculous.')

[325] StadtA Munich, Hist. Ver. Urk. 2050.   [326] Geyer, 'Hexen', 18.

was supported by influential citizens of Freising, a councillor of the Prince-Bishop felt in early 1591 that great care must be taken

> that not too much should be done in the matter and wrong done to no one, especially because in such doubtful cases it is better to acquit the guilty than to condemn the innocent. I am moved to this opinion and view by the following causes. Firstly because under the law accomplices in crime are not usually to be believed without other accompanying [circumstantial evidence; WB] and secondly that the guilty witches and sorceresses often wish . . . that all women must be condemned to death through their statements.[327]

But it was just this additional evidence that caused the greatest difficulties. At the beginning of the persecutions, the authorities had relied heavily on the skills of the executioners, and great weight had been attached to the reputations of the accused, even when it was known from the hearings that these had in most cases only been given credibility by the manipulations of the soothsayers. Generally torture was readily resorted to.

Critics of persecution concentrated more and more on the influence of the executioners in the course of the persecutions, and their arguments began to have a noticeable effect on the governments, with regard to the magical practices of the headsmen, the alleged infallibility of the witches' mark, and the inhuman severity of the tortures, which went far beyond the normal bounds. In Ansbach a faction formed within the government itself, strengthened by criticism from Nuremberg, which openly criticised the procedure applied and demanded that the Margrave should end the 'improper procedure and forbidden methods' which, in their view, had been used in the persecution. They were relatively frank in telling the Margrave that his councillors felt he had been misled by false advisers.[328] It was easier to make these criticisms in the Margravate because the tortures had been inflicted by the executioner of Eichstätt, so that the difference of opinion on the right procedure could be represented as a confessional conflict.

The use of consecrated salt and water, the preparation of the meal by the executioner and the search for the witches' mark were themselves a kind of sorcery in the eyes of the councillors of Ansbach, and one which could not possibly be used in trials for witchcraft.

> Since a foreign executioner was called in here, who is not only objectionable, as being of the popish religion, and, as the common rumour goes, a finder of devils or witches . . . and also uses improper and forbidden

---

[327] HStAM, Hexenakten 9a, fol. 412v, 413.
[328] 'Bedenken, die Unhulden betreffend', 538.

methods, searching for the witches' mark, and is said to have used more of the same kind of sorcery, in as much as information reaches us that among some popish authorities the same is also said to be undertaken. But if such a way is not the right and proper means to bring the truth to light, or to reach a verdict, and it is unheard of among the other Evangelical estates elsewhere that one should tolerate and authorise such idolatrous headsmen and popish ceremonies, and thus drive out one devil with another, or use sorcery against sorcery . . .

So we would humbly and kindly be pleased to see that your Illustrious Princely Grace should dispense with the present idolatrous executioner here and his sorcerous ceremonies and deceitful tricks . . .[329]

Though this criticism was presented as confessional, exactly the same problem exercised the governments of the Catholic territories. There too people were increasingly troubled by the influence of the executioners, though in this case less by their 'popish ceremonies' than by the alleged significance of the witches' mark. In October 1590, at the request of the government in Freising, the University of Ingolstadt issued a statement of principle that the witches' mark could not be regarded as a safe proof, since 'such a common and despised person' as an executioner could be mistaken in recognising it.[330] This was, it is true, no change from the first opinion on witchcraft of April 1590, as that had not taken up any position on the witches' mark. But by way of explanation it ruled out the mark as evidence, which had not been the case six months earlier. In subsequent opinions the University restated this position.[331]

The increasingly frequent intervention of respected persons with the governments, the denunciations of judges or their wives, the misery of the hearings under torture, and of course the popular mood, all wore down the persecuting zeal of the governments. Above all the 'social expansion' of the persecutions, their tendency to jump to the higher ranks of society, made it difficult for the governments, if it was not to be claimed that they lacked any sympathy for the fate of the lower orders. Not just the common folk, but the upper classes as well saw clearly that the persecutions would come to a halt if they themselves were threatened with being drawn into them. In every persecution women from the lower classes exploited this knowledge for their own benefit. The judges and governments were powerless against this, unless they were willing to adopt overt class justice and exclude those of higher rank from all charges in advance.

The problem for the governments, which for their part were willing to

---

[329] *Ibid.*, 541f.
[330] HStAM, Hexenakten 9a, fol. 456–71. Schrittenloher, 'Aus der Gutachter- und Urteilstätigkeit', 324.
[331] HStAM, GR 323/16, fol. 3–16 (opinion of 18.7.1592).

continue the persecutions, was that they saw fewer and fewer possibilities of testing the truth of the suspicions, and thus distinguishing the 'truly guilty' from the 'maliciously accused'. It was not a fundamental, principled criticism of the paradigm of witchcraft that was required in 1590 – the criticisms began at different times in the individual territories – but at first merely a pragmatic testing of the methods of torture which had come to be recognised as inadequate. This soon confronted them with the dilemma that was to characterise the later debates in the years 1600–30 (cf. chapter 4). As soon as they began to bring the procedure back into the normal channels, and apply the usual criteria to circumstantial evidence as grounds for arrest or torture, or to restrict the use of impermissible evidence, such as soothsayers, unsupported denunciations, the witches' mark etc., the persecutions were over. In 1591 this was presumably not yet realised, or if the opponents of persecution already knew it, they did not shout it from the rooftops. The changes demanded were minimal, but their effects were profound.

REGULATORY EFFORTS AT THE END OF THE PERSECUTIONS

The breakdown of consensus resulted in attempts to regulate the matter in principle and to guarantee that the persecutions would take their proper course, so that not only would witches be rooted out, but the innocent would be protected against torture and burning. The blind persecuting zeal of the *Malleus*, of Bodin and Binsfeld, had been discredited by the persecutions themselves, and now an effort was made to bring order to the witch trials within the respective territorial contexts.

These attempts at regulation were doomed to fail in advance, if they tried to reconcile ruthless persecution and extreme caution, which were mutually exclusive. Fundamentally, the opinions from Höchstädt, Ingolstadt and Ansbach[332] represent curious 'hermaphrodites', which can only be explained if we understand that they attempted to integrate differing opinions within the ruling bodies of the territories. The honourable efforts of some of the drafters of these opinions to avoid the persecution of the innocent are not in question:

for in such very important matters, which concern the body, honour and life, yes even the soul and salvation of man, one should not proceed in passion, thoughtlessly, hastily and seeking vengeance, but it is vitally necessary that one should proceed cautiously, in accordance with the Common Law and the well-considered and reasonable ordinances, so

---

[332] Cf. above p. 118, note 12.

that the innocent are not molested, imprisoned, cruelly tortured and punished as if they were guilty, by which an authority will incur wide notoriety; yea, most of all so that God's fifth commandment is not broken, and the blood of a human being made in God's image is not shed.[333]

Even though the considerations in all the territories tended in the same direction, they were oriented, so far as can be recognised, along confessional lines towards certain examples. For the moderate party in the Margravate of Ansbach this was the Franconian metropolis, Nuremberg; for the Protestant authorities in Swabia, the attitude of Württemberg or of the University of Tübingen counted for more.[334] The Catholic territories of southeast Germany, the Duchy of Bavaria, the Bishoprics of Freising, Eichstätt and presumably also Augsburg, were oriented towards the opinions of the University of Ingolstadt, which can thus be taken as an index of the cautious change of attitude in the Catholic territories of the region.

The opinion in principle, issued on the instructions of Duke Wilhelm V of Bavaria in April 1590, already contained severe terms against two grave abuses in the trials: firstly, the suggestion of falsehoods by the interrogator, which Bodin had declared permissible,[335] and secondly the use of other superstitious means to confirm a suspicion of witchcraft. This term opposed the 'water test', which in any case was not very common in Bavaria, and thus reveals its dependence on Binsfeld.[336] More important was the exhortation not to found any suspicion of witchcraft on the statements of soothsayers:

nor is any soothsayer or black magician to be believed, who identifies a witch through his black and diabolical arts, unless such sorcery or witchcraft witnesses to things that human reason can also understand . . .[337]

When we recall that consulting a soothsayer was the most important means of proving witchcraft in popular magic, and the role it had still played at the beginning of the persecutions in 1586–9, we can appreciate the importance of this rule. Later opinions were even more specific. An opinion of 22 May 1592, prepared for the Bishopric of Eichstätt, stipulated

---

[333] 'Bedenken, die Unhulden betreffend', 539.
[334] Kunstmann, *Zauberwahn*, 186–211; Midelfort, *Witch Hunting*, 36–56. In 1588 the parish priest Moses Pflacher interpreted the great inflation for the citizens of Kempten, entirely in line with the Württemberg orthodoxy, as a sign from God, who caused all injustice directly – without witches – to move people to mend their ways and show penitence. Midelfort, *ibid.*, 41f. and note 54, from M. Pflacher, *Weinthewre (...)*, Tübingen 1589.
[335] HStAM, Hexenakten 1, Prod. 1, fol. 7v.   [336] *Ibid.*   [337] *Ibid.*

that in each case the origin of a slander or rumour had to be investigated, since it was not always immediately possible to recognise its source.

> We therefore obediently give your Princely Grace to understand that . . . no person should be arrested . . . on a mere tale . . . whose grounds and actual origin, from which it comes, are not known. . .[338]

This opinion would not accept as circumstantial evidence an accusation emanating from the 'common populace', from malicious people, those who readily repeated evil tales, enemies or those who were themselves under suspicion.

As we have already shown, the University of Ingolstadt also tried to restrain the influence of the executioners, by declaring the witches' mark to be doubtful evidence, in two opinions for the government of the Prince-Bishopric of Freising.[339] Also very important was the change in attitude to the use of torture in trials for witchcraft, which was becoming apparent: the opinion in principle of April 1590 had still permitted a quick application of torture 'in this vice, which is very difficult to test', when the accused was too uncommunicative. On the other hand, the opinion of 1592 said that torture should not be lightly undertaken and

> not be applied on too little or very slight circumstantial evidence, by which a suspect is wronged. . .[340]

This opinion explicitly states that 'everyday experience' had shown

> that often the witches name pious and innocent people out of pure hatred, spite and at the instigation of their master, so that, if the same innocent people are tortured, they might become desperate and, as they must burn for the dreadful vice they have committed, they are glad to see the whole world burn with them.

Fundamentally, however, the opinion of 1592 did not escape from the dilemma, that in principle there was a demand for the burning of the 'really guilty'. It therefore concluded by remarking that the judges should not demand too much circumstantial evidence for the admission of torture, for otherwise 'for lack of the same the whole trial would be hindered . . . and in this lack, the evil must remain unpunished'.[341]

The University therefore moved toward a more cautious attitude but did not break completely with the procedure employed hitherto. For that, political decisions were necessary, which could only be taken by the governments.

---

[338] HStAM, GR 323/16, fol. 9v.   [339] Cf. note 330.
[340] HStAM, Hexenakten 1, Prod. 1, fol. 8v–9. For evidence to the contrary *ibid.*, GR 323/16, fol. 10v.   [341] *Ibid.*, fol. 10.

In fact a more or less open breaking off of the persecutions can be demonstrated in several territories. In general one could say that until the summer of 1590, the crest of the wave of persecution, a relatively unbroken mood of persecution is recognisable among the governments. In the autumn of 1590 the persecutions in several territories in Swabia and Bavaria came to a halt, though in almost all the places where persecutions had been held there were still prisoners suspected of witchcraft. They had been denounced by the witches already executed, and the governments could not make up their mind to release them.[342] New arrests were already being carried out, in general, with more caution, as was the use of torture. Attempts were also made to prevent the persecutions spreading. The government at Dillingen ordered that parish priests should 'forbid the outcry against witches from the pulpit'[343] and thus calm the mood of the people. In the Bishopric of Freising no new arrests were undertaken in 1591, nor were there any in Schongau or Munich. In the second half of the year a few women under particular suspicion, on whose release it had not yet been possible to decide, were executed in Freising and Ingolstadt, and then the persecution lapsed. The Bavarian Governor in Ingolstadt received an order from the Duke forbidding him to arrest any more witches.[344] In November 1591 the government at Dillingen forbade the county court judge of Schwabmünchen to make any more arrests; in summer 1592, apparently because of the plague, the persecution at Oberdorf, the last great persecution south of the Danube, was stopped.[345] After the end of the plague the trials were not resumed in the Bishopric of Augsburg, although, of course, the lists of names of suspects and those denounced were still on file wherever persecutions had been held.

Even in the Bishopric of Augsburg great caution was exercised about accusations of witchcraft after 1592. When further accusations were brought in the courts of Zusmarshausen and Schwabmünchen the government in Dillingen had the origin of the suspicion very thoroughly investigated. Credence was no longer given to mere suspicions, for they had become too common. A minute of the Court Council puts it into context in a remark that a woman had accused another 'as so many others have done'.[346] As in Bavaria the accused were no longer simply arrested, but the denunciation or the accuser was very thoroughly investigated first. As

---

[342] This was the case even at Höchstätt in Pfalz-Neuburg, where no further executions were carried out after 1588, but a decision to release the remaining prisoners was not taken until a year later. HStAM, Hexenakten 16, fol. 337. A further Neuburg recognisance for a witch of 1588 is found in HStAM, SV 2225, no. 60.
[343] HStAM, Hochstift Augsburg, NA, Akten no. 1200, fol. 301v.
[344] Geyer, 'Hexen', 26.
[345] HStAM, Hochstift Augsburg, NA, Akten no. 1205, fol. 153.
[346] *Ibid.*, no. 1210, fol. 196f.

before the beginning of the great persecutions, now again accusations rebounded on the accusers. They, and not the accused, were interrogated in detail by the court, and were forbidden on pain of punishment to utter further accusations, or else they were directly punished for their unprovable suspicions.[347] But how could the alleged victims have substantiated their suspicions when the traditional proof through popular magic and soothsayers was forbidden, and torture was only applied by the authorities when very strong circumstantial evidence was present to justify it?

The most important document for the breaking off of the persecution comes from the small Free City of Kaufbeuren in Swabia. After the persecutions in the neighbouring knightly territory of Osterzell and the Guardian's court of Oberdorf had led to an increase in accusations of witchcraft in the city, several women were arrested and burned as witches in July 1591. But popular excitement did not decline after the executions, on the contrary it only grew even greater. The council, which had meanwhile begun to feel doubts about the correctness of its actions, resolved on a bold step: on 25 June 1591 it adopted a decree, 'On the outcry against the work of witches', which was published on the following two days. It forbade further accusations of witchcraft and threatened the severest penalties 'in person and property'. The council criticised the fact that

among men and women, young and old, there is much wicked, slanderous and disgraceful talk, yes even among married couples such unseemly, undesirable and reprehensible offensive remarks are made that some accuse the others of the accursed and pernicious work of witches, when no probable grounds can or may be represented or brought before the authorities. But everything is the thoughtless result either of untimely spite and anger or otherwise of frivolous and wilful insolence.

To take timely steps to prevent such evil before it spreads alarmingly, so that death or other wrongs result from it, the Honourable Council hereby strictly and most earnestly commands . . . on pain of punishment of person and property, that from henceforth everyone, whoever he may be, young or old, rich or poor, man or woman, married couple, servants, whoever they may be, shall wholly refrain and abstain from thoughtless, frivolous, dishonourable outpourings of complaints, evil talk and crying out suspicions of the work and name of witchcraft, and shall not undertake anything further in the same matter . . .[348]

As in Munich and Freising, the persecution was also broken off in the Free City of Donauwörth, after accusations against the rich or patrician citizens had become more frequent. A wealthy apothecary's wife, a burgomaster's

347 *Ibid.*, fol. 209f.   348 StadtA Kaufbeuren, B 106, fol. 164v–6.

daughter, was executed; another patrician, the daughter of the burgomaster Hans Buecher who had once introduced the Reformation into the city, was under severe suspicion and took her own life after some years in prison.[349] In the County of Oettingen, the persecutions ended after the Countess herself had fallen under suspicion of being a witch.[350]

The breaking off of the persecutions by no means meant that the new idea of witchcraft had been abandoned, or that persecution was no longer acknowledged to be necessary. On the contrary. The persecutions had been discontinued because people had become convinced that innocent victims had suffered; this was seen as a particularly treacherous device of the Devil, who not only brought harm on humanity through the witches, but also compromised the authorities, who were incapable of distinguishing the innocent from the guilty. The belief in the existence of witches had, however, been cemented by the numerous confessions and executions. With the breaking off of the persecutions in the years after 1590, the last word had not been spoken.

[349] Zelzer, *Geschichte*, 208, 395; Grohsmann, *Geschichte*, 256.
[350] Riezler, *Geschichte*, 239.

4 The struggle for restraint, 1600–30

THE WITCH CRAZE AT ITS PEAK

Far from closing the debate on witchcraft, the end of the wave of persecution in 1590 made it even more explosive. A hundred years earlier, the persecutions of the papal Inquisitors had set an example, and now the witch burnings of 1590 did the same. Even though many criticised the burning of the 'innocent', and though the danger that the persecutions would spread to the upper classes had been revealed, these were not unanswerable arguments against further persecution. On the contrary; the persecutions of 1590 had to some extent met long-cherished popular demands for persecution and seemed to have vindicated those who had long been warning of the great danger from witches. The confessions read out in public at the executions – if several witches were being executed it often took hours to read the full details[1] – anchored the belief in witchcraft even more firmly in the consciousness of the people. A witness told the court in Augsburg that she had 'never believed before that there were such people, until she had now seen that it was open and public'.[2]

While the radical critic Weyer had repeatedly criticised the persecutions as a 'bloodbath of the innocents'[3] in the numerous editions of his works published during the last third of the century, after 1590 people were unwilling to believe that thousands could have been judicially murdered. Even decided critics like Montaigne or Goedelmann did not directly question the existence of witches, but used covert arguments, and only challenged parts of the elaborated concept of witchcraft and the judicial procedure.[4] The suppression of the uncompromising critic Cornelius Loos

[1] *Erweytterte Unholden Zeyttung*, in Behringer, 'Hexenverfolgung', 351.
[2] StadtA Augsburg, Urgichtenakten 1590 (Anna Gsellin).
[3] Weyer, *De praestigiis Daemonum*, foreword.
[4] Montaigne, in Becker, *et al., Aus der Zeit*, 385–9; J.G. Goedelmann, *Tractatus de magis, veneficiis et lamiis*, Nuremberg 1584; J.G. Goedelmann, *Von Zauberern, Hexen und Unholden Warhafftiger und Wolgegründter Bericht (. . .)*, Frankfurt am Main 1592. The Protes-

in 1592 left other critics in no doubt that their room for manoeuvre had been restricted.[5]

Finally, in many places a party of outright persecutors was formed, who pressed for the resumption of persecutions, which in their eyes had been a success.

THE PROTESTANT SOLUTION

THE SCOPE OF THE DISCUSSION: BETWEEN WEYER AND BODIN

Midelfort has rightly pointed out that until about 1590 there were no unambiguous differences between the confessions on the question of witchcraft. There were hard-liners and representatives of more moderate views in all confessions. The Reformers had not done away with the belief in witches. In Luther's Wittenberg and Calvin's Geneva, women had been burned as witches in the 1540s, and the Zwinglian Bullinger also commended such activities as pleasing to God. The role of Protestant preachers in disseminating the fully developed theory of witchcraft, for example in Scotland or Transylvania, is well known. Some of the earliest post-Reformation persecutions – in Denmark in the 1540s, in Württemberg in the 1560s – were undertaken by Protestant authorities. The Protestant wave of persecution of 1562–3 probably provoked the anti-persecution polemic, already mentioned, *De Praestigiis Daemonum* of the Johann Weyer.

Both opponents and supporters of persecution could look back on their own tradition in the sixteenth century. The *Malleus Maleficarum* ('Hammer of Witches') was regarded as an authority by many Protestants too. Yet besides this tradition, which went back to the *Malleus*, Reformation theology had also incorporated an older and wider tradition, which admitted that the Devil was active on Earth, but in fact excluded his 'bodily' contact with depraved people, and denied that he carried them through the air or copulated with them. In this view real cases of witchcraft were non-existent or very rare miracles. The evil deeds only took place in the imagination of those whom the Devil had deluded. This *Episcopi* tradi-

tant jurist Goedelmann came from Württemberg, studied at Tübingen and taught at the University of Rostock in the 1580s. He was particularly opposed to Bodin and to the scholastic doctrine, adapted by Bodin, of *crimen exceptum*, for which the *Carolina* offered no foundation. Lea, *Materials*, II, 761–88; Thorndyke, *History*, VI, 535–7; Janssen and Pastor, *Culturzustände*, VIII, 571–4. Paulus, *Hexenwahn*, 125, is wrong to assume that Goedelmann's admonitions in favour of milder treatment of witches were 'die Stimme eines Predigers in der Wüste'. Even in distant Catholic Bavaria, after 1582 when the writings of Johann Weyer were placed on the Index, Goedelmann was cited as the most important witness for the opponents of witch hunting.

[5] E. Zenz, 'Cornelius Loos – ein Vorläufer Friedrich von Spees im Kampf gegen den Hexenwahn', *Kurtrierisches Jahrbuch*, 21 (1981), 147–53; Baschwitz, *Hexen*, 147–53.

tion[6] had been strongly represented at the University of Tübingen even before the Reformation, and was continued by the Reformer Johann Brenz and his followers. In Brenz's opinion controlling the weather by spells or the like was impossible, and only the spiritual crime of forsaking God and willing evil was real.[7] When persecution was resumed in Germany in 1560 the discussion was radically polarised: the Calvinist Weyer flatly denied the existence of witchcraft and stigmatised the burnings as a 'bloodbath of the innocents'. The Catholic Bodin reformulated and rationalised the assumptions of the *Malleus*, and demanded the merciless persecution of witches. Both authors were regarded as authorities by the Lutherans of southeast Germany and served, for example in Ansbach,[8] as starting points for the discussion of the opposing points of view. The south German Protestants displayed a persistent affinity for the *Episcopi* tradition,[9] which triumphed in the reaction to the wave of persecution of 1590.

CONFESSIONALISATION OF CRITICISM IN THE REGION

In the debates, critics in the Protestant territories of southeast Germany were remarkably quick to take the line of confessional polemic when they had to find arguments for the ending or restriction of persecution. In principle the Pfalz-Neuburg jurist Mumprecht was already following this line in a legal opinion of 1588, when he urged theologians to consider the implications of the fact that this crime was not mentioned in the Bible:

> Thus if this *atrocissimum facinus* is not included as a sin in the Holy Scriptures, then indeed it must not be far from it ... which I leave to the theologians to dispute ...[10]

During the persecutions, confessional polemic came increasingly to the fore as an argument against the apologists of persecution within the polemicists' own ranks. This is most clearly expressed in an Ansbach opinion of 1591, which attacks the adoption of the 'Catholic' paradigm of persecution. The Margrave is advised that

> as it appears to some of our coreligionist lords and friends that they ought to adopt and understand such, so we, as our duty bids us, cannot conceal from Your Illustrious Princely Grace that there is already some evil speech of this from other Evangelical persons and it is also demanded that in these countries, where, God be praised, preaching is still

---

[6] Midelfort, *Witch Hunting*, 65. So called from the *canon Episcopi* which denied the possibility of flight through the air.   [7] *Ibid.*, 34–8.   [8] Muck, *Geschichte*, II, 59.
[9] Midelfort, *Witch Hunting*; 36–56. Kunstmann, *Zauberwahn*, 176f., 186f., 197, but esp. 54–73.   [10] HStAM, Hexenakten 16, fol. 140v.

pure and clear, that the same irregular procedure . . . should be admitted.[11]

The 'irregular' procedure was identified by Protestant critics with the witchcraft trials of the Catholic authorities, which, following the doctrine of the *crimen exceptum*, had gone well beyond the rules laid down in imperial legislation for arrest and torture. Many Catholic rites (exorcism, the use of consecrated objects, benedictions etc.) were sorcery in the eyes of orthodox Protestants, who drew far-reaching conclusions from this point of view: the Superintendent of Pfalz-Neuburg, Jacob Heilbronner, described several Catholic scholars as sorcerers; Tübingen Lutherans[12] found it as self-evident as the theologians of the Free City of Nuremberg that the 'detestable idolatries' of 'popery' had first provoked the growth of witchcraft,[13] and a pastor from Schwäbisch Hall said in 1589 that Catholicism in general had a tendency to witchcraft because it led to superstitious rites.[14]

During the years immediately after 1590 this confessional criticism of persecution became more firmly established. It was a specific feature of Protestant criticism that it did not simply object to abuses of procedure, but that it repeatedly questioned parts of the elaborated concept of witchcraft *per se*. This helped to maintain the great variety of opinions that had existed in the period before the great persecutions of the later sixteenth century. Protestants denied, for example, that witches could change into animal shapes, that they copulated with the Devil, and even that it was possible for them to fly through the air – which meant denying the witches' sabbaths – as well as denying the reality of harmful sorcery. This perspective left nothing but a purely spiritual crime, that of forsaking God, of making a pact with the Devil, and of wishing to use witchcraft to cause harm. The offence was thereby 'dematerialised' to such an extent that many theologians wondered if a mere will could be punished by a death sentence.[15] The Protestant attitude after 1590 was characterised by a strong emphasis on the deceitful machinations of the Devil, who tricked the witches into believing that they had been to witches' sabbaths and had caused harm. This emphasis can be demonstrated in nearly all the Protestant areas: in the Free Cities of Kaufbeuren, Nördlingen and Nuremberg as well as in the territories of Oettingen-Oettingen, Pfalz-Neuburg or the Franconian Margravates. The key words that provided an explanation even for self-delusion were 'trickery', *phantasma, praestigia daemonum*.[16]

---

[11] 'Bedenken, die Unhulden betreffend', 543.   [12] Midelfort, *Witch Hunting*, 63.
[13] Kunstmann, *Zauberwahn*, 184.   [14] Midelfort, *Witch Hunting*, 63.   [15] *Ibid.*, 50.
[16] Kunstmann, *Zauberwahn*, 180f., mentioned here as representative of numerous other pieces of evidence.

THE IMPORTANCE OF THE PROTESTANT ATTITUDE

The cities and territories under Protestant rule largely suspended persecutions after the end of the wave of persecution of 1590,[17] albeit without disputing the existence of witches, or the necessity of punishing them. Suspicions of witchcraft were still investigated, as is shown by evidence from the Free Cities and the Principality of Pfalz-Neuburg (before its recatholicisation was begun in 1614). But sentences of execution were not passed as readily as before, and an expansion of the trials into a persecution was avoided. In this perspective a witchcraft trial at Hemau in Pfalz-Neuburg in 1610–11 is particularly informative. Only the main defendant, a seventy-seven-year-old man, was executed, while eight other accused were released on bail or on recognisances, although the charges against them were serious, they were relatives of the old man and were regarded with distrust by the local deacon.[18] The decline in Protestant witch burnings in southwestern Germany corresponded with developments at the same time in the southwest.[19]

As far as we can conclude from the literature and the researches of the *H-Sonderkommando*, a broad belt of territories (the Margravate of Ansbach, Bayreuth, Electoral Upper Palatinate, the Free Cities of Rothenburg, Nuremberg and Dinkelsbühl, and Pfalz-Neuburg until 1614) remained free from persecution in the subsequent period. Protestant influence was, however, continuously eroded by the territorial gains of the Counter-Reformation. In addition, the debate on witchcraft was polarised as certain arguments came to be regarded as 'Protestant' and could no longer be used by Catholic opponents of persecution.

THE CATHOLIC STANCE HARDENS

REJECTION OF PROTESTANT VIEWS

In the Catholic territories the objections to the holding of witch trials were well known. The nobleman von Randeckh wrote, in self-justification, that

> as in this case the most learned theologians, jurists and philosophers engage in the most violent polemics against one another, as can be seen from their published writings, in which it is found that some of them even hold the old wives' tales and confessions to be a dream and fantasy; and so they consider the same not liable to punishment, or that the crime is not worthy to be punished by death by burning.[20]

[17] In the territory of the present Federal State of Bavaria, only Saxony-Coburg was an exception. Film 494.   [18] Film 1160, from HStAM, Hexenakten 17, fasc. 3.
[19] Midelfort, *Witch Hunting*, 204ff.
[20] HStAM, SV 2243, fol. 190ff. According to Bosl, *Bayern*, 601f., the author may have been Count Alexius Fugger.

Weyer and other moderate authors had numerous followers among the Catholics. Just as in southwestern Germany, we can say of Bavaria that an official theory of witchcraft did not exist before 1590 and moderate positions remained possible until into the 1580s.[21] An explicit appeal to the Protestant authors, who were now on the Index, was of course no longer possible.

In 1590 positions in the debate on witchcraft became polarised, as a result of criticism of the content of the elaborated concept of witchcraft and the decline in the readiness of Protestant authorities, e.g. Pfalz-Neuburg, to carry out persecutions. The impetus came from a generation of jurists and theologians brought up in the spirit of the Counter-Reformation; many of the ruling princes, but fewer townsmen and nobles, were also imbued with this ideology. An opinion given by the Court Council at Munich on 2 April 1590 was one of the first to draw the classical distinction between Catholics and heretics. The Council had discussed the principles that were to decide the proper attitude to questions of witchcraft. During the discussion it came to

a statement of the opinion on the part of some, especially on the Scholars' Bench, who did not think much of this vice and scarcely believed that the Evil One could do such things with human aid, but that they were *praestigia, imaginationes* and strong *impressiones*, and this opinion, which in our time is said to be that of the greater part of the heretics, *in specie* Weyerus and Brenzius, was refuted and confuted *atque tam ex profanis quam ex sacris historiis et libris*, and indeed through everyday experience which cannot mislead and in all things is certain proof, was demonstrated to be an heretical opinion . . . [22]

The drawing of a distinction from the chief critics, Weyer and Brenz, was carried out with remarkable radicalism. The Catholic tradition that was critical of trials for witchcraft, and had been handed down from the *Canon Episcopi* through Ulrich Molitor to the age of the persecutions – we may mention the Freiburg theologian Lorichius and the Ingolstadt pastor Wegmann[23] – was simply denied. It was asserted, quite contrary to the truth, that

all Catholic and approved authors *tam recentiores quam antiqui*, unanimously write that whoever does not believe and holds it doubtful that such a vice is imposed on humanity by God, the same is not only to be held a heretic but *pro mago*.[24]

---

[21] Riezler, *Geschichte*, 139f., 233; Midelfort, *Witch Hunting*, 33f., 58.
[22] HStAM, Hexenakten 1, Prod. 4, fol. 1v.
[23] Midelfort, *Witch Hunting*, 60; Riezler, *Geschichte*, 234.
[24] HStAM, Hexenakten 1, Prod. 4, fol. 2.

Thus the only possible Catholic position in Munich was declared to be the acceptance of the *Malleus* with the additions and refinements of Bodin and Binsfeld, as the Ingolstadt opinion of principle of April 1590 confirmed.

The elaborated concept of witchcraft becomes a virtual 'dogma'

Contrary to what is sometimes stated in the literature, the Catholic Church never raised the elaborated concept of witchcraft to the rank of a dogma in canon law. *De facto*, however, it became a dogma in 1590 as critics of the five most important components of the theory were branded as heretics. In south Germany the attitude of Bavaria or of the University of Ingolstadt was especially important in this, since it subsequently influenced the attitude of the other Catholic universities. Gregor von Valentia, whom Duhr names as the author of the opinion, was one of the most important Catholic theologians of his time and also enjoyed great authority at Dillingen, where he had been employed before his appointment at Ingolstadt; the theologian Albert Hunger[25] had a significant influence on the views of the Freiburg jurist Friedrich Martini, who himself had taught at Ingolstadt in 1582–9 before becoming the chief spokesman of the University of Freiburg for four decades.[26] The University of Würzburg, a new foundation in the 1580s, was of no importance in questions of witchcraft but seems to have taken the same line as the other Catholic universities of south Germany.

It was to be characteristic of the Catholic position that even though the pact with the Devil was regarded as the central spiritual core of the crime of witchcraft, intercourse with him, witches' flight, witches' sabbaths and harmful sorcery were not dismissed as fantasies but their reality was insisted on, against 'Protestant' critics.[27] Other opinions were no longer publicly professed in Catholic Germany in the seventeenth century, and in southern Germany not until the middle of the eighteenth century. Even the most important Catholic critic of the witchcraft trials, Friedrich Spee, whom Thomasius regarded as a Protestant because of his radicalism, admitted the existence of witches without reservations, and merely hinted vaguely at additional truths, for which the time was not ripe.[28]

---

[25] Bosl, *Biographie*, 800; *ibid.*, 379f.
[26] Bosl *Biographie*, 509; Midelfort, *Witch Hunting*, 61–3; C. Schott, *Rat und Spruch der Juristenfakultät Freiburg im Breisgau*, Freiburg 1965, 63.
[27] Midelfort, *Witch Hunting*, 62.   [28] Spee, *Cautio*, 35, 135.

CONCENTRATION OF APOLOGISTS OF PERSECUTION IN BAVARIA

Midelfort argues that in the Catholic southwest, 'formal witchcraft theory seems to have virtually dried up' after Martini.[29] We cannot say the same of southeast Germany. Though the debates on witchcraft were not distinguished by great originality, the theme remained contentious enough to provoke apologists of persecution into publishing their arguments. The concentration of the authors in the Duchy of Bavaria, especially Munich and Ingolstadt, is especially striking. Apart from the witch sermons of the suffragan Bishop of Bamberg, Friedrich Förner, a treatise on child witches published at Aschaffenburg, and a Dillingen dissertation,[30] all the publications before the last third of the seventeenth century came from Bavaria, and their authors are to be placed either in the circle of the princely court at Munich or in that of the University of Ingolstadt.

Even before 1590, on the instructions of the President of the Court Council Wiguläus Hund, the Ingolstadt Professor Hieronymus Ziegler had translated into German the well-known answers of Abbot Trithemius to eight questions of Emperor Maximilian I (questions 5–7 concerning witchcraft); the interest of the ducal family had been behind this.[31] The Princes' tutor and Court Councillor, Johann Babtist Fickler, had already published a tract on witchcraft in 1582, when he had been in the service of the Archbishop of Salzburg.[32] Fickler's son Johann Christoph, who was a Court Councillor at Munich from 1600, had qualified

---

[29] Midelfort, *Witch Hunting*, 62.
[30] F. Förner, *Panoplia armaturae dei adversus omnem superstitionem, divinationem, excantationem, daemonolatriam (. . .)*, Ingolstadt 1626; (anon.) *Tractat von der verführten Kinder Zauberey*, Aschaffenburg 1629; J.J. Lang, *Daemonomagia (. . .)*, Dillingen 1630.
[31] J. Trithemius, *Antwort Herrn Johan Abts von Spanheim auff acht fragstuck, ime von weylandt Hern Maximilian Roem. Kayser etc. hochlöblichster gedachtnuss, fürgehalten (. . .)*, Ingolstadt 1556. In the mid-1550s Trithemius' treatises on witchcraft suddenly enjoyed a revival of interest. His *Antipalus Maleficiorum* was printed for the first time in 1555, though it had been written in 1508 at the command of Elector Joachim of Brandenburg. J. Trithemius, *Antipalus Maleficiorum*, Ingolstadt 1555 (on this see Janssen and Pastor, *Culturzustände*, VIII, 515–17; Lea, *Materials*, I, 369f.). Trithemius' answers to eight questions put by Emperor Maximilian had been printed in Latin at Oppenheim in 1515. After more than forty years of latency they were now not only reinterpreted by the Ingolstadt professor Ziegler (Bosl, *Biographie*, 875), but translated into German by the President of the Bavarian Court Council, Hundt (Bosl, *Biographie*, 379). The translation was dedicated to Princess Anna of Austria, Duchess of Bavaria (1528–90), the wife of Duke Albrecht V (1528–79). Sheet A i verso bears the Bavarian coat of arms, which would hardly have been possible without the permission of the court.
[32] J.B. Fickler, 'Judicium generale de poenis maleficiorum, magorum et sortilegiorum utriusque sexus', Ms. Salzburg 1582. (It is not clear whether this Ms. was ever printed.) On this see J. Steinruck, *Johann Babtist Fickler. Ein Laie im Dienst der Gegenreformation*, Münster 1965, 258–60. The corresponding witch trial in Salzburg in Byloff, *Hexenglaube*, 52ff. On Fickler as the tutor of Duke Maximilian of Bavaria see Dotterweich, *Maximilian*, 113, 123.

in 1592 with a *Disputatio iuridica de maleficis et sagis* supervised by the famous Ingolstadt jurist and co-signatory of the opinion, Andreas Fachineus.[33] The date of this printed disputation is not surprising: the wave of persecution of 1590 was the start of the lasting interest in the theme of witchcraft.

The Ingolstadt opinion of April 1590 was the work of the Jesuits Gregor von Valentia and Petrus Stevartius, the theologians Albert Hunger and Matthias Mairhofer, and the jurists Vitus Schober, Kaspar Lagus, Andreas Fachineus and Leonhard Zindecker, though it is not possible to identify their individual contributions.[34] Hunger and Gregor von Valentia were hard-line persecutors, who pressed for persecutions. Valentia restated his views on the need for the persecution of witches in 1595 in his *Commentariorum Theologicorum Tomi IV*, in which he again pleaded for harsh measures, and followed the arguments of Binsfeld.[35] In the case of Stevartius, Schober and Fachineus we know only that they shared an unconditional belief in the fully developed theory of witchcraft.[36] We have been unable to find any information on the views of Mairhofer, the Dean of the faculty of theology, while Lagus' critical attitude has already been mentioned.

Opinions on witchcraft have been preserved in the collected legal opinions of the Ingolstadt jurists Everhard, Chlingensberg and Schiltenberger.[37] Under the chairmanship of the jurist Ferdinand Waizenegger, a legal disputation was held in 1629 – dedicated to the Prince-Bishop of Bamberg (!) – *de maleficis et processu adversus eos instituendo*; only a few years later a further treatise on witchcraft by Waizenegger was published posthumously. A few years later still, the Ingolstadt jurist Caspar Manzius, who was one of the most respected academic jurists of his time, also concerned himself with the trials of witches.[38]

---

[33] J.C. Fickler, *Disputatio juridica de maleficis et sagis*, Ingolstadt 1592. On J.C. Fickler, Heydenreuter, *Der landesherrliche Hofrat*, 326.

[34] Riezler, *Geschichte*, 188. Duhr, *Geschichte der Jesuiten*, I, 746, names Gregor von Valentia as the author of the opinion, on the basis of internal information from the Jesuit order.

[35] Duhr, *Die Stellung*, 35–9; On Hunger, Midelfort, *Witch Hunting*, 61.

[36] Fachineus because of the disputation on witchcraft, which differed not an iota from Binsfeld's arguments; Schober was later repeatedly mentioned as a reliable ally by the persecution party in Munich, e.g. HStAM, Hexenakten 4, Prod. 25. All attempts to promote him to higher honours, however, were failures. The Jesuit Stevartius, the founder of the Ingolstadt orphanage, had no objections to witch hunting. Riezler, *Geschichte*, 221; Geyer, 'Hexen', 18.

[37] G. Everhard, *Consilia*, 2 vols., Munich 1618; H.A.M. Chlingensberger, *Consilia et responsa criminalia*, 2 vols., Ingolstadt 1738; J.P. Schiltenberg, *Consilia seu responsa (. . .) super diversis materiis*, Ingolstadt 1739. Cf. Schrittenloher, 'Aus der Gutachten- und Urteilstätigkeit', 345–51.

[38] F. Waizeneggeer (1580–1634). He was not wholly uncritical of the witch craze; his enemies alleged this was because his wife had been accused of witchcraft. Riezler, *Geschichte*, 237. The fact is that in a disputation held under his chairmanship, doubt had been cast on the

As the ideologist of the harsh persecution of witches after 1590 we might name the Jesuit Jacob Gretser, a pupil of Gregor von Valentia, and described in the literature as 'the most important German Jesuit after Canisius'.[39] Gretser did not write a treatise of his own on witchcraft, but his influence can be seen in many places. In 1612 he dedicated his work on the Christian festivals to the Prince-Provost of Ellwangen, Johann Christoph von Westerstetten, and several passages of this were explicitly devoted to the local persecutions. The relevance of this statement is that the persecutions at Ellwangen in 1611–13 exceeded all others in southern Germany at that time in their ferocity, for several hundred witches were burned in one place in a short time.[40] The Bavarian Court Chancellor Wagnereckh was in close contact with Gretser, as were the Court Councillor and Secretary of the Privy Council Gewold, and the author and Secretary of the Court Council Albertinus, all of whom distinguished themselves as zealous persecutors. All four men enjoyed the particular confidence of Duke Maximilian I of Bavaria, and Gewold, a protégé of the Ingolstadt theologian Hunger, whom we have already mentioned, stood

value of denunciations in trials for witchcraft. F. Waizenegger, praeside, *Disputatio juridica de maleficiis et processu adversus eos instituendo. Ad publicam disputationem proponit Joannes Neydecker, Bambergensis Franco*, Ingolstadt 1629 (with afterword by Wolfgang Gravenegg SJ and Dr Joachim Denich IUD). Thesis 39 states: 'Haec questio pracipuam difficultationem continet et in usu forensi apud prudentissimos adeo dubia est, ut vix ullus sine offensa suam explicare possit sententiam.' The explosive nature of this statement is clear from the contemporary witch hunts in Bamberg led by the 'witch Bishop' J.G. II Fuchs von Dornheim, in which several members of the prominent Bamberg family of Neudecker were involved: Film 205, 32–41: Anna Neudecker, 51, denounced by fifteen persons, imprisoned 1628–30, put to harsh torture in 1629, confessed in 1630, soon afterwards died in prison. She was the wife of the Burgomaster. Georg Neydeckher, c. 50, Burgomaster of Bamberg, arrested on 28 April 1628, tortured from May, executed as a warlock in June 1628 (episcopal commissioners: Schwarzkonz, Herrn-berger). Anna Barbara Neudecker, 15, arrested in March 1629, executed as a witch on 1 February 1630. Imprisoned at the monastery of Banz. Magdalena Neudeckerin, nee Viehheiner, denounced by twenty-two persons, confessed 1630, not clear if she was burned as a witch, but probable. Ursula Neydeckherin, confessed amicably and under torture, c. 1628–30. The estate of the Burgomaster was valued at 100,000 gulden. *Ibid.* Thirty years later newsletters were still mentioning the case: *Kurtzer und warhafftiger Bericht und erschreckhliche neue Zeitung von 600 Hexen (. . .) welche der Bischoff zu Bamberg hat verbrennen lassen (. . .)*, Bamberg 1659, in: E.D. Hauber, *Bibliotheca acta et scripta magica*, cap. CCLXVII: 'Der Bürgermeister Neidecker hat mit seiner teufflischen Gesellschaft bekennet, wie sie die Brunn vergifftet haben. Wer davon getruncken, hat alsbald die Beul oder Pestilentz bekommen, und viel Menschen [haben] dadurch gesterbet.' *Ibid.*, 446. The background was the great plague of 1628. The disputation chaired by Waizenegger at the University in 1629 was certainly a political gesture against this background. Waizenegger's *Dissertatio VI de servitudine daemoniaca, hoc est maleficio et processu contra maleficos instituendo*, Ingolstadt 1630, was published posthumously. Around 1630 Waizenegger occupied a position midway between those of Binsfeld and Tanner. Duhr, *Geschichte der Jesuiten*, II/2, 542. Manzius, *Commentarius.* [39] Bosl, *Biographie*, 273. Cf. note 41.

[40] Duhr, *Geschichte der Jesuiten*, II/2, 514; Midelfort, *Witch Hunting*, 212; H. König, 'Jacob Gretser', 160.

for a particularly hard line in his unpublished opinions on witchcraft.[41] In 1602, at Gretser's suggestion, Albertinus translated the Spanish treatise on witchcraft *Flagellum Diaboli* and later published *Lucifers Königreich und Seelengejaid*, a detailed treatise on the power of the Devil.[42]

It was not the jurists or the lay Councillors, however, but the Jesuits who made the most outstanding contributions to the discussion of witchcraft in Bavaria. We will refer to the moderate Jesuits Tanner, Laymann, Cusan, Gobat, Manzin and Haunold later.[43] The unbroken chain of unconditional and politically highly influential apologists of persecution stretched for almost a century in Bavaria, from Petrus Canisius through Gregor von Valentia and Jacob Gretser to Adam Contzen, Jeremias Drexel, Georg Witweiler and Georg Stengel.

Contzen, a close associate of the moving spirit behind the great persecutions in Bamberg, suffragan Bishop Förner, urged an implacable persecution of witches in his political romance *Methodus civilis* of 1628. In the kingdom of the Christian King of Abyssinia, in Contzen's tale, there had been an enormous increase of sorcery, with witches flying through the air, witches' sabbaths and the raising of storms and damage to the crops. The judges had all kinds of objections to a great persecution – many of them thought it was a dream or a fantasy (!) – others shirked the difficulties of the investigation, others again feared the great number of those who might be guilty, who would all have to be executed, while yet others feared that the persecution would spread to the upper classes. The just and righteous prince, however, was not to be put off by objections and cautiously set about eradicating witchcraft.[44] In 1637 the preacher Drexel published a tract urging a persecution, justifying all the previous persecutions and

---

[41] A. Dürrwächter, *Christoph Gewold. Ein Beitrag zur Gelehrtengeschichte der Gegenreformation (. . .)* Freiburg 1904, 13–18. Like Gregor von Valentia, Gretser, Hunger and Wagnereckh, Gewold defended the view that denunciations were *indistincte admittendae*, since without them trials for witchcraft could not be held at all. *Ibid.*, 18, 113. He was a close dependant of Gretser, with whom he was in almost daily contact. *Ibid.*, 16. It is almost unnecessary to mention that he also kept up a regular correspondence with F. Förner in Bamberg. *Ibid.*, 1, 38, 61–3 *passim*. In 1614 Gewold edited the speeches of his patron Hunger, *ibid.*, 4. On Albertinus, Gewold and Wagnereckh see also Heydenreuter, *Der landesherrliche Hofrat*, 127f., 330f., 358. On the relationship between Wagnereckh and Gewold see the essay by M. Kunze, which needs much supplementing: 'Johann Simon Wangnereck. Ein Jurist in der Zeit der Hexenprozesse', *Journal für Geschichte* (1983), 9, 4–11. *Ibid.*, 6.

[42] A. Albertinus, *Lucifers Königreich und Seelengejaid (. . .)*, Munich 1616; (on this Janssen and Pastor, *Culturzustände*, VI, 510ff.); F. de Ossuna, *Flagellum Diaboli, oder des Teufels Gaissl*, Munich 1602.   [43] See chapter V.1.

[44] A. Contzen SJ, *Methodus Civilis Doctrinae, oder Wunder-Seltzame Geschichte des grossen Abissini, Königs der Mohren (. . .)*, Sulzbach 1672, 277–80; (first edition in Latin, Cologne 1628); on this see Duhr, *Die Stellung*, 67–9. According to R. Bireley SJ, *Maximilian von Bayern, Adam Contzen SJ und die Gegenreformation in Deutschland 1624–1635*, Göttingen 1975, 106, Contzen's political romance was written with a direct application to the controversies in Munich. Contzen's religious extremism greatly influenced the Bavarian princes. Bireley, *ibid.*, 143, 226.

calling for the resumption of the merciless destruction of the alleged servants of the Devil:

O ye enemies of God's honour! Does not God's law expressly command: thou shalt not suffer a witch to live? Here I cry as loud as I can at God's behest to the bishops, lords, princes, and kings: 'Suffer not the witches to live.' With fire and sword this terrible plague must be rooted out. This weed must be torn out, so that it does not shoot up with excessive vigour, as we – alas – see and lament. The godless must be got rid of, so that the plague does not spread further, and those who rebel against God must be burned . . . [45]

At this time the apologists of persecution were already clearly on the defensive. Yet even later there were ardent apologists to be found. The Jesuit Georg Witweiler spoke up for harsh persecutions in his popular *Katholisch Hausbuch*,[46] while the Ingolstadt jurist Georg Stengel defended the burning of witches in 1651 in his *Opus de iudiciis divinis*, in which he followed the arguments of Binsfeld and Delrio. In this book, dedicated to Emperor Ferdinand III, the example of the Bishop of Würzburg, Philipp Adolf von Ehrenberg, was expressly cited: without any regard for social ties, the Bishop had had his own nephew executed as a witch, a deed which should serve as an example to all other authorities.[47]

In this connection we must also mention the dedications of famous treatises on witchcraft to the princely house of Bavaria. The most important Catholic author on witchcraft after Binsfeld, the Jesuit polymath Martin Delrio, dedicated his *Disquisitionum Magicarum Libri Sex* to the Wittelsbach Elector Ernst of Cologne, Duke of Bavaria, Bishop of Freising etc., in 1600, 1603 and 1612.[48] The Munich translations of Binsfeld's

[45] J. Drexel SJ, *Gazophyliacum Christi Eleemosyna, quam in aula Maximiliani explicavi*, Munich 1637; here cited in translation from Duhr, *Die Stellung*, 69–71; cf. also Duhr, *Geschichte der Jesuiten*, II/2, 511.
[46] G. Witweiler SJ, *Katholisch Hausbuch*, Munich 1631, 269–71. On this Duhr, *Geschichte der Jesuiten*, II/2, 514. Witweiler, *Hausbuch*, 270, defends the view that the power of the Devil cannot be compared with any other power on earth.
[47] G. Stengel SJ, *Opus de iudiciis divinis, quae Deus in hoc mundo exercet*, 4 vols., Ingolstadt 1651 (German edn, Augsburg 1712). *Ibid.*, II, 857ff. Stengel (1584–1651), born in Augsburg, entered the Society of Jesus in 1601, and spent his whole life in the region studied here: he was a novice at Landsberg, studied at Ingolstadt and taught in Munich, became a professor at Ingolstadt in 1618, Rector of the College in Dillingen in 1640 and returned to Ingolstadt in 1643. Bosl, *Biographie*, 752. All the punishments of God seemed to him to point to the need for an implacable persecution of witches on the Franconian model.
[48] M. Delrio, *Disquisitionum Magicarum Libri Sex*, Louvain 1599/1600. The twenty-five editions of this work published up to 1755 have now been exactly described by E. Fischer, 'Die *Disquisitionum Magicarum Libri Sex* von Martin Delrio als gegenreformatorische Exempelquelle', PhD thesis, Frankfurt am Main 1975. *Ibid.*, 156–75 for data on the dedications to the Bavarian princes. The Mainz edition of 1603 is the first to bear the title engraving of the plagues of Egypt from Exodus 7–11, in which the public was intended to recognise the signs God had given in their own time.

treatise of 1591 and 1592 were dedicated to Duke Ferdinand, the brother of the reigning Duke Wilhelm, and the ruler of the district of Schongau.[49] Bavarian Dukes continued to be particularly credulous about witchcraft: after his abdication Wilhelm V remained a staunch supporter of the persecution party in Bavaria, Maximilian I was always inclined to lend an ear to the blandishments of the persecutors in his circle and Duke Albrecht, the heir presumptive until the birth of the Electoral Prince Ferdinand Maria in 1636, also favoured the persecution party.[50] The early restriction of persecutions in Bavaria certainly owed nothing to the princely family.

EXCURSUS: EXCESSIVE PERSECUTION IN THE CATHOLIC AREAS
OF FRANCONIA.

Although the Duchy of Bavaria was a constant source of theoretical treatises and ordinances on witchcraft, it was not there but in the ecclesiastical territories in Franconia that persecution reached a new order of magnitude. Together with the persistent tendency to persecution in the neighbouring Bishopric of Augsburg, these excessive persecutions formed the background to the discussions on the subject in Bavaria, and for that reason they deserve a brief examination here.

Between 1600 and 1605 western and northern Lower Franconia suffered a wave of persecution, the chief participants being the Upper Archbishopric of Mainz (Aschaffenburg), the Prince-Bishopric of Fulda, the *Freigericht* of Alzenau (a condominium of Electoral Mainz and the County of Hanau), and the County of Hanau. The literature speaks of 250 witches burned in Fulda, 139 in the *Freigericht*, more than a hundred for the Calvinist County of Hanau, and the victims in the Upper Archbishopric must have reached three figures as well – the research has yet to be done.[51] Witches were already being burned again in the Bishoprics of Augsburg and Eichstätt around 1600, though not in the same numbers as in Lower Franconia.[52]

From 1610 a series of Franconian territories was again shaken by major

---

[49] Binsfeld, *Tractatus*, foreword.

[50] On Duke Albrecht (1584–1666), younger brother of Maximilian, see below, p. 293; on Wilhelm V's activities long after his abdication and on Maximilian's suggestibility to the influence of the witch hunting party, cf. chapter 4, pp. 291–311.

[51] On Fulda, Spielmann, *Die Hexenprozesse*, 167–73; on Alzenau, Grebner, 'Hexenprozesse', 223; on Hanau, Spielmann, *Die Hexenprozesse*, 138; on the Upper Archbishopric, Film 173 and 135.

[52] On Eichstätt Film 668–9; for the Bishopric of Augsburg: the minutes of the Court Council 1598–1606 are unfortunately missing but references to an increase in executions are found in HStAM, Hochstift Augsburg, NA, Akten no. 1210; HStAM, Hexenakten 15.

persecutions. In Aschaffenburg at least sixty-six witches were burned at nine executions in 1611–14, and this time the greatest persecutions took place in the little Prince-Provostship of Ellwangen (now in Baden-Württemberg), which bordered the County of Oettingen on the east. There the witch burnings lasted without interruption from 1611 to 1618; as early as July 1612, after the twenty-ninth mass burning, 167 persons had been executed as witches. In January 1613 the thirty-fourth burning was recorded, in October 1615 the sixtieth, in August 1618 the seventy-third.[53] Midelfort's estimate of approximately 400 witch burnings in Ellwangen in this period may in fact be too low. After the thirty-seventh burning in September 1613, the Jesuit Johann Flinck, who came from Dillingen, reported that 303 persons had already been burned at the stake.

> Where these things will lead or what end they will have, I cannot see, as this detestable evil has so gained the upper hand and has touched so many like a plague, that if the magistracy goes on with the performance of its office, the town will be miserably desolate after some years.[54]

In 1612 Johann Christoph von Westerstetten, who had begun the persecution at Ellwangen as Prince-Provost, was elected Prince-Bishop of Eichstätt, and this was the signal for witch trials to begin in Eichstätt. In the Bishopric of Augsburg, too, there was a major witchcraft trial in the Bishop's capital of Dillingen in 1612–13.

In 1616 the persecutions spread to all the Franconian Prince-Bishoprics. While the authorities in Ellwangen were already conducting their sixty-fifth to seventy-first burnings of witches (January to December 1616), persecutions began in the Bishoprics of Würzburg, Bamberg and Eichstätt. The famous reforming Bishop Julius Echter von Mespelbrunn had more than 300 witches burned in the Bishopric of Würzburg between July 1616 and June 1617,[55] while in Bamberg Prince-Bishop Johann Gottfried von Aschhausen began widespread persecutions at the same time. Aschhausen had been installed in Bamberg as a counter-reformer in 1609, on the recommendation of Duke Maximilian I of Bavaria and Echter, the Bishop of Würzburg.[56] Friedrich Förner, suffragan Bishop of Bamberg and an

---

[53] Midelfort, *Witch Hunting*, 212–14; Film 694–5 (Ellwangen).
[54] Duhr, *Geschichte der Jesuiten*, II/2, 489.
[55] Merzbacher, *Die Hexenprozesse*, 43; Kerler, 'Julius', 60.
[56] In general Spindler, *Handbuch*, III/1, 222 (Endres); Bauer, 'Die Bamberger Weihbischöfe', 443f. recognises the close connection between change of office and witch hunting in the Bishopric of Bamberg. Possibly witchcraft was also discussed at the League negotiations in 1609–10, for the coincidence in time of the mandates on superstition and witchcraft is astonishing: the first was the Bamberg *Mandat der Zauberer, Wahrsager und deren, welche sich des verbottnen Segens gebrauchen* of 30 March 1610 (StA Bamberg, Bamberger Verordnungen, Rep. B 26 no. 44, fol. 53v–4v). Then in October 1610 the decrees of the Synod of Dillingen for the Bishopric of Augsburg, in which *veneficium, incantationes*

associate of the Bavarian court, who is said by the literature to have 'worked beneficially for the diocese', seems rather, from the perspective of persecution, to have been the evil genius of the region, and to have been a persistent advocate of persecution. In the Bishopric of Bamberg too, between 1616 and 1618, about 300 witches must have been executed. In Bamberg alone in 1617 102 persons were burned, but dozens more were executed at Hallstadt and Zeil.[57] The small Bishopric of Eichstätt occupied an exceptional position even in Franconia; the persecutions began there in 1617, but unlike the Bishoprics of Würzburg and Bamberg the trials did not diminish in 1618. The practised persecutioner Johann Christoph von Westersetten had witches burned every year from 1617 to 1630. The estimates in the literature for the number of persons burned in the Bishopric in this period range from 122 to 274,[58] but more exact studies have not been made. The figure of 274 goes back to the statement of the witch commissioner of Eichstätt, Dr Kolb, who in 1629 claimed that he had 'examined' 274 witches who had been executed. Kolb was active in Eichstätt from 1624 to 1628 but according to the researches of the *H-Sonderkommando* the first three peaks of persecution had been in 1617–18, 1620 and 1623, and there were others in 1627 and 1630.[59]

The persecutions in Franconia were at their most savage in 1626–30. In the Bishopric of Bamberg during these five years, under Bishop Johann II Fuchs von Dornheim, still assisted by his suffragan Friedrich Förner, no fewer than 600 persons were burned as witches.[60] At the same time the persecutions in the Bishopric of Würzburg under Bishop Philipp Adolf

magicae, maleficium were declared to be reserved to the Bishop's courts and all magic, charms, etc. were forbidden 'bei aller strenge', while the relevant terms of the mandate on religion of 1600 were also renewed. J. Spindler, 'Heinrich V, Fürstbischof von Augsburg (1598–1646)', *Jahrbuch des Historischen Vereins Dillingen*, 24 (1911), 1–139; 28 (1915), 1–255; 24 (1911), 39, 51, 110. Then in February 1611 the printing of the Bavarian *Landtgebott wider die Aberglauben, Zauberey, Hexerey und andere sträffliche Teufelskünste*, the effectiveness of which, however, was greatly restricted by resistance within Bavaria. On Eichstätt cf. note 58.

[57] In Spindler, *Handbuch*, III/1, 222 (Endres), Förner is quite unreasonably described as 'überaus segensreich für die Diozese' of Bamberg. But we must set to Förner's account not only the witchcraft mandate of 1610 but above all the witch hunts of 1616–18, during the double episcopate (Würzburg and Bamberg) of Bishop J.G. von Aschhausen, the incitement to preach against witches (cf. note 30), the building of the 'witch house' at Bamberg (Bauer, 'Die Bamberger . . .', 456), and finally the the execution of at least 600 persons in the Bishopric of Bamberg between 1626 and 1630. Even Förner's well-disposed biographer L. Bauer, 'Friedrich Förner', *Fränkische Lebensbilder*, 1 (1967), 182–209, recognises this connection. On the witch hunts, Wittmann, 'Die Bamberger Hexenjustiz', 182ff.; Film 3085–6.

[58] See below. Prince-Bishop Johann Christoph von Westerstetten (1565–1637, Bishop 1612–36) had had hundreds of witches burned while he was still Prince-Provost. Förner dedicated his witchcraft sermons to him in 1616 (note 30). On the figures: Riezler, *Geschichte* (1896), 221, 226.   [59] HStAM, GR 323/16, fol. 28. Cf. Film 668–9.

[60] Much evidence of this. Cf. note 38; Wittmann, 'Die Bamberger Hexenjustiz', 188f.

von Ehrenberg reached their peak. Here, in fact, 900 'witch folk' are said to have been burned.[61] The persecutions in the Upper Archbishopric of Mainz, in the district courts of Aschaffenburg, Miltenberg and Amorbach, again assumed significant proportions. Grebner believes that the number of executions there was 'almost as great . . . as in the territories of Würzburg or Bamberg', but the researches of the *H-Sonderkommando* suggest that this estimate may be too high.[62]

Although more detailed historical research still has to be done on almost all the Franconian Bishoprics, the older works and the material collected by the *H-Sonderkommando* make it clear that the persecutions in the region between 1600 and 1630 were quite exceptional in their character. A veritable centre for specialists in persecution was formed; trained jurists were employed exclusively to conduct persecutions. With other councillors they belonged to so-called *Malefizkommissionen*, which had their own clerks and extraordinary powers, and almost developed into regular bureaucratic institutions. These bodies existed in the bishoprics of Eichstätt, Würzburg and Bamberg, and from 1628 for a short time in the County of Oettingen-Wallerstein and the Principality of Pfalz-Neuburg while the beginnings of them are also found in the Duchy of Bavaria.[63] The Catholic Prince-Bishoprics collaborated with one another in hunting witches, though they were not above poaching one another's specialist persecutioners. In 1598, for example, the Oettingen councillor Dr Paulus zum Ackher was appointed to the government of the Bishopric of Augsburg, from where he also gave advice to the persecution party in Munich. The Eichstätt witch commissioner Dr Wolfgang Kolb was recruited by the Count of Oettingen-Wallerstein in 1628 and not long afterwards entered Bavarian service. Another Eichstätt commissioner, Dr Schwarzkonz, transferred to the service of the Bishop of Bamberg in 1628.[64]

---

[61] Merzbacher, *Die Hexenprozesse*, 45.

[62] Grebner, 'Hexenprozesse', 223. To many historians, e.g. Kamen, *Iron Century*, 236, the figures for the Franconian witch hunts between 1600–30 have appeared very improbable. 'It seems likely', wrote Kamen, that the 600 in Bamberg and the 900 in Würzburg 'may all be gross exaggerations'. But the personal index of the *H-Sonderkommando* shows that these orders of magnitude can all be verified, for the later 1620s alone, that is, not including the witch hunts of 1600, 1610 and 1616–17.

[63] Wittmann, 'Die Bamberger Hexenjustiz', 186ff., names the members of the witch commission at Bamberg. The members of the Pfalz-Neuburg commission are listed in Henker, 'Zur Prosopographie'. The moving spirit and leader of the commission in Neuburg was Dr Hieronymus Dickhell (?–1667), son of a Saxon superintendent (a convert). In 1628–30 he coordinated the witch hunts in Eichstätt, Pfalz-Neuburg and Oettingen-Wallerstein. Under Count Palatine Wolfgang Wilhelm he rose to become Director of the Court Council and Privy Councillor. Henker, 'Zur Prospographie', 103f. On Würzburg, Merzbacher, *Die Hexenprozesse*, 134.

[64] UBM, Cod. Ms. 214, fol. 208f. (Kolb); fol. 139f. (Schwarzkonz). Cf. chapter 3, note 65 (zum Ackher). See below, pp. 298–9 (zum Ackher); p. 299 (Kolb), p. 318 (Schwarzkonz). Cf. note 68.

The Franconian persecutions realised the sombre dream of unconditional persecution, of persecution without regard for political, social or
humanitarian obstacles, but only for the logic of the persecutions themselves. Numerous new tortures were devised, which went far beyond the
usual torments of the thumbscrew, the footscrew and the rack.[65] During
the persecutions at Eichstätt some individuals were interrogated for so
long that they denounced hundreds of alleged witches. A fishwife from a
village near Eichstätt finally denounced 223 persons, a peasant woman
from the same place even denounced 261.[66] It was also characteristic of the
Franconian persecutions that there was no longer any taboo to prevent the
'social' expansion of the trials into the upper classes.

The 150 victims of the persecutions at Eichstätt whose names and social
standing are known included three former burgomasters, eight burgomasters' wives, four councillors, the master of the hospital and his wife, five
innkeepers and four women brewers, nine women innkeepers and brewers,
the wife of the Town Clerk, the widow of the judge of the monastic court of
Rebdorf, the Treasurer of Herrieden, the wife of the Treasurer of Dolln-
stein, three court craftswomen, the wife of the *Registrator* of Herrieden,
the *Domkapitelsdepositarin*, the daughter of the Bishop's provincial administrator and Maria Richel, the wife of the Chancellor Bartholomäus
Richel, who transferred to Bavarian service after his wife was burned at the
stake in 1621.[67] The parish priest Johann Reichard, though often accused,
never admitted guilt and was kept under house arrest for twenty years,
until his death in 1644.[68]

The social barriers were breached even more flagrantly in Würzburg and
Bamberg. In the first twenty-nine witch burnings alone, in the Bishop's
capital Würzburg (from 1627 to February 1629), several young nobles, two
learned theologians, five canons, fourteen vicars, the wife of the former
Chancellor, a burgomaster's wife, the wives of three councillors, and

---

[65] Film 668, 669; Film 2709
[66] Film 3844.
[67] Film 668, Film 669; on Maria Richlin see Heydenreuter, *Der landesherrliche Hofrat*, 352;
Film 669, 92.
[68] Film 669, 89f. Johann Reichard (1573–1644) was the son of a woman burned as a witch at
Wemding in 1609 (see Schneid, 'Das Rechtverfahren', 164). From 1589 he studied at
Ingolstadt, where he took his master's degree in 1597, attended the seminary at Eichstätt
and became town priest in Spital. In 1624 he was denounced by his housekeeper and her
daughter, who had already confessed witchcraft. In spite of his priesthood Reichard
was harshly tortured, but confessed nothing. No fewer than ten commissioners attended
his interrogations, four clerics and six laymen, among them Dr Schwarzkonz and Dr
Kolb. Film 669, 89f. Parts of the record of the hearing are in UBM, Cod. Ms. 214, fol.
55–83; formerly HStAM, Hexenakten 47, now in StA Nuremberg. See also A. Hirschmann, 'Johann Reichard. Ein Sittenbild aus der Zeit der Hexenverfolgungen', *Hist. Pol.
Blätter*, 161 (1918), 679–81.

several other dependants of high officials and citizens were burned as witches.[69]

The persecutions at Bamberg have not yet been systematically studied, but there is no need to doubt the word of a Bamberg *Hexenzeitung*, which reports that 'eight councillors and two burgomasters with their wives and several daughters' had been burned at Zeil. In Bamberg itself, the Bishop's residence, the persecutions even attacked the government and the court: even the Chancellor of the Bishopric was executed as a witch:

> The Chancellor and Doctor Horn, the Chancellor's son, his wife and two daughters, and also many prominent gentlemen and members of the Council, in particular some persons who had sat at table with the Bishop, were all executed and burned to ashes.[70]

The persecutions in the Prince-Provostship of Ellwangen, the Prince-Bishoprics of Eichstätt, Würzburg and Bamberg, which claimed more than 3,000 victims in all, represented the absolute peak of persecution in south Germany. The proceedings in the ecclesiastical territories of Franconia made an enormous impression on the persecution party in Bavaria. Gradually they replaced the witch trials in the Bishopric of Augsburg in their paradigmatic significance. Whereas the Ingolstadt opinion of 1590 had still pointed to the persecutions in the Bishoprics of Augsburg and Eichstätt as examples, an opinion produced by the Chancellor of the Bavarian Court Council, Wagnereckh, in 1615, urged that attention should be paid to the example of other 'princes who proceed against witches, and have also had many of them executed, as at Dillingen, Eichstätt, Ellwangen . . .'[71] In 1629 the former witch commissioner of Eichstätt Dr Kolb, who had been recruited to the Bavarian service at the request of Elector Maximilian I to conduct the persecutions at Wemding and Ingolstadt, praised his method of procedure:

> For as the witch trials were conducted at Bamberg, Würzburg and Eichstätt, so they say he has adopted the same procedure in Ingolstadt and Wemding . . .[72]

The great persecutions in Franconia became a standing example for the apologists of persecution in Bavaria. They are the background against which the discussions of witchcraft in southeast Germany must be understood.

---

[69] Soldan *et al., Geschichte der Hexenprozesse*, III, 17–20.   [70] Cf. note 38.
[71] HStAM, Hexenakten 1, Prod. 3, 'Capita Deliberationis Quoad Processum contra Maleficos vel Sagas Instituendum'; on this *ibid.*, Prod. 7, fol. 6 (passage quoted).
[72] HStAM, GR 323/16, fol. 27v.

FORMATION OF AN OPPOSITION PARTY IN BAVARIA

NEW ATTEMPT AT PERSECUTION

A few years after the plague of 1592 and the minor inflation of 1594, Bavaria and Swabia were hit by the next agrarian crisis. The years 1597–1601 were characterised in southeast Germany by harvest failures, inflation (back to the price level of 1589) and high mortality in many places.[73] Complaints of witchcraft increased again, and in Dillingen the wife of a town councillor was burned as a witch in 1597; in Nördlingen, Tölz and Dinkelscherben (in the lands of the chapter of Augsburg cathedral) there were isolated witch burnings, as there were in the County of Oettingen. Discussions of witchcraft revived but this time they showed even more dangerous tendencies. In correspondence between the Bishop of Augsburg and the chapter in 1599, we read:

> although because of the arduous continuation of the witch trials in our lands, doubts have arisen and all kinds of arguments *pro* and *contra* have been raised *in deliberatione causa*, it has been decided both *resolutione privatim* in the presence of our lord the Dean, and also *capitulariter*, that the proceedings begun should not be stopped . . .

The newly elected Bishop Heinrich V von Knöringen (1598–1646) confirmed the chapter's view and referred to the successful persecutions of his predecessors.[74]

In Bavaria too there had been an important change of ruler in 1598, when Maximilian I (1598–1651) succeeded Duke Wilhelm V. The young Duke had been educated by apologists of persecution, and had followed the persecutions at Ingolstadt as a student at the University.[75] Like the neighbouring Bishops of Augsburg and Eichstätt, and the kindred spirit who held the see of Würzburg, the Duke of Bavaria was a hard-line counter-reformer and an active supporter of persecution. As will become clear below, a persecution party had formed in Bavaria after the suspension of persecutions in 1590, and urged a resumption of witch trials on a wider basis, that is throughout the Duchy.

The occasion for such a resumption seemed to present itself in 1600, when there were serious grounds for suspicion of sorcery and witchcraft against a family of vagrants in the north Bavarian county court of Abensberg-Altmannstein. The whole family of six was brought to Munich on the Duke's orders, where their trial was conducted with exemplary severity by

[73] Cf. chapter 2, note 164. Now also Clark, 'Inversion', 6–9; Souden, 'Demographic Crisis', 233.   [74] HStAM, Hexenakten 15, fol. 1. List of trials in the German edition.
[75] Dotterweich, *Maximilian*, 100f., 111ff., 123; Riezler, *Geschichte*, 194ff.

Kurtze Erzöhlung vnd Fürbildung der vbelthatten/welche von Sechs personen/als einem Mann/seinem Eheweib/zweyen jrer beiden Söhnen/vnd zweyen anderen Jhren Gesellen/begangen/was massen sie auch/an dem 29. Tag deß Monats Julii/in dem 1600. Jar/der Fürstlichen Haupstatt München/von dem Leben zum Tod gebracht worden / den Bösen zu einem Schröcken/den Frommen aber zu Wahnung/für die Augen gestellt.

Schröcklich vnd Erbärmlich ist es anzuhören/das Sechs so geringe vñ vnansehenliche Personen/so vil junger vnd alter Leüth/abgöthisch verzaubert/erkrümbt/getödtet/vnnd etwan andere grosse Sünden vnd Vbelthatten/die sie mit Raub/Siebstal vnd anderen sachen begangen haben/das der Vatter Paulus Gämperle sonst Pappenheimer genaÿt/seines alters 58. Jar/hat allein Hundert junge Kinder/vñ Zehen alte Leüth/mit grewlicher Zauberey erkrümbt/vnd erbärmlich vmbgebracht...

Getruckt zu Augspurg/bey Michael Manger/in Jacober Vorstatt.

8. *Kurtze Erzöhlung und Fürbildung der übelthatten (...)* Augsburg 1600. Text and pictures show stages of the Munich witch trial in the same year. Four coloured woodcuts: pact with the Devil, torture before the execution, the procession to the place of execution, and the burning of the witches before the gate of the city.

some of the committed members of the Court Council. Using the doctrine of *crimen exceptum* as a basis, all the desired confessions were soon obtained by harsh torture, and the protests and recantations of the accused were ignored. In a short time several hundred alleged accomplices were denounced in many places, which opened up the possibility of expanding the trial into a persecution. Arrests were made in many places and further suspects were brought to Munich. Six persons were burned as witches with the utmost cruelty in July, and six more in November; nine of them were men. These executions had an extraordinarily dramatic impact; woodcuts and printed broadsheets, chronicles and poems reported the events; a chronicler of Freising included them in his world chronicle a few years later among the most important events of the century; and a Munich Jesuit sent an account of them to the polymath Delrio, who mentioned the trial in the next edition of his *Disquisitiones Magicae*. As late as 1744 they were referred to in a book published at Leipzig. As this key Bavarian trial has recently been the subject of a monograph dissertation,[76] we need not go into the details here.

In November 1600 all the original suspects had been executed and the question of the value of the denunciations obtained under torture was raised again. At this time there were already persons under arrest at Munich, Abensberg, Dingolfing, Ingolstadt, Riedenburg, Vohburg, Landshut and Kelheim; once again the higher social classes had been affected in the persons of the wife of Michael Mair, a wealthy innkeeper in Abensberg, and the wife of Burgomaster Simon Paur of Kelheim.[77] The leader of the witch trial at Munich, Court Councillor Wagnereckh, pressed for an expansion of the proceedings to the whole of the Duchy after the second burning of witches in Munich in November 1600. An opinion on the trial of the witches referred rhetorically to the endless damage caused to the country by witchcraft:

and the *modi nocendi* specified . . . have been found by experience, so that it is to be presumed that if there were no such *mancipia* and *instrumenta diaboli*, we could hope for greater fruitfulness in the land . . .

For this reason, and of course in order to save God's honour, the authorities had 'causes in plenty' to take the severest action against witches. The example in the mind of the author was the persecution in the Electorate of Trier in 1590, at that time the greatest persecution in the Empire. The first step would be for all those denounced by the witches executed in Munich to be arrested, especially in the district courts of Abensberg, Kelheim,

[76] Kunze, 'Der Prozess'; *idem, Der Prozess; idem, Die Strasse;* Riezler, *Geschichte*, 198–201; Leuchtmann, 'Zeitgeschichtliche Aufzeichnungen', 158; Mayr, *Epitome*, 272ff. Trial records: HStAM, Hexenakten 2. Information of Delrio: Duhr, *Die Stellung*, 43; Gregorius, *Gemüths Hand-Buch*, 512–14.
[77] HStAM, Hexenakten 4, Prod. 1, Prod. 25; StA Munich, Hofkammer Ämterrechnungen, GR Abensberg, GR Vohburg; Markmiller, 'Verhandlungen', 68. Cf. list of trials in the German edition.

Riedenburg and Vohburg, so far as they had not already been arrested, and interrogated:

and it should be ensured that whatever these persons have made known, especially other witches and accomplices, so these proceedings would be spun out and there would be no end of them in sight for a long time . . . as experience in other places makes sufficiently plain, especially in the Archbishopric of Trier in the year 90, when proceedings were taken against the witches there.

The heavy expenses were not to be shunned, because 'of the good of the common fatherland'. To reduce the costs of the proceedings, and above all to speed up and rationalise the persecution, it was suggested that special commissioners be appointed to conduct them on their own authority, independently of the local authorities and without the need for constant reference back to the *Regierungen*. Besides Wagnereckh himself, three other named jurists were to be appointed to this office. The county court judges, after all, did nothing to promote persecutions and the *Regierungen* in Landshut, Burghausen and Straubing took no steps on their own initiative to follow the example of the Court Council in Munich.[78]

SHARP CRITICISM OF THE WITCH TRIALS

Witchcraft trials were proceedings of such exceptional importance that by 1600 attendance at them was almost a part of the basic training of all members of the government, especially jurists, in the Catholic territories. This meant that trials could not be conducted by any obscure official, executioner or untrained county court judge on his own initiative. In Bavaria, every larger trial after 1590 had to be attended by at least one commissioner from one of the *Regierungen* or the Court Council, who was responsible for guiding and supervising the proceedings. The Falkenturm, the ducal criminal prison in Munich, offered every member of the government the opportunity to form an impression of the trial for himself. This opportunity was also used by non-jurists – nobles, clerics and members of the princely house. The nobleman Heinrich von Haslang set down his impressions of Wagnereckh's witch trials; he found:

that the denunciations, and much else, are extorted from them [the alleged witches; WB] by irregular torture, and in many other ways the procedure is quite wrong. As I myself attended an examination not as a commissioner but as a private person, in which those executed were

---

[78] HSTAM, Hexenakten 4, Prod. 25 and 25a, 'Gutachten wegen der Unholden Process', 4 fols. The passages quoted are on fol. 2 and 1.

interrogated about their accomplices and those who lodged them, and I may say on my oath that I have never seen such procedure, nor heard of it . . . [79]

The opponents of persecution in Munich did not stop at mere expressions of their concern, but raised objections of principle. The apologists of persecution were attacked on two fronts: the first was the 'evil procedure' in the current trial of witches in Munich; the second was the denunciations, which in principle were not accepted as grounds for imprisonment and torture.
One of these principled criticisms claimed that

Several Councillors have stoutly defended the idea that the denunciations *in ordine ad torturam* are not valid and are to be disregarded, and that by virtue of the same . . . the court could in no way proceed to torture.

In fact, a person might not even be arrested on such a denunciation, while torture might not be inflicted until the guilt of the accused had been 'infallibly' proven by other, 'certain' evidence. The reputation of the denouncer also had to be considered. If it was not too bad, the denunciations did not even count as additional pieces of circumstantial evidence. This principle had to apply in witchcraft trials as in others, and it made no difference whether a person had been denounced once or a hundred times.

Item it is all one and makes no difference . . . if there are such denouncers and they name someone as their accomplice and say he is a witch, or other, and has helped to commit this or that crime, or if there are two, three or as many as are willing or able to say the same, for this *concursus* is of no effect . . . *Cum id, quod nihil est, nullum recipiat supplementum.*[80]

By attacking denunciations in witchcraft trials the opponents of persecution were targeting the central mechanism of the persecutions. For the apologists of persecution, who had recently asserted that 'the authorities had reason in plenty to proceed *in hoc crimine . . . ad denunciationes complicum*, which is all that such pernicious people recognise',[81] this must have been a slap in the face. The criticism in principle also attacked the excessive use of torture, the disregard of the rules laid down in imperial legislation and the disregard of the fundamental axiom that 'it is better to let many accused go free than to condemn a single innocent person'.[82]
The opponents of persecution scored their first success in securing the abandonment of the persecution at Munich. A ducal decree castigated the

[79] EOAM, Akt Varia 516, fol. 178r–v.
[80] HStAM, Hexenakten 4, Prod. 15, 18 fols., fol. 1v–6.
[81] HStAM, Hexenakten 4, Prod. 25, fol. 2.   [82] *Ibid.*, Prod. 15, fol. 1v-6.

faults in procedure, behind which, however, if one started from the theory of *crimen exceptum*, as the apologists of persecution did, there was a system.

And as moreover the trial was said to be somewhat irregularly conducted, his aforesaid Princely Grace was not only greatly alarmed by such irregularity but also with good reason displeased . . . and so his aforesaid Princely Grace has given orders to cease the abovementioned irregularities and to do that which the law and the Emperor's Criminal Ordinance require and demand.[83]

THE PRO-PERSECUTION PARTY

So Your Grace has on the Scholars' Bench . . . conscientious, upright people . . . only some of them, in my opinion, wish to be too hot and sharp *in Criminalibus* . . . and in their opinion Justice should be administered *secundum Rigorem iuris absque omni Benignitate et Clementia* . . .[84]

The question of the composition of the two opposing parties[85] is one of the most interesting problems of this study. During our research some old views were soon shown to be untenable, while numerous new questions were raised. For example, the current picture of Duke Maximilian of Bavaria as 'the most indefatigable persecutioner among all the German Electors'[86] was not confirmed. Bavaria's 'Iron Elector', the leader of the Catholic League and one of the most decisive and forceful figures among the German princes of the early seventeenth century, revealed himself to be a paper tiger in the question of witchcraft, for all his strong language. In spite of his personal interest in the witchcraft question, which can be documented from his unexpected interventions in the discussions of the authorities and numerous personal initiatives,[87] his position remains remarkably vague and undecided. The Prince's decisions were unpredictable, sometimes he followed the advice of the apologists of persecution, at other

---

[83] EOAM, Akt Varia 516, fol. 27–30, 'Decretum Serenissimi Ducis, Datum 29 Martii 1601', fol. 27r–v. This decree was the first great success of the opponents of witch hunting during the reign of Duke Maximilian (1598–1651). For the apologists of persecution it was the greatest reverse since the end of the great witch hunt of 1589–91.

[84] HStAM, HR 401/2, s.f., opinion of the *Hofoberrichter* Wolf Höhenkircher on the occasion of the visitation of the Court Council of 1605. Höhenkircher held this office from 1604 to 1606. See Heydenreuter, *Der landesherrliche Hofrat*, 338.

[85] In contemporary terminology *politici* and *zelanti*. Cf. notes 57, 98 and 99.

[86] Becker *et al.*, *Aus der Zeit*, 288 (Brackert).

[87] For advice on the question of witchcraft in 1602–4, Duke Maximilian turned, among others, to Pope Clement VIII (Riezler, *Geschichte*, 204), the Electors of Mainz, Cologne and Trier and the authors Nicolas Rémy (Remigius) in Lorraine and Martin Delrio SJ in Graz.

times that of their opponents. This vacillation was not the result of tactical political calculation, but an expression of his own deep uncertainty. Both parties distanced themselves remarkably from their ruler, who was unable to reach a decision, during the discussion of witchcraft in Bavaria. In December 1601, after a year of hard and fruitless arguments, the spokesman of the moderate party urged the Prince to ask the advice of an impartial university, 'as through this exchange of opinions Your Grace can only be drawn deeper into doubt'.[88] A few years later the spokesman of the persecution party was to use unusually hard language about the Prince: 'They had thought that they served a highly intelligent Prince, but now for the first time they realise that they are in the service of an idiot . . .'[89]

Only the indecisiveness of Maximilian explains why such a long and constant struggle between the two parties in Bavaria was possible.

For various reasons it is not easy to determine the composition of these two parties. The most important reason is that they did not act as parties in the modern political sense, but apparently operated without a coordinated plan. Not until the discussion of witchcraft had been analysed over a longer period did it become clear that beneath the apparently individual expressions of opinion there was an informal group or party structure which went beyond mere affinities of kindred spirits but cannot be reduced to a system of clienteles. Shedding light on the make-up of the parties is even more difficult because their debates were conducted, as it were, by proxy in the competent body – the Court Council – while it seems that in fact other forces were grappling with one another. But there were limits to the willingness of those involved to name names, when they had to refer to their superiors in an absolutist court. While inferior opponents could be openly identified, the 'patrons' of the parties are only revealed with difficulty – of course, they were known to contemporaries. The analysis is even more diffucult because no one in Counter-Reformation Bavaria dared to omit paying at least lip-service to the necessity of persecuting witches under the criminal law. The actual oppositions do not become apparent until the practical discussions of witchcraft.

The spokesman of the persecution party in Munich was the jurist Dr Johann Sigmund Wagnereckh, a citizen of the provincial town of Neuötting, who had risen rapidly thanks to his legal talent and patronage. After studying at Ingolstadt (1585–92) he was brought to Munich as a Court Councillor in 1592, appointed an Ecclesiastical Councillor in 1593, Chancellor of the Court Council in 1606, and Privy Councillor in 1607. Wagnereckh combined all these offices until his death in 1617. In 1600 Wagnereckh distinguished himself as the leader of the exemplary witch

---

[88] EOAM, Akt Varia 516, fol. 127–43, 'Responsio pro negativa' (author: 'H.v.H.'), fol. 142v–3.   [89] Heydenreuter, *Der landesherrliche Hofrat*, 148.

trial in Munich and in the following years as the spokesman of the persecution party in the lengthy debates about the problem of witchcraft. In his numerous opinions he combined legal skill, confessional zeal and rhetorical flair, though a certain limitation in finding arguments against the objections of his opponents was masked by a readiness to depict them as enemies, and by the exertion of his personal authority.

Wagnereckh was one of those who plotted to bring down the old Chancellor of the Court Council, Gailkircher, in 1606, and afterwards he dominated the debates in the Court Council as Gailkircher's successor; several of the other members were attached to him as his clients.[90] Exploiting all the sources of power at his command, the Chancellor and his close confidant Dr Vagh[91] tried to suppress all opposition, especially on questions of witchcraft, in the most authoritarian style. Like Wagnereckh, Vagh was a high-flyer in the Bavarian service, had studied at Ingolstadt in 1590, and was a brilliant jurist and zealous (converted) Catholic. Both men recruited their followers chiefly from the Scholars' Bench on the Court Council.

If we examine Wagnereckh's closest contacts, we can reconstruct the broad outlines of the persecution party. The protection of Christoph Gewold, a close confidant of Duke Maximilian, had played some part in his early transfer from Ingolstadt to the service of the Court Council.[92] Gewold himself was a protégé of the Ingolstadt professor and apologist for persecution, Albert Hunger, who had smoothed his path into the government in Munich. Hunger and Gewold were on close terms with the Jesuit Jacob Gretser, a pupil of Gregor von Valentia, and a committed apologist of persecution in Ingolstadt.[93] Like the Jesuit Adam Contzen later, Gewold was also in close contact with the suffragan Bishop of Bamberg, Friedrich Förner, one of the leaders of the persecutions in Franconia.[94] With the author of works on witchcraft, Fickler, as the Prince's tutor, the

---

[90] *Ibid.*, 358; Kunze, *Der Prozess*; Kunze, 'Wagnereckh'; Behringer, 'Hexenverfolgung', 62–78 *passim*.   [91] Heydenreuter, *Der landesherrliche Hofrat*, 324.
[92] *Ibid.*, 320; Kunze, 'Wagnereckh', 6.
[93] Dürrwächter, *Christoph Gewold*, 4, 16. Cf. note 4. J. Gretser dedicated his work on the Christian festivals, published in 1612, to the witch-hunting Bishop of Eichstätt J.C. von Westerstetten, of whose radical witch hunting in the Prince-Provostship of Ellwangen he wrote: 'The stubborn plague of sorcerers and witches is trying to attain unconquerable strength. The more hidden it is, the more pernicious and dangerous is this creeping evil. Against this plague of sorcerers, your Highness, inflamed by godly zeal and love of the welfare of your subjects, can use no other or more serviceable means than steadfastness in the execution of justice. In this good work, which you have already steadfastly and tirelessly continued for many years, you cannot displease reasonable, good people. And if ever it applied to an evil or an illness, then the saying is true here, that a wound which will not heal is to be cut out with a knife, so that the healthy part is not infected.' J. Gretser, *De festis christianorum*, Ingolstadt 1612, cited from the German translation in Duhr, *Geschichte der Jesuiten*, II/2, 514.   [94] Bauer, 'Die Bamberger Weihbischöfe', 405.

Jesuit confessors Buslidius and Contzen, the court preacher Drexel and the Secretaries Gewold and Albertinus, the influence of the apologists of persecution penetrated into the immediate circle of the ruler.[95] The Duke was usually willing to listen to the religiously inspired eagerness of the persecution party for a persecution, as his father Wilhelm V and his uncles Duke Ferdinand and Ernst, Prince-Bishop of Cologne, Freising etc., had been before him.

In this connection Bireley's study of Contzen's role in the internal debates in Bavaria in the later 1620s is most interesting, for it allows us to recognise the same party formations which were already so clearly defined in the great witchcraft discussion at the beginning of the century and may have gone back to the 1560s. As in the other south German Catholic principalities, on the one hand there was an intransigent 'Jesuit party',[96] headed in the 1620s by Adam Contzen. Following a line which Bireley calls 'religious extremism', in foreign policy this interest group pushed the princes into blind alleys in the religious war, while in domestic policy it pressed for the enforcement of rigorous social discipline and persecution. Themselves possessed by the radical spirit of penitential asceticism, such Jesuit leaders of opinion as Gregor von Valentia, Contzen and Gretser knew how to use religion to reinforce their own political inclination, and to propagate it as a 'holy struggle';[97] a group of like-minded lay Councillors, Fickler, Gewold, Albertinus, Preysing, Wagnereckh and others, drew support from the theological arguments of the Jesuits and added 'secular' motives of their own.

The religiously motivated confrontation politicians and the apologists of persecution regularly clashed with another party, headed by the 'moder-

---

[95] Steinruck, Fickler; Bireley, Maximilian, 19; Bauer, 'Die Bamberger Weihbischöfe,' 403ff.

[96] Bauer, 'Die Bamberger Weihbischöfe', 410. This description seems justified, even though later dissidents such as Tanner, Hell and Spee broke ranks with the 'Catholic phalanx' created by Gretser (König, 'Jacob Gretser', 150).

[97] Bireley, Maximilian, 62, 143, 152–6. The verdict of 'extremism' passed by Bireley on his fellow Jesuit, 143. Bireley regards Contzen and Dr Jocher as the spokesmen of the two opposing parties at the end of the 1620s. On the very similar crusading spirit of Förner and Gretser cf. Bauer, 'Die Bamberger Weihbischöfe', 368; H. König, who uses the terms 'radikale Buss- und Sühnegeist' and 'heiliger Kampf', ibid., 144 and 150. On the 'worldly' partisans see the literature already cited; Steinruck, Fickler; Dürrwächter, Christoph Gewold; Kunze, 'Wagnereckh'; on Preysing: J. Sturm, Johann Christoph von Preysing. Ein Kulturbild aus dem Anfang des Dreissigjährigen Krieges, Munich 1923. Bireley, Maximilian, 32, 154. Contzen's reflections on the causes of the Thirty Years War and the oppression of the Catholic Church are found in his opinion 'De persecutione Ecclesiae Christi per Germaniam', in HStAM, Jesuitica no. 81. Failure to hunt down witches was said to be one of the causes of this punishment from God, the blame being laid on the politici. Cited in Duhr, 'Zur Geschichte', 141–3. Contzen was in no way troubled by the fact that leading Jesuits were by now found among the critics. In this connection it is not without interest that Contzen had studied in Trier around 1590, and then in Mainz around 1600 (Bireley, Maximilian, 25f.), and had witnessed the great witch hunts in both places.

ate majority in the Privy Council', led in the later 1620s by the Privy Councillors Dr Wilhelm Jöcher and Dr Joachim Donnersberger, as well as Dr Bartholomäus Richel. These men tried to keep the damage within bounds by using political arguments, and urged timely reconcilation and a cautious line in questions of witchcraft. Contzen mocked his opponents as *politici*, and did not even shrink from blaming them for the military reverses in the war.[98]

THE ANTI-PERSECUTION PARTY

Fourthly, the Councillors on the Knights' Bench, several of whom are cited *pro testibus*, have been not a little offended by the report in the witchcraft case, as their votes have been set aside in such consultation. And their *affectus carpendi* appears so strong, that those who have sometimes spent hours *in examinibus*, or attend them *ex curiositate* and as *privati*, can judge of the proceedings as much as a blind man can judge of colours, since they know nothing either *procedendi* or of the *sequentia*. From which it is to be inferred that those who talk so much nonsense about the trial themselves do not know where they are or what they are doing ... thus as a thing pleases or displeases these people, so they praise or blame a case, as they please.[99]

(Wagnereckh on his political opponents, 1602–3)

Two of Wagnereckh's rhetorical tricks were to disqualify the opponents of persecution by decrying them either as unreliable Christians ('cold and political Christians') or as incompetent idlers; in both cases there was an unmistakably anti-feudal overtone: against the people of standing, the old country nobility or the city patricians, Wagnereckh upheld the work ethic

[98] Bireley, *Maximilian*, 143, 152–4. As other moderates and opponents of Contzen Bireley names the Councillors Wolkenstein, Hohenzollern, Peringer and Schuss, *ibid.*, 152. The extremism of the intransigents, to whom the Bishop of Augsburg Heinrich V von Knörin-gen and the Bishop of Osnabrück and son of Duke Ferdinand of Bavaria, F.W. von Wartenberg, also belonged in 'externals', was so great that even the Pope spoke slightingly of *zelanti*, Bireley, *Maximilian*, 226. On Knöringen, Spindler, 'Heinrich'; on Wartenberg, Heydenreuter, *Der landesherrliche Hofrat*, 359f. and Schwaiger, *Kardinal Franz Wilhelm*. On the 'question of war guilt' cf. note 97.

[99] EOAM, Akt Varia 516, fol. 179v–81v. Like Contzen Dr Wagnereckh also described his enemies as *politici* or as 'kalte und politische Christen': HStAM, Hexenakten 1, Prod. 6, fol. 6r–v. (in a letter to ex-Duke Wilhelm V in 1615, about the topic of witchcraft. In general the militant counter-reformers stigmatised their opponents as *politici*, accusing them of being devoid of or lacking in religious principle. R. Bireley, *Religion and Politics in the Age of the Counterreformation. Emperor Ferdinand II, Wilhelm Lamormaini SJ and the Formation of Imperial Policy*, Chapel Hill 1981, 23 (example from 1625). Bireley, like Engel, 'Respublica', 145, refers to the party of the *politiques* in the French Wars of Religion, which is not altogether unproblematical in view of the position of Bodin.

of the rising bourgeois, the absolute ideological reliability of the servant of the Prince and friend of the Jesuits. Erudition and zeal for persecution were unscrupulously equated as all the standard Catholic authors – Sprenger and Institoris, Bodin, Binsfeld, Remy and Delrio – followed the same line of argument.

In fact the opponents of persecution were recruited from the very social groups that Wagnereckh ridiculed: the higher patriciates of Ingolstadt and Munich, and the Bavarian nobility, while most of the apologists of persecution were 'foreigners' (Valentia, Gretser, Contzen, Fickler, Albertinus and Fachineus; Gewold and Vagh were also converts).[100] At the beginning of the discussions, however, Wagnereckh had to suffer serious disappointments, with respect to both the competence of the opponents of persecution, and the extent of their influence.

The nobles in the government were in fact shocked by the Munich witch trial conducted by Wagnereckh in 1600. They criticised not only the offensive discrimination against them in the debates, as Wagnereckh attempted to suggest, but above all the form of procedure. In January 1601, that is at the decisive moment for the expansion of the Munich witch trial into a general persecution, one of their representatives was appointed President of the Court Council. Heinrich (II) von Haslang[101] did not understand his position in the usual sense, but, unlike the Court Chancellor Gailkircher, who had been uninterested in the witchcraft question, emerged as the spokesman of the anti-persecution party. Though Haslang came from an old Bavarian noble family, he had studied law in France and Italy. His legal opinions are terse and to the point, and show that he was a competent jurist and doughty polemicist.

Yet there were other hidden forces ranged behind Heinrich von Haslang, with whom he was closely associated in his capacities as Chamberlain, Commissioner of the Estates, and ducal commissioner. Behind Haslang stood the office-holding elite of the principality, namely the Privy Councillors Dr Hans Georg Herwarth von Hohenburg[102] and Dr Joachim Donnersberger,[103] who had had a hand in the appointment of Haslang as

---

[100] Gregor von Valentia from Spain, Gretser from Baden, Contzen from the Duchy of Jülich, Fickler from Württemberg, Albertinus from Deventer in the United Provinces, Fachineus from Italy, Vagh from Flensburg, Gewold from the Electoral Upper Palatinate (data from Bosl, *Biographie*). For similar remarks on France, cf. Soman, 'Parlement', 39.

[101] Little is known of Haslang (?–1606). His father was the Privy Councillor Rudolf von Haslang, and the family belonged to the high Bavarian nobility. Heydenreuter, *Der landesherrliche Hofrat*, 334; Lanzinner, *Fürst*, 358; Dürrwächter, *Christoph Gewold*, (1904), 7; Sturm, *Preying*, 206f., 333, 345 (*passim*).

[102] (1553–1626). Heydenreuter, *Der landesherrliche Hofrat*, 335f.; *ADB*, 13 (1881), 169–75; *NDB*, 8 (1969), 720f.; Spindler, *Handbuch*, II, 801 (Kraus); M. Caspar, *Johannes Kepler*, Stuttgart 1948, 90–2 *passim*, 102, 200.

[103] Heydenreuter, *Der landesherrliche Hofrat*, 319f.; *ADB*, 5, 337f. Lived from 1565 to 1650.

President of the Court Council. Donnersberger came from a Munich patrician family and had experienced the persecutions of 1590 as a member of the Court Council. From 1599 to 1650 he was the most important political official in the Duchy, as Supreme Chancellor. Herwarth came from the patriciate of Augsburg, and his father had been raised to the Bavarian nobility in 1566. Herwarth too had experienced the persecution of 1590 as a member of the Court Council, and in the same year had been nominated as Supreme Chancellor, as Donnersberger's predecessor, but, while retaining his seat in the Privy Council, had transferred to the post of Chancellor of the Estates. In this post he collaborated with the Commissioner of the Estates Haslang; together with Haslang, Donnersberger and the Privy Councillor and High Chamberlain Wolf Konrad von Rechberg,[104] Herwarth led an investigation in 1602 into suspicions of corruption against the Chancellor of the Court Council Dr Gailkircher. Herwarth is one of the most interesting figures in early modern Bavaria, not only because of his key political role – he led the joint finance committee of government and Estates which brought about the abdication of Duke Wilhelm V when the state was threatened with bankruptcy – but also because of his scholarly work as a classical philologist, historian, astronomer and mathematician. His *Tabulae arithmeticae* contributed to the development of logarithms and between 1597 and 1611 Herwarth carried on an extensive correspondence with Johannes Kepler, whose advancement in Prague he had helped to promote.[105]

Herwarth and Donnersberger had been the guarantors of the moderate attitude in questions of witchcraft in the Duchy of Bavaria since 1590, although by 1600 this attitude was not yet securely established, and still had to be fought for again and again. As early as December 1601 Haslang mentioned that 'the learned Privy Councillors were already of my opinion before my report'.[106] Wagnereckh held them responsible for the changing attitude of the University of Ingolstadt, which was becoming apparent in 1601.[107] After Haslang's death in 1608 it was again Herwarth and

---

[104] Heydenreuter, *Der landesherrliche Hofrat*, 351; Dürrwächter, *Christoph Gewold*, 7.

[105] Cf. note 102. An interesting detail: J.G. Herwarth was, in spite of the difference in faith, a godfather of a daughter of Kepler. The godfather of a son of Kepler was J.G. Goedelmann, a publicist who opposed witch hunting (Goedelmann, *Tractatus*; Goedelmann, *Von Zauberern*). Caspar, *Kepler*, 186, 200. Goedelmann's writings were repeatedly cited by the Bavarian opponents of witch hunting, greatly to the irritation of the persecution party, since he was a Lutheran 'heretic'.   [106] EOAM, Akt Varia 516, fol. 143.

[107] *Ibid.*, fol. 116v–17: 'Ist nit ohne verdacht, dass sie [the University of Ingolstadt] etliche Argumenta, welche allhie [Munich] pro negativa starck getrieben worden sein, in specie auf die Pan bringen . . . [examples; WB]. Darauss nit wenig zu besorgen, es sein von Jemandt alhier rationes negativae hinyber geschrieben worden und die facultas Juridicae mecht in diesem werckh etwas respectiert haben . . .' ('It is not without suspicion that they bring forward in this case several negative arguments which have been strongly urged here. It is not a little to be feared that negative reasons have been written by someone here and sent to them, and the faculty of law might have shown some respect in this work.')

Donnersberger, with the President of the Court Council Gundaker von Tannberg and the later Privy Councillor Dr Wilhelm Jocher,[108] who were subjected to the stinging criticisms of the new Chancellor of the Court Council, Wagnereckh. In 1611 they prevented the publication of the mandate on superstition and witchcraft prepared by Dr Vagh. Donnersberger and von Rechberg also intervened directly in the business of the Court Council to oppose Wagnereckh on the question of the punishment of the 'witch judge' of Wemding, which would signal their intentions to the world. This is the light in which we must see the indignation of Wagnereckh and Vagh:

> the Count [Rechberg] is an idiot, the Supreme Chancellor [Donnersberger] is no jurist and also stinkingly lazy. The Chancellor of the Estates [Herwarth] is an open sorcerer [! WB]. Dr Jocher does not understand the custom of the country . . .[109]

The resistance to the apologists of persecution was not confined to the Privy Councillors and representatives of the Estates in Munich, but had its roots in the not very submissive patriciates of the cities of Ingolstadt and Munich. Time and again the importance of social and family relationships becomes apparent. This can be illustrated from the two Ingolstadt jurists Dr Joachim Denich[110] and Dr Kaspar Hell, who dominated the faculty of law around 1600. Kaspar Hell[111] was regarded, even by his enemies, as the most brilliant mind in the University, but his boldness in advocacy had earned him the reputation of being willing to defend the Devil for money. That was just one of the usual exaggerations but Hell was unorthodox

---

[108] On Jocher, Heydenreuter, *Der landesherrliche Hofrat*, 340f.; *ADB*, 14, 102f; above all Bireley, *Maximilian*, 62, 143, 192f. for Jocher's importance as the opposite pole of the 'extremists' in the 1620s. His dates were 1565–1639.

[109] Heydenreuter, *Der landesherrliche Hofrat*, 148. For the opinion of 1608 cf. Behringer, 'Hexenverfolgung', 73f.

[110] On Denich (1560–1633), Bosl, *Biographie*, 132; Henker, 'Zur Prosopographie', 101f; *ADB*, 5, 50f. Dr J. Denich became a professor at the University of Ingolstadt in 1590, when his stepfather Dr Kaspar Lagus resigned in his favour. Denich's opinions were in great demand in both Munich and Nuremberg. At the time of the Ingolstadt opinion of 1601 Denich was Dean of the faculty of law.

[111] Dr Kaspar Hell of Aichach was a professor at Ingolstadt from 1586 to 1601. Wilczek, 'Die Universität', 24. He is not highly praised in university histories, biographical and prosopographical works, presumably because of his dismissal in 1601 in connection with the second Ingolstadt opinion on witchcraft; the accusations against him ranged from corruption to high treason and favouring witches. Our knowledge of Hell comes mainly from the proceedings which he brought against Bavaria in the Imperial Chamber Court, demanding compensation after his dismissal: HStAM, RKG 6519. Dr Fasold of Ingolstadt, himself a partisan of Wagnereckh, said of Hell in 1601: 'Man halte ihn für einen prächtigen Mann, der Jedermann aussrichte, und sonderlich sein kein gelertter als er, und seien die alten Everhardi nichts gegen ihn, haben keine Fundamenta . . .', *ibid.*, s.f. (cross-examination of 15 Nov. 1601).

enough to represent the Protestant Counts of Ortenburg against the Dukes of Bavaria.[112] While Prince Maximilian was a student at Ingolstadt Hell had been able to chair two of his legal disputations, one against Heinrich von Haslang, the other against the later Town Clerk of Munich Dr Georg Locher, both of whom could be regarded as Hell's pupils and ranged themselves among the moderates (*politici*) in the discussions of witchcraft.

Locher, who married a daughter of Professor Hell, several times represented the interests of the city of Munich against the Duke's Court Council in questions of witchcraft. In 1601 he was approached by one Mair, an innkeeper of Abensberg, to help his sister, who had been arrested as a witch. Hell agreed and represented the interests of the woman in the University, while Locher was active at Munich. We must assume that they were in contact with Haslang or one of the Privy Council. In the same year, when the government in Munich asked the University for an opinion which was to state a general line on questions of witchcraft with reference to the case of three particular women, Hell took on the task of preparing the opinion for the Dean of the faculty of law, Dr J. Denich. The opinion argued that none of the women should be tortured, and that 'Mairin of Abensberg', in particular, ought to be released.[113]

Professor Denich was a friend of Hell's and a brother in law of the former Court Councillor Dr Kaspar Lagus, who had warned against trials of witches as early as 1590. J. Denich had a son by Maria Lagus who, as Dr Kaspar Denich, was later to be the centre of resistance to further witch trials in Ingolstadt.[114] Dr Kaspar Hell, who was suspended from his professorship in 1601, also had a son, Kaspar, who in the 1620s stirred up the Jesuit college at Eichstätt against the persistent persecutions of the Bishop Johann Christoph von Westerstetten.[115] In this light it is not without interest that the sons of the Councillors Haslang, Donnersberger and Herwarth were able to assert themselves in the inner circles of power in Munich,[116] while this was not the case for any of the hard-line advocates of persecution.

---

[112] HStAM, RKG 6519, *ibid.*

[113] *Ibid.*, s.f. (and not numbered). The Ingolstadt opinion on witchcraft of 1601 is in HStAM, Hexenakten 4, Prod. 1, 9 fols. Essentially it follows the arguments of Goedelmann and indirectly distances itself from the former position of the University, which had been based on Binsfeld's hard line. It is apparent from RKG 6519 that Hell was the only professor who appeared at the discussion with a written draft, and that he dominated the discussion. Only the Jesuit Gretser turned a deaf ear to Hell's arguments. On Dr Georg Locher cf. Spindler, *Handbuch*, II, 587; Behringer, 'Hexenverfolgung', 64f.

[114] (1591–1660), from 1614 a professor at the University of Ingolstadt. Bosl, *Biographie*, 133; *ADB*, 5, 50f.; Prantl, *Geschichte*, I, 421f.; Schrittenloher, 'Aus der Gutachter-...', 343–5. On the impressive activities of Denich cf. chapter 4, pp. 269–90.

[115] (1588–1634). Duhr, *Geschichte der Jesuiten*, 488. Cf. chapter 4, pp. 291–309.

[116] Heydenreuter, *Der landesherrliche Hofrat*, 320, 335–8.

We cannot go into the numerous petty acts of defiance of the magistracies of Ingolstadt and Munich here. More important, in their capacities as Receiver and *Hofoberrichter* or superior judge, were the Councillors Christoph Elsenheimer and Bernhard Barth, both of whom came from Munich patrician families; the latter was an important counterbalance to Wagnereckh especially in the first years of Wagnereckh's Chancellorship of the Court Council (1606–10), as he did not shrink from any conflict and tried to ensure that investigations of sorcery and witchcraft were properly conducted, in spite of the constant encroachments of the Chancellor.[117] From 1612 the Court Councillor Christoph Tanner took over this function, supported after 1614 by Dr Johann Georg Brugglacher.[118] Three years later Brugglacher succeeded Wagnereckh as Chancellor on the latter's death.

The high officials were most troubled by executions of witches in their own families. Johann Christoph Abegg was Court Chancellor of Bavaria from 1625 to 1644. In 1626 a relation of his wife, Margarethe Bittelmayerin, wife of the Town Clerk of Eichstätt, was executed as a witch. In the years 1628–30 Abegg was considered an enemy of persecution.[119] From 1651 to 1667 the Court Chancellor was Dr J. Ernst, a son-in-law of the former Chancellor Dr Brugglacher. Magdalena Mack, a relation of his wife, had been burned as a witch at Wemding in 1630.[120] Dr Bartholomäus Richel was deputy of the Supreme Chancellor Donnersberger from 1623 to 1649. Previously he had been Chancellor of the Bishopric of Eichstätt, where his wife Maria Richel, née Bonschab, had been burned as a witch in December 1620. Richel's swift move to the Bavarian service was also advisable in view of the fact that six other members of the patrician family of Bonschab were burned as witches in the Bishopric of Eichstätt between 1617 and 1627, the last victims being Burgomaster Lorenz Bonschab and his wife and daughter.[121]

We can regard it as the greatest triumph of the opponents of persecution in Bavaria that at the end of the 1620s, for the first time, a reputable

[117] On Elsenheimer (1563–1630): Bosl, *Biographie*, 174; on Barth (1560–1630): Heydenreuter, *Der landesherrliche Hofrat*, 304f.

[118] Heydenreuter, *Der landesherrliche Hofrat*, 313 (Brugglacher, ?–1620), 318. Tanner (?–1665). Cf. Behringer, 'Scheiternde Hexenprozesse', 63–6.

[119] Heydenreuter, *Der landesherrliche Hofrat*, 302. Film 668, 64; Snell, *Hexenprozesse*, 43; Schrittenloher, 'Aus der Gutachter- und Urteilstätigkeit', 344.

[120] Schneid, 'Das Rechtsverfahren', 170. Magdalena Mack (1582–1630), daughter of the Town Clerk Johan Lang of Rain on the Lech, was married to Martin Mack, a rich brewer and landlord of the 'Stern' inn in Wemding. Two of her brothers were Town Clerk and Burgomaster of Rain. Her father was married to the sister of the Chancellor of the Bavarian Court Council, Dr Johann Georg Brugglacher (cf. note 118). *Ibid.*, 188.

[121] Heydenreuter, *Der landesherrliche Hofrat*, 352. Film 669, 92 (Maria Richel). Film 668, 7–5 (Bonschab family).

Catholic theologian took an authoritative stand against the 'Catholic' practice of persecution and laid a solid foundation for further resistance to it. This was the Jesuit Adam Tanner,[122] the most important precursor[123] of Friedrich Spee. During his student years at Dillingen, 1587–90, Tanner had experienced the persecutions in the city, while as a novice in Landsberg and Munich in 1590–2 he had probably seen the persecution at Schongau and the trials in the Bavarian capital. In spite or because of these experiences, Tanner was less marked by his studies under the Ingolstadt Jesuits Gregor von Valentia and Jacob Gretser, than by the following six years he spent in Munich, where he witnessed the discussion in the Bavarian government on the principle of witchcraft. Influenced by this debate in Munich, Tanner developed a relatively sharp criticism of the current procedure in trials for witchcraft, to which he continued to adhere firmly even after the persecutions in Catholic Franconia became more intense. In the years 1603–27, when Tanner was lecturing at Ingolstadt, a group of decided opponents of persecution was formed in the city.[124] Tanner made

[122] (1572–1632). For his biography and theological positions: W. Lurz, *Adam Tanner und die Gnadenstreitigkeiten des 17. Jahrhunderts. Ein Beitrag zur Geschichte des Molinismus*, Breslau 1932. Also interesting is Tanner's early defence of Trithemius, who had fallen under suspicion of sorcery: A. Dürrwächter, 'Adam Tanner und die Steganographie des Trithemius', in *Festgabe Herrmann Grauert*, Freiburg im Breisgau 1910, 354–76. Literature on Tanner's attitude to the witchcraft question: A. Tanner SJ, *Theologia Scholastica (. . .)*, 4 vols., Ingolstadt 1626–7, vol. III, col. 981–1022; Spee, *Cautio*. Spee relies on Tanner as an authority in nearly thirty decisive passages. Tanner's criticism of trials for witchcraft, much less radical than that of Spee was thus preserved like a fly in amber; H. Loeher, *Hochnöthige, Unterthanige, Wehmütige Klage der Frommen Unschüldigen worin . . . zu lesen. . ., wie arme unschüldige fromme Leut durch Fahm- und Ehrenrauben von den falschen Zauberrichtern angegriffen (. . .)*. Welches auch die Herren Tannerus, Cautio Criminalis, Michael Stapirius härtlich bekräftigen, Amsterdam 1676. Rapp, *Die Hexenprozesse*, 47–71; Janssen and Pastor, *Culturzustände*, VIII, 655–60; Riezler, *Geschichte*, 250–60; Soldan *et al., Geschichte der Hexenprozesse*, II, 178–84; Duhr, *Die Stellung*, 45–53; Lea, *Materials*, 647–70; Baschwitz, *Hexen*, 290; Lurz, *Tanner*, 24–8.
[123] Spee, *Cautio*, 9, 11, 21–4 *passim*, 29–32 *passim*, 39, 48, 56, 66f., then 77, 99, 102, 109, 150, 159f., 198, 218, 232, 234, 238, 264, 270–2 *passim*. Even if Spee cites Tanner for tactical reasons, where he develops a more far-reaching criticism, it is impossible to overlook the fact that Tanner was basically the only Catholic authority whom Spee could quote in support of his argument. Tanner's role as a pathfinder becomes clear when Spee goes into the details of the hostility which Tanner aroused through his criticism.
[124] Tanner, *Theologia*, III, col. 981, writes: 'Et quia mihi quoque adhuc Monachii Theologiam moralem docenti, iam ante annos 24 ea ipsa quaesita circa hanc materiam resolvenda proposita fuerunt, quae postea ad Martinum Delrium delata. . .'; *ibid.*, col. 988, 990–2, 995, 998–9, 1002–5 and 1012 for Tanner's references to the discussions in Munich and to the opinions framed by the foreign sources consulted (cf. chapter VI.5 of the German edition of this book). Tanner's opinion of 1602, which he mentions in *ibid.*, col. 981, has either not been preserved or did not differ from the opinion of the secular opponents of witch hunting, e.g. von Haslang or von Herwarth. A 'Tractatus theologico-canonicus Jesuitae cujusdam Theologicae Professore de criminis exceptis, praefatim in causis veneficarum', SBM, Cgm. 2625, fol. 265–316, is a copy of the witchcraft chapter

his views known to a wider public in his *Theologia Scholastica*, an influential standard work on moral theology in the seventeenth century.[125] Yet Tanner was perhaps less the spokesman of the Bavarian opponents of persecution than their mouthpiece. Resistance was rooted in society itself, and these roots were wide and deep. While the city magistrates, the Estates and the officials who had risen from these bodies gave voice to this resistance, it was Tanner's thankless but important task to reconcile it with scholastic theology.[126]

in Tanner, *Theologia*, III, col. 981–1022. The groups of opponents of witch hunting around Tanner: Spee, who often shows himself well informed about events in Eichstätt (cf. e.g. the incident in Duhr, *Geschichte der Jesuiten*, II/2, 488 with the version, with names suppressed, in Spee, *Cautio*, 253f.) and also on conditions in neighbouring Ingolstadt as the counter-pole in the question of witchcraft (cf. below p. 389f.), writes of 'Tanner selbst und guten gewissenhaften Christen die ihm anhängen', Spee, *Cautio*, 21. Mention must be made above all of P. Laymann, *Theologia Moralis*, Munich 1630, who largely associated himself with Tanner's arguments in the third edition of his moral theology. Laymann took over whole passages verbatim from Tanner and clearly distanced himself from Delrio (*Theologia*, I, 524) and Binsfeld. See Duhr, *Die Stellung*, 53–9. Laymann was also taken over by Spee. Spee, *Cautio*, 15, did not yet know the third edition of Laymann's moral theology at the time of the composition of the *Cautio Criminalis*; this third edition was the first to reveal Laymann as a decided opponent of witch hunting. The old controversy about a treatise attributed to Laymann can now be regarded as closed: S. Riezler, 'Paul Laymann und die Hexenprozesse', *Historische Zeitschrift*, 84 (1900), 244–56; versus B. Duhr, 'Paul Laymann und die Hexenprozesse', *Zeitschrift für katholische Theologie*, 23 (1899), 733–44; see Duhr, *Geschichte der Jesuiten*, II/2, 521–4; and Lea, *Materials*, II, 670–89. Laymann, like Tanner, came from the Tyrol, was a novice at Landsberg on the Lech, a student at Ingolstadt and then taught at the gymnasium in Dillingen. From 1603 to 1609 he was a lecturer at Ingolstadt, from 1609–25 at Munich and from 1625 to 1632 a professor of canon law at Dillingen. He lived from 1575–1635. Bosl, *Biographie*, 468, contains serious errors, e.g. in ascribing to Laymann the Cologne treatise of a witch hunter (Goehausen), the subject of the controversy between Riezler and Duhr. Besides Laymann the following influential Bavarian Jesuits were themselves influenced by Tanner: Georg Gobat SJ (Duhr, 'Zur Biographie', 330), court confessor in Munich; Sebastian Denich SJ (*ibid.*, 328), Ingolstadt; Christoph Haunold SJ (Duhr, *Geschichte der Jesuiten*, II/2, 540–2), professor and director of studies at Ingolstadt; Nikolas Cusan SJ (*ibid.*, 515); Kaspar Hell SJ (*ibid.*, 487f.), Ingolstadt, Eichstätt, later Rector of the colleges in Neuburg and Amberg (Bireley, *Religion*, 256). Cf. chapter V.1.
[125] Cf. notes 122, 124. But it was not until his *Theologia Scholastica* that Tanner dealt authoritatively and in principle with the question of witchcraft trials. This bold move must be seen in connection with the excessive persecutions raging at the time in the four Franconian Prince-Bishoprics. Friedrich Spee shows how bold it was, even for a theological authority of Tanner's standing, to raise this subject; he reports that 'zwei Inquisitoren eines gewissen mächtigen Fürsten, nachdem sie kürzlich das kluge, gelehrte Buch des hochbedeutenden Tanner SJ gelesen hatten, zu sagen gewagt haben, wenn sie diesen Menschen zu fassen bekämen, dann würden sie ihn ohne langes Zögern foltern lassen', Spee, *Cautio*, 23. Tanner's breach with the usual method of treating the subject is clear when one compares his approach with comparable treatises, e.g. that of the Molinist L. Lessius SJ, *De Iustitia et Iure*, Antwerp 1609. It was only the discussions in Bavaria in the early seventeenth century that made it possible for Tanner to deviate from this beaten path.
[126] Cf. note 125. Cf. also Behringer, 'Scheiternde Hexenprozesse', 72–8 and chapter 4,

LEARNED DEBATE, 1601–4

And so it would be most advisable that the *quaestiones emergentes in causa Maleficarum*, which are sent to Ingolstadt (and to which several might be added) should also be sent to other *Universitates Catholicas Germaniae, Galliae, Italiae, Hispaniae*, and *responsa* to them desired. So it would serve not a little for greater consideration and better information, if, in the main questions, in which there have been different opinions here, each party should deduce its *rationes et allegatione*, and such a deduction were to be sent to the universities with the *Questionibus*.[127]

THE DESIRE FOR A SETTLEMENT IN PRINCIPLE

Wagnereckh, as a tactician who knew his own strength, was clearly well aware that he could no longer limit the damage to his cause by defaming individual opponents, or by intrigues and threats, after the criticism of the Munich witch trials had taken the form of a manifesto. Now he had to bring other battalions into the field to support his own views, of whose rightness he was firmly convinced, by external authorities, and to be able to force their adoption as domestic policy in Bavaria. In view of the literature on witchcraft Wagnereckh could expect his opinions to be shared by all the Catholic authorities in Germany and beyond. In 1599 the polymath Delrio had published his *Disquisitiones Magicae*, in which he proved in detail that to doubt the accuracy of the fully developed theory of witchcraft was not only wrong but heretical; he demonstrated from two cases how those who had been led astray were to be dealt with. The theologian Cornelis Loos had had to abjure his errors, the Rector of the University and Privy Councillor Dr Flade had even been unmasked as a witch himself, and burned. Both cases had left a deep impression in Bavaria and Swabia as elsewhere.[128] The opinion of 1590 and the presence in the faculty of the theologians Hunger and Gretser seemed to guarantee the attitude of the University of Ingolstadt.

At first, however, Wagnereckh tried to eliminate all objections to his trial in Munich itself. In a detailed 'reckoning and answer' he pointed to the careful preparation of the *Interrogatoria*, their approval by the Court

pp. 247–68.

[127] EOAM, Akt Varia no. 516, fol. 114v–21, 'Notabilia ad Responsum Ingolstadiensis'; fol. 118r–v (Dr Wagnereckh).

[128] Zenz, 'Flade'; Zenz, 'Loos'. Impression in Bavaria: HStAM, Hexenakten 4, Prod. 16, fol. 5; HStAM, Hochstift Augsburg, NA, Akten no. 1222, fol. 427–9v. Obviously it was always the hard-line apologists of persecution who referred to these cases, e.g. Wagnereckh in Munich, zum Ackher in Dillingen. *Ibid.*

Council under the chairmanship of Dr Gailkircher, the obtaining of authorisation for torture in every case and the proper keeping of the court record. The only delicate point seemed to be that Wagnereckh had decided on his own authority as commissioner that a new torture was not to be classed as a repetition but as a continuation, if the catalogue of questions had not yet been exhausted. In this way he had created for himself the possibility of avoiding the duty to refer back to the Court Council, until the suspects persisted in their confessions for fear of further torture. Nevertheless, in early April 1601 the Court Council approved Wagnereckh's procedure, and a little later Duke Maximilian also expressed himself satisfied with this apparent supervision of the proceedings.[129] Yet, as we shall see, the critics in the government continued to accuse Wagnereckh of irregular procedure.

Even more serious were the principled objections of the opponents of persecution to the lawfulness of arrest and torture on the grounds of denunciations. In a rhetorically polished opinion, Wagnereckh appealed to the Duke not to pay any attention to such objections. We should particularly note the high value he attached to denunciations in trials for witchcraft. Without them, so Wagnereckh wrote, in most cases the trials simply could not be carried on:

> And this is all the more so, because we are dealing *in crimine plusquam excepto, atrocissimo et occultissimo*, so that otherwise it would be hard or impossible to bring them to trial . . . unless a sorcerer or witch were revealed by the special will of God, or the case was so flagrant that it brought sorcery into the open before the people, so that they were caught, *quod rarissimo vel nunquam contingit*[130]

Wagnereckh also tried to counter objections to the treatment of witchcraft as an exceptional crime (*crimen plusquam excepto*) by claiming that there was no fear that the innocent would be found guilty in trials for witchcraft.

> Experience and daily example shows that the *inculpationes* and statements of the witches against their accomplices are almost always true and very seldom is any innocent person denounced . . .
> And even assuming that once, by God's doom, an innocent person should be at risk and thus executed, a judge would do no wrong . . .

---

[129] EOAM, Akt Varia 516, fol. 30 (5/12 April 1601).
[130] HStAM, Hexenakten 4, Prod. 15, 18 fols. *Ibid.*, fol. 7.

But one would like to know where, when and how such a thing in fact happened, and whether a thousand cases could not be cited when such denunciations and statements have been found to be true, while on the other hand there is not a single case that could be alleged *in contrarium*.[131]

In fact the possible arguments open to the opponents of persecution were weak on some points, for they could hardly claim that thousands of judicial murders had been committed during the wave of persecution of 1590 in Trier and southeast Germany. Once again, the witch burnings themselves proved the strongest arguments for the persecutioners.

In spite of the objections of the opponents of persecution, Court Councillor Wagnereckh, who had risen to the leading position in the persecution party in Munich in 1600, by his programmatic apologies for persecution, again pressed for an unconditional persecution; nor did he shrink from threatening the Duchy of Bavaria and its ducal house with the gravest consequences if his advice were ignored. All the objections of the opposing party were mere 'inconsiderable *impedimenta*':

And so it is proper for an authority to take strong measures to root out this detestable vice, let it hit as many of them and the most exalted persons as it will . . . but especially if the authorities are negligent, God himself will severely punish rulers and subjects, city, country and *in summa* all together . . .[132]

Wagnereckh's gloomy visions may have influenced the Duke, but they did not move the opponents of persecution in the government of the Duchy. As no consensus could be reached in Munich under these circumstances, both parties pressed for an authoritative decision by the University of Ingolstadt, as a way out of the impasse in Munich.

This meant a consideration in principle of the role that denunciations, torture, revocations and so on ought to play in witch trials. The crucial question was whether the normal rules of legal procedure ought to apply or whether the courts were to be given a free hand in arrest and torture, because of the exceptional character of the offence of witchcraft, as the leading Catholic authors on the subject demanded. The basic issue was what had been the right course: helping the persecution to expand in 1589–90 or stopping the trials in 1590–1?

[131] *Ibid.*, fol. 7v.   [132] *Ibid.*, fol. 13.

A NEW OPINION OF PRINCIPLE FROM INGOLSTADT (2 APRIL 1601)

His Grace desires *informationem juris*, first and *in specie*, in what way to proceed against the said three persons on the denunciations given . . . and for the rest Your Servants desire from the two faculties of *Theologica* and *Juridica* a detailed joint information *et quoad totum processum in hoc crimine instituendum*[133]

The great question put to the University of Ingolstadt in 1601 was as fundamental as that of April 1590. A covering letter did not omit to point out that the opinion of 1590 had given a positive answer to the question of whether denunciations alone, without further circumstantial evidence, were sufficient grounds for arrest and torture. But now that doubts had arisen about the justice of this procedure, the two faculties were 'to give more detailed grounds for their view in the present response'.[134] Their task was thus clear: it was not new principles, but a clarification of the convictions expressed before, that was wanted.

Yet the enquiry took the form of a question of principle. Besides a decision on the individual fates of three women in Kelheim and Abensberg, whose cases were explained in detail (*facti species*), the request also included twenty-two generally formulated questions (*Quaestiones emergentes in causa maleficarum*), the answers to which would make it possible to set a new course for future proceedings. The first and most important question was: 'An denunciatio plurium per se sit sufficiens indicium ad torturam, absque aliis indiciis aut adminiculis?' All the other questions touched on the same complex of problems. The answer, as always in such weighty matters, was to be delivered into the hands of the Prince himself.

The Ingolstadt opinion of April 1601 caused a sensation in Munich, especially among the persecution party, because it broke with the opinion of 1590 on decisive points. Moreover, it fell into two clearly distinct parts: the first was given by both faculties and was obviously closer to the opinion of 1590 than the second part, which was concerned with the particular fate of the three women. The general part of the opinion was jointly written by the apologists of persecution in the faculty of theology, Albert Hunger, Petrus Stevartius SJ and Jacob Gretser SJ. In principle the doctrine of *crimen exceptum* was confirmed, albeit with minor modifications.[135] The theologians declined to cooperate in the second part of the opinion because

---

[133] *Ibid.*, Prod. 10, 40 fols., 'Facti Species et Quaestiones Emergentes in Causa Maleficarum', fol. 3v. The same representation also in EOAM, Akt Varia 516, fol. 38–48v.
[134] HStAM, Hexenakten 4, Prod. 10, fol. 4v.
[135] HStAM, Hexenakten 4, Prod. 1, 10 fols., Ingolstadt opinion on witchcraft of 2.4.1601. *Ibid.*, fol. 2.

they were unwilling to decide on the fate of individuals, that is on the death penalty. This means that the opinion clearly revealed the difference between the views of the theologians on the one hand, and those of the jurists on the other – especially the two Professors Dr J. Denich and Dr Hell, whom we have already mentioned. With the aid of imperial legislation (articles 6, 31, 44, 182 and 189 of the *Carolina*), Italian commentaries on criminal law,[136] and opinions on witchcraft of the Rostock jurist J.G. Goedelmann and the Frankfurt jurist J. Fichard,[137] the jurists refuted the views of Binsfeld and the Ingolstadt opinion of 1590. Like the opponents of persecution in Munich the jurists of Ingolstadt believed that denunciations alone were of no effect, and they were unwilling to exclude the crime of sorcery from the general legal principles of the *Carolina*. The opinion of the jurists criticised the arrest of two of the three women (the innkeeper Mair in Abensberg and the burgomaster's wife Paur of Kelheim), and in the case of the third (a poor old inmate of a hospice in Kelheim) they demanded a closer examination of the circumstances. Generalising, they stated that even if, like the Ingolstadt theologians, one took the view

that this *crimen* is *occultum* and *exceptuatum*, then it does not follow that one should transgress the *regulas iuris* in all things, *maxime modo procedendi* . . . As Emperor Charles in his Criminal Ordinance does not exempt this vice of witchcraft *in modo procedendi vel circa indicia*, but in Art. 44 demands special *indicia*. . .[138]

The persecution party in Munich was taken completely by surprise by the tendency of the opinion. In an extremely sharp counter-opinion (*Notabilia ad responsum facultatis juridicae Ingolstadiensis*), which bears all the marks of being written by Wagnereckh himself, every possible objection is listed: the opinion of 1601 was diametrically opposed to that of 1590. This *inconstantia* alone was dangerous and objectionable.

To point the finger at this, in the said response of the year 90 both faculties decided *quod denunciatio plurium sufficiat ad torturam absque*

---

[136] The usual commentators were cited: Julius Clarus (1525–75), a Councillor of Philip II in Milan (on him Zedler, *Grosses Lexikon*, 233); Prosper Farinacius (1554–1618), *procurator fisci* of the Pope (Zedler, *Grosses Lexikon*, 253–4); Petrus Folerius, a Neapolitan jurist of the sixteenth century (Zedler, *Grosses Lexikon*, 1430); Anton Gomez, a jurist in Salamanca, sixteenth century (Zedler, *Grosses* Lexikon, 163); Robert Maranta, a jurist in Salerno, early sixteenth century (Zedler, *Grosses Lexikon*, 1169).

[137] J. Fichard, *Consilien*, Frankfurt am Main, 1590; Goedelmann, *Tractatus*; *Von Zauberern*. Cf. notes 4 and 105. In its most essential parts this opinion is based on Goedelmann.

[138] HStAM, Hexenakten 4, Prod. 1, fol. 6v–9 (Ingolstadt opinion on witchcraft 1601). The interpretation in Schrittenloher, 'Aus der Gutachten- und Urteilstätigkeit', 329, should be corrected from this.

aliis indiciis, et quod in huiusmodi criminibus alioqui occultis pluris faciendae sint denunciationes quam indicia. But in this current response the *facultas Juridica* demands diffamation as well as denunciation. *Cum tamen in occultis raro aut nunquam diffametur delinquens. Et hoc esset securim ad arborem ponere*, that the *denunciationibus in effectu* would be of no value.[139]

It was revealing that Wagnereckh only attacked the jurists, for he was well aware that he could rely on the views of Gretser and the other theologians. If the new opinion had 'laid an axe' to the roots of the fully grown theory of witchcraft and its procedural outgrowth, this was the fault of the jurists alone, who had deviated from the principles of the Catholic theory of witchcraft. Wagnereckh was particularly indignant that the opinion 'explicitly concluded *contra Binsfeldium*', and made matters worse by its appeal to the Rostock Lutheran Goedelmann.

> It is strange and unusual that Catholics do not shrink from citing a heretic, such as Goedelmann, *in tali causa et materia, quae etiam theologica est.* That this Godelmannus does not believe *translationem corporalem sagarum*, as Delrius writes of him.[140]

Besides the charge made here, which sounds like one of heresy, Wagnereckh made three further accusations, each of which alone was very grave. First, he indirectly accused the Privy Councillors in Munich of having given the jurists in Ingolstadt their instructions for the drafting of their opinion; secondly, he accused the Ingolstadt jurists, and indirectly the opponents of persecution in Munich, of taking bribes; and thirdly he directly accused the Ingolstadt jurist Dr Kaspar Hell of having represented the interests of two parties, namely 'Mayrin of Abensberg' and the Duke of Bavaria, that is of having acted in breach of his duty of service, which in such a serious matter as witchcraft bordered on high treason.

The case of Professor Hell spotlights the harshness of procedure in cases of witchcraft. Wagnereckh managed to get Hell removed from his office, and ultimately even had him arrested and brought to Munich. There he was first kept in the Count's Room of the Old Court, but was finally thrown into the Falkenturm, which was reserved for serious offenders. When the hearing was entrusted to a hard-liner, Dr Vagh, Hell seemed to be facing the same fate as the Trier Councillor Dr Flade, with which the persecution party in Munich regularly threatened its opponents. The Town Clerk of Munich, Dr Locher, immediately protested against this turn of events. Finally he was assured that he had nothing to fear from

---

[139] EOAM, Akt Varia no. 516, fol. 144v ('Notabilia').   [140] *Ibid.*, fol. 115.

Vagh for Dr Hell. No charges of high treason or sorcery were brought, and Vagh was assigned other Councillors, including the anti-persecution Councillor Bernhard Barth, to assist him. Not until fourteen months later was Hell released from the Falkenturm, on humiliating recognisances. The outcome of the proceedings against Hell had been in doubt throughout the whole period of intensive discussion of witchcraft, 1601–3.

Nevertheless, it became clear during Hell's trial that though he had had a decisive influence on the drafting of the opinion, all the jurists had shared his views, and that even of the theologians only Jacob Gretser had argued for the execution of the three women, while Stevartius had abstained and the Jesuit Eiselin had voted with the jurists.[141] The charges of heresy and corruption were thus beside the point.

As far as we can see, Wagnereckh continued to maintain his charge that the Ingolstadt jurists had been influenced by the members of the government in Munich, for otherwise, in his opinion, it would be impossible to explain why the jurists had used the same arguments as the opponents of persecution in Munich (Art. 44 of the *Carolina*, Goedelmann, Fichard). Wagnereckh wanted to have Dr Gewold and the *Patres Societatis* investigate the leak.[142] Though in the end Wagnereckh could do nothing to alter the majority in the University of Ingolstadt, the reputation of the University was permanently damaged by his severe and partially justified attacks on it. This brought within his grasp Wagnereckh's goal of further expanding the debate, which now seemed to offer the only guarantee of allowing the persecution party to enforce its intention.

Now it was above all a matter of warding off the consequences of the interpretation of the Ingolstadt opinion of 1601, which were correctly foreseen by Wagnereckh:

Thirdly they draw from *eodem fonte*, if *discretio* and caution are demanded in a *crimine*, so that the innocent may not be put at risk, it is necessary in this. *Et per hoc tacite insinuant* that we must have *fortiora indicia* than in other *Criminibus*.[143]

---

[141] HStAM, RKG 6519.

[142] EOAM, Akt Varia 516, fol. 118. This suggestion of Wagnereckh's is also interesting because it reveals that the 'Jesuit party' was still solid in 1601. Tanner's dissidence did not become apparent until 1601–2. Cf. note 125.

[143] EOAM, Akt Varia no. 516, fol. 115 (Wagnereckh's 'Notabilia'). In fact the tactician recognised at once what was at stake: though the Ingolstadt opinion of 1601 seemed to differ only in nuances from earlier opinions, in fact it questioned the whole trial procedure. Only in this way can the bitterness of the discussions, so incomprehensible at first sight, be understood.

The planned expansion of the debate on principle

The persecution party, which had been thrown on the defensive by the unexpected tenor of the Ingolstadt opinion, now concentrated on the crucial issue. The release of the three suspected women in Abensberg and Kelheim was approved, because 'the *salus reipublicae* was not at stake, if they had to be released'. What was wanted now was a definitive ruling on how cases of witchcraft were to be handled. As the majorities in Munich and Ingolstadt were unfavourable and the Duke undecided, Wagnereckh intended to carry out a planned enquiry at the *Universitates Catholicas Germaniae, Galliae, Italiae, Hispaniae,* to obtain an authoritative decision in favour of the necessity of persecution and repudiating the Ingolstadt opinion as erroneous.

In a masterly paper Wagnereckh suggested to the Duke that this solution would not only be fair, just, thorough, God-fearing and for the public good, but would also save expense, if the money spent on asking the opinion of the universities were regarded as an investment which would help to avoid much greater damage in future, that is God's punishments and the harmful sorcery of the witches. According to the scenario sketched in this opinion, the witches were increasing in numbers every day, so that 'if this evil is not suppressed, the whole country can expect nothing more certain than the punishment and curse of God'.[144] Incidentally, it was also pointed out that the objections of the opponents of persecution would inevitably bring down God's punishment if they were followed.

The expansion of the discussion was to follow a plan. Each university was to receive the same material, which had been the basis of the Ingolstadt opinion of 1601. The cases of the three women were left in this material as the theoretical basis for the discussion of the admissibility of torture on the evidence present; once again, the main question was the value of denunciations. In addition, each of the parties in Munich was to set down its views in a written opinion, and add the queries as an aid to decision. This should ensure that the universities did not, as so often, evade giving a direct answer to the main questions by resorting to nebulous formulations. The presentation of alternatives was to lead to a clear decision for a hard or a moderate line in the question of witchcraft. It was probably Wagnereckh himself who, in a forty-page *Deductio opinionis affirmativa,* argued in detail that torture might be applied in a *crimen exceptum* where the denunciations were in broad agreement but differed on details (place, time, circumstances). Further evidence or eye-witnesses were not to be demanded, contrary evidence (e.g. *bona fama*) or revocations out of court (e.g. to confessors) were not to be valid. Following Binsfeld, two denunciations

---

[144] *Ibid.,* fol. 118r–v.

were to be sufficient for repeated torture, among the recognised conditions of the witchcraft trials (silence = *maleficium taciturnitatis*; lying = a possible sign of the presence of the Devil; distinction between continuation and repetition of torture). This was a programme for the harshest persecutions.[145]

The opposition drew up an eighty-page *Deductio negativa* in reply. It began by restating the fundamental difference of opinion between Weyer and Bodin, and left no doubt that Weyer was to be rejected because of his uncatholic views. It also admitted that witches caused harm. Yet witch trials were so difficult to conduct that the greatest caution had to be used. The integrity of the innocent had to be protected and only the multiplicity of evidence required by Article 44 of the *Carolina* could entail the necessity of arrest and torture. The author of the *Deductio negativa*, the President of the Court Council Heinrich von Haslang, concluded, unlike the author of the *Deductio affirmativa*, that none of the three women ought to have been tortured.[146]

OPINIONS FROM DILLINGEN, INGOLSTADT AND FREIBURG

The discussions in Munich during the summer and autumn of 1601 were characterised by the debates on the opinions of the south German Catholic universities. The persecutioners in Munich expected particular support from Freiburg, since the faculty of law there, under the former Ingolstadt Professor Friedrich Martini, held particularly rigid views on the issue of witchcraft.

The University of Dillingen at this time was still a purely Jesuit academy, and had no faculty of law. Its staff were still recruited predominantly from the larger Jesuit establishments in Bavaria.[147] The Bavarian Jesuits, especially Jacob Gretser, still enjoyed the unrestricted confidence of the

[145] HStAM, Hexenakten 3, Prod. 12; *ibid.*, Prod. 13; EOAM, Akt Varia 516, fol. 4–8v (in three copies), 'Deductio Opinionis Affirmativa in causa trium Feminarum Denunciatarum Super Maleficio. Quoad contra eas ad Torturam Procedendi Possit.' The protagonist of the persecutors opens his opinion with 'IHS – Adiutorum nostrum a Domino.' Cf. note 16.

[146] EOAM, Akt Varia 516, fol. 49–66. HStAM, Hexenakten no. 3, Prod. 20; *ibid.*, Prod. 35, 40 fols., 'Deductio Negativa'. The protagonist of the anti-witch hunting party opens his opinion with the words 'Deo bene favente'. Both opinions are anonymous. Their authors have been identified on the basis of later opinions, in which 'W.' (Wagnereckh) and 'H.v.H' (von Haslang) have been written on the opinions of the two parties in the collection, EOAM, Akt Varia 516. That 'H.v.H.' is not to be interpreted as Herwarth von Hohenburg is shown by a textually identical opinion, which is marked 'H.v.H.' in EOAM, Akt Varia 516, fol. 118v, but 'Heinrich von Haslang' in HStAM, SV 2063, no. 3. This was the 'Negativa Assertio ex Consilio Friburgensis' of 2 January 1602.

[147] T. Specht, *Geschichte der ehemaligen Universität Dillingen*, Freiburg im Breisgau 1902; Spindler, *Handbuch*, III/2, 928f., 1153f. (Layer, Kraus).

apologists of persecution at this time, as Wagnereckh's remarks reveal. The very cautious opinion given by the University of Dillingen on 30 August 1601 was therefore unexpected. It stated that it was within the competence of the Duke to follow either the hard line or the *Deductio negativa* in the case of the three women. If the circumstantial evidence was weak, torture should not be too severe and might not be repeated. In view of the contradictory explanations, the opinion comes to a surprising conclusion:

> After ripe consideration of all the circumstances it appears to be better, if the judge and the prince decide that torture is not admissible ... for the case is such that the public good commands that not only the innocence of these three private persons, but that of very many persons, be protected. But this is in grave danger if arrest and torture are undertaken on such weak evidence. The protection of the innocent must be as close to the heart of the judge and the prince as the care of the public good against the sorcerers.[148]

These formulations are all the more startling since they decide against the authority of Gregor von Valentia, Martin Delrio and Jacob Gretser, without authoritative bases. The Rector of the University was appointed directly by the General of the Jesuits, and his immediate superior was the Provincial of the Upper German province of the Jesuit order.[149]

In September 1601 the Faculty of Law at Ingolstadt gave an opinion on the case of five women suspected of witchcraft at Mergentheim. This opinion is important, for it was the first to adopt a line on the question of witchcraft after the dismissal of Dr Hell, and the discussions have to be understood in the context of the debate in Bavaria. After making several far-reaching admissions about the existence of witches and the possibility of their flight through the air, the opinion comes to the heart of the matter: the question of denunciations. Once again Binsfeld's hard line was refuted by the authority of the Lutheran jurist Goedelmann, and in such an ingenious form that no clear guidelines for procedure could be deduced from the remarks in principle. In Munich, it was bound to seem to confirm the opinion of April, and in other places it was not enough to save the lives of the accused women. An attentive observer in Munich was later able to mark small crosses against the names of two of the five women.[150]

The arrival of the first Freiburg opinion in October 1601 caused great

---

[148] HStAM, Hexenakten 4, Prod. 7 (request for the opinion). The opinion: *ibid.*, Prod. 3, 3 fols. Partly printed in Duhr, 'Zur Geschichte' (1904), 167; here cited from the translation in Duhr, *Geschichte der Jesuiten*, II/2, 506. The authors of the opinion could not be identified.   [149] Spindler, *Handbuch*, II, 1165 (Böhm).

[150] UBM, Cod. Ms. 230, fol. 382–96.

excitement in Munich. This forty-page document claimed that the Duke of Bavaria ought to have had the women tortured without hesitation. The opinion confirmed the views of Wagnereckh's *Deductio affirmativa* on all points: the combination of two simple denunciations without agreement on the details (place, time, particulars) was enough for torture. *Mala fama* was not required as well, and *bona fama* was as unable to prevent torture as a revocation of the evidence out of court. No regard need be paid to the ill repute of the denouncers in witchcraft trials.[151]

Duke Maximilian at once ordered the Freiburg opinion to be discussed in his Councils, and this time the anti-persecution party was expected to justify itself. Its representative, Heinrich von Haslang, put forward an argument which the apologists of persecution must have found rather audacious or even an outright provocation. In a *Negativa assertio ex consilio Friburgensis* of 2 January 1602, Haslang asserted that he had no occasion to change his view but felt that the Freiburgers' opinion strengthened him in it. In principle, he wrote, the faculty of law at Freiburg was quite of his opinion, as was the famous author Delrio,

for although they conclude *generaliter, quod denunciatio plurium per se sola, absque aliis adminiculis indicium sit sufficiens ad torturam in criminibus exceptis*, such a *regula* must be understood *sano modo*, and not so *rude et crude*, but so that the natural *defensio* through the *generalia indicia et praesumptiones* is not denied to the *denunciatis . . . Cum iuris naturalis sit . . .*[152]

This was an astonishing argument, but not particularly far-sighted, since both Delrio and the University of Freiburg could be asked for their opinion at any time. This was done in both cases, with the predictable result that the second Freiburg opinion of March 1602[153] fully confirmed the hard position already stated. We shall return to Delrio's opinion later.

In his commentary on Haslang's opinion (*Ulterior deductio affirmativa*

[151] HStAM, Hexenakten 3, Prod. 1; *ibid.*, Hexenakten 4, Prod. 8, 20 fols.; EOAM, Akt Varia 516, fol. 70–82. The Freiburg opinions begin: 'Divino auxilio humiliter implorato'. The author of the opinion was Dr Friedrich Martini (c. 1550–1630), to whom Duke Maximilian had sent the request. HStAM, Hexenakten 4, Prod. 2. Martini had been a professor at Ingolstadt from 1573 to 1589, and then spent more than forty years in Freiburg. On the question of witchcraft he adhered to the viewpoint taken by the University of Ingolstadt at the beginning of the wave of witch hunting in 1590. After 1590 Martini took his line from Binsfeld, Gregor von Valentia and his Ingolstadt colleague Hunger, and was one of the most implacable spokesmen for persecution in the Empire. Midelfort, *Witch Hunting*, 61–5 *passim*, 117, 120, 165–70 *passim*. The Freiburg opinions sent to Duke Maximilian of Bavaria are also mentioned in C. Schott, *Rat und Spruch der Juristenfakultät Freiburg im Breisgau*, Freiburg im Breisgau 1965, 226.
[152] EOAM, Akt Varia No. 516, fol. 118v–121.
[153] HStAM, Hexenakten 3, Prod. 30. EOAM, Akt Varia No. 516, fol. 202–21.

opinionis) Wagnereckh remarked, quite rightly, that it was 'very strange and odd to hear' this, for it was

> as clear as daylight that the *Consilium* of Freiburg was quite contrary to the *negativa* opinion, and cannot be reconciled with the same by any declaration or limitation.

The Freiburg opinion confirmed the Ingolstadt opinion of 1590 and the *opinio affirmativa*, which was the only one

> to be defended before the strict judgement seat of God, and the *opinio negativa* is in no way to be justified.[154]

Wagnereckh also goes on to say explicitly that the leading Jesuit Jacob Gretser himself had advised the Duke to resume trials on the basis of the Ingolstadt opinion of 1590, that is to revert to the hard line.

Following this a ducal decree ordered a new opinion from Freiburg and a new statement of position from Haslang on the same case.[155] Haslang explained that he was still firmly of his previous opinion. Obviously, however, he recognised the danger it involved, and therefore decided to produce a detailed refutation which aimed to expose the internal contradictions in the arguments of the apologists for persecution. This time Haslang did not appeal to Protestant authorities like Goedelmann and Fichard, but based his argument exclusively on the terms of the *Carolina*, the recognised commentaries on criminal law, and 'natural justice'. Haslang attempted to shake the authority of Binsfeld and Delrio by making it clear that in many places they themselves favoured a more complicated presentation of evidence, so that in the end they too had wavered and could not be used as a solid foundation for an argument on the difficult question of witchcraft. If one had to assume, even in criminal cases, that people accused themselves falsely, how much more must one take into account the probability that they would denounce others falsely, all the more so when the denunciations came from sorcerers, who were a notorious danger to the public. It would also be *mille absurda* to accept that multiple denunciations were better circumstantial evidence than a single one, when the single denunciation on its own was of no value. Gretser's view could only be based on his inadequate information – a clear dig in the

---

[154] HStAM, Hexenakten 4, Prod. 21, fol. 1–10; *ibid.*, fol. 1v. In his 'Ulterior Deductio Affirmativa Opinionis' Wagnereckh wrote that the prince ought to ask the Jesuit Gretser who was right in this dispute.

[155] EOAM, Akt Varia 516, fol. 82v–5v. The most recent opinion of Haslang is in *ibid.*, fol. 127–43, 'Responsio pro Negativa ad praecedens Scriptura'.

ribs at Gretser's poor performance in the religious Colloquies of Regensburg in December 1601.[156] Haslang therefore suggested that

> both the Freiburg *Responsum* and the *deductiones* drawn up by both sides should be submitted to an impartial university in the Empire or outside it.[157]

The other party again had its say on Haslang's counter-opinion. Wagnereckh produced a consideration, which is of interest for its concern with the theory of knowledge, and which dealt with one of the chief arguments of the anti-persecution party. They had argued that those denounced ought to be considered innocent, for if the witches had 'really' seen them at witches' sabbaths, it was impossible to be sure that they had really been physically present and had taken part, and that their presence was not a hallucination caused by the Devil, through *fascinationes*, *illusiones* and delusions. For this reason alleged eye-witness statements were not to count as evidence. Wagnereckh now turned this argument on its head and denied that the human mind could know anything about the question of witchcraft. Hence, there could be no witnesses to exculpate the accused or to provide them with an alibi.

> It is necessary to produce several eye- witnesses for this apparent vision (by which the world is commonly imposed on, but all that glisters is not gold) and *ratione autoritate et experientia*, to assert that it is impossible to prove a negative in the matter of witchcraft because of its form and nature, and not to be permitted by a Christian authority. For firstly this vice is so covert that many things can be done so that those who are with the said person do not notice them, or are so blinded and deluded in their senses that they take one thing for another . . . (Delrio lib. 2, q. 8 et 18). For the foundation of all evidence is *in sensibus*, and everyone who has the least understanding can judge that in such cases, in which the senses of the witnesses may be deceived, little reliance can be placed on their testimony, especially *ad probationem negativam* . . .[158]

[156] *Ibid.* Haslang excused the delay in the drafting of his opinion (his third) on the grounds that he had been 'mit anderen, sonderlich Landschafftlichen sachen nit wenig beladen'. *Ibid.*, fol. 143. For Gretser's poor performance in the Colloquies of Regensburg cf. Lurz, *Tanner*, 7–9; König, 'Jacob Gretser' 157–9. The decisive point is that when the ill-prepared Gretser put up such a poor showing, Adam Tanner SJ leapt into the breach for him and gave a bravura performance. This was a good position from which to oppose Gretser on the question of witchcraft. For the Colloquies of Regensburg see now B. Bauer, 'Das Regensburger Kolloquium 1601', in Glaser, *Um Glauben*, II/1, 90–9. Duke Maximilian's Jesuit confessor, the Lorrainer Buslidius, sent the General of the order, Aquaviva, a disparaging report on Gretser's failure, König, 'Jacob Gretser', 159.

[157] EOAM, Akt Varia 516, fol. 143.

[158] *Ibid.*, fol. 143v–56, 'Brevis Responsio ad Argumenta Opinionis Negativa', cited here from the textually identical copy in HStAM, Hexenakten 4, Prod. 16, fol. 1r–v.

But if the reliability of the evidence of the senses as a whole was to be questioned, there could be no further possibility of defence for those denounced, for all the evidence in their favour could be based on deceptions of the senses.

Yet Wagnereckh went on to conclude, illogically, that the senses of witnesses for the prosecution could not be deceived, or that, if this were the case, God would not permit the Devil to create the illusion that the innocent had been present at witches' sabbaths. Once again, the authority for this bold assertion was Binsfeld, speaking of the exemplary case of the Burgomaster of Trier and Privy Councillor Dr Flade, who had been burned as a witch in 1590:

> Thirdly and lastly it may be that a witch does not come *corporaliter* to the witches' sabbath, but his or her presence is pretended *a Daemone*, as the example, notorious throughout the Empire, of Dr Flade, former Councillor of the Elector of Trier, shows, and it is *doctissime* explained by Binsfeld, that *ex providentia Dei ordinaria* only the guilty can be pretended by the Evil spirit . . . [159]

To be able to measure the intensity of the struggle in Munich in early 1602, one must realise that Flade had belonged to a moderate opposition party in Trier, and that as a learned Privy Councillor he had occupied a position similar to that of the opponents of persecution in the government at Munich. Delrio, the most important contemporary author on witchcraft, represented the view that the defenders of witches – their so-called 'patrons' – themselves had an affinity for the crime of witchcraft, and so were to be suspected of it in advance. At the same time the persecution party in Munich pressed forward the criminal proceedings against Dr Kaspar Hell, which were entrusted to the outright advocate of torture, Dr Vagh, as commissioner.[160] In his opinions Wagnereckh did not shrink from demonising his enemies in the government to the best of his ability. In his second opinion, on the Freiburg *Consilium*, he used the imagery of the broad path that led to Hell and the narrow path to Heaven. The narrow path also led to the truth, the broad one to heresy, the narrow one had God as its source, the broad one was in the Devil's care; the *Deductio affirmativa* led to the narrow path, the *Deductio negativa* to the broad one.

> And thus the Evil One, if this opinion . . . should gain the upper hand *in Tribunalibus*, would make even more use of his well known delusions,

---

[159] *Ibid.*, fol. 5
[160] HStAM, RKG 6519. The sweeping denunciation of the enemies of witch hunting as 'patrons of witches' goes back to Delrio, who naturally cited the case of Dr Flade in Trier as his conclusive example. Duhr, *Die Stellung*, 43, from Delrio, *Disquisitionum* (Mainz edition 1603), III, 66, 77; Fischer, 'Die "Disquisitionum"', 107.

which are easy for him, and so would propagate his tyranny even more securely . . . and to fight and suppress this evil the error which has taken root is to be rooted out and extirpated *ex animis hominum*.[161]

OPINIONS OF THE UNIVERSITIES OF PADUA AND BOLOGNA

While the debate on the first Freiburg opinion was still under way, early in 1602 the opinions of the two Italian universities reached Munich, where they again caused confusion. While the University of Padua in essence argued on the basis laid by Delrio and ranged itself alongside the hard-line apologists of persecution,[162] the *Consilium* of the jurists of Bologna defended precisely the opposite view.[163] While Padua believed that multiple denunciations were sufficient for the application of torture without further circumstantial evidence, the Bologna opinion stated, without allowing the possibility of a contrary interpretation, that the denunciation of alleged accomplices, who were said to have been seen at the witches' sabbaths, could never be admitted as grounds for the infliction of torture (*nullum probant indicium*).[164] Fundamentally, the Universities of Padua and Bologna reproduced the front lines in south Germany, which ran between the Catholic Universities of Freiburg and Ingolstadt, or between the various factions in Bavaria: Wagnereckh, Freiburg and Padua against Haslang, Ingolstadt and Bologna.

Particular interest was aroused in Munich by the comment of the Bologna jurists that their explanations corresponded to the practice of the Holy Office, that is the Inquisition in Italy.[165] The court confessor of Duke Maximilian, the Jesuit Johannes Buslidius,[166] showed such irritation at this that in 1602 he approached Martin Delrio, who was then in Graz, with the following question:

The professors of imperial law in Bologna have . . . answered that no credence is to be given to statements on the meetings of witches and that they do not provide grounds for torture; all the Italian courts, they say, follow this line, especially the Inquisition in Rome and Bologna. But as the decision on the nature of the diabolical influence is a matter for theologians and the Pope has placed theologians at the head of the Inquisition, who defend the opinion that the statements of the witches give no grounds for torture, must not we too follow their opinion, or

[161] HStAM, Hexenakten 4, Prod. 16, fol. 4v–5v.
[162] EOAM, Akt Varia 516, fol. 221–50; HStAM, Hexenakten 3, Prod. 29.
[163] EOAM, Akt Varia 516, fol. 89–106v; HStAM, Hexenakten 3, Prod. 12, 14 fols. See on this Duhr, *Geschichte der Jesuiten*, II/2, 506; Fischer, 'Die "Disquisitionum"', 117f.
[164] EOAM Akt Varia 516, fol. 96v.   [165] *Ibid.*, fol. 96.
[166] (1554–1623), Bosl, *Biographie*, 105.

must the Duke not be advised to obtain . . . certain information on the procedure of the Inquisition?[167]

Delrio replied that he did not believe the assertions on the practice of the Inquisition to be true. But even if they were, the practice of trials for witchcraft in Germany, France and Spain ought not to be altered to bring it into line.[168] The repeated references to the Catholic authorities on the question of witchcraft by the protagonists in the conflict over policy in Munich, as well as the question put by the Duke's confessor to Delrio, already pointed to the next step in the debate: after the consultation of the south German and Italian universities had failed, it was time to approach the contemporary theoreticians of witchcraft themselves. Binsfeld had died in 1598 but Delrio and the Lorraine Privy Councillor Rémy were still alive and could be asked for their opinion.

THE OPINIONS OF REMY AND DELRIO

There could be no doubt, even before they were asked, what the opinions of Rémy and Delrio would be. In his *Daemonolatria*,[169] first published in 1595, translated into German in 1596, and reissued in five printings in Germany between 1595 and 1600, Rémy had openly boasted of his share in the burning of 800 witches in Lorraine in sixteen years; and as many again had fled or had died under torture before the verdict was pronounced. The numerous cases described from Rémy's practice contributed significantly to the success of the folio, which was the most comprehensive compendium of examples of persecution between Bodin's *Daemonomania* of 1580 and Delrio's *Disquisitiones Magicae* of 1599. As with Bodin, Rémy's main object was to refute Weyer by arguments drawn from the trials themselves. In his proceedings Rémy interpreted everything to the detriment of the accused (e.g. rare attendance at church, but also frequent attendance at church). A healthy zeal in persecution was always to be preferred to pernicious clemency.[170] In his opinion for the Duke of Bavaria Rémy pleaded for the necessity of torture in the case of the three women denounced.[171]

The Jesuit polymath Martin Delrio enjoyed a greater authority in Munich than the judge from Lorraine; he was described as *miraculum*

---

[167] HStAM, Oefeleana, 44; quoted from the German version in Duhr, *Geschichte der Jesuiten*, II/2, 506f.   [168] *Ibid.*; Fischer, 'Die "Disquisitionum"', 117.
[169] N. Remigius, *Daemonolatria, Das ist von Unholden und Zauber-Geistern (. . .)*, Frankfurt am Main 1598; on this see Janssen and Pastor, *Culturzustände*, VIII, 610; Lea, *Materials*, 604–24.   [170] Janssen and Pastor, *Culturzustände*, VIII, 612,
[171] EOAM, Akt Varia 516, fol. 252v–4; HStAM Hexenakten 3, Prod. 32.

nostri aevi by Justus Lipsius, who was held in great esteem at the Bavarian court and was certainly above suspicion as a witness in questions of witchcraft.[172] Haslang too had repeatedly appealed to Delrio's *Disquisitiones Magicae*, for besides the most rigid views on the right method of dealing with witches and those who defended them, Delrio had also admitted that it was better to let ten guilty persons go free than to condemn a single innocent person.[173] It was this apparent impartiality and his vast reading that made Delrio the outstanding authority of the seventeenth and early eighteenth centuries, repeatedly cited by both Protestant and Catholic authors.[174] Yet most contemporaries read Delrio's works as a call to hunt down witches. In two of his opinions for Duke Maximilian I of Bavaria, and in his reply to the queries of Buslidius, the Duke's confessor, Delrio did not disappoint those who read him in this sense. He argued for torture without restriction.[175] Even when the opinion of the University of Bologna was sent to him from Munich, he did not change his point of view. Like Wagnereckh, Delrio argued that if no credence were given to denunciations of participation in witches' sabbaths, the axe would be laid to the root of the trials, and every possibility of discovering the truth would be blocked. He had dealt with this problem in detail in the new Mainz edition of his *Disquisitiones Magicae*.[176]

Delrio's opinion set the familiar mechanism of the debate in motion again in Munich: Duke Maximilian ordered the authors of the *Deductio affirmativa* (Wagnereckh) and of the *Deductio negativa* (Haslang) to restate their positions in writing. The well-known arguments were rehearsed

---

[172] Fischer, 'Die "Disquisitionum"', 13. The first edition of Delrio's *Disquisitionum magicarum libri sex* was preceded by a 'Carmen Justi Lipsi' recommending the work to the reader; *ibid.*, 156.

[173] Duhr, *Die Stellung*, 45. In neither of his two opinions for Duke Maximilian is there any question of such reticence in witch hunting.

[174] For example in Saxony-Coburg, where a curious conflict took place: the apologists of witch hunting, chief among them the Lutheran General Superintendent and court preacher Hugo, appealed to the Jesuit Delrio (Janssen and Pastor, *Culturzustände*, VIII, 614; Kretz, 'Der Schöppenstuhl', 72–8) while the opponents of witch hunting, on the other hand, jurists who sat on the *Schöppenstuhl*, appealed to the Bavarian Jesuit Laymann (Janssen and Pastor, *Culturzustände*, VIII, 656). The Saxon jurist Benedict Carpzow (1595–1666) also relied on Delrio to support his rigid attitude, and Thomasius, the enemy of the witch craze, admitted that he had been influenced by Delrio until the 1680s. Delrio was still considered a reliable authority in witch trials in Styria until the 1740s (Fischer, 'Die "Disquisitionum"', 144f.), and Zedler too still accepted the deductions of the Jesuit polymath as current (Zedler, *Grosses Lexikon*, LXI (1749), col. 38–142, *s.v.* 'Zauberey').

[175] First opinion of Delrio: HStAM, Hexenakten 3, Prod. 25; *ibid.*, Prod. 26; EOAM, Akt Varia 516, fol. 160–77v. Second opinion of Delrio: HStAM, Hexenakten 3, Prod. 24; EOAM, Akt Varia 516, fol. 198v–201. See Duhr, *Geschichte der Jesuiten*, II/2, 506.

[176] Duhr, *Geschichte der Jesuiten*, II/2, 507f., from HStAM, Hexenakten 4, Prod. 34; *ibid.*, Prod. 24, 29, 30, 34, 38; also contains correspondence between Duke Maximilian and Delrio.

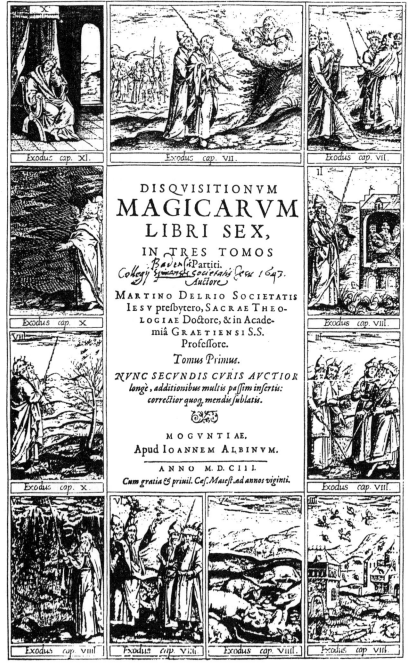

9. Martin Delrio, *Disquisitionum Magicarum libri sex*, Cologne 1657. Title page with engraving after Exodus 7–11, the Egyptian sorcerers and the punishments of God: the plagues of Egypt.

again, with even greater acrimony. Haslang again accused Wagnereckh of 'bad conduct of the trials', while Wagnereckh dismissed his noble opponent as a complete incompetent who had as much right to express an opinion on the trial of witches as a blind man had of colours.[177] Now, at any rate,it began to become clear that the anti-persecution party would hold inflexibly to its 'negative' attitude, against the authority of the learned Catholic authors Bodin, Binsfeld, Gregor von Valentia, Rémy and Delrio. At about this time Wagnereckh remarked bitterly in a polemic that there was 'no hope that these people will change their opinion, even if one can show them the truth and point to it'.[178]

After the Chancellor of the Estates Herwarth von Hohenburg and the Supreme Chancellor Donnersberger had ranged themselves in writing behind their champion, Heinrich von Haslang, the President of the Court Council,[179] the front lines were finally drawn in the government in Munich, or at least they solidified in the form they had assumed at the end of the wave of persecution in 1590. However many 'refutations' Wagnereckh might write, he could do nothing more to alter this. New, and therefore interesting, however, were the signs of a split within the Jesuit block, of which we learn chiefly from Adam Tanner's reminiscences of his time in Munich, and from a letter of the court confessor Buslidius to Delrio.[180] While in 1601 Wagnereckh had still been able to regard the attitude of his kindred spirit Gretser as characteristic, in 1602, after Tanner had stated his views, there was an unambiguous opposing position, which in its consequences was no different from that of the lay opponents of persecution. Tanner conceded that many authorities, among them Delrio,

[177] The discussion became positively hectic: Haslang composed a 'Deductio Negativa' on the first opinion of Delrio, HStAM, Hexenakten 4, Prod. 17; EOAM, Akt Varia 516, fol. 178–9. Wagnereckh replied to this 'Deductio Negativa', numbered 'A', in his 'Notae ad L.A.', *ibid.*, fol. 179–81v. Haslang retorted with a refutation, 'B', *ibid.*, fol. 181v–6; which Wagnereckh countered in 'Notae ad B.', *ibid.*, fol. 186–8. A further 'Deductio negativa', 'C', was evidently not composed by Haslang but by 'D.I.D.', *ibid.*, fol. 188–93. In the circumstances these initials can only be those of the Privy Councillor and Supreme Chancellor Dr Joachim Donnersberger, who had also been instructed by Duke Maximilian to work through the trial records, as had the Chancellor of the Estates Dr Johann Georg Herwarth von Hohenburg. HStAM, Hexenakten 3, Prod. 21 c (letter of Donnersberger to Gewold). The considerations of 'D.I.D.' were answered by 'Notae ad C.' EOAM, Akt Varia 516, fol. 193–5v. An unnamed author then wrote a 'negative' explanation in reply to this (*ibid.*, fol. 196–7), which provoked a further affirmative answer: 'Notae ad D.', *ibid.*, fol. 197–8. The Court Councillor Dr Forstenhäuser, who appeared particularly qualified as a former notary of the Imperial Chamber Court and son of the Chancellor of the Bishopric of Augsburg, then had to give his opinion. *Ibid.*, fol. 198r–v. On Forstenhäuser, see Heydenreuter, *Der landesherrliche Hofrat*, 327f. Cf. also notes 179 and 180.   [178] EOAM, Akt Varia 516, fol. 181v.
[179] HStAM, Hexenakten 4, Prod. 23, 4 fols. Herwarth von Hohenburg expressed himself unequivocally: 'negativam partem subscribo'. The opinion of Donnersberger is in EOAM, Akt Varia 516, fol. 188–93 (cf. note 177).   [180] Cf. note 125.

Binsfeld, Julius Clarus, Farinacius, the Ingolstadt opinion of 1590, the Freiburg opinion of 1601, the opinion from Padua of 1602 and Gregor von Valentia, only required limited grounds for torture in trials for witchcraft. But they were opposed by the views of Baldus, Bossius and Marsilius, the Ingolstadt opinion of 1601 and that of Bologna of 1602.[181] He differed from Binsfeld in believing that a trial for witchcraft was not to be undertaken lightly, for otherwise the public good might be greatly endangered. Judges were to be prevented from acting on their own initiative[182] and the innocent were to be protected from every risk of injustice.[183] But this was just what was practically impossible in trials for witchcraft.

OPINIONS FROM BADEN, MAINZ, COLOGNE AND TRIER

After Delrio's second detailed opinion was received at the end of May 1603[184] Wagnereckh was able to obtain a further five opinions on the case of the three women, all by now long released, and the questions of principle, which had now doubled in number to forty. On 18 June 1603 the questions were sent to five Catholic territories, where great persecutions had been held in the previous fifteen years: Lorraine (Rémy), Electoral Mainz, Electoral Trier, Electoral Cologne and the Margravate of Baden. Besides the materials that had already been sent to the Universities of

---

[181] Tanner, *Theologia*, III, col. 987ff., 992, 1002ff., 1012. On the tradition cf. note 124.

[182] Tanner, *Theologia*, III, col. 984. Cf. on this also Riezler, *Geschichte*, 252ff.; Duhr, *Die Stellung*, 52. Spee again follows the argument of Tanner: Spee, *Cautio*, 159.

[183] Tanner, *Theologia*, III, col. 983 practically lays an axe to the current procedure: 'Tertium principium est . . . ita procedendum a iudicibus esse, ut ne ex eo processu, secundum imprudens iudicium morale & frequens creetur periculum ipsis etiam nocentibus.' Tanner then cites (*ibid.*, col. 984) the famous parable of the tares among the wheat (Gospel according to St Matthew 13:24–30). This was taken up and developed by Spee (Spee, *Cautio*, 39) who refers explicitly to Tanner as the first to apply the parable to the problem of witchcraft trials. The argument is also clear in Tanner: where guilt cannot be 100 per cent proven before torture, torture may not be applied; for without torture guilt was practically unprovable, unless the accused incriminated herself. The second stage in making a trial impossible was to disqualify denunciations, if a person was still accused of witchcraft. Tanner, *Theologia*, III, col. 993, develops the following dilemma: if the denouncers are not guilty, then *a priori* they cannot have seen anyone at the witches' sabbaths; but if they are guilty, their statements are not to be believed, because by the nature of their crime they wish to harm others. This completely undermined the evidential value of denunciations, which, as the apologists of witch hunting constantly repeated, offered the only possibility of tracking down the bands of witches. Here too Spee follows Tanner almost verbatim, but without indicating his dependence on him. Spee, *Cautio*, 219. Even when Spee finally went beyond Tanner, his frequent recourse to him and the value he attached to him as a source, must be taken seriously; for all his conservatism it was Tanner who had opened up the way to the fundamental criticism of trials for witchcraft.

[184] EOAM, Akt Varia 516, fol. 198v–201; HStAM, Hexenakten 3, Prod. 24, 4 fols. (Graz, 21 May 1603).

Ingolstadt, Freiburg, Padua and Bologna, a new and comprehensive statement of the case was added to the questions, sketching the course of the debate up to that point. Each of the sets of questions sent to the ecclesiastical territories was accompanied by a personal letter from Duke Maximilian, in which he expressed his confidence that

> almost the same *dubia* and doubts will have arisen in such witchcraft trials, at which nonetheless *Iustitia* has been administered and such a great number of witches burned and executed. Therefore we hereby kindly request Your Graces to inform us confidentially which of the two opinions has been followed by your *Judices Criminales* in such cases as have arisen, and what proceedings are taken against those denounced . . .[185]

None of the authorities consulted, apart from Rémy, found it easy to answer the questions from Bavaria, and their replies were slow in coming, not arriving in Munich until May to July 1604. The reason for this delay was partly that those responsible had changed to some extent since the time of the persecutions, and partly that they were unwilling to admit that they no longer held their former views with such conviction. Again apart from Rémy, their answers did not satisfy the persecution party in Munich.

It was true that all the answers were rather pragmatic in character, but it was easy to recognise that torture was no longer being inflicted on the basis of mere denunciations in any of the former scenes of the persecutions. The reply from Mainz explained in detail how reports on the reputation of the denounced person were gathered, which was always a necessary precondition for the use of torture. People of good reputation and those in higher positions were no longer arrested there even after multiple denunciations, as 'occasionally' the denunciations had been made out of spite or hatred. In any case other evidence beside mere denunciations was required.[186] The reply from Trier also showed that there too the current rulers had dissociated themselves from the measures of the suffragan Binsfeld, who was now dead. *Denunciationes nudae* could not be relied on *propter fraudem Daemonis.* Yet they still defended the dangerous view that several concurring denunciations, especially when they agreed on time, place and other particulars, could provide grounds for torture. Revocations out of court were not invalid in principle but they were if they had only been made privately

---

[185] HStAM, Kurbayern Urkunden no. 9444 (letter of Duke Maximilian of Bavaria to Elector and Archbishop Johann Schweikhardt of Mainz, Munich, 18 June 1603, written by Gewold, signed by the Duke in his own hand). The other letters are practically identical to this.

[186] HStAM, Hexenakten 4, Prod. 14, 'Mainzisch Bedenken in Causa Sagarum', 6 fols. (copy).

to a confessor.[187] The faculty of law at Cologne no longer considered that unsupported denunciations were sufficient grounds for torture. The authorities in Baden (Margravate of Baden-Baden) also inclined to the 'milder and safer side', that is to the views of the enemies of persecution in Munich.[188]

It must have seemed to those in Munich that, apart from Lorraine, none of the most important Catholic territories in the Empire was following the hard line of those who argued for persecution. After this the outcome of the debate on the principle in Munich was no longer in question, all the more so since the views of the anti-persecution party in Munich were backed by the authority of the faculty of law at Bologna. In Bavaria itself, the opponents of persecution were dominant in the University of Ingolstadt and in the ducal Privy Council in Munich, while among the Jesuits and in the Court Council the apologists of persecution faced eloquent opponents in Adam Tanner and Heinrich von Haslang. The battle had been won.

THE SIGNIFICANCE OF THE EXEMPLARY DISCUSSION 1601–4

The exemplary discussion in Munich not only prevented the witchcraft trial of 1600, mentioned above, growing into a persecution as the persecution party had intended. It permanently influenced the situation in Bavaria, where not only did the personnel composition of the ruling bodies show a certain continuity over the next few decades, but there was also a constant reference back to the opinions exchanged in the discussions of the early years of the century, whenever disputed questions cropped up again. We can trace this direct recourse to the exemplary discussion through the whole reign of Maximilian I, that is well into the middle of the century and beyond.[189] Its extensive documentation has survived in the archives, a clear sign that even afterwards it was still regarded as an issue of importance.

In addition, Adam Tanner helped to carry the effects of the Munich discussions into a much wider field. Tanner transplanted the moderate attitude of the opponents of persecution in Munich to the theological faculty of the University of Ingolstadt, where he taught scholastic theology

---

[187] HStAM, Hexenakten 4, Prod. 26, 'Trierisch Bedenken in der Hexensach', 5 fols. (copy).
[188] Ibid., Hexenakten 3, Prod. 27, 26 fols. Opinion of the law faculty of the University of Cologne. Ibid., Prod. 18, 30 fols., 'Consilium Badensis'. The key sentence is on fol. 22: 'Et ita in praesentia concludimus tamquam in mitiorem et securiorem partem.'
[189] Chapter 4, pp. 291–309. This also explains why the full documentation of the Catholic debate on the issue of principle has been preserved. The questions discussed by way of example here remained current until the complete abolition of witch trials in the age of the Enlightenment.

from 1603 to 1617, and where, after his return from Vienna in 1619, he was able to work on his *magnum opus*, the *Theologia Scholastica*, until 1627.[190] By their incorporation in this standard work, the arguments in the Munich debate gained an influence throughout the Empire. Tanner was the first to fix an authoritative moderate attitude in the question of witchcraft. He was followed in Bavaria by a whole school of Jesuit opponents of persecution, who, like Kaspar Hell in Eichstätt or Paul Laymann in Dillingen, helped to make his views widely known. After the Thirty Years War a group of Bavarian Jesuits appealed to Tanner to justify their moderate attitude to the trial of witches.[191] Tanner's section on the witchcraft trials appeared as a separate publication in Cologne as early as 1629, and at the same time he became the chief authority of the radical opponent of persecution Friedrich Spee SJ, who was able to rely largely on him in his *Cautio Criminalis* of 1631. With the Catholic Spee, the Lutheran Meyfahrt and Hermann Löher, the most important German opponents of persecution in the seventeenth century all appealed to Tanner.[192]

CONFLICT OVER THE MANDATE AGAINST SUPERSTITION AND WITCHCRAFT OF 1612

THE DEMAND FOR THE MANDATE

Whereas 'white magic' had been specifically excluded from punishment under Perneder's *Halsgerichtsordnung* in the 1570s, it too fell within the sphere of criminal justice as the attitude to witchcraft hardened. The Ingolstadt opinion of 1590 had demanded a general ordinance to make it clear to the people, contrary to the older view, that all forms of magic were liable to punishment.[193] The breaking off of the persecutions in 1591–2, and the ensuing political turbulence in Bavaria, forced the witch question

---

[190] Lurz, *Tanner*, 14–20, 24–8. It is not implausible to assume that Tanner also argued in support of his view of the current controversy about witchcraft during his year's stay in Vienna – where he was invited by Cardinal Khlesl – in 1618 and during his Chancellorship of the University of Prague in 1627. [191] Cf. note 124.

[192] Baschwitz, *Hexen*, 286, and Lea, *Materials*, II, 647, mention separate reprints of the chapter on witchcraft from Tanner's *Theologia Scholastica*. A. Tanner, *Tractatus Theologicus de processu adversus Crimina excepta, ac speciatim adversus Crimen Veneficii*, Cologne 1629 (from Lea, *ibid.*); on Spee and Löher cf. notes 122 and 123. J.M. Meyfartus, *Christliche Erinnerung an gewaltige Regenten (. . .)*, Schlensingen 1635. On Meyfahrt see Janssen and Pastor, *Culturzustände*, VIII, 687–94; Lea, *Materials*, II, 729–43, esp. 734. Heinrich Schultheiss, *Eine ausführliche Instruction, wie in Inquisitions sachen des grewlichen Lasters der Zauberey (. . .) zu procediern*, Cologne 1634, also opposes Spee and above all Tanner. Lea, *Materials*, II, 727f.

[193] HStAM, Hexenakten 1, Prod. 1, fol. 3v.: '§3 Wie ein Inquisition soll angestellt werden'. On Perneder's *Halsgerichtsordnung* cf. above, p. 81. According to Bosl, *Biographie*, 579, Perneder's *Halsgerichtsordnung* retained its validity until the seventeenth century. But on the question of magic this changed in the years before 1590.

into the background. During the debates of 1601–4 Wagnereckh pointed to the necessity for a set of legal rules, while the opposition party, which ultimately triumphed, strove to play down the importance of the whole subject. Only when Wagnereckh became Chancellor of the Court Council did the need for a mandate on superstition and witchcraft become plausible again. The Chancellor pressed for witches to be brought to trial and, in the spirit of 1590, he demanded the launching of a general persecution backed by the authority of a mandate. Instead of denunciations, popular magic was now to provide sufficient grounds for the holding of a systematic inquisition into witchcraft. Seen in this light the opponents of persecution also had an interest in a mandate, for they believed it essential to separate the issues that the apologists of persecution wished to combine. After discrediting denunciations, distinguishing popular magic from witchcraft was the next step in their efforts to restrain persecution. This was the way recommended by the political elite of the Duchy (Herwarth, Donnersberger, Jocher) in 1608. The significance of the famous or notorious mandate against superstition and witchcraft of 1611–12 lay in its meaning for the two opposing parties; at the time of its composition it was highly contentious, and in the following account it will be taken as the point of reference for the discussions during Wagnereckh's Chancellorship of the Court Council. This struggle was the direct continuation of the debate on the issues of principle of the years 1601–4.

WAGNERECKH'S CHANCELLORSHIP OF THE COURT COUNCIL 1606–17

Two years after the close of the debate on the principle of the role of denunciations in trials for witchcraft, the political leader of the persecution party was appointed Chancellor of the Court Council. Even if we bear in mind that Wagnereckh had already been the leading figure in the discussions in the Council before this, his promotion can only be seen as a deliberate political calculation on the part of Duke Maximilian. If the Privy Council and the Estates operated as a brake on the persecution of witches, it might well seem to the Duke, who was tormented by religious anguish, that it was appropriate to create a counterpoise by elevating the decided advocate of persecution, Wagnereckh, to the head of the competent authority. This would ensure that no punitive measure which appeared necessary was neglected. As disputed points were in any case submitted to the Duke for decision, this move also restored an element in the absolutist balance of power.

Wagnereckh's Chancellorship of the Court Council deserves examination here not only because these ten years saw the high point of the debates on the treatment of supposed witches, but also and above all because they offer a case study of political struggle at its most bitter. The theme of witchcraft was at the heart of most of the debates, implicitly or explicitly, even though we must assume that other conflicts were fought out around this issue: personal power rivalries played a role, as did the conflict between the nobles and the learned jurists. The battle to enforce persecution was Wagnereckh's *idée fixe*, and this explains why his attitude on this point was so crucial; the formation of parties within the administration followed the front lines drawn in the battle over the policy on witches.

Even before 1606 Wagnereckh and Dr Vagh had risen to such a position of power in the Court Council that they had had a decisive share in the overthrow of Dr Gailkircher, the former Chancellor.[194] After Wagnereckh's rise to the Chancellorship, the two jurists, who were friends, egged each other on in a kind of hybrid intoxication of power, which appeared to bring the fulfilment of their personal and political wishes within sight. Vagh even saw himself as the future Supreme Chancellor, that is as the successor of Donnersberger. They regarded the existing political elite (Donnersberger, Herwarth, Rechberg, Jocher, Gewold and Duke Maximilian himself) as incompetent, the patricians of Munich as 'braggarts', and the professors of the University of Ingolstadt as 'mere schoolboys and children', whose judgement could be disregarded. The two learned Councillors dismissed the nobles as simply ignorant of the matter and therefore incompetent. But Wagnereckh and Vagh even accepted the views of learned European jurists only when they coincided with their own, and reinforced each other in their views.

Although not without often hearing from both of them, that to Vagh no one was a learned, upright, reasonable, zealous Catholic except Wagnereckh himself, and so *e contra* Vagh for Wagnereckh.[195]

Thanks to their 'learning', and even more their highly authoritarian behaviour, Wagnereckh and his henchman Vagh dominated the discussions of the Court Council. Through personal contacts and promises they were able to attach several other Court Councillors to their cause.

They attempted to bring the rest of the Court Council into line by concentrated arguments, by manoeuvring them into isolation, or even by outright intimidation. Anyone who contradicted the Chancellor made himself unpopular and had to fear the consequences. Any reports that differed from their preferred line were barracked by Wagnereckh and

[194] Heydenreuter, *Der landesherrliche Hofrat*, 145
[195] HStAM, HR 401/3; *ibid.*, 403/3 (records of the visitation of the Court Council).

Vagh, who made remarks to each other and interrupted the reporters with comments and interjections that were often loud and accompanied by violent gestures. Private pressure was put on such Councillors, who were threatened with 'subtle ruin'. Wagnereckh also retained his old habit of denouncing his political opponents as heretics.

> Inasmuch as he has recently, in his vote in the case of the Council of Riedenburg [a trial for sorcery; WB] gone around with great fanfare, saying that those who were of another opinion (namely contrary to his own) were not Christians, irrespective of the fact that, as I believe, the Provincial Administrator and many leading Councillors joined in the vote.[196]

Under such circumstances the discussions in the Court Council became very acrimonious and were often avoided by the Councillors. The fact that, nevertheless, the years of Wagnereckh's Chancellorship were years of especially hard-fought and frequent discussions is explained by the fundamental differences on the question of witchcraft trials, and the courage of some individuals who stood up to the opinions of the Chancellor in spite of enormous pressure.

THE WITCHES AS A STANDING THEME IN THE COURT COUNCIL

While the central authorities could hardly control the number of accusations and reports of witchcraft/sorcery in individual county courts, their influence was involved as soon as a case was reported to Munich from the district courts. This became noticeable as soon as Wagnereckh took office, in a tightening up of procedure. A decision of 1601 forbade the Chancellor to bring trials for witchcraft on the basis of denunciations, but Wagnereckh attempted to nullify this restriction by more severe torture (harsher and more frequent) and by using popular magic as circumstantial evidence for witchcraft. Almost at the same time as Wagnereckh's appointment as Chancellor, however, Bernhard Barth, a formidable opponent of persecution, had been appointed *Hofoberrichter*. In this function, besides being responsible for supervising the Falkenturm, Barth was able to claim the second seat on the Knights' Bench and was thus in fact the spokesman both of the nobles and of the anti-persecution party in the Court Council, at a time when the President was a rather vague figure.[197]

[196] *Ibid.*, 401/3.
[197] Gundaker, Baron von Tannberg (?–1625), was President of the Court Council from 1607 to 1623, but was never able to get his way against the opposition of the Chancellor Wagnereckh. Heydenreuter, *Der landesherrliche Hofrat*, 318f. On Barth: *ibid.*, 304f. and

In the years 1607 and 1608 in particular the Court Council was shaken by very acrimonious debates, which led in the end to the visitations of the Council in 1608 and 1609. Four trials for witchcraft in Riedenburg and Munich played especially important roles in this. In 1607 Dr Vagh was appointed commissioner for the case of an alleged witch in Munich. The woman had been accused of preparing a love charm by a client of Wagnereckh, and a search of her house had found circumstantial evidence in the form of writings on sorcery. As the city magistrates showed no sign of bringing proceedings against the woman, the case was brought directly before the Court Council. As the woman would not confess to witchcraft in spite of repeated torture, Vagh stated his intention to 'torture the prisoner until she confessed, even if the sun shone through her'.[198] Not only did the *Hofoberrichter* Barth protest vehemently against this illegal procedure, but the Secretary of the Privy Council Dr Gewold, himself an apologist of persecution, at the request of relatives from Freising, informally approached the Chancellor of the Court Council and submitted a petition to the Duke. These countermeasures probably saved the woman's life.[199]

The case of an alleged sorcerer from Riedenburg, in which the council of Riedenburg was also implicated, again revealed the deep gulf between the two parties in the Court Council in 1608. In themselves, the investigations were only based on superstitious acts or soothsaying, but widely differing opinions were held about the seriousness of these offences. The minutes of the Court Council observed that

> there were several opinions on this matter. Some held that the prisoner Riedmüller should be racked 2 or 3 times and examined seriously *pro discretione* of the district judge, *praeservativa grassantibus delictis*, and [as] sorcery is becoming so common, and such cases *de jure communi* may be punished *capitaliter* . . . Some, however, thought those of Riedenburg were simple poor people who have very little, and because they were interested themselves, had done it out of sheer simplicity. They should be

note 117. The long struggle over the witches finally led to the visitation of the Court Council in 1608, on which see Heydenreuter, *Der landesherrliche Hofrat*, 145–50. This investigation, led by the Supreme Chancellor Donnersberger, in which all the members and secretaries of the Court Council were heard, revealed the depth of the differences of opinion and the extent to which parties had formed. All the records in HStAM, HR 401/3. It is quite clearly stated: 'Were also Canzler [Wagnereckh] ein, Barth die ander Parthey.' Practically every member of the Court Council could be allocated to a party: 'Herr Cantzler, wie ich vermuete, favoriert die folgenden Herrn, Alss Dr Vaghen, von Tandorff, Rieger, Dr Reisacher, Dr Schobinger und Dr Aurelio [Gilg].' These persons were described as 'gut Cantzlerisch'. Barth had fewer suppporters: 'Dr Balthasar und [Dr] Aurbach dem HofOberRichter anhengig gewest.'
[198] Heydenreuter, *Der landesherrliche Hofrat*, 149.
[199] HStAM, HR 401/3 (statement of Dr Vagh).

examined *in loco*. Some, to save expense, were for sending commissioners to examine the matter thoroughly, or to refer it to Ingolstadt.[200]

While the Councillors around Wagnereckh wanted to begin the proceedings with harsh torture, on the grounds of general prevention, and as they regarded sorcery as circumstantial evidence for witchcraft, the group around Barth distinguished between sorcery and witchcraft, and believed those under arrest deserved milder treatment on the grounds of their 'simplicity'. The trial finally ended in fines for several citizens of Riedenburg.[201]

The third serious dispute also took place in 1608, when the accused was a relatively highly placed ducal official, the *Pflegsverwalter* or district administrator of Schwaben. Besides defalcation of money he was also accused of favouring a 'witch'. After 'books of sorcery' were found when his house was searched, an accusation of witchcraft against him gained weight in the eyes of the persecution party. In fact, during his interrogation in the Falkenturm, actions were brought to light which Wagnereckh judged to be circumstantial evidence, for example the ritual eating of a hoopoe's heart or painting a plate with signs used in sorcery.[202] Wagnereckh took over the case himself and assigned four other Court Councillors to conduct the hearings, which Barth also had to attend *ex officio*. The administrator, who had been suspended from his post, refused to admit witchcraft, and Wagnereckh was unwilling to cease torture. This led to a heated argument in the torture chamber itself between Wagnereckh and Barth, who in the end stopped the torture on his own initiative, backed by two of the Court Councillors, who were otherwise supporters of Wagnereckh.[203] Once again this quarrel reveals the differences: Barth accused the Chancellor of inhumanity in the torture ('there was no *modus* and satisfaction for him in inflicting torture'), while Wagnereckh in turn accused Barth of understanding nothing of the trials because he was not a scholar. The suspected administrator was released after almost five months of imprisonment and after being tortured three times. Wagnereckh managed to persuade the Court Council to impose a sentence of 'perpetual banishment from the country' with a previous humiliating punishment. This decision was overturned by the Supreme Chancellor Donnersberger,

[200] HStAM, KHR 66, fol. 165v–6. According to the minutes those present at the discussion were: on the Knights' Bench, the President of the Court Council von Tannberg, *Hofoberrichter* Barth, von Preysing, von Kirchberg, Hundt, the *Rentmeister* Elsenheimer; on the Scholars' Bench, the Chancellor Dr Wagnereckh, Dr Balthasar, Dr Schobinger, Dr Gilg, Dr Aurbach, Dr Reisacher, Dr Faber, Dr Vagh.   [201] HStAM, KHR, 67, fol. 7, 18v.
[202] *Ibid.*, KHR 66, fol. 115. The *Pflegsverwalter* of Markt-Schwaben was Lorenz Niedermayr. Ferchl, 'Bayerische Behörden', II, 969.
[203] HStAM, HR 401/3. Five Councillors, among them the Chancellor and the *Hofoberrichter*, attended the tortures. Even Dr Hundt and Dr Gilg, two partisans of Wagnereckh, voted in this case with Barth for the ending of the tortures.

allegedly at the request of the Duke, and commuted to banishment for three years without the humiliating penalty.[204]

The fourth dispute, and the one which was richest in consequences, was the unsuccessful trial for witchcraft of 'Beyerin of Winden' in 1608. She was a woman from the district of Schwaben, who took her own life after several months of imprisonment and repeated torture in the Falkenturm at Munich. At first there had seemed to be grave grounds for suspicion against her, as she had been discovered *in flagrante* performing sorcery in the church, by the parish priest. Witnesses' statements revealed that she had not been directly accused of witchcraft by the people, but that they remembered her committing previous acts of sorcery, charming the cattle, healing spells, weather spells, none of which, after all, was to be classed as 'black magic'. Wagnereckh himself took on the case at once, had the woman brought to the Falkenturm in Munich, and persuaded the full Court Council to grant a 'contingent decision' which was supposed to allow him to have her tortured without reference back to the Council, in effect a blank cheque to do as he wished.

Yet it seems that Barth, the *Hofoberrichter*, refused to allow the torture to be inflicted. In his view popular magical practices were by no means adequate grounds on which to apply severe torture. Moreover, he believed that the accused woman was a 'foolish, silly or senseless person' who was 'giddy, in the head and simple minded'. Barth's open resistance to the decision of the Court Council led to vehement discussions in the usual emotionally charged atmosphere of these central governing bodies. The Court Councillor Dr Aurbach, later Chancellor of the Bishopric of Freising, who showed some understanding for the cautious attitude, reported in the visitation of the Court Council:

> When I now said *in meo voto*, it would be acting *per postero ordine, cum fama debeat procedere ipsam torturam et non e contra, Item* it seemed from all the facts of the case, that this woman was a pure simpleton, he, Dr Wagnereckh, tore into me in the meeting of the Council, attacked my vote, and said I should not presume to give advice to a Princely Court Councillor, and no one knew what sort of people such sorcerers were, how they posed as simple, and one had to deal coolly with them, one should read the commentators on Criminal law on them . . . finally, the matter was so dealt with that once again the same conclusions were drawn.[205]

Wagnereckh appointed one of his followers as a 'counter-commissioner' to Barth, and so the two parties prevented each other taking action in the

---

[204] HStAM, KHR 67, fol. 3, 14, 18, 30.
[205] HStAM, HR 401/3. On Dr Hieronymus Aurbach, Heydenreuter, *Der landesherrliche Hofrat*, 303. On the controversy Behringer, 'Scheiternde Hexenprozesse', 72ff.

case. The *Hofoberrichter* publicly refused to deal with the case any further as long as the Chancellor's supporter was acting as a direct 'supervisor', and added that there was a suspicion in the Court Council that some of the Councillors did not draw up their own opinions but had them drafted for them by Wagnereckh.[206] Barth's refusal led to the case dragging on, and thus played an indirect part in the suicide of the prisoner. The impasse in the Court Council about trials for witchcraft and the old woman's suicide ultimately led to the case becoming notorious, and helped to bring about the holding of a visitation of the Court Council. A commission also concerned itself with the case, and raised questions of principle about the role of popular magic as circumstantial evidence in trials for witchcraft (cf. chapter 2, pp. 65–88).

These trials of suspects from Schwaben, Riedenburg and Munich were only the tip of the iceberg. During a regional agrarian crisis, prices in 1607–8 reached their highest level since 1600–1. The number of trials for sorcery and witchcraft also rose to a new peak in 1608, previously exceeded only during the wave of persecution in 1590. Besides the district courts already named, there were trials in those of Pfaffenhofen, Geisenfeld, Vohburg, Kranzberg, Dingolfing, Dachau, Mainburg, Landshut, Landsberg, Reichenhall, Rosenheim and the Free City of Donauwörth, then under Bavarian occupation, that is in fifteen district courts in all. Executions were held only in Landshut, which was not directly under the Court Council in Munich but subject to the *Regierung* in Landshut.[207] As the number of trials increased, they became a burden on the Court Council, since each trial was allocated to at least one Councillor as commissioner, who had to deal with the documents, and report back to the full Court Council before every decision. This happened seventy-two times in 1608. In addition, every report contained the germ of a dispute in itself, since there was no possibility of agreement on questions of principle.

In this situation the old plan for a mandate on superstition and witchcraft surfaced again. On 12 April 1608 Wagnereckh circulated to the Court Councillors the first draft of a mandate he had composed, the object of which was

to root out with public punishments in these dangerous times when great sins prevail, superstitions, superstitious arts, spells and casting of lots and soothsaying too . . .[208]

---

[206] HStAM, KHR 65, fol. 190. Wagnereckh nominated his partisan Dr Schobinger as commissioner. On Schobinger cf. Heydenreuter, *Der landesherrliche Hofrat*, 354. In HStAM, Hexenakten 4, Prod. 25 and 47 and in HStAM, GR 323/16, Schobinger is referred to as a supporter of witch hunting.

[207] HStAM, KHR 65, 66, 67, 68, 69. Cf. list of trials in the German edition.

[208] HStAM, KHR 66, fol. 17v.

Several Councillors were critical of the severity of the mandate, and suggested that the less serious cases of superstition in particular should not be treated as *Viztumshändel* from the beginning but, at first, as offences punishable in the ecclesiastical courts. Otherwise the mandate was welcomed, and it was resolved to submit it to the Duke.

THE VERDICT OF THE 'POLITICAL CHRISTIANS'

The suicide of 'Beyrin of Winden' gave the moderate party in the government the opportunity to state its position in principle on Wagnereckh's conduct of the witch trials. The members of the investigating committee were the Supreme Chancellor Dr Donnersberger, the Chancellor of the Estates Dr Herwarth, the President of the Court Council von Tannberg and Dr Wilhelm Jocher, who was later to become a trusted adviser of Duke Maximilian. The committee's findings sharply criticised the 'improper form of the procedure'. The documents in the case gave reason to doubt whether the circumstantial evidence had been enough to inflict torture at all, to say nothing of repeated torture. Mitigating statements by witnesses had not been sufficiently taken into account.

In two opinions the committee dealt with the eight alleged items of circumstantial evidence, which Wagnereckh had used to justify torturing the woman. Two of them concerned unusual but real events (the sickness of a neighbour's daughter, a hail shower) which, however, seemed quite normal to the members of Donnersberger's committee. Three other pieces of evidence had been superstitious or sorcerous practices of the old woman. The committee recognised these as normal practices of popular superstition: while they admitted that using sorcery on livestock or to influence the weather or heal the sick was to be deplored, it was far from a sign of witchcraft,

but much rather a *vana superstitio* (of which the like is very common and among the common people, before admonition and warning, is held no sin or a very minor one) than a downright work of witchcraft or sorcery *in processu*, if proceedings are taken[209]

---

[209] *Ibid.*, fol. 98v (16 May 1608) for Barth's report of the suicide of the accused. *Ibid.*, fol 141v–2v for the reports in the plenum of the Court Council. HStAM, KHR 68, fol. 145v, Donnersberger's report on the disorder in the Court Council. HStAM, GR 323/16, fol. 51–76 and fol. 78–83 for the opinions of the investigative committee (Dr Donnersberger, Dr Herwarth, Dr Jocher, von Tannberg). Dr Wilhelm Jocher (1565–1639), who studied at Ingolstadt 1586–92, was an assessor at the Imperial Chamber Court before becoming a Councillor in 1604 and a Privy Councillor in 1610. When Donnersberger withdrew from politics on the grounds of age, Jocher became the leader of the *politici*. On his political function see Bireley, *Maximilian*, 62, 143, 192f. For his biography Bosl, *Biographie*, 393.

Barth had therefore acted quite properly in opposing the torture of the prisoner. The last two pieces of evidence, which concerned the old woman's reputation, were also dismissed by the committee, as the alleged *mala fama* was not sufficiently well founded, but rested only on the statements of a neighbour who bore her ill will.

In its opinion the committee stated its objection in principle to

> proceedings being brought out of excessive zeal without sufficient circumstantial evidence against those who are accused only *ex observationibus vanis*, when not a single sign of *maleficii, magiae, heresi affecta, vel sortilegii pacti expressi* is brought forward.[210]

The easy acceptance of popular magic as evidence for witchcraft would bring countless persons all over the country under suspicion. It was known that even parish priests used spells to influence the weather, and how should their flocks be punished for something when errors existed even among the clergy? Moreover, it was open to question whether crimes could be punished if they were not yet forbidden by a public mandate. In connection with the discussion of the planned mandate on superstition and witchcraft, therefore, Donnersberger's committee went beyond the case of 'Beyrin of Winden' to demand

> that in future in such cases *observationis seu superstitionis vanae*, the procedure be more cautious, torture not so lightly repeated, *contraria indicia* be regarded and a distinction be made with sorcery which admits of ordinary purgation. The trial is to be held in such a way that it does not appear as if we wish to extort a confession from common suspicions, which would easily happen if, on common evidence of *vanae superstitionis*, we seized the persons, tortured them, collected all kinds of statements, heard witnesses about the same, from which further suspicions arose, again put the prisoner to torture, and finally obtained *confessionem quamcumque*; that would bring countless persons in Your Grace's country into the highest danger because of common superstition, of which every place is full.[211]

This was another clear rejection of the plans of the persecution party by the moderate group and a demonstration that the latter was also ready to defend its view in public. At a rather later phase of the debate the Court Chancellor complained to the old Duke Wilhelm V of these 'cold and political Christians' who thought that popular magic was 'the work of

---

[210] HStAM, GR 323/16, fol. 59v–68v. (circumstantial evidence); *ibid.*, fol. 80 (quotation).
[211] *Ibid.*, fol. 81ff. In more detail Behringer, 'Scheiternde Hexenprozesse', 72ff.

children and fools', and excused it on the grounds of the alleged simplicity of the 'common folk'.[212]

The visitation of 1608 revealed the extent to which the Court Council was divided between the parties. The ducal decrees of November 1608 that concluded the visitation followed the opinions of the Donnersberger committee almost verbatim. They criticised Wagnereckh's 'untimely zeal' in the conduct of the trials, but did not draw personal consequences from this. They announced the proclamation of a mandate against superstition and witchcraft, which was to distinguish between the various forms of magic, 'both *in principio processus* and in torture and punishment'. Torture was not to be lightly undertaken, confessions were not to be 'extorted by force', and in doubtful cases the decision was to go in favour of the accused. There were no special rules in trials for witchcraft, but procedure was to be strictly in accordance with the 'general law'.[213] As he had done seven years earlier, the Duke followed the arguments of the moderate party.

The triumph of the anti-persecution party was even greater because another mandate explicitly condemned the conduct of Dr Vagh, severely censuring both his personal attacks on other members at the sessions of the Court Council and his persistent pressure for excessive torture. Referring explicitly to the rebuke Vagh had received in 1607 because of his behaviour in the trial of 'Khepserin of Munich', he was told that 'there were grounds enough to dismiss Dr Vagh from the service . . .'[214] A third ducal decree was concerned in a general way with the conditions in the Court Council, and particularly condemned the formation of factions, whose increasing hostility had hampered the work of the administration and had been the indirect cause of the suicide of 'Beyrin of Winden'. It is striking that the written text of the decree makes no personal reference to Wagnereckh, who was obviously spared by Duke Maximilian. Nevertheless this decree must have made a great impression, as it was read out and commented on in the Court Council by Supreme Chancellor Donnersberger, in the presence of the High Chamberlain Count von Rechberg.[215]

THE WITCHCRAFT TRIALS AT DONAUWÖRTH AND WEMDING

The triumph of the opponents of persecution was diminished when Bernhard Barth, the protagonist of the moderate party in the Court Council,

[212] HStAM, Hexenakten 1, Prod. 6, fol. 6r–v (letter from Chancellor of the Court Council Wagnereckh to ex-Duke Wilhelm).
[213] HStAM, GR 323/16, fol. 84–90 (decree of Duke Maximilian, 30 November 1608). This says explicitly that procedure in such trials should be 'in dubio in mitiorem partem'.
[214] HStAM, HR 401/3 (decree of 28 November 1608). Parts quoted in Heydenreuter, *Der landesherrliche Hofrat*, 148.
[215] *Ibid.*, HR 401/3 (decree of 28 November 1608). See HStAM, KHR 68, fol. 145v.

was called to account for his opposition to the Chancellor. He was told that although, as a nobleman, he took precedence over the Chancellor, it was not for him to set himself above decisions of the Court Council, to take over the direction of the Council in the absence of the President, or to intervene on his own initiative in the course of its deliberations.[216] Barth felt so insulted by this reprimand, which, after the visitation, ought in fact to have been administered to his opponent Wagnereckh, that he resigned the post of *Hofoberrichter* and reverted to his previous post of provincial administrator.[217] This created a dangerous situation, for the members of the persecution party had been able to retain their places while the leader of the opposition had stepped down. Vagh, who had been much more severely censured and even threatened with dismissal, had managed to retain his place thanks to a letter to the Duke which could hardly have been more abject.[218]

Two months after the occupation of Donauwörth by Bavarian troops, the old suspicions of witchcraft of the years around 1590 revived.[219] At the request of the Bavarian Governor Konrad von Bemelburg the elder, the Court Council decided by a majority vote in October 1608 to grant an unrestricted power to inflict repeated torture,[220] which in itself was quite unlawful. Of the two accused, one, a man accused of using sorcery to cause impotence, was strong enough to bear the torments, and was released. An accused woman confessed and denounced four other women, who were then arrested. Wagnereckh himself had taken on the judicial appraisal of the trials at Donauwörth. After the trial was under way, he transferred it to his follower Dr Schobinger as commissioner. The 'first witch' (Brigitha Schusterin) was executed at the end of November 1608.[221] At the beginning of March 1609 denunciations were made from Donauwörth against several women of Wemding in Bavaria, where the administration was in the hands of Konrad von Bemelburg the younger, son of the Governor of Donauwörth and a man who enjoyed the esteem of Duke Maximilian. At Wagnereckh's request the Court Council granted him too an open power to torture the prisoners. This time, it is true, there was some resistance on the part of the nobles in the Council, The *Jägermeister* von Wensin, President von Tannberg and the provincial administrator (Eisenheimer or

---

[216] HStAM, HR 401/3 (decree of 2 December 1608).
[217] Heydenreuter, *Der landesherrliche Hofrat*, 148ff., 304.
[218] HStAM, HR 401/3. Vagh did not spare effects; he submitted his request 'magno affectu usque ad lacrimas', and loudly complained that proceedings were not being taken against the witches, as they ought to be.
[219] Duhr, *Geschichte der Jesuiten*, II/2, 497.
[220] HStAM, KHR 68, fol. 64v (23 October 1608).
[221] *Ibid.*, fol. 90r–v.

perhaps already Barth) complained that there were no adequate grounds for torture and that mitigating statements by witnesses had been disregarded.[222] Even so, the majority of the Court Council, the Scholars' Bench led by Wagnereckh, voted down the opposition.

At the beginning of April 1609 the trials of witches began at Wemding, and during the year they were to expand quite rapidly into a minor persecution. At Donauwörth too more and more women were arrested on suspicion of witchcraft, so that the same danger was threatened there. Two women had already been burned at Donauwörth by August 1609, and eight more were in prison, while seventeen had been denounced. In Wemding fifteen women were in prison, and for some of them the 'strict day of justice' had already been set. Several more women were tried in both Donauwörth and Wemding up to July 1610, before pressure from various sides in Munich could be detected. The Estates objected to the way in which the accused were denied the opportunity to defend themselves, and the *Hofkammer* or Court Chamber complained of the high costs of the proceedings.[223]

As later events show, there was wide resistance to these two persecutions as well, but it was not recorded in any extant source. For five years after the resignation of Barth, the Court Council itself was rarely the forum for debate, as the Councillors qualified to speak were all to be found on the side of the advocates of persecution. During the years of the persecutions at Donauwörth and Wemding, 1609–11, the Court Council was dominated by Wagnereckh. Barth's successor as *Hofoberrichter*, Dr Georg

---

[222] HStAM, KHR 73, fol. 151v. At about this time, in 1607, Lorenz von Wensin (?–1626), Guardian of the County of Werdenfels for the Bishop of Freising, averted a witch hunt there. Although the chief suspect, as in the case of 'Beyrin of Winden', had been caught in the act of performing sorcery in the church, Wensin reported to Freising that such circumstantial evidence had to be treated with care. An order for the woman's release was sent from Freising. Kuisl, *Die Hexen*, 40f. As Bavarian Governor at Amberg in 1623 Wensin was a supporter of balance. Heydenreuter, *Der landesherrliche Hofrat*, 361.

[223] J. Schneid, 'Das Rechtsverfahren wider die Hexen zu Wemding im ersten Drittel des 17. Jahrhunderts', *Oberbayr. Archiv*, 57 (1913), 118–95. Schneid did not use the minutes of the Munich Court Council, in which the witch hunt at Wemding takes up much space. HStAM, KHR 74, fol. 26v (10 April 1609), and from there almost continuously until KHR 108, fol. 76 (13 August 1613, questions concerning the estate of the victims). The reporter in the Court Council was Dr Schobinger, a partisan of the Chancellor Wagnereckh (cf. note 206). The Estates complained of the lack of a defence (HStAM, KHR 73, fol. 3v, 131f.), while the *Hofkammer* criticised the costs (*ibid.*, KHR 87, fol. 45). A minority in the Court Council had criticised, from the beginning, the fact that 'es mangle schier bei allen an genuegsame erfahrung und haben die Commissarii nur das jenig, wider die personen taugt, khainesswegs aber, was zu ihrer liberation und ihnen zu gutem geraichen mag, bericht[et]'. HStAM, KHR 73, fol. 151v–2. ('In the case of almost all [suspects] there were not enough grounds for suspicion and the Commissioners only reported that which was to the detriment of the persons and never that which would lead to their release and be to their advantage.')

Hundt zu Lauterbach, came increasingly under the influence of the Chancellor.[224]

In general we can say that Wagnereckh's political intentions with regard to a general inquisition against witchcraft received a strong impetus in these two years. A whole series of reasons may have been responsible for this development, but their relative importance can hardly be estimated. In the political sphere we can think of the formation of the Catholic League, in the socio-economic sphere of the agrarian crisis of 1610–11, the associated rise in accusations of witchcraft, or the beginning of great persecutions in some of the ecclesiastical territories in Franconia, which also belonged to the Catholic League. It was no coincidence that the League developed in the next few years into a gathering of the harshest apologists of persecution in south Germany. Though there were no firm agreements between the Catholic princes, it does not seem too far-fetched to assume an informal understanding on the question of trials for witchcraft.[225] The number of those involved was relatively small and we must think in terms of very direct links between them: the political elite was occupied in negotiations, and the danger of great persecutions seemed to have declined since the debate on the issue of principle in 1601–4.

Wagnereckh seized this favourable moment. In an opinion, composed jointly with five of his partisans, on the possible political consequences of the negligent attitude of the Munich magistrates towards the matter of an inquisition against witches, he restated the goal of a systematic persecution in Bavaria. In passing, he also discussed the most important obstacles to such a persecution, illustrating them from the example of Munich. This important matter was to be removed in advance from the competence of recalcitrant lower authorities, because they could create 'all kinds of hindrances if any prominent citizens came into the hands of the Inquisition'. As early as 1590 the witchcraft trials had been 'directed' by the ducal Councils in order to eliminate such hindrances. The Prince ought to bring such witch trials directly before himself, by virtue of his supreme judicial authority, and commit them to suitable learned jurists for 'it would be an *absurdum* if *in tali casu inferior magistratus* should compete *cum superiore*'. As in many of his earlier and later opinions Wagnereckh combined propo-

---

[224] This is expressed in the visitation of the Court Council of 1612. HStAM, HR 401/3. In 1611 Wagnereckh recommended Hundt to Duke Maximilian together with the Court Councillors Dr Schobinger, Dr Bonet, von Preysing and Dr Aurbach as witch commissioners for a systematic inquisition into witchcraft among the citizenry of Munich. HStAM, Hexenakten, 3, Prod. 4, textually identical with HStAM, Hexenakten 4, Prod. 46, 'Defectum ordinarii Iurisdictionis in Inquirendo Crimine Sortilegii betr.' (20.1.1611).

[225] Spindler, *Handbuch*, II, 372f. (Albrecht). Cf. note 56.

sals for measures with suggestions for personnel, which were intended to place his reliable partisans in the key positions.[226] Wagnereckh also strove to bring about a resumption of the debate on the basic principles of the years after 1600, in the hope that this time it would lead to a different result – one he could exploit for practical persecution.

> But since this trial might spread far and wide, the *modus procedendi* however *propter varias Doctorum opiniones* is rather doubtful, and the *indicia* are not sufficiently understood by many of them, Your Grace should send the *Consilia* produced some years ago by several reputable universities and jurists, who framed opinions at your command, to both the theological and legal faculties of Ingolstadt for their detailed *Responsum*, and thereafter frame *statuta* from them and send them to all *iudicibus* in the country, commanding them to regulate their conduct in trials for witchcraft and to proceed in accordance with them.[227]

This opinion failed both in its particular object – the resumption of an investigation for witchcraft against a woman who had been suspected since 1590 – and in its general intention. The Chancellor was more successful in his efforts to bring about the mandate against superstition and witchcraft. Its drafting was entrusted to the keenest apologist of persecution in the country, Dr Cosmas Vagh.

THE SCANDALOUS MANDATE (1611–12)

The famous, or infamous, Bavarian mandate against superstition and witchcraft, the *Landtgebott wider die Aberglauben, Zauberey, Hexerey und andere sträffliche Teufelskünste*, was first submitted to the full Court Council by Vagh in January 1611.[228] But Wagnereckh was just as much its intellectual father as Vagh; together they had led the persecution party for more than a decade and had left the permanent stamp of their personalities on it. The Court Council approved the mandate with a few minor proposed alterations, and was in favour of sending it to the neighbouring bishops. It may seem incredible, but it was quite in tune with the Chancellor's calculations in power politics: the mandate was printed in Munich on 12 February 1611 without the prior consent of the Duke or of the Privy Council. Not until March, as a *fait accompli*, was the mandate presented to

---

[226] M. Kunze, 'Zum Kompetenzkonflikt zwischen städtischer und herzoglicher Strafgerichtsbarkeit in Münchner Hexenprozessen, *Zeitschrift der Savigny-Stiftung für Rechtsgesc-hichte. Germanistische Abteilung*, 87 (1970), 305–14.
[227] HStAM, Hexenakten 4, Prod. 46, fol. 5–6.   [228] HStAM, KHR 91, fol. 58–9.

Er Fürstl. Durchl.
Hertzog Maximilians in Bayern/rc.
vnsers gnädigsten Landtsfürsten vnd Herrens.

Landtgebott wider die Aberglauben Zauberey
Hexerey vnd andere sträffliche Teufels/
künste.

Gedruckt in der Fürstlichen Hauptstatt München/
Bey Anna Bergin Wittib.

ANNO   M. DC. XI.

ad Academiam

10. *Landtgebott wider die Aberglauben, Zauberey Hexerey und andere sträffliche Teufelskünste*, Munich 1611. Title engraving with the chequered Bavarian coat of arms.

Duke Maximilian for his signature.[229] One of the numerous paradoxes that surround the mandate may be mentioned right away: it was indeed printed in 1611 but it was not published.

In many of its parts the form and content of the mandate corresponded to the compromises that had been reached in Bavaria in the previous twenty years, but in other parts its content was scandalous. A detailed analysis of the terms of the extensive document would go beyond the scope of this book, and will be given elsewhere. Here we can only go into the terms that were of importance in the preceding or subsequent discussions. In form the mandate consisted of three parts: a general text, which was also available separately as a large pamphlet, a 'part number 1', which sum-marised individual manifestations of sorcery and superstition in fifty-two articles on twenty-one folio pages; and a 'part number 2', which took sixteen articles and twelve pages to list the penalties for the individual offences. In total the mandate occupied forty pages.[230]

The mandate abided by the results of the previous debates on witchcraft in Bavaria to the extent that it no longer questioned the necessity of circumstantial evidence as required by article 44 of the *Carolina* (dis-cussions of 1601–4) and drew a clear distinction between superstition and witchcraft/sorcery (discussions of 1607–8). Torture was not prescribed as obligatory in 'normal' cases of superstitious practices, and the penalty for some of these forms of superstition was within the bounds of what was thought tolerable at the time, even by comparison with other territories (penances in church, a month's imprisonment). There were possibilities of commuting a sentence from banishment to a fine, or even to a penance in church, the lightest penalty. Particularly important was the mild punish-ment of the very common offence of simply handling superstitious objects.

Yet in its baroquely violent language the whole tenor of the mandate recalled the position of the rigid apologists of persecution of the previous two decades. The general part of the mandate again invoked the fear of witchcraft gaining the upper hand, and did not omit to point to the frightful consequences of laxness in hunting down witches, as

if proper and carefully considered measures are not taken to abolish such superstition . . . Almighty God will be moved to righteous anger

---

[229] *Ibid.*, fol. 194 (8 March 1611). Even before it was signed, the mandate had been printed in Munich at the press of Anna Bergin, Widow: *Landtgebott wider die Aberglauben, Zauberey Hexerey und andere sträffliche Teufelskünste*, Munich 1611. *Ibid.*, fol. VIII, says: 'Geben und geschehen in unser Stadt München 1611 . . . den zwölfften Tag Monats Februarii, Anno MDCXI.'

[230] *Ibid.*; an account of the mandate is given by Riezler, *Geschichte*, 208–12; but he was not clear either about the prehistory of the mandate or about the problems which it posed even for contemporaries, and the associated controversies.

against us and will punish and chastise our country and people with dearth, war and pestilence and manifold other plagues.

The introduction reminds the reader or hearer of the horrors of simple superstition, which was not a simple procedure, but the 'first step or degree, also a *pactum si non expressum, tamen tacitum et implicitum cum Daemone* . . . [which] commonly goes with it'.[231] Once again the two spheres of popular magic and witchcraft, which the Donnersberger committee of 1608 had sought to distinguish, were deliberately confused. In its introduction the mandate stated that

unfortunately the superstitions, such as suspicious charms for diseases of livestock and people and *in summa* the *sortilegia* and soothsaying or the revelation of secret, hidden and future things (knowledge of which belongs to Almighty God alone), not without great suspicion of sorcery and *expressae invocationis*, that is explicit invocation of the Evil One, are spreading and gaining the upper hand, above all among the common folk, so that it is to be feared that some of them will gradually be drawn into the forbidden and damnable vices of witchcraft and sorcery . . .[232]

These views were also reflected in several articles in parts numbers 1 and 2, as for example that ascribing the effectiveness of rhymed spells (a chief element in popular magic) to the 'secret help of the Evil One', or that which branded the common sorcerers' signs (pentagrams, circles, triangles, etc.) as the work of the Devil. For soothsayers, interpreters of dreams and sorcerers who had not made a pact with the Devil, the obligatory death penalty was exceptionally harsh.[233]

Burning at the stake without the possibility of commutation was imposed for pacts with the Devil, prayer to the Devil, and – with a reference to article 109 of the *Carolina* – for harmful sorcery. In cases of calling up the Devil, or using sorcery to cause love, impotence or disease, the burning could be mitigated by previous decapitation.[234]

If one of the enormities of the mandate was that it again declared certain forms of popular magic to be evidence of the crime of witchcraft, by invoking the old theory of the tacit pact with the Devil,[235] the specification

---

[231] *Landtgebott wider die Aberglauben, Zauberey, Hexerey und andere sträffliche Teufelskünste* (1611), fol. 2–3.   [232] *Ibid.*, fol. 2.

[233] For example the magical 'charakteres' were described as 'Haupt Superstition', which could not achieve anything without the aid of the Devil; *ibid.*, fol. XX. Also, 'alle die jenige [were] ins gemain der Zauberey verdächtig, welche mit verdächtlichen Geberden, Worten und Wercken umbgehen', *ibid.*, fol. XIII. Soothsaying was to be punished by death (by the sword, not by fire), as it implied a pact with the Devil. *Ibid.*, fol. XXXI.

[234] *Ibid.*, fol. XXXff.

[235] Once again it was of course Binsfeld (1591), *Tractat*, who was cited as the authority for the mandate, composed by the apologists of persecution. For the the legal roots of the semiotic theory of the pact with the Devil see Harmening, *Superstitio*, 303–17.

of individual forms of superstition, which all parties had originally demanded, was just as objectionable in its printed form. It was hardly possible to punish an act when its perpetrator had never been told, in binding terms, that it was liable to punishment; the Donnersberger committee of 1608 had made this point in its opinion. On the other hand the government had so little trust in its subjects that it feared that listing the forms of superstition would only arouse their interest in possibilities of sorcery of which they had not previously been aware.

PERSISTENT CONFLICTS ON THE MANDATE

The Bavarian mandate on superstition and witchcraft, printed in 1611, renewed in 1665 and 1746, and nominally in force until the reform of the criminal law in 1813,[236] got off to a difficult start. Although the Court Councillors in Wagnereckh's circle were thinking of submitting it as early as March 1611, the Duke did not sign it until almost a year later, so that in reality the mandate ought to be dated 1612. In the first half of the seventeenth century, as long as the details were still remembered, it was in fact always referred to as the mandate of 1612.[237]

The Duke and his Privy Councillors refused to pass the already printed mandate in the form in which it was submitted. They objected to the detail and to the severity of some of the penalties. A ducal command of 21 January 1612 ordered the mandate to be corrected in accordance with the objections notified.

> Because in this mandate and pamphlet, for the better information of the subordinate authorities who are inexperienced in this matter, certain *circumstantia* and things, which might easily give occasion to the curious for vain ponderings, are rather too fully explained and specified, and there are also changes to be made to the penalties.
> And so His Grace sends his Court Council a specially corrected copy, from which you are to have one or more learned [Councillors; WB] correct and delete the others enclosed herewith in the appropriate places . . .[238]

As a surviving copy of the mandate with handwritten corrections shows, the corrections concerned chiefly the severity of the punishments. All the capital sentences were retained, but the banishments, imprisonments or

---

[236] Riezler, *Geschichte*, 272f.
[237] Thus for example in HStAM, KHR 230, fol. 179–80, where the General Mandate of 2 November 1629 refers to the mandate against witchcraft and superstition of 1612. Likewise HStAM, KHR 366, fol. 40v, where the General Order of 13 April 1665 refers to the mandate printed in 1611 but amended and issued in 1612.
[238] SBM, Cgm. 258, fol. 107; HStAM, KHR 97, fol. 210.

humiliating penalties were relaxed or left at the judges' discretion,[239] on the unspoken assumption that the judges on the spot regarded popular magic as a less serious offence than the learned but credulous theoreticians, who were eager to pin the guilt of a tacit pact with the Devil on everyone who wore an amulet. The command to all the learned Councillors to insert the corrections by hand may be seen as a subtle rebuke for the overhasty printing of the mandate.

The learned Councillors were even more indignant at a ruling which restricted the publication of the mandate, if it did not prevent it altogether. Originally the the mandate had been intended for the information of all the Estates and subjects, as the text itself makes clear. Supreme Chancellor Donnersberger, however, found the mandate produced by Vagh so explosive that he felt 'that such mandates should only be sent to the county courts', and ought not to be made accessible in print to a wider public. The scholars in the Court Council could scarcely believe such a decision and queried it with the two highest political officials, Donnersberger and von Rechberg. Vagh also objected that the relevant decision had not been signed.[240] The attempts of the Court Council to challenge this order were fruitless. The mandate in its corrected form was sent to the county courts (one copy for each of them) between 10 March and 20 April 1612. At the explicit request of the *Regierung* in Straubing, some extra copies were sent in May 1612, but the principle that the number of copies was to be limited was confirmed.[241] It was clear to everyone involved, supporters and opponents of persecution alike, that an unpublished mandate was of little value.

The chief task of the county court judges was to file the mandate among their archives. They were not allowed to release it, to have it transcribed or to duplicate it in any other way. Not even the noble or ecclesiastical holders of lower judicial rights were to receive copies of the text. The only compensation for the practical keeping secret of the mandate was its annual reading from the pulpit at Christmas and Whitsun,[242] but it was hardly possible to verify that this rule had been observed unless the local county court judge used his own initiative and reported to the Court Council. Moreover, the clergy, in their clerical functions, were in no way subject to the government in Munich, but to their bishops. The territory of

---

[239] HStAM, Mandatensammlung; *Landtgebott wider die Aberglauben, Zauberey, Hexerey und andere sträffliche Teufelskünste*, Munich 1665. The penal terms of article VI (fol. XXXIII), article VII (fol. XXXIV–XXXV) and article VIII (fol. XXXVI) were moderated; they were chiefly concerned with the dealings with soothsayers common in popular magical culture. A proof copy of the mandate of 1611–12 is in HStAM, SV 2063.
[240] HStAM, KHR 97, fol. 130r–v.   [241] *Ibid.*, fol. 210; HStAM, KHR 98, fol. 66, 117.
[242] *Landtgebott wider die Aberglauben, Zauberey, Hexerey und andere sträffliche Teufelskünste* (1611), fol. VII.

the Duchy of Bavaria fell within several dioceses: Augsburg, Freising, Regensburg, Passau, Salzburg, Chiemsee and Eichstätt. Where a county court judge who served the Duke insisted on the reading of the mandate, this caused conflict. As early as Whitsun 1612 it was clear that difficulties would be created, 'as the priesthood are opposed to it'.[243] The problem was by no means confined to the level of the local clergy, for the resistance originated with the bishops, 'who did not wish to have it read from the pulpit'.[244] In the summer of 1612 the Court Council was already beginning to prepare opinions 'on the poor observance of the mandate issued on superstition'.[245]

As the debates and attempted revivals of later years show, we should not imagine that the mandate was particularly effective. The limitations imposed by the Privy Council had greatly restricted its effect. In 1615 the *Capita Deliberationis* of the persecution party said that

> the mandate and order against superstition and *sortilegia*, issued some years ago, has still not only not been published *ordinario modo*, as is usual with other mandates, or sent to all the Estates, and has only been read before the Prince's county courts, and a single copy has been sent to each county court judge. And so it has remained unpublished in the estates, court countys and lordships which fall under the Estates . . . so that many are of the opinion that such a mandate is to some extent in doubt and respectively revoked and abolished in most of the articles and points.[246]

During the visitation of the Court Council of 1617, when the Councillors were asked why the mandate had had so little effect, they placed all the blame on the county court judges.[247] In 1625 it was stated at a session of the Court Council that there was the greatest negligence in the observation of the mandate.[248] A general order of March 1625, intended as a reminder, did not help either. In June 1625 the University of Ingolstadt claimed that it had never heard of the mandate. When it was finally sent a copy – thirteen years after it had been issued – in order to give an opinion on the mandate, the University wrote to Munich, asking if the verdict was in fact to be given according to this mandate. Under article 4 of the mandate, the

---

[243] HStAM, KHR 99, fol. 91.   [244] *Ibid.*, fol. 180; cf. note 252.
[245] *Ibid.*, fol. 190f., 293; KHR 100, fol. 280.
[246] HStAM, Hexenakten 1, Prod. 6, fol. 5v (letter of Wagnereckh to ex-Duke Wilhelm V).
[247] HStAM, HR 401/3, opinion of the Privy Councillors, no date. The visitation took place after the death of Wagnereckh. A Court Councillor expressed the view that 'der vorige Canzler sey etwas rigeros sonderlich in Malefizsachen gewesen', and saw a connection between this and the failure to observe the mandate. Another Court Councillor said bluntly: 'Seines Erachtens geschehe der Mandatis genuege.'
[248] HStAM, KHR 197, fol. 367–8.

sorcerer Reinboldt, who was a prisoner in Munich, ought to have been executed, although he denied a pact with the Devil and there was no proof that he had practised harmful sorcery. Indeed, it was a question whether an unknown mandate could be enforced at all!

> In the contrary case, however, and as the abovementioned Electoral mandate is not *in observantia*, as we are unable to remember it, but in the opinion of those learned in the law, only the common law and the Criminal Ordinance of Emperor Charles V ought to be regarded, we have unanimously decided that the said Reinboldt, as he has not caused any harm or detriment to the people by sorcery and forbidden means ... should be publicly placed in the pillory, and further beaten with a rod, and then banished from the country in perpetuity.[249]

We may take it as significant that the Court Council itself no longer kept to Wagnereckh's mandate after his death, and followed the milder vote of the University of Ingolstadt. In October of the same year the same problem arose again in the case of a 'sorceress' from Burghausen, who had not only acted as the leader of a band of treasure-seekers, but was openly regarded as an expert in the black arts; soothsaying and charms formed the provable core of her offences, while of course witchcraft could not be proved against her without a confession. Here too the University decided in favour of banishment, against the mandate.[250] Under the impression of the persecutions in Franconia, a new general order of 1629 again gave a reminder of the mandate of 1612.[251]

In 1665 there was even a new impression of the corrected text of the mandate, but in the same year the Court Council refused to send the county court judge in Landsberg more than one copy.[252] In 1677 another

[249] HStAM, SV 2218, no. 16.
[250] *Ibid.*, no.17. Cf. Schrittenloher, 'Aus der Gutachter- und Urteilstätigkeit', 329; Schmid, *Altertümer*, 43.
[251] SBM, Cgm 2542, fol. 123. HStAM, KHR 230, fol. 179–80.
[252] HStAM, KHR 3676, fol. 40v. The request of the *Regierung* in Amberg for further copies of the mandate was refused, on the grounds that it 'seye umb soviel weniger solche allen Gerichten zuschickhen, Zumahlen dergleichen Process ohnedess in die Reg[ierung] gezogen werden'. KHR 367, fol. 124. The county court judge of Kranzberg wanted to have forty copies sent to him, but was told that it would be enough for him to have a single copy in his registry. *Ibid.*, KHR 366, fol. 288. The *Regierung* in Landshut complained that parish priests were unwilling to read the mandate from the pulpit. They were told that 'obwohlen in dem Mandat herkhomme, dass solches auf der Canzel verlesen werden solle, so gehe doch die Intention mehrers dahin, dass man sich deren bey Gericht ... bedienen solle, dahero die Regierung die verwaigerte ablesung auf der Canzl zu dissimulieren wissen werde'. *Ibid.*, KHR 367, fol. 165v (3 August 1665). ('Although it said in the mandate that it was to be read from the pulpit the intention was rather that the courts should make use of it, and so the government would know how to play down the refusal to read it from the pulpit.') Cf. below, p. 299.

Table 11 *Witch trials and executions of witches in Bavarian county courts (1608 – 1616), based on analysis of the minutes of the Court Council in Munich* [253]

Half year	Courts with witchcraft trials	Courts with executions of witches	Number of those executed as witches	Remarks
1608 I	5	–	–	Agrarian crisis 1607–8
1608 II	11	2	3	
1609 I	9	1 or 2	1 or more	Resignation of Barth
1609 II	6	2	8 or more	
1610 I	5	1 or 2	2 or more	
1610 II	6	1	2	
1611 I	4	–	–	Agrarian crisis 1611–12
1611 II	4	1	1	
1612 I	4	–	–	Witchcraft mandate
1612 II	4	–	–	
1613 I	4	–	–	Execution of Sattler
1613 II	2	–	–	
1614 I	6	–	–	
1614 II	4	–	–	Agrarian crisis 1614–15
1615 I	5	–	–	
1615 II	12	1	1	
1616 I	7	–	–	
1616 II	4	–	–	

general order again recalled the memory of the mandate, which was said to have been forgotten.[254]

PREDOMINANCE OF THE MODERATES IN BAVARIA

EXECUTION OF THE WITCH-JUDGE OF WEMDING

Neither the number of witch trials nor their severity was immediately influenced by the mandate of 1612. In both cases other factors were more important. If we look at the total figures for the witchcraft and sorcery trials that can be proven from the minutes of the Court Council between 1608 and 1615, the picture is as shown in Table 11.

While we can detect an increase in the number of accusations of witchcraft in the autumn of the second year during the agrarian crises of 1607–8 and 1614–15, no such development took place in the agrarian crisis of

[253] Cf. above, p. 223, note 45.
[254] HStAM, KHR 415, fol. 192v–3 (5 November 1677). A very similar reason was given in the reprint of the mandate in 1746. Then too it was stated that the mandate was 'dermassen in absezung gekhommen' that it was ineffective. HStAM, GR 323/16, fol. 139 (order of Elector Maximilian III Joseph, 29 November 1746).

1611–12, although it too was characterised by relatively high inflation (back to the level of 1590 or 1600), harvest failures, livestock diseases and an epidemic of plague.[255] Conversely, in the years 1609 and 1610, which saw the first persecution at Wemding and the second at Donauwörth, we find a high level of prices but not the other typical signs of an agrarian crisis. The persecution at Donauwörth went back, in fact, to the agrarian crisis of 1607–8, and that at Wemding had been caused by denunciations from Donauwörth, but both reached their peak in the second half of 1609 and the beginning of 1610.

In the absence of better explanations we can explain this lack of synchronicity by the outcome of the debates in Munich and the shock effect of the persecution at Wemding: with the resignation of Bernhard Barth, who had already stayed away from the Court Council since mid-1608 because of the intolerable situation, the persecution party no longer faced any direct opposition, so that at first it was free to escalate individual witchcraft trials. As the persecution in Wemding expanded and the tendency to persecution in Munich was recognisably invigorated by it, the cases of suspected witchcraft reported to the Court Council rapidly fell back to the very low average of four investigations for sorcery/witchcraft per half-year. Even during the agrarian crisis of 1611–12, when the first persecutions began in the Bishopric of Augsburg and in Franconia, the number of new trials in Bavaria remained low, while the persecutions at Donauwörth and Wemding were again brought under control. The number of accusations of witchcraft reported fell to its absolute low point in the second half of 1613, when investigations were carried out in only two district courts, Pfaffenhofen and Reichenhall.

The favourable food situation of the year 1613 in Bavaria certainly provides part of the explanation for the decline in investigations into witchcraft. It can also be sensibly connected, however, with the exemplary punishment meted out to the judge who had instigated the persecution at Wemding: the administrator Gottfried Sattler.[256]

The escalation of the witch trials in Donauwörth, but above all in Wemding, and the controversy about the mandate against superstition and witchcraft, had again turned the attention of the political elite to the topic. From September the commissioner at Munich in charge of the Wemding persecution, Dr Schobinger, a partisan of Wagnereckh, was replaced by the commissioner Dr Leuker. At about the same time ten suspected witches were ordered to be brought to the Falkenturm in Munich. The hearings in Munich revealed a very different picture from that painted in

---

[255] Cf. chapter 2, pp. 89–114, and note 165.

[256] The name and the case of Sattler have long haunted the literature, but the context has never been reconstructed. Cf. Ferchl, 'Bayerische Behörsden', II, 1297; Schneid, 'Das Rechtsverfuhren', 158; Riezler, *Geschichte*, 244; cf. below, pp. 293–5.

the previous reports of the local officials. The arbitrariness of the procedure adopted became clear. As early as October 1611 the district judge Konrad von Bemelburg the younger was officially reprimanded for his failure to exercise control over his officers:

> And the district judge of Wemding is to be told that he has entrusted his judge and subordinates with the said trial and has not looked into it himself.[257]

A few weeks later the persecution at Wemding was described in the minutes of the Court Council as 'an irregular witch trial'. A few weeks later still, a man was sent to Wemding who had already made a name for himself in the earlier discussions of witchcraft in Bavaria: the former *Hofoberrichter* and now Provincial Administrator Bernhard Barth. Barth collected such damaging evidence on the spot against the judge in charge, Sattler, that the Court Council at once ordered him to be arrested and brought to Munich. In the meantime the remaining prisoners at Wemding had been released on the recommendation of Dr Leuker. Barth and Leuker were instructed to investigate the witch-judge of Wemding, Gottfried Sattler.[258]

They made rapid progress. Stronger and stronger evidence accumulated that Sattler had filed fictitious reports, and had ordered arbitrary arrests and torture in order to enrich himself from the property of the accused. Soon after Sattler was arrested, the conditions for arrest were tightened; in September 1612 he himself was tortured and in December his execution was considered for the first time. Yet there was resistance to this idea: the council of Wemding pleaded for clemency, as did his family, some unnamed petitioners, Duke Albrecht, a younger brother of the reigning Duke, and of course Chancellor Wagnereckh, who was well aware of the signal that such a precedent would send. As a death sentence could not be imposed in the teeth of such opposition, the Court Council was again unable to take a decision. With the approval of the Privy Councillors Dr Jocher and Count von Rechberg, it was decided to put the question to the University of Ingolstadt. In two opinions the University confirmed that the witch-judge himself was to be executed. Duke Maximilian, however, still hesitated to agree to such a step.[259]

Wagnereckh now went into action. He surprised the Court Council into

[257] HStAM, KHR 90, fol. 67.
[258] *Ibid.*, KHR 98, fol. 9, 11v, 253v–4. On Dr Esaias Leuker of Augsburg see Heydenreuter, *Der landesherrliche Hofrat*, 343.
[259] The minute books HStAM, KHR 99, KHR 100 and KHR 107 are full of discussions on the Sattler case. The most important stages: transfer to Munich (KHR 99, fol. 16); torture (*ibid.*, fol. 260v–1); decision to execute; consent of Privy Councillors Dr Jocher and Count Rechberg (*ibid.*, fol. 236v, 240); seven intercessions on Sattler's behalf, including that of Duke Albrecht (KHR 107, fol. 4, 42); two Ingolstadt opinions (*ibid.*, fol. 52); proclamation of the death sentence on Sattler (*ibid.*, fol. 240).

voting, by a majority and against the opinions of the University, that the death sentence against Sattler should be commuted to exile. Once again the opponents of persecution were to be presented with a *fait accompli*. To the public, Sattler's banishment was bound to seem a much less serious penalty than his execution. For the persecution party, the political damage would be contained.[260] Yet Wagnereckh's attempt to steamroller his opponents failed because the principle at stake was too important. After only two days the Court Council was prevailed upon to revoke its decision, by the direct intervention of the Supreme Chancellor Donnersberger.[261] The Court Council, the University and the Privy Councillors thus argued in favour of the execution of the judge. In May 1613 Duke Maximilian finally brought himself to decide on the execution of Sattler. At the end of June or early in July 1613 Sattler was beheaded in Schwaben (the present Markt-Schwaben). Two other officials from Wemding were sentenced to perpetual exile from Bavaria. Their posts were to be filled by new men appointed by Barth. The noble district judge of Wemding, Bemelburg, had long since distanced himself from the machinations of his former subordinates. He had read the signs of the times, and aligned himself with the right side in good time. No doubt as a sign of his remorse, Bemelburg now wished to appoint the former administrator Niedermayr as Sattler's successor. The Court Council voted by a majority against Niedermayr's appointment, but the High Chamberlain Count von Rechberg ordered that its decision be revoked. Niedermayr, once under suspicion and exiled from the country, was appointed administrator and thus fully rehabilitated in the eyes of the public.[262]

The criminal trial of the witch-judge of Wemding bears all the hallmarks of a key event. Between July and December 1612 the Court Council discussed this case on average ten times a month. The man in charge of the proceedings, Dr Leuker, was appointed Privy Secretary in the same year. Once again the conflict between the Privy Councillors and Chancellor Wagnereckh came out into the open. It was hardly a coincidence that the Jesuit Gretser openly sided with the persecution party at the same time.[263] The execution of the witch judge was more than a symbolic defeat for the persecution party. For all those who had believed that God would not permit the innocent to be burned as witches, Sattler's execution was an unparallel debacle that came near to a public refutation of a false theory. Years later suspects in the persecutions at Eichstätt were still appealing to

---

[260] *Ibid.*, fol. 104v–5.   [261] *Ibid.*, fol. 106v–7.

[262] *Ibid.*, KHR 107, fol. 280, 287. On Niedermayr's case cf. above, chapter 4, pp. 269–90 and notes 202–4. Ferchl, 'Bayerische Behörden', II, 1297.

[263] Duhr, *Geschichte der Jesuiten*, II/2, 514. Gretser emphatically approved of the contemporary witch hunts at Ellwangen (cf. note 93).

this case. The execution of Sattler followed the execution in 1618 of the witch-judge Ross in Fulda, after thirteen years' imprisonment. Both cases were made known to a wide public by the Jesuit Adam Tanner. Friedrich Spee took over these precedents from Tanner:

> Frequently the judges to whom these witchcraft trials are entrusted are shameless and base people. Excessive and cruel torture is often applied. Many pieces of circumstantial evidence are unlawful and dangerous and the procedure is not seldom against law and reason ... Tanner relates that in earlier years in Germany two bloody judges who had had to deal with cases of witchcraft, were condemned to death by a judgement of the faculty of law at Ingolstadt and executed, because they had held trials contrary to law, in which innocent persons had been endangered ... Who will still doubt that many innocent people have been burned by these judges?[264]

THE PERSECUTION PARTY STRIPPED OF ITS POWER

Major changes were not confined to the district court at Wemding in 1613; they also affected the Court Council at Munich, which had become a stronghold of the persecution party during Wagnereckh's Chancellorship. Though the Chancellor was retained in his office, he was kept occupied with such honourable tasks that his name is hardly to be found in the Council's attendance lists of the next few years. His most important duty was to prepare the Bavarian law code (*Codex Maximilianeus*, 1616) in cooperation with the Privy Councillor Dr Gailkircher and the Town Clerk of Munich Dr Locher, a grouping of personnel which gains point when seen against the background of the controversies about witchcraft. The terms of the ordinance on procedure in trials for witchcraft of 1616 were neutral with respect to these controversies.[265] An honourable 'sideways promotion' (Heydenreuter) was also found for the other hard-liner in the Court Council, Dr Cosmas Vagh, who was 'promoted' to the Chancellorship of the provincial administration of Burghausen in July 1613.[266] The framing of the controversial mandate against superstition and witchcraft was thus Vagh's last great task in the central government.

The third decisive new appointment concerned the *Hofoberrichter*'s administrator Dr Georg Hundt. Hundt, who felt that the superintendence

---

[264] The parish priest Johann Reichard, for example, appealed to Sattler's case during the witch hunts of 1624 at Eichstätt. UBM, Cod. Ms. 214, fol. 65v, 71v. Tanner, *Theologia*, III, col. 1005, followed by Spee, *Cautio*, 32.

[265] Spindler, *Handbuch*, II, 586ff. (Albrecht); Christel, 'Die Malefizprozessordnung', 70f.; Riezler, *Geschichte*, 212f.

[266] Heydenreuter, *Der landesherrliche Hofrat*, 148, 324.

296 WITCHCRAFT PERSECUTIONS IN BAVARIA

of the ducal criminal gaol was not a very honourable task for a nobleman, had shown little commitment, and had thereby become an agent of the persecution party. As early as the visitation of the Court Council of 1612 Hundt had been very severely censured. The *Jägermeister* Wensin described him as '*uno verbo*, the most incompetent Councillor', because he had 'little discretion', usually a shorthand term for willingness to allow too easy or excessive use of torture. On the same occasion the Provincial Administrator Barth had demanded that Hundt be replaced by the Court Councillor Hans Christoph Tanner, a moderate in questions of witchcraft. A prisoner's escape in 1614 supplied a pretext for this change of personnel.[267] In 1613 another partisan of Wagnereckh, the Court Councillor Dr Reisacher, was demoted to Straubing, from where he had been called to the Court Council in 1607. In the visitation of 1612 Reisacher had been reproved for aligning himself too closely with Wagnereckh and Vagh.[268] The Court Councillor von Dandorf, who had long been close to the persecution party, transferred to the service of Pfalz-Neuburg in 1613. None of the new men appointed to the Court Council can be described as a member of the hard-line persecution party. They included the sons of the Privy Councillors Herwarth and Donnersberger, and the two later Chancellors Dr Brugglacher and Dr Abegg, both of whom sided with the moderates.[269] The persecution party reached its lowest point in 1617, when, with the death of the Chancellor Wagnereckh and Court Councillor Rieger, as well as Dr Gewold's move to Ingolstadt, and Dr Bonet's to Brixen, all the old representatives of the hard line in witchcraft questions had left the Court Council.[270]

The shift in the balance of the Court Council came at just the right time. A new persecution of enormous dimensions had begun in south Germany with the agrarian crisis of 1614–15. Witches were being hunted in the Prince-Bishoprics of Passau and Augsburg,[271] in the Principality of Pfalz-Neuburg, now under Catholic rule, in the Prince-Provostship of Ellwangen and in four of the Franconian Bishoprics. In Bavaria too the number of accusations of witchcraft reached a new peak. Trials for witchcraft were held in 1614–16 in the county courts of Abensberg (twice), Aibling (twice), Aichach (three times), Burghausen, Dachau (three times), Friedberg, Hohenschwangau, Ingolstadt, Kling, Kötzting, Landsberg, Landshut,

---

[267] HStAM, HR 401/3. Heydenreuter, *Der landesherrliche Hofrat*, 318, 329. HStAM, KHR 114 (8–14 March).   [268] Heydenreuter, *Der landesherrliche Hofrat*, 152, 351.
[269] Henker, 'Zur Prosopographie', 97f.; Heydenreuter, *Der landesherrliche Hofrat*, 301–63 on the prosopography of the persons named. For their line on witchcraft questions in the Court Council cf. above, p. 244.
[270] Heydenreuter, *Der landesherrliche Hofrat*, 309, 330f., 352, 358.
[271] Cf. list of trials in the German edition.

Marquartstein, Munich (five times), Murnau, Pfaffenhofen, Regen, Rosenheim, Stadtamhof, Starnberg,Tölz, Traunstein (twice), Wasserburg (twice), Weilheim (twice), Wemding and Wolfratshausen.[272] At least fifty-one persons were involved in these forty trials over three years (seventeen men, thirty-two women, two children). Of these fifty-one persons, a man was probably executed at Tölz in 1615 for sorcery, and a woman suspect died in prison at Wemding, but without making a confession. Five others (two men and three women) were banished, twelve (five men and seven women) received lighter punishments (short prison sentences, the pillory or a pilgrimage as penance), twenty-four were acquitted (eight men, fifteen women and one child), and the fate of eight others could not be discovered, but their cases suggest at least that they were not executed. As one can recognise from the mere figures, such a large number of trials entailed a great risk, for each individual trial could grow into a persecution if the procedure was harsh enough. When we look at the individual witch trials, as they are reflected in the minutes of the Court Council, we can see a difference from the period when the Council had still been dominated by Chancellor Wagnereckh, who now rarely attended. The *Hofoberrichter* Hans Christoph Tanner, who was coming increasingly to the fore, acted with what contemporaries regarded as 'discretion'. He took a personal interest in individual trials, did not allow the hearings to be twisted against the suspect, was satisfied in most case with 'amicable' questioning, confirmed at the most by 'territion' (the showing of the implements of torture) or a short torture. Even though these distinctions may seem absurd from our modern perspective, we are on the right track to assume that for the radical advocates of persecution torture was a means to extort confessions, but for moderates like Tanner it was used to rehabilitate the suspect. If the accused stood up to torture he or she was 'purged' of suspicion, and the basis for acquittal was laid.[273] Sentences were now nominally decided by the Court Council in accordance with the mandate of 1612, but in practice this left considerable leeway in all cases of sorcery where there was no pact with the Devil or alleged ensuing death. This leeway was exploited by the moderates on the Council to release many suspects without punishment or with no more than a light sentence.[274]

---

[272] Compiled from HStAM, KHR 114, 115, 116, 119, 120, 121, 124, 125, 126, 127, 128, 129, 130, 131, 132.

[273] Examples of this in HStAM, KHR 119, fol. 174; KHR 120, fol. 257, 260v; KHR 128, fol. 10v, 39. The admission of 'ordentlichen purgationes' had been a crucial demand of the investigative committee of 1608.

[274] Examples in HStAM, KHR 119, fol. 139, 188v; KHR 128, fol. 39, 48, 122, 205; KHR 130, fol. 258, 277v; KHR 131, fol. 234v.

THE INTRIGUE OF 1615

The agrarian crisis of 1614–15, the 'manifest need with which Almighty God has visited Bavaria this year, in that almost everywhere the corn and rye has spoiled in the winter',[275] the hunger in many districts, cattle sicknesses, numerous diseases such as plague, the 'headache sickness', the 'Hungarian sickness', the 'bloody flux', numerous 'infections' and here and there a 'rare disease', as well as wolves penetrating into populated areas, seem to have created a strange tension in the countryside, though of course it is not possible to quantify such a mood. Some indicators nevertheless reveal the unusual situation: wolves were taken for werewolves, 'little men' were seen in the Bavarian forest, more diseases than usual were regarded as 'unnatural'.[276] Such fears were by no means confined to the ordinary people, but were also felt more often at the ducal court in these years. The death of the wife of Duke Ferdinand was blamed on sorcery, the old Duke Wilhelm V felt that he had been bewitched, there were accusations and counter-accusations of sorcery at court, and a black chest with secret objects inside was found behind the stove in the Ecclesiastical Council Chamber, which Wagnereckh and the Secretary of the Privy Council Albertinus identified as a deposit of objects for use in sorcery, sorcerer's clothing and 'many other things, books and letters, which are frightful to see and grim objects of sorcery'.[277]

In this mood there was renewed pressure for the resumption of the persecutions. The old Duke Wilhelm V, who had abdicated in 1597, took the opportunity of an audience which Duke Maximilian gave Dr Paulus zum Ackher, the leader of the persecution party at Dillingen,[278] to 'order' Wagnereckh to confer with the Dillingen Councillor on the question of witchcraft:

How and in what form such highly pernicious vice should not only be inquired into, but also what kind of proceedings should be held and

---

[275] HStAM, KHR 114, s.f. (19 April 1614).

[276] *Ibid.*, KHR 115, fol. 74v. The *Regierung* in Straubing reported 'grassierender Sucht' and 'Waldmännlein' seen in the district of the court of Kötzting. The *Regierung* at Landshut reported an 'infection' in Passau (KHR 116, Index 'L'), where the witch hunt began not long afterwards. In 1615 the strange phenomena became more frequent, while cattle diseases and every possible kind of sickness were reported to the Court Council (numerous entries in KHR 120). There were occasional points of contact with trials for witchcraft and sorcery. In the district of Aichach, for example, a 'seltsame Krankheit' occured from September. In early December a witchcraft trial investigated whether a woman had used 'natürliche Mittel' (or sorcery) to cause the death of cattle. HStAM, KHR 120, fol. 257. The increasing sensitivity to such news was only evident in a very indirect form and did not lead to a general witch hunt.

[277] On the bewitchment of Duke Wilhelm and Maria Pettenbeckh, HStAM, Hexenakten 1, Prod., 6, fol. 1; on the accusations in the Court Council *ibid.*, Prod. 3, Caput 3; on the 'erschröckhenlichen' findings in the Ecclesiastical Council: HStAM, KHR 119, fol. 189v.

[278] Cf. note 65 to chapter 3.

undertaken in such a case, and also what procedure has been used in Dillingen in such cases hitherto . . . and above all, how to go about it, so that such a trial may be continued as long as is necessary and does not have to be suspended right away as soon as it is begun, because of the difficulties arising, and contrary opinions.[279]

The results of Wagnereckh's discussions with the Court Councillor from Dillingen took the form of twenty-four *Capita Deliberationis quoad processum contra maleficos vel sagas instituendum*, which once again strove to achieve the favourite goal of the persecution party, a general and systematic persecution, the 'General Inquisition against Sorcerers and Witches'. A systematic search was to be made throughout the whole country by a 'Council deputed' for this purpose. The mandate of 1612 was at last to be generally published, a public proclamation was to call on the people to collaborate in the search for witches, and letter boxes for anonymous denunciations were to be placed in every church, while the clergy were to preach sermons on the subject.

Because of the immovability of the Bavarian Councillors, foreign jurists were to be brought in from the Prince-Bishoprics of Augsburg or Eichstätt, or from the Prince-Provostship of Ellwangen, and only those Bavarian Councillors whom experience had shown to be reliable allies of the persecution party were to be entrusted with the task.[280] The aim, in a nutshell, was to reverse all the previous gains of the discussions on witchcraft in Bavaria: popular magic was again to be valid as evidence of witchcraft, unsupported denunciations were to suffice for torture to be ordered, and torture was to be allowed to be applied at will and repeated in trials for witchcraft. Wagnereckh also wanted to start the discussion on principle of 1601–4 all over again, but this time excluding the opponents of persecution, the 'cold political jurists' and 'cold and political Christians' who considered all these questions 'more as politicians than as Christians'.[281]

---

[279] HStAM, Hexenakten 1, Prod. 6, fol. 1. *Ibid.*, Prod. 3. 'Capita Deliberationis Quoad Processum contra Maleficos vel Sagas Instituendum.' The addressee is revealed by the passage 'E.D. geliebter Herr Son Herzog Maximilian in Baiern', the author by a comparison of the style with numerous earlier opinions of Wagnereckh, the dating by the proposal to appoint doctors Schobinger, Götz and Bonet as witch commissioners. Götz was not appointed to the Court Council until 3.12.1615, Bonet went to Brixen in 1617. Heydenreuter, *Der landesherrliche Hofrat*, 309, 332. HStAM, Hexenakten 1, Prod. 6, fol. 1, speaks of the death of Maria Pettenbeckh as a recent event. She died on 4.12.1614. Bosl, *Biographie*, 581. Not only her death was attributed to bewitchment, but in the city of Munich numerous persons had 'solche Krankheiten an sich gehabt welche nit natürlich, oder von der medicis zu erkennen gewest, sondern ex maleficio herkommen zu sein von den medicis dafür gehalten worden'. HStAM, Hexenakten 1, Prod. 6, fol. 1.

[280] *Ibid.*, fol. 2–3.

[281] *Ibid.*, fol. 2v. The 'kaltsinnigen politischen Juristen' are referred to in a second associated letter, *ibid.*, Prod. 7, fol. 2v–3.

But it will be very important, what kind of Councillors and jurists are involved in such deliberations, for it is not advisable to bring in those who have opposed this *denunciatione complicum* (through which most witches and wizards are revealed), so strongly that even after the response was received from Delrio, they still persist firmly in their opinion and presumably will continue to do so.[282]

FAILURE OF WITCHCRAFT TRIALS

The *Capita Deliberationis* did not give any decisive impetus, and the debate on the principle of witchcraft was not resumed until the eighteenth century. Only for a short time around 1629, when Dr Kolb was appointed witch commissioner, were some of its proposals followed. Otherwise the moderate Councillors retained their dominant position. This was clearly illustrated by several unsuccessful trials at Ingolstadt and Munich in the years between 1615 and 1630, which caused increasingly serious conflicts between the pro- and anti-persecution parties; in the end the moderate party always had its way. Because both parties shared a belief in the principle that pacts with the Devil and harmful sorcery were possible, there were repeated cases in which very harsh measures were taken against individual suspects, but every attempt to force the trials was regarded with deep suspicion by the opponents of persecution. Precise investigation of the statements of witnesses, and the contradictions in confessions, led to greater scepticism in particular cases, often reinforced by the tenacious resistance of the accused. As a detailed account of the complications of specific cases would go beyond the confines of this book, we shall merely refer to special studies.[283]

While the city council of Munich and its highest official, the Town Clerk Dr Locher, pressed for moderation in questions of witchcraft, Professor Kaspar Denich the younger rose to a position of recognised authority in the University of Ingolstadt and beyond; his influence extended to the magistracy and the Duke's Governor. The unanimous rejection of intentions of persecution – in spite of constant investigations of suspicions of witchcraft – was described by a follower of the persecution party in 1629:

They are not eager to burn [witches] at Ingolstadt, it does not need much, they are not eager. For all the witches who have had to be arrested

[282] *Ibid.*, Prod. 7, fol. 1v–2.
[283] Geyer, 'Hexen'; Geyer, 'Die Ingolstädter Hexenprozesse'; W. Behringer, 'Scheiternde Hexenprozesse', 42–79, 218–25.

at Ingolstadt in the last twelve years have been released again, and the Elector's Councillors wish to hinder the trials.[284]

THE FRANCONIAN PERSECUTION PARADIGM IS AVERTED

From the social-historical point of view the third decade of the seventeenth century surpassed all the catastrophes of the previous hundred years, including the hunger crisis of the early 1570s. In south Germany it was not the war itself that was the real problem, but an unprecedented series of harvest failures. The 'great need and dearth' of 1621 was followed without a break by the 'Kipper- und Wipper' inflation, and in 1623 there was again 'great need, dearth and misery'; 1624–5 was not much better and infectious diseases were widespread; 1625 saw another harvest failure and hunger, which of course affected only the lower classes. The situation remained grim in 1627, a cold, rainy year when an epidemic of plague began which was to reach catastrophic proportions in 1628. Constant rain and cold weather, a poor grain harvest and inflation increased susceptibility to disease. A whole folio volume, in effect a special volume, of the minutes of the Court Council of Bavaria, now an Electorate, is made up almost exclusively of reports from the Bavarian towns and villages hit by the plague.[285] These were the years in which the Catholic Bishoprics went over to continuous persecution. In the Bishopric of Eichstätt the burnings had not ceased since 1617, in Würzburg, Bamberg and Mainz they resumed after a pause of a few years, in 1625–6 and reached a scale that far exceeded anything known before (cf. chapters, 2, pp. 35–64, and 4, pp. 216–29). Official 'criminal commissions' led the persecutions in these territories. In 1628 the Catholic territories of Pfalz-Neuburg and Oettingen-Wallerstein set up similar institutions. Denunciations, the credibility of which had been greatly shaken in Bavaria since 1600, helped the persecutions to expand southwards.

---

[284] HStAM, GR 323/16, fol. 27v. Dr Gewold, who had transferred to Ingolstadt, expressed himself similarly in a letter to Duke Maximilian of 1616, which must refer to the period 1590–1616: 'Wann schon der Verdacht auf etliche Personen (die ohne dess der Häxerei, Kellerfahren . . . übl beschrait . . .) sehr scharf gehet, so fragt man doch nichts darnach unnd ist man diss orths plind und taub'; SBM, Cgm. 2210, fol. 119–21. Likewise, an autograph opinion of Wagnereckh for Duke Maximilian says that the civic authorities in Munich had 'nit vleissig nachgeforscht [witchcraft] noch auf den rechten grundt gesehen' since 1590. 'Defectum Ordinarii Jurisidictionis in Inquirendo Crimen Sortilegii betr.', HStAM, Hexenakten 4, Prod. 46, fol. 1f. It is beyond dispute that the apologists of persecution in Bavaria tried again in 1615–16, as they had in 1600–1, 1608–9 and 1611, to realise their *idée fixe* of a general eradication of witches, in parallel with the great witch hunts of Julius Echter in Würzburg and those of the other Franconian bishops. But in the Duchy of Bavaria this was not so easily achieved.

[285] HStAM, KHR 216 (Jan.–Sept. 1628)

11. *Druten Zeitung 'Schmalkalden'*, Nuremberg 1627

In the Electorate of Bavaria two district courts were particularly affected by denunciations: the exclave of Wemding, which lay between the territories of Pfalz-Neuburg and Oettingen-Wallerstein, and Ingolstadt, which formed a peninsula between the Prince-Bishopric of Eichstätt and the Pfalz-Neuburg towns of Reichertshofen and Neuburg on the Danube, both scenes of persecutions. In 1629 Elector Maximilian appointed the former Court Councillor of Eichstätt and Oettingen Dr Kolb as 'witchcraft commissioner', to conduct trials at Wemding and Ingolstadt.[286] This new model of persecution, the introduction of which in Bavaria had been the long-standing demand of Wagnereckh, was important and not only for Wemding and Ingolstadt: the fear was much rather that the Franconian paradigm of persecution would spread from these two courts to the whole of the Electorate, if it 'proved itself' in them. A follower of the Bavarian persecution party from Ingolstadt commented on Dr Kolb's procedure in 1629:

> I know for certain that he conducts the witch trials at Ingolstadt in such a way that he can answer for it at the Last Judgement . . . inasmuch as he has soon brought four women to confess at Wemding . . . but I have never heard that his procedure was unlawful in anything, for they say that he has used the same procedure at Ingolstadt and Wemding as that which is always applied in Bamberg, Würzburg and Eichstätt.[287]

The persecution spread rapidly in the exclave of Wemding, once Kolb had replaced the hesitant Professor Schmid of Ingolstadt in the conducting of the trials.[288] Now, under the leadership of a practised persecutioner, not only were denunciations from Eichstätt, Reichertshofen and Neuburg looked into, but even those of the first persecution at Wemding in 1609–10 were raked up again as well. Under these circumstances socially prominent people were affected by the persecution from the start: at the very first witch burning (14 March 1629) the victims executed included, besides three women, a rich innkeeper and butcher whose mother had been denounced from Donauwörth and executed at Wemding in 1609. Four of the five executed in the second witch burning were wealthy, one of them being the mother of a town councillor. In the third witch burning, the Burgomaster Epple, one of the wealthiest and most respected men of the town, was burned, as well as a relation of the former Chancellor of the Bavarian

---

[286] HStAM, KHR 225, fol. 221v. In HStAM GR 323/16 fol. 33, the *Pflegsverwalter* of Wemding was issued with an order for payment of sixty *Reichstaler* to Dr Kolb, for the preparation of an 'Instruction über die Hexenprocess' (7.2.1629). This does not appear to have been preserved. For the Wemding trial in general, Schneid, who however underestimates the role of Kolb ('Das Rechtsverfahren', 155–9).

[287] HStAM, GR 323/16, fol. 27v.

[288] To be corrected: Schneid, 'Das Rechtsverfahren', 159.

Court Council Dr Brugglacher. In total this persecution claimed thirty-nine victims, twenty-nine women and ten men, who were burned at nine executions.[289] The second persecution at Wemding was the greatest in the Duchy or Electorate of Bavaria since 1590. While the timid protests of the Council of Wemding against the persecutions had no recognisable effect, the old fronts emerged again in the fortress and university city of Ingolstadt, after Elector Maximilian, urged on by the Bishop of Eichstätt Johann Christoph von Westerstetten, ordered trials to be begun. Even the persons involved in the controversies at Ingolstadt were drawn to some extent from the old parties: the spokesman of the persecution party was the Councillor Dr G. Fasold, whom Wagnereckh had wished to appoint as a special witchcraft commissioner as long ago as 1601.[290] The leader of the opponents of persecution was Professor

[289] The course of the witch hunt can be reconstructed from the minutes of the Court Council in Munich, HStAM, KHR 225, 226, 227, 228, 229, 230, 231, 232, 233, 234. It is clear from these that the five great witch hunts in the Bavarian–Franconian–Swabian frontier region influenced one another: the witch hunt in the Bishopric of Eichstätt, those in the Pfalz-Neuburg districts of Reichertshofen and Neuburg, the witch hunt in Oettingen-Wallerstein, and that in the Bavarian exclave of Wemding. Ingolstadt was marginally affected (denunciations from Wemding, Eichstätt, Reichertshofen and Neuburg), while in other places in Bavaria, according to the minutes of the Court Council for these years, it did not reach the stage of executions, although the *Regierungen* or middle tiers of government at Amberg and Straubing were urged to show greater vigilance (*ibid.*, KHR 231, fol. 155, 170r–v.) Trial records of the second witch hunt at Wemding are in SBM, Cgm. 2197a-b; and in the Stadtarchiv Wemding (cf. Schneid, 119). A list of those executed in Schneid, 163–75. Schneid's view that the trial was not supervised from Munich (*ibid.*, 138) needs correction. In HStAM, KHR 29, fol. 153–4v., 26 July 1629, it is expressly stated, with a reference to the corresponding order of 2 October 1628, 'das ihr iederzeit, so offt ihr mit ain oder ander person aintweders zu der captur oder tortur zu schreiten vorhabens [! WB] solch euer vorhaben iederzeit alhero underthenigist berichtet und on unser einstimmen und gemessnen bevelch in diesem laster der Hexerey niemand gefenckhlich einkhert, viel weniger weiter verfaret, sondern iederzeit unser resolution gehorsamst erwartet'. ('That whenever you intend to arrest or torture someone or other you should always humbly report your intention here and not arrest anyone, still less take further steps, in this vice of witchcraft, without our unanimous and appropriate order, but should at all times obediently await our resolution.')

[290] HStAM, KHR 230, fol. 323–4. As early as 1601; HStAM, Hexenakten 4, Prod. 25. Otherwise the apologists of persecution had to be brought in from outside: the Ingolstadt professor Dr Valentin Schmid came from Bregenz in the Vorarlberg and had been an episcopal Councillor in Würzburg and Bamberg during the wave of witch hunting in Franconia in 1616–17 (Bosl, *Biographie*, 863). Dr Kolb (origin and biography unknown), had been witch commissioner in Eichstätt and Oettingen-Wallerstein (UBM, Cod. Ms. 214). Also asked for their advice were two other witch commissioners from outside Bavaria: Dr Hieronymus Dickhel of Neuburg (HStAM, KHR 233, fol. 44v; on him Henker, 'Zur Prosopographie', 103f: 'treibende Kraft der Hexenprozesse') and Hans Martin Staphylo von Nottenstein, witch commissioner in Eichstätt (HStAM, KHR 232, fol. 171–3v). In this connection it is interesting that Dr Dickhel wrote, and the Chancellor of Pfalz-Neuburg Dr Zeschlin corrected, the instruction for trials for witchcraft of 1630: 'Ihs – Memorial und Instruction nach wellicher sich irer F.D. Räthe und zum Malefizwesen deputierte Commissarii zu richten', in HStAM, Hexenakten 53, 6 fols. Another outside instruction on trial procedure played a part in the witch hunts in Bavaria; it had

Kaspar Denich, whom we have already mentioned, the son of the Dean Dr Joachim Denich, who had been responsible for the moderate opinion given by the University of Ingolstadt in 1601.[291] The Bavarian Governor Count von Tilly stood between the two parties.

The trials at Ingolstadt in 1629 were provoked by the case of the court seamstress Catharina Nickhlin of Eichstätt, who had fled to relatives in Ingolstadt after numerous denunciations. When she was to be arrested and tortured on the orders of the Elector, there were heated debates in Ingolstadt:

> The younger Dr Denich at once spoke out, and said he thought nothing of these 25 denunciations, someone or other could say I don't know what, and were we then to believe such people? And because the Elector's command had not specified what kind of torture was to be applied to the seamstress, he had wished to spin out the case *tacite*, so that further information could be obtained, but only to this end, that the Dr [Kolb; WB] should again be dismissed by this means and the trial completely hindered. Which those on the Knights' Bench, who have studied little of this trial for witchcraft, would readily have followed, if Your Grace's Count von Tilly, aforementioned, and Dr Fasold and he [Dr Kolb; WB] too had not put up resistance and opposition, so that according to the order the old court seamstress should be tortured according to her bodily constitution. Thus these three gentlemen won the first round against this mighty hero, young Denich.[292]

The opponents of persecution were not well placed to resist an unequivocal order from the Elector, although the majority of the Elector's Councillors in Ingolstadt evidently supported Denich, as did the City Council. Even among the people, after the arrest of the old woman, there was 'muttering and grumbling, that they should treat people like this'. Several citizens of Ingolstadt who attended the hearing, and saw the methods used by the commissioner, who had his instructions to apply them, were 'greatly altered and looked grimly at the Doctor'. Though they frowned on the harsh procedure they could do nothing to prevent the old woman confess-

---

been constantly referred to by Wagnereckh and Gewold (e.g. HStAM, Hexenakten 1, Prod. 6, fol. 3v) and was directly connected with Bavarian inquiries to the Catholic territories in 1600. We refer to the 'Kurkölnische Hexenordnung' of 1607, HStAM, Hexenakten 53, 9 fols. This had been drafted in Bonn around 1604, in connection with the inquiries from Munich to Ferdinand of Bavaria. Siebel, 'Die Hexenverfolgung', 43–6; also Decker, 'Die Hexenprozesse', 206f.

[291] (1591–1600); from 1614 professor at Ingolstadt, Bosl, *Biographie*, 133.

[292] HStAM, GR 323/16, fol. 23v. The electoral order of 10 April 1629: HStAM, KHR 227, fol. 103v.

ing her 'witchcraft' under torture.[293] Now, however, new conflicts arose, as the persecution party wished to ask about those who had been her accomplices at the witches' sabbath, as in Wemding.

In the session of the Council Denich, with unusual excitement, asked explicitly, what should be done about the denunciations. If two or three named him in their confessions, would he therefore be a witch? Everyone was shocked by this insolent speech . . .[294]

The result of Denich's drastic intervention was that a decision in favour of the persecution party could once again only be obtained after great effort and only with the support of the Elector's order, which tied the Governor's hands when it came to a decision. There were further arrests even before the execution of Catharina Nickhlin.

In Ingolstadt and Wemding resistance now took a wide variety of forms, albeit not that of overt opposition to the Prince's orders. In the first place, the witch commissioner and long-time princely household Councillor Dr Kolb was exposed to public scorn. At first he was made to sit below the three Ingolstadt Councillors in the hearings, and was then left to sit outside the closed door of the council chamber for hours, excluded from the discussions and ultimately refused all payment for his services; 'and if he had not had good acquaintances at Ingolstadt who advanced him money, it would have been a great humiliation for him'.[295] After these unpalatable experiences Kolb again withdrew to Wemding and Wallerstein, where his work had met with more support. There is no doubt that the opponents of persecution could not have scored such a success if they had not had backing from Munich. In fact both the Council of Wemding and Dr Denich had arranged the relevant contacts.

The Doctor [Kolb; WB] had hardly come to Ingolstadt when the young Denich, unsummoned and uninvited, waited on the Chancellor Dr Abeckh, who was also at Ingolstadt, and spoke to him about witchcraft. And the other day here in the Electoral Council [at Ingolstadt; WB] he said without fear that he had been with the Chancellor of Munich yesterday and the same also thought nothing of the denunciations, whomever they might be aimed at, and the other Electoral Councillors at Munich, especially the younger gentlemen, would readily follow his opinion.

---

[293] HStAM, GR 323/16, fol. 23ff. According to an order of 6 July the court seamstress of Eichstätt was executed at Ingolstadt. HStAM, KHR 229, fol. 60–1. She had been arrested on the grounds of a request from Eichstätt to Munich. Cf. HStAM, GR 323/16, fol. 92–103.

[294] HStAM, GR 323/16, fol. 25v. A similar argument is found in Tanner, *Theologia*, III, col. 996. It was certainly usual among the opponents of witch hunting.

[295] HStAM, GHR 323/16, fol. 25v.

And through this so harmful means even the trial at Wemding might be stopped, which the leading men in the Council at Wemding would be heartily glad to see done, considering that they had already made use of various doctors, with no other intention than to hinder this trial. To this end they had bribed many important people at Munich with much money. And the Elector's Councillors at Ingolstadt would bravely help them in this, just as Calvinus and Zwinglius had helped Luther . . .[296]

In spite of repeated orders from the Elector the trials at Ingolstadt went forward only sluggishly. If we may believe the minutes of the Court Council, during the whole persecution phase only two persons (one woman and one man) were burned as witches, while it is certain that at least fifty faced grave accusations. Forty denunciations from Reichertshofen in Pfalz-Neuburg alone pointed to neighbouring Ingolstadt in Bavaria, including its newly elected Burgomaster Wolf.[297] Another witch commissioner from Eichstätt, Hans Martin Staphylo von Nottenstein, appointed by Elector Maximilian as a household Councillor, was unable to give any help here. From June 1630 the persecution at Wemding also slowed down. Although five more persons were executed as witches after this date, the intervals between executions widened.

The number of accusations of witchcraft in Bavaria reached its absolute peak in 1629 and 1630. If we ignore the persecution at Wemding, that leaves forty-one investigations into suspected witchcraft in twenty-three district courts. Those most affected were above all Bavarian district courts in the neighbourhood of the persecution zones along the Danube and the Altmühl, namely Ingolstadt (five times), Pfaffenhofen (three times), Kranzberg (three times), Friedberg (four times), Schrobenhausen (twice), Dachau (twice), Mainburg (twice), Donauwörth (twice) and finally Gerolfing, Rain, Rottenburg and Vohburg. Beyond this particularly affected area, the district courts of Schwaben (three times), Marquartstein (twice) and Rosenheim (twice) stood out. There was one investigation each in the county courts of Diessen, Mindelheim, Munich, Straubing, Traunstein and Weilheim, while general investigations were also carried out from Munich in Amberg, Straubing, Kötzting, Viechtach and Mitterfels, though their outcome cannot be determined. In July 1630 the Bavarian government at Heidelberg (in the Electoral Palatinate) was ordered to appoint a qualified person to conduct trials for witchcraft (the Franconian model of persecution!) and to conduct the trials independently.

More astonishing than the relative frequency of investigations into suspicions of witchcraft at this time, when persecutions in Catholic south

---

[296] *Ibid.*, fol. 30. The Ingolstadt jurist Dr F. Waizenegger also rejected torture on the grounds of mere denunciations. Cf. note 38. A decisive passage from Waitzenegger, *Disputatio*, is reprinted in Schneid, 'Das Rechtsverfahren', 177.

[297] HStAM, KHR 232, fol. 43, 171v–3.

Table 12 *Trials and executions of witches in Bavarian county courts (1629–31), based on analysis of the minutes of the Court Council in Munich*[298]

Half year	Courts with witchcraft trials	Courts with executions	Number of those executed as witches	Those executed in Wemding alone
1629 I	9	2 (W,R)	5	4
1629 II	9	2 (W,I)	6	5
1630 I	14	2 (W,I)	26	25
1630 II	10	2 (W,I)	4	3
1631 I	–	1 (W)	2	2
	42	Wemding ⎫ Ingolstadt ⎬ 43 Rosenheim ⎭	43	39

Germany were reaching their peak, is the outcome of all these trials: once again excepting the events in Wemding, the trials reveal that forty-six persons were under suspicion of witchcraft (twenty men, nineteen women, seven children). Four of them were executed (three men and one woman). One of the three men, originally suspected of sorcery, was actually executed for theft (Mindelheim). Another was convicted of a real attempt at sorcery using a host, and would have been executed irrespective of whether or not he admitted a pact with the Devil (Rosenheim). Catharina Nickhlin and a baker of Ingolstadt were burned on the grounds of denunciations from outside, but these were connected with local causes of suspicion and their confessions under torture.[299] Of the other forty-two accused, twenty-one were released, eight received lighter sentences (penance in church, pilgrimage, the pillory), the fate of thirteen is unclear, but there is nothing to suggest that they were executed. None of the forty-two was sentenced to banishment. The moderation of the sentences was partly the result of the way in which the real 'offences' (popular magic) were offset against the torture undergone during the investigation ('computed *in poenam*'). In no case was any compensation paid for the imprisonment or torture, and those released only received the costs of their imprisonment. It is remarkable that persons who accused others of witchcraft without solid proof were relatively frequently and severely punished: ten such denouncers were punished in 1629–30, and it was characteristic that half of these slanders had emanated from children. As a rule children were 'beaten with the rod'

---

[298] According to an evaluation of the minute books referred to in note 289. For the regional distribution cf. the list of trials in the German edition.

[299] HStAM, KHR 229, fol. 60–1.; KHR 234, fol. 139–40. Two other persons faced such serious accusations that an execution cannot be ruled out.

and handed back to their parents.[300] While a woman slanderer escaped with a 'severe reprimand', harsher sentences were imposed on men; the minimum was a public recantation, and a 'swingeing' fine, while an over-zealous bailiff was confined in the same cell as the woman he had falsely suspected; in two cases the slanderers themselves were tortured and exposed in the pillory, and in another an additional sentence of perpetual banishment was imposed.[301]

If we bear in mind the size of the territory of the Electorate of Bavaria, these figures justify us in saying that the Franconian paradigm of persecution was successfully warded off at the height of the witch craze in southern Germany. This resistance is to be attributed to the decades of controversy on the role of denunciations, popular magic and torture in witchcraft trials, which had persisted with undiminished vehemence from the great wave of persecution in 1590 until 1630, although the debates had been more intense in some years than in others. It may be mentioned in passing that the discussions followed the rhythm of the fluctuations in agriculture, as they were concentrated in the years when accusations of witchcraft were most numerous: 1601, 1608, 1611, 1615, 1629–30. Today it is hardly possible to understand that the Franconian paradigm was averted when belief in the possibility of witchcraft was so intense. The crime of witchcraft was so grave, but at the same time criminal proceedings against it were so hazardous, that the trials in Bavaria were led by the *Regierungen* themselves, although the work was very time-consuming and disagreeable. The boundless misery of the witch trials was a psychological burden on most of the commissioners, and the assumption that the trials were mostly brought for 'base' motives (the hope of enrichment etc.) seems absurd. Such cases were harshly punished when they became known. It is clear from numerous internal complaints that the treasury did not profit from the trials.[302] When they were held it was solely because of the alleged harmful sorcery and 'for the greater honour of God'.

---

[300] Trials of children included those at Rosenheim in 1629, and at Friedberg, Kranzberg and Rain in 1630. For the full references see the list of trials in the German edition.

[301] Apart from the trials of children, the trials at Dachau, Kranzberg, and Pfaffenhofen in 1639 ended in the punishment of the denouncers or accusers, as did the trial at Bärnstein in 1629 and the Swabian trials in Augsburg in 1630 and Lauingen 1631, which were not in Bavarian territory (cf. list of trials in the German edition).

[302] Of course possessions were confiscated, but some account was taken of the social position of the survivors, since it was not desirable to drive them to despair and into the arms of the Devil. At least in the Bishopric of Augsburg, in Pfalz-Neuburg and in the Duchy/Electorate of Bavaria, the procedure resembled that outlined in Merzbacher, *Die Hexenprozesse*, 178ff. The decisive point is that except in the case of the executed *Pflegsverwalter* Sattler and the Guardian Kracker of Reichertshofen, self-enrichment by the judges seems never to have been involved (see Riezler, *Geschichte*, 240). The deficit to the treasury, which is almost always referred to in every witch hunt, and seems credible, excludes this hackneyed explanation for witch hunting in southeast Germany.

'Institutional' reasons also helped to create the background for the persecution in Wemding. Because of the war and the associated 'conquests' (Upper Palatinate, Electoral Palatinate, Upper Austria) the Court Council in Munich was much more fluid and its personnel overworked. This may have favoured the appointment of a special witch commissioner. The persistent scepticism towards denunciations and unrestricted torture continued to be beyond the comprehension of the persecution party:

> Now it is well known that the *Contrarium* is performed at Bamberg and Würzburg and several other places, for otherwise no witch would ever be taken . . . and if the denunciations were not followed up, the trials would soon . . . have to be abandoned. And one could conclude that wrong has been done to the justified . . .[303]

TRIUMPH OF THE MODERATES IN SOUTHERN GERMANY

END OF THE PERSECUTIONS BEFORE THE SWEDISH INVASION

> The Swedish army that marched into Bavaria in 1632 suppressed the witch burnings here as it did everywhere it penetrated . . .[304]

One of the oldest and most persistent *topoi* of German witchcraft research asserts that the army of Gustavus Adolphus put an end to the persecutions in southern Germany. The kernel of truth in this story is that war and persecution did not go together, in general, and that the sober Swedish Protestants were even less willing to believe tales of witchcraft than their German counterparts.[305] But otherwise this traditional view of events will not stand up to examination. After their victory over the army of the Catholic League at Breitenfeld in September 1631, the Swedish forces marched southwards and occupied Würzburg in October, Aschaffenburg in November and Bamberg at the end of January/early February 1632.[306] After the troops of Gustavus Adolphus defeated Tilly's army at Rain on the Lech in April 1632, Swabia and parts of Bavaria were also occupied. We can hardly assert that the Swedish armies had any effect in south Germany before these dates.

If we look at the chronology of the persecutions in southern Germany, we make several astonishing discoveries. On the one hand, the persecutions

[303] HStAM, GR 323/16, fol. 26v–7.
[304] Baschwitz, *Hexen*, 288, representing numerous others who repeat this prejudice. Criticised, on the other hand, by Midelfort, *Witch Hunting*, 75: 'a Swedish solution will not work for the German Southwest'. One may add: nor for the whole of south Germany!   [305] Baschwitz, *Hexen*, 269.
[306] Spindler, *Handbuch*, III/1, 226 (Endres); Wittman, 'Die Bamberger Hexenjustiz', 222.

continued unchecked in several Protestant noble territories, e.g. the County of Löwenstein-Wertheim, during the 'Swedish period'.[307] On the other hand the persecutions in the Catholic territories had ended more than a year before the Swedish invasion. The great block of territory formed by the Electorate of Bavaria had not experienced any persecutions for some time, nor had the Prince-Bishopric of Freising.[308] In the Prince-Bishopric of Augsburg, too, the persecutions had abated since the mid-1620s.[309] If we look at the territories where persecution was most pronounced, we notice that in Pfalz-Neuburg the last executions of witches took place in July 1630 (Neuburg) and August of the same year (Reichertshofen).[310] The last documented burnings of witches in the Prince-Bishopric of Eichstätt took place on 30 July 1630.[311] In the County of Oettingen-Wallerstein they ceased on 23 August 1630, except for one woman who was burned in early June 1631.[312] In Wemding, the persecution was in rapid decline from mid-June 1630; in October and November 1630 three more witches were executed, the last two following in March 1631.[313] The persecutions in the Prince-Bishopric of Würzburg also ended in 1630.[314] In the Prince-Bishopric of Bamberg, where more than 600 witches had been burned between 1625 and 1630, the executions ceased in 1630. In September 1631, before the Swedes marched into the city, the last ten prisoners under suspicion of witchcraft were released from the 'witch house' in Bamberg. New arrests had already been suspended since June 1630.[315]

In the light of these data, which are collected here for the first time, it is no longer possible to invoke an external explanation for the end of the persecutions in southeast Germany, at least in the traditional form. Gustavus Adolphus may have seemed a *deus ex machina* to contemporary Protestants, but his appearance did not have the effect on the persecutions in the region which has been attributed to it. This is also illustrated by the fact that the persecutions were not revived after the Swedes departed.

THE CRITICAL POTENTIAL IN THE REGION

In general we can say that since the wave of persecution in 1590 the Free Cities had declined to take part in further persecution. This applies in particular to the great cities of Augsburg, Memmingen, Ulm, Regensburg, Rothenburg and Nuremberg. Nuremberg above all played a role as a

---

[307] Midelfort, *Witch Hunting*, 218ff.
[308] Weber, 380f., *Veit Adam Gepeckh* 505, 569; cf. list of trials in the German edition.
[309] *Ibid.*   [310] Film 2234, 50, 85, 91; Film 3716, 31f.
[311] Film 668, 114 (Elisabeth Fingerin); Film 669, 198 (Sabina Walchin).
[312] Film 2869, 5,12,33.   [313] Schneid, 'Das Rechtsverfahren', 166.
[314] Merzbacher, *Die Hexenprozesse*, 47f.
[315] Wittmann, 'Die Bamberger Hexenjustiz', 188f., 231, 214, 216. On Zeil, Film 3085–6.

leader of opinion; several of the city's opinions on questions of witchcraft even made their way into contemporary literature.[316] The situation was more difficult in the Protestant territories, for here, as in Bavaria, more clearly defined parties had been formed. In the small Principality of Coburg there were vigorous debates at the end of the 1620s between the Lutheran clergy, who were ready to persecute, and the *Schöppenstuhl* or bench of jurors under the *Ordinarii* Winter and Drach, who insisted on an orderly procedure and refused to countenance a persecution on the pattern of the surrounding Bishoprics. They appealed to the example of the first *Ordinarius* of Coburg, Wesenbeck, and the faculties of law at Tübingen, Marburg, Altdorf and Jena.[317] As Prince Johann Casimir supported the persecutions, a special witch commissioner with wide powers was also appointed in Coburg, and more than thirty witches were burned on his authority in 1628–32.[318] According to Lory the Margravates of Ansbach and Bayreuth rejected the 'Catholic' practice of persecution,[319] but more recent studies are lacking here, as they are for the numerous Protestant noble territories. Only in the case of the Protestant County of Oettingen-Oettingen is it known that there was sharp criticism of the persecution in neighbouring Ellwangen.[320]

The hardening of confessional positions left Catholic critics at a great disadvantage, for since 1590 they had no longer been free to express open doubt of the possibility of witches' flight through the air, witches' sabbaths, intercourse with the Devil or harmful sorcery. In procedural questions too, except in Bavaria, the view that witchcraft was a *crimen exceptum* gained wide acceptance. In the Bishopric of Augsburg, for example, in the 1620s, there were constant debates about the treatment of particular suspects, for although it was agreed in principle that witches deserved special treatment, there was a certain hopelessness about these discussions.[321] In Pfalz-Neuburg, on the other hand, a critical tendency

---

[316]   Weyer, *De praestigiis daemonum* (1586 enlarged fourth German edn of 1563 original), 292; A. Praetorius, *Von Zauberey und Zauberern gründtlicher Bericht*, Heidelberg 1613, 216ff. (The second reference from Kunstmann, *Zauberwahn*, 183.) In the other cities this can be inferred from the 'absence' of executions.

[317]   Kretz, 'Der Schöppenstuhl', 72–9. *Ibid.*, 35f. biographical details on Winter and Drach. Dr Anton Winter, to whom we shall return later, is particularly interesting. Before he was called to Coburg Winter had been a professor at Tübingen. In 1621 he became *professor ordinarius* in Coburg, changed confession and employer in 1627 and became a councillor of the Bishop of Bamberg. In 1630, however, he spoke out against his employer at the Regensburg meeting of the Electors, and then, as an imperial commissioner, arranged the ending of the witch hunt in Bamberg.   [318]   Kretz, 'Der Schöppenstuhl', 65; Film 494.

[319]   Lory, 'Hexenprozesse', 303; Film 3709, 613–17.

[320]   Midelfort, *Witch Hunting*, 110–12.

[321]   HStAM, Hochstift Augsburg, NA, Akten no. 1219, 1220, 1221, 1222, 1223, 1224, 1225. The discussions always followed the same pattern. The protagonist of the persecution party, Dr Paulus zum Ackher, voted in every case for torture or execution, as in most

seems to have survived the change of confessions, and a few Catholic priests took a stand against the 'extremely questionable method of procedure'.[322] We have only indirect information, sometimes from the trial records, on the critical tendencies in the Franconian Prince-Bishoprics, since all attempts at resistance were nipped in the bud there. At any rate it is clear from the records of hearings that the witchcraft trials must have been seen as a huge injustice by some of the citizens of the towns. In the Archbishopric of Mainz, for example, a man is on record as saying

> he was amazed that people should believe such superstitious things, for they are quite impossible, and it cannot be proved from any writings, that they are to be believed . . . They should read Goedelmann . . . If he was burned, God himself must be able to practise sorcery.[323]

The priest Johann Reichard, arrested on suspicion of witchcraft in Eichstätt, also replied evasively to the urgent questions of the witch commissioners, as to whether he believed in the existence of witches and the reality of their dances and gatherings: 'I have never studied such matters; it may be so and it may not be . . .'[324] A woman beltmaker of Eichstätt complained to the witch-judge before she was burned:

> If everyone were as little a witch as she was, then there would not be a single witch in the whole town, but all of them had been wronged.[325]

Although the authorities made an effort to keep the procedure in witchcraft trials as secret as possible, the truth leaked out through many chan-

cases did the Court Councillor Johann von Gemmingen. The more cautious Chancellor of the Bishopric Dr Matthäus Wanner raised objections, mostly supported by the learned Councillor Dr Knor. The moderates used very defensive arguments, often with reservations (e.g. *ibid.*, no. 1219, fol. 258; *ibid.*, fol. 641–2, fol. 501, 524f., 547.) The persecution party knew that it could count on the support of the Prince-Bishop Heinrich V von Knöringen (1598–1646); it was sure of itself in its arguments, and regularly won the vote, even when the Chancellor voted against. Also interesting in the Bishopric of Augsburg is the attention that the government paid to the 'public opinion' that obviously existed. During the discussions on the execution of the Burgomaster of Dillingen, Conrad Schmid, as a warlock in 1624 the decisive argument was: 'Zu deme werd jedermann insgemein sagen, "Wanns ein armer Tropf gewesen, hett man seiner nit verschont."' HStAM, Hochstift Augsburg, NA, Akten no. 1222, fol. 427–9v.

[322] Schneid, 'Das Rechtsverfahren', 176. (The town priest Leonhard Mayr of Neuburg.) Here too the population allowed itself to have an opinion of its own. After the execution of a witch in Neuburg in 1630 Mayr noted in the death registers: 'Habens viele für unschuldig gehalten', Schneid, 'Das Rechtsverfahren', 142. The tendency to justify the trials in Neuburg in 1630 (cf. note 290) as in Bavaria in 1590 clearly indicates tensions; one may cite Dr Hieronymus Dickhel (see Henker, 'Zur Prospographie', 103f.) on the one hand and perhaps the Supreme Chancellor Dr Johann Zeschlin (1566–1639) (see *ibid.*, 362–6) on the other as the protagonists of these tensions. Cf. note 290.

[323] Film, 3701, 13.

[324] UBM, Cod. Ms. 214, fol. 69 (14 Sept. 1624); Spee, *Cautio*, 274, may have had this case in mind.   [325] Film 3709, 625 (Walburga Knäbin).

nels: confessors, prison warders, executioners and secret messages smuggled out of prison.[326] Prisoners also managed to escape amazingly often, which suggests that they had support from outside. Finally, as had already been the case in the persecutions of 1590, there were spectacular recantations at the executions, as at Neuburg in early 1630;[327] once again these helped to prepare the great shift in public opinion. Bavaria played a special role, at least in south Germany, for it was the scene of prolonged debates on the issues of principle between supporters and opponents of persecution. The outcome was that an 'orthodoxy' was formed among the opponents of persecution, which gained an authority far beyond southern Germany, by preparing the way for more radical critics.

THE INFLUENCE OF BAVARIA AND NUREMBERG ON THE PERSECUTIONS IN FRANCONIA

The Council is said to have stated that if so many petitions were in vain, the Court of Bamberg would be like Hell, from which there was no escape . . .[328]   (A Capuchin of Nuremberg, 25 January 1630)

Two examples will briefly illustrate the influence of the two greatest powers of the region, both of which tended to side with the opponents of persecution.

In the case of Bavaria, this influence must be thought of as more informal. Elector Maximilian, persuaded by the radical Jesuit Contzen, believed that he had to play the part, at least outwardly, of the vehement apologist of persecution.[329] Yet below the official level of the state there were possibilities of influence open to both Contzen and the so-called *politici*, of whom the Privy Councillor Dr W. Jocher was widely regarded as the leader in the 1620s (see the work of Bireley). The opinions of the University of Ingolstadt formed one of the channels of such influence. In 1625 the faculty of theology issued a sharp criticism, although with some saving clauses, of the witch trials in Eichstätt, which had already lasted for several decades, extended far beyond Middle Franconia and represented the greatest problem of the time in southern Germany. The usual procedure in Eichstätt, based on denunciations, was categorically rejected in

---

[326] Cf. on this chapter 3, pp. 194–205. We may recall the moving letter of farewell of the Burgomaster of Bamberg Junius to his daughter. Soldan *et al., Geschichte der Hexenprozesse*, II, 6–13.
[327] Schneid, 'Der Rechtsverfahren', 142 (public recantation in Neuburg). See the passage in Spee, *Cautio*, 274. Examples of escape from prison in Gänstaller, 'Zur Geschichte', 17f., Merzbacher, *Die Hexenprozesse* (2nd edn), 83f., 121.
[328] Wittmann, 'Die Bamburger Hexenjustiz', 200.
[329] Riezler, *Geschichte*, 215–20; influence of Contzen: Bireley, *Maximilian*, 143, 226.

the opinion, on the grounds that 'the guilty are hardly to be distinguished from the innocent in the very covert crime of sorcery, because of the delusions of the Devil'. 'All this excuses the judge, especially in the German Empire, if he shows himself unwilling to launch such persecutions.'

A milder form of procedure is decidedly to be preferred, for not only does it correspond more closely to the *Carolina* but it is much better at preventing great evils, such as the slandering of whole families and provinces. In places where the stricter procedure is followed, it has gone so far that it seemed as if whole towns and villages must be burned. But what would happen if, in every country of Europe, especially in the populous towns, the procedure were so conducted? How many people, especially women, would not have to be executed then? And would not people of good reputation and the really innocent also be endangered, yes even plunged into despair, because they did not feel safe from the malevolent witches?[330]

A little later critical voices were raised in Eichstätt itself. The former Ingolstadt Professor Kaspar Hell SJ, probably a son of the distinguished opponent of persecution Dr Kaspar Hell,[331] openly condemned the persecution and did not spare the Prince-Bishop himself from criticism. The ripples of this unusual event extended to Vitelleschi, the General of the Jesuit Order, who in 1629 informed the Provincial of the Upper German province:

I hear that the Prince was recently not a little insulted by the imprudent zeal of Father Kaspar Hell, who is said to have been too free in condemning that which is done on the orders of the Prince in the examination and punishment of witches and sorcerers. And I hear that the Father is so firmly convinced of his opinion that in spite of the serious warning he has had, he in no way leaves off his criticism of the Prince's measures, and his efforts to win others round to his opinion . . . [332]

---

[330] Duhr, *Geschichte der Jesuiten*, II/2, 508f. A similar opinion for Freising is found in HStAM, Hexenakten 9a, fol. 475–85, 'Consilium Juridica Facultatis Ingolstadiensis in causa der Ränersedlin wittib alhier bezichtigten Häxerey' (4 Dec. 1631). See Schrittenloher, 'Aus der Gutachtenr und Urteilstätigkeit', 326–9. The opinion admits neither denunciations nor bad reputation, nor an unusual way of life and deviant behaviour, as circumstantial evidence for the crime of witchcraft, and urges the government of the Bishopric to release the accused without torture.

[331] On Professor Kaspar Hell cf. chapter 4, pp. 230–68, and notes 111 and 115. On Kaspar Hell SJ (1588–1634) cf. notes 115 and 124. The Jesuit Hell may be identical with the Caspar Hell who was appointed professor of philosophy at Ingolstadt in 1621. Wilczek, 'Die Universität', 31. In any case Kaspar Hell SJ, after his dramatic intervention at Eichstätt, which shows little sign of slavish obedience, held important positions in Neuburg and Amberg. His contact with W. Lamormaini SJ, the confessor of Emperor Ferdinand II, also points to extensive relationships. Bireley, *Religion*, 256.

[332] Duhr, *Geschichte der Jesuiten*, II/2, 508.

We may take it as certain that the political elite in Bavaria was opposed to the persecutions in Eichstätt. The Privy Councillors Herwarth, Donnersberger and Jocher had already chosen their sides in the Bavarian controversy, as had Vice-Chancellor Richel, whose wife had been burned at Eichstätt in 1620, Abegg, the Chancellor of the Court Council, and Bittelmair, the Chancellor of the *Regierung* of Landshut, who had been powerless to prevent their close relations being burned at Eichstätt.[333] Even though there is no documentary proof, we may assume that these interested *politici* exerted some influence.

The Free City of Nuremberg became the centre of resistance to the persecutions in the Franconian Prince-Bishoprics, and the chief refuge of fugitives, especially those from the neighbouring Bishopric of Bamberg. The way in which this resistance was organised is illustrated by the activities of the Bamberg Councillor Flöckh, who fled to Nuremberg to take refuge with relatives of his wife Dorothea, nee Hofmann, who was under arrest in Bamberg. With other relatives and patricians of Nuremberg he managed not only to get a message to the Emperor through the Infanta in Brussels, but also to induce numerous imperial officials, among them the Imperial Court Councillor J.A. von Popp, to use their influence with the Prince-Bishop Johann Georg II Fuchs von Dornheim. Through the Nuremberg Capuchin Father Paris van Griepen, the Guardian of the Capuchins in Würzburg and the Guardian of the Franciscans in Bamberg were also persuaded to exert themselves on behalf of Dorothea Flöckhin. Finally a formal complaint was addressed to Emperor Ferdinand II, attacking the trials of witches in Bamberg in principle.[334]

THE END OF THE PERSECUTIONS IN SOUTH GERMANY

Fugitives from the persecution areas of Franconia fled to places where they hoped to be safe from further persecution and able to influence the fate of their relatives imprisoned at Eichstätt, Würzburg and Bamberg: besides Ingolstadt and Nuremberg, these included Vienna, Prague, Speyer and Rome.[335] Not infrequently, the campaigns of the refugees and those who took up their cause, at first for personal motives, went beyond their original occasion and took on an exemplary character. In the case of

[333] Cf. above pp. 228, 244, 270, 288.
[334] Wittmann, 'Die Bamberger Hexenjustiz', 197–202; Kunstmann, *Zauberwahn*, 173–6.
[335] Duhr, *Handbuch*, II/2 484; Wittmann, 'Die Bamberger Hexenjustiz', 209; Schrittenloher, 'Aus der Gutachten- und Urteilstätigkeit', 326; Merzbacher, *Die Hexenprozesse*, 47; Film 3726, 96 (Archive of the Ministry of the Interior, Prague, Litt. Z.J. 28, 'Schriften in Betr. dern aus dem Bisthum Bamberg in Königreich Böhmen einschleichenden Zauberinnen und Hexen de Anno 1629' – autograph letter of Emperor Ferdinand II to the Governor of Bohemia).

Dorothea Flöckhin, early in April 1630 an imperial mandate was issued calling the Prince-Bishop of Bamberg to account for the particular and general charges levelled against him. Shortly afterwards, the aged Cardinal-Archbishop of Vienna Melchior Khlesl, and Count von Fürstenberg, the President of the Imperial Court Council, also intervened with the Bishop, appealing to this mandate.[336]

The Prince-Bishop resisted not only the petitions but also the imperial mandate and 'begged' the Emperor to pay no heed to the petitioners, and in future 'most graciously to spare him in his just and very necessary work . . . from any innovations'. The case of Dorothea Flöckhin became an increasingly important precedent as a result of this confrontation. On 28 April 1630 the Bishop had the proceedings against her resumed in even harsher form. Her relations from Nuremberg, who had been warned of the impending danger, again turned to the Emperor and Pope for help. On 11 May a second and more emphatic imperial mandate was issued, forbidding the Bishop, on pain of punishment, to undertake any further proceedings against Dorothea Flöckhin. On 16 May the Prince-Bishop was informed that 'His Holiness the Pope . . . had taken steps so that her sister and relations should be granted grace . . .', and an authenticated copy of the document was enclosed with this letter. The witch Bishop of Bamberg now rushed the proceedings through: Dorothea Flöckhin was executed in the early hours of 17 May 1630, before the imperial mandate and the papal petition had arrived.[337] In two letters of protest the Nuremberg relations expressed their rage at this arbitrary act. They equated the Bishop with the murderers of Christ, and said that he had acted on the maxim, 'hasten her to the cross'. The 'voluntary' confessions of Dorothea Flöckhin were dismissed as the result of torture. It was also made clear that the Emperor and the Pope would in future 'know of ways of getting their rescripts and commands better obeyed'. This sounded like one of the many empty threats that could have been heard in those recent years, but it was soon to prove more substantial.

The opponents of persecution achieved their breakthrough at the Electoral Diet of Regensburg of 3 July–12 November 1630, which was important for the political situation in the Empire. The persecutions in Franconia, with their thousands of witch burnings, had involved so many families in suffering that the chorus of petitioners and advocates had grown to unprecedented dimensions. As early as 6 July 1630 the Prince-Bishop of Bamberg was given the alarm in a letter from a man in his confidence:

all kinds of unexpected and outrageous things are being practised against Your Grace, some of them against Your Grace's execution of

---

[336] Wittmann, 'Die Bamberger Hexenjustiz', 202f.   [337] *Ibid.*, 207f.

justice, some against your person ... humble and miserable petitions are being presented to His Imperial Majesty and the Electors and Princes present, at the special instigation of prominent and leading persons of rank, by G.H. Flöckh and two of the fugitives from the witch house in Bamberg and others . . . Now it is high time that the Prince-Bishop sought to frustrate the intrigues of his enemies, if his reputation is not to suffer irrevocable damage.[338]

Two leading witch commissioners from Bamberg, Dr Schwarzkonz and Dr Harsee, were then ordered to Regensburg to defend the inquisition against witches in Bamberg in August and September. However, their first conversation with Father Wilhelm Lamormaini SJ, the confessor of Emperor Ferdinand II, and Count von Fürstenberg, the President of the Imperial Court Council, showed them that both these men were aware of the character of the justice meted out to witches in Bamberg, and would not be reliable allies. Fürstenberg had already spoken out against the procedure applied in Bamberg, saying that where human lives were at stake, procedure should be 'all the more cautious'.[339] Lamormaini had known of the problems of the trials at Bamberg since 1628, when a letter from the Bishop of Bamberg had unexpectedly mentioned that the Vicar-General Dr Förner had several times been denounced as a witch by 'slanderous tongues', and consequently the usual procedure of imprisonment and torture was not to be applied in his case. In Munich, too, the court and Adam Contzen SJ had been informed of these events. Lamormaini was also adamantly opposed to the efforts of the witch commissioners on political grounds, as the widespread unease about the attitude of the Emperor to persecution was harming the House of Habsburg, not least in the question of the election of the King of the Romans. Lamormaini is said to have threatened the Emperor in September 1630 with refusal to give him absolution after confession, if he continued to tolerate the breaches of the law practised at Bamberg.[340]

The moving spirit behind the persecutions at Bamberg, Dr Förner, also travelled to Regensburg to defend the trials. On 5 October 1630 he explained the viewpoint of the hard-line advocates of witch burning to the 'leading Privy and other Councillors of the Empire'. Dr C. Hildebrandt, an Imperial Court Councillor, had been entrusted with the duty of reporting on the events at Bamberg,[341] and the Bamberg witch commissioners

---

[338] *Ibid.*, 210. The Bavarian delegation included the moderate Councillors Richel, Wolkenstein, Peringer and Zollern, but also the protagonist of the other party, Contzen SJ. Bireley, *Maximilian*, 114.   [339] Wittmann, 'Die Bamberger Hexenjustiz', 203.

[340] This last is asserted by Baschwitz, *Hexen*, 267, without evidence. In general Wittmann, 'Die Bamberger Hexenjustiz', 191, 210; Bauer, 'Die Bamberger Weihbischöfe', (1965), 457f. Cf. note 331 for Lamormaini's contacts with Bavarian 'dissidents'.

promised themselves a 'prospect of . . . a good handling' of the affair from him. Their optimism proved premature, since it was opposed not only by the countless influential people who petitioned on behalf of the victims, but also by the evidence of a witchcraft trial record from Bamberg which was circulated in Regensburg, and finally by the testimony of a member of the government of Bamberg, Dr Anton Winter. Winter, a former jurist at Tübingen and later at Coburg, who had converted to Catholicism in 1627, and had been appointed a Court Councillor at Bamberg, confirmed the charges of the petitioners and bore witness against the 'witch justice' practised at Bamberg.[342] Under these circumstances the representatives of the Bishop had difficulties in bringing their 'very odious and disreputable business' to a conclusion. At the end of October 1630 they had to return empty-handed.

Now the machinery was set in motion for intervention in the proceedings at Bamberg. On 20 September 1630 a third imperial mandate was issued, which sharply rebuked the failure to obey the second mandate of 1 May, and demanded that trial documents should be handed over to the Imperial Court Councillor von Popp. Once again the readiness to apply torture, the 'unusual and outrageous pain and torment' and the reckless extortion of confessions were criticised. Apart from the case of Dorothea Flöckhin this mandate also referred to three others. Early in 1631 further serious complaints had reached the Emperor, which were even clearer than their predecessors:

It is known to all the world, and a report will be produced about it from the list of prisoners submitted at Regensburg, how bloodthirstily, unchristianly and mercilessly the princely witch commissioners of Bamberg have caused such a great number, six hundred persons, to be executed without proper justice, in such a short time, as a result of an irregular procedure . . . the petitioners beseech His Imperial Majesty by the bonds of Christ to order the said witch commissoners, on pain of severe penalty, to release those who are imprisoned for alleged witchcraft . . .[343]

---

[341] Wittmann, 'Die Bamberger Hexenjustiz', 211. Dr Konradt Hildtbrandt (Hüldbrand, Hillebrand) was an Imperial Court Councillor 1619–44, and had previously been advocate of the nunnery of Rottenmünster in Swabia. His report on the Bamberg witchcraft question is also mentioned in O. von Gschliesser, *Der Reichshofrat. Bedeutung und Verfassung, Schicksal und Besetzung einer obersten Reichsbehörde von 1559–1806*, Vienna 1942, 37, 205, 214.

[342] Wittmann, 'Die Bamberger Hexenjustiz', 210; Kretz, 'Der Schöppenstuhl', 35 (cf. note 317).

[343] Wittmann, 'Die Bamberger Hexenjustiz', 214f. Dr Johann Anton Popp had been an Imperial Court Councillor since 1625. For his involvement in the Bamberg witchcraft question see Gschliesser, *Der Reichshofrat*, 214. Cf. also the Ingolstadt criticism of the

It is true that no further witches were executed at this time, but no steps were taken to release the prisoners, some of them very old, and who as a rule were confined in foul conditions. In a fourth imperial mandate of June 1631 Dr Winter was appointed President of the Witch Commission, which was now supposed to guarantee the proper conduct of the further proceedings. In subsequent letters the Prince-Bishop showed no sign of complying, so that the release of all the prisoners was delayed until the Bishop finally fled.[344] The procedure ordered in this mandate resembled that recommended by Tanner: no arrest or torture without solid grounds, the most scrupulous testing of the accusations on the spot, exact times and detailed circumstances of the alleged offence, ability to prove the accusations etc. The procedure thus imposed on the Bishop of Bamberg was exactly that which had been agreed in Bavaria thirty years earlier after tough internal discussions. In practice it corresponded to the procedure in Protestant territories and must have been well known to the imperial commissioner Dr Winter from his time in Tübingen and Coburg.

Developments in the Bishopric of Würzburg almost paralleled those at Bamberg. The excesses there had become such a byword that in northwest Germany excessive persecution was called 'Würzburgish work'. A syndic who had escaped from prison in Würzburg brought proceedings against the persecution before the Imperial Chamber Court in Speyer. According to Merzbacher, the outcome of this was a *mandatum inhibitorium* of around 1630, forbidding the Prince-Bishop von Ehrenberg to continue the inquisition against witches.[345] A fuller account of these events would be desirable. The correspondence about the persecution in Bamberg reveals that the last prisoners were released on bail in September 1631, a few weeks before the Swedish invasion.[346] As we have mentioned above, without exception all the Catholic persecutions in south Germany had already ended before the arrival of the Swedes, after being halted around the middle of the year 1630.

It may be thought fortuitous that the end of persecution in south Germany coincided with the passing of the generation of unconditional apologists for persecution whose outlook had been formed in their youth by the wave of persecutions in 1590. In Bavaria the Jesuits Gretser and Contzen died in 1625 and 1635, Duke Wilhelm V in 1626. The leading witch commissioners Dr zum Ackher (Dillingen) and Dr Kolb (Eichstätt/

witch hunts in Bamberg: note 38.

[344] For the appointment of Dr Winter: Wittmann, 'Die Bamberger Hexenjustiz', 220ff; Gschliesser, *Der Reichshofrat*, 37; Cf. also note 317. On the delaying tactics of the Bishop of Bamberg, see von Lamberg, *Criminalverfahren* 20ff.; Wittmann, 'Die Bamberger Hexenjustiz', 220f.

[345] Merzbacher, *Die Hexenprozesse*, 47; 'Wirtzbürgisch werck': Decker, 'Die Hexenprozesse', 217.   [346] Wittmann, 'Die Bamberger Hexenjustiz', 220.

Wallerstein) died in 1628 and 1630, the Vicar-General of Bamberg Dr Förner in 1630. All the witch bishops of Franconia ended their lives in exile: von Ehrenberg (Würzburg) in 1631, Fuchs von Dornheim (Bamberg) in 1633 and von Westerstetten (Eichstätt) in 1636. If the initiative in questions of witchcraft passed to the moderate forces in the region in 1630, however, 'biological' reasons ultimately played only a minor role. It was much more a case of a general shift in mentalities, as in the years before 1590. In future natural law and reason of state would limit the excesses of faith. The actual ending of the south German persecutions at the Diet of Regensburg must be seen in this context.

5 *Perpetuation through domestication 1630–1775*

CONVERGENCE OF TRIAL PROCEDURE

THE CATHOLIC POSITION AFTER 1630

Even after 1630, Catholic opinion remained divided. Supporters of persecution explicitly favoured excessive witch hunts following the pattern
imposed in the Prince-Bishoprics of Würzburg and Bamberg, as illustrated
by a broadsheet published in the latter town with episcopal approval in
1659.[1] Eight years earlier, an Ingolstadt theology professor, Georg Stengel
SJ, had criticised the secular authorities for their lethargy. He sided with
Binsfeld and Delrio, urging merciless persecutions modelled after the
conduct of Prince-Bishop Philipp Adolf of Ehrenburg in Würzburg.[2] The
reputation of Delrio as an encyclopaedic Jesuit scholar went untarnished
well into the eighteenth century and even moderate authors like Tanner
had to defer to him on certain points. Although the article on witchcraft in
Zedler's *Universal-Lexikon*, published in the mid-eighteenth century, took
an otherwise dim view of Delrio, it nevertheless affirmed the need to
execute 'magicians' in accordance with his teachings.[3]

The horror of the Franconian persecutions did usher in a mood of
caution among many Catholic authors, who took their lead from Adam
Tanner. Of course, they challenged neither the actual existence of witches
nor the elaborated concept of witchcraft. However, as these extremely
virulent persecutions had obviously claimed many innocent victims, they
agreed that the struggle against the diabolical conspiracy could no longer
be entrusted to human judgement. Tanner supported this central tenet as
well, citing the biblical parable of leaving the weeds to grow until harvest
time (i.e. the day of judgement) before separating the chaff in order to

---

[1] Hauber, *Bibliotheca*, III, 441–9. Cf. note 38 to chapter 4.
[2] Duhr, *Geschichte der Jusuiten*, II/2, 512f.; on G. Stengel SJ (1584–1651), cf. Bosl, *Biographie*, 752. Also see note 47 to chapter 4.
[3] Zedler, *Grosses Lexicon*, LIV, 38–141, article on 'Zauberey'.

avoid accidental damage to the good grain (i.e. the innocent).[4] Another Imgolstadt theologian, Paul Laymann SJ, added a full chapter on witch-craft trials to his own writings in April 1630, consciously adopting the controversial stance of his fellow Jesuit, Tanner, in 'this exceedingly im-portant matter'.[5] The plea of Bavarian Jesuits opposing persecutions lost none of its urgency in the coming decades. In his 'Christian School of Discipline', the Ingolstadt theologian, Nikolaus Cusan SJ, pleaded with preachers to douse the flame of witchcraft accusations spreading rampant-ly among the general populace. His sermons admonished listeners in no uncertain terms to imagine themselves in the position of an innocent person falsely accused who, beset with torture, had no hope of escape. Cusan reprimanded the people for blaming all their misfortunes on the activities of sorcerers and accusing others of witchcraft: 'one should sooner bite one's tongue, than say such a thing'.[6] Convinced of the innocence of many victims of the persecutions, the preacher at the court in Munich, Leopold Manzin SJ, advised that judges who ordered suspects scourged should themselves be tortured for half an hour to acquaint them with the full horror of their intention. Another Jesuit, Georg Gobat, suggested one must assume natural, rather than magical causes in cases with reasonable doubt. He personally knew of an innocent woman accused of witchcraft and sentenced to burn at the stake. He was present when the imperial delegate dispatched by Ferdinand II to end the Franconian persecutions, Dr Winter (chapter 4, pp. 319–20), reviled the uncritical acceptance of any denunication as grounds for suspicion. Gobat, quoting Tanner, also noted 'multum lenis in hac materia'.[7] In the 1660s, Bernard Frey SJ, father confessor to Elector Ferdinand Maria of Bavaria, referred for the first time to the *Cautio Criminalis* of a Roman theologian (=Friedrich Spee), as well as Tanner, to prevent the proliferation of an isolated witchcraft trial. The estate records of the Ingolstadt Jesuit, Sebastian Denich, listed a copy of the *Cautio Criminalis* among his books and his family had already sided with the opposition party for three generations. First editions of Spee's *Cautio Criminalis* made their way into the estates of other Bavarian Jesuits as well (Rinteln, 1631).[8] In 1631, the Bavarian moderate party gained a measure of administrative support as well. A noteworthy Decree of 12

---

[4] Tanner, *Theologia*, III, 984; Spee, *Cautio*, 39.
[5] Duhr, *Geschichte der Jesuiten*, II/2, 521–3. On the Laymann discussion, cf. note 124 to chapter 4.
[6] N. Cusan, *Christliche Zuchtschul*, Ingolstadt 1627, 494, 497; quoted according to Duhr, *Geschichte der Jesuiten*, II/2, 515f.
[7] L. Mancini, *Passio D.N. Jesu Christi nova-antiqua*, Munich 1663, 817–21; quoted according to Duhr, *Geschichte der Jesuiten*, III, 775. G. Gobat, *Opera Omnia*, Munich 1681. Gobat often commented on witchcraft, e.g. *ibid.*, I, 292f.; II, 709f.; quoted according to Duhr, *Geschichte der Jesuiten*, II/2, 776.   [8] Duhr 'Zur Biographie', 228–31.

January 1631 issued by Elector Maximilian promised clemency and discretion to those who voluntarily confessed to a priest and turned themselves in to the authorities as witches.[9] Naturally, this was a slight gesture and even pious individuals like Tanner and the Tyrolean Jesuit, Rochus Pirchinger, while favouring a bloodless alternative in the struggle against witches, remained convinced of their existence.[10]

Heated debate on witchcraft in Bavaria precluded persecutions as virulent as those in other Catholic territories, so that the shift after 1630 was lasting and less abrupt. The climate of opinion on the question of witchcraft changed during the 1630s and 1640s. In Bavaria, Tanner's success encouraged the publication of more drastic, indeed radical demands in the early 1630s, among them polemic tracts by Spee, the Jesuit, and Meyfahrt, a Lutheran.[11] While Tanner vaguely alluded to Nero's persecutions of the Christians, Spee publicly declared that witchcraft trials targeted 'countless innocents daily' and one might doubt whether there were really any witches at all. Spee employed all of Tanner's arguments, including references to letters drafted by the faculties of German and Italian universities for use in the Munich debates of 1601 and 1602 and to the execution of the witch-judge of Wemding in 1613.[12] His head-on style attacked hypocritical clergymen, ivory-tower intellectuals oblivious to the terrible realities of the trials (here he meant his fellow Jesuit, Delrio), uncritical jurists and incompetent princes, an unusual method of presentation, originating as it did from a Catholic perspective. In Jesuit circles, Spee's authorship of the *Cautio Criminalis* of 1631 was undisputed from the onset and a 1641 bibliography of the order notes that the work had been received with enthusiasm.[13]

The advent of critical public opinion necessitated deliberations on tactical issues. In 1626, Suffragan Förner of Bamberg could view virulent witch-hunting as a badge of honour; in his opinion, it enhanced the purity of the faith. However, after the great wave of persecutions from 1626 to 1630, many influential Catholics concluded that such excesses actually damaged the reputation of their religion, since some zealous theoreticians

[9] HStAM, Hesenakten 9 a, fol. 488–91. Suspicions of witchcraft in the capital at Munich again provided motivation for this decree. Cf. also Riezler, *Geschichte*, 266f.

[10] Duhr, *Geschichte der Jesuiten*, II/2, 497. Rapp, *Die Hexenprozesse*, has already noted that many leading Catholic opponents of persecution came from Tyrol: Tanner, Laymann, Tartarotti, Sterzinger. Interestingly, penal procedure was generally milder there than in Germany: Bücking, *Kultur*, 133.

[11] Cf. note 122 to chapter 4. Even Riezler noted the prudent reaction to the great plague of 1634. Riezler, *Geschichte*, 269. Cf. also A. Bechthold, 'Hexen im bayrischen Lager bei Durlach 1643', *Alemannia* 44 (1917), 138–44. when an epidemic among livestock resulted in reports of witchcraft to Munich. Orders from Munich managed to calm the enthusiasm of the local officials. Around the same time and without reference to the central authorities, Bavarian troops burned witches near Schwäbisch Hall. Midelfort, *Witch Hunting*, 76f.   [12] Spee, *Cautio*, 66, 32.

[13] Duhr, *Geschichte der Jesuiten*, II/2, 531.

of persecution even identified frequent churchgoing, apparent piety, as well as inadequate religiosity all as signs of witchcraft. The ecclesiastical advisers pressuring Emperor Ferdinand II were certainly motivated by tactical considerations.[14] As mentioned previously, complaints from ecclesiastical territories also found a receptive audience in Pope Urban VIII. The Bolognese letter of opinion of 1602 referred to milder judicial procedures employed by the Italian Inquisition and, shortly thereafter, witchcraft persecutions in Spain met with massive critique, resulting in their eventual suppression by the Inquisition itself. A papal constitution of 1623 (*Omnipotentis Dei*) ordered that sorcerers might only be executed if they caused the death of another person and never for lesser offences.[15] Instructions were also released criticising previous trial procedures in a fashion reminiscent of the Munich debates after 1600: denunciations were accepted too quickly, as were rumours, the application of torture was undertaken too lightly in the absence of hard evidence, the penchant to associate all manner of apparitions or events with witchcraft was to be avoided, differentiations needed to be made between superstition and witchcraft, legal defense was permitted, the approval of the higher authorities had to be sought before applying torture, torture should not be repeated without sufficient cause, etc.[16] At first, all these instructions were distributed in manuscript form, but then, in 1657, a printed papal instruction appeared, not as radical as Spee's recommendations, but in precise accordance to the views of the moderate party in Germany, particularly those of Tanner. Made public in the 1630s, these admonitions to moderation manifested a decisive partisanship and, by 1657, supporters of persecution could not theoretically oppose them. They might ignore them in practice, as some-

---

[14] Tanner, *Theologia*, III, 984f. Baschwitz, *Hexen*, 267 (to Ferdinand II).

[15] Rapp, *Die Hexenprozesse*, 28; Riezler, *Geschlichte*, 267.

[16] Riezler, *ibid.*; Baschwitz, *Hexen*, 285; German translation in A. Dettling, Die Hexenprozess im Kanton Schwyx, Schwyz 1907, 42–54; 'Grundlicher Underricht, wie ein rechtlicher Process mit den Unholden, Zauberen und Teuffelbeschweren solle angestellt werden', with the annotation 'getruckht in der Päpstlichen Truckery 1657'. The meaning of this instruction has been widely considered in secondary literature. Riezler, *ibid.*, claimed that this instruction was meaningless outside Italy. Dettling, Hexenprozesse, 42, could establish the contrary for Switzerland; Paulus, *Hexenwahn*, 273–6, could prove its efficacy in Germany, adding that this instruction circulated outside Italy as early as the 1630s. In 1641, it was quoted by a papal Inquisitor, Carena, in his *Tractatus de officio S. Inquisitionis*. Lea, *Materials*, II, 950–2, gives evidence that the instruction must have been composed at the beginning of the reign of Pope Urban VIII (1623–44), in an attempt to counter the bull *Omnipotentis Dei*, decreed by Gregory XV (1621–3) in 1623, which, though mild for Germany, was quite severe for Italian conditions. Under these circumstances, an early copy in the SBM, Cgm. 6051b is particularly interesting since it suggestions reception southeast Germany. It carries the title *Instructio pro Formandis Processibus in Causis Strigarum, Sortilegiorum et Maleficiorum*. Cf. Lea, *Materials*, II, 950; Paulus, *Hexenwahn*, 274, note 1. The instruction was later reprinted in the appendix of a regional edition of Spee's *Cautio Criminalis*, Augsburg 1731.

times happened in the south where the Inquisition's stance was also moderate, but one can reasonably assume that the German Catholic Church, still looking to Rome for its lead, was liable to have recourse to such a document or to direct inquiries toward Rome.

Subsequent Prince-Bishops in Freising, Regensburg and especially the Schönborn-Bishops of Franconia harboured little conviction toward persecutions. Johann Philipp of Schönborn, heavily influenced by Spee, ensured that the Prince-Bishoprics of Würzburg and Mainz remained free of persecution in the mid-seventeenth century.[17] When the County of Isenburg-Büdingen inquired of the University of Würzburg in 1651 whether, after a twenty-year hiatus, persecutions should be initiated again, the jurists distanced themselves from previous practices. Despite some thirty denunciations presented against the accused, the Würzburg jurists could 'find neither grounds nor sufficient cause in any of the matters considered here to advise arrest, much less torture, with an untainted conscience'. Theoretically, they supported their position with the same dilemmas already present in Spee, Tanner and the Munich debates. They held that the persons denounced and executed for witchcraft in 1630 were either innocent, in which cause denunciations arising from torture were untrustworthy, or were actually witches. However, in the latter case, the accusations were all the more untrustworthy, because the devil was the greatest liar on earth and his minions, the witches, simply learned this trait from their master. 'And so, it truly follows that no such legal methods or evil persons should or can be very likely to produce witches or sorcerers.'[18]

The legal opinion delivered by the jurists of Würzburg in 1651 demonstrates that even the authorities in the Franconian bishoprics had assumed the posture of other moderate Catholics following the forced conclusion of the persecutions in the 1620s, resulting in an end to large witch trials, despite the continued survival of the elaborated concept of witchcraft.

To wit that this trial . . . is also so couched with errors to the extent that even all the most intelligent men are unable to trust in their understanding, and all wit and reason is held captive. Therefore, it can actually be held that once one has embarked on such witch trials and afforded several years to them, that the number of those who should be punished

---

[17] The famous quote from Leibniz's *Theodizee* concerning Spee's influence on Johann Philipp of Schönborn (1605–73). Schönborn experienced the persecutions of 1629 as a member of the cathedral chapter in Würzburg; had contact with Spee during exile in Cologne, 1631–4; 1642–73, Bishop of Würzburg, from 1647 Bishop of Mainz as well; Bosl, *Biographie*, in extended form in Soldan *et al.*, *Geschichte der Hexenprozesse*, II, 189f. The findings of the *H-Sonderkommando* confirm the absence of witch executions in the areas ruled by Schönborn. On Freising, Weber, *Veit Adam Gepeckh*, 380f., 505, 569; on Regensburg, Schwaiger, *Kardinal*, 77f., 251f., 290.   [18] Film 3784, 5–19.

mounts more and more, to the point that there is no hope of an end to the burnings, until the entire country would be burned and executed . . . And just as no prince or lord has ever been found, who has not been forced to put an end to witch trials, so has there never been anyone able to end them, even when he wanted to do so; instead, the fires themselves have had to end the affair. And since this is such a difficult and demanding task, whose end is not easy to bring about, it is all the more difficult to consider this at the beginning with the ignition of the flame.[19]

The uppermost priority had shifted from the reckless elimination of a diabolical conspiracy to the defence of the innocent from the clutches of over-zealous authorities. Naturally, investigations conducted against persons suspected of witchcraft continued. Nonetheless, at least in so far as we can tell from the research of the *H-Sonderkommando*, spot-checks in the Court Council protocols of Munich and the secondary literature, the number of executions for sorcery and witchcraft declined dramatically in all larger Catholic territories after the mid-third of the seventeenth century.[20] Trial procedures began to resemble those in Protestant regions and executions limited to individual persons became the order of the day.

CONVERGENCE OF TRIAL PROCEDURES

The advent of relative moderation on the Catholic side meant conformity in dealing with witchcraft. The novel disregard for denunciations made trial proceedings more uniform, whether or not this occurred because the belief in witches' flight had fallen into disrepute or simply because the authorites no longer believed the testimony of accused sorcerers. The fear expressed by supporters of persecution, that persecutions would be rendered untenable if denunciations lost their credibility, bore itself out. After 1630, only isolated individuals tended to be burned as witches, while related trials arising from denunciations ended in lesser punishments or in clemency. Surprisingly, a general convergence of trial procedures was as much the result of moderation on the Catholic side as of the new hard line among some Protestant authorities, who displayed a greater willingness to execute witches than before the Thirty Years War.

This change is clearly discernible in the imperial cities during the early decades of the seventeenth century,[21] where the willingness to execute individual witches increased just as the absolute number of executions began to decline.[22] There were executions in Schweinfurt and Nuremberg

---

[19] *Ibid.*, 11f.   [20] Cf. chapter 2, pp. 35–64.   [21] *Ibid.*
[22] Absolute figures for executions in Augsburg and Memmingen are found in Schuhmann, *Der Scharfrichter*, 142–4.

during the second decade of the century, as well as in Rothenburg and Augsburg during the third decade and in Memmingen and Dinkelsbühl in the sixth decade.

All told, twenty-one witch trials leading to executions occured in the thirteen imperial cities located in what is today the *Bundesland* of Bavaria, while only eleven such trials have been identified for the preceding 150 years.[23] Although urban Protestants viewed the possibility of witches' flight and witches' sabbaths with growing scepticism, the number of trials and executions related by denunciations increased. Apart from individual trials and major persecutions, a third type of trials made its appearance, referred to in recent literature as 'chain-reaction trials'.[24] Chain-reaction trials placed a premium on the collection of additional evidence while reviewing the guilt or innocence of any persons denounced. Even if the testimony of the 'first witch'[25] failed to achieve the necessary evidential standards, other persons were incriminated by their confessions or by third-party testimony. In this fashion, spontaneous concentrations of executions occurred in several places, though to speak of them as actual persecutions is a misnomer. Dinkelsbühl (1656–8) and Memmingen (1663–8) witnessed just such chain-reaction trials. The same pattern appeared in Augsburg, demographically depleted after the War, and events in Wasserburg on Lake Constance in the Catholic territories of the Fuggers justify reckoning its trials among the chain-reactions rather than the persecutions.[26]

In addition to the quantitative convergence in terms of executions, the opposing confessions also began to conform to a similar qualitative model. Catholic authorities like Tanner persisted in their acceptance of the elaborated concept of witchcraft, but admitted that witches' flight, shape-changing and other controversial components of the cumulative concept were actually rare. Therefore, confessions to that effect were, more often than not, the product of a diabolical illusion. After the War, Protestant authorities apparently placed greater value on traditionally abhorrent signifiers of witchcraft, e.g. the *stigma diaboli*. Some Protestant magistrates, like those in Memmingen, also took account of confessions implicating other co-conspirators ostensibly spotted at a witches' sabbath.[27]

[23] Hesse, 'Der Strafvollzug', 43–6; Kunstmann, *Zauberwahn*, 88–102; Schmidt, 'Vordringender Hexenwahn', 86ff.; Riezler, *Geschichte*, 226f.; Eggmann, *Geschichte*, 147; Freiner, 'Hexenprozesse'.   [24] Unverhau, Akkusationsprozess', 115.
[25] On the term 'first witch' cf. chapter 3, pp. 158–82.
[26] Wiedemann, 'Hexenprozesse'; On the chain-reaction trials in Augsburg 1685/86 and Memmingen 1663–8 cf. the list of trials in the appendix to the German edition. On Dinkelsbühl, Greiner, 'Hexenprozesse'.
[27] Kunstmann, *Zauberwahn*, 99; Eggmann, *Geschichte*, 147. StadtA Memmingen, Schubl. 354/6.

12. *Warhaffte Historische Abbild: und kurtze Beschreibung, was sich unlangst in (. .) Augspurg (. . .) zugetragen (. . .)* Augsburg 1654. Fifteen woodcuts describe the pact with the Devil, exorcism, the trial and execution as a witch of Maria Bihlerin (4).

This rapprochement on the question of witchcraft opened avenues for the ideological exchange of expert opinion across confessional boundaries and it was by no means clear from the onset which side would adopt the harsher and which the milder stance. For example, an opinion drafted by the town council of the imperial city Lindau legally supported trial proceedings in the Catholic territory of the Fuggers in Wasserburg,[28] legal opinions were requested from Ulm, Ingolstadt and Tubingen for a 1649 trial in Biberach,[29] and from Marburg and Ingolstadt for a trial in the County of Löwenstein-Wertheim.[30] The imperial city Kempten sought advice from the councils in Augsburg and Ulm in 1665; the authorities in Ulm favoured clemency and those in Augsburg recommended torture.[31] The Catholic town council of Lauingen in the Palatinate-Neuburg consulted authorities in Dillingen and Ulm in 1664. In this case, the scholars of the imperial city spoke out in favour of torture, while the jurist from episcopal Dillingen opposed that severity, stating that 'human blood is not calves' blood'.[32] In 1673, a woman was burned in the Prince-Abbacy of Kempten, but some years later, in 1687, the Prince-Abbot forbade the extradition of a peasant woman to a Protestant imperial city, as he felt that proper evidence was lacking.[33]

These cases suffice to elucidate the nature of the shift and although it meant little for those tried and/or executed, the earlier threat to whole communities had been removed. Apart from a few chain-reaction trials, individuals from the urban and rural underclasses tended to be victimised – in this case, exceptions did validate the rule.[34] One can only guess at the social-psychological effects of these developments, since an absence of trials produced little documentation. It seems likely that the ruling elites lost interest in trials as soon as they themselves became targets, although this is just one of several possible configurations. However, this was a decisive aspect of the continuation of trials in greatly reduced form: the ecclesiastical and secular authorities were no longer threatened because of the restrictive trial procedures. Additionally, the conformity of trial procedure reduced the potential for social conflict. In that sense, the domestication of trials simultaneously facilitated their perpetuation.

[28] Wiedemann, 'Hexenprozesse', Nos. 2 and 3.   [29] Film 3636, 1–4.
[30] Midelfort, *Witch Hunting*, 142.
[31] O. Erhard, *Ein Hexenprozesse in der Reichstadt Kempten von 1664–1665*, 17–21.
[32] Rückert, 'Der Hexenwahn', 17–21.
[33] Schuhmann, *Der Scharfrichter*, StA Neuburg, Reichsstift Kempten No. 110, fol. 195–234.
[34] Cf. chapter 5, pp. 331–43.

NOVEL POLARITIES AND STRUCTURAL CHANGES OF TRIALS

CONJUNCTURES OF THE WITCHCRAFT THEME 1630–1750

Researchers generally agree that the major European witchcraft persecutions from 1580 to 1630 were followed by another minor wave of persecutions beginning in the early 1660s. A gradual ebbing of persecutions is also assumed for the period after 1680 and it has even been suggested that major works opposing persecution published at the end of century by Bekker and Thomasius were too late to have any real impact.[35] However, this view ignores the fact that developments in the west and north of Europe during the seventeenth century – naturally not just in the area of witchcraft – took a different course from those in central and southeast Europe, where, to some degree, time appeared to stand still. The electoral Saxon jurist, Benedict Carpzow, confirmed trial procedures along the lines prescribed in the *Malleus Maleficarum* and the writings of Bodin and Delrio,[36] followed by Kaspar Manzius in Bavaria and, in the early eighteenth century, Christoph and Hermann Anton von Chlingensberg,[37] as well as the Tyrolean instructor of law, Frölich von Frölichsburg.[38] Fundamental attitudes were only transformed in southeast Germany and the neighbouring Habsburg territories after 1750–60.

The German southeast witnessed a re-activation of the witchcraft theme after the 1660s, especially conspicuous in the years around 1665 and 1670. The Bavarian Mandate on Sorcery and Witchcraft was reprinted at these times.[39] The next temporal concentration of trials occurred in the years from 1677 to 1681 and, once again, the electoral authorities re-issued a general order in 1677 designed to direct the attention of county judges to the threat

---

[35] Schormann, *Hexenprozesse* (1981), 52–63; *Hexenprozesse* (1977), 158f.
[36] Soldan *et al.*, *Geschichte der Hexenprozesse*, II, 211–14.
[37] Schneid, 'Das Rechtsverfahren', 139ff. Schrittenloher, 'Aus der Gutachter- und Urteil-stätigkeit', Manzius (1606–77) was one of the most important legal scholars of the seventeenth century. On his life, see Spindler, *Handbuch*, II, 805 (Kraus); Bosl, *Biographie*, 505; Henker, 'Zur Prosopographie', 211–13; *ADB* 20, 281–5. Court Councillor in Dillingen 1630, Professor at Ingolstadt 1636, 1653 Chancellor in Neuburg, 1660 succeeded Dr Kaspar Denichs (cf. note 114, chapter 4) as Ordinarius at the University of Ingolstadt. v. Chlingensberg (1651–1720) taught law from 1677 to 1720 at the University. His son, H. A. v. Chlingensberg (1685–1755) succeeded him from 1707 to 1755. Bosl, *Biographie*, 113.
[38] Soldan *et al.*, *Geschichte der Hexenprozesse*, II, 215–18; Riezler, *Geschichte*, 272; Byloff, *Hexenglaube*, 128, 144. Lived from 1657 to 1729.
[39] *Landtgebott wider die Aberglauben, Zauberey, Hexerey und andere sträffliche Teufelskünste*, Munich 1665. This matter frequently occupied the Court Council: HStAM, KHR 366, fol. 40v, fol. 288; KHR 367, fol. 124, 148, 165v.

13. *Warhaffte Beschreibung des Urthels (...)* Augsburg 1666. Witch trial of Simon Altseer of Rottenbuch. Six woodcuts show the pact with the Devil, the witches' flight and witches' sabbath, 'weather cooking', bewitchment of humans and animals, exorcism of the Devil, torture inflicted on the way to the execution, and execution before the gates of the city of Munich.

of sorcery.[40] During those five years, witches were also hunted in the Prince-Bishoprics of Salzburg and Freising, the Imperial Cities of Augsburg and Memmingen and the Protestant principalities of Coburg and Ansbach[41] making it impossible to associate this wave of trials solely with the publication of the Mandate.

Additional concentrations followed in 1685, 1689–94, 1699–1703, 1710–16, 1720–2, 1724, 1728–30, 1740, the mid-1740s, and 1749–56. Only thereafter were trials for witchcraft and sorcery so infrequent that concentrations can no longer be identified. Temporal concentrations still appeared between 1730 and 1760 and, even if these trials only targeted single individuals, they continued to end in executions. There were isolated incidents of mass trials involving more than ten arrests and numerous burnings until 1730. The last major persecution took place in Freising in 1721/22, when some 200 persons fell under suspicion of witchcraft, more than 20 were arrested and, in the end, 11 were executed.[42] Protestant authorities in the region executed their last witch in 1699,[43] while Catholics burned witches in the years 1749–56, 1766 and 1775.[44]

A comparison of conjectures in the witchcraft theme with agricultural prices reveals close, if not complete agreement. In Munich and Augsburg, rye prices were quite high during the years 1660–6, but not in 1670. Similarly, prices were high in 1674–80, 1688–94, 1698–1704, 1709–13, 1716–17, 1719–21, 1724, 1726–31, 1738–42, 1749–51, 1755–8, 1762, 1768–72.[45] In relation to figures presented by Abel and Goubert, one recognises that many of these maximum-price years are actually supraregional or international events and Goubert emphasises the high rates of mortality in the 1660s, the early 1690s and around 1710.[46] Local sources could offer

---

[40] 'Generale an alle Regierungen und Gerichte dieses Rentamts die Zauberey und abergläubische Sachen betr', in: HStAM, KHR 415, fol. 192v–193 (5 Nov. 1677). On the wave of trials in these years cf. chapter 5, pp. 344–54, as well as the list of trials in the appendix to the German edition.

[41] *Ibid.* On Coburg, see Films 494 and 1955 (Neustadt bei Coburg). On the Margravate Ansbach, Film 773 (Feuchtwangen).

[42] HStAM, Hexenakten 9, 9b, 9c, 93, 9f. Film 803. Cf. in general the list in the appendix to the German edition.

[43] *Ibid.*, list of trials. However, this is only true of the German southeast, with its small proportion of Protestant authorities. The University of Tübingen did sanction one execution for witchcraft in the second decade of the eighteenth century (Gehring, 'Der Hexenprozess', 15–47) (1938). In Schweinfurt, a serious witch trial ensued in 1723 (R. Rösel, 'Die letzte Hexe in Schweinfurt anno 1723' in *Schweinfurter Heimatblätter* 12 (1929), No. 9), though it ended in acquittal. As late as 1766 an old woman suspected of witchcraft died in the jail of imperial Nuremberg. Bock, *Zur Volkskunde*, 64.

[44] Cf. chapter 5, pp. 344–54. Only southeast Germany!   [45] Elsas, *Umriss*, I, 562–5, 596–9.

[46] P. Goubert, 'Demographische Probleme im Beauvaisis des 17. Jahrhunderts', in Honegger, *Schrift*, 198–219, esp. 209ff. and 213–17; W. Abel, *Agrarkrisen und Agrarkonjunktur. Eine Geschichte der Land- und Ernährungswirtschaft Mitteleuropas seit dem hohen Mittelalter*, Hamburg/Berlin 1966, 152–81.

more precise information on the background to concentrations of trials without necessarily suggesting a mechanistic derivation of witchcraft accusations resulting from general crisis conditions (climatic adversity, crop failure, famines, epidemics, etc.).[47]

The nearly unbroken persistence of witch trials into the fourth decade of the eighteenth century is remarkable, even at a markedly decreased rate. Here we can differentiate the Catholic southeast from those areas affected by the Enlightenment early on.

NEW 'CATHOLIC' MASS TRIALS

Protestants ceased executing witches in the Imperial Cities and smaller territories at the end of the seventeenth century. Protestant proponents of persecution who had played an important role in the trials of the 1670s and 1680s, like the Augsburg theologians Ehinger and Spitzel, had died. The next generation of Lutheran theologians and jurists came from universities which either did not entertain traditional witchcraft theories at all or, if so, then did so only in a very restrictive form. Even before this great transformation around the year 1700, which is identified with the University at Halle and the person of Thomasius, the academies of west and north Germany had already been heavily influenced by progressive ideas coming from the countries of western Europe. After 1680, the number of death sentences authorised by these universities fell dramatically, ending completely within a surprisingly short period of time, e.g. in Tübingen after 1717.[48]

The end of executions by 'Protestants' stood in stark contrast to the renewed escalation of witch trials on the part of Catholic authorites. In this region, two important persecutions took place between 1675 and 1680. The presence of Catholic princes willing to persecute helped bridge the difficult gap between legal and illegal persecutions. Since both cases are of primary importance, but still relatively unknown, they are presented here in abridged form:

Case 1   In the County of Vaduz, persecutions in the years 1648–51 and 1677–80 claimed over 300 victims, about 10 per cent of the population. The first wave of persecutions was ended endogenously, when accusations threatened the family of the official in charge. With no apparent end in

---

[47] Cf. above, chapter 2, pp. 158–82.

[48] Gehring 'Der Hexenprozess' (1938), 32. Protestant universities are compared in Schormann, *Hexenprozesse* (1977), 9–44. On the Augsburg theologian: L. Lenk, *Augsburger Bürgertum im Späthumanismus und Frühbarock (1580–1700)*, Augsburg 1968, 54–9. Cf. also note 43 above.

14. *Relation oder Beschreibung (...)*, Augsburg 1669. The trial of Anna Eberlerin for witchcraft. Six woodcuts show the pact with the Devil, witches' flight and a witches' sabbath, the hearing, the abduction of two children, the witch being led to her execution, and her execution itself (6).

sight, the second persecution was finally terminated dramatically. The territorial estates and clergy turned to the Emperor, who sent Prince-Abbot Rupert Bodman of Kempten as acting commissioner to preside over the matter. The Prince-Abbot was soon convinced of the unlawful nature of the proceedings, much influenced by the sadistic inclinations and fiscal interests of the territorial prince, Ferdinand Carl Franz von Hohenems. The Prince-Abbot, working closely with the Tyrolean administration in Innsbruck, the University of Salzburg and the Imperial Court Council in Vienna, arranged to depose and arrest the imperial count of Vaduz, who spent the rest of his life in a prison in the territory of Kempten. Prince-Abbot Bodman administered the estate from 1681 until 1712 and his initiative put a radical end to the persecution. Among other things, he criticised the use of trials for personal enrichment, arrests without sufficient evidence and the infliction of 'unchristian torments'.[49]

Case 2   A persecution was conducted in the Bishopric of Salzburg from 1677 to 1681 which claimed some 140 lives. A number of victims originated from Tittmoning, Laufen and Teisendorf, Bavarian locales which fell under the jurisdiction of the Prince-Bishop at that time. Several other areas in neighbouring Bavaria were also affected, such as Reichenhall, Traunstein, Trostberg and the princely provostship of Berchtesgaden, all drawn in on the basis of denunciations produced by the mass trials in Salzburg.[50] In contrast to the trials in Vaduz, the persecution in Salzburg was 'legitimate'. The criminal-law commentator, Frölich von Frölichsburg, ensured that this persecution would go down in the annals of criminal history as the 'Zauberer-Jackl' (Little-Sorcerer Jack) trials, cited approvingly by the article 'Sorcery' in Zedler's Universal-Lexikon in 1749 as a 'most recent example'.[51] The secret of this persecution's success lie in the choice of targets, who were primarily beggars or indigent children rather than respected burgers or peasants. The actual or ostensible leader of the band of child-beggars, 'Zauberer-Jackl' or Jakob Koller, was the son of a skinner. The victims lacked influential patrons, rich relations or access to other networks of social support, which explains how some 140 persons could perish at the stake around 1680 without any opposition.[52]

[49] O. Seger, 'Der letzte Akt im Drama der Hexenprozesse in der Grafschaft Vaduz und Herrschaft Schellenbert', in Jb. d. Hist. Ver. d. Fürstentums Liechtensteins 57 (1957), 137–227, esp. 156–69; 59 (1959), 331–49. HHStA Wien, Bestand Reichshofrat, Denegata Antiqua, Karton 96.   [50] Nagl, 'Der Zauberer-Jackl Prozess', I, 522–39.
[51] Zedler, Grosses Lexicon, LXI (1749), 84, 90, 123, 135; Rapp, Die Hexenprozesse, 33.
[52] Byloff, Hexenglaube, 116ff. For a list of those executed, see Nagl, 'Der Zauberer-Jackl Prozess', I, 522–39.

The 'Zauberer-Jackl' trials in Salzburg made a resounding impression on all of the surrounding regions; in Tyrol, Bavaria, Carinthia, Styria and, naturally, many tiny territorial fragments. 'Zauberer-Jackl' became a legend in his own lifetime and, although the authorities hunted for him throughout the region, he was never found.[53] This Salzburg persecution differed greatly from all earlier ones: more than 70 per cent of those executed were younger than twenty-two years and the same proportion of victims were males. Over 90 per cent of those arrested, including all of those executed, were beggars, mostly members of vagrant bands of children, supposedly lead by 'Zauberer-Jackl'.[54]

THE NEW WITCHES: FROM OLD WOMAN TO YOUNG MAN

The 'Zauberer-Jackl' trials in Salzburg guided future developments in southeast Germany. The pattern of these trials was repeated again and again in form, if not extent, between 1680 and 1730. The largest of the later persecutions took place in the Prince-Bishopric of Freising in the years 1720–2, confirming the pattern of the 'Zauberer-Jackl' trials: all the old women were set free, three middle-aged female beggars and eight 'boy-sorcerers' between the ages of fourteen and twenty-three (average age: sixteen) were executed as witches.[55] Statistically speaking, the victims of this period contrasted sharply with those of the major persecutions: young men or 'boy-sorcerers' were targeted rather than old women.

A few 'traditional' trials continued to target old women, but popular interpretations of magic had fallen into such disrepute that one can identify three other stereotypes which explain the drastic rise in suspicion directed at men: apart from the boy-sorcerer trials, there are also repeated

---

[53] *Ibid.*, 407; Moser, *Chronik*, 219f.; Schattenhofer, 'Beiträge', 133; StadtA Memmingen, Schubl. 354, No. 7, *Copia Schreibens . . . sub dato 7. Dezember 1678, den Zauber Jackele betreffend.* Feared was an infiltration by 'Little Sorcerer Jack', already referred to as the 'most famous sorcerer, witch master and seducer of youth'. A reward of 100 to 500 Reichsthalers was offered for his apprehension by the Elector of Bavaria.

[54] Nagl, 'Der Zauberer-Jackl Prozess', I, 522–39. However, the hunting of vagrants and beggars as sorcerers has a longer tradition in Austria than in Germany. Byloff, *Hexenglaube*, 48 (which mentions the connection of sorcery and vagrancy in 1580), 67, 70f., 76, 80ff., 88, 91f., etc. In 1654, a female beggar in Carinthia admitted: 'All beggars can make weather; if she got off, then she intended to make use of this art in revenge.' *Ibid.*, 92. A close connection between begging and sorcery was also noted by V. C. B. Ave-Lallemant, *Das deutsche Gaunertum in seiner sozialpolitischen, literarischen und linguistischen Ausbildung zu seinem heutigen Bestande*, 1916, 65f., 70f., 196–201. In Bavaria, both themes were connected for the first time in the great witch trial of 1600 at Munich. Kunze, *Der Prozess*.

[55] Cf. note 42 above. In general, chapter 5, pp. 344–54.

examples of trials targeting families[56] and treasure-seekers. All three share a common, real and verifiable link between the 'first witch' and those persons denounced by him/her, far less tenuous than unifying concepts like mutual attendance at a witches' sabbath.

Trials for treasure-seeking Trials for treasure-seeking were already being conducted in the sixteenth century, but the crime became very fashionable in the last third of the seventeenth and first half of the eighteenth centuries, as judges confronted growing numbers of diviners in their courts. It was associated with witchcraft since treasure-seeking involved all manner of arcane formulations, spells and the invocation of demons. According to demonologists, this crime implied a tacit pact with the devil rather than a formal one.[57] The crime of treasure-seeking is characterised by the existence of actual groups of people, mostly middle-aged men, who acted in common. Most groups were led by an 'educated' individual, a schoolteacher, town councillor, etc., and usually included a person acquainted with magic, perhaps a white witch, fortuneteller or executioner.

Several examples may illustrate the significance of trials for treasure-hunting during this period. According to Court Council protocols, investigations of suspected witchcraft were conducted in sixteen counties of the Electorate of Bavaria in 1670; six cases related to treasure-seeking. The largest trial involved seventeen people from the counties of Vohburg and Neustadt/Donau, among them a town councillor, a judge and a schoolmaster.[58] Thirteen counties conducted inquiries in 1677, nine for treasure-

---

[56] Nagl, 'Der Zauberer–Jackl Prozess', I. This tendency is reflected in the titles of relevant monographs, e.g. R. M. Pleyer, 'Der Prozess Schuster (1728–1734)', MA thesis, Munich 1983; or M. Kunze, *Der Prozess Pappenheimer*, Ebelsbach 1981. Contemporary terminology corresponded to this usage: the protocols of the Munich Court Council referred to the major witch trials in the provincial administration of Straubing, County Haidau, of 1689–94 as a 'Grueberischer Hexenprozesse'. HStAM, KHR 469, fol. 21v; KHR 470, fol. 106v–107; KHR 473, fol. 47–9.

[57] *Landgebott wider die Aberglauben, Zauberey, Hexerey und andere sträffliche Teufelskünste* (1611), fol. X, para. 4: 'Es beschehe nun das angemast Wahrsagen durch Spiegel oder Glass, durch Christall oder Parillen, durch Ring, durch Sieb oder Schär, oder durch Beckh, oder auf was weiss und weeg es immer beschehen kan oder mag, so kan es nit wol anders als per spiritus familiaren und heimbliche vermeintliche gefangene oder beschworne böse Geister zuegehen, und seyn solche Leuth der Zauberey und gemeinschafft mit dem bösen Geist, . . . hoch verdächtig.' *Ibid.*, fol. XII, para. 8: 'Zum achten seyn alle diejenige, welche sich understehen, die böse Geister . . . zu beschweren und zu bannen, darmit sie ihren willen erfüllen müssen, gar für Zauberer zu halten.' Burning at the stake with confiscation of goods was ordered for soothsaying, and for banishing or indirect invocation of the devil according to part II, para. 1–2. *Ibid.*, fol. XXX–XXXI. Treasure-seeking, though not identical with witchcraft, was legally treated in the same fashion.

[58] HStAM, KHR 387, fol. 331–2; 485 (Vohburg); *Ibid.*, 401, fol. 504–5 (Neustadt/Donau). All the authorities involved forfeited their office and sixteen were dishonoured or interred according to the *Landgebott*, part II, para. 6 (KHR 387, fol. 504–5; curiously, the

seeking. The two largest trials took place in the counties of Pfaffenhofen and, again, Neustadt/Donau. Fourteen men were charged in Pfaffenhofen, while authorities in Neustadt/Donau requested the construction of a new jail, since there were only enough cells to detain the 'ringleaders' and the counties of Abensberg, Mainburg and Landshut had to be called upon to incarcerate additional suspects. Ultimately, it appears that five men paid with their lives for either ostensibly or actually invoking the devil in this particularly egregious episode. A noble suspect, Count Lodron, was among those questioned during a trial for treasure-seeking conducted in Landshut in that same year. Indeed, a rise in treasure-seeking was one of the reasons mentioned for the release of a general order to all provincial and county administrations in the Electorate on 5 November 1677, which explicitly referred to the recently republished *Mandate on Superstition and Witchcraft* of 1665 and noted how delinquents regularly disputed that treasure-seeking was a crime:

> Faithful subjects, we have learned with great misgivings that magical practices long held at bay and even eliminated in our land of Bavaria are now taking hold once again and gaining the upper hand among the common peasantry, so that they try to locate monies with the help of the vile devil and then attempt to excuse themselves through ignorance . . . [59]

Treasure-seeking remained virulent well into the eighteenth century. The Imperial City of Memmingen had its treasure-seeking trial in 1721 and the

paragraph mentioned, even in the revised version of 1665, actually prescribed internment only – *Landgebott*, fol. XXXIIf.). In one case, it almost appears that execution for playing a leading role was unavoidable, since the file was referred to the electoral high judge to confer on the sentence (KHR 387, fol. 401). A subsequent report notes, however, that this punishment was remitted in favour of territorial exile (KHR 388, fol. 306–v, fol. 353–4). The need to exercise caution against forming hasty conclusions is emphasised by another case from 1670: although everything pointed to an execution in the case of a woman from Pfaffenhofen, the next entry in the protocols indicates that she received a sentence in the pillory, followed by banishment. KHR 386, fol. 43–4, 377. A smith from Wasserburg/Inn was actually executed; he possessed a magic book over 100 pages in length, 'full of incantations', probably for the purpose of treasure-finding. In this trial, the high judge was sharply reprimanded for ignoring the newly published (1665) decree on witchcraft in this important witchcraft trial (*sic*). In the county Wasserburg/Inn, the decree was also never publicly proclaimed, thereby allowing subjects to fall back on ignorance as their typical defense. KHR 388, fol. 10, 268, 277, 397, 455, 520. Further trials for treasure-seeking were conducted in Dachau, Reichenhall, Landshut and Landau in 1670 (cf. list of trials in the German edition).

[59] HStAM, KHR 415, fol. 192v–3. In this year alone, trials for treasure-seeking were conducted at Neustadt/Donau, Abensberg, Pfaffenhofen, Kranzberg, Teisbach, Landshut, Straubing, Munich and Rain. In the case of the five treasure-seekers from Neustadt, the high judge was personally issued a copy of the decree on witchcraft in 1667 to ensure his compliance (KHR 415, fol. 303v).

Imperial City of Kempten was rocked by trials in 1727 and 1733 involving members of the town council.[60] Mandates against treasure-seeking were issued in the Prince-Bishopric of Eichstätt in 1731 and in the Prince-Bishopric of Bamberg as late as 1776, though the latter recommended that this 'error' be punished mildly.[61] Nonetheless, in Catholic areas, treasure-seeking remained a capital crime related to witchcraft until the mid-eighteenth century.

Familial witchcraft trials   This type of trial had also taken place in the past. As previously mentioned, denunciations were often levelled against close relatives at the beginning of major persecutions and because of the expectations of inquisitors, female relations were particularly threatened. This gender-specific selection tended to unravel in the second half of the seventeenth century. Entire families were targeted again and again, as in Amberg in 1655, Memmingen in 1656, Reichertshofen in 1661, etc. Familial witch trials reached their apex between 1690 and 1730, with severe trials in the Bavarian district courts of Haidau and Rain, as well as the Swabian district of Schwabmünchen in the Bishopric of Augsburg. There were two familial trials in lower Bavarian Haidau (1689–94 and 1700–2), in the course of which twenty persons were involved and eventually executed.[62]

---

[60]   Treasure-seeking at Memmingen in 1721 is mentioned in Unold, *Geschichte*, 367f. On the trials for treasure-seeking in the imperial city of Kempten: StadtA Kempten, Ratsprotokolle 1726–8, fol. 178v–80; fol. 222–3. The leaders were the two councillor Abraham Gufer and his son Tobias Gufer (*Ibid.*, fol 64, 139v–40, 159v–60, 170–v, 173–v, 193). The city requested a legal opinion from Ulm. In the final verdict, the town councillor was held accountable as the primary leader because of his education. However, in light of his old age and years of service, he was only sentenced to a fine of several gulden and then 'wider ad sessionem ac votum zugelassen'! StadtA Kempten, RP 1726–8, fol. 223. Just a few years later, T. Gufer was caught engaging in sorcery again, this time acting as a soothsayer with a 'divining rod' made of brass. Other magical writings, symbols and objects were also discovered in his house. Despite the intercession of his family, he was interred in a workhouse (probably in Langenegg), the magical objects were burned by the executioner, and the 'divining rod' was ceremoniously broken and thrown into the river Iller. StadtA Kempten, RP 1732–4, fol. 232v–3v, 248v, 398. Indications of later trials against treasure-seekers in the area are found in Riezler, *Geschichte*, 205–10; H. Böhm, 'Strafverfahren gegen Schatzgräber in Dillingen und Lauingen', in: *Jb. d. Hist. Ver. Dillingen* 79 (1977), 195–209; Rückert, 'Der Hexenwahn', 77. Trials for treasure-seeking were also conducted in Abensberg (1680), Traunstein and Wasserburg/Inn (1700), Riedenburg (1701), Mainburg (1702), Abensberg (1710), Neumarkt/St Veit and Landshut (1691), and Augsburg (1714).

[61]   StA Bamberg, Bamberger Verordnungen, B26c, No. 42. Riezler, *Geschichte*, 206; E. Schubert, *Arme Leute, Bettler und Gauner im Franken des 18. Jahrhunderts*, Neustadt/Aisch 1983, 253.

[62]   The exceptional importance of major witch trials in Haidau in the province of Straubing is witnessed by the voluminous records present in five archives: HStAM, Hexenakten 7; *Ibid.*, GR 324/16 1/2; *Ibid.*, KHR 467–69, 473, 475. SBM, Clm 26493, fol. 383v–6v. StA Landshut, Rep. 97 c, Fasc. 614 No. 1a (1273 fol.!). BZA Regensburg, Geisling Malefiz Proz. No. 1–8. StA Amberg, Landshuter Extradition No. 1497. Relevant literature is also

All told, the Haidau trial eliminated four families, but left others unaffected. Familial trials always began with the testimony of children and might be considered a variant of children's witchcraft trials. It was not unusual for the trials to open as an investigation of neighbourhood crimes and judges employed leading interrogatories to direct the fantasies of children toward the *crimen magiae*. Authorities initially questioned young Maria Schuster on suspicion of incest, concealed pregnancy, and either abortion or infanticide at the start of the Schwabmünchen trial of 1728–34. Then she was directed to confess to copulating with the Devil and sealing a Devil's pact, implicating her parents and siblings as well.[63] The major witchcraft trial at Haidau from 1689 to 1694 originated with reports of ghostly apparitions to a twelve-year-old girl named Katharina Gruber, whereupon her parents literally turned the house into a pilgrimage shrine, allowing the girl to act as a medium and give advice for a fee. At the insistence of the Capuchins of Regensburg and the Administrator of Haidau, who condemned the visions as a staged trick, the girl was arrested two months later, putting an end to her fortunetelling activities. Initiated for fraud, the trial took a turn when the girl, incarcerated for two months, told her jailer that she, her mother and a third woman were all witches, they had entered into pacts with the Devil and flew regularly to the sabbath.[64] The Haidau trial eventually engulfed three families; all of the parents as well as eight of ten children aged twelve to nineteen were executed as witches. At the time of arrest, the children, four girls and four boys, were between seven and sixteen years old. A girl three years of age (!) confessed that she too had copulated with the devil, but went unpunished. One daughter had been a servant away from home for many years and for that reason the commissioners discounted her testimony as implausible. The same was true of the other denunciations which invariably resulted from the trial. Like the chain-reaction trials, familial trials were a form of persecution restricted by the narrow application of criteria to verify denunciations, just as had occured before 1630.

plentiful: M. Raab, 'Grosser Hexenprozess zu Geislingen 1689–1691. Als Beitrag zur Geschichte der Hexenprozesse in Bayern aus Originalakten dargestellt', in: *Verhandlungen d. Hist. Ver. Oberpfalz* 65 (1915), 73–99; Huber, *Hexenwahlin*, 16–52; Riezler, *Geschichte*, 286f.; Franz Xaver von Altötting, OFMCap, 'Konrad von Monheim OFM (1643–1712) als Seelsorger bei den Geislinger Hexen', in: *Miscellania Melchor de Pobladura* 2 (1964), 377–91. On the witch trial in the county of Rain 1711–14, cf. anon., 'Der Hexenprozesse von Etting. Das tragische Schicksal der Bauernfamilie Pölz', in: *Aichacher Heimatblätter* 4 (1956), No. 5; Film 3710, 54ff. Files are found in HStAM, Pfleggericht Rain No. 163; StAM, AR 14/236 (according to Film 3710, 54ff.). This trial took place during the Austrian occupation and Emperor Charles VI intervened on numerous occasions.
[63] Pleyer, 'Der Hexenprozess', 17–24.
[64] Raab, 'Grosser Hexenprozess', 94; Huber, *Hexenwahn*, 16–19.

Trials of Child-Witches   As with familial trials, these were another variant of the children's witchcraft trials already in practice during the persecutory wave of the 1590s ('children and fools'). Children's witchcraft trials played a significant role in the seventeenth century: numerous 'Protestant' persecutions in Württemberg (Esslingen 1662–5, Reutlingen 1665–6, Calw 1683–6), the major persecution at Mora in Sweden, as well as the events in Salem, Massachusetts, occurred in the wake of surprising testimony volunteered by children.[65] Both secular and ecclesiastical authorities found the handling of such voluntary confessions very problematic. In southeast Germany, they were usually able to recognise the fantasy of children's accounts and the court ordered an education with the clergy or gave the children back to their parents with strict instructions for their upbringing.[66] Nevertheless, children were occasionally executed for witchcraft. The authorities encountered special difficulties if the voluntary testimonies of several children or youths supported each other. Such cases originated predominantly in educational institutions (orphanages, boarding schools, Jesuit schools). After 1670, the absolutist authorities in southeast Germany turned their attention to a new group of children who appeared naturally suspect to them: vagrant children.

Social-historical analyses of the circumstances among the lower classes in the seventeenth century are so rare[67] that this peculiar phenomenon has received little mention in the literature of the field. However, the 'Zauberer-Jackl' trials indicate the urgent necessity to confront this problem. The mass trial in Salzburg was only the prelude to a whole series of similar trials for which 'Zauberer-Jackl' played little more than a tangential role as a legendary figure. Evidently, these youth bands were common and consisted of young men between the ages of fifteen and twenty-five. Unfortunately, it proved impossible to gauge the formation of this subculture against the backdrop of troop raising and quartering for the military

---

[65] Midelfort, *Witch Hunting*, 154–63; Baschwitz, *Hexen*, 318–30, 388–429.

[66] The trials of children in Ingolstadt indicate the relative caution exerted when examining such accusations in the seventeenth century. Beyer, 'Hexen', 26–30. There are numerous examples of the lenient treatment of children. Even during the climax of trials in Pfalz-Neuburg in 1629/30, apprehensions about the treatment of minors were vocal. Chancellor Zeschlin corresponded with all important Catholic territories in southeast Germany and Franconia (Bavaria/Ingolstadt, Augsburg/Dillingen, Eichstätt, Würzburg, Bamberg, and Oettingen-Wallerstein) in 1629 regarding one of six persons denounced, a ten-year-old girl. In the end, it was decided to remand the girl to a proper upbringing under ecclesiastical supervision. Film 3709, 520–3 (according to HStAM, Hexenakten No. 26). Any adult would surely have been executed, or at lest severely tortured under the same circumstances.

[67] The older work of Ave-Lallemant and the observations (unfitting for the eighteenth century) of Schubert, *Arme Leute* or C. Küther, *Räuber und Gauner in Deutschland. Das organisierte Bandenwesen im 18. und frühen 19. Jahrhundert*, Göttingen 1976, notwithstanding.

during the Turkish wars and the War of Spanish Succession. The number of boy-witches' and children's witch trials from 1680 to 1740 demonstrates that the problem was principally a regional one.

The life-style of these bands resulted in the intermingling of real delinquency, from harmless begging to picking pockets, and an elaborated conception of their potential to engage in sorcery and witchcraft. Whenever the authorities arrested and tortured boy-sorcerers (mostly by whippings with 'consecrated' switches), they produced spontaneous confessions of sorcery, evoking the impression that real attempts at sorcery may have been behind their confessions. If young charges of the Jesuits displayed a remarkably evolved fantasy regarding witches' flight, demonic copulation and the celebration of sabbaths, the fantastic imaginings of these undisciplined youth-bands were even more highly developed, especially in regards to lycanthropy and shape shifting to 'swine and mice', as well as highly unusual notions about sodomy.[68]

In the wake of the 'Zauberer-Jackl' incident in Salzburg, boy-sorcerer trials spread to Styria (1678), southern Tyrol (1679), eastern Tyrol (1679/80), back to the Archbishopric of Salzburg (1680–90), to east Styria (1700), Carinthia (1705/6), etc.[69] The events of the Salzburg incident involved neighbouring Bavaria from the outset. Five men were executed as witches at Burghausen as early as 1685 and again in 1690, when twelve boy-sorcerers were incarcerated and one executed, and in 1698 when three were probably executed. In 1700, child-beggars were arrested in the districts of Dingolfing, Landau and Haidau and later in Diessenstein and Vilshofen (1705), Kelheim (1706), Bärnstein and Regen (1707), Bogen (1710) and Straubing (1712). This persecution resulted in the execution of boy-sorcerers throughout the greater portion of eastern Upper and Lower Bavaria[70] and, for the first time, a systematic inquisition of witchcraft emerged in the region. The question of whether or not similar procedures had existed in this eastern area prior to that time remains unanswered. In any case, the serial examinations of Markmiller, Wagner and Schmid indicate that they did and one should not lose sight of the fact that persecutions in the Austrian Alpine territories first reached their peak between 1675 and 1695.[71]

In 1715, the boy-sorcerer trials expanded to the west. From 1715 to 1717 there were actual waves of trials, which incorporated the Bavarian districts of Moosburg, Wasserburg, Haag, Mühldorf (in the Bishopric of Salzburg), Teisbach, Dingolfing, Erding, and perhaps others as well. The nine

---

[68] Byloff, *Hexenglaube*, 116–18.
[69] *Ibid.*, 123–6, 134f., 146ff.; Nagl, 'Der Zauberer-Jackl Prozess', I, 463–76.
[70] Cf. list of trials in the German edition.
[71] Byloff, *Hexenglaube*, 160; Nagl, 'Der Zauberer-Jackl Prozess', I, 391.

trials targeted fifty-six males, almost all of them under twenty years of age, and four adults, among them two women.[72] A successive wave of boy-sorcerer trials followed immediately thereafter, from 1719 to 1722. Once again, Freising led the pack, while the Bavarian counties of Burghausen, Deggendorf, Erding, Kranzberg, Dachau, Moosburg and Munich were affected, with trials in Salzburg as well. In Freising, eleven persons were executed for witchcraft in 1721–2.[73] There were additional trials of boy-sorcerers in the region in 1740 and 1755, but these did not end in executions.[74]

Furthermore, 'traditional' witch trials of old women and 'village witches' suspected of weather-making and maleficent magic added to the list of trials of boy-sorcerers, families and treasure-seekers. In isolated cases, these charges of magic did result in the execution of women for witchcraft. However, one is justified in stating that the traditional view of the 'old witch' ceased to play its earlier role in these trials. The authorities were better able to differentiate between popular magic and witchcraft, so that only voluntary confessions presented them with difficulties.

THE LAST EXECUTIONS FOR WITCHCRAFT 1749–75

The later history of witchcraft executions is also a history of repressed consciousness, because the age of the Enlightenment cared little for its own witch trials. We know that Colbert restricted witch trials in France in 1670, but few realise that a sorcerer was executed in Paris as late as 1745. We know that Friedrich Wilhelm I restricted witch trials in Prussia in 1714, but did he actually end them? We know that the article on 'Witchcraft' in Zedler's *Universal-Lexikon* reproached Delrio's belief in witches' flight, but are we aware that the 1749 entry on 'Sorcery' still cited Delrio and Carpzow, as well as Frölich von Frölichsberg's uncritical commentary on the 'Zauberer-Jackl' trials in Salzburg and that it approvingly mentioned the burning of the Devil's conspirators according to Article 109 of the

---

[72] 'Unständlicher geistlicher Vortag über einen Hexenprozesse aus der ersten Hälfte des XVIII. Jahrhunderts (Freising 1715–17)', in C. Frhr von Aretin, *Beyträge zur Geschichte und Literatur vorzüglich aus den Schätzen der pfalzbaierischen Centralbibliothek zu München*, vol. IV, Munich 1805, 273–327; Baader, 'Zur Geschichte', 296ff.; on the Moosburg trial, J. Metz, 'Ein Moosburger Hexenprozess,' in *Der Isargau* 1 (1927), 64–8. On the other child sorcerer trials, cf. trial list in the German edition.

[73] HStAM, Hexenakten No. 9, 9b–f (Freising); No. 12 1/2 (Tittmoning/Salzburg); No. 13 (Schwabmünchen). See also: StadtA München, Hist. Ver. Bibl. 13010 (Moosburg). Boader, 'Zur Geschichte', 296ff; J. Metz, 'Ein Moosburger Hexenprozess', in *Der Isergau*, 1 (1927), 64–8.

[74] Other child-sorcerer trials in Erding (1740), Regensburg (1746) and Burghausen (1755). Apparently, the trials against child-sorcerers lost their volatility earlier than the remaining trials against 'children and fools'.

standing imperial law code, the *Carolina*?[75] Certainly, the term 'witchcraft' had fallen from grace. Even the boy-sorcerers executed for witchcraft were generally referred to as *pueri venefici* or *malitiose Pettel-Buben* and charged for *veneficium* (poisoning) as their primary offence, in other words, a real criminal offence. However, when one examines trial records closely, the issue of whether or not we are dealing with poisoners, who actually existed, or accusations of witchcraft, becomes apparent rather quickly.

Trials for sorcery and witchcraft continued until well into the eighteenth century, even in places that we might describe as enlightened. Even where witches were not burned, the ideological preconditions existed and only a catalyst was lacking. In Free-Imperial Nuremberg, for example, which executed its last witch in 1660, a woman died in prison during her interrogation on charges of witchcraft in 1766! In Memmingen, a tobacco producer brought an accusation of witchcraft against a woman before the city council in 1790.[76] The loci of the last major persecutions, Salzburg and Freising, were also centres of the early Catholic Enlightenment and home to the Benedictine academies, which played a significant role in the regional Enlightenment. The same holds true of Würzburg, a port of entry for the early Catholic Enlightenment into southern Germany.[77] Naturally, the ideological separation of West from East and, especially important for Germany, of the Protestant North from the Catholic South, was significant. Clearly however, the complete elimination of trials for sorcery and witchcraft was a very different matter from simply restricting or halting them, and this without ever fundamentally challenging the belief in the existence of witches. Several essential components of the Christian worldview were related to a belief in the existence of witches and only the bravest free-thinkers dared to challenge them: the existence of angels, the Devil and other supernatural powers. The ultimate question of the existence of God as an actual force in world affairs loomed in the background. Contextually, the last witch trials have to be viewed with reference to the confrontation of these beliefs with Deism.

In this confrontation, Catholic southeast Germany lagged somewhat behind, shielded from the northwest European Enlightenment until after 1740, when Maria Theresia of Austria restricted witch trials, seriously eroding one of the last ideological strongholds for the necessity of executing witches. Perhaps this very lack of coincidence contributed to the tenacity of the ideology, since there had been a regional tendency toward restriction for some time. The authorities in the southeast brought the

[75] Baschwitz, *Hexen*, 238; Zedler, *Grosses Lexikon*, LXI (1749), 62–141, article on 'Zauberey'.
[76] Bock, *Zur Volkskunde*, 64; StadtA Memmingen, Schubl. 354/8.
[77] Spindler, *Handbuch*, II, 987ff. (Hammermayer).

problems associated with witch trials under centralised control far earlier than in many other areas, even if the literature usually awards credit to Colbert, Friedrich Wilhelm I and Maria Theresia for such measures.[78] In the sixteenth century, this goal became reality in the microcosm of southeast Germany and after the shock caused by the persecutions of the 1620s, witch trials were effectively restricted throughout all the territories of the region. Here, the elaborated witchcraft paradigm had been domesticated early on. However, social stagnation prevented a follow-up on these initial gains and probably facilitated the perpetuation of minor witch trials.

A CLOISTER BEWITCHED (WÜRZBURG 1749)

The last Franconian execution needs to be mentioned here for two reasons. First, it is incorrectly considered the last execution for witchcraft in Germany. Second, an address delivered in commemoration of the burnings in Würzburg pleaded aggressively for the necessity of further executions, unleashing the final Catholic debate in southeast Germany, the subject of the next chapter.

Our knowledge of the Würzburg trial still derives from the analysis of Memminger,[79] but our interest in his account is limited to two important points. The accusations of witchcraft arose in an institutional setting, a nunnery, where several cases of 'hysterical' possession were blamed upon a senile subprioress who, as a witch, was held responsible for all the evil-doings. Over the course of three years, numerous exorcisms took place at the nunnery until, in a moment of adversity, the old woman confessed. Furthermore, the Würzburg trial demonstrates that this evaluation was controversial among the authorities. A group of high secular officials attempted to hinder the execution of Subprioress Maria Renata Singer of Mossau and the interrogations reveal a difference of opinion concerning the physical activities of the Devil, implying a degree of doubt regarding the reality of the Devil's pact, demonic copulation, witches' flight and the sabbath, even if no actual doubt was expressed about the reality of witchcraft as a crime. The group fighting the executions was opposed by a town councillor from Würzburg and members of the clergy, among them the Deacon of the cathedral chapter and members of the Benedictine, Premonstratensian and Jesuit orders. The reactionaries, led by the abbot

---

[78] Soldan et al., Geschichte der Hexenprozesse, II, 262; Baschwitz, Hexen, 445, 449. Here, it becomes obvious that the hierarchy of structure was only advantageous if an 'enlightened' monarch was located at its head.

[79] A. Memminger, Das verhexte Kloster. Nach den Akten dargestellt, Wurzburg 1904; thereafter all standard works, such as Soldan et al., Geschichte der Hexenprozesse, II, 284–93; Baschwitz, Hexen, 454–7.

of Oberzell, Oswald Loschert (O. Praem), were able to gain the upper hand during a vacancy in the see, acting against the warnings of an enlightened faction under the leadership of the Würzburg professor and privy councillor, Dr J. C. Barthel. The newly appointed Bishop, K. P. H. von Greiffenklau, granted approval for the witch burning.[80]

THE LAST SERIES OF EXECUTIONS IN SOUTHEAST GERMANY 1749–56

Although no one was executed for witchcraft in the capital, Munich, after 1722, executions persisted in the other provinces of the electorate. Witches were burned in 1740, 1749 and 1751 at Burghausen, in 1749, 1752, 1754 and 1756 at Landshut and in 1750 in Straubing.

Neighbouring ecclesiastical principalities took part in this series of executions as well: the flames of persecution claimed victims in Dillingen in 1745, in Würzburg in 1749, in Salzburg in 1750 and in Kempten in 1755.[81] Naturally, these late trials all received approval from the electoral regime in Munich; it intervened in the affairs of the subordinate administrative provinces, approving the execution in Landshut in 1752, for example. The authorities in Landshut made the initial decision to execute a witch, but it was confirmed by Munich 'ex intimo consilio selbsten'.[82] Witches from other parts of the electorate were also incarcerated in the Falkenturm in Munich, like a woman from Stadtamhof, who was handed over by the authorities in Straubing in 1753.[83] These trials and executions must be

[80] The newly elected Prince-Bishop was Karl Philipp Heinrich von Grieffenklau (1749–54). Interesting details of the advice of Würzburg can already be found in contemporary literature, e.g. Rübel, *Systematische Abhandlung*, 134ff. The Catholic luminary in Würzburg, Canon Johann Casper Barthel (1697–1771) (on him, Bosl, *Biographie*, 43; Spindler, *Handbuch*, II, 988 (Hammermayer)) as well as the ecclesiastical councillor Herr von Weinbach and his brother-in-law, Johann Adam Frhr von Ickstatt (1702–76) (on him, cf. Bosl, *Biographie*, 382) displayed noticeable opposition toward the machinations of the monks, above all Premonstratensian abbot Oswald Loschert, who continued to play a role in later controversies. A comment on the important textual reference by Rübel is found in C. F. v. Kautz, *De cultibus magicis (. . .)*, Vienna 1767, 191. Cf. Duhr, *Geschichte der Jesuiten*, IV, 315–20.   [81] Cf. list of trials in the German edition.

[82] HStAM, Kurbayern Geheimer Rat No. 166, fol. 25–v. The capital sentence of the electoral high judge concerning the case of Landshut 'puncto Magiae verhaffte Maria Anna Amerin, vulgo, "Geist-Nandl"', was confirmed by the Privy Council of the 'enlightened' Elector Maximilian III Joseph. In 1752, the Privy Council still believed that the 'Laster des Teufflischen Beyschlaffs' was possible! On the same case, cf. HStAM, Kurbayern Geheimer Rat No. 165, fol. 269v. which expressly refers to the new *Codex Juris Bavarici Criminalis* of Kreittmayr. This case is also mentioned in anon., 'Merkwürdiger Rechts- oder Unrechtsspruch, welcher am 2. April 1756 zu . . . [=Landshut; WB] an einer par force als Hexe demonstrierten und behandelten dreizehnjährigen unglücklichen Waise auch Vollzogen ward', in *Landshuter Wochenblatt* (1818), 204–53 (the continuation); *Ibid.*, 237.

[83] HStAM, HL Freising No. 320/15.

348 WITCHCRAFT PERSECUTIONS IN BAVARIA

viewed against the backdrop of simultaneous legislative activity in electoral Bavaria, i.e. the re-release of the Mandate on Superstition and Witchcraft in 1665 and 1746, as well as the stiff penalties for sorcery and witchcraft incorporated into Kreittmayr's *Codex Juris Bavarici Criminalis*, which replaced the *Carolina* in 1751.[84] As late as 1751, Kreittmayr's legal reforms provided justification for the execution of a fourteen-year-old girl, which served as a precedent for a series of children's trials over the next five years.[85] Bavarian legislation of the mid-eighteenth century served as a practical guide for conducting trials and was not limited to theoretical exegesis.

As far as one can tell, the last witch trials leading to executions always targeted young women, and children between the ages of 9 and 17, who either accused themselves or close acquaintances of witchcraft. The average age of the six girls at the centre of trials in Landshut, Straubing, Burghausen and Mühldorf/Salzburg was thirteen and one-half. The present state of research indicates that, between 1749 and 1756, neither men, boy-sorcerers nor old women were targeted.

The largest of the recognised patterns of trials at this late date in the witchcraft problem began in Mühldorf am Inn, an exclave of Salzburg. The fifteen- or sixteen-year-old illegitimate daughter of a washer women, originally from the lower Bavarian town of Neumarkt who served at the home of a smith at the time, stood accused. Marie Paurin (this was her name) rattled her employer by staging a scene of a ghostly apparition.

---

[84] Spindler, *Handbuch*, II, 1074f. (Hammermayer); W. Peitzsch, *Kriminalpolitik in Bayern unter der Geltung des Codex Juris Bavarici von 1751*, Munich 1967, 28. *Ibid.*, 7–13 on the later Bavarian witchcraft trials. Also Riezler, *Geschichte*, 272–8. The Mandate on Superstition and Witchcraft of 1611/12 and 1665 was almost literally renewed in 1746. The order of Elector Maximilian III Joseph of 29 November 1746 is found in: HStAM, GR 323/16, fol. 139. The 'Landgebot wider die Aberglauben, Zauberey, Hexerey und andere sträfliche Teufelskünste', Munich 1746, is found in *ibid.*, fol. 122–38. The order 'Die Auflegung der alten Decreti in pcto. sortilegi betr. Sothanes decret ist also nach der Hof Cammer Meynung zum Druck zu befördern', HStAM, KHR 886, s.f. (13 April 1746). The referee is Court Councillor J. C. v. Dulac, a long-standing councillor (Court Council 1717–51). T. Münch, *Der Hofrat unter Kurfürst Max Emanuel von Bayern (1679–1726)*, Munich 1979, 166. Riezler, *Geschichte*, 273, suggests that the new Chanceller of the Court Council, Kreittmayr (1706–90, studied in Leiden and Utrecht, elevated to Court Councillor in 1725, from 1746 Chancellor, from 1758 Chancellor of the Privy Council) took a critical stance on the witchcraft mandate. Actually, Kreittmayr writes that the possibility of the devil's pact had always been doubted. Nevertheless, he lined himself up with the legislation of the Tyrolian legal scholar, Fröhlich, who based his knowledge on the Salzburg 'Little Sorcerer Jack' trial. Riezler, *Geschichte*, 275f. Although Kreittmayr became a key figure in Bavarian politics in 1749 (Spindler, *Handbuch*, II, 1075), witchcraft, a central theme for luminaries, was for him unworthy of any potential conflict, since witches continued to be burned in Bavaria, albeit not within the provincial administration of Munich. There is presently no proper examination of the internal relations of power in the government during this critical juncture.

[85] *Landshuter Wochenblatt* (1818), 251 (cf. note 82 above).

When all the local Benedictines proved unable to drive the ghost off, suspicion fell on the servant-girl. In court, she initially stated that a deceased relative appeared to her and encouraged her to stage the apparition. During the next interrogation, she confessed, without torture or threat thereof, that the ghost was actually the 'evil Enemy', i.e. the Devil.[86] In subsequent interrogations, the girl became increasingly inconsistent in her statements, which were uttered freely, but in accordance with a leading interrogatory produced by the civic judiciary. In February 1749, superiors at the Court Council of Salzburg and the Bavarian county court in Neumarkt were notified. The girl denounced two other women in Neumarkt for witchcraft, her mother, Maria Zötlin, and her employer's wife, Maria Elisabeth Goglerin, known locally as 'Gusterer Liesl'. Several persons in Neumarkt already suspected that the latter was a witch after she received an open wound on her breast during a carriage accident that would not heal. It was said that 'someone' visited her constantly, who 'sucked on her breast until it bled'. This woman of some forty years also suffered from epileptic fits and she despaired of 'assaults, as if black men wanted to fornicate with her'. The county court of Neumarkt also procured testimony to that effect without the application of torture.[87]

The trial gained impetus. In April 1749, the authorities began collecting evidence. Marie Paurin was transferred to Salzburg, while 'Gusterer Liesl', along with Marie Paurin's mother and a ten-year-old girl from Neumarkt, were transported to Landshut. There also appear to have been arrests in the districts of Neuötting and Burghausen after Marie Paurin and the other women from Neumarkt denounced two other individuals. After 'Gusterer Liesl' admitted her relationship to the devil during three interrogations, interrupted by recurring epileptic fits, she was finally executed at Landshut in August 1749.[88] In September 1749, the *Vossische Zeitung* newspaper in Berlin reported on another announcement from Regensburg detailing the execution of a witch in Landshut, an eighteen-year-old girl whose wrists had been slit.[89] Marie Paurin was executed in Salzburg one year later, a woman denounced by her was burned at the stake at Burghausen in 1749, and another fourteen-year-old girl was executed there two years later, although it is uncertain whether she had also been denounced by Marie Paurin. In 1751, a trial directly related to the events in Neumarkt was conducted in Vilsbiburg against a ten-year-old girl and an older woman simply referred to as 'Geistnandl'. The girl managed to

[86] A. F. Neumeyer, *Der Mühldorfer Hexenprozess der 16 jährigen Dienstmagd Marie Pauer von der Katharinenvorstadt Anno 1749/50, Bearbeitet nach den Original-Prozessakten*, Mühldorf 1980 (originally 1926); *Ibid.*, 15–23.

[87] F. Byloff, 'Die letzten Zaubereiprozesse in Mühldorf und Landshut', in *ZBLG* 11 (1938), 427–44. *Ibid.*, 438; Neumeyer, *Der Mühldorfer Hexenprozesse*, 24–44.

[88] *Ibid.*, 46–59.   [89] Film 1543, 4. Lüers, 'Hexen', 179.

escape, but the woman was executed in Landshut in 1752.[90] In 1754, a fourteen-year-old girl was executed there as a witch, another trial commenced during the following year, though its outcome is unknown, and the last known execution of a witch on Bavarian soil took place in Landshut in 1756. The files of this trial have been lost, but the closing legal remarks of the electoral high court judge in the administrative province of Landshut survive in a file that appears to have been the second in a series of three such documents. The referee listed all the classic authorities of the past two centuries who supported persecutions: Bodin, Binsfeld, Delrio, Carpzow, Manz, Haunold, Frölich and the instructions of the *Codex Juris Bavarici Criminalis* of 1751. However, he obviously knew the traditional 'Catholic' critics of the trials in their most radical form as well:

Whereby it appears that the well-known *Cautio Criminalis contra sagas* intended to cease and desist with all inquisitions directly, for no other reason than the subtleties of the matter had demonstrated through experience that so many innocents fell under suspicion, so that the surest proof against this method was held to be, *illud decantum Evangelii Matthaei 13. finite utrumque crescere, propter scil. evellendi tritici cum zizaniis.* Therefore, one is given to understand, that there is great danger of damning someone innocent and the matter must be left in the status quo . . . as it is always better *in dubio nocente dimittere, quam innocentem condemnare.*[91]

The analogy with the weeds among the grain was taken from Spee and the high court judge did not fail to mention the caveats in Kreittmayr's *Codex Criminalis* which gave credence to Friedrich Spee's apprehensions. Additionally, the mitigating circumstances of the accused's poor socialisation were taken into account, which was not generally the rule for the later witchcraft trials:

The accused, Veronica Zerritsch, the daughter of a braider from Landshut, was about thirteen or fourteen at the time of the trial in 1755/56. Her father had been dead for some time and her mother had remarried. When her mother died in 1753/54, her stepfather drove all the children from home and remarried as well. The girl, eleven or twelve at the time, lived 'on the street' as a homeless child sleeping it the market stalls at night. She left Landshut, first for Freising and then Mühldorf, finally settling with relations in distant Straubing. The legal reference mentions little about her circumstances at that time, except for a general comment on the bands of

---

[90] Byloff, 'Zaubereiprozesse', 440; *idem, Hexenglaube*, 156; cf. note 82 above.
[91] *Landshuter Wochenblatt* (1818), 220. It is noteworthy that the argument of the weeds among the grain was no longer accredited to Tanner, but to the more radical formulation of Spee. Cf. Tanner, *Theologia*, III, 984; also chapter 5, pp. 322–30.

children wandering about the Bishopric of Freising collecting alms. Her relatives in Straubing referred the orphan-girl to the Holy Spirit Hospice, where she cut an unpleasant figure because of her lack of piety, her swearing, her inability to adapt and, above all, for stealing consecrated hosts. Consecrated hosts were often employed in popular magic but, according to the views of demonologists, the Devil and witches sought to profane the sacred wafers. When questioned, the girl admitted that she 'suffered severe torments from the evil enemy'. Benedictions delivered by Franciscan monks summoned in on the case accomplished little, and 'the threat of beatings' only drove the now thirteen-year-old girl to run away from the hospice. This time she sought shelter with a 'Lady Lieutenant' in Landshut, who took the girl into her home as a servant. After a short time, the girl-sorcerer fell into a condition of 'confusion' after being 'assailed' by demons, attempted suicide and practised magic, which she learned during her wanderings in Freising from a 'man with a white skirt and red facings' (i.e. the Devil). Apparently, she bewitched a student and two small children, among them the child of her stepfather, causing them to become ill. Her aspirations now mixed with actual crimes: the 'Lady Lieutenant' caught the girl red-handed, as she was about to 'cut off the head' of her own child with a knife. The women no longer wished to keep the possessed girl at her home and the mayor of the city ordered her confinement in a workhouse – at age thirteen, Veronica Zerritschin remained a legal minor. The girl also expressed the desire to undergo exorcism. The mayor ordered her to name the cause of her condition and she recalled the stolen hosts, which were actually found at the place where the girl-sorcerer had buried them, wrapped in a piece of paper. She was immediately arrested and interrogated – without the application of torture. There was no mention of physical force, which proved unnecessary with the labile child. Confessions of a Devil's pact, copulation with the devil, flight and maleficent magic passed lightly from her lips, indeed she could recite a twenty-verse magical incantation for weather magic to members of the civic court, learned once again from the 'evil enemy' in Freising.

It was a simple matter to convict the witch: like so many other children, she confessed voluntarily to the wildest crimes, the court possessed physical evidence in the form of the hosts and all of her maleficent practices were verifiable, excluding her confessions of weather magic 'performed' in the region round Freising and Mühldorf. The 'bewitched' persons in Landshut had actually fallen ill and some had even died. Therefore, the formal trial critique of the *Cautio Criminalis* did not apply in this witchcraft case and there was no danger of uprooting the grain with the weed, since the guilt of the young witch seemed so obvious.

The electoral high court judge displayed his willingness to grant leniency, because the girl had come forward to confess the crime and had expressed her remorse. He also took the child's social-psychological background into account, admitting that she had all reason to despair after her 'merciless treatment at the hands of her stern stepfather' and her circumstances as a child 'on the street', and that 'it is truly no wonder that she . . . fell into thoughts of desperation and was led into misdeeds by the evil enemy of mankind'. Therefore, 'in the present case, there is much in favour of showing mildness in the degree of punishment for these things', and not to execute her, but instead to remand her to a good Catholic upbringing.[92] On the other hand: if one was not to execute those surely guilty of witchcraft, then when should witches be executed at all? For that reason, it proved necessary to burn the girl as a witch,

> that which has just been mentioned to the contrary notwithstanding, unless one wishes to completely end inquisitions into such clandestine crimes, and simply let witches be witches.[93]

It was a matter of principle!

THE LAST EXECUTION FOR WITCHCRAFT (11.4.1775)

Fiat iustitia! – Honorius, Prince-Abbot
(Signature of Prince-Abbot Honorius Roth of Schreckenstein
on his Court Council's sentence for witchcraft, 1775)

The classification of the last execution for witchcraft in the Holy Roman Empire presents certain difficulties, since investigations of the internal conditions in the Prince-Abbey of Kempten are conspicuously lacking in all branches of historical writing.[94] The thousand-year jubilee of the Prince-Abbey represents the most relevant occurrence there during the reign of Prince-Abbot Honorius Roth von Schreckenstein (1760–85), generally remembered as a benefactor of the poor. He ordered the celebration of the jubilee with great pomp in 1777.[95] Just as the Enlightenment achieved a breakthrough in the once great Catholic powerhouse of Bavaria in the 1760s (see chapter 6), several neighbouring ecclesiastical territories became the last strongholds of anti-Enlightenment thought. This situation reached a head at the beginning of the 1770s during the Gassner controversy (chapter 6, pp. 381–7) when several ecclesiastical Princes, above all the Prince-Bishop Fugger of Regensburg and the Prince-Abbot of Kempten, supported the activities of this exorcist, just as several other territories,

---

[92] Chapter 3, pp. 206–11.   [93] Chapter 4, pp. 213–15.
[94] Spindler, *Handbuch*, III/2, 963–8.
[95] F. L. Baumann, *Geschichte des Allgäus*, III, Kempten 1894, 426.

among them the Bishopric of Augsburg, took in members of the Jesuit order, dissolved in 1773, and ensured this continued influence. This last series of witchcraft executions coincided with the onslaught of the Enlightenment and the executions in Kempten in 1775 represented a new conservative reaction which, although it ultimately damaged the limping image of Christianity, stubbornly defended certain principles, manifest in the figure of the faith-healer, Gassner.[96] Surprisingly, the executions in Kempten never led to any great controversy. Only the next and last execution in a German-speaking area, which took place in the reformed Swiss canton of Glarus in 1782, resulted in an international outcry that finally ended persecutions once and for all.[97]

Once again, the background to the Kempten executions is preserved in a single legal reference. The target was a female inmate of Kempten's disciplinary poorhouse in Langenegg, an orphaned daughter of a day-labourer in her thirties, who fought her way through life in a variety of menial jobs, suffering numerous personal disappointments and was finally lamed in an advanced stage of leprosy. After a stay in a leprosarium in Günzburg, she managed to gain admittance to the poorhouse in Langenegg. Maria Anna Schwägelin suffered severe bouts of conscience, leading to her conversion to evangelical Lutheranism in Memmingen, in part motivated by her betrothal to a servant which never came to fruition. Her conversion necessitated a denial of the power of Mary and the saints, just as might have been required of a witch by the Devil. An Augustinian friar eventually absolved her, but immediately thereafter, he too abandoned Catholic orders, whereupon a parish priest informed her that only Rome could absolve her for such a serious indiscretion.

The feelings of guilt harboured by Maria Anna Schwägelin induced mounting 'assaults' which she suffered at the hands of a demon. She found herself in good company in the poorhouse in Langenegg, where a five-year-old girl developed fantasies of demonic possession. A local pastor undertook a benediction on the child's behalf, but arrived at a diagnosis of bewitchment.[98] Other inmates at the poorhouse were convinced 'that something was amiss there', noting mysterious noises. Another inmate responsible for the distribution of food beat Schwägelin with a rope until she admitted that she was the witch and had entered into a Devil's pact. At first, the 'Master of Discipline' at the poorhouse was reluctant to file a complaint with the princely authorities, because Schwägelin denied the

[96] Weitnauer, *Chronik* III, 104.
[97] Soldan *et al.*, *Geschichte der Hexenprozesse*, II, 327–31; Baschwitz, *Hexen*, 463–7.
[98] StadtA Kempten, A IV 8. Employed by Haas, *Die Hexenprozesse*, 108–19; but above all G. F. v. Wachter, 'Der letzte Hexenprozess des Stiftes Kempten', in *Allgäuer Geschichtsfreund* 5 (1892), 8–63 (continuation).

accusations in his presence as a result of the beatings. Nonetheless, the 'Master of Discipline', who forbade further beatings, eventually felt obligated to report the incident to the authorities, as he became convinced of her guilt.

The administration of the Prince-Abbey of Kempten never appears to have doubted witchcraft and its criminal nature, embracing the reality of the pact and copulation with the Devil whole-heartedly. Four days after the accusation was filed on 16 February 1775, Schwägelin was handed over to the authorities in Kempten. Two weeks later, on 8 March, interrogations commenced after initial observations by the 'Master of Irons'. According to the testimony of other prisoners, they too heard unusual noises in the jail after her arrival. The interrogations of 8–10 March proceeded without torture, but the woman proved labile enough to provide voluntary confessions. The protocols of the interrogations reached the Court Council and county judge, Treichlinger, whose legal referral was dated 30 March 1775; a copy is still to be found in the archives.[99] Treichlinger cited all the classic literature of witch trials from Bodin to Carpzow, as well as some critics of persecutions, such as Weyer and Goedelmann, but he ignored the enlightened works of Thomasius, Maffei, Jordan, Simon and Sterzinger, to name but a few. He countered Weyer's explanation of demonic copulations as mere imaginings of women who confess with the argument that 'throughout the centuries, one regularly finds the most thorough and detailed confessions of such people about these matters'.[100] Although the suspect committed no maleficent magic, never attended a sabbath and had no suspicious marks on her body, he maintained that the admission of the Devil's pact, according to Carpzow the most fundamental element of the crime of witchcraft, provided sufficient grounds under article 109 of the *Carolina* to order her execution.

The other Court Councillors concurred 'with the well-presented opinion of the referee' and handed the approved sentence over to the Prince-Abbot. At the announcement of the sentence, the date of execution was set for 8 April 1775, the following Tuesday. The sentence contains this comment: '*Actum et publicatum*, Abbey of Kempten, on April 11, 1775', so there can be little doubt that the order was actually carried out.[101]

---

[99] StadtA Kempten, A IV 8. Treichlinger was also involved in the trial of 1755.
[100] Wachter, 'Der letzte Hexenprozess', 62.   [101] *Ibid.*, 63.

6 The final Catholic debate[1]

FROM TANNER TO SPEE

Adam Tanner's arguments retained their significance for opponents of persecution in southeast Germany until the end of the seventeenth century, perhaps to an even greater degree than those of the more radical *Cautio Criminalis* of Friedrich Spee. In the 1630s, authors consciously referred to them in an attempt to limit the scope of persecutions in Bavaria and Tyrol, while the Tyrolean supporter of persecution, Frölich von Frölichsburg, castigated Tanner as a 'patron of witches' in the early eighteenth century.[2] One ought to keep in mind that the Jesuits Tanner and Laymann, also Tyroleans, lived in Bavaria and authored standard works on moral theology purchased by virtually every important Catholic library; indeed, they can still be found in surviving monastic collections. Spee's *Cautio Criminalis*, on the other hand, was published anonymously. The author was generally assumed to be Protestant, although two original editions of 1631 mention an *Incerto Theologo orthod.* and an *Incerto Theologo Romano.*[3] Indeed, Spee's initial influence was greater in Protestant regions of Germany. Only Protestant authors mentioned or reproduced portions of the

---

[1] On the final Protestant debate in England, Holland and north Germany (Thomasius), cf. Baschwitz, *Hexen*, 181–204, 344–87, 439–47. Within the framework of Catholic Europe, the debate was also much more advanced in France, Spain, Italy and Austria than in the region considered here. The particular attraction and peculiar value of the 'Bavarian witchcraft war' lies with the fact that a decisive frontal assault against witchcraft beliefs was dared here, despite the hesitance of the luminaries and in the face of relative social underdevelopment sustained by partisan political powers-that-be. Naturally, one can assume that even in Bavaria there were many behind-the-scenes developments before the onset of public debate – the *de facto* ending of witchcraft executions several years previously testifies to this. Nevertheless, the quality and intensity of the regional debate can be correctly interpreted as part of the climax and end of a conflict that had been mounting throughout Catholic Europe for some time.
[2] Rapp, *Die Hexenprozesse*, 33. Cf. Lea, *Materials*, II, 727f.
[3] Duhr, 'Zur Biographie', 329, 332.

Cautio Criminalis in the mid-seventeenth century, among them Seyfert, Meyfahrt and finally Thomasius.[4]

Catholics in southeast Germany preferred to reference the less-radical traditionalist, Tanner, even when they knew the *Cautio Criminalis*, or, as in the case of Johann Philipp von Schönborn, when they were ardent adherents of Spee's ideas. In 1670, an important Bavarian Jesuit mentioned the *Cautio Criminalis* alongside Tanner, for the first time in an official referral. Bernhard Frey SJ, father confessor to Elector Ferdinand Maria, condemned a renewed and devastating series of persecutions as the 'dangerous and dreadful trials against witches':

> Certe in presenti casu ac processu timendum est . . . ne ex sola fama, denuntiationibus Magicorum et Sacrilegorum Impostorum contra Complices maxime tot Ecclesiaticos, aut indiciis non satis firmis, ad Inquisitionem, Capturam, Torturam, et denique ad Sententiam procedatur, cum plurium forte innocentium quam nocentium praejudicio et totius Bavariae gravissima ac atrocissima diffamatione. Quam vero id periculosum, et quam multis hac in re sit cautelis, passim apud Theologos et maximae Tannerum et incertum Theologum Romanum in sua Cautione Criminali facile videri potest.[5]

One might take this first public reference to the *Cautio Criminalis* as an indication of broad reception in southeast Germany. Midelfort goes so far as to suggest that Spee's work, received at such a late date, had already been superseded in importance by the early luminaries, i.e. Thomasius and his followers.[6] However, Thomasius himself admitted that he incorporated many of Spee's ideas into his own writings. Furthermore, this interpretation is particularly misleading for the Catholic south. Legal referrals indicate that Spee's radical critique of trials gradually replaced Tanner's moderate stance. In 1695, a new edition of the *Cautio Criminalis* was published at Sulzbach in the Upper Palatinate, the residence of a theosophically oriented Catholic Prince, Christian August. It was reprinted there in 1718[7] and at Augsburg in 1731 in reaction to a major children's trial and family trials in nearby Schwabmünchen, thus expositing Spee as its author to a broad audience for the first time with the addition of the aforementioned papal instructions on the witch trials of 1623/57 as an appendix.[8] Any mention of Tanner's work in southeast Germany during the early eighteenth century by opponents of persecution was subsidiary, probably motivated by Spee's own frequent references to Tanner in the *Cautio Criminalis*. Nonetheless, the employment of the older

---

[4] Baschwitz, *Hexen*, 294–6, 299f., 439ff.   [5] Duhr, 'Zur Geschlichte', 331.
[6] Midelfort, *Witch Hunting*, 28f.   [7] Baschwitz, *Hexen*, 295.   [8] *Ibid.*, cf. 335f.

arguments put forward by opponents of persecution during the apex of witchcraft persecutions from 1560 to 1630 proved inadequate in the later seventeenth and early eighteenth centuries, because later trials had less in common with their precursors. Early opponents still made frequent concessions to the dominant ideas of the witch craze. Even if Weyer did not believe in witches, he still insisted on the need to execute allies of the devil. Fichard and Goedelmann, as well as other authors, may well have doubted the possibility of shape-changing, witches' flight and the sabbath, but they never denied the existence of witches, and they recommended execution for those entering into a Devil's pact or committing maleficia. Finally, Tanner and Laymann primarily warned against the threat to innocent victims, while ultimately confirming the necessity of eliminating witchcraft. As the execution of witches became an issue of principle in the eighteenth century, these authors were just as liable to be cited by proponents of persecution to support their case.

Naturally, some supporters of persecutions and executions simply ignored all of their arguments. The Saxon criminologist, Carpzow, whose opinions decisively influenced Manz and Frölich, merely refused to take the criticisms of Tanner and Spee into account. In a similar fashion, neither the Ingolstadt jurist, von Chlingensberg, nor the capital judge of Freising, Rumpfinger, in his legal reference of 1717, nor Court Councillor Treichlinger of Kempten was deterred by opposing points of view.[9] However, in conflict situations, Spee remained the major authority cited until the issuance of the Bavarian legal reference of 1756, rather than Bekker, Thomasius, Tanner or Goedelmann.[10] The comment was often made, quite rightly, that the type of trial Spee had criticised really belonged to the past.[11] Spee's formal critique had reached its efficient limits. The abolition of executions for witchcraft required other arguments than those previously explicated in Catholic literature.

THE ONSET OF CATHOLIC DEBATE

Of all executions for witchcraft in the eighteenth century, the burning of subprioress Maria Renata Singer in Würzburg in 1749 stands out for many reasons. The centuries-old rule exempting elites and members of the clergy from initial accusations of witchcraft broke down; the old woman was a nun in a prominent cloister and belonged to the lower nobility. A local

---

[9] Lea, *Materials*, II, 813–50; v. Aretin, 'Umständlicher geistlicher Vortrag', 273–327; v. Wachter, 'Der letzte Hexenprozess'. Cf. 360f.

[10] *Ibid.*, cf. Pleyer, 'Der Hexenprozess', 14. Similarly A. U. Mayer, *Nichtige (. . .) Verantwortung (. . .)*, *Vom Moldaustrom*, Straubing 1767, 7f.

[11] Legal opinion of the electoral high judge 1756 in *Landshuter Wochenblatt* (1818), 227.

Jesuit, Georg Gaar, conducted two public sermons promoting the necessity of burning witches, exemplifying the case of the subprioress as proof positive for the existence of a dangerous sect of witches, transforming the case into a rallying-cry. The legality of the trial was relegated to secondary consideration. Both sermons appeared under the widely published title: *Christliche Anred nächst dem Scheiterhaufen, worauf der Leichnam Mariae Renatae, einer durchs Schwert hingerichteten Zauberin, verbrennt worden.* This provocation caused a furore in the Catholic south, e.g. at the court of Maria Theresia in Vienna, as well as in the north.[12]

However, publicised condemnation appeared first in northern Italy and not in southern Germany. The Italian abbot, Hieronymus Tartarotti, had just confronted witch trials first hand. His book, *Del congresso notturno delle lammie*, took the position that witches were actually a creation of inquisitors. It was composed in 1748, but its publication was delayed by the Venetian Inquisition until 1750. In opposition to Delrio, who claimed that the burning of witches testified to their existence, Tartarotti offered proof that the milder trial procedures in Italy, in Spain and, after 1672, in France actually resulted in declining numbers of witches. He also cited Spee as the primary authority of the danger of witch trials.[13] The leading proponents of the Italian Enlightenment, Ludovico Muratori and Scipio Maffei, were enthused by Tartarotti's presentation and maintained that Delrio had been finally and authoritatively disproved.[14] Maffei did criticise Tartarotti, since Weyer had already come to the same conclusions in the sixteenth century; although both doubted the existence of witches, they agreed with the execution of demonic conspirators and sorcerers. Maffei recognised the weakness of this argument and declared the natural impossibility of all forms of supernatural intervention. Maffei's conclusions were the most progressive of any Catholic in Italy or Germany up to that time. He associated himself with the European Enlightenment in its highest form and it is hardly surprising that Maffei also quoted northern German authors. He referred to E. D. Hauber's *Bibliotheca acta et scripta magica*, where Delrio's *Disquisitiones Magicae* was condemned as 'an insufferable, worthless book filled with the most Godless heresy', as 'una grandissima raccolta di scritti, per dimostrar la vanita, e insussistenza della Magia'.[15] Now, Tartarotti had to defend himself against both sides in public debate: from Maffei's enlightened critique on the one hand and, on the other, from the comments of the Franciscan Provincial of Trent, Bonelli, who defended the belief in witches on principle.[16]

[12] Rübel, 'Systematische Abhandlung', 134ff. Baschwitz, *Hexen*, 456ff.
[13] Rapp, *Die Hexenprozesse*, 71–108; however, Tartarotti reported his doubts on the content of the elaborated concept of witchcraft, citing Malebranche and Protestant authors. Lea, *Materials*, III, 1441–7.   [14] Soldan *et al.*, *Geschichte der Hexenprozesse*, II, 296.
[15] Hauber, *Bibliotheca*, XX. *Stück* (1740), 522–44 (cit. 542); S. Maffei, *Arte Magica Dileguata*, Verona 1750, 17.   [16] Soldan *et al.*, *Geschichte der Hexenprozesse*, II, 296f.

The sermons conducted in Würzburg by the Jesuit Gaar burst upon the scene of the Italian debate. Tartarotti had them translated into Italian and published them in Verona, attaching his own scathing commentary. As a result, the Italian debate was intensified and Gaar felt obliged to respond, claiming that Tartarotti 'had shied from antagonising neither this preacher nor all the tribunals of Europe'. In turn, a German-speaking teacher at the *gymnasium* of Rovereto, Johann Babtist Graser, composed a new polemic attacking Gaar's reply.[17]

This 'Franconian–Italian' debate motivated a south-German Catholic author to take a firm stance in print for the first time. The Franconian Augustinian hermit, Jordan Simon from Neustadt/Saale in the Bishopric of Würzburg,[18] translated and adapted the works of Maffei. Simon, a professor of church history and canon law in Erfurt, published a book in 1761 sporting the provocative title *The Great Internationally Fraudulent Nothing* under the pseudonym 'Ardoino Ubbidiente Dell'Osa', its title already revealing the content of this voluminous work. It was republished in 1766 with the title *Contemporary Witchcraft and the Art of Sorcery*, indicating its initial popularity.[19] Jordan Simon's polemic represents the point of departure for the final debate on the witchcraft question in south Germany.

PUBLIC DEBATE AND THE VICTORY OF THE ENLIGHTENMENT, 1766–70

The extensive 'final Catholic debate' in southeast Germany is a peculiarity of the region's history, as well as of the general history of witch trials. It began in Munich and engulfed the entire area. In conjunction with debates in late-seventeenth-century England and in early-eighteenth-century Prussia, the 'Bavarian witchcraft war' was one of the great controversies marking the end of the era of witch burnings.[20]

On 13 October 1766, an ecclesiastic member of the historical class of the

---

[17] *Ibid.*, 297f. J. B. Graser, *Verteidigung der kritischen Anmerkungen über des Pater Gaars Rede von der Hexe Maria Renata*, Bayreuth 1754.

[18] On Jordan Simon (1719–76): S. Strüber, *P. Jordan Simon aus dem Orden der Augustiner-Eremiten. Ein Lebensbild aus der Aufkärungszeit*, Würzburg 1930. Simon had already fought against the Würzburg witch trials of 1749, reputedly publishing a polemic (*ibid.*, 144, 204). He had been strongly influenced by the writings of Muratoris and Maffei during a previous journey to Italy (*Ibid.*, 28ff., 151).

[19] J. Simon, *Die heutige Hexerei und Zauberkunst*, Frankfurt/Leipzig 1766.

[20] Riezler, *Geschichte*, 297–312. All further depictions relied more or less on Riezler, arriving at no singular conclusions: H. Fieger, *P. Don Ferdinand Sterzinger (. . .). Ein Beitrag zur Geschichte der Aufklärung in Bayern unter Kurfürst Maximilian III. Joseph*, Munich 1907, 97–150; Soldan et al., *Geschichte der Hexenprozesse*, 299–306; Lea, *Materials*, III, 1459–64; Baschwitz, *Hexen*, 458–60; H.-P. Kneubühler, 'Die Überwindung von Hexenwahn und Hexenprozess' (Diss. Zurich), Diessenhofen 1977. The following explication recapitulates the debate on the basis of original publications and other contemporary sources.

Bavarian Academy of Sciences, the Theatine father, Don Ferdinand Ster-zinger, held an *Akademische Rede von dem gemeinen Vorurtheile der wirkenden und thätigen Hexerey.*[21] Its message was inherent to the forum chosen for presentation: article one of the Academy's rules forbade the treatment of religious topics.[22] Since the Academy was willing to treat the topic in the presence of the Elector and the presentation defined witchcraft beliefs as 'common prejudice', the intent was clear from the onset. Anyone wishing to investigate the matter further need simply examine the printed version of Sterzinger's presentation to discover that he considered witch-craft an old wives' tale, which 'the common rabble, especially in our beloved Bavaria', still believed on account of their lack of education, but which must seem 'an absurd chimera, or a fabled matter' to any reasonable thinking person. Sterzinger contested the existence of the devil's pact, thereby relegating theological authority from Augustine and Thomas Aquinas into the present era to the realm of fairytales. The Theatine pater treated previously accepted components of the cumulative concept of witchcraft with unabashed irony: is it possible for a spirit to assume corporeal form in order to consummate a written contract with humans? Are we to believe that naked women ride on brooms smeared with oint-ment up chimneys at midnight to attend some sort of festive banquet where the food is repugnant? All of these imagining could only result from the 'prejudices of inept souls'.

> I was unable to restrain my laughter after reading about these comical witches' jaunts in the work of that famous defender of witchcraft, Del Rio, or in an old witch trial.[23]

In his treatment of witchcraft, Sterzinger often admitted his full accord with the 'good Catholic books' of Tartarotti, Maffei and Dell'Osa (Jordan Simon). His presentation represents an obvious frontal assault on witch-craft beliefs.

Nevertheless, Sterzinger was tactful enough to establish certain reserva-tions, for example the mitigating influence of the ruling Prince of Bavaria in 1756, as well as the draconian criminal laws against witchcraft still in effect in 1746 and renewed in 1751. Furthermore, he admitted that some biblical citations pointed to the 'existence' of sorcerers, supported by papal

---

[21] F. Sterzinger, *Akademische Rede von dem gemeinen Vorurtheile der wirkenden und thätigen Hexerey*, Munich 1766 (reprinted twice in 1767).

[22] L. Hammermayer, *Gründungs- und Frühgeschichte der bayerischen Akademie der Wissen-schaften*, Kallmünz 1959, 254; Riezler, *Geschichte*, 297.

[23] Sterzinger, *Betrügende Zauberkunst*, 11. In the later editions, Sterzinger softened the term *Schlechtdenkenden* to *Seichtdenkende Seelen* at the urgings of ecclesiastical supervisors.

decrees and the utterances of numerous prominent theologians, all of which suggested the dangers of witchcraft, to include witches' flight, the Devil's pact, the sabbath, and copulation with paramours. Of course, he had to make these concessions to avoid compromising past Electors and the Catholic Church. His concessions reveal some of the fundamental paradoxes of the early Catholic Enlightenment, considerably more tradition-bound than its Protestant counterpart. Sterzinger could not dare the decisive step of rehabilitating all victims of persecutions as innocents. On that point, he reminded his listeners of the reality of poisoning and the subjective reality of apastosy, lese-majesty, the temptations of the Devil, and the goal of practitioners of sorcery, all of which continued to require the death penalty. However, these concessions did not diminish Sterzinger's resilient insistence, that 'witchcraft is . . . in and of itself an empty and vain nothingness, a prejudice and imagining of unstable minds'.[24] Nor did Sterzinger dare openly to criticise the participation of Catholic authorities in the genesis of the cumulative concept of witchcraft, instead attributing the possibility of a Devil's pact to the 'wondrous ruminations' of Caesarius von Heisterbach ('a fantasising monk of the Cistercian order'), a reference quite obvious to anyone initiated in the literature of witchcraft.[25]

Despite these argumentative weaknesses, Sterzinger's presentation was well received in all German-speaking regions. Klopstock in Hamburg and Nicolai in Berlin displayed an interest in it, while learned periodicals in Hamburg, Berlin, Dresden, Leipzig, Jena, Frankfurt, Langensalza and Vienna[26] all reacted positively to the Munich Theatine father. The Imperial Councillor, von Senckenberg, wrote approvingly from Vienna that he was pleased on behalf of Bavaria by the destruction of superstition in the Empire.[27] Positive resonance from other Bavarian locales is recorded, such as from Neuötting and Viechtach, although it brings to light the pressures to which supporters of the Enlightenment in Bavaria were exposed. The majority of the common populace held tooth and nail to their beliefs in witchcraft, supported by the better part of the Catholic clergy. Just as the pastors in Munich had thundered earlier against 'free-thinkers', so too could contemporary pastors count on a receptive audience for their opinions on the question of witchcraft, because it continued to hold practical validity in the sphere of everyday life.

---

[24] *Ibid.*, 24. Lea, *Materials*, III, 1462f., also notes this contradiction.
[25] Opponents did not miss the opportunity to point this out.
[26] Riezler, *Geschichte*, 312; Fieger, *Sterzinger*, 215; R. Messerer, 'Briefe an den Geheimen Rat Johann Caspar v. Lippert (1758–1800). Ein Beitrag zur Geistes- und Kulturgeschichte Bayerns in der 2. Hälfte des 18. Jahrhunderts', in *Oberbayr. Archiv* 96 (1972), 1–803; *ibid.*, 101 (1976), 129–282; *ibid.*, 104 (1979), 259–426. *Ibid.*, (1972), 631ff.; F. N. Blocksberger (pseudonym for A. U. Mayer), *Sechs Sendschreiben and den Hochwürdigen H. P. Agnellus Merz (. . .)*, Straubing 1767, I, 9.   [27] Messerer, 'Briefe', 631f.

In Bavaria and the neighbouring bishoprics, resistance to the ideas of Sterzinger, referred to as the 'Hexenstürmer', emerged quickly. Sermons on witchcraft were delivered in the episcopal city of Salzburg, the pilgrimage centre at Altötting, and the administrative capitals of Burghausen and Straubing. The Administrator of Straubing, Freiherr Franz Xaver von Lerchenfeld, organised polemics against Sterzinger, while the Jesuits of Altötting recorded actual tests of the Devil's power[28] and theologians of the monastic orders in the centre of the region (the Benedictines of Scheyern, Oberaltaich, Nideraltaich and Innsbruck, the Premonstratensians of Oberzell near Würzburg, and the Augustinian hermits and Pauline monks in Munich) sharpened their quills in opposition to the heretical views of the Munich academician.[29] Contemporaries reported on the unusually excited reaction throughout the region to Sterzinger's speech.

There was no palace, hut, nor cell, no matter how still, which did not raise its voice with enthusiasm, as if it was up to them to decide the issue.[30]

The broad range of responses became a popular topic of conversation. Apart from scholars and elite circles, debates were conducted in cafes and ale-halls; one author complained that even his barber had troubled him with his opinions. The peasants in the countryside, goaded on by charismatic preachers, complained of Sterzinger's denial of the existence of witches. One observer from Innsbruck concluded: 'There was a general commotion in Munich involving not only scholars, but the common rabble as well.'[31]

Published resistance to Sterzinger followed immediately. Two oppositional treatises were already in print in November 1766, only one month after Sterzinger's presentation, and they significantly influenced the manner in which the subsequent conflict was conducted. For example, the first, composed by a 'lover of the truth', boasted 'Sterzingen in Tyrol' as its place of publication. The resultant 'Bavarian witchcraft war' developed into a tenacious debate between conflicting social forces. Tactically, the parties

[28] Ibid., 136, 177, 207, 250, 342, 502, 631–3, 648, 664.
[29] The following monastical theologians participated: F. Durich (OSF de Paula, Munich), B. Ganser (OSB, Oberaltaich), O. Loschert (OPräm, Oberzell bei Würzburg), A. März (OSB, Scheyern), A. Merz (OSA, Munich), A. Planch (OSB, Innsbruck), B. Schallhammer (OSB, Niederaltaich). There were also many monastic theologians who sided with the luminaries: B. Mayr (OSB, Donauwörth), J. Simon (OSA, Erfurt), F. Sterzinger (OTheat, Munich), J. Sterzinger (OTheat, Innsbruck) and H. Braun (OSB, Gengenbach). Naturally, the published polemics only scrape the tip of the iceberg.
[30] L. Westenrider, Geschichte der Baierischen Akademie der Wissenschaften, I, Munich 1784, 232.
[31] [J. Sterzinger], Der Hexenprozess – ein Traum, Innsbruck 1767, 7 (published under a pseudonym).

sought to spread uncertainty by disguising their own identity, intentions and place of origin, as well as the exact place of publication. Therefore, the debate was characterised by a constant guessing game in an attempt to identify shadowy opponents. The 'lover of the truth' was at work in one place, the 'lover of decent freedom' in another. Some authors included a 'healthy sane mind from this side of the Danube', 'a Godly scholar', 'a non-partisan pen', a certain 'F. N. Blocksberger', a 'Eutychius Benjaminus Transalbinus', an 'honourable scholar and lover of Christian truth', a 'Bavarian', and others known as 'J.F.Z.', 'F.L.', or simply 'A.E.I.O.U.' Their polemics appeared along 'the banks of the Lech' or 'the banks of the Main', 'on the River Tauber', 'from the stream of the Danube' or 'from the stream of the Moldau', in 'Sterzingen', 'Lappendorf', 'Report-town' (*Berichthausen*), from 'Disbelief', or merely without reference to place of publication or to author. In some cases, their identity has never been established, while in others several contemporaries gave conflicting reports, all of which seem plausible. Despite intense efforts, two of the almost forty polemics defy all conjecture and several others retain certain unsolvable mysteries.[32]

The 'lover of the truth' criticised Sterzinger's presentation at the academy in his '*Urtheil ohne Vorurtheil*', which assumed the standpoint of traditional scholastic theology. Like Sterzinger, Agnellus Merz, OSA, was a member of the Bavarian Academy of Sciences and a theologian of his order stationed in Munich.[33] Merz was no country bumpkin and the burning of witches was not his primary concern. Indeed, his 1784 obituary in the *Journal von und für Deutschland* described him as a 'very sublime man, beyond the caprices of monks'. In addition to the classic theological authorities, Merz, OSA, knew the luminaries – Muratori, Tartarotti, Maffei and Dell'Osa – as he pointed out himself. He was even prepared to accept their arguments up to a point, in fact just as far as Tanner and Spee had distanced themselves from a belief in witchcraft in the seventeenth century:

> I also believe that such nightly journeys . . . are usually imagined . . . however, I cannot accept . . . that all aspects [of witchcraft] are untrue.[34]

His stance reflects the boundary that traditional Catholics refused to cross: the authority of scripture, the fathers of the Church, the scholastic theolo-

---

[32] On the resolution of his pseudonym, cf. the bibliography. The determined authors are mentioned in the notes with a reference to the form of publication (cf. note 31 above).

[33] [A. Merz], *Urtheil ohne Vorutheil über die wirkend- und thätige Hexerey. Abgefasset von einem Liebhaber der Wahrheit. Gedruckt zu Sterzingen in Tyroll. Mit Erlaubnis der Obern.* Munich 1766 (second edition, probably also Munich, 1767). [34] *Ibid.*, 41.

gians (i.e. Aquinas), ecclesiastical and secular law codes, as well as the evidence from the confessions of witches during the previous three hundred years, many of which were reproduced in the relevant works of theological authorities.

I am further unconvinced that the author [Sterzinger] actually accepts that he lives among people who have read the appropriate literature . . . In fact, we too have examined the evidence provided by these authors [Maffei, etc.] just as the honourable author, but still could not accept their evidence as unchallenged . . . Second, against these aforementioned authors I refer to holy scripture, the teachings of the church fathers, most venerable ordinances and traditions of the church, ecclesiastical and secular law, a disproportionate number of theologians and, indeed, common sense; in addition, it seems to me that the aforementioned authors simply claim that these sources contain very much which is false and erroneous . . . with which we would agree, however, not that everything which they contain is false and void . . .[35]

Taken from his own point of reference, Merz was undoubtedly correct. If one oriented oneself along the lines of Catholic authorities (and what else could a Catholic theologian be expected to do?), then one had to admit that the possibility of sorcery and the power of the Devil on earth had never been principally called into question prior to Maffei and, in particular, that the Augustinian and Thomistic teachings on the devil's pact remained beyond all critique. The authors of the fifteenth, sixteenth, seventeenth and early eighteenth centuries avoided any confrontation with these authorities.[36]

Obviously, Merz, OSA, argued for the existence of witches defensively in the form of an intellectual retreat. One has the impression that, at times, he was less concerned with the existence of witches than with the premises legitimising their existence: the physical existence of the Devil and his potential for intervention in the material world and, ultimately, the role of the Christian God – a question of his *Weltanschauung* in its broadest sense. The contemporary struggle against Deism formed the backdrop to his approach. The essential arguments of Sterzinger, Maffei, and even Protestant opponents of witchcraft beliefs such as Bekker and Thomasius, included a refutation of the traditional power attributed to the Devil. Christ's passion had taken away any powers attained by the Devil after the fall. This theological line of argumentation, based on the Revelation of John,[37] theoretically undermined all components of the cumulative con-

---

[35] *Ibid.*, 55.   [36] Cf. the conflict outlined in chapter 5.
[37] F. Sterzinger, *Geister- und Zauberkatechismus*, Munich 1783, 10f. (based on Revelation 20: 1–3). On Bekker's and Thomasius' argumentation, cf. Lea, *Materials*, III, 1380–406.

cept of witchcraft by eliminating the physical Devil and the necessary precondition of his material existence: according to the authorities of the Church, the Devil's pact written in blood, witches' flight and corporeal transportation through the air, the reality of copulation with paramours and, ultimately, maleficent magic itself were only possible with the physical assistance of demons.

The weakness of these beliefs, based on the categorical acceptance of 'Godly omnipotence', was a need to concede in principal that Devil's pacts were possible, even if not in the present age. However, this view was logically inconsistent with Sterzinger's conclusion that the Devil's pact was simply 'an absurd chimera'. Merz, OSA, recognised this inconsistency:

> Just prior to this, our author stated that, if God had not limited Satan's power to hard us by exercising his free will, who on earth would then be safe from the evils perpetrated by squadrons of witches armed with the support of the Satan? Even if he admits that this support is subject to the omnipotence of God, said support can only arise from a promise or confederation between the two parties and so, how then can this confederation be a chimera, a fabled matter?[38]

Merz, OSA, operates along the Binsfeld premise, established at the end of the sixteenth century, that the Devil's pact must fulfil three preconditions: human free will, the permission of God, and the power of the Devil. The fact that God permitted the Devil to intervene in the material world time and again to test the good and punish the wicked was well established in examples found in the writings of church fathers and in the Bible, i.e. Revelation, and therefore was beyond dispute. The treatment of biblical passages intended to prove the power of the Devil and the existence of sorcerers assumes a prominent role in Merz's polemic *Urtheil ohne Vorurtheil*, the 'Egyptian sorcerers' of the Pharaoh, the 'witch of Endor', Simon Magus, the sorcerer Elymas, the temptation of Christ by the Devil, the exorcisms in the Evangelists, as well as relevant commentary by the church fathers and scholastic theologians.[39] Locating these passages was hardly difficult, since the 'disproportionate number of theologians' (Merz, OSA) continued to cite them in recent years – always with a view to substantiating the possibility of demonic activities which, ultimately – even if this seems paradoxical to us – all testified to the undisputed omnipotence of God.

---

[38] Merz, *Urtheil*, 36.
[39] A compilation of pertinent biblical passages is found in Sterzinger, *Geister- und Zauberkatechismus*, 16–24, along with the critique of the corresponding luminary. Treated are: Exodus 22: 18; Leviticus 20: 27; Deuteronomy 18: 10–11 (legislation on sorcery); Exodus 7: 10–12 (Egyptian sorcerers); I Samuel 28: 7–25 ('witch' of Endor); Mathew 4: 5; Luke 4: 5 (temptation of Christ); Acts of the Apostles 8: 9–11 (Simon Magus); Acts of the Apostles 13: 8 (sorcerer Elymas).

Agnellus Merz, OSA, from Munich was not alone in this line of argumentation. Other vocal advocates of the existence of witches included Angelus März, OSB, of Scheyern, Fortunat Durich, OSF de Paula, of Munich, Benno Ganser, OSB, from Oberaltaich, Oswald Loschert, Premonstratensian abbot of Niederaltaich and Pastor Premb from Lower Bavaria. Even the anonymous 'from the river Tauber' or the example of the Munich lawyer, Model, strengthened the argument by offering the added emphasis of juridical literature or concrete examples.[40] The preferred literary form of their oppositional writings was, not coincidentally, a learned polemic. Of thirteen tracts, twelve followed this scheme and attempted to convince the reader of the existence of witches by citing learned authorities.

In the eyes of traditional theologians in the region, witchcraft beliefs were never a tangential matter which might be discarded without damage to the Christian religion. The assaults of the luminaries against Christian demonology ushered in a tendency to question the entirety of the antiquated Catholic corpus of learning by establishing arguable doubt about individual biblical texts or their interpretation by patristic and scholastic authorities. The credibility of scholastic theology hung in the balance of witchcraft beliefs, because it had authoritatively fixed the cumulative concept of witchcraft. Even though Sterzinger left this heated issue out of his speech before the academy, his polemic tract of January 1767 entitled *Betrügende Zauberkunst und träumende Hexerey*, which met with the approval of enlightened theologians in Bavaria, put the arguments of theological authorities to the test of their own reason as the singular criterion of proof. Questionable biblical passages were reinterpreted and even the authenticity of the Book of Revelation was subjected to scrutiny on individual points. Sterzinger coolly wrote of the 'holy fathers' whose commentary had given rise to the cumulative concept of witchcraft in the high and late Middle Ages:

> that they were led so far astray by pagan demonology and platonic teachings on the spirit, and that we may, in all reverence, deviate from their opinions . . .[41]

Although Sterzinger, and after him Mayer, Kautz, Simon and Kollmann, all took pains to discuss each traditional reference the Bible at length – with an ensuing side-debate between Sterzinger, Merz, OSA, F. Durich and the Viennese Professor of Hebrew, von Sonnenfels, on the proper

---

[40] Cf. bibliography.
[41] F. Sterzinger, *Betrügendeu Zauberkunst*, 26f. Still clear is Sterzinger, *Geister- und Zauberkatechismus*, 53 whence the quote originates).

rendition of Hebrew words[42] – Sterzinger still made clear in his second publication that the foundation of his argument consisted of an abstract system of reason along Wolff's parameters, according to which the haunting presence of a physical Devil in the material world appeared a priori as an absurdity, rather than relying on an alternative form of biblical exegesis. Sterzinger, himself a theologian, hardly contested the omnipotence of God, but it appeared to him that the scholastic construction used to prove the existence of criminal witches was absurd, indeed ridiculous. Sterzinger summed up the main argument of the traditionalist, Merz, OSA, as follows:

For some reason unknown to us, but justifiable, God the almighty permitted the spirit of hell to enter into an express and secret pact with sorcerers or witches and to appear to them offering aid and support: whereby, whether or not the devil might be coerced to appear through words, circles or signs, he nevertheless did so with the permission of God to punish the wicked and inverted will of such persons. This conclusion of his, the fundamental substance of which is vexing and idle talk, is supposed to provide the indefatigable battering-ram with which he proposes to shatter my corpus of learning.[43]

The quintessence of Sterzinger's argument – though not so poignantly formulated – relegated the scholarly opinions of ecclesiastic authorities to the level of subjective opinion to be disproved simply by reason alone. He facilely configured a comparative synopsis of many ecclesiastic authorities into 'vexingly idle talk', unable to withstand the test of a tribunal of 'rational conclusions'. The 'lover of truth' (Merz, OSA) merely dodged the tribunal, moving around it 'like a cat in hot porridge'.[44]

In his second tract of February 1767, the *Vertheidigung wider die geschwulstige Vertheidigung der betrügende Zauberkunst und träumenden Hexerey*, Merz, OSA, makes his accusations against Sterzinger more obvious: 'If the spirit of hell is completely and totally bound, then it can not longer tempt anyone . . . All admonitions of the church . . . are for nothing and in vain. My congratulations, Sir! This is precisely the language

[42] [F. Durich], *Eutychii Benjamini Transalbini Dissertatio Philologica de vocibus Hartymin et Belahateham*, [Munich] 1767. A. v. Sonnenfels, *Sendschreiben . . . an den hochgelerhten Herrn P. Ferdinand Sterzinger . . . über zwey hebraeische Wörter Chartumim und Belahateham: nochmals zur nothwendigen Belehrung des sogenannten Liebhabers der Wahrheit, und seiner lateinischen Eutychii Benjamin Transalbini in ihrem Zauber- und Hexereystreite (. . .)*, Vienna 1767.
[43] Sterzinger, 43. Almost coincidentally, Sterzinger refers to the authority of Christian Wolff in his argumentation (*ibid.*, 75f.). In his speech to the Academy, he still refrained from citing Protestant authors.　　[44] *Ibid.*, 42f.

of a free thinker . . .'[45] Free-thinking and 'materialism', a given, if one claims that spiritual beings – Angels and Devils – cannot assume corporeal form, were central to Merz's second contribution to the witchcraft debate, which also openly raises the charge of heresy.[46] The fear of similar authors for the ultimate legitimacy of existing religion became even more obvious in a further contribution to the debate in November 1766. The author of this tract, the *Kurze Vertheidigung der thätigen Hex- und Zauberey wider eine dem heiligen Kreuz zu Scheyern nachtheilige akademische Rede*, was the benedictine theologian Angelus März, OSB, of Scheyern, who, like Sterzinger and the theologian with a similar name, Agnellus Merz, OSA, was also a member of the Munich Academy.[47] Naturally, März, OSB, dealt with the respective biblical passages and supported his defense for the existence of witches with authority. Above all, he was concerned with the practical consequences of Sterzinger's presentation. Like many other monasteries, the abbey of Scheyern operated a booming business in devotional articles, among them the regionally famous 'little cross of Scheyern', tiny, double-beamed, lead crucifixes, which supposedly derived their power as functional aids and defence mechanisms against witchcraft from direct contact with the relics of the true cross at the monastery. If the arts of sorcery and witchcraft were mere fraud and imaginings, then this held direct consequences for the reputation of the cloister:

> Most honourable academicus! If witchcraft and sorcery are fables, simple idiocy, a 'prejudice of unreasonable souls', then we paters of Scheyern are shameful swindlers and exaggerators . . . Not only in Bavaria, Swabia, Bohemia, Austria, Moravia and Hungary, but in Saxony and Poland as well, the little crosses of Scheyern are successfully employed, so that seldom fewer than 40,000 are distributed in a single year . . .[48]

---

[45] [A. Merz], *Vertheidigung wider die geschwulstige Vertheidigung der betrügenden Zauberkunst und träumenden Hexerey* [Munich] 1767 ('Mit Erlaubnis der Oberen'), 13.

[46] Martin Delrio is still recognisable as the irrefutable authority. Fischer, *'Die "Disquisitionum"'*, *107, 115.* Delrio was also the one who posed the suggestive question: If one follows the argumentation of the opposing party ('Weyer oder einem anderen Ketzer'), 'hiesse das nicht, alle katholischen Gerichte der Unwissenheit, Ungerechtigkeit und Grausamkeit zu beschuldigen?' (*Ibid.*, 115, according to Delrio, *Disquisitionum*, 804ff.) The negation of witches' travel was a sin against the Church. 'Nam Ecclesia Catholica non punit crimina, nisi certa & manifesta.' Ergo, either the Church or the doubters were in error. Längin, *Religion*, 140. Fischer, 'Die "Disquisitionum"', 39, from Delrio, *Disquisitionum*, 182.

[47] A. März, *Kurze Vertheidigung der thätigen Hex- und Zauberei wider eine dem heiligen Kreuz zu Scheyern nachttheilige akademische Rede*, Freising 1766 (Ingolstadt 1767).

[48] Soldan *et al.*, *Geschichte der Hexenprozesse*, II, 303f. Delrio represents the primary authority for März as well.

Countless occurrences from daily life supposedly testified to the efficacy of the 'little crosses', above all a witch trial at Mainburg in 1713, during which a 'little cross' melted down into the church bells had hindered a witch from succeeding in weather magic ordained by the Devil.[49] Sterzinger's speech at the Academy demeaned the activities of the Benedictines at Scheyern to the level of 'public fraud' and such speeches generally 'inhibited devotion'; in other words, they damaged the reputation of the Church. März, OSB, described Sterzinger as a 'half-Catholic' in his tract, and the accusations of heresy and witchcraft were less than subtle. Beyond that, his speech was perpetrated 'to please evil-thinkers'. This represented a direct attack against the luminaries in the Academy, Lori, Osterwald and Pfeffel, who were connected by März, OSB, with Sterzinger's official presentation.[50]

The representatives of the monastic Enlightenment in Bavaria were reluctant to accept the argumentation of the Scheyern Benedictine on behalf of the Church. The prelate of the Augustinian-Choir cloister of Polling, Töpsl, wrote to his brother-in-orders in Rome, Steigenberger, that this tract was the most absurd and patently stupid that he had ever read.[51] The luminaries assumed their characteristic literary form in their rejoinders to März, OSB: satire. Sterzinger's speech to the Academy repeatedly ridiculed the cumulative concept of witchcraft and his rejoinder to Merz, OSA, also comically parodied the bitter seriousness of traditional theologians. He described this fellow-member of the Academy as 'our purveyor of sorcery' and 'the witches' patron', in jesting references to traditional demonologists like Delrio, who himself had earlier patronised the 'defenders' of witches – e.g. Tanner and Spee – as 'witches' patrons'. Sterzinger simply inverted the charge, applying the title to the successor of demonology, precisely because they defended the existence of witches.

The first mocking satire appeared at the end of January 1767, in Straubing, Lower Bavaria. The author was Andreas Ulrich Mayer, palace chaplain of an Upper Palatine nobleman, who addressed a public 'well-wishing' to the Benedictine of Scheyern, März, under the pseudonym 'Blocksberger'.

---

[49] *Ibid.*, 31.   [50] *Ibid.*, Vorrede (Preface).

[51] R. van Dülmen, 'Aufklärung und Reform in Bayern I. Das Tagebuch des Pollinger Prälaten Franz Töpsl (1744–1752) und seine Korrespondenz mit Gerhoh Steigenberger (1763–1768)', in *ZBLG* 32 (1969), 606–747, 886–961. The enlightened monastics were unhappy about the initiation of the debate, dubbed the 'Guerre des Sorcières' by Steigenberger in Rome (letter of 11.3.1767), because they were caught between the lines. Still, they clearly renounced the argumentation of the region's clerical reactionaries, the laughable utilitarian arguments of März, OSB, as well as the theological deductions of Merz, OSA ('non minus cruda'). *Ibid.*, 911, 913, 915f., 918, 921, 923, 924f. 927, 935, 942, 944. They were aware of the Italian role model: 'Controversiae de magia ex Italia nunc in Bavariam translatae.' *Ibid.*, 924.

In your case, I would simply note the benefit of experience used to repudiate Sterzinger through all manner of stories about witches. You cannot lack this kind of weapon, and I wager, can summon up enough stories of witches solely in our district courts to provide materials . . . for a book.

Despite the polemics and irony, Sterzinger insisted upon retaining the form of the academic conflict and concentrated on the theological arguments of the Augustinian Merz, but the pragmatic approach of März, OSB, called for a different sort of reply, one which corresponded more closely to the intentions of the luminaries. Their goal was to avoid theological disputation, concentrating instead on practical reform, in particular to counteract the influence of monks like März, OSB, who actively fuelled popular beliefs – one of their primary concerns. März's explanations were not only given over to merciless ridicule, but also received criticism for their social orientation.

Our Chaplain . . . laughed himself half to death over your hare-brained fantasies, and said, you knew well how to orient yourself to accord with the tastes of your readers, becoming at once a brewer's apprentice for the brewer's apprentice and a fruit-vendor to the fruit-vendor, just to win them over to your side.[52]

Naturally, the background to this criticism was the considered attempt on the part of a greater portion of the clergy to turn the people against the luminaries in Munich by employing the issue of witchcraft. We know from numerous contemporary sources that this strategy did not fall on deaf ears, even though it is impossible to quantify the actual degree of their success. Sterzinger made a point of noting the positive reaction to his speech in scholarly journals and the court in Vienna and 'Blocksberger' repeated this argument in a more scathing fashion:

Your tract is really a masterpiece: too bad that it won't find its way past the porter in the contemporary world of great free-thinkers: otherwise, one could still hope that . . . witch-burnings, now forbidden – unfortunately – in all places, would greatly add to the confidence of the faithful and might begin again.[53]

Mayer edited the correspondence of two members of the upper nobility as evidence, in which the enlightened Elector, Maximilian III Joseph, was

[52] Mayer, *Glückwunschschreiben*, Vorrede (Preface). On the 'Book' topos, cf. Sprenger and Institoris, *Malleus* II, 132. Mayer still considered it a nursery story.
[53] *Ibid.* März belonged to that party which '. . . vor lauter Mägden und Handwerksgessellen wider die Freygeister predigen. Man weys schon, *wen sie meynen . . .'*

praised for freeing his subjects from the 'yoke of superstition'. The letters went on to recommend that it would well suit the Benedictine order to put an end to the 'witch beliefs of Scheyern'.

In February 1767, two further clergymen produced satires lampooning the polemics of Merz, OSA, and März, OSB: Heinrich Braun, a Benedictine from Tegernsee, co-opted into the Bavarian Academy of Sciences in 1765, and the Innsbruck Theatine, Josef Sterzinger, a younger brother of Don Ferdinand Sterzinger; both published under assumed names.[54] In J. Sterzinger's satire, *Der Hexenprozess – ein Traum*, witch beliefs take the form of a scurrilous dream from which one is rudely awakened into reality. A fourth satire was delivered by the academic printer, Ott at the beginning of March 1767.[55] From January to April 1767, twelve polemic tracts were contributed to the 'Bavarian witchcraft war', not including new editions of the publications of 1766 and commentaries in journals. In addition to Sterzinger's own contribution, the *Betrügende Zauberkunst*, and the other four satires already mentioned, two further polemics took up the cause of the Munich luminaries against the 'unenlightened' Bavarian monks, relying on satire as well. Blocksberger/Mayer dedicated over 200 additional pages to the refutation of all arguments employed by the supporters of the existence of witches, arriving at the conclusion that torture, the fear of death and fantasy were solely responsible for the content of earlier confessions to crimes of witchcraft, apart from the guilt of judges, whose blindness he demonstrated with the example of the Salzburg 'Zauberer-Jackl' trials.[56] The Munich publisher Finauer outlined the antagonistic background to the partisanship of both sides in his *Gedanken über die Werke des Liebhabers der Wahrheit* – for Sterzinger, the fame of appearing in learned journals, for Merz, OSA, and März, OSB, the lure of a public audience in Munich beer-halls – refusing to compose yet another satire against the two monks: 'They have suffered enough by having their works printed . . .'[57]

The opposing party held a different opinion. Merz, OSA, and März, OSB, composed new polemics, a certain A. Planch from Innsbruck fundamentally 'proved' the existence of witches, the Catholic publisher, Benno Ganser, OSB, from Oberaltaich stood up for Merz, OSA, as did another

---

[54] Cf. note 31 above. [H. Braun], *Drey Fragen zur Vertheydigung der Hexerey. 1. Ob P. Angelus März die Rede des P. Sterzinger gründlich und 2. bescheiden widerleget habe, 3. und ob wohl diese akademische Rede dem heil. Kreuze von Scheyern in der Tat Nachtheilig sei? Mit einem sichern JA beantwortet und dem P. Angelus selbst dediziert, von J.F.Z.*, [Munich] 1767.

[55] [F. Ott], *Gespräche von verschiedenem Inhalte, unter einer munteren Fastnachtscompagnie, verfasset von einem Liebhaber einer anständigen Freyheit. Gedruckt vor baares Geld, im Jahr, als noch im März Fasching war. Verfasst am unsinnigen Donnerstag, Lappendorf 1767*, Munich 1767.   [56] Mayer, *Sechs Sendschreiben*, 66.

[57] [P. P. Finauer], *Gedanken über die Werke des Liebhabers der Wahrheit von der Hexerey*, Munich 1767, 18.

clergyman by the name of Premb from Lower Bavaria.[58] Apart from the seven tracts already directed against Sterzinger, five further products appeared on the market before 1770, among them a 240-page dissertation by Beda Schallhammer, OSB, from Niederaltaich, which led the pack in terms of sheer volume. Even a Munich jurist and the Premonstratensian abbot, Oswald Loschert, took up their pens; the latter had participated in the Würzburg burning of 1749.[59] All these tracts shared common proofs for the existence of witches, citing evidence from Revelation and theological and juridical authorities, especially the standing legal codes of the Empire and its territories, in order to legitimise witch trials. Continued resistance to ending the trials, expressed in tracts as well as in actual attempts to revive them,[60] resulted in four more serious attempts to convince readers through philological, theological, historical and political argumentation. However, three of the four publications, among them the two most extensive, were not produced by Bavarian authors, coming instead from neighbouring Catholic regions. In an impressive treatment entitled *De cultibus Magicis*, an Imperial Councillor in Vienna, von Kautz, reflected on all previous enlightened debates concerning the theme of witchcraft, granting particular pride of place to the public appearance of Sterzinger in Munich.[61] The Viennese Professor, von Sonnenfels, a mem-

---

[58] A. März, *Verantwortung über die von P. Don Ferdinand Sterzinger bey dem hochfürstlichen hochlöbl. geistlichen Rat zu Freysing freywillig wider ihn gestellten Fragen*, Ingolstadt 1767. Prince-Bishop Klemens Wenzeslaus von Sachsen (Bishop of Freising 1764–8) forbade both sides further libels and writings on the witchcraft issue. Cf. van Dülmen, 'Aufklärung', 927. A. Planch, *Dissertatio critico-scripturistica de Magia diabolica et Magorum prodigiis*, Innsbruck 1767. [B. Ganser], *Sendschreiben an einen gelehrten Freund, betreffend die hitzigen Streitschriften von der Hexerey, Vom Donaustrom*, [Straubing] 1767. [D. Premb], *Drei wichtige Fragen über das Hexensystem, von einem gesunden unverrückten Kopf diesseits der Donau*, n.p. 1767.

[59] B. Schalhammer, *Aliquid ex Theologia contra grande Nihilum seu Dissertatio de Magia nigra*, Straubing 1767. [O. Loschert], *Vorgängiger Versuch zur Erwirkung eines Vertrages zwischen den in dem bisherigen Hexereykriege verwickelte Gelehrten (. . .), An dem Maynstrome*, [Würzburg] 1767. Loschert, directly involved with the Würzburg burnings of 1749, demonstrates just how hypocritical the claims of mildness of the clerical reactionaries actually were. J. M. Model, *Beantwortete Frage: Ob man die Ausfahrt der Hexen zulassen könne? Wider den heutigen Hexenstürmer P. Ferdinand Sterzinger*, Munich 1769. [Anon.], *Sieben abenteuerliche Sätze zu der Geisterlehre dieses aufgeklärten Jahrhunderts, Am Tauberfluss*, 1770.

[60] Cf. a Bavarian witch-trial instruction of 1769 (not official) from Lower Bavaria: 'Eine kurze Einleitung zum Malefiz-Inquisitions-Prozess, wie solche in praxi nach der churbayer. Malefizordnung und der neuen Cod. Crim. bei den churfürstl. Gerichten auf dem Lande geführt werde, de Anno 1769.' In book II, title 3, a Kelheim copy deals with 'de crimine sortilegii seu Magiae, von dem Laster der Zauberei, Hexerei oder Schwarzkunst', naturally making reference to the now legendary 'Little Sorcerer Jack' trial. The sources of this 'instruction' are given as Kreittmayr's *Codex Iuris Bavarici Criminalis* and the works of the Saxon jurist Carpzow; the electoral mandate on witchcraft of 1746 and the commentaries of Frölich on the Salzburg trials loom in the background. Cf. R. Schuegraf, 'Zum Hexenprozess', in: *Zeitschrift für deutsche Kulturgeschichte* 3 (1858), 764–73.

ber of the Imperial/Regal Learned Society in Rovereto, defended Sterzinger against the accusation of inaccurate translations.[62] The intervention of Jordan Simon, OSA, was more immediate to the Bavarian debate, as he took a renewed stance on the diminished importance of the power of the Devil in theological and historical discourse. Sterzinger had already pointed to Simon as his model and spiritual rector in the Bavarian debate, because of his receptive attitude toward Maffei and his book on *Das grosse weltbetrügende Nichts*, and his anonymous contribution in the 'witchcraft war' was held by contemporaries to be the most important yet.[63]

Once again, Jordan Simon dedicated his tract to the theological-philosophical refutation of the arguments of Bavarian supporters for the existence of witches, as well as to the interpretation of a recently discovered document which had come to the attention of the participants in the debate in November, 1766: *Sr. Kaiserlich-königlich-Apostolischen Majestät allergnädigste Landesverordnung, wie es mit den Hexenprozessen zu halten sey.*[64] Maria Theresia systematically limited witch trials from the onset of her reign, effectively ending executions in the German-speaking portions of the Habsburg lands. Later witch trials in Hungary and Siebenburgen in Romania led to the isssuance of the Territorial Ordinance in 1766, which was designed to render executions for witchcraft untenable.[65] However, the Territorial Ordinance of 1766 still avoided the ultimate question of the existence of witches. Theoretically, the penalties for witchcraft remained in place. Although it was enthusiastically praised by the luminaries in Bavaria, its lack of clarity on this point could still be cited by supporters of witchcraft persecutions. Merz, OSA, properly pointed out that although Maria Theresia personally withdrew her support for the punishment of witches, the Ordinance never specifically stated that, in principle, they were immune from sanctions.[66] Jordan Simon provided a contrary interpretation, citing the Territorial Ordinance passage for passage with extensive

[61] v. Kautz, *De Cultibus*.   [62] v. Sonnenfels, *Sendschreiben*. Cf. note 42 above.
[63] As per the comments of the *Churbayrischen Intelligenzblats* of 16 July 1767 and 20 August 1767. Correspondingly, the following is meant: [J. Simon], *Anpreisung der allergnädigsten Landesverordnung Ihrer Kaiserl. Königl. apostolischen Majestät, wie es mit dem Hexenprocesse zu halten sei, nebst einer Vorrede, in welcher die kurze Vertheydigung der Hex- und Zauberey, die der P. Angelus März der akademischen Rede des P. Sterzinger entgegengesetzet, von einem Gottesgelehrten beantwortet wird*, Munich 1767.
[64] Decree of Maria Theresia of 5 November 1766: Byloff, *Hexenglaube*, 161. Whether the contents of the forthcoming decree were known to the circle of Bavarian luminaries around Osterwald and Sterzinger and thereby influenced the conceptualisation of Sterzinger's speech is unclear. In Bavaria, it was first made public in the *Churbayrische Intelligenzblatt* 2/1767 (30 January), though some interested circles had been apprised since November. The decree was circulated with informed commentary in the work of Simon (note 63 above).
[65] Soldan *et al.*, *Geschichte der Hexenprozesse*, II, 274–80; Baschwitz, *Hexen*, 440–51; Byloff, *Hexenglaube*, 160ff.   [66] Merz, *Vertheidigung*, 40ff., 97–100.

commentary. At the end of his interpretation, he left no doubt as to the intent of the mandate. More radically than Sterzinger and his other compatriots in the debate, Simon declared that the witchcraft persecutions were nothing more than a terribly erroneous interpretation of all previous secular and ecclesiastical authorities:

> For what reasons were witch trials conducted so frequently and so unfortunately? I wish to elaborate upon them sincerely to the horror of those who still feel justified in the defence of these foolish arts of witchcraft. Certain clergymen have hitherto been granted the power to conduct trials for what they believed was witchcraft, because witchcraft was viewed as heresy. And these clergymen subordinated secular courts to their purposes. The rest was achieved through the terrors of torture. Secular courts deferred to the decisions of the inquisitors out of hand and were only tasked with carrying out executions.[67]

Even if this depiction deviates somewhat from actual historical circumstances, since witch trials were conducted exclusively by secular courts after the Reformation, it nevertheless touches upon the core of the taboo: the guilt of the Catholic Church for authorising judicial murder on a gigantic scale. Simon, unlike Sterzinger and Tartarotti, closed all the cracks through which any of the enduring arguments for the guilt of witches might seep. Simon's claim that all those executed for witchcraft had been innocent was more insistent than either Sterzinger or the Territorial Ordinances of Maria Theresia.

Sterzinger's adherents in Bavaria reacted with irritation to subsequent writings that supported witch trials. As late as February 1767, the *Churbayerische Intelligenzblatt* regarded the sudden and unexpected 'author's feverishness' with humour and irritation over the next several issues, reacting against the productions of those 'bewitched minds', who continually employed the same arguments to defend the existence of witches. Finally, in 1768, it published a satire directed against monastic academicians, the *Stossseufzer eines gelehrten Ignoranten*, depicting their uneasiness at living in a changed world devoid of witches.[68] In another Munich periodical edited by Braun, Osterwald and Pfeffel, the *Baierische(n) Sammlungen zum Unterricht und Vergnügen*, terms such as 'superstition', 'foxy scholar', 'learned fool', 'pedant', 'scholastic', etc., entered into the stock repertoire of themes directly relating to the 'Bavarian witchcraft war'. Shortly before Sterzinger's speech at the Academy, a short satire appeared

---

[67] Simon, *Anpreisung*, 237f.
[68] *Churbayrisches Intelligenzblatt* (1767); 18 February 1767, 'Authorfieber'; 30 August 1767, 'Verhexte Köpfe'; 16 August 1767, 'Stossseufzer eines gelehrten Ignoranten'. In 1767, the editor was J. S. Kohlbrenner.

in the *Sammlungen*, which might be viewed as a harbinger of the enlightened debate: in the 'Elysian fields', several philosphers dispute the efficacy of so-called 'thunder stones', ostensibly deriving their power from superstitious forces. 'A Thomist' supported their efficacy with learned scriptural authorities, while Descartes vehemently denied these properties, even after the proponent of the older philosophy proceeded to beat him with a 'thunder stone'. The locus of the debate in Elysium is characteristic for a conflict over philosophic principles between a scholastic and a luminary, i.e. between the 'old' and the 'new':

All the venerable bowed their heads in reverence when they heard this. The innovators laughed, as is customary among these birds of scorn, and the judge was so partisan that he joined them. He could hardly pronounce the sentence, having lost his breath from laughing so hard at the silliness of these good people. Until he was finally heard to say: The mere authority of someone venerable, were he a saint . . . had no weight in matters philosophical.[69]

The judge in Elysium represented the enlightened Elector, Maximilian III Joseph, or at least his idealised image as perceived by the luminaries in numerous references to him. The enlightened judge presented the learned public with a proper example for dealing with scholastic 'pedants', who persisted in traditional interpretations against all reason: he could hardly restrain his laughter.

Additional satires ensured that the public could also hardly help but laugh. In 1768, a 'Quill which loves the Truth' composed *Fünf bewehrte und wahrhaffte Hexen- und Gespenstergeschichten, die sich unlängst zugetragen,* ostensibly to support the 'defenders of witches' against Sterzinger. The reason: one should be able to cite incidents more recent than the 'Zauberer-Jackl' trials. However, of the pieces of 'evidence' it provided, each proved less useful than the last: a suspected poltergeist turns out to be a servant courting his sweetheart in a nocturnal visitation, a weather witch is actually a pair of pants blown onto a bell tower by the wind. The mayor has the pants arrested and subsequently exorcised by monks, until a carpenter appears in the council chambers to reclaim his trousers.[70] Beda Mayr, OSB, from Donauwörth, who later became a follower of Kant, took the defenders of witchcraft to task with no less severity. In his satire about

---

[69] *Baierische Sammlungen zum Unterricht und Vergnügen,* 11 (1766), 872–87 (anonymous). Thunder stone: Beitl, *Wörterbuch,* 140.

[70] F.L., *Fünf bewehrte und wahrhaffte Hexen- und Gespenstergeschichten, die sich unlängst zugetragen. Zur Bestätigung der letzten Hexengeschichte von Ingolstadt, herausgegeben und dem P. Sterzinger dediciert von einer die Wahrheit liebenden Feder,* Ingolstadt 1768. On the connection to the Salzburg 'Little Sorcerer Jack' trials, *ibid.,* 26; for the story of the trousers, 27f.

a trip to the moon, published in 1770, he criticised the theologians 'on the moon', who still pray according to the standards of the theologian 'Sturus Pemolbard', who died 600 years before. Whoever denied the existence of witches on the moon was denounced as a heretic, contrary to practices in enlightened Bavaria.[71]

The luminaries increased their criticisms of the educational system during the 'witchcraft war', pointing out that it was administered by just those institutions which persisted most adamantly in witchcraft beliefs, i.e. the monasteries. Many satires characterise them as stubborn pedants or learned fools, who argue against all reason for atavistic views. In January 1767, Sterzinger had already directed attention to those scholars who, 'chained to prejudice, slumber obliviously'. Blocksberger/Mayer made explicit mention of the 'vulgar education' received by monks, which he blamed on universities still directed by the Jesuits. The belief in witchcraft could be curtailed sharply over the next ten years, if 'the inefficacy of witchcraft' was taught publicly 'at the universities'.[72] These remarks were not simply directed at the universities, but at the entire educational system, which was largely in the hands of the monasteries and badly in need of reform.

Peter von Osterwald delivered the decisive blow in the 'Bavarian witchcraft war' in 1767. Exactly one year after Sterzinger's speech, Osterwald appeared before the Academy and the Elector to discuss the *Nutzen der logikalischen Regeln, besonders wider die Freigeisterei und den Aberglauben*.[73] In scholarly terms, the topic of his speech may seem trivial and, indeed, it received little attention in later literature. However, in the context of the 'Bavarian witchcraft war', its political and social implications were explosive and justify its characterisations as the climax and denouement of enlightened debate in Bavaria, even though a whole series of tracts was published subsequently. The subject of the speech was neither 'logical rulings' in general, nor free-thinking in particular, but rather the erroneous precision of traditional Catholic theology and the application of

---

[71] [B. Mayer], *Johann Kehrwischens Reise in den Mond, samt dem Realregister über die Merkwürdigkeiten derselben*, in H. Braun (ed.), *Ein Päckchen Satiren aus Oberdeutschland*, Munich 1770, 94–127.

[72] Sterzinger, *Betrügende Zauberkunst*, Vorrede (Preface); Mayer, *Sendschreiben*, III, 72. In the *Baierischen Sammlungen und Auszüge zum Unterricht und Vergnügen*, the numerous contributions all pointed in this direction. The following contributions appeared: in the second year (1766), 566, the 'Grabschrift eines Scholastikers' ('. . . Wer war er denn? Ein Narr . . .'); in the third year (1767), 73, a poem with the little 'Der Pedant'; in year four (1768), 190–2, the poem, 'Der Schulfuchs', celebrating the coming of the new philosophy: '. . . Jetzt stützt nur der Beweis die Sätze, das andre heisst man ein Geschwätze, und nichts als leere Grübeley.'

[73] P. v. Osterwald, *Rede vom Nutzen der logikalischen Regeln, besonders wider die Freigeisterei und den Aberglausen*, Munich 1767.

an untenable belief in witchcraft, which had sunk to the level of common superstition for Osterwald and other luminaries, an obsolete and long-recognised 'prejudice', against which 'reason' must finally arise victorious. The representative teachings of Augustine and Aquinas on the 'pactum tacitum', by which God allowed Satan to appear manifestly to a sorcerer, 'are false and opposed all rules of logic'.[74] Witches' flight and the Devil's pact were 'old wives' tales' for Osterwald and a theology or scholarship that allowed itself to admit to such fictions had to be condemned in the harshest terms possible:

> The peripatetic logic practised by our scholastics over the past four centuries is a very useless form of scholarship, which can neither lead to the discovery of new truths, nor prove established ones: it derives from twisted logic and for that reason it deserves all our contempt. . .[75]

Formally, Osterwald's speech was imbued with a conciliatory stance which fitted the official occasion. The by-products of theological superstition were juxtaposed with the dangers of free-thinking, scholasticism was not criticised wholesale but only in its exaggerations, and Osterwald avoided direct criticisms of the Bible, focusing instead on its exegesis ('Do you alone possess a correct understanding of Revelation? You must not search for anything more than that which is stated explicitly therein'). To this extent, his 1767 speech before the Academy is analogous to Sterzinger's of the previous year.

However, Osterwald went several steps further. Although he exhibited consideration for scholastic authorities and standing penal codes, he hardly stopped there. He couched his views in rhetorical questions, but left no doubt among his contemporaries that he, like Maffei and Jordan Simon, was completely convinced of the criminal innocence of the victims of witch trials. For Osterwald, confessions of witchcraft were products of 'madness' or 'fear of inhumane torture'. The judges were consumed 'by the superstitious prejudices of their times'.[76] Osterwald, less concerned with the witch trials in a bygone era, concentrated his attention on the present advocates of the possibility of witchcraft and the need for witch trials. He appealed to them directly with these closing remarks:

> In a word, simply re-examine these alleged stories . . . according to the rules of sound logic. I request, however, that you first discard your prejudice . . . Soon you will surely see that you are caught up by reasonable conclusions and must ultimately recognise that you have accepted old wives' tales as credible stories . . .[77]

---

[74] *Ibid.*, 32.   [75] *Ibid.*, 23.   [76] *Ibid.*, 33.   [77] *Ibid.*, 34.

The 'Bavarian witchcraft war', the final Catholic debate concerning the theme of witchcraft, has previously been viewed in isolation. In order to appreciate its full range of implications, it is necessary to broaden our horizons. In 1766–7, Bavaria stood on the brink of important political reforms directed primarily against the powerful territorial monasteries. The Church possessed 56 per cent of all property[78] and enjoyed considerable immunity from taxation. The extravagant policies of the Electors Maximilian Emanuel and Karl Albrecht in the first half of the eighteenth century consequently resulted in a rising state deficit. Even after imperial ambitions were abandoned following the Peace of Füssen in 1745, the debt continued to increase during the Seven Years War. Although the debt mounted to a staggering thirty-two million gulden and state bankruptcy could only be avoided with the help of French subsidies and papal authorization for a 'decimal' contribution from monastic property, the monasteries tenaciously and successfully resisted all forms of direct taxation.[79] The resistance of the wealthy cloisters and the dependence of the state on papal approval increased pressure for a fundamental reform of legal relations between state and Church after 1760, in order to secure state authority over the monasteries by breaking down traditional immunities. In 1761, Court Councillor Peter von Osterwald was named Director of the Ecclesiastical Council. In 1766, Osterwald published a 'revolutionary tract' (Hammermayer) entitled *Veremund von Lochsteins Gründe sowohl für als wider die geistliche Immunität in weltlichen Dingen*. Based on a rationalised understanding of natural law as well as Jansenist and early Josephine examples, the tract propounded the programmatic repression of church influence in 'secular matters' in favour of the state.

Osterwald's 'Lochstein' tract immediately resulted in excited debate, taken up by targeted clergy. Some bishops banned the tract, various theologians of the orders composed oppositional tracts and, at the beginning of 1767, Rome placed the tract on the Index.[80] Despite this formidable resistance, the Bavarian legal reforms proposed by Osterwald were initiated in the autumn of 1768: the reform of the Ecclesiastical Council, the so-called 'Klostermandate' of 1768–70, and the creation of the electoral censorship authorities in February 1769 (the elimination of the ecclesiastical censorship board). Apparently, these far-ranging plans were

---

[78] Spindler, *Handbuch*, II, 1092 (Hammermeyer); Pfeilschifter-Baumeister, *Der Salzburger Kongress*, 111.   [79] Spindler, *Handbuch*, II, 1092f. (Hammermeyer).
[80] *Ibid.*, 990; Pfeilschifter-Baumeister, *Der Salzburger Kongress*, 107ff.; R. Bauer, *Der kurfürstliche geistliche Rat und die bayrische Kirchenpolitik 1768–1802*, Munich 1971, 50f. [P. v. Osterwald], *Veremund von Lochsteins Gründe sowohl für als wider die geistliche Immunität in weltlichen Dingen*, Munich 1766. Osterwald's 'Lochstein' tract appeared about six months before Sterzinger's speech; the 'Lochstein' debate was already underway in the autumn of 1766. Observant contemporaries made the connection between the two themes.

intended to erode the position of the surrounding episcopates, in addition to mediating the power of the territorial monasteries.[81]

Without intending to detract from the importance of Sterzinger's role in the 'Bavarian witchcraft war', it must nevertheless be admitted that the debate on witches fits quite snugly into the state reform plans of the 1760s. It opened a 'second front' alongside the 'Lochstein' debate, not only chronologically, but in terms of content as well: the fiscal motives behind state attacks on the immunities of the cloisters are readily visible and no issue was better suited to discredit the monasteries in the eyes of luminaries than their support for witch trials. The defence of witch burnings by monastic theologians simultaneously called their theology, the legitimacy of their monopoly over the educational system and their immunities into question. One hundred and sixty years after the high point of persecutions, witchcraft again became the focus of heated political debate: as in the past, witchcraft again polarised the forces of confrontation among the forces of religious dogmatism and those of a pragmatic 'reasonable' Realpolitik at the state level, though for novel reasons. The employment of witchcraft as a symbol of political and social progress testifies to the tactical aptitude of the luminaries in Munich.

Even contemporaries suspected that Sterzinger's speech was commissioned by Osterwald or some other luminary of the Academy of Sciences.[82] At the very least an inner circle, most probably the Elector, Osterwald and Pfeffel, was appraised of the contents of the speech since September 1766. The speech was approved on 2 October 1766.[83] Sterzinger's opponents, including the academic members Merz, OSA, März, OSB, and Ganser, OSB, were unaware of its content, since they were only able to commence their oppositional tracts after the public hearing. This lends credence to the suggestion of a deck stacked by the luminaries against their potential opponents. One can assume that Sterzinger's unique provocation was actually planned as a parallel to public debate on the 'Lochstein' programme, because it offered the luminaries the only means to discredit monastic theologians before a large German-speaking audience. As Westenrieder put it: otherwise, the 'pedants' could not be made 'shy and cautious'.

In part, the circle of combatants in the immunity/witchcraft debate overlapped. The monastic theologians felt targeted by both debates. From 1766 to 1770, Benno Ganser, OSB, of Niederaltaich, composed no fewer than four polemics against 'Lochstein'/Osterwald, while, on the other side,

---

[81] Spindler, *Handbuch*, II, 1093ff. (Hammermayer); Bauer, *Der kurfüstliche Rat*, 55–125.

[82] Messerer, 'Breife', I, 250; Ott, *Gespräche*, n.p.; F. Sterzinger, *Bemühung, den Aberglauben zu stürzen*, Munich 1787, 88.

[83] L. v. Westenrieder, *Beytäge zur vaterländischen Historie (. . .)*, I, Munich 1788, 342f.

Andreas Ulrich Mayer retorted with as many in favour of the legal reforms, receiving approval from Sterzinger.[84] While the circle of authors willing to play 'advocatus diaboli' was tightly knit – evoking polemic comments from the luminaries that affirmed the critique of 'vulgar' education of monastic theologians by 'Lochstein'[85] – Sterzinger's adherents were more heterogeneous: professors from Vienna and Erfurt and secular publishers like Finauer and Kohlbrenner stood side by side with monks, members of the secular clergy, and possibly Pfeffel in Munich, a direct confidant of Osterwald. The Bavarian clergy who publicly sided with the Munich luminaries from 1767 to 1770 later received generous promotions from Osterwald. Sterzinger assumed the post of Director to the Historical Class of the Bavarian Academy of Sciences after Pfeffel's departure in 1768; Braun and Kollmann were rewarded with canonical prebends in Munich and co-opted onto the Ecclesiastical Council. Both were tasked with areas central to the luminaries' goals, namely the reform and restructuring of the educational system in Bavaria. The appointments of Braun and Kollmann in this area were very consistent with the Enlightenment in Bavaria, since the luminaries attributed the roots of all superstition and witchcraft beliefs to improper education at the hands of monks.[86]

The 'Bavarian witchcraft war', located in an over-arching political movement, marks the victory of the Bavarian luminaries against the representatives of a surviving social system at a point when the probability of victory was already assured. Nevertheless, the 'witchcraft war' was more than a symbolic struggle, since it was directly related to the reality of witchcraft beliefs, which were reawakened among the populace by the numerous sermons of theological supporters of witch trials. Even though many participants in the debate noted that the age of major witchcraft persecutions lay 130 years in the past,[87] the last witch burning in Bavaria

[84] On Ganser's publications, cf. J. G. Meusel, *Lexikon der vom Jahre 1750–1800 verstorbenen teutschen Schrifsteller*, 15 vols., Leipzig 1802–16, IV, 19; on Mayer's work, *ibid.*, V, 82–4. On Sterzinger's position, Fieger, *Sterzinger*, 160–9. More generally, Bauer, *Der kurfürstliche Rat* 41ff., 52, 101f.; Pfeilschifter-Baumeister, *Der Salzburger Kongress*, 108. Enlightened monks recognised the parallel with unease; v. Dülmen 'Aufklärung', 918.

[85] Mayer, *Sendschreiben*, III, 34f. Another parallel to the 'Lochstein' debate.

[86] J. Gebele, *Peter von Osterwald. Ein Beitrag zur Geschichte der Aufklärung in Bayern unter Kurfürst Max III. Joseph*, Munich 1891, 117–30. Kollmann participated in the debate of 1768: [J. A. Kollmann], *Zweifel eines Bayers über die wirkende Zauberkunst und Hexerei, An dem Lechstrom*, (Augsburg) 1768. The connection between engaged publications and entrusting school reform is more apparent in Westenrieder, *Beyträge*, I, 376–81; also K. A. Baader, *Das gelehrte Baiern oder Lexikon aller Schriftsteller, welche Baiern im 18. Jahrhundert erzeugte oder ernährte*, I (A–K), Nuremberg/Sulzbach 1804, 617f. Braun entered into the witchcraft debate on numerous occasions: through his polemics (cf. note 54), as well as satires which he either edited or wrote (cf. note 71). The forum was provided by his monthly periodical *Der Patriot in Bayern*. On Braun and Kollmann in general, Bauer, *Der kurfüstliche Rat*, 92ff., 104ff.; Spindler, *Handbuch*, IV/2, 951f.

[87] [A. U. Mayer], *Nichtige unbegründete, eitle, kahle und lächerliche Verantwortung des H. P.*

in 1766 had been scarcely a decade earlier. The last series of burnings from 1749 to 1756 occurred during a time when the luminaries Ickstatt and Lori were already members of the law faculty of the University of Ingolstadt, during the reign of the enlightened Elector, Maximilian III Joseph. In 1752, the Privy Council in Munich responded to inquiries from the provincial administration in Landshut that a woman should be burned according to the provisions of Kreittmayr's reformed penal code for copulating with the Devil.[88] A sorcerer was executed in the Bishopric of Augsburg in 1766 and another in the Prince-Abbey of Kempten 1775.[89] Although the last great debate occurred at a relatively late date, it still impacted on current affairs. Only a legitimate prospect for an official end to witchcraft trials was required to initiate it.

COMBATING SUPERSTITION AFTER THE 'WITCHCRAFT WAR'

Neuester Hexenprozess aus dem aufgeklärten heutigen Jahrhundert, oder: So dumm liegt mein bayrisches Vaterland noch unter dem Joch der Mönche und des Aberglaubens   (Anonymous polemic, 1786)

The raging persistence of witchcraft beliefs among the populace was as little affected by the 'Bavarian witchcraft war' as was the insatiable desire of many clergymen to continue with their usual exorcisms and anti-magic directed against demons, ghosts and witches. The physical reality of evil was still publicly preached to hold the flock of believers together. The 'witch fathers', those outspoken specialists fought by representatives of the Enlightenment and still commonly found in the monasteries of the territory, were more than mere straw men to be burned in effigy to achieve the political goal of diminishing the influence of the church on society.[90] Only three years after the ebbing of the 'Bavarian witchcraft war', the

---

Angelus März, Benedictiner in Scheyern, über die von P. Don Ferdinand Sterzinger bey dem hochfürstlichen geistlichen Rat in Freysing gestellten Fragen, Vom Moldaustrom, [Prague] 1767, 7f. Similarly, F. Sterzinger, *Betrügende Zauberkunst,* 42: 'Nachdem verschiedene Autoren tapfer wider die Hexenprozesse geschrieben, wurden die Verbrennung der Hexen so selten, dass man sie von hundert Jahren her leicht zählen kann.' Cf. Rübel, *Systematische Abhandlung,* (1759), 127, 131.

[88] HStAM, Kurbayern, Geheimer Rat No. 165, fol. 269v.

[89] J. Pezzl, *Faustin oder das philosophische Jahrhundert,* Zurich 1783 (republished: W. Griep (ed.), Hildesheim 1982). Despite its exaggerations, the novel provides interesting insights on the confrontation between luminaries and the defenders of the traditional witchcraft beliefs in southeast Germany at the time of the 'witchcraft war'. *Ibid.,* 26–34, 44–51. Film 416; on the Kempten witch trial of 1775 cf. chapter 5, pp. 344–54.

[90] Soldan *et al., Geschichte der Hexenprozesse,* II, 313ff.; Riezler, *Geschichte,* 317ff.; C. Wehn, Der Kampf des Journals von und für Deutschland gegen den Aberglauben seiner Zeit, Diss. Phil., Cologne 1937, 81f., 87.

flames of the witchcraft debate were fanned anew by the appearance of the faith healer, J. J. Gassner,[91] on the scene, who accorded the origins of illness to the influence of demons and witches rather than to natural causes. This pastor from the Vorarlberg won sensational success as a faith healer after 1774, quickly gathering a strong following throughout southern Germany and beyond that included adherents in the highest social circles. He was summoned in that same year to Regensburg and Ellwangen to treat Prince-Bishop Ignaz Anton von Fugger for blindness, celebrating a major success through his treatments. The luminaries displayed animosity toward these events from the first, because Gassner's 'wonders' offered new evidence to support the physical efficacy of witchcraft and demons. When his *Nützlicher Unterricht wider den Teufel zu streiten* appeared in Kempten in 1774, the enlightened party in Munich went on the offensive again. Sterzinger wrote a review in the *Churbayrisches Intelligenzblatt*, that justified Osterwald, then serving as a member of the college of censors, in banning the work in Bavaria.[92]

This conflict took a fundamental turn, because Gassner was praised by portions of the clergy and the public 'as the Apostle sent to oppose free thinkers'.[93] Thousands of his followers travelled to Ellwangen in the coming weeks to be cured by Gassner and his disciples or simply to view the sensational exorcisms. Among Gassner's adherents were numerous Protestants, including the Duke of Württemberg and the famous Lavater from Zurich, in addition to members of the clergy and the imperial aristocracy. Gassner received public support from the Bishops of Regensburg, Eichstätt and Freising, as well as from the Prince-Abbot of Kempten. The secular authorities in the Upper Palatinate, the court at Sulzbach and the electoral Bavarian administration in Amberg all called upon Gassner to demonstrate his talents. The party of ex-Jesuits[94] in Augsburg and Ingolstadt justified Gassner's activities, and the personal physician of

[91] J. Hanauer, Der Exorzist Johann Joseph Gassner (1727–1779). Eine Monographie, Diss. Phil., Würzburg 1950; G. Pfeilschifter, Des Exorzisten Gassner Tätigkeit in der Konstanzer Diözese im Jahr 1774, in *Historisches Jb. d. Görres-Gesellschaft* 52 (1932), 401–41; Soldan et al., *Geschichte der Hexenprozesse*, II, 311–13; Riezler, *Geschichte*, 314f.; Rapp, *Die Hexenprozesse*, 133ff.; Fieger, *Sterzinger*, 169–234. Pezzl's satirical report *Faustin*, (pp. 34–44) is also informative.

[92] J. J. Gassner, *Nützlicher Unterricht wider den Teufel zu streiten*, Kempten 1774 (twelve editions by 1782! Hanauer, 'Der Exorzist'); Spindler, *Handbuch*, II, 990f. (Hammermayer).

[93] v. Dülmen, 'Aufklärung', 64, on the correspondence between the Augustinian Steigenberger and Töpsl from Polling. Steigenberger reported to his abbot concerning his audience with Elector Maximilian III Joseph, who once again took the side of the luminaries. The reactionary propaganda evoked by Gassner's activities led Steigenberger 'to fear grave consequences'.

[94] v. Dülmen, 'Angkläning', 111, 121f., 129. Steigenberger speaks of the 'Wolterisch-Gasnerische(n) Parthey', *ibid.*, 111, as well as the 'Jesuitische(n) Parthey' and its 'patron v. Wolter', *ibid.*, 121. More generally, Spindler, *Handbuch*, II, 993 (Hammermayer).

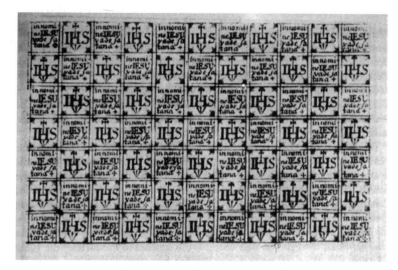

15. Peasant magic: charms against bewitchment of the cattle, as used in the eighteenth century.

16. Gassner's *Weise wider den Teufel zu streiten*, a work by the exorcist J.J. Gassner, who ascribed most illnesses to witchcraft or the work of the Devil, published in 1774.

the Elector, Wolter,[95] was just as impressed by the efficacy of Gassner's 'wondrous cures' as were many other high officials from Bavaria, indeed from the entire region. When one considers the essential importance of the Gassner conflict against the backdrop of the witchcraft debate, it offers interesting insights into the mentality, as well as the geography and sociological formation, of conservatism (Epstein) in Germany, which has received inadequate treatment in the past. Only a rough outline of the resistance to Gassner can be offered here. Sterzinger travelled with a delegation to Ellwangen and observed the suggestive activities of the exorcist, documented and commented upon in his *Die aufgedeckten Gassnerischen Wunderkuren.*[96] Between 1774 and 1777, a published debate on Gassner ensued, during which Sterzinger and Johann Salomo Semler from Halle[97] emerged as the leaders of the enlightened party. The Gassner conflict resonated throughout the entire German-speaking press with more than one hundred publications,[98]

[95] Cf. note 94. Fieger, *Sterzinger*, 179ff.; Hanauer, 'Der Exorzist', 81–7.

[96] F. Sterzinger, *Die aufgedeckten Gassnerischen Wunderkuren. Aus authentischen Urkunden beleuchtet und durch Augenzeugen bewiesen*, Munich 1775. See also Fieger, *Sterzinger*, 198; Pfeilschifter, 'Des Exorzisten', 402; Hanauer, 'Der Exorzist', 92ff.

[97] J. S. Semler, *Sammlungen von Briefen und Aufsätzen über die Gassnerischen und Schröpferischen Geisterbeschwörungen, mit eigenen vielen Anmerkungen*, Halle 1776. On Semler: *ADB* 33, 698–704. However, Semler's influence on the Gassner conflict was much less than Sterzinger's. Cf. note 98.

[98] Pfeilschifter, 'Des Exorzisten', 432, underestimates the number of the polemics exchanged. Hanauer, 'Der Exorzist', II–X, counts 113 tracts for or against Gassner. Although Hanauer was unable to decode many anonymous tracts, the fronts remain quite clearly divided: leading the side of Gassner's opponents was F. Sterzinger with five (of thirty-three) tracts. He was followed by J. F. Graf von Auersperg (1743–95), head of the cathedral chapter of Passau and an engaged luminary, councillor of Emperor Joseph II and later Prince-Bishop of Passau, who published three. Two tracts each were composed by the Augsburg notary G. W. Zapf (1747–1810), later electoral privy-councillor of Mainz and Palatine Count of the imperial court, as well as a privy councillor of Wallerstein and later provincial director F. M. v. Schaden (1726–90). Other pro-Sterzinger authors included Protestant pastors of Memmingen and Leipzig, Catholic Court Councillors from Würzburg and Vienna and as yet unidentified authors from Berlin and Prague. The official stance of the luminaries had, by then, advanced: Emperor Joseph II and Elector Maximilian III Joseph (as well as his councillor v. Osterwald) both made their support for the enlightened faction known, as did the Archbishops of Salzburg, Prague, Trier and Mainz, and the Bishops of Würzburg, Augsburg and Constance. However, the supporters of Gassner were just as visible: of fifty-five tracts, seven each were composed by the personal physician of the Princes of Palatine-Sulzbach, Dr B. J. Schleiss von Löwenfeld, and by the Premonstratensian abbot Oswald Loschert, who had already joined in the witchcraft debates of 1749/50 and 1766/70. A councillor of Ellwangen, v. Sartori, and the Augsburg ex-Jesuit Alois Merz (1727–92) also published five tracts each. It is also worth mentioning the two pieces composed by another Augsburg ex-Jesuit, Zeiller (*alii Savonarolam Exjesuitam esse credunt*), the scandalous testimony of the Ingolstadt ex-Jesuits M. Gabler and B. Stattler (1728–97) on Sterzinger's behalf. The initial exuberance of the Zurich pastor, J. K. Lavater (1741–1801), is also well known. Gassner received direct support from the Prince-Bishops of Regensburg, Eichstätt and Freising, the Prince-Abbot of Kempten, the court in Palatine-Sulzbach, as well as the Prince K. A. v. Hohenlohe-Schillingsfürst and Duke Ludwig Eugen von Württemberg.

making it one of the major debates of the German Enlightenment. The Enlightenment in Catholic Germany had established enough credence to move some authorities to proceed against Gassner administratively. The Archbishops of Trier, Salzburg, Mainz and Prague turned against the faith healer, as did the Bishops of Augsburg (personally united with Trier), Constance and Würzburg. The Elector of Bavaria forbade the publication of his writings in 1774, reprimanding the provincial administration in Amberg and four Ingolstadt professors, among them the ex-Jesuit Stattler, in 1775 for their support of Gassner.[99] The Catholic campaign against Gassner reached its climax with the intervention of Emperor Joseph II, who forbade the promotion of Gassner's activities by the Prince-Bishop of Regensburg, especially his exorcisms. Finally, the newly elected Pope, Pius VI, criticised Gassner's views on the origin of illnesses.[100] The channels of the decision-making process in the Gassner affair have yet to be researched fully, but the little material examined thus far indicates that some threads spun in Munich ultimately obstructed and finally ended his activities.[101]

The struggle over witch beliefs and superstition continued undiminished even after the conclusion of the Gassner conflict. Sterzinger published a number of tracts right up to his death in 1786, summarising in school-book fashion the knowledge necessary to carry on the fight against superstition.[102] The last legal execution of a witch in the canton of Glarus in Protestant Switzerland in 1782 resulted in broad public condemnation for the first time.[103] Catholic periodicals, like the *Journal von und für Deutschland*, published in Fulda, dedicated itself to a permanent supra-confessional struggle against witch beliefs and superstition.[104] At the end of the 1780s, the Dillingen professor of physics, Joseph Weber, opened a minor debate with his *Die Nichtigkeit der Zauberey*, which once again forcibly emphasised the persistent cleft of world-views between the ex-Jesuit party and the moderate Catholic luminaries against the backdrop of monasticism in the age of the persecution of the Illuminati and the French

---

[99] Fieger, *Sterzinger*, 204–16; Pfeilschifter, 'Des Exorzisten', 427ff.; Hanauer, 'Der Exorzist', 140–219, with further details.

[100] Fieger, *Sterzinger*, 218; Hanauer, 'Der Exorzist', 206–19. The intervention of Catholic authorities against the ex-Jesuit party and their prophet, Gassner, was deeply satisfying for 'enlightened' monks: 'Wir lachen unterdessen und fühlen ein süsses Vergnügen.' Dülmen, 'Aufklärung', 111.

[101] Pfeilschifter, 'Des Exorzisten', 427f.; Fieger, *Sterzinger*, 225, points out the connection with Sterzinger's pastoral letter to the Archbishop of Prague contra Gassner.

[102] Sterzinger, *Geister* . . .; F. Sterzinger, *Bemühung*. Sterzinger's impact was praised throughout Germany. *Journal von und für Deutschland* 5 (1786), 273; Westenrieder *Geschichte*, 233f.

[103] Soldan et al., *Geschichte der Hexenprozesse*, II, 327–31; Baschwitz, *Hexen*, 466f. As in the Gassner controversy, there was great engagement by the Swabian publicist C. F. D. Schuhbart (1739–91).   [104] Wehn, *Der Kampf*, 66–88, 169ff.

Revolution.[105] The political restoration at the end of the eighteenth century still did not bring about a resurrection of the witchcraft question. Even persons of the ilk of Westenrieder, newly converted to conservatism through the honours bestowed upon him, looked back with emotion upon the conflict of world-views in the mid-eighteenth century that brought an end to witch burnings. Sterzinger was elevated to the level of a national hero and his death in 1786 was unanimously mourned from Hamburg to Vienna. The 'witchcraft war' was subsequently featured as an irretrievably pioneering achievement at the dawn of a new age:

> These events belong to others of that age which no thinking Bavarian can recall without tears. Oh, you pleasant unrest! Oh, you days filled with deeds of healing struggles, how sweet and powerful is your memory! How often will you be remembered by our descendants as the example of happy times of better thinking and the courage of our brave nation![106]

Obituaries of and memorials to Sterzinger called the question of superstition into balance, demonstrating the existence of a pronounced town–country dividing line in the repression of witchcraft beliefs which were generally opposed by the learned strata of society. Critical commentary by contemporaries demonstrates, however, that the optimism was conjoined with goal orientation.[107] Superstition remained rampant among the general populace. One of the motivating factors mentioned in plans for the secularisation of the monasteries at the end of the eighteenth century under Elector Maximilian IV Joseph and his Privy Councillor, Montgelas, was that they were a burden to society, 'because they survive at its cost and they spread ignorance and superstition'.[108] Even at the beginning of the nineteenth century, the state-administrative struggle against popular superstition was incomplete. The fight against superstition was now entrusted to the newly educated class of teachers. The process of 'disenchanting the world' might have speeded up, but it remains undecided to the present day.[109]

---

[105]   J. Weber, *Ungrund des Hexen- und Gespensterglaubens*, Dillingen, n.d.; *idem, Die Nichtigkeit der Zauberei*, Salzburg 1787. Opposition was raised: Anon., *Über die Hexen Reformation des Professors Weber zu Dillingen. Von einem katholischen Weltmanne*, n.p. 1787. (The author was probably part of the ex-Jesuit circle in Augsburg.) 'Ein anderer katholischer Weltmann zu Augsburg' came to Weber's aid with the satirical title: Anon., *Was hält man anderswo von Hexerei, Zauberei, Gespenstern, Amuletten, Ignazibohnen und geweihten Kräutern*, Augsburg 1787. This theme was too passé for the luminaries. Riezler, *Geschichte*, 315ff.; Messerer, 'Briefe', 674.   [106]   Westenrieder, *Geschichte*, 342f.
[107]   Wehn, 'Der Kampf', 159; Sterzinger, *Geister . . .*, 32; Riezler, *Geschichte*, 315.
[108]   Spindler, *Handbuch*, IV, 41 (Weis).
[109]   O. Schmidt, 'Brauchtum und Aberglauben in der Oberpfalz i.J. 1809', in *Verhandlungen d. Hist. Ver. Oberpfalz u. Regensburg* 121 (1981), 489–502, provides provisional results of

Nevertheless, the first two decades of the nineteenth century represent a watershed, with which this work can usefully conclude. Under the 'all-powerful' Minister, Montgelas (1799–1817), all of southeast Germany, including the Imperial Cities and territories examined here, were consolidated into 'greater' Bavaria, elevated to the status of a Kingdom by Napoleon in 1806. At this time, all the monasteries were secularised, the monastic orders were eliminated and a secular educational system with comprehensive attendance requirements for the whole population was established. The smaller secular territories and the ecclesiastical territories, among them the Prince-Bishoprics of Freising, Regensburg, Bamberg, Würzburg, Passau, Eichstätt and Augsburg, as well as portions of the Archbishoprics of Salzburg, Mainz and the Prince-Abbey of Kempten, were subjugated. This centralised state was ruled from Munich according to the new French model and those reforms initiated by the luminaries in the eighteenth century, then limited by the dictates of balancing precarious internal politics, were finally pushed through. In 1808, torture in criminal procedure was ultimately eliminated. Legally limited and less applied during the preceding century, its application came to an end in the Electorate in 1803 and, shortly after its elevation to the status of kingdom, in the rest of the region in 1808.[110]

The abolition of penalties for witchcraft and sorcery first came into being with the legal reforms of Feuerbach in 1813.[111] Long an absurd irritation for the supporters of the Enlightenment, controversial even during the high point of the 'witch craze', the power of tradition-bound forces had finally receded to the point that this crime, now only nominally existent on paper, could at long last be extinguished.

this process shortly after the social and state upheaval. On the persistent acceptance of witchcraft beliefs, cf. E. Wagner, 'Hexenglauben in Franken heute,' in: *Jb. f. fränk. Landesforschung* 30 (1970), 343–356; H. Fink, *Verzaubertes Land*, Vienna/Innsbruck/Munich 1973; I. Schöck, *Hexenglaube in der Gegenwart. Empirische Untersuchungen in Südwestdeutschland*, Tübingen 1978.

[110] Spindler, *Handbuch*, II, 1074–6 (Hammermayer).
[111] *Ibid.*, 1075; Riezler, *Geschichte*, 319.

7 Conclusions

A multi-levelled, problem-oriented and comparative regional analysis of early modern witchcraft beliefs, trials, persecutions and contemporary perceptions does not lend itself to simple summarisation. With this in mind, the next three sections offer a brief critical overview of this study and raise questions for future research. We begin with witchcraft trials and learned discourse in Bavaria, then compare southeast Germany with other regions and conclude in the attempt to abstract fundamental causes of major persecutions in early modern Europe by integrating our regional findings into the current discussion on witchcraft as a whole.

WITCHCRAFT TRIALS AND LEARNED DISCOURSE IN SOUTHEASTERN GERMANY: A SUMMARY

Our efforts at quantification demonstrate the irregularity of trials and executions, which peaked at some times and faded at others. Witchcraft might be considered a two-tiered problem: upon a relatively constant and ubiquitous foundation of beliefs in the reality of magic, sorcery and witchcraft, a conjunctural layer of accusations fluctuated over time, linked to the agrarian crises that recurred at frequent intervals in early modern Europe.[1] Contrary to common opinion, only a minority of these accusations ever culminated in witch trials or burnings. Since almost 75 per cent of the witch burnings documented here occurred within a period of less than fifty years – between 1586 and 1630 – no direct correlation between popular beliefs, executions and agrarian crises can be established. Indirectly, however, they always provided the backdrop; every denunciation or accusation[2] of witchcraft was fuelled by popular beliefs in magic and even

---

[1] Cf. on this chapter 2, pp. 89–114. In view of the extent of this work, a single reference is made here to the passages on which the summary is based.

[2] The contrast between adversarial and inquisitorial procedure, so often made in the older secondary literature, played practically no role of importance, because even in inquisitorial

those rare major persecutions conducted by the authorities –those in 1590, 1600, 1610, 1614 and 1629 –occurred during crises, above all the devastations of 1585–9 and 1626–8. And, even in years of severe crisis, executions were limited to relatively few districts, if the region is considered as a whole. Apart from several administrative centres (e.g. Dillingen, Munich, Landshut and Wallerstein), executions were rare events from a local standpoint. Conjunctures first stand out at the regional level. This is especially true of excessive witchcraft persecutions which, in spite of their rarity, encompassed the vast majority of total executions. In all, fourteen major and thirty-six minor persecutions, fifty in all, were spread over a period of two centuries in a region of 38,000 square kilometres with a population of over one million around the year 1600. These fifty persecutions were concentrated in only thirty-six districts; the Duchy of Bavaria alone (excluding the Upper Palatinate) contained over one hundred counties. Even if several additional trials are discovered in the future,[3] these proportions indicate that witch hunts were uncommon occurrences above and beyond the normal volume of accusations or trials for sorcery and witchcraft.

Witchcraft persecutions were conducted when the interests of the authorities coincided with those of their 'subjects'. If the population actively opposed a witch hunt, it ended quickly. If the authorities opposed a persecution, it never even started. Two factors were decisive in the region studied here. First of all, the judicial apparatus was characterised by an advanced state of centralisation, guaranteeing that the dictates of the central authorities guided witchcraft policy. Local officials, regularly accused by authors since Friedrich Spee of supporting trials for reasons of financial, sexual or personal gain, did not play a deciding role in this region. In fact, the central authorities were quick to punish any excesses they uncovered.[4] Secondly, strict evidential criteria were imposed during most trials for sorcery or witchcraft, resulting in incalculable risks for accusers or denunciators. Supporters of persecution constantly lamented these regrettable conditions. Furthermore, judicial procedure was expensive and time-consuming, requiring messengers to travel back and forth, local judges to appear at the central court, administrative commissions to conduct investigations at the scene of the trial, expert executioners to be called in to torture witches properly and legal briefs to be obtained from

procedure (*ex officio* establishment of the facts) at least one person had to make a denunciation, and in practice had a status similar to that of a plaintiff: he was made liable if he brought a false charge. Cf. on this Unverhau, 'Akkusationsprozess', who has devoted a detailed essay to this subject.
[3] Cf. for a discussion of the results of quantitative investigation, the summary at the end of chapter 2, pp. 89–114.
[4] Cf. chapter 4, execution of the witch judge of Wemding, pp. 292–5.

foreign jurists or universities. Despite confiscations,[5] trials usually ended in a deficit for the state budget or local judges, who were seldom reimbursed for expenses. Only the executioners profited greatly. Generally, when a trial for witchcraft was held, it was motivated by a sincere desire to investigate suspicions of witchcraft.

In recent years, the evolution of suspicions has attracted much attention from international scholars.[6] Our study demonstrates that none of the schematic explanations of the selective process satisfactorily indicates why certain persons were ultimately executed as witches. Most overlook the fact that only a tiny percentage of suspects actually ended their lives at the stake. Trial records frequently comment on the heredity of witchcraft in certain families, even though no charges had ever been brought. The rarity of trials can be explained by the self-regulation of the magical folk culture,[7] the relative difficulty of proving accusations, the risk for the accuser, and even a certain reluctance on the part of judges to conduct trials for fear of conflict with the local populace, the central government, or both. Supporters urged persecutions on the grounds that there were so many witches, they could be found in the tiniest hamlet, but our study indicates that only exceptional circumstances could unleash a persecution. After 1590, the application of stricter criteria for defining such exceptional circumstances resulted in a decline in persecutions.[8]

The great wave of persecutions around 1590 was the central, formative event in the history of witchcraft persecutions in southeast Germany. Until that time, no regional body of legislation dealt specifically with witchcraft and reports of executions were extremely rare. Though there are signs that the elaborated concept of witchcraft had gained some acceptance since the beginning of the fifteenth century (Nider, Hartlieb), it had obviously failed to establish itself firmly until the eve of the major persecutions. Influenced by Petrus Canisius, chroniclers in Augsburg followed the witch trials in southwest Germany with astonishment and, with the onset of regional persecutions in the 1590s, expert executioners had to be called in from

---

[5] This is another hackneyed motif of the secondary literature: the enrichment of the judges. Schormann, *Hexenprozesse* (1981), 80–9, has examined the validity of this thesis and has rightly presented the evidence against it. In the present regional study the accounts, which are preserved in part and are very extensive, have not been examined. The negative cost balance for the tax authorities emerges unambiguously from the numerous internal memoranda of the governments. Cf. for example chapter 4, where the high costs of proceedings are balanced against the expected increase in harvests, if those who were alleged to have damaged the crops are destroyed.

[6] The contributions to the collection of articles in Degn *et al., Hexenprozesse*, show how Macfarlane's microsociological approach found a school of followers.

[7] Cf. chapter 2, Witch trials and popular magic, pp. 65–88.

[8] Cf. chapter 3, pp. 158–82 on the triggering events, chapter pp. 269–90 on the tightening of the criteria. The whole discussion of the following forty years revolved around these criteria. Individually inconspicuous, collectively they were decisive.

areas where the papal Inquisitors Sprenger and Institoris had once been active.[9] In view of the broad circulation of Tengler's *Layenspiegel*, the tacit disregard for inquisitorial theories demonstrated by Pfalz-Neuburg jurists such as Mumprecht or the Bavarian criminal law commentators Perneder, Hunger and Schrenck can only be interpreted as a sign of conscious rejection.[10] Legal and theological reflection on the crime of witchcraft only began after the persecutions of the 1590s were well under way, bursting the seams of established procedure. Catholic jurists referred to the persecutions of Sprenger and Institoris as precedents, while Lutheran theologians and jurists stressed the novelty of the trials or linked them to apocalyptic fears of the imminent end of the world.

We might caricature the wave of persecutions in the 1590s as a regional test of fire. Bavarian authorities lacked a great deal of prior experience and soon adopted the policies of the Prince-Bishop of Augsburg, Marquard vom Berg,[11] who began massive persecutions in two counties of his territory in 1587. Independent, or at least relatively independent of confessional, political, economic and social structures, persecutions set in during the next three years in the following territories: the Protestant Principalities of Pfalz-Neuburg and Ansbach-Bayreuth, the Catholic Prince-Bishoprics of Freising and Eichstätt, the Duchy of Bavaria, the Teutonic Order's territory of Ellingen and the Free-Imperial cities of Nördlingen, Kaufbeuren, Weissenburg and Windsheim, the Catholic and Protestant noble territories of the Counts of Oettingen, of Rechberg, and the Fuggers, the territories of the Marshal of Pappenheim, the Lords of Kaltenthal, of Geyern, of Randeckh, the lands of the cathedral chapter of Augsburg, the possessions of the monastery of the Holy Cross at Donauwörth, and the city of Donauwörth itself. Even in places where there were no executions for witchcraft, such as the imperial cities of Augsburg, Regensburg or Nuremberg, the imperial abbey of Irsee, the princely monastery of Kempten, or courts in the territories of Pfalz-Neuburg and Bavaria, trials were hastily orchestrated in the frenzied atmosphere of these years. This first and greatest regional wave of persecution extended from the Alps in the south to the river Main in the north, reaching far into the neighbouring region of Franconia, which thus came into contact with the problem of witchcraft almost as soon as did southeast Germany. During later persecutions in the Upper Archbishopric of Mainz and the Prince-Bishoprics of Würzburg and Bamberg, we come across the first reports of executions for witchcraft, as in the Lutheran Principalities of Ansbach and Coburg.[12] In

---

[9] Cf. chapter 2, pp. 65–88, chapter 3, pp. 115–20.

[10] Cf. chapter 2, Rejection of the paradigm of witche-hunting, pp. 79–83.

[11] Cf. chapter 3, pp. 121–57.

[12] The regional reconstruction of the wave of witch hunting in chapter 3, pp. 121–57.

southeast Germany, ten of the fourteen major persecutions and fifteen of the thirty-six minor ones, about half of all those discovered in this region thus far, took place in the years around 1590. Of the more than 900 executions for witchcraft known to date in southeast Germany, almost half fell within the decade around 1590. In that year alone no fewer than 250 witches were burned at the stake – the absolute high point of witch hunting in this region.[13]

Somewhat paradoxically, the onset of persecutions coincided with their climax. This curious phenomenon is explained by the mass of criticism provoked by this first great wave of persecution, which, as many contemporaries recognised, had claimed the lives of countless 'innocent' victims. In most territories and cities, this recognition caused a breakdown of consensus and, in turn, helped to bring about the end of persecution. Opponents of persecutions did not criticise trials as such, but attacked the traits of the catastrophic persecutions around 1590: the ease of arrest for mere suspicion, lax criteria dictating the application of torture, excessive freedom apportioned to executioners who specialised in witch trials, and a general application of the exceptional measures that made witch hunting possible in the first place.

A decisive shift is obvious in Protestant territories and Free-Imperial cities, where the persecutory paradigm was applied for a short time, but was soon abandoned. Sharp criticism indicates that the authorities in Nördlingen and Ansbach enjoyed greater latitude than Catholic authorities. The town council of Kaufbeuren publicly and distinctly distanced itself from the persecutions, and in Nuremberg, a city of leading importance, no witches were executed; indeed, when the former assistant of the executioner of Eichstätt tried to incite trials there, he was put to death. Supported by confessional polemics, an aloofness toward persecutions was maintained for several decades; so far as we know, no further persecutions began at this time. Persecutions did not resume in Donauwörth and Pfalz-Neuburg until after their recatholicisation and persecutions in the region came increasingly to be viewed as a Catholic affair. The existence of witches was certainly never denied by Protestants, but some elements of the elaborated concept of witchcraft lost their influence; Goedelmann and the representatives of Lutheran orthodoxy in Württemberg associated themselves with Weyer, thereby casting doubt on the so-called 'witches' mark' (a mole or 'witches' teat'), the 'weeping test' (pricking a mark to see if pain resulted), the possibility of flight through the air and nocturnal sabbaths; in short, those elements which fanned the individual conflagra-

[13] Cf. chapter 3, The wave of persecutions around 1590.

tions of witchcraft trials into full-blown persecutions. Consequently, Protestant authorities tended to reduce charges of witchcraft to simple maleficium or pacts with the Devil. The pattern of confessional polarisation observed by Midelfort in southwestern Germany is confirmed for southeast Germany.

The success of the Counter-Reformation transformed southeast Germany into an almost purely Catholic region after 1590. Only several small noble territories and – apart from Donauwörth – the Free Imperial cities were capable of withstanding pressure from the leading Catholic power, Bavaria. Therefore, Catholic policies heavily influenced the resolution of the witchcraft question, especially the policies of Bavaria. Nevertheless, after 1590, a breakdown of consensus over the legality of persecutions followed in Catholic territories too, and they came to a halt soon thereafter. However, unlike Protestant areas, the elaborated concept of witchcraft remained intact, ensconced in scholastic theology and thus protected against substantive attack. Regional Jesuit theologians (Petrus Canisius, Gregor von Valentia, Jacob Gretser and, later, Adam Contzen and Jeremias Drexel) were completely enamoured of the elaborated concept of witchcraft, campaigning actively at court and in the universities in support of an unwavering stance on the witchcraft issue. Under their influence, the Catholic position stiffened and to doubt the witchcraft orthodoxy elaborated by Binsfeld, suffragan Bishop of Trier, was equated with Protestant heresy.[14] Given this tension, a showdown between Catholic supporters of persecution and their opponents became unavoidable.

A major trial conducted with exemplary severity by the supporters of persecution inflamed this conflict of principles in 1600. Several high officials in Munich and Ingolstadt, both nobles and jurists, resisted pressures to expand the trial into a general persecution. The opposition was headed by the Privy Councillors Herwarth, Donnersberger and Rechberg, holders of the highest political offices in the country (Supreme Chancellor, Chancellor of the Estates and Major Domo respectively). The persecution party suspected the opposition leaders Donnersberger and Herwarth of coordinating resistance by manipulating opinion in Munich and at the University of Ingolstadt.[15] Dr Johann Georg Herwarth von Hohenburg was a key political adviser, and his studies in mathematics and natural science (his correspondence with Kepler is well documented), provoked such hostility that supporters of persecution labelled him a 'sorcerer'. Since Catholic opponents of persecution could hardly challenge the content of witchcraft theory with any hope of success, they concentrated their efforts

---

[14] Cf. chapter 4, The Catholic stance hardens, pp. 216–29.
[15] Cf. chapter 4, Formation of the opposition party in Bavaria, pp. 230–46.

on judicial procedure. Appealing to natural law and 'reason', they fought for more stringent guidelines on arrests, torture and executions, arguing that even some theologians regarded many alleged acts of witchcraft as demonic delusions which only existed in the minds of so-called witches.[16] The persecution party countered, claiming that stricter guidelines would make trials nearly impossible, defeating the purposes of persecutions.

To resolve the stalemate in Bavaria, systematic inquiries were made among Catholic authorities in 1601 in order to establish an authoritative ruling on the issue. Assistance was requested from the Universities of Ingolstadt, Dillingen, Freiburg, Padua and Bologna, the learned demonologists Rémy and Delrio, and Catholic authorities in the ecclesiastical Electorates of Mainz, Cologne and Trier, as well as the Margravate of Baden. To the great disappointment of the persecution party in Bavaria, these inquiries offered little support; by 1600, a gulf between supporters and opponents of persecution divided all of Catholic Europe. The struggle for an appropriate policy on witchcraft in Bavaria found no recognised arbiter and continued through the first decade and a half of the seventeenth century. Incessant disputes, reflected in conflicting instructions, briefs and decrees on witchcraft, have long been cited in the secondary literature to give the impression of a ferocious persecution in Bavaria. In fact, the persecutions were not nearly as ferocious as the debate about the trials themselves. The Munich Court Council, the competent authority on witch trials, debated on issues of principle between 1601 and 1604, and was split by especially fierce internal conflicts between 1607 and 1612. With three minor persecutions at Donauwörth, Wemding and Landshut, the persecution party appeared to be gaining the upper hand in 1609, but it suffered a series of painful setbacks between 1611 and 1613: the persecutions ended amidst allegations of improper conduct in Wemding which had prevented the publication of the territorial witchcraft mandate and led to the execution of the witch judge himself.

Resistance to persecutions in Bavaria originated among local burgers and the nobility, perhaps even among segments of the population at large.[17] The spokespersons of resistance represented the provincial nobility like Haslang, the urban patriciate like Herwarth (Augsburg), Donnersberger and Barth (Munich), and Jocher (Mauterndorf), Ingolstadt jurists such as Hell and the two Denichs, the magistrates of Munich and Ingolstadt, and political officials such as the Munich Town Clerk, Dr Locher. Later, resistance was even championed by Bavarian and Tyrolean Jesuits. In 1601, while the Jesuits were still regarded as reliable allies by the

[16] Tanner, *Theologia*, I, 994.
[17] Cf. chapter 3 'breakdown of consensus', pp. 194–205.

persecution party, Adam Tanner became the first leading Jesuit openly to break ranks. Tanner experienced the regional wave of persecutions in Swabia and Bavaria in 1590 and achieved prominence in 1601 after his stunning performance during important religious disputations at Regensburg, facilitating a change in stance. In most respects, his arguments matched those of the anti-persecution party in Munich. In the 1620s, many Bavarian Jesuits opposed persecution, including the Ingolstadt professors Hell and Denich the younger. The more moderate Bavarian attitude toward witchcraft assumed supra-regional significance after the publication of tracts on moral theology written by Tanner and Laymann in the 1620s. These books, widely regarded as authoritative, influenced Friedrich Spee, as well as Meyfahrt, a Lutheran. Tanner and Laymann won a host of followers in southeast Germany, providing the authority needed to moderate attitudes toward witchcraft in the seventeenth century.[18]

To claim that the opposition originated in Bavaria itself may appear tautological, until one considers the origins of supporters of persecution, ideologues recruited from all over Europe: the Jesuits Canisius, Gregor von Valentia, Delrio and Gretser came from Holland, Spain, Belgium and Baden, the jurists Fachineus and Gilg from Italy, the Court Councillors Fickler and Vagh from Württemberg and Schleswig, the Secretaries Gewold and Albertinus from the Upper Palatinate and Hesse. Vagh and Gewold were converts to Catholicism. Persecutions certainly found native champions, like the radically accommodating Court Chancellor Wagnereckh. Nevertheless, contemporaries recognised that native councillors who sat on the Noble Bench of the Court and Privy Councils appeared less inclined to favour persecution than councillors of the Learned Bench, who tended to favour theoretical and authoritarian solutions. Supporters of persecution repeatedly emphasised the advantages of employing foreign commissioners, who were unhindered by familial ties or other close relationships.[19] In the end, their clerical, ideological and ivory-towered theories of a witch conspiracy imagined a demon behind every superstitious peasant woman, alienating them from local realities. Whereas generations of local opponents recurred among town councils, local authorities, Jesuits

---

[18] Cf. chapter 4, pp. 230–46, of this book and chapter 5, pp. 322–30.

[19] An opinion of 1628 explained in detail that the Ingolstadt Professors Waizenegger and Denich were against witch trials, because they feared for their dependants. The Eichstätt witch commissioner Dr Kolb, on the other hand, because he 'weder Vatter noch Muetter, Schwester noch Brueder und kheine Kinder habe . . . dannenhero sowohl jetzo als ins khünftig kein affectus bey ihm nit so bald zu besorgen . . .', HStAM, GR 323/16, fol. 28r–v. ('He had neither father nor mother, sister nor brother and no children locally, therefore he has no affections to care about now or in the future.')

17. Adam Tanner, *Theologia Scholastica*, Tomus 3. Ingolstadt 1627.

and other scholars at the University of Ingolstadt, none of the supporters of persecution was ever able to plant lasting roots.[20] When we examine the victims of witch trials and persecutions, those who fell prey to the first wave around 1590 and another around 1630 correspond largely to the cliche of inquisitorial theory harmonised with popular beliefs: most were old women.[21] However, the initially uncompromising position around 1590 meant that persecutions quickly expanded socially, as well as geographically. Soon prominent local families were targeted and even nobles were denounced. Although wealth was a factor, the fundamental principle of equality before the law was not abandoned;[22] otherwise, persecutions would most certainly have been criticised by the poor as discriminatory. In fact, social solidarity among different classes and estates was so great that accusations of witchcraft had to be treated with caution and soon conformed to previous patterns. Though torture was still applied frequently – as in all other criminal proceedings – the problems arising from confessions extracted under torture were well known, so they counted for less than voluntary statements. As a rule, confessions obtained under torture did not suffice for conviction without other evidence – agreement among witnesses' statements, circumstantial evidence, or remarkable incidents pointing unequivocally to the suspect.

Of course, there were exceptions to these rules, such as the persecutions at Wemding in 1608 and 1630, at Neuburg and Reichertshofen in 1630, in the Fuggers' territory of Wasserburg in 1656–60 and in the Protestant Free City of Memmingen in 1663–8. However, the fact remains that witch trials were generally conducted with relative caution and the proceedings were

---

[20] Cf. chapter 4, The pro-persecution party, and The anti-persecution party, pp. 235–46. We must make an exception for the Bavarian Court Council Chancellor Wagnereckh, whose three sons all joined the Society of Jesus. Heinrich Wangnereckh SJ (?–1664) at times played a very prominent role in the Jesuit academy at Dillingen. We find him following in the footsteps of his incorrigible father: 'Weniger durch wissenschaftliche Fundierung als durch kirchenpolitische Wirkung zeichneten sich aus die vielen Streitschriften des unversöhnlichen Heinrich Wagnereck aus München, des entschiedenen literarischen Vorkämpfers der Gegenreformation während des Dreissigjährigen Krieges', Spindler, *Handbuch*, III/2, 1155 (Kraus). ('The many polemical works of the irreconcilable Heinrich Wagnereckh of Munich, the outspoken literary champion of the Counter-Reformation during the Thirty Years War, are distinguished less by their scholarly substance than by their effect on ecclesiastical politics.') An identical opinion in Duhr, *Geschichte der Jesuiten*, II/1, 479; Riezler, *Geschichte Baierns*, VI, 382f.

[21] An exact percentage and an average age cannot be deduced from the available source material, but the contemporary stereotype speaks for itself. There are also figures for several witch hunts: of thirty-one women executed in Nördlingen (less the young insane woman who had provoked the trials) the average age was fifty, but at the beginning of the witch hunt (in the first two burnings, omitting the mentally ill people) sixty-eight. The average age of forty-seven women burned at the stake in the County of Werdenfels in 1590 was fifty-seven, but the average age of the twelve oldest was seventy-seven. In other witch hunts of 1590, several women said that they had been alive at the time of the Peasants' War. [22] On the mechanism of persecution, cf. chapter 3, pp. 183–93.

certainly no harsher than for other offences; in contemporary eyes, maleficent magic was a very real offence, on a par with poisoning. Investigations
still seemed warranted in many cases and although scepticism undoubtedly
existed among some of the educated in the seventeenth century about the
reality of supernatural power, most people continued to believe in witchcraft without hesitation. Social contempt for the persecutors, efforts to
restrain overzealous judges and the execution of the witch-judge of Wemding all testify to the narrow limits confining supporters of persecution.[23]
Eventually, relative caution altered the targets of persecutions. If old
women of all social backgrounds had been chiefly at risk around 1600, the
circle of victims gradually shifted during the seventeenth century onto the
lower classes, especially children and youths, above all, young men (!). The
reason may well be that roving bands of young vagabonds claiming the
power to cast spells admitted their guilt 'amicably' (i.e. without torture).
These claims were common among children, a phenomenon enlightened
luminaries attributed to insufficient education. Witchcraft trials against
children, including bands of young magicians and the families of suspected
witches, were conducted only with difficulty, since they raised fundamental
questions of criminal responsibility. Not uncommonly, courts waived
punishment and ordered children to submit to a Christian education.
Jurists confronted another problem here: if they were unwilling to execute
witches who confessed, then whom should they execute at all?[24]
Surprisingly, 'popular magic' was fairly unaffected by all this, even if
orthodox representatives of all confessions never tired of inveighing
against popular magical practices, such as conjuring the Devil to find
buried treasure, to say nothing of the wearing of amulets, love charms, and
countercharms against bewitchment, or the use of spells against disease or
to promote fertility among human beings, animals and crops –but all
proved intractable. They were just as fashionable in the eighteenth century
as they had been in the preceding three centuries; some customs and
practices were probably older than the Christian Church itself. In spite of
attempts by ecclesiastical reformers, magical practices permeated culture
at all levels. Muchembled's depiction of 'high' religion and magical folk
culture as a one-way process of acculturation[25] was really a two-way

---

[23] Cf. chapter 4.
[24] Cf. chapter 5, pp. 331–43. The spokesmen of the Enlightenment were well aware of this
historical trend: Sterzinger, *Betrügende Zauberkunst*, 42, wrote that for a hundred years
witch burnings had never been so rare that they could be so easily counted. Mayer,
Glückwunschschreiben, 7f., wrote that for 130 years the rules of the *Malleus* had rarely
been less often applied. Rubel, *Systematische Abhandlung*, 131, points to the reduction of
the 'Hexen Gesellschaft' to 'lauter Canaillenvolk, Bettler oder armer Leute Kinder von
zehn, zwölf und fünfzehn Jahren'.
[25] Muchembled, *Kultur*, 232–76, speaks of the 'cultural conquest of the rural areas' (*ibid.*,
233) and the 'intellectual subjection of the countryside' (*ibid.*, 241).

dialectic, at least in the rural areas. For enlightened Catholic theologians, even accepted eighteenth-century Christian practices in the Bavarian countryside, the weather magic (firing bullets into the air or ringing bells), and processions to promote fertility, charms to combat illness among livestock, 'benedictus pennies' and consecrated fragments from the cross of the Abbey of Scheyern to guard against witchcraft, were scarcely distinguishable from unofficial magic.[26]

The ultimate lines of the Catholic debate over witchcraft in the 1760s were drawn along both themes: luminaries attacked superstitious religious practices related to witchcraft, while conservative theologians defended them. Witchcraft was debated very differently than in the early seventeenth century. At the peak of the witchcraft persecutions, opponents struggled to distinguish popular magic from the crime of witchcraft to prevent a devastation of the countryside through continuous witch burnings. They could not dispute the existence of witchcraft, since sentiments in that direction had to bow to religious pressure. In the eighteenth century debate, however, real executions of witches played a subordinate role. Enlightened theologians, politicians and publicists were concerned to prevent executions for witchcraft in the future, since they were still possible in theory (Kempten 1775!), but the scornful tactics in their argumentation lumped beliefs in witches together with magical practices sanctioned by the Church and had a more fundamental goal. The reform of state ecclesiastical law promoted by Osterwald, among others, aimed at a general reduction of the Church's influence on society as a whole, on the grounds that it restricted the ability of the state, not to mention the enlightened thinkers themselves, to intervene effectively. Witchcraft was ideally suited to this issue. The early Enlightenment in Bavaria found fertile soil in many monasteries, whose theologians formed the traditional backbone of the territorial Church, and an explosive debate within the ranks of the Church ensued. To view this debate as a clever gambit in the interest of secularisation underestimates the personal interest of its enlightened intellectual proponents (Jordan Simon, Sterzinger, Braun etc.), but, in the end, this was the precise effect of the Bavarian 'witch war', as some perceptive contemporaries realised.[27]

On a more abstract level, there are similarities between the debates of the early seventeenth century and the mid-eighteenth century. The 'frigid' and 'political' Christians of 1600 strove to restrain authoritarian religious

---

[26] Cf. chapter VI.3.
[27] *Ibid.* Interesting in this connection are the commentaries of H.C. Freiherr von Senckenberg (1704–68) of Vienna, who not only refers to Lochstein and the witch debate in the same breath but writes in general terms about the aims of the enlightened thinkers: 'Das Reich des Aberglaubens wird nun auch in Baiern mit Macht zerstöret.' Messerer, 'Briefe' I, 631–3.

fanaticism, the hallmark of many zealots in the service of their faith. Rather than scholastic authority or the consistent application of theologically determined truths, opponents of persecution were motivated by a secular capacity to distinguish according to the principles of reason and natural law, even if these concepts meant different things in 1600 than in the mid-eighteenth century. However, as a legal brief of 1608 shows, opponents of persecution successfully employed reasons of state and common sense as valid arguments against ideologically motivated demands for persecution.

STRUCTURES AND REGIONS IN COMPARISON

This study has examined two areas usually treated separately by historians because of their divergent evolutions and contrasting natures. It was precisely this heterogeneity that facilitated a historical experiment to determine whether certain structural aspects of any one area necessarily resulted in a greater propensity to persecute witches.[28] The discovery was astonishing: essentially, both Free-Imperial cities and rural territories in 'southeast Germany' followed a uniform pattern of persecution! Naturally, there were differences within the region, heterogeneous in so many ways, but they were slight in comparison to neighbouring lands: the persecutions coincided, beginning and peaking around 1590, but falling off drastically thereafter.

There are clear differences from the neighbouring regions in the west, south and north. Southwestern Germany had already witnessed its first major persecutions a century earlier, inheriting this tradition intact. Subsequent persecutions began there almost a quarter of a century earlier than in the southeast and were on a markedly different order of magnitude.[29] To the south, in the Austrian Alpine territories, persecutions initiated by the papal Inquisition around 1485 failed to establish a precedent and were opposed by the inhabitants of Innsbruck, the Estates of Tyrol, the Bishop of Brixen, etc.[30] Persecutions were rare after 1560, only attaining larger proportions much later indeed – from 1675 to 1690.[31] In the north, the first Franconian persecutions began around the same time as those in southeast Germany, but increased during the first half of the seventeenth century until – like southwestern Germany – they were four times as virulent as in Austria or southeast Germany.[32] If we compare the dimensions and chronological distribution of intense

[28] Cf. chapter 1, Witch trials in historiographic context, pp. 1–16.
[29] Midelfort, *Witch Hunting*.   [30] Byloff, *Hexenglaube*.
[31] On this the see the survey graph in Byloff, *Hexenglaube*, 160.
[32] Cf. above, pp. 35–64, 121–57, 216–29, 310–21.

Table 13 *Intensity of witch hunting in four neighbouring regions of southeastern Germany and Austria*[33]

Region	Witches burned (Min. = 100%)	Intensity of witch hunting	
SE Germany	900	1562–1600	55%
		1601–1650	26%
		1651–1700	11%
		1701–1775	9%
Austria	900	1562–1600	6%
		1601–1650	15%
		1651–1700	63%
		1701–1750	7%
SW Germany	4,000	1562–1600	33%
		1601–1650	60%
		1651–1700	13%
		1701–1757	1%
Franconia	4,000	1562–1600	9%
		1601–1650	85%
		1651–1700	5%
		1701–1749	1%

persecutions in the four neighbouring regions, we notice that Franconia and southwestern Germany figured among the 'heartlands' of persecution in the Empire, both witnessing a peak in the first half of the seventeenth century (between 1600 and 1630), at a time when persecutions in southeast Germany and Austria were more restrained. In southeast Germany, persecution waned. In Austria, no real 'wave' of persecution ever occurred, only a few local, unrelated persecutions. Furthermore, victims of the trials in Austria and southeast Germany between 1650 and 1750 came from another social group, mostly young men rather than old women.[34] Taken together, these factors indicate significant regional differences.

The secondary literature often reduces distinctions to structural factors – economic and social structure, political and administrative systems and confession. In short, a scheme is sought to explain divergent patterns. But scholars are really scraping the bottom of the barrel for an interpretative model when they enlist topographical differences between regions as explanations.[35] Undoubtedly, sociological explanations of the European witchcraft persecutions are useful, they may even hold out some slight hope of a historical interpretation within the realm of the politically explicable. Ingenious journalists have long taken this approach, albeit without troubl-

[33] Cf. notes 29–32.
[34] On the change in the victims of the trials see note 24 and above, pp. 331–43. For the periodisation of the great witch hunts in Germany and the differentiation between 'heartlands' of witch hunting and the areas less affected, see Schormann, *Hexenprozess* (1981), 52–71. [35] Cf. note 41 to chapter 1.

ing to support their views with evidence; one could quote numerous examples from popular literature.[36] But the historical evidence resists such generalisations, a problem for which the deficits of social history are not solely to blame. This is true even of the coarsest of comparative analyses. In southwestern Germany and eastern Swabia, for example, finance capitalism and proto-industrial crafts thrived, distinguishing these areas from the agrarian economies of Bavaria and Austria. Schematically, an implicit connection with intense persecutions might seem to verify the 'capitalism theory' of Macfarlane.[37] Indeed, a superficial illustration is offered by the Free-Imperial city of Kaufbeuren, troubled by crises and the scene of a witch hunt in 1591. However, other regional examples prove the opposite, demonstrating that the apparent connection is tenuous at best. Other commercial centres hit by export crises, such as Kempten, did not persecute witches at all, even if enough suitable victims were available among a population of several thousand. On the other hand, witches were persecuted in places with no recognisable social or economic problems, like the Free Imperial city of Nördlingen. Even more troubling is the fact that no recognisable connection can be demonstrated between allegations of witchcraft and the Swabian craft and textile 'proto-industries', as in the counties of the Bishopric of Augsburg. The 'backwardness' hypothesis, which claims that persecutions were related to economic underdevelopment, is even more difficult to maintain. Although structurally disadvantaged areas suffered more severely from recurrent subsistence crises, they did not result in more intense persecutions, at least not in southeast Germany. Although witchcraft beliefs persisted more stubbornly in such areas, they were regulated by the rules of 'popular magic' and mitigated by the central authorities to the point that executions were quantitatively negligible. Witchcraft really only became a hallmark of economic backwardness during the eighteenth century.

Any attempt to correlate witchcraft trials and confessional allegiance faces similar problems. Generally, Midelfort's hypothesis of confessional polarisation has been confirmed: Catholic authorities clung more rigidly to the elaborated concept of witchcraft (witches' sabbaths, flight, etc.) than did Lutherans and Calvinists. The confessional dichotomy is especially

---

[36] Cf. note 6 to chapter 1.
[37] The thesis was put forward by Macfarlane, *Witchcraft*, 205f. The originator of the thesis soon found himself compelled to qualify it: A. Macfarlane, *The Origins of English Individualism*, Oxford 1978, 1–2, 59. Larner, *Enemies*, 21 rightly remarked: 'Macfarlane has now rejected the idea that there were important changes in social structure at the beginning of the period of the witch hunt, but it has taken root in witchcraft analysis.' The thesis was in any case adopted rather tentatively by more cautious authors, because it does not lend itself to direct application; cf. Wunder (1983), 'Hexenprozesse', 194f.

marked in Franconia, where the 'witch-bishops' are credited with more than 90 per cent of executions, while Lutheran Nuremberg, the Margravates of Ansbach and Bayreuth after 1590, and the partly Lutheran and partly Calvinist Upper Palatinate all rejected witch hunting, stigmatising it as a Catholic peculiarity.[38] However, long before this reputation hardened into a Protestant historical legend in the eighteenth century, it was quite possible for a persecution party to exist in Lutheran territories as confessional policy on persecutions was initially dictated by internal political concerns.[39] Protestant authorities played a significant role in the resumption of persecutions after 1560 and, in Free Imperial cities, trials first peaked in the later seventeenth century. At a glance, the confessional model is confirmed by the experience of southeast Germany, where a disproportionate number of witches were executed in the Prince-Bishoprics of Augsburg and Freising, a fact associated with the personal proclivities of the bishops themselves. Closer investigation reveals that many ecclesiastical territories persecuted no witches at all – e.g. the Abbey of Kempten, the lands of the Swabian monasteries and the domains of the Bishop of Regensburg. Even the Bishops of Augsburg and Freising did not repeat the great witch hunts of 1590. In Bavaria, vanguard of the Counter-Reformation, a whole school of Catholic opponents of witch hunting emerged, analysing the internal contradictions of witchcraft theory to refute paradigmatically demands for persecution at any price raised by Binsfeld and other Catholic zealots. Nor were Catholic authorities in Austria inclined to participate in the ostensibly Catholic proclivity to persecute. Even if the risk of persecution was greater among Catholics

---

[38] Cf. chapter 4, 'The Protestant solution', pp. 213–15.

[39] *Ibid.* Especially interesting are the relationships in the Lutheran state of Saxony-Coburg in the 1620s, where the party of witch hunters, led by the Superintendent, looked to the savage witch hunts of the neighbouring Bishopric of Bamberg for its model, and theoretically explicitly took its line from Martin Delrio SJ, while the opponents of witch hunting were inspired by the moderate attitude of Catholic Bavaria, especially the authority of the Bavarian theologians Tanner and Laymann. Cf. Janssen and Pastor, *Culturzustände*, VIII, 614f., 656. The taking over of Tanner's arguments is recognisable right down to the details. *Ibid.*, 686f. Kretz, 'Der Schöppenstuhl', 74–7. The example of Coburg is further proof of the great importance of the discussions at Munich in the years after 1600. The alleged exceptional severity of the witch hunts in Bavaria is thus revealed as a Protestant myth of the later seventeenth or eighteenth century; at that time, when southeastern Germany was economically backward, witch burnings still persisted when they were scarcely imaginable any longer in northern and western Germany. It should be pointed out that southeastern Germany never had a witches' meeting place of more than regional importance, like the Blocksberg in northern Germany or the Heuberg in southwestern Germany. The lack of a continuity in persecution, such as was found in Saxony or the southwest, had the result that the concept of a witches' dancing place was not so widespread in comparable form in Bavaria, although prominent mountains were often thought to be secret meeting places in local legend (e.g. the Peissenberg near Schongau, the Auerberg near Oberdorf).

owing to papal and scholastic authorisation, the connection between confession and persecution was not automatic.

More tenable is the connection to political and administrative structures. Schormann observed that major persecutions occurred less frequently in larger territorial units – e.g. Electoral Brandenburg and Saxony and the Welf principalities – than in politically fragmented ones.[40] The cases of Bavaria and the Habsburg lands confirm his observation. This may have resulted from the complex political and administrative structures of these territories. All too often, witchcraft studies overemphasise centralised judicial systems, inquisitorial procedure,[41] or legal exceptions as culprits, although none of them was directly related to the intensity of persecution. The interaction of opposing social groups or political institutions within a territory might exercise a retarding influence, especially when these groups and institutions were linked with one another in the political administration. The Bavarian example discussed in this book demonstrates the complexity of political debate. Nobles possessing private justice, civic councils in Imperial Cities and Prince-Bishops all exercised judicial fiat in their own territories,[42] but, in Bavaria, 'checks and balances' operated despite its early absolutist government. The Duke had to deal with his political officials (Privy Council, Court Council, Court Chamber), as well as representatives of the Estates, the magistrates of the towns, the representatives of bishops whose religious jurisdiction penetrated his territories, the regional clergy, the Jesuits in Munich and Ingolstadt, the University, other members of the dynasty, the local patriciate and nobility who were closely tied by kinship and from whose ranks judges and the middling officials were co-opted and, finally, with advisers independent of princely favour, such as Count von Rechberg or the scholar J.G. Herwarth von Hohenburg. Despite an absence of institutionalised channels for protest, this multiplicity allowed opponents of persecution to put their arguements to good use. Occurrences such as the execution of whole town councils, ecclesiastical dignitaries or princely officials, as we find in the Franconian Prince-Bishoprics,[43] were hardly imaginable in the political culture of Bavaria. Reasons of state alone prohibited a policy of uncompromising persecution in a territory of this size.

Midelfort's main argument for the decline in witch hunting in south-

---

[40] Schormann, *Hexenprozesse* (1981), 65.   [41] Cf. note 2.

[42] At least in the present state of research the witch trials reveal no trace of any involvement of the cathedral chapters, as is assumed in the literature (Spindler, *Handbuch*, III/1, 355–8; III/2, 955f. and 961). Even during vacancies (e.g. Augsburg 1591, Bamberg 1591, Eichstätt 1590), the chapters were not politically active, in the sense of a change of course. One may see the correspondence between the Bishop and chapter of Augsburg from 1599 as symptomatic. HStAM, Hexenakten 15.

[43] Cf. chapter 4, 'Excursus: excessive persecution in the Catholic areas of Franconia'.

western Germany, especially the Duchy of Württemberg with its Lutheran university at Tübingen, is based on certain assumptions of a Lutheran orthodoxy in harmony with the Reformer Brenz's admonitions against exaggerating the power of the Devil and of witches.[44] However, the question remains whether other motives were concealed behind theological statements. The Bavarian example demonstrates that, apart from theological arguments, a secular critique of misplaced zealotry took the interests of the state into account along with the peculiarities of popular magic; though it never condoned them, neither did it demonise them.

WITCH TRIALS AND SOCIAL CRISES

Like Calvinist Scotland with its demonologist King James VI, the largely Catholic territories of southeast Germany were dominated by the stature of the 'Iron Elector', Maximilian I of Bavaria, himself a passionate opponent of witches. Both occupied an intermediate level between regions where persecutions were very intense and those where they were rare.[45] Otherwise, Scotland and Bavaria appear to have little else in common, apart from their political and confessional opposition during the Thirty Years War. However, similarities in the area of witchcraft ran much deeper than one might suppose. It was no mere coincidence that the intensity as well as the chronology of events in Scotland corresponded to those in southeast Germany: the growing threat posed by the exceptional crime after 1562 (Witchcraft Act, 1563), unusually harsh treatment of accused witches after an agrarian crisis in 1570 and major persecutions in 1590/91 (a 'national panic'). After a rapid decline, executions of witches resumed during subsistence crises in the mid-1620s and peaked during another 'national panic' in 1629–30.[46] Indeed, the Scottish chronology is only symptomatic of a larger phenomenon. It applies with only minor variations to England, parts of France, northwestern Germany, Franconia, southwestern Germany and the region examined here, southeast Germany – in other words, a major portion of all regions studied to date.[47] The increase and apex of the western European enthusiasm for persecuting witches was not perfectly synchronic, but did follow an unmistakable

---

[44] Midelfort, *Witch Hunting*, 36–56.   [45] Larner, *Enemies*, 192–204.
[46] Cf. the useful survey in Larner, *Enemies*, 204f.
[47] Midelfort, *Witch Hunting*, 202–19; Muchembled, *Kultur*, 232–41; Soman, 'Parlement', 33–6; Schormann, *Hexenprozesse*, (1977), 158; Schormann, *Hexenprozesse* (1981), 52–62; Lehmann, 'Hexenglaube', 14. Of course there was no automatic connection between agrarian crisis and witch hunting, and many regions, e.g. Austria, came through the chronic crises of the later sixteenth century relatively unscathed. But where more serious witch hunts took place they were almost always related to one of the major supraregional agrarian crises.

rhythm, achieving its first common peak in Bavaria, Swabia and Scotland around 1590. The European climax in these years is reflected by frenzied publication of demonological tracts,[48] but thereafter the witch craze broke down into regional patterns.

In order to explain the astonishing uniformity of this supra-regional phenomenon, particular historical events and regional/national peculiarities have to be ruled out as causal factors. From a geographic perspective, these include the old Counter-Reformation theory, Macfarlane's capitalism hypothesis and the opposing theory on backward regions.[49] The great complexity of endogenous social structures in early modern Europe renders monocausal explanations unsatisfactory as well, e.g. the hackneyed theme of divergent judicial procedures.[50] Nor can the cause of mounting witch trials be sought in 'confessional strife and the rise of absolutism', described as the 'most important historical forces at work in that epoch'.[51] All confessions concurred on the need to burn witches, but rigid administrative structures might just as soon restrain persecutions as unleash them. Nor should we overemphasise social disciplining like Muchembled, who views trials as mere tools instrumentalised by ruling authorities to acculturate the rural populace.[52] The authorities were not alone in calling for persecutions in the second half of the sixteenth century; the 'common' people clamoured for them too, if for other reasons.

On the other hand, all western European societies experienced a period

---

[48] This applies both to the dates of the original editions and to the reprints, as can be shown from the large holdings of the Staatsbibliothek in Munich and the Herzog-August-Bibliothek at Wolfenbüttel. Of course the trend in demonological literature followed the rhythm of agrarian crisis, as mediated through the actuality of the witch theme in those years. The first wave of persecution in 1562–3 was marked by the fundamental criticism of J. Weyer. The hunger crisis of 1570–1 was followed not only by a reprint of Weyer's *De praestigiis daemonum* but also by new editions, after more than fifty years, of Sprenger and Institoris' *Malleus Maleficarum* and the old treatises on witchcraft of Jacquier and Trithemius. At the same time L. Daneau (Danäus) and T. Erastus opened new fronts within Calvinism. The crisis year 1580 saw J. Bodin's *Daemonomania*, the first great witch hunting manifesto of the sixteenth century. Not long afterwards it was followed in England by a defence of Weyer against Bodin, R. Scot's *Discovery of Witchcraft*, and in Germany by J.G. Goedelmann's *De Magia*. The beginning of the great wave of persecution of 1590 was preceded in 1586–7 by the *Theatrum de Veneficiis* and the first German translation of Weyer's anti-witch hunting book of 1563, as well as the Faust book of Spiess. In 1589–92 there were five editions of Binsfeld's treatise on witches in Trier and Munich (two in Latin and three in German), four editions of Goedelmann's *De Magia* (two in Latin and two in German). These examples could be multiplied at will. All the great works of demonology had appeared by 1630, after which date not only was the theme exhausted, but the number of reprints fell off abruptly. Comparable heights were never reached again after the great wars, although many of the older printings must have been destroyed during these. It is almost unnecessary to say that the demand for demonological literature was less in regions where witch burnings were less common.

[49] Cf. chapter 1, witch trials and their associated events as a theme of historiography, pp. 1–16.   [50] Cf. note 2.   [51] Lehmann, 'Hexenverfolgung', 31.

[52] Muchembled, *Kultur*, 267, 276, 315.

of secular inflation once referred to as a 'price revolution' of the sixteenth century. Today, there is general consensus on Abel's conclusions that gradual inflation reflected a demographic trend during the 'long sixteenth century' and a relative scarcity of resources, rather than a sharp increase in the money supply.[53] The origins of social crisis in the latter half of the sixteenth century are too complex and far too little understood to allow for a full accounting here of the 'iron century' (Kamen) or the 'crisis in Europe, 1560–1600' (Aston). These terms are employed to characterise the inflation, increasing scarcity of resources, breakdown of traditional crafts, unusual climatic phenomena, subsistence crises, extreme social polarisation, the shift of the economic core from Germany and the Latin countries to northwestern Europe, the formation of the absolutist state and more rigid social structures and the hardening of lines between social classes, political groups, confessions and states, all culminating in a series of revolts and civil and international wars around mid-century, marking the end of demographic growth during the first half of the seventeenth century.[54] It is abundantly clear, however, that European witchcraft persecutions coincided with the end of that long upward trend and with growing tensions within and between societies.[55] Long-term connections between inflation and witchcraft persecutions have often been noted. 'Taking the long view', writes Henry Kamen, 'the equation of crisis and witchcraft becomes even more striking. It was the very period of the greatest price rise – the late sixteenth and early seventeenth century – that saw the most numerous cases of accusation and persecution of witches.'[56]

His formulation is not only valid for the 'long view'. In the short term, agrarian crises were far more important than inflation, even if they only figure statistically as sharp outlyers. That agrarian crises played an important role in agrarian societies is self-evident. The increasing scarcity of resources (or their unequal distribution) following recurrent harvest failures in central Europe after 1562 caused acute malnutrition and famine. Harvest failures brought on by climatic or other 'natural' causes led to acute subsistence crises, higher infant mortality and disease among people and livestock. Hence, hunger went hand in hand with devastating epidemics which claimed victims among substantial portions of the popula-

---

[53] A crisis of the later sixteenth century? Cf. chapter 2, pp. 89–114.

[54] An excessive concentration on political crises marks many of the contributions in Aston, *Crisis*, Parker and Smith, *General Crisis*, although here too social aspects are discussed and the connection with the theme of witchcraft is repeatedly raised. A greater weight is placed on mentalities and cultural historical dimensions in Kamen, *Iron Century* or Rabb, *Struggle*. The increasing multiplicity of perspectives has opened up many 'new' possible connections in the theme of witchcraft, which at first seems so exotic.

[55] Expressed in lapidary form by Stone, 'Disenchantment', 17f.

[56] Kamen, *Iron Century*, 249f.

tion. Goubert once wrote that 'Crises of enormous dimensions must have characterised the close of the sixteenth century',[57] a view confirmed here. Higher-than-average, short term price rises clustered chronologically in the region during the second half of the sixteenth century (1559–63, 1566, 1569–75, 1579–80, 1585–94, 1598–1602), and accusations of witchcraft were more frequent in these periods of dearth; in the final analysis, virtually every major persecution was rooted in agrarian crisis.[58] The two worst waves of persecution (1586–91 and 1626–31) corresponded to the two worst periods of crisis, namely those of 1585–94 and 1624–9. One manifest connection between agrarian crises and witchcraft was harvest failure, since the peasantry held witches accountable for unusual weather (hail, storms, frost, prolonged rains, drought). The sequence of harvest failures, 'unnatural' infant mortality and human and animal diseases contributed to the surge of accusations for harmful sorcery so typical of the initial phases of witch trials. Finally, the tense mood in crisis years increased popular receptiveness to metaphysical explanations for unusual occurrences, altering popular expectations.[59] The great agrarian crises of the later sixteenth century affected large parts of western Europe and were made more acute by the dynamic of secular social developments. These facts explain why the rhythm of persecution was the same all over western Europe. For analogous, but independent reasons, people in diverse regions began persecuting witches.

But the complex subject of witchcraft cannot be explained from one side alone. Harvest failures hit the rural population first, but the resulting subsistence crises affected the lower classes in town and country. We might assume that the upper classes of society, themselves responsible for the conduct of the witch trials, were unaffected by the potential dangers of crises and might simply retire to their country estates to avoid epidemics, like the Florentines in Boccaccio's *Decameron*. But it should not be forgot-

---

[57] Pierre Goubert, 'Demographische Probleme im Beauvaisis des 17. Jahrhunderts', in Honegger, *Schrift*, 198–219 (German translation of 'En Beauvaisis: Problèmes démographiques du XVIIe siècle' in *Annales E.S.C.*, 7 (1952), 453–68).

[58] Cf. chapter 2, 'Witch trials and agrarian crises'.

[59] The pan-European crisis of 1590, hitherto inadequately illuminated and overshadowed by the great wars that followed, has now been properly spotlighted by the contributions in Clark, *European Crisis*. It is generally assumed that at times of crisis the level of anxiety in the population increases, but it is hard to grasp this almost undefinable factor. Many authors generalise feelings of anxiety to whole societies and/or periods, with almost comical effect, e.g. J. Kuczynski, *Geschichte des Alltags des deutschen Volkes*, I, Cologne, 1981, 145; similarly Muchembled, *Kultur*, 19–45. A general feeling of anxiety can hardly be detected in the sources, probably because every age knows its own problems well enough, but it cannot be denied that at the height of the witch hunts an extremely pessimistic world-view prevailed and a certain nervousness can be read between the lines of the sources during the great agrarian crises. Cf. chapter 2, pp. 89–114, and chapter 3, pp. 115–20.

ten that the belief in witchcraft bonded divergent social elements. If sorcery was the weapon of the weak against the strong, and if the strong shared in these beliefs, then they were bound to fear the vengeance of the weak. When an indebted weaver of Augsburg tried to extort money from Count Jacob Fugger amidst the persecutions in 1590, purporting to warn him against bewitchment, Fugger was deeply alarmed and pondered whom he might recently have offended.[60] Spells against grain speculators have already been mentioned and we might also note the remarks of Hippolytus Guarinoni, who wrote of old women who

> are so wrongly and unfairly despised and rejected by all, that no one shields and protects them, much less loves and keeps faith with them: Good God, is it any wonder that they often resort to wickedness out of poverty and want, grief and despondency, and even yield themselves up to the evil one, the Devil, and dabble in sorcery? Even strong men, the rich, the young, those in high places have committed such and still greater evils with less cause.[61]

More than one powerful ruler lived in constant fear of sorcery and enchantment, like Emperor Rudolf II, Elector Maximilian I of Bavaria, Count Wolfgang Wilhelm of the Neuburg Palatinate, who converted to Catholicism, or Augsburg Prince-Bishop Johann Egolf von Knöringen, whose death was attributed to an inmate of a hospital in Dillingen by witchcraft.[62] The fear of bewitchment played a role in persecutions, but it is only mentioned here as one aspect of a much deeper insecurity felt at the upper echelons of society and described as a 'crisis of religious consciousness'.[63]

What is meant is a transformation of mentality among the social elite in the decades after 1560, extending across confessional boundaries. Their 'gloomy' world-view dramatically coincided with the growing potential for social conflict and with frequent natural catastrophes. The optimistic mood of the first half of the sixteenth century, characterised by joyous sensuality, zesty vivacity and largesse, yielded to a pessimistic outlook more in tune with harsher living conditions and social rigidity. Almost simultaneously, John Knox and Petrus Canisius delivered sermons designed to heighten the consciousness of sin in Scotland, Swabia and Bavaria,

---

[60] StadtA, Augsburg, Urgichtenakten 1590 (Paulus Meirat).

[61] H. Guarinoni, *Von Grewel der Verwustung menschlichen Geschlechts,* Ingolstadt 1610, fol. 314.

[62] Evans, *Rudolf II,* 65f., 135, 201, 206; Riezler, *Geschichte,* 196f.; Duhr, *Geschichte der Jesuiten,* II/2, 481; Zoepfl, 'Hexenwahn', 240. Similar examples could probably be multiplied, but reference can be made to the suspected bewitchment of the Archbishop of Trier during the great witch hunts there in 1587. Duhr, *Geschichte der Jesuiten,* I, 742.

[63] Van Dülmen, *Kultur,* 289.

shocking high society with all the force of medieval penitentials and planting the suggestion that unusual events – comets, monstrous births, harvest failures and climatic disasters – were signs of God's wrath or the imminent return of Satan to Earth. The wording of a Bavarian general decree,

> that the anger and wrath of God is not diminishing in this age of wars, privations, pestilence and all manner of dangerous epidemics and sicknesses, but instead grows fiercer and more dreadful in many places, including our own principality, because all manner of sins and vices are gaining the upper hand from day to day in the present, crazy, Godless world . . . [64]

was no mere exuberant rhetoric or some ideological framework for the social disciplining of the population, which certainly began in earnest at this time, but reveals a deeply felt fear of the 'harsh anger and wrath of God', above all in the leading circles of society. Free from the everday cares of mere survival, they still could afford the luxury of a spiritualised or mystical religious experience. And yet, the social elite submitted themselves to the rigours of harsh self-discipline and the strictest moral code; the new age was marked by asceticism, the continual practice of religious austerities intended to appease God, courtly self-discipline and hard work. The sombre, brooding seriousness of this transformation of all habits, this 'new modelling of the affective personality' (Norbert Elias), penetrated the most private spheres, as exemplified by hairshirts and whips for self-flagellation mentioned in estate inventories of the ruling classes. The Bavarian Electors wrote letters in their own blood dedicating themselves to the Madonna of Altötting which represented, as the literature rightly observes, a direct counterpart to witches' pacts with the Devil. [65]

The rigid internalised piety of the upper classes changed their world-view dramatically. As in the lives of the saints, we often read of sudden conversion experiences. [66] Since confessionally motivated chroniclers were interested in fixing the date of these experiences, they can be established with relative precision. If we take the Dukes of Bavaria as an example, we find that Albrecht V experienced a 'conversion' to internalised religious piety in 1570 and Wilhelm V in 1575. [67] As the gulf between the culture of the elite and that of the masses widened, the latter appeared particularly 'sinful' and thus liable to provoke the wrath of God: their moral laxity, their intractable this-worldliness and, above all, their popular magic were all thorns in the side of the authorities. Here, the urge to purify man's relationship to God by 'rationalising' traditional forms of behaviour, at

---

[64] *Ernewerte Mandata und Landtgebott* (1598), 2.
[65] Elias, *Über den Prozess*, II, 372–97. Hubensteiner, *Vom Geist*, 117.   [66] *Ibid.*, 110ff.
[67] *Ibid.*

the very heart of the reformation of manners and conduct, revealed its more unpleasant side. A rigid demonisation of deviant views and practices was the price paid to purge society of popular animistic beliefs, along with a pandemonium of spirits, ghosts, elves, wild huntsmen, fiery dragons, lost souls, walking dead, spectres and demons, as well as polytheistically tinged cults of the saints and magical rituals, all diametrically opposed to the new religious attitude. This new piety also changed attitudes toward nature, which was exorcised of 'secret' forces, leaving only God, man and the Devil as active players. Representatives of high Renaissance magic, like Faust or Agrippa of Nettesheim, were retrospectively damned as the Devil's associates – even Trithemius and Albertus Magnus fell into disrepute – since magic without a Devil's pact was unimaginable in the new religious ideology. In this context attitudes toward 'white magic' changed between 1560 and 1590; it was no longer accepted as 'natural' but was feared since it signalled either a pact with the Devil, or a preliminary stage to witchcraft, or was considered endemic to the crime itself. Even harmless superstition was criminalised by this interpretation and had to be repressed with every available means – otherwise 'Almighty God would be roused to righteous anger against us, and punish and chastise our land and people with dearth, war and pestilence and manifold other plagues.'[68] Naturally, this was especially true of witchcraft, regarded as the worst of all imaginable sins. When 'righteous' God punished his people by inflicting a succession of crop failures, famines and diseases as signs of his discontent, only the pitiless persecution of witches seemed to offer any hope of attaining the goal dearest to the people: 'the propitiation of Almighty God to avert the punishment with which he threatens us'.[69]

There are multiple connections between the rise of trials for witchcraft and the social crisis that began in Europe in the second half of the sixteenth century and culminated in the well-known 'crisis of the seventeenth century',[70] a lengthy phase of decline or stagnation between two extended periods of economic and demographic growth. Two different developments coincided decisively at this time. On the one hand, a population plagued by frequent subsistence crises felt the need to persecute witches, understood essentially as sorcerers (men or women) who raised storms, damaged crops and brought disease on people and livestock. The rise in accusations of witchcraft corresponded to relevant agrarian crises. Per-

[68] *Landtgebott wider die Aberglauben, Zauberey, Hexerey und andere sträffliche Teufels-künste* (1611), fol. IIf. Guarinoni, a pupil of the Jesuits, vehemently criticised the popular fixation with this world and the people's ineradicable attachment to an 'unholy life of sensual enjoyment'. In his opinion superstition among the people was stronger than belief. Bücking, *Kultur*, 118, 181. If one reads the relevant trial records, this contemporary view gains in plausibility.

[69] *Landtgebott wider die Aberglauben, Hexerey und andere sträffliche Teufelskunste*, fol. IV.

[70] Cf. note 54.

haps the number of real attempts at sorcery also rose in times of want,[71] but this cannot be verified. Contemporaries certainly held this opinion. On the other hand, radical changes in the mentality of the upper classes also inclined them to perceive the deterioration in living conditions as a sign of God's wrath and as proof of demonic activity, either as the result of greater sinfulness or in the context of eschatological interpretations (Revelation 12:12 or 20:7). The world seemed turned upside-down. In 1591, a Lutheran noted that the Devil was raging with his witches 'as if he . . . wished to ruin man and beast once and for all and even cast God down from Heaven'.[72] Under these circumstances, Christian authorities were charged with the merciless persecution of witches, from whom the rural population as well as the ruling elite of all confessions expected immediate relief, above all to ease the dearth among their subjects![73]

Since the 1970s, sociological and socio-psychological research has stressed the reconstruction of microstructures in village or neighbourhood communities, in order to understand the process of 'scapegoating' and the personal, mental and social tensions behind it. This is certainly of great interest, since, until recently, penetrating analyses of 'our' past for its inherent anthropological-historical interest would have been dismissed as untenable. Of course, it should be said that this kind of microhistorical approach only partially explains European witch trials in the early modern period. Without a doubt, far-reaching fields of motivation underlie many witch trials, with social tensions dispersed among them, but two factors remain decisive. First, the chain of events behind individual accusations and trials for witchcraft were so multifarious that they cannot be squeezed into one explanatory model. We can, however, distinguish certain constellations of events that often – though for various reasons and on different levels – led to charges of witchcraft. Several unambiguous events may have 'triggered' the trials, but one cannot force them into a comfortable theoretical framework.[74]

Second, this broad regional study clearly demonstrates that, even under

---

[71] As Kamen, *Iron Century*, 241 suggests.

[72] 'General Instruction von den Truten' (1591), fol. 1. Cf. on this Mandrou, 'Das europäische Barock', 384: 'Ist die Verbindung zwischen der mentalen, fast physiologischen Gleichgewichtsstörung und der unterschwelligen sozialen Krise nicht offensichtlich? . . . Die Welt steht auf dem Kopf.'

[73] Cf. chapter 3, Contemporary interpretations, pp. 115–20.

[74] Cf. chapter 3, 'Triggering factors', pp. 183–93, on the typical constellations of events that triggered the great witch hunt of 1590. But this must be compared with the quantitative part of our investigation, which shows that witch trials in no way formed a normal model of the resolution of conflict. Cf. chapter 2, 'Quantification synchronic and diachronic juxtaposition', pp. 35–64. Probably microsociological models are more promising for the explanation of suspicions of witchcraft, but witch trials were a political matter and their success depended on factors outside the microsociological sphere, perhaps particularly in the region studied here, which was one of the earliest centralised states.

microstructurally similar conditions (as far as these can be determined at all), witch trials were rare events. An apparently decisive causal relationship studied in the isolation of one or two trials loses its significance when examined at the regional level. For every trial ending in the execution of an alleged witch, there were a hundred other trials for sorcery or witchcraft that resulted in a lesser sentence or even in the punishment of the accuser. Analysing the records of these trials reveals a strong affinity to 'magical' modes of thought, and one can assume that the majority of suspicions were never brought before a court, as the contemporary supporters of witch hunting ceaselessly lamented.[75] To comprehend this fully, one must accept the normalcy of magical beliefs in early modern Europe. As in the ethnological studies of Evans-Pritchard, the analysis of European witchcraft files proves that the seriousness of the crime of witchcraft was ameliorated within the context of the popular magic. People did not run to the authorities with every suspicion, and even when they were certain, they sought solutions outside the law courts, perhaps in a counterspell. Sociological assumptions about the exclusion of unpopular persons from local communities may or may not be correct, but they do not explain why common discrimination was unlikely, in the long run, to lead to trials and executions of witches.[76]

Although this book demonstrates that most witchcraft persecutions occurred when the interests of the local populace and the authorities coincided, it is undeniable that the attitude of the authorities in places where they had absolute jurisdiction determined when witch hunts would begin and end. The region studied provides many examples of officials who refused to stage persecutions in the early 1580s, only to swing to the opposite extreme at the end of the decade. Fading optimism and a gloomy world-view in these years, 'crucial years if ever there were', as Mandrou wrote,[77] marked a general trend toward a multi-faceted transformation in this territorially fragmented region. In southeast Germany and its northern neighbour, Franconia, a direct connection can often be made between the mentality of the rulers and the handling of witchcraft accusations. Freely adapting the principle of *cuius regio eius religio*, rulers who took less interest in religion or were more 'traditional' were less interested in witch hunting. Notorious 'concubine keepers' like the anti-reform Prince-Abbots of Kempten displayed as little persecuting zeal as the Bishop of Bamberg Johann Philipp von Gebsattel, who earned the enmity of ideo-

---

[75] For dabbling in witchcraft in popular magical culture cf. pp. 65–88. Sprenger and Institoris had already been willing to see a witch even in the smallest village, *Malleus*, II, 147. All the apologists for persecution, who saw the world as threatened by a conspiracy of huge dimensions, found it hard to stomach the lack of persecuting zeal of most of their contemporaries.   [76] Cf. pp. 65–88.   [77] Mandrou, 'Das europäische Barock', 384.

logues.[78] On the other hand, almost all zealous religious innovators of both regions are found among the witch hunters: Dukes Wilhelm V and Maximilian I of Bavaria, the Prince-Bishops Marquard vom Berg and Heinrich V von Knöringen at Dillingen (Bishopric of Augsburg), Martin von Schaumburg and Johann Christoph von Westerstetten in Eichstätt, Johann Gottfried von Aschhausen and Johann Georg II Fuchs von Dornheim in Bamberg, Julius Echter von Mespelbrunn and Philipp Adolf von Ehrenberg in Würzburg.[79] All the zealous ideologues and supporters of persecution were intransigent champions of religious reform, both externally and internally: the suffragans Förner in Bamberg and Binsfeld in Trier, the Ingolstadt theologian Albert Hunger – all three graduates of the Collegium Germanicum – the Jesuits Petrus Canisius, Gregor von Valentia, Gretser, Contzen and Drexel, the writers Fickler, Gewold and Albertinus. The eschatological obsessions of the princely house of Ansbach and its Lutheran advisers also point in the same direction.[80]

Ultimately, whether one links witchcraft persecutions in western Europe to a social crisis remains a question of interpretation, but the evidence favours it. If persecutions are a serious indicator of social crises, then the decisive break or climax occurred in the years immediately before and after 1590, not in the mid-seventeenth century. It was no coincidence that the Faust legend assumed its literary form at that time. In those years, when the world seemed out of joint,[81] social and political conflicts became more

[78] Cf. Bauer, 'Die Bamberger Weihbischöfe', on the opposition between Gebsattel and the reform party in Bamberg (Förner), Würzburg (Echter) and Munich (Gewold, Maximilian I). There is much information in the Kempten chronicle in UBM, 2 Cod. Ms. 500: Abbot Erhard vom Stein (1571–84) was, it says, a kindly ruler, who did not overburden his subjects, liked to drink, and had four children by his concubine in Kempten. Abbot Albrecht von Hohenegg (1584–7) was 'ein geschickt hochverständiger Herr schier mehr weltlich als geistlich', who had four children by his concubine in the Free City. Abbot Johann Erhart Blarer von Wartensee (1587–94) had four children by his concubine in the Protestant town of Isny and left the government of his abbey to his capable Chancellor Ulrich Deggelin. *Ibid.*, fol. 139ff. But lack of interest in religion and mere lust for life were probably less decisive than a rejection of the fanatical yet at the same time rational and calculated religiosity of the confessional reformers in all camps, for whatever reason. The hard-working Bishop of Freising, Veit Adam Gepeckh (1618–51), certainly worked in the spirit of the Counter-Reformation, but his vitality was directed into different channels from those of the Prince-Abbots of Kempten. The son of a country nobleman of Dachau, born in 1584 and educated at Dillingen and Ingolstadt, he was remote from the fanaticism and sombre world-view of many of his educated contemporaries. He saw no automatic connection between sins and divine punishment, and took action against religious zealotry (miracles, pilgrimages etc.). The Bishop was concerned to maintain a balance in his treatment of the very heterodox practices of his flock, e.g. the veneration of an earthenware lion by women as part of a local fertility cult. So far as is known, no witches were burned during his long episcopate. Weber, *Veit Adam Gepeckh*, 380–5, 568–77. It should be emphasised that the persecuting zeal of many contemporaries was less a question of confession than one of mentality.

[79] A special role may have been played by the Catholic League, in which the Catholic movement combined in 1610.   [80] Cf. p. 76.   [81] Cf. note 72.

acute as the secular trend of the 'long sixteenth century' drew to a close and tens of thousands died of famine and epidemics in almost all regions of Western Europe every few years. The institutional framework proved incapable of coping with subsistence crises on such an unprecedented scale and it became urgent to ascertain whether these phenomena were 'natural' or were signs of God's wrath. Schemes to resolve the problem were informed by one's inherent assumptions. On the one side, between 1560 and 1610 Europe witnessed a boom of demonological literature and the most intense debate on the supposed intervention of supernatural powers in worldly affairs. On the other side, astronomers and scientists like Kepler, Galileo, Bacon, Scheiner or Herwarth did not gaze to the heavens to observe angels or witches in flight. Even those who still believed in an older cosmology, such as the Jesuit Adam Tanner, began admitting that 'real' cases of flight by witches were quite exceptional.[82] After 1600, many lands drastically scaled down witch-hunting activities and persecutions, among them Spain, Holland, Italy, England – and Bavaria.[83]

[82] Tanner, *Theologia*, I, col. 994. On Tanner's cosmology, cf. his dispute with the more progressive Bavarian Jesuit Christoph Schreiner (1575–1650), who was prominent as an inventor and natural scientist. Schreiner not only disputed with Galileo the priority in the discovery of sunspots but also ventured to correct several points in traditional cosmology that did not agree with observations. Schreiner was violently criticised for this by Tanner. Cf. Lurz, *Adam Tanner*, 18f. Literature on Schreiner in Spindler, *Handbuch*, II, 800f. (Kraus).

[83] The resumption of witch hunting in southeastern Germany at the end of the seventeenth century and its long persistence into the middle of the eighteenth is a phenomenon that must be treated separately from the earlier developments. Because of the scantier sources for the region at this time by comparison with the decades around 1600 – in itself a sign of the relative state of society – the basis for a resumption is not easy to understand. It is possible that many and varied factors combined, which in turn require interpretation. A mandate of 11 July 1673 in Bavaria generally allowed less stringent conditions for torture, for reasons of costs (SBM, Cgm. 2545, fol. 276), and this may have relaxed the supervision of the central government to some extent. It appears that the witchcraft mandate of 1665 was actually read from the pulpit in the 1670s (Moser, *Chronik*, 219f.). Finally, this period also saw the return of hunger crises, while a rise in population exacerbated the latent problem of beggars. The protective veil drawn against early rationalist philosophy led to a partial regression, and a renewed willingness to allow executions of witches.

Sources and Literature

SOURCES

Bundesarchiv Aussenstelle Frankfurt (BundesA ASt Frankfurt)

F 215–Zsg. 2/1–f (Films)
(These are the microfilmed materials of the socalled *H-Sonderkommando*. The originals are now in the Provincial Archives of Poznan, Poland, which kindly advised me of the current programme of microfilming. All the material relevant to the present Federal State of Bavaria was used. It is listed below. Instead of the full reference, I give merely the number of the relevant microfilm in the footnotes.)

Film	Place	Film	Place
68	Abenberg	340	Bogen
69	Abensberg	416	Buchloe
90	Aibling	442	Burgau
107	Altdorf	444	Burgebrach
117	Altheim	445	Burghausen
127	Alzenau	447	Burglengenfeld
128	Amberg	448	Burgrain
135	Amorbach	453	Burkheim
153	Apfelbach	483	Cham
165	Arnstein	494	Coburg
173	Aschaffenburg	521	Dachau
180	Aufkirchen	538	Deggendorf
181	Augsburg	572	Dillingen
188	Babenhausen	574	Dingolfing
190	Bachgau	575	Dinkelsbühl
204	Bamberg A–L	576	Dinkelscherben
205	Bamberg K–Z	596	Donauwörth
206	Banz	641	Ebermannstadt
221	Baunach	642	Ebern
226	Bayreuth	668	Eichstätt A–K
269	Bärnstein	669	Eichstätt L–Z
285	Bezenstein	693	Ellingen
300	Birk	699	Eltmann
305	Bischofsheim	714	Ensdorf

Film	*Place*	*Film*	*Place*
718	Erding	1308	Iphofen
721	Erlabrunn	1310	Ismaning
724	Erlenbach	1342	Kälberau (?)
740	Eschau	1354	Kallmünz
773	Feuchtwangen	1378	Kaufbeuren
778	Fischbach	1382	Kelheim
783	Fladungen	1389	Kempten
790	Forchheim	1418	Kleinheubach
803	Freising	1427	Klingenberg
847	Fulda Bishopric	1446	Königsberg
861	Garmisch	1449	Königshofen
876	Geisling	1465	Kötzting
883	Gemeinfeld	1491	Kranzberg
885	Gemünden	1503	Kronach
901	Gerolzhofen A–J	1517	Kupferberg
902	Gerolzhofen K–Z	1530	Laber
962	Gräfenberg	1541	Landsberg
963	Gräfendorf	1543	Landshut
982	Greussendorf	1557	Langenzenn
1017	Grosslangheim	1566	Laudenbach
1059	Günzburg	1570	Laufen
1063	Gundelfingen	1574	Lauingen
1096	Hallstadt	1605	Leuchtenberg
1104	Hammelburg	1617	Lichtenberg
1124	Hassfurt	1620	Lichtenfels
1141	Heidenfeld	1634	Lierheim
1143	Heidingsfeld	1641	Lindau
1156	Hellmitzheim	1647	Lindheim
1160	Hemau	1667	Lohr
1165	Hengersberg	1714	Mainaschaff
1183	Herrieden	1715	Mainberg
1187	Hersbruck	1716	Mainbullau (?)
1188	Herschfeld(?)	1750	Marktbibart
1192	Herzogenaurach	1751	Marktbreit
1199	Heydau (= Haidau)	1752	Marktheidenfeld
1200	Heydeck	1779	Mellrichstadt
1203	Hilckersdorf	1782	Memmelsdorf
1218	Höchstädt	1783	Memmingen
1222	Hörstein	1814	Miltenberg A–G
1230	Hohebach	1815	Miltenberg H–Z
1232	Hohenburg	1820	Mittelsinn
1250	Hollfeld	1821	Mitterfels
1262	Horbach	1828	Möhrn
1295	Igersheim	1839	Monheim
1300	Impfingen	1843	Moosburg
1302	Inchenhofen	1848	Mosbach
1304	Ingolstadt	1865	Munich
1305	Innenthal	1870	Münnerstadt

Film	Place	Film	Place
1871	Münster	2589	Spalt
1874	Münster	2603	Stadelschwarzach
1914	Nennslingen	2609	Stadprozelten
1919	Neubrunn	2611	Stadtschwarzach
1945	Neumark (?)	2612	Staffelstein
1955	Neustadt/Coburg	2640	Steinwiesen
1958	Neustadt/Main	2655	Stockenberg
1962	Neustadt/Saale	2664	Stopfenheim
1992	Nördlingen	2677	Straubing
2000	Nuremberg	2687	Stüffenberg
2003	Neunkirchen	2695	Sugenheim
2006	Oberaltenbernheim	2708	Tambach
2011	Oberdorf (=Marktoberdorf)	2711	Tapfheim
2022	Obernburg	2730	Thüngen
2029	Oberscheinfeld	2735	Tilsberg (?)
2031	Oberschwarzach	2740	Tölz
2034	Oberstdorf	2775	Uissigheim
2044	Ochsenfurt	2783	Unteraltenbernheim
2060	Oettingen	2784	Untereisenheim
2104	Passau	2788	Unterzell
2160	Poppenlauer	2829	Vilsbiburg
2162	Pottenstein	2836	Vötting
2197	Rain	2837	Vohburg
2214	Rattenberg	2843	Volkach
2230	Regen	2848	Vornheim
2231	Regensburg	2853	Wachenroth
2232	Regenstauf	2856	Wechterswinkel
2234	Reichertshofen	2860	Waischenfeld
2241	Reichenberg	2866	Wallenburg
2260	Remlingen	2869	Wallerstein
2266	Rettenberg	2872	Walsheim (?)
2267	Retzbach	2898	Wasserburg/Bodensee
2291	Rieneck	2899	Wasserburg/Inn
2296	Rimbach	2900	Wassertrüdingen
2303	Ritzisried	2908	Weiden
2349	Rothenberg	2912	Weilheim
2351	Rothenburg ob der Tauber	2920	Weissenburg
2353	Rothenfels	2926	Weissenhorn
2356	Rottenbach(?)	2939	Wemding
2358	Rottenburg	2944	Wenschdorf
2367	Rüdenhausen	2947	Werdenfels
2479	Schlüsselfeld	2983	Willanzheim
2480	Schmachtberg	2996	Windsheim
2485	Schmidmühlen	3027	Wörth/Main
2516	Schongau	3042	Wolfmannshausen (?)
2527	Schwabach	3064	Würzburg
2530	Schwabmünchen	3065	Würzburg
2546	Schweinfurt	3085	Zeil A–K
2580	Sommerach	3086	Zeil L–Z

Film	*Place*
3633	StadtA Aschaffenburg, StiftsA Aschaffenburg
3634	StaatsA Bamberg, Staatsbibliothek Bamberg
3662	Staatsbibliothek Eichstätt
3676	StadtA Günzburg
3691	StaatsA Coburg
3706	StadtA Mergentheim
3709	Hauptstaatsarchiv Munich (Hexenakten nos. 10–54; Staatsverwaltung; Oefeleana; Hochstiftsliteralien Passau, Augsburg and Freising; Reichsstädte Literalien Memmingen, Augsburg, Dinkelsbühl, Lindau, Regensburg; Gerichtsliteralien Wemding)
3710	Hauptstaatsarchiv Munich (Hochstiftsliteralien Freising; MarktA Garmisch; Generalregistratur nos. 20/5, 21/7, 22/8, 113/5, 139/5, 139/60, 139/61, 139/62, 140/64, 140/65, 318/1, 318/2, 320, 322/8, 322/9, 323/16, 324/16, 1/2, 518/83, 1210; Amtsrechnungen 14/236, 530/38, 2066/203; Gerichtsliteralien Amberg, Burghausen, Dingolfing, Dorfen, Erding, Haag, Haidau, Ingolstadt, Landau, Landsberg, Landshut, Mainburg, Mitterfels, Murnau, Rosenheim, Schongau, Schwabeck, Straubing, Tölz, Vilshofen, Wasserburg, Weilheim; Geheimes HausA)
3711	StadtA Munich
3712	Stadtmuseum Munich
3713	Universitätsbibliothek Munich
3716	Staatsarchiv Neuburg/Donau
3718	StadtA Nördlingen
3721	StadtA Passau
3747	Fürstl. Löwenstein-Wertheim-Rosenb.A, Wertheim
3748	Haus-, Hof- und Staatsarchiv, Vienna
3750	StaatsA Würzburg
3751	StaatsA Würzburg
3784	Copy of an opinion of the University of Würzburg
3840–3844	Copy of the draft of a long treatise on witch trials at Eichstätt by Brems
3852–3854	Copy of the record of the hearings of a Munich witchcraft trial of 1615–16, StadtA Munich
3865	Replies of Bavarian archives to the inquiries of the *H-Sonderkommando* of the *Reichssicherheitshauptamt*, 1936 (HStAM, Staatsarchive Nuremberg, Amberg, Munich, Coburg, Landshut, Neuburg, Bamberg (with Staatsbibliothek) and Würzburg)
3866–3878	Picture archives
3883	Index

Hauptstaatsarchiv Munich (HStAM)

Hexenakten, nos. 1, $1\frac{1}{2}$, 2, 3, 4, $4\frac{1}{2}$, 5, 6, 7, 7a, 7b, 8, 9, 9a, 9b, 9c, 9d, 9e, 9f (from searches of the *H-Sonderkommando*: 10a, 10b, 10c, 11, 12, $12\frac{1}{2}$, 13, 14, $14\frac{1}{2}$), 15, 15a, 16 (from searches of the *H-Sonderkommando*: 17, 18, 19, 20, 21, 22, 23, 24, 25, 26, 27, 28, $28\frac{1}{2}$, 29, 30, 31, 32, 33, 34, 35, 36, 37, 38, 39, 40, 41, 42, 43, 44, 45, 46, 47, 48, 49), 50, 51, 52, 53, 54.

(The Eichstätt records, nos. 42–49, have since been transferred to the StA Nuremberg. The other numbers concern:

nos. 1–7b Duchy of Bavaria

nos. 8–9f Bishopric of Freising

nos. 10–12½ Bishopric of Salzburg

nos. 13–15, 16 Bishopric of Augsburg

nos. 15a–41 Pfalz-Neuburg

nos. 42–49 Bishopric of Eichstätt

nos. 50–54 miscellaneous.)

Kurbayern Hofrat (KHR)

Nos. 1, 4, 5, 6, 7, 16, 17, 18, 19, 41, 42, 43, 44, 45, 59, 60, 61, 62, 63, 64, 65, 66, 67, 68, 69, 70, 71, 72, 73, 74, 75, 76, 77, 78, 79, 80, 81, 82, 83, 84, 85, 86, 87, 88, 89, 90, 91, 92, 97, 98, 99, 100, 101, 102, 107, 108, 109, 110, 111, 112, 113, 114, 115, 116, 117, 118, 119, 120, 121, 122, 123, 124, 125, 126, 127, 128, 129, 130, 131, 155, 157, 158, 159, 160, 161, 162, 163, 172, 173, 174, 175, 176, 177, 178, 179, 225, 226, 227, 228, 229, 230, 231, 232, 233, 234, 266, 267, 268, 269, 305, 306, 307, 308, 309, 310, 345, 347, 348, 349, 365, 366, 367, 368, 386, 387, 388, 412, 413, 414, 415, 424, 425, 426, 428, 464, 466, 467, 468, 469, 470, 471, 472, 473, 474, 475, 476, 504, 505, 506, 507, 508, 509, 510, 511, 543, 544, 546, 547, 583, 584, 585, 588, 623, 624, 625, 626, 663, 664, 665, 666, 687, 688, 689, 690, 703, 704, 705, 706, 743, 744, 745, 746, 880, 884, 886, 893, 894, 913, 914, 915.

Kurbayern Geheimer Rat, nos. 163, 164, 165, 166, 167, 168, 169, 170, 175.

Kurbayern Äusseres Archiv, nos. 1330, 4826.

Gerichtsliteralien (GL): cf. Film 3710

Generalregistratur (GR), nos. 318/1, 323/16, 324/16 1/1, 324/19, 324/23, 324/24, 1210/20.

Hofamtsregistratur (HR), nos. 288/1, 400 1/2, 401/1, 401/2, 401/3

Kurbayern Hofkammer, nos. 93, 94, 95, 96, 97, 98.

Hofzahlamtsrechnungen (HZR), nos. 35, 36, 37, 38, 39, 40, 41.

Kurbayern Urkunden, nos. 9444, 36227.

Staatsverwaltung (SV), nos. 2063, 2218, 2222, 2243, 2281, 3221.

Reichskammergericht (RKG), nos. 4230, 5973, 6069, 6519, 10688.

Oefeleana, nos. 44,2; 48.

Kasten Schwarz, no. 8692.

Hochstift Augsburg, Neuburger Abgabe (NA), Akten (minutes of the Court Council of the Bishopric of Augsburg at Dillingen), nos. 1183, 1184, 1185, 1186, 1187, 1188, 1189, 1190, 1191, 1192, 1193, 1194, 1195, 1196, 1197, 1198, 1199, 1200, 1201, 1202, 1203, 1204, 1205, 1206, 1207, 1208, 1209, 1210, 1211, 1212, 1213, 1214, 1215, 1216, 1217, 1218, 1219, 1220, 1221, 1222, 1223, 1224, 1225, 1226, 1227, 1228, 1229, 1230.

(other records in this class) 799, 800, 806, 819, 831, 2629, 2816, 2920, 6737, 7228, 7229, 7472, 7485, 7488.

Hochstift Augsburg, Münchner Bestand (MB), Literalien, no. 572.

Hochstift Freising, Hochstiftsliteralien (HL), III, no. 320/39.

Klosterliteralien (KL) Benediktbeuren, no. 16.

Fürststift Kempten, Neuburger Abgabe (NA), Literalien, nos. 2661, 2667, 2750, 2751, 2770 (minutes of the Court Council); nos. 1422, 2052.

Fürststift Kempten, Neuburger Abgabe (NA), Akten nos. 1605, 1606, 1607 (nos. 2036, 2037, 2039, 2040, 2071 – material on the trials at Vaduz, collected by Prince-Abbot Rupert Bodmann).

Fürststift Kempten, Urkundenarchiv (UA), nos. 1261, 3223.
Mediatisierte Fürsten, no. 28, Reichsherrschaft Wasserburg/Bodensee (Fugger),
Akt 73, 74, 75, 76, 77.
Plansammlung, nos. 19896, 19897, 19898.

Erzbischöfliches Ordinariatsarchiv Munich (EOAM)

Protokolle, Geistlicher Rat, Protokolle (GR Prot.) nos. 3, 4, 5, 6, 7, 8, 9, 10, 11, 12.
Verschiedene Akten
Akt Varia no. 516.
Akt Aberglaube (old no. 141)
Akt Magiae
Akt Unzulässige Benediktionen
Akt Varia no. 1513
Heckenstaller-Sammlung, nos. 298, 310, 730.
Klosterbestände, no. 50 (Gars/Inn)
Hochstift Salzburg (S), no. 133.

Staatsbibliothek Munich (SBM), Manuscript department

Cgm. nos. 1251, 1307, 1516, 1732, 1771, 1985, 2025, 2026, 2197, 2198, 2210, 2538,
2542, 2545, 2574, 2586, 2587, 2588, 2614, 2622, 2625, 2811, 3116, 3126, 3148, 3252,
3313, 3731, 3891, 4235, 4387, 4421, 4608, 4914, 4972, 5145, 6051, 6596.
Clm, nos. 1607, 1608, 4795, 8554, 26469, 27219.
Oefeleana, nos. 343, 414.

Universitätsbibliothek Munich (UBM), Manuscript department

2° Cod. Ms. 214
2° Cod. Ms. 230
2° Cod. Ms. 500

*Institut für Volkskunde (IV) der Kommission für bayrische Landesgeschichte bei
der Bayr. Akademie der Wissenschaften, Munich*

Card index of customs (BK) cabinets: 'Religion – Kirche – Geistlichkeit – Volksglaube'; cabinets 'Obrigkeit – Rechtspflege - Volksrüge'.

Staatsarchiv Munich (StAM)

Hofkammer Ämterrechnungen (accounts (GR) of the district courts). References
are to years.
Abensberg-Altmannstein 1590, 1600, 1610, 1620, 1625, 1629
Auerberg 1590
Dachau 1560, 1581, 1582, 1589, 1592, 1593, 1594, 1595, 1596, 1597, 1598, 1602,
1603
Diessen 1590
Gerolfing 1590

Kösching 1590
Kranzberg 1590
Landsberg 1589
Marquartstein 1590
Pfaffenhofen 1590
Rain 1590
Reichenhall 1590, 1610, 1620, 1630
Riedenburg 1590
Rosenheim 1590
Schongau 1566, 1572, 1575, 1576, 1599, 1600, 1610, 1616, 1620, 1630, 1640, 1650,
1660, 1670, 1680, 1690, 1700, 1710, 1720, 1730, 1740, 1750, 1760, 1770
Schrobenhausen 1590
Schwaben 1590
Starnberg 1590
Traunstein 1560, 1570, 1580, 1590
Vohburg 1590
Wasserburg 1590, 1610, 1620, 1630
Weilheim 1599
Wemding 1590, 1610, 1620, 1630
Wolfratshausen 1570, 1580, 1590, 1600, 1605, 1629, 1630
Rentmeisterliteralien (RL)
Fasc. 24 nos. 96, 97, 98, 99
Fasc. 25 nos. 100, 101.

Staatsarchiv Landshut (StAL)

Gerichtsrechnungen (GR)
Moosburg (years) 1550, 1560, 1570, 1580, 1590, 1600
Dingolfing (years) 1671, 1763, 1764, 1765, 1766
Erding (years) 1507, 1508, 1511, 1514, 1520, 1530, 1540, 1542, 1543, 1549, 1551,
1560, 1565, 1570, 1580, 1590, 1600, 1610, 1620, 1630, 1640, 1650, 1660, 1670, 1680,
1690, 1700, 1710, 1720, 1730, 1740, 1750, 1760, 1770.

Staatsarchiv Bamberg (StAB)

Bamberger Verordnungen
Rep. B 26c, no. 42 (mandate against treasure hunting 1776), no. 44 ('General-
Instruction von den Truten' (Ansbach), instruction on trials of witches (Landshut),
mandate against superstition and witchcraft (Bamberg).

Staatsarchiv Neuburg

Augsburger Pflegämter, no. 61
Reichsstadt Kempten, no. 110.
(The Pfalz-Neuburg witch trial records in the Depot Heimatverein and the Grass-
egger-sammlung were included in the researches of the *H-Sonderkommando*.)

Staatsarchiv Nuremberg
Staatsarchiv Amberg
Staatsarchiv Coburg
Staatsarchiv Würzburg

The witchcraft trial records in these archives were included in the researches of the *H-Sonderkommando* in 1936 (Film 3865: evaluation in the card index of places).

Staatsbibliothek Augsburg (SBA)

2° Cod. Aug. nos. 127, 130, 203, 268, 284, 285, 286, 287, 288, 289, 324
2° Cod. S. 20, 21, 23, 24, 25, 49, 50, 51, 52, 114, 123, 124, 125, 126, 127, 128.

Stadtarchiv Augsburg (StadtA Aug)

Strafbücher 1563–71, 1581–7, 1588–96, 1596–1605, 1608–15, 1615–32, 1632–53, 1693–1703.
Register der Urgichtenakten, 5 vols.
Urgichtenakten (UA) (380 fascicles from 1492 to 1722, of which I consulted, as indicated by the Strafbücher and the Register der Urgichtenakten, the years): 1589, 1590, 1591, 1592, 1605, 1625, 1630, 1639, 1643, 1650, 1654, 1666, 1669, 1670, 1680, 1685, 1686, 1687, 1690, 1692, 1694.
Anschläge und Dekrete, 1. (1522–1682), 2. (1490–1649)
Baumeisterbücher 1590, 1625.
Ratsprotokolle, nos. 45, 46, 71.
Chroniken, nos. 27, 27a, 33.
Geheimer Rat. Rat und andere Reichsstädte nos. 12, 23, 59.
Manuscripts: Haid, 'Hexenprozesse von dem Jahr 1525 bis zum Jahr 1728 (. . .)', Augsburg 1828 (practically unusable because of its numerous errors; WB);
Weng, 'Extractus der Stadt Augspurgischen Raths -Erkenntnussen 1392–1734', Augsburg 1734;
Anon., 'Verzeichnis derjenigen Personen welche allhier in Augsburg vom Leben zum Thod verurtheilt (. . .) (1513–1800)';
J. Bausch, 'Verzeichnis derer Maleficanten welches in Augsburg von Anno 1353 bis zu diesen unsern Zeiten (. . .) vom Leben zum Thod gebracht worden sind', Augsburg 1755.

Stadtarchiv Kaufbeuren (StadtA Kau)

W.L. Hörmann, Versuch einer General- und Special Registratur über die in (. . .) Kauffbeurer Cantzley-Archiv befindlichen Acta und Protocolla', 3 vols., 1773.
Archivbände B4, 7, 8, 9, 14, 23, 103, 106, 112.
Stadratsprotokolle 1543–1811 (the volume for 1585–91 is missing) (searched using index volume B 7).

Stadtarchiv Kempten (StadtA Kem)

Anon., 'Material-Index über Sämtliche Reichs Stadt Kemptische Raths-Protocolla von Anno 1477 bis Annum 1789 in 78 Tomis' (undated Ms.)

Stadtratsprotokolle 1477–1789 (searched using the Material-Index)
Akten IV, 8 (the trial of 1775, for which the trial records are not preserved).

Stadtarchiv Lindau (StadtA Lin)

Ratsprotokoll 1589–91
Akten 49, 7 (Scharfrichter); 57, 7 ('witch trial' of 1730).

Stadtarchiv Memmingen (StadtA Mem)

Urgichtenbücher 1551–73, 1574–1614, 1615–83
Prozessakten Schubl. 132/3, 132/9, 134/10, 138/3, 138/4, 146/1, 146/2, 344/9, 354/5, 354/6, 354/7, 354/8
Chroniken
2,84 (Schorer-Büchele)
2,53 (Schorer, anonymous continuator)
2,61 (D. Engler)
2,49 (J.G. Unold)
2,19 (Kimpel)
Stadtratsprotokolle 1518, 1566, 1570, 1589, 1591, 1592, 1656, 1663, 1665, 1668, 1696, 1697, 1701, 1702, 1703, 1704, 1705.

Stadtarchiv Munich (StadtA Mun)

Stadtgericht nos. 865/1–2, 866/1–11, 22,25 (Malefizprotokolle); 867/1–31, 880, 893, 911, 926, 952 A 2, 896.
Bürgermeister und Rat, no. 60 B 2
Ratssitzungsprotokolle, nos. 16, 17, 18, 19, 20, 21, 29, 230, 231, 232, 233.
Kämmerei, nos. 198, 199, 200, 226, 227, 228, 229, 230, 231, 232.
Hist. Ver. Urk. 1996–2088, 621c.
Mss. 183/1–8
Bibl. 1310
Elaborate 1872.

Haus-, Hof- und Staatsarchiv Vienna (HHSTA Vienna)

Reichshofrat, Denegata Antiqua, Karton 96.

Österreichische Nationalbibliothek Vienna (ÖNB Vienna)

Manuscript and incunabula collection
Cod. 8959, 8960, 8961, 8962, 8963, 8964, 8965 (Fugger *Zeitungen*)

Note
To capture as much as possible of the regional source material, written requests for information were sent to numerous other archives. The class references of relevant archives given in their replies are indicated in the appropriate places in the footnotes. In all, the following archives were consulted in my research:

Outside the region of the study:
Haus-, Hof- und Staatsarchiv Vienna; Österreichische Nationalbibliothek Vienna; Oberösterreichisches Landesarchiv Linz; Landesarchiv Salzburg; Konsistorialarchiv Salzburg; Tiroler Landesarchiv Innsbruck; Vorarlberger Landesarchiv Bregenz; StadtA Schärding; StadtA Hall/Tirol; Fürstl. Liechtenstein. HausA Vaduz; Hauptstaatsarchiv Stuttgart; StadtA Biberach; StadtA Wangen; StadtA Ulm; SchlossA Zeil; Staatsarchiv Amberg; Staatsarchiv Bamberg; Staatsarchiv Würzburg; Staatsarchiv Coburg; Staatsarchiv Nuremberg; StadtA Eichstätt; DiözesanA Eichstätt; StadtA Hof; StadtA Kulmbach; StadtA Rothenburg ob der Tauber; Provincial Archive Poznan; Bundesarchiv Koblenz; Bundesarchiv Aussenstelle, Frankfurt.

In the region studied:
Hauptstaatsarchiv Munich; Erzbischöfliches Ordinariatsarchiv, Munich; Staatsarchiv Munich; StadtA Munich; Staatsbibliothek Munich; Universitätsbibliothek Munich; Institut für Volkskunde d. Kommission für bayr. Landesgeschichte bei der Bayr. Akademie der Wissenschaften Munich; StaatsA Neuburg; StaatsA Landshut; StadtA Augsburg; Staatsbibliothek Augsburg; Bistumsarchiv Augsburg; MarktA Berchtesgaden; StadtA Burghausen; StadtA Deggendorf; StadtA Dillingen; Fuggersches Familien- und StiftungsA Dillingen; StadtA Dingolfing; StadtA Donauwörth; StadtA Freising; StadtA Füssen; StadtA Garmisch; StadtA Günzburg; StadtA Ingolstadt; StadtA Kaufbeuren; StadtA Kelheim; StadtA Kempten; StadtA Landsberg; StadtA Landshut; StadtA Lauingen; StadtA Lindau; StadtA Memmingen; StadtA Mindelheim; MarktA Mittenwald; StadtA Mühldorf; StadtA Neuötting; StadtA Nördlingen; Fürstl. Oettingen-Spielbergsches Archiv Oettingen; AbteiA Ottobeuren; BistumsA Passau; StadtA Passau; StadtA Pfaffenhofen; StadtA Rain; Bischöfl. Zentralarchiv Regensburg; StadtA Regensburg; Fürstl. Thurn- und Taxissches ZentralA Regensburg; StadtA Bad Reichenhall; StadtA Riedenburg; StadtA Rosenheim; StadtA Sonthofen; StadtA Straubing; StadtA Bad Tölz; StadtA Traunstein; StadtA Vilshofen; Fürstl. von der Leyensches Archiv Waal; Fürstl. Oettingen-Wallersteinsches Haus- und Familienarchiv Wallerstein; StadtA Wasserburg; StadtA Weilheim; StadtA Wemding.

LITERATURE
Literature before 1800

Baierische Sammlungen und Auszüge zum Unterricht und Vergnügen (ed. H. Braun, P. von Osterwald, C.F. Pfeffel), Munich 1764–7.
'Bedenken, die Unhulden betreffend. Ein merkwürdiges Aktenstück aus dem 16. Jahrhundert', *Ansbachische Monatsschrift*, Jahrgang 2 (1794), 534–48.
Cautio criminalis seu de processibus contra sagas liber (. . .) auctore incerto theologo romano, Rinteln 1631.
Eigentliche und Warhaffte Vertzaichnus, was sich in diesem 1563. Jar (. . .) zu Augspurg (. . .) zugetragen, Augsburg 1563.
Ein Christliche und nutzliche Erinnerung uber gegenwertige Tafel, Darinnen kurtzlich angezeigt wirdt der Ursprung, Ursach und Grewel des schändtlichen Lasters der Zauberey, Cologne 1595.
Ernewerte Mandata und Landtgebott, Munich 1598.
Erschreckhenliche newe Zeyttung (. . .) wie das Wetter in Wirttenberger Land so

grossen Schaden gethan, n.p. 1562.

Erweytterte Unholden Zeyttung, Ulm 1590.

Gründtlicher Bericht, ob Zauberey die ärgste und grewlichste Sünd auf Erden sey, Würzburg 1627.

Historia von D. Johann Fausten, Frankfurt am Main 1587.

Kurzer und warhafftiger Bericht und erschreckhliche Neue Zeitung von sechshundert Hexen, Zauberern und Teufels-bannern, welche der Bischof zu Bamberg hat verbrennen lassen (...) Auch hat der Bischof zu Würzburg über die neunhundert verbrennen lassen (...) Mit Bewilligung des Bischofs und ganzen Thum-Capitels in Druck gegeben, Bamberg 1659.

Landtgebott wider die Aberglauben, Zauberey, Hexerey und andere sträffliche Teufelskünste, Munich 1611 (1612).

Landtgebott wider die Aberglauben, Zauberey, Hexerey und andere sträffliche Teufelskünste, Munich 1665.

Landtgebott wider die Aberglauben, Zauberey, Hexerey und andere Sträffliche Teufelskünste, Munich 1746.

Mandat der Zauberer, Wahrsager und deren, welche sich verbottenen Segens gebrauchen, Bamberg 1610.

Newe Zeittung von den Hexen oder Unholden, so man verbrendt hat, n.p. 1580.

Newer Tractat von der Verführten Kinder Zauberey (...), Aschaffenburg 1629.

Theatrum de Veneficiis, das ist: Von Teuffelsgespenst, Zauberern und Gifftbereitern, Schwarzkünstlern, Hexen und Unholden (...), Frankfurt am Main (Basseus) 1586.

Theatrum Diabolorum, Frankfurt am Main (Feyerabend) 1569.

Warhafftige und erschreckliche newe Zeitung von einer jungen Dienern, welche sich dem Teufel sechs Jahr lang ergeben (...), Item von grewlichen ungestümen Wettern, so den 12. Maii dieses 1582. Jars in Baiern (...) grossen Schaden an Menschen und Viehe gethan haben, Dresden 1582.

Warhafftige und erschreckhliche Thatten und Handlungen der 63 Hexen und Unholden, so zu Wiesenstieg mit dem Brandt gerichtet worden seindt, n.p. 1563.

Warhafftige Zeytung von 134 Unholden, so umb irer Zauberey halben verbrennet worden, Strasbourg 1583.

Warhafftige Zeytung von dem grausamen Wätter und Schaur (...), Munich 1582.

Zwei Hexenzeitung, die erste von Dreyen Hexen-Pfaffen und einem Organisten zu Ellwangen, wie dieselben Christo abgesagt (...), Nuremberg 1615.

Zwo Hexen Zeitung, Die erste: aus dem Bisthumb Würtzburg, Das ist, Gründliche Erzählung, wie der Bischoff zu Würtzburg das Hexenbrennen im Franckenlande angefangen (...), Die Ander aus dem Herzogtum Würtenberg, wie der Herzog zu Wirtenberg in unterschiedlichen Stätten das Hexenbrennen auch angefangen, Tübingen 1616.

Zwo newe Zeittung, die erste welcher gestalt zween falsche Juden durch Zauberey zuwegen gebracht, dass vil tausend Stückh Vihe (...) gestorben ist. Welche auch 1599. Jars ihren gebührenden Lohn empfangen haben, Vienna 1599.

Zwo newe Zeitung, was man für Hexen oder Unholden verbrendt hat, n.p. 1580.

Zwo warhafftige newe Zeittung, die erste ist ein warhafftige Propheceyung, was sich diss 1628. Jar wird verlauffen und zutragen (...). Die ander Zeittung ist aus dem Bistumb Würzburg und Bamberg, auch sonst aus anderen Herrschaften, wo man viel Hexen und Gabelreuteren verbrennen lest, und noch viel gefangen liegen (...), Würzburg 1627.

Agricola, F., *Gründtlicher Bericht, ob Zauber- und Hexerei die aergeste und grewlichste sünd auff Erden sey (...)*, Cologne 1597 (Dillingen 1613, Ingolstadt 1618).

Agricola, S. and Wittmerus G., *Erschröckliche, ganz warhafftige Geschicht, welche sich (...) zu Spalt inn dem Ey[ch]stätter Bistum (...) verlauffen hat*, Ingolstadt 1584.

Albertinus, A., *Der Welt Tummelplatz und Schawplatz*, Munich 1612.

Lucifers Königreich und Seelengejaid, Munich 1616.

Albrecht, B., *Magia, das ist: christenlicher Bericht von der Zauberey und Hexerey (...)*, Leipzig 1628 (Albrecht was a priest in Augsburg).

Althusius, J., *Vermahnung an die Richter* [in witch trials; WB], in J.G. Goedelmann, *Von Zauberern (...)*, Frankfurt 1592, 142–55.

Am Wald, G., *Gerichts-Teuffel, darin angezeigt und gehandlet wird, wie und was massen der leydig Sathan bissweilen unordnung und zerrüttung in Gerichten (...) anrichten thut*, St Gallen 1580 (dedicated to the Town Council of Memmingen).

B., H.A., *Informatio Juris in causa poenali utrum tres mulieres maleficii et veneficii (...). Rechtliches Bedencken in Malefitzsachen, Ob drey weyber der Zauberey halber angegeben in Gefängliche Verhafft genommen und peinlich befragt werden können oder nicht?*, Frankfurt am Main 1590.

Baurer, F., Schmid, Franz, Josef und der Satz: Teuflische Magie existiert, besteht noch. In einer Antwort des kathol. Weltmannes auf die von einem Herrn Landpfarrer herausgegebene Apologie der Professor Weberschen Hexenreformation, Augsburg 1791.

Bayle, P., *Peter Baylens Historisches und critisches Wörterbuch, 4 Bde.*, Leipzig *1741–1744 (Hg. J. Ch. Gottscheid)*.

Bechmann, J. V., *Discursus juridicus de crimine maleficii. Von der Zauberey*, Halle 1749.

Beer, J. Ch., *Der höllische Intelligenz-Zettul (...)*, Augsburg 1753.

Bekker, B., *Die bezauberte Welt*, 4 vols., Amsterdam 1693.

Biermann, M., *De magicis actionibus disquisitio succincta, elegans et nervosa (...)*, Frankfurt am Main 1629.

Binsfeld, P., *Tractatus de confessionibus maleficorum et sagarum*, Trier 1589 (2nd edn 1591, 3rd edn 1596).

Tractat von Bekanntnuss der Zauberer und Hexen, Munich 1591 (2nd edn 1592).

Bodin, J., *De Daemonomagia Magorum*, Strasbourg 1581 (translated by J. Fischart).

Braun, H., Drey Fragen zur Vertheydigung der Hexerey. 1. Ob P. Angelus März die Rede des P. Sterzinger gründlich, und 2. bescheiden widerlegt habe, 3. und ob wohl diese akademische Rede dem heil. Kreuze von Scheyern in der Tat nachtheilig sei? Mit einem sichern Ja beantwortet, und dem P. Angelus selbst dediziert von J. F. Z., o.O., o.J., (München 1767).

Bucher, J., *Ein gross wunderbarlich und unerhörtes Mirackel (...) von einer jungen Magd, welche unschuldig zum Tod verurtheilt (...) ist worden*, Augsburg 1589.

Chlingensberger, H.A.M., *Consilia et responsa criminalia super diversis casibus et delictis*, 2 vols., Ingolstadt 1738–9.

Contzen SJ, A. *Methodus doctrinae civilis seu Abissini regis historia*, Cologne 1628 (German tr., Sulzbach 1672).

Cusan SJ, N., *Christliche Zuchtschul*, n.p. 1627 (2nd edn Lucerne 1645).

Delrio SJ, M., *Disquisitionum Magicarum libri sex*, Mainz 1603 (first edition

1599–1600; the (eighteenth) Cologne edition of 1633 has been used).

Drexel, SJ, J., *Gazophyliacum Christi Eleemosyna quam in aula Maximiliani explicavit*, Munich 1637.

Durich, F., *Eytychii Benjamini Transalbini Dissertatio Philologica de vocibus Hartymin et Belahateham*, o.O. (München) 1767.

Echard, M.S., *Des leidigen Teuffels Kunst- und Bubenstücklen*, Nuremberg 1645.

Ehinger, C., *Daemonologia oder etwas neues vom Teufel*, Augsburg 1681.

Ellinger, J., *Hexen-Coppel, darinnen derer Hexen und Unholden uhralte Ankunfft und seltzame Gattung auff den Schauplatz geführet werden*, Frankfurt am Main 1628.

Everhard, G., *Consilia*, 2 vols., Augsburg 1618.

Ewich, J., *De sagarum (. . .) natura*, Bremen 1584 (German tr., Bremen 1585; *Theatrum de Veneficiis* (1586), 325–55).

Fachineus, A. (praeside), *Disputatio juridica de maleficis et sagis*, Ingolstadt 1592 (cf. J.C. Fickler).

Farinacius, P., *Praxis et theoria criminalis*, Frankfurt 1597.

Fichard, J.C., *Consilia*, Frankfurt am Main 1597.

Fickler, J.C., *Disputatio juridica de maleficis et sagis*, Ingolstadt 1592.

Finauer, P. P., *Gedanken über die Werke des Liebhabers der Wahrheit von der Hexerey*, München 1767.

Fornerus, F., *Panoplia armaturae dei adversus omnem superstitionem, divinationem, excantationem, daemonolatriam (. . .)*, Ingolstadt 1626.

Geiler, J., *Die Emeis. Dies ist das Buch von der Omeissen*, Strasbourg 1516.

Glaser, P., *Gesindteufel. Darin acht stück gehandelt werden, von des Gesindes untrew*, Leipzig 1564.

Gobat, SJ, G., *Accusatio canonica ebriosa*, Munich 1681.

Goedelmann, J.G., *Tractatus de magis, veneficis et lamiis*, Nuremberg 1584.

Von Zauberern, Hexen und Unholden warhafftiger und wolgegründter Bericht (. . .) Allen Beampten zu unsern Zeiten, von wegen vieler ungleicher und streittigen Meynung, sehr nützlich (. . .) zu wissen, Frankfurt am Main 1592.

Graser, J. B., *Verteidigung der kritischen Anmerkungen über des Pater Georg Gaars Rede von der Hexe Maria Renata*, Bayreuth 1754.

Gräter, J., *Hexen- und Unholdenpredikt*, Tübingen 1589.

Gregorius, J.G., *Gemüths vergnügendes Historisches Hand-Buch für Bürger und Bauern (. . .)*, Frankfurt/Leipzig 1744.

Gretser SJ, J., *Bavius et Moevius (. . .)*, Ingolstadt 1605.

De festis Christianorum, Ingolstadt 1612.

Grillandus, P., *Tractatus de sortilegiis*, Geneva 1536.

Grossens, J. M., *Gewisse Macht und Ohnmacht des Fürsten der Finsternis*, Regensburg 1734.

Guarinonius, H., *Die Grewel der Verwüstung menschlichen Geschlechts (. . .)*, Ingolstadt 1610.

Hauber, E.D., *Bibliotheca acta et scripta magica. Gründliche Nachrichten und Urteile solcher Bücher und Handlungen, welche die Macht des Teufels in leiblichen Dingen betreffen (. . .)*, Lemgo 1736–45.

Haunold, SJ, C., *Controversiae de justitia et jure privatorum*, 6 vols., Ingolstadt, 1671–4.

Heerbrand, J., *Ketzer Katzen*, Tübingen 1589.

Heiden, C., *Practica auff das 1570. Jar (. . .) Regenten diss Jars Saturnus und Mars*, Nuremberg 1570.

Heilbrunner, J., *Daemonomania pistoriana seu Antidotum prophyliacticum contra S. Pistorii Daemonomaniam seu magicam cabalistam curandorum morborum curationem*, Lauingen 1601.

Henischius, G., *Kurze Erinnerung von dem Cometen, Welcher im October dieses 80. Jars erstlich erschinen und noch am Himmel zu sehen ist*, Augsburg 1580.

Hocker, J., *Wider den Bannteufel. Das ist eine getrewe, wolmeinende Christliche Warnung wider die gottlosen Teuffelbeschwerer oder Banner, so in diesen örtern herumbherschleichen*, Magdeburg 1564.

James VI, *Demonologie*, Edinburgh 1597.

Kautz, K. F. von, De Cultibus Magicis eorumque perpetuo ad acclesiam et rempublicam habitu, Wien 1767[1], 1771[2].

Keyser, G. A., Uhuhu Hexen-Gespenster-Schatzgräber- und Erscheinungsgeschichten, Erfurt 1785–92.

Khueller, S., *Kurtze und warhafftige Historia von einer Junckfrawen, welche mit etlich und dreissig bösen Geistern leibhaftig besessen (. . .)*, Munich 1574.

Kohlbrenner, J., Stoßseufzer eines gelehrten Ignoranten zu Pau in Bearn, in: Ders. (Hg.), Churbayrisches Intelligenzblatt 16/1768.

Kollmann, J. A., Zweifel eines Bayers über die wirkende Zauberkunst und Hexerei, An dem Lechstrom (Augsburg) 1768.

Kuntz, H., *Newe Zeittung von einer erschrecklichen Tat, welche zu Dillingen von einem Ihesuwider und einer Hexen geschehen ist, welche dann offenlich durch strenge Martern bekand haben, wie sie es getrieben und was sie für grossen Schaden getan. Auch in Sonderheit von diesem grossen Gewitter, welchen sie den 2. Augustii dieses 1579. Jars durch ihre Zauberey gemacht (. . .) Auch ist die Hexe (. . .) den 8. Oktober zu Dillingen zum Fewr verurtheilet worden. Aber erschrecklicherweise von dem Teufel aus dem Fewer in den Lüften hinweg geführet worden*, Basel 1579 (largely fictional; WB).

Lancre, P. de, *Wunderbarliche Geheimnussen der Zauberey (. . .)*, n.p. 1630 (1st edn Paris 1612).

Lang, J.J., *Daemonomagia*, Diss. Dillingen 1630 (could not be consulted).

Lauch, J., *Einunddreissig Türkenpredigten*, Lauingen 1599 (2nd edn 1609) (the fourteenth sermon deals with witches).

Laymann SJ, P., *Theologia Moralis*, 3rd edn Munich 1630.

Lehmann, H. L. Freundschaftliche und vertrauliche Briefe den sogenannten sehr berüchtigten Hexenhandel zu glarus betreffend, Zürich 1783.

Leib, J., *Consilia, responsa ac deductiones juris variae (. . .), wie und welcher Gestalt der Process wider die Zauberer und Hexen anzustellen (. . .) Mit beygefügten unterschidlicher Universitäten über verschiedene schwere Fälle Bedencken und Informationen*, Frankfurt am Main 1666.

Leonicius, C., *Prognosticon und Weyssagung der fürnemsten Dingen so vom 1564. Jar bis auff das 1607 sich zutragen werden*, Bern 1563.

Lercheimer, A., *Christlich Bedencken und Erinnerung von Zauberey (. . .)*, Heidelberg 1585 (*Theatrum de Veneficiis* (1586), 261–98).

Lessius SJ, L., *De iustitia et iure compendium*, Antwerp 1609.

Levenwald, A. von, *Tractätel von des Teufels List und Betrug*, Salzburg 1680.

Loeher, H., *Hochnöthige, Unterthanige, Wehmütige Klage der frommen Unschüldigen; worin (. . .) Augenscheinlich zu sehen und zu lesen ist, wie die arme unschüldige fromme Leut (. . .) von den falschen Zauberrichtern angegriffen (. . .) Welches auch die Herren Tannerus, Cautio Criminalis, Michael Stapirius härtlich bekräftigen*, Amsterdam 1676.

Lorichius, J., *Aberglaub. Das ist kurtzlicher bericht, von verbottenen Segen (. . .)*, 2nd edn Freiburg im Breisgau 1593.

Loschert, O., *Vorgänger Versuch zur Erwirkung iened Vertrages zwishcen den in dem bisherigen Hexereykriege verwickelten Gelehrten, von einem Verehrer der gelehrten und Liebhaber der christlichen Wahrheiten, An dem Maynstrome* (Würzburg 1767).

Maffei, S., *Arte Magica Dileguata*, Verona 1750.

Mancini, SJ, L., *Passio D.N. Jesu Christi nova-antiqua*, Munich 1663.

Mantzel, E. J. F., *Ob wohl noch Hexenprozesse entstehen möchten?* Rostock 1738.

Manzius, C., *Commentarius rationalis in (. . .) Carolinam*, Ingolstadt 1650.

März, A., Kurze Vertheidigung der thätigen Hex- und Zauberei wider eine dem heiligen. Dreuz zu scheyern nachtheilige akademische Rede, Freising 1766[1], Ingolstadt 1767[2].

– Verantwortung über die von P. Don Ferdinand Sterzinger bey dem hochfürstlichen hochlöbl. geistlichen Rath zu Freysing freywillig wider ihn gestellten Fragen, Ingolstadt 1767.

– Kurze, doch gründliche Abhandlung von dem Hl. Kreuz Christi und dessen wunderthätigen (sic) Partikel, welcher zu scheyern O. S. Bened. in Oberbayern schon über 600 Jahr mit großer Andacht verehrt wird, Freysing 1770.

Mayer, A. U., (F. N. Blocksberger), Glückwunschschreiben an den hochwürdigen P. Angelus März über seine Vertheidigung der Hex- und Zauberey, von F. N. Blocksberger, Benefiziaten zu T., Straubing 1767.

Mayr, J., *Epitome Cronicorum seculi moderni, Das ist: Kurtzer Begriff und inhalt aller gedenckwürdigen Sachen, so von 1500. biss zu dem 1604. Jar Christi auff dem gantzen Erdenkreis sich verlauffen*, Munich 1604.

Meder, D., *Acht Hexen-Predigten von der Hexen schrecklichen Abfall und Üblthaten*, Leipzig 1605.

Merz, A., *Urtheil ohne Vorurtheil über die wirkend- und thätige Hexerey*. Abgefasset von einem Liebhaber der Wahrheit, Sterzingen in Tyroll 1766. Mit Erlaubniß der Obern. (München 1766).

– Vertheidigung wider die geschwulstige Vertheidigung der betrügenden Zauberkunst und träumenden Hexerey. (o.O), Müchen 1767.

Meyfartus, J.M., *Christliche Erinnerung an gewaltige Regenten (. . .) wie das abscheuliche Laster der Hexerey mit Ernst auszurotten*, Schlensingen 1635.

Model, J. M., Beantwortete Frage: Ob man die Ausfahrt der Hexen zulassen könne? Wider den heutigen Hexenstürmer P. Ferdinand Sterzinger, Müchen 1769.

Molitor, U., *De lamiis et phitonicis mulieribus Teutonice unholden vel hexen*, n.p. 1489 (in German, Strasbourg 1575).

Müller, S., *Astronomische Beschreibung dess Cometen, so zu ende dises verloffenen 1577. Jars erschinen, sampt seiner bedeutung*, Augsburg 1578 (dedicated to the Prince-Abbot of Kempten).

Neydecker, J., *Disputatio juridica de maleficis (. . .)*, Ingolstadt 1629 (cf. F. Waitzenegger).

Nider, J., *Formicarius*, 3rd edn Strasbourg 1517.

Osa, A.U. Dell', *Das grosse weltbetrügende Nichts oder die heutige Hexerei und Zauberkunst*, Frankfurt am Main 1761 (= J. Simon).

Ossuna, F. de, *Flagellum Diaboli, oder dess Teufels Gaissl*, Munich 1602.

Osterwald, P., Rede vom Nutzen der logikalischen Regeln, besonders wider die Freigeisterei und den Aberglauben, München 1767.

Ott, F., Gespräche von verschiedenem Inhalte, unter einer munteren Fastnachts-compagnie, verfasset von einem Liebhaber einer anständigen Freyheit (A.E.I.O.U.), Gedruckt vor baares Geld, im Jahr, als noch im März Fasching war. Verfaßt am unsinnigen Donnerstag, Lappendorf, 1767. (München).

Pererius, B., *Adversus (. . .) magia, de observatione somniorum et divinatione astrologica libri tres*, Ingolstadt 1591.

Perneder, A., *Von Straff und Peen aller und yeder Malefitzhandlungen (. . .)*, Ingolstadt 1551 (ed. W. Hunger).

Pezzl, J., *Faustin order das philosophische Jahrhundert*, Zürich 1783.

Planch, A., *dissertatio critico-seripturistica de magia diabolica et Magorum prodigiis*, Innsbruck 1767.

Praetorius, A., *Von Zauberey und Zauberern gründtlicher Bericht*, 2nd edn Heidelberg 1613.

Premb, D., Drei wichtige Fragen über das Hexensystem, von einem gesunden unverrückten Kopf diesseits der Donau, o.O., März 1767.

Reiche, J., Unterschiedliche Schriften vom Unfug der Hexenprozesse, (. . .), Halle 1703.

Remigius, N., Daemonolatria. Das ist Von Unholden *und Zauber Geistern (. . .)*, Frankfurt (EA Lyons 1595).

Rinder, J. Ch., Kurtze doch nachdrückliche Abfertigung an den Würtzburgischen Pater Herrn Gaar, Lojoliten (. . .), Jena 1750.

Rübel, J. F., Systematische Abhandlung von denen fast allgemein eingerissenen Irrthümern betreffend die Besizung des Menschden vom Teufel, Hexerey (. . .), o. O. 1758.

Saur, A., *Eine kurtze treuwe Warnung, Anzeige und Underricht, ob auch zu dieser unser Zeit unter uns Christen Hexen, Zauberer und Unholden vorhanden: und was sie ausrichten können*, Frankfurt am Main 1582 *(Theatrum de Veneficiis*, 202–14).

Schallhammer, B., Aliquid ex Theologia contra grande Nihilum seu Dissertatio de Magia nigra, Straubing 1769.

Scherer SJ, G., *Postill der sonntäglichen Evangelien*, 3rd edn Munich 1608 (a sermon on witchcraft, 430–5).

Schiltenberger, J. P., Consilia et Responsa, Ingolstadt 1739.

Schorer, C., *Memminger Chronik*, Memmingen 1660.

Schultheiss, H., *Eine ausführliche Instruction, wie in Inquisitionssachen des grewlichen Lasters der Zauberey (. . .) zu procediern*, Cologne 1634.

Schwager, J.M., *Versuch einer Geschichte der Hexenprocesse*, Berlin 1784.

Scot, R., *The Discoverie of Witchcraft*, London 1584.

Scultetus, J., *Gründtlicher Bericht von Zauberey und Zauberern*, Lich/Solms 1598 (pseudonym of A. Praetorius).

Simon, J., Anpreisung der allergnädigsten Landesverordnung Ihrer Kaiserl. Königl. apostolischen Majestät, wie es mit dem Hexenprocesse zu halten sei, nebst einer Vorrede, in welcher die kurze Vertheydigung der Hex- und Zauberey, die der P. Angelus März der akademischen Rede des P. Sterzinger entgegengesetzet, von einem Gottesgelehrten beantwortet wird, München 1767.

–, Nun ja – oder kleine Zweifeln über zwey Berichte von einer Hexen- oder Studentengeschichte, die sich im Jahr 1768 den 10., 11., 12. und 13. Junius zu Ingolstadt in Baiern soll zugetragen haben. Gedruckt zu Unglauben (!), mit der Akademiker Schriften (München, 1768).

–, Nicht doch – oder Auflösung der kleinen Zweifel über zwey Berichte von einer Hexen- und Studentengeschichte . . . aus einem dritten Berichte ses Herrn Direktors gezogen, Berichtshausen 1767 [München 1768].

Spee, F., *Cautio Criminalis*, Augsburg 1731 (German tr. Weimar 1939, cited here from the reprint, Munich 1982).

Spitzel, G., *Die gebrochene Macht der Finsternüss, oder zerstörte teuflische Bundes- und Buhl-Freundschaft (. . .)*, Augsburg 1687.

Sprenger, J. and Institoris, H., *Malleus Maleficarum*, Strasbourg 1587 (German tr.: *Der Hexenhammer*, tr. and ed. J.W.R. Schmidt, Berlin 1906, reprint Darmstadt 1974).

Stengel SJ, G., *Opus de iudiciis divinis, quae Deus in hoc mundo exercet*, 4 vols., Ingolstadt 1651. (German tr. Augsburg 1712).

Sterzinger, F., *Betrügende Zauberkunst und träumendeHexerey, oder Vertheidigung der akademischen Rede von der gemeinen Vorurtheil der wirkenden und thätigen Hexerey wider das Urtheil ohne Vorurtheil*, Munich 1767 (January).

Sterzinger, J., *Der Hexenprozeß – ein Traum. Erzählet con einer unparteyischen Feder im Jahre 1767* (Innsbruck).

Stetten, P. von, *Geschichte der Heyl. Röm. Reichs Freyen Stadt Augsburg*, 2 vols., Frankfurt/Leipzig, 1743–58.

Tanner SJ, A., *Disputatio Theologica de iustitia et iure*, Ingolstadt 1609.
Theologia scholastica, 4 vols., Ingolstadt 1626–7.
Tractatus Theologicus de Processu adversus Crimina excepta ac speciatim adversus Crimen Veneficii, Cologne 1629.

Tengler, U., *Der neu Layenspiegel*, Augsburg 1511.

Thomasius, C., *De crimine magiae*, Halle 1701 (German tr., Weimar 1967).

Trithemius, J., *Antipalus Maleficiorum*, Ingolstadt 1555.
Antwort Herr Johan Abts von Spanheim auff acht fragstuck, ime von weylandt Herrn Maximilian Roem. Kayser (. . .) fürgehalten, Ingolstadt 1556 (*Theatrum de Veneficiis*, 355–66).

Ursinus, G., *Zwo Practicken Vom 1580. Jar biss man schreiben wird 1600. Jar (. . .)*, Augsburg 1580.

Valentia, SJ, Gregor von, *Commentariorum Theologicorum, Tomi IV*, Ingolstadt 1591–7.

Valentin, *End-Urthel und Verruf (. . .) Aller derjenigen (. . .) so von Augsburg Von Anno 1649 bis Anno 1759 (. . .) justificiert (. . .) worden*, Augsburg 1760.

Wahrlieb, G., Deutliche Vorstellung der Nichtigkeit der vermeynten Hexereyen und des ungegründeten Hexenprocesses, Halle 1720.

Waitzenegger, F. (praeside), *Disputatio iuridica de maleficis et processu adversus eos instituendo*, Ingolstadt 1629 (ad publicam disputationem proponit J. Neydecker).
Dissertatio VI de servitudo daemoniaca, hoc est maleficio et processu contra maleficos instituendo, Ingolstadt 1637.

Weber, J., Die Nichtigkeit der Zauberei, Salzburg 1787.

Wechner, L. A., *Consilia seu Responsa (. . .)*, Frankfurt/Lipzig 1725.

Westenrieder, L. v., Geschichte der baierischen Akademie der Wissenschaften, Bd. 1, München 1784.

Weyer, J., *De praestigiis Daemonum*, Basel 1563 (cited from the fourth German edition, Frankfurt 1586).
De Lamiis, Basel 1577 (German tr. Frankfurt 1586).
Etliche newe Zusätz (. . .) von den Hexen und Unholden, so der Bodinus mit gutem

grund nicht widerlegen kann, in *De praestiguiis Daemonum*, 555–75.

Winkler, N., *Bedenken von künfftiger Verenderung Weltlicher Policey und Ende der Welt, auss heyliger Göttlicher Schrift unnd Patribus, auch auss dem Lauff der Natur dess 83. biss auf des 88. und 89. Jars beschrieben*, Augsburg 1582.

Witweiler, SJ, G., *Katholisch Hausbuch*, Munich 1631.

Zedler, J.J., (ed.), *Grosses vollständiges Universal-Lexikon*, 63 vols. and 4 supplementary vols., Leipzig/Halle 1732–54 (reprint Graz 1961–4).

Literature since 1800

Abdruck aktenmässiger Hexenprozesse, welche in den Jahren 1590, 1626, 1628 und 1637 gerichtlich verhandelt worden, Eichstätt 1811.

Abel, W., *Agrarkrisen und Agrarkonjunkturen in Mitteleuropa vom 13. bis zum 19. Jahrhundert*, 2nd edn Hamburg 1966.

Massenarmut und Hungerkrisen im vorindustriellen Europa, Hamburg/Berlin 1974.

Massenarmut und Hungerkrisen im vorindustriellen Deutschland, 2nd edn Göttingen 1977.

Albrecht, H., 'Oberdorfer Hexen', *Heimat und Welt. Wochenbeilage zum Marktoberdorfer Landboten*, Jg. 6 (1929), no. 18.

Allgäuer, E., 'Zeugnisse zum Hexenwahn des 17. Jahrhunderts. Ein Beitrag zur Volkskunde Vorarlbergs', *Archiv. f. Gesch. und Landeskunde Vorarlbergs*, 11 (1915), 29–52; 12 (1916), 61–72.

Allgemeine deutsche Biographie (ADB) (ed. by the Historical Commission of the Bavarian Academy of Sciences), 56 vols., Munich and Leipzig 1875–1912.

Alt, S., *Reformation und Gegenreformation in der freien Reichsstadt Kaufbeuren*, Munich 1932.

Altötting, F. X. von, (OFMCap), Konrad von Monheim OFM (1643–1712) als Seelsorger bein den Geislinger Hexen, in: Miscellania Melchor de Pobladura 2 (1964), 377–391.

Amman, H., 'Der Innsbrucker Hexenprozess von 1485', *Zs. des Ferdinandeums für Tirol und Vorarlberg*, 34 (1890), 1–87.

'Die Hexenprozesse im Fürstentum Brixen', *Forschungen und Mitteilungen zur Geschichte Tirols und Vorarlbergs*, 11 (1914), 9–18, 75–86, 144–66, 227–48.

Anglo, S. (ed.), *The Damned Art. Essays in the Literature of Witchcraft*, London 1977.

Ardener, E., 'Witchcraft, economics and the continuity of belief', in Douglas, *Witchcraft* (1970), 141–60.

Aretin, I. Chr. von, (Hg.), Umständlicher geistlicher Vortrag über einen Hexenprozeß aus der ersten Hälfte des 18. Jahrhunderts, in: Ders., Beyträge zur Geschichte und Literatur vorzüglich aus den Schätzen der pfalzbairischen Centralbibliothek zu München, Bd. 4, 273–328, München 1805.

Arnold, H., 'Der Auerberg im Allgau', *Zs. d. Hist. Ver. für Schwaben und Neuburg*, 9 (1882), 285–357.

Aston, T. (ed.), *Crisis in Europe 1560–1660*, New York 1965.

Aubin, H. and Zorn, W. (eds.), *Handbuch der deutschen Wirtschafts- und Sozialgeschichte*, vol. I, Stuttgart 1971.

Baader, C. A., Das gelehrte Baiern oder Lexikon aller Schriftsteller, welche Baiern im 18. Jahrhundert erzeugte oder ernährte, Bd. 1, A–K, Nürnberg/Sulzbach

1804.

Baader, J., *Eine bayrische Verordnung gegen Zauberer, Hexen und Wahrsager vom Jahr 1611*, n.p., n.d.

'Zur Geschichte des Hexenwesens', *Anzeiger des German. Museums*, 23 (1876), cols. 225–30, 259–70, 292–9.

Bacherler, M., 'Über Eichstätter Hexenprozesse', *Heimgarten* (1929), nos. 43–7.

Bächtold-Stäubli, H., *Handwörterbuch des deutschen Aberglaubens*, 10 vols., Berlin/Leipzig 1927–42.

Bader, G., 'Die Hexenprozesse in der Schweiz', Dr. jur. thesis, Zürich 1945.

Baschwitz, K., *Hexen und Hexenprozesse. Die Geschichte eines Massenwahns und seiner Bekämpfung*, Munich 1963.

Bath, B.H. Slicher van, *The Agrarian History of Western Europe 500–1850*, London 1963.

Bauer, L., 'Die Bamberger Weihbischöfe Johann Schöner und Friedrich Förner. Beiträge zur Gegenreformation in Bamberg', *Berichte des Hist. Vereins (. . .) Bamberg*, 101 (1965), 305–530.

Bauerreiss, R., *Kirchengeschichte Bayerns*, vols. VI–VII, Augsburg 1965–70.

Baumann, F.L., *Geschichte des Allgäus*, vol. 3, Kempten 1894.

Baumann, W., *Ernst Friedrich von Baden-Durlach. Die Bedeutung der Religion für Leben und Politik eines süddeutschen Fürsten im Zeitalter der Gegenreformation*, Stuttgart 1962.

Baxter, C., 'Johann Weyer's "De Praestigiis Daemonum": Unsystematic Psychopathology', in Anglo, *The Damned Art*, 53–75.

'Jean Bodin's "De la Démonomanie des Sorciers". The Logic of Persecution', in Anglo, *The Damned Art*, 76–105.

Bayerl, H., 'Die letzte Hexe von Regensburg', *Die Oberpfalz*, 33 (1939), 180–3.

Bechthold, A., 'Hexen im bayrischen Lager bei Durlach 1643', *Alemannia*, 44 (1917), 138–44.

Beck, P.P., 'Zwei Hexenprozesse aus dem Fränkischen', *Jahresberichte d. Hist. Ver. Mittelfranken*, 43 (1889), 7–25.

Becker, G., Bovenschen, S., Brackert, H. *et al.*, (eds.), *Aus der Zeit der Verzweiflung. Zur Genese und Aktualität des Hexenbildes*, Frankfurt am Main 1977.

Behringer, W., 'Scheiternde Hexenprozesse. Volksglaube und Hexenverfolgung um 1600 in München', in van Dülmen, *Kultur*, 42–79, 218–25.

'Hexenverfolgung im Spiegel zeitgenössischer Publizistik. Die "Erweytterte Unholden Zeyttung" von 1590', *Oberbayerisches Archiv*, 109 (1984), 339–60.

Beitelrock, J.M., *Geschichte des Herzogthums Neuburg oder der jungen Pfalz*, Aschaffenburg 1858–67.

Beitl, R., *Wörterbuch der deutschen Volkskunde*, 3rd edn Stuttgart 1974.

Bergdolt, J., 'Hexenprozesse in Windsheim', *Heimatkundlicher Lesebogen für den Landkreis Uffenheim* (1950), Heft 9.

Bezold, F., 'Jean Bodin als Okkultist und seine Demonomanie', *Historische Zeitschrift*, 105 (1910), 1–64.

Biedermann, H., *Handlexikon der magischen Künste von der Spätantike bis zum 19. Jahrhundert*, 2nd edn Graz 1973.

Bilgeri, B., *Geschichte Vorarlbergs*, vol. III, Vienna 1977.

Binz, C., Augustin Lercheimer (Prof. H. Witekind) und seine Schriften wider den Hexenwahn, Straßburg 1888.

Doktor Johannes Weyer, ein rheinischer Arzt, der erste Bekämpfer des Hexenwahns, 2nd edn Berlin 1896.

Bireley, SJ, R., *Maximilian von Bayern, Adam Contzen SJ und die Gegenreformation in Deutschland 1624–1635*, Göttingen 1975.

Religion and Politics in the Age of the Counter-Reformation. Emperor Ferdinand II, William Lamormaini SJ and the Formation of Imperial Policy, Chapel Hill 1981.

Birlinger, A., 'Ein Donauwörther Zauberer', *Alemannia*, 8 (1880), 122.

Bisle, M., *Die öffentliche Armenpflege der Reichsstadt Augsburg. Mit Berücksichtigung der einschlägigen Verhältnisse in anderen Reichsstädten Süddeutschlands*, Paderborn 1904.

Blaufuss, D., 'Gottlieb Spitzel (1639–1691)', Dr. Theol. thesis, Erlangen 1971.

Blickle, P., *Deutsche Untertanen. Ein Widerspruch*. Munich 1981.

Bloch, E., *Christian Thomasius, ein deutscher Gelehrter ohne Misere*, Frankfurt am Main 1967.

Bock, F., *Zur Volkskunde der Reichsstadt Nürnberg, Lesefrüchte und Untersuchungen*, Würzburg 1959.

Böck, K., *Johann Christoph Beer. Ein Seelsorger des gemeinen Volkes*, Kallmünz 1955.

Böhm, H., 'Strafverfahren gegen Schatzgräber in Dillingen und Lauingen', *Jb. d. Hist. Ver. Dillingen*, 79 (1977), 195–209.

Böhm, R., *Sagt Ja, Sagt nein – Getanzt Muess Sein. Der Fuessener Totentanz*, Füssen 1978.

Borst, A., *Lebensformen im Mittelalter*, Frankfurt/Berlin/Vienna 1979.

Bosl, K. (ed.), *Bayern. Handbuch der historischen Stätten Deutschlands*, vol. VII, 3rd edn Stuttgart 1981.

Bosls bayerische Biographie, 8000 Persönlichkeiten aus 15 Jahrhunderte, Regensburg 1983.

Bossy, J., 'The Counter-Reformation and the People of Catholic Europe', *Past and Present*, 47 (1970), 51–70.

Braudel, F., 'Europäische Expansion und Kapitalismus 1450–1650', in: E. Schulin (ed.), *Universalgeschichte*, Cologne 1974, 255–94.

Braun, P., *Geschichte der Bischöfe von Augsburg*, vol. IV, Augsburg 1815.

Breitenbach, J. 'Ein Hofmagd als Zauberin. (Leuchtenberg 1638)', *Die Oberpfalz*, 7 (1913), 112–15.

Brischar, J.N., *Die katholische Kanzelredner Deutschlands seit den letzten drei Jahrhunderten*, 5 vols., Schaffhausen 1867–71.

Brodrick, J., Petrus Canisius (1521–1597), 2 Bde., Wien 1950.

Carsten, F. L., Was there an economic Decline in Germany before the 30 years War?, in Economic History Review 71 (1956), 240–247.

Chaunu, P., Europäische Kultur im Zeitalter des Barock, München 1968.

Clark, S., Inversion Misrule and the Meaning of Witchcraft, in: Past & Present Nr. 87 (1980), 98–128.

Cohn, B. S., Anthropology and History in the 1980s. Toward a Rapprochement, in: Journal of Interdisciplinary History 12 (1981\1982), 227–252.

Davis, N. Z., Anthropology and History in the 1980s. The Possibilities of the Past, in: Journal of Interdisziplinary History 12 (1981), 267–275.

Brodrick, J., *Petrus Canisius (1521–1597)*, 2 vols., Vienna 1950.

Brunnhuber, J., *Chronik des oberen Leizachtales*, Fischbachau 1928.

Buchner, E., *Medien, Hexen und Geisterseher, Kulturhistorisch interessante Dokumente aus alten deutschen Zeitungen und Zeitschriften*, Munich 1926.

Buck, R., 'Malefizgericht und Ordnung', *Alemannia*, 11 (1883), 101–8.

'Hexenprozesse aus Oberschwaben', *Alemannia*, 11 (1883), 108–35.

Bücking, J., *Kultur und Gesellschaft in Tirol um 1600*. *Des Hippolytus Guarinonius' 'Grewel der Verwüstung Menschlichen Geschlechts' (1610) als kulturgeschichtliche Quelle des frühen 17. Jahrhunderts*, Lübeck/Hamburg 1968.

Buff, A., 'Verbrechen und Verbrecher zu Augsburg in der zweiten Hälfte des 14. Jahrhunderts', *Zs. d. Hist. Ver. f. Schwaben und Neuburg*, 4 (1878), 160–231.

Burke, P., *Popular Culture in Early Modern Europe*, London 1978.

Butler, E.M., *The Myth of Magus*, Cambridge 1979.

Butler, J., 'The People's Faith, in Europe and America: Four Centuries in Review', *Journal of Social History*, 12 (1978), 159–67.

Byloff, F., *Hexenglaube und Hexenverfolgung in den österreichischen Alpenländern*, Berlin 1934.

'Die letzten Zaubereiprozesse in Mühldorf und Landshut', *ZBLG*, 11 (1938), 427–44.

Byr, R. 'Hexenprozesse in Bregenz', *Schriften d. Ver. f. Gesch. des Bodensees*, 15 (1886), 215–26.

Cappelli, A., *Lexicon Abbreviaturarum*, 2nd edn Leipzig 1928.

Caro Baroja, J., *Die Hexen und ihre Welt*, Stuttgart 1971 (1st edn Madrid 1964; Eng. tr. *The World of the Witches*, Chicago 1964).

Carsten, F.L., 'Was there an Economic Decline in Germany before the 30 Years War?', *Economic History Review*, 71 (1956), 240–7.

Caspar, M., *Johannes Kepler*, Stuttgart 1948.

Cassirer, E., *Individuum und Kosmos in der Philosophie der Renaissance*, Leipzig/Berlin 1927. (Eng. tr., *The Individual and the Cosmos in Renaissance Philosophy*, New York 1964).

Caulfield, E., 'Pediatric Aspects of the Salem Witchcraft Tragedy', *American Journal for the Diseases of Children*, 65 (1943), 788–802.

Chaunu, P., *Europäische Kultur im Zeitalter des Barock*, Munich 1968.

'Sur la fin des sorciers au XVIIᵉ siècle', *Annales E.S.C.*, 24 (1969), 895–911.

Christel, G. 'Die Malefizprozessordnung des Codex Maximilianeus von 1616 dargestellt in ihrem Verhältnis zur Carolina und den Rechtsquellen des 16. Jahrhunderts in Bayern', Dr. jur. thesis, Regensburg 1975.

Clark, P. (ed.), *The European Crisis of the 1590s*, London 1985.

Clark, S., 'Inversion, Misrule and the Meaning of Witchcraft', *Past and Present*, 87 (1980), 98–128.

Cohn, B.S., 'Anthropology and History in the 1980s. Toward a Rapprochement', *Journal of Interdisciplinary History*, 12 (1981/2), 227–52.

Cohn, N., *Europe's Inner Demons*, London 1975.

Croissant, W., 'Die Berücksichtigung geburts- und berufsständischer und soziologischer Unterschiede im deutschen Hexenprozess', Dr. jur. thesis, Mainz 1953.

Davis, N.Z., 'Anthropology and History in the 1980s. The Possibilities of the Past', *Journal of Interdisciplinary History*, 12 (1981), 267–75.

Decker, R., 'Die Hexenprozesse im Herzogtum Westfalen und im Hochstift Paderborn', in Degn *et al., Hexenprozesse*, 204–18.

Degn, C., Lehmann, H. and Unverhau, D. (eds.), *Hexenprozesse. Deutsche und skandinavische Beiträge*, Neumünster 1983.

Dengler, R., 'Das Hexenwesen im Stifte Obermarchthal von 1581 bis 1756', PhD thesis, Erlangen 1953.

Denzinger, J., 'Auszüge aus einer Chronik der Familie Langhans in Zeil', *Archiv d.*

Hist. Ver. Unterfranken, 10 (1850), 143–8.

'Der Hexenprozess von Etting. Das tragische Schicksal der Bauernfamilie Pölz', *Aichacher Heimatblätter*, 4 (1956), no. 5.

Dertsch, R., 'Hexenglaube am Bodensee', *Bayerischer Heimatschutz* (1929), 65–71.

Dettling, A., *Die Hexenprozesse im Kanton Schwyz*, Schwyz 1907.

Diefenbach, J., *Der Hexenwahn vor und nach der Glaubensspaltung*, Mainz 1886 (reprint 1969).

Diepolder, G., Das Volk in Kurbayern zur Zeit des Kurfürsten Max Emanuel. Beobachtungen zur Demographie, in: H. Glaser, (Hg.), Kurfürst Max Emanuel – Bayern und Europa um 1700, München 1976, 367–405.

Diethelm, O., 'The Medical Teaching of Demonology in the 17th and 18th Centuries', *Journal of the History of the Behavioral Sciences*, 6 (1970), 3–15.

Döberl, M., *Entwicklungsgeschichte Bayerns*, vol. I, 3rd edn Munich 1916.

Dollinger, H., 'Kurfürst Maximilian von Bayern und Justus Lipsius. Eine Studie zur Staatstheorie eines frühabsolutistischen Fürsten', *Archiv für Kulturgeschichte*, 46 (1964), 227–308.

Dömling, M., *Heimatbuch von Marktoberdorf*, Marktoberdorf 1952.

Dotterweich, H., *Der junge Maximilian. Jugend und Erziehung des bayrischen Herzogs und späteren Kurfürsten Maximilian I. (1573–1593)*, Munich 1962.

Douglas, M. (ed.), *Witchcraft Confessions and Accusations*, London 1970.

'Das Problem des Bösen', in *idem, Ritual, Tabu und Körpersymbolik*, 2nd edn Frankfurt 1981, 152–72 (1st edn London 1970: *Natural Symbols, Explorations in Cosmology*).

Dudik, B., 'Kaiser Ferdinand II und P. Lamormaini', *Hist. Pol. Blätter* 78 (1876), 6–09.

Duerr, H.P., *Traumzeit. Über die Grenzen zwischen Wildnis und Zivilisation*, Frankfurt am Main 1978.

(ed.), *Der Wissenschaftler und das Irrationale. Beiträge aus Ethnologie und Anthropologie. Beiträge aus Philosophie und Psychologie*, 2 vols., Frankfurt am Main 1981.

Duhr SJ, B., *Jesuitenfabeln*, 3rd edn Freiburg im Breisgau 1899.

Die Stellung der Jesuiten in deutschen Hexenprozessen, Cologne 1900.

'Zur Geschichte des Jesuitenordens. Aus Münchner Archiven und Bibliotheken', *Hist. Jb. der Görres-Gesellschaft*, 25 (1904), 126– 67; 28 (1907), 61–83, 306–27.

'Zur Biographie des P. Friedrich Spee', *Hist. Jb. der Görres-Gesellschaft*, 26 (1905), 327– 33.

Geschichte der Jesuiten in den Ländern deutscher Zunge, 4 vols., Freiburg im Breisgau (and elsewhere), 1907–28.

'Paul Laymann und die Hexenprozesse', *Zeitschrift für katholische Theologie* (1899), 736ff.; (1900), 585ff.

Dülmen, R. van, *Entstehung des frühneuzeitlichen Europa 1550–1648*, Frankfurt am Main 1980.

'Formierung der europäischen Gesellschaft in der Frühen Neuzeit. Ein Versuch', *Geschichte und Gesellschaft*, 7 (1981), 5–41.

(ed.), *Kultur der einfachen Leute. Bayerisches Volksleben vom 16. bis zum 19. Jahrhundert*, Munich 1983.

and Schindler, N. (eds.), *Volkskultur. Zur Wiederentdeckung des vergessenen Alltags (16.–20. Jahrhundert)*, Frankfurt am Main 1984.

'Das Schauspiel des Todes. Hinrichtungsrituale in der frühen Neuzeit', in Dülmen and Schindler, *Volkskultur*, 203–46.

Dürr, O., 'Philipp Adolf von Ehrenberg, Bischof von Würzburg (1623–31)', PhD thesis, Würzburg 1935.

Dürrwächter, A., *Christoph Gewold. Ein Beitrag zur Gelehrtengeschichte der Gegenreformation* (...), Freiburg im Breisgau 1904.

'Adam Tanner und die Steganographie des Trithemius', in *Festgabe Herrmann Grauert*, Freiburg im Breisgau 1910, 354–76.

Dürrwanger, L., *Nesselwang in Kultur und Geschichte*, Marktoberdorf 1954.

Dussler, H., *Magister Hieronymus Tauler. Leben und Umwelt eines Augsburger Pfarrers vor und während des Dreissigjährigen Krieges. Nach Taulers Tagebuch beschrieben*, Kempten 1961.

Easlea, B., *Witch-Hunting, Magic and the New Philosophy. An Introduction to the Debates of the Scientific Revolution 1450–1750*, Brighton 1980.

Eco, U., *Der Name der Rose*, Munich 1982.

Eggmann, G.F., *Geschichte des Illertales. Ein Beitrag zur Geschichte Oberschwabens*, Ulm 1862.

Elias, N., *Über den prozess der Zivilisation. Soziogenetische und psychogenetische Untersuchungen*, vol. II, *Wandlungen der Gesellschaft, Entwurf zu einer Theorie der Zivilisation*, 5th edn Frankfurt am Main 1978.

Elsas, M.J., *Umriss einer Geschichte der Preise und Löhne in Deutschland vom ausgehenden Mittelalter bis zum Beginn des 19. Jahrhunderts*, vol. I (Munich, Augsburg, Würzburg), Leiden 1936.

Engel, J., 'Von der spätmittelalterlichen respublica christiana zum Mächte-Europa der Neuzeit', in Schieder, *Handbuch* (1971), 1–444.

Epplen, H., *Obergünzburger Chronik*, Kempten 1968.

Ernst, C., *Teufelsaustreibungen. Die Praxis der katholischen Kirche im 16. und 17. Jahrhundert*, Bern 1972.

Eschbaumer, G., *Bescheidenliche Tortur. Der ehrbare Rat der Stadt Nördlingen im Hexenprozess 1593/94 gegen die Kronenwirtin Maria Holl*, Nördlingen 1983.

Eschenröder, W., 'Hexenwahn und Hexenprozess in Frankfurt am Main', PhD thesis, Frankfurt 1932.

Estes, L., 'The Medical Origins of the European Witch-Craze: A Hypothesis', *Journal of Social History*, 17 (1983), 271–84.

Ettelt, R., *Geschichte der Stadt Füssen*, Füssen 1971.

Geschichte der Stadt Kelheim, Kelheim 1983.

Evans, R.J.W., *Rudolf II. Ohnmacht und Einsamkeit*, Graz/Vienna/Cologne 1980 (first published as *Rudolf II and His World: A Study in Intellectual History*, Oxford 1973).

Evans-Pritchard, E.E., *Hexerei, Orakel und Magie bei den Azande*, Frankfurt am Main 1978 (1st published as *Witchcraft, Oracles and Magic among the Azande*, Oxford 1937).

Theorien über Primitive Religionen, 2nd edn Frankfurt am Main 1981.

Febvre, L. 'Sorcellerie, sotise ou révolution mentale', *Annales E.S.C.*, 3 (1948), 9–15.

Ferchl, G., 'Bayerische Behörden und Beamte 1550–1804', *Oberbayerisches Archiv*, 55 (1908/12); 64 (1925). (Each article comprises a whole volume.)

Fina, O. (ed.), *Klara Staigers Tagebuch. Aufzeichnungen während des dreissigjährigen Krieges im Kloster Marienstein bei Eichstätt*, Regensburg 1931.

Fink, H., *Verzaubertes Land*, Vienna/Innsbruck/Munich 1973.

Fischer, E., 'Die "Disquisitionum Magicarum Libri sex" von Martin Delrio als gegenreformatorische Exempel-Quelle', PhD thesis, Frankfurt am Main 1975.

Foucault, M., *Überwachen und Strafen. Die Geburt des Gefängnisses*, 3rd edn Frankfurt am Main 1979.

Franck, J., 'Geschichte des Wortes Hexe', in Hansen *Quellen und Untersuchungen*, 614–70.

Franz, J., 'Von in der Fronveste zum Amberg inhaftierten Hexen und Dieben', *Die Oberpfalz*, 13 (1919), 153–5.

Franzen, A., *Der Wiederaufbau des kirchlichen Lebens im Erzbistum Köln unter Ferdinand von Bayern*, 1612–50, Münster 1941.

Freud, S. 'Eine Teufelsneurose im Siebzehnten Jahrhundert', in *idem, Studienausgabe* vol. VII, 3rd edn Frankfurt am Main 1982, 283–322 (1st edn 1923; *Gesammelte Werke* (1940), XIII, 317–53).

Friedrichs, C., *Urban Society in an Age of War: Nördlingen 1580–1720*, Princeton NJ 1979.

Fuchs, A., *Geschichte des Gesundheitswesens der freien Reichsstadt Kaufbeuren*, Kempten 1955.

Funk, Ph., Von der Aufklärung zur Romantik. Studien zur Vorgeschichte der Münchner Romantik, München 1925.

Gabler, A., *Altfränkisches Dorf- und Pfarrhausleben 1559–1601. Ein Kulturbild aus der Zeit vor dem Dreissigjährigen Kriege. Dargestellt nach den Tagebüchern des Pfarrherrn Thomas Wirsing von Sinbronn*, Nuremberg 1952.

Gänstaller, R., 'Zur Geschichte des Hexenwahns: Der Fall Barbara Reuterin in Eichstätt', dissertation, Nuremberg 1974.

Gebele, J., Peter von Osterwald. Ein Beitrag zur Geschichte der Aufklärung in Bayern unter Kurfürst Max III. Joseph, München 1891.

Geertz, H. and Thomas, K., 'An Anthropology of Religion and Magic. Two Views', *Journal of Interdisciplinary History*, 6 (1975), 71–110.

Gehring, P., 'Der Hexenprozess und die Tübinger Juristenfakultät. Untersuchungen zur Württemberger Kriminalrechtspflege im 16. und 17. Jahrhundert', *Zs. f. Württembergische Landesgeschichte*, 1 (1937), 157–88, 370–405; 2 (1938), 15–47.

Gertrudis, M., 'Aus dem Tagebuch der Äbtissin Magdalena Haidenbucher', *Studien und Mitteilungen aus dem Benediktiner- und Cistercienserorden*, 28 (1907), 122–42, 379–92, 559–76.

Geyer, H., 'Hexen und ihre Verurteilung in den Beschlüssen des Ingolstädter Rates zu Ende des 16. und Anfang des 17. Jahrhunderts', unpublished dissertation, Munich 1964.

'Die Ingolstädter Hexenprozesse um 1600', *Ingolstädter Heimatblätter*, 28 (1965), nos. 5–8 (series).

Gillies, E., 'Introduction' to Evans-Pritchard, *Hexerei*, 7–38.

Ginzburg, C., 'High and Low: The Theme of Forbidden Knowledge in the Sixteenth and Seventeenth Centuries', *Past and Present*, 73 (1976), 28–41.

Der Käse und die Würmer. Die Welt eines Müllers um 1600, Frankfurt am Main 1979.

Die Benandanti. Feldkulte und Hexenwesen im 16. und 17. Jahrhundert, Frankfurt am Main 1980 (1st edn, *I benandanti. Ricerche sulla stregoneria*, Turin 1966).

'Volksbrauch, Magie und Religion', in E. Maek-Gérard (ed.), *Die Gleichzeitigkeit des Ungleichzeitigen. Studien zur Geschichte Italiens*, Frankfurt am Main 1980, 226–304.

Glaser, H. (ed.), *Um Glauben und Reich – Kurfürst Maximilian I. Ausstellungs-*

kataloge Wittelsbach und Bayern, II/1 and II/2, Munich 1980.

Gosler, S., *Hexenwahn und Hexenprozesse in Kärnten von der Mitte des 15. bis zum ersten Drittel des 18. Jahrhunderts*, Graz 1955.

Gould, J.D., 'The Crisis in the Export Trade 1586–1587', *English Historical Review*, 71 (1965), 212–22.

Grassinger, J., *Geschichte der Pfarrei und des Marktes Aibling*, Munich 1857.

Grassl, H., *Aufbruch zur Romantik. Bayersn Beitrag zur deutschen Geistesgeschichte 1765–1785*, München 1968.

Grebner, C., 'Hexenprozesse im Freigericht Alzenau (1601–1605)', *Aschaffenburger Jahrbuch*, 6 (1979), 137–240.

Greiner, J., 'Hexenprozesse in Dinkelsbühl', *Alt-Dinkelsbühl*, 16 (1929), no. 6.

Grohsmann, L., *Geschichte der Stadt Donauwörth*, vol. II, Donauwörth 1978.

Gschliesser, O. von, *Der Reichshofrat. Bedeutung und Verfassung, Schicksal und Besetzung einer obersten Reichsbehörde von 1559–1806*, Vienna 1942.

Gumpelzheimer, C.G., *Regensburg's Geschichte, Sagen, und Merkwürdigkeiten*, 4 vols., Regensburg 1830– 8.

Gurjewitsch, A., 'Probleme der Volkskultur und Religiosität im Mittelalter', in *Das Weltbild des mittelalterlichen Menschen*, Munich 1982, 352–401 (1st edn Moscow 1972).

Gwinner, H., Ein Hexenprozeß aus der Reichsstadt Lindau im bodensee aus dem Jahr 1730, in: bodensee-Heimatschau 17 (1937), Nr. 1–2.

Haan, H., 'Prosperität und Dreissigjähriger Krieg', *Geschichte und Gesellschaft*, 7 (1981), 91–119.

Haas, C., *Die Hexenprozesse. Ein cultur-historischer Versuch nebst Dokumenten*, Tübingen 1865.

Hammermayer, L., gründungs- und Frühgeschichte der bayerischen Akademie der Wissenschaften, Kallmünz 1959.

Hampe, T., 'Der Trudenbanner von Abenberg', *Die Heimat. Beilage zum Schwabacher Tagblatt* (1931), no. 5.

Hanauer, J., *Der Exorzist J. J. Gaßner. Eine Monographie*, Diss. phil. Würzburg 1950.

Hansen, J., *Zauberwahn, Inquisition und Hexenprozess im Mittelalter und die Entstehung der grossen Hexenverfolgung*, Leipzig 1900.

Quellen und Untersuchungen zur Geschichte des Hexenwahns und der Hexenverfolgung im Mittelalter, Bonn 1901.

Hansmann, L. and Kriss-Rettenbeck, L., *Amulett und Talisman. Erscheinungsform und Geschichte*, Munich 1966.

Harke, W., 'Das Strafrecht des Münchner Blutbannbuches unter Berücksichtigung der anschliessenden Malefizprotokolle 1574–1617', Dr. jur. thesis, Munich 1950.

Harmening, D., *Superstitio. Überlieferungs- und theoriegeschichtliche Untersuchungen zur kirchlich-theologischen Aberglaubensliteratur des Mittelalters*, Berlin 1979.

Hartmann, F.S., 'Über schwarze und weisse Kunst in den Bezirken Dachau und Bruck', *Oberbayer. Archiv*, 18 (1881), 119–52.

Hauschild, T., Staschen, H. and Troschke, R., *Hexen. Katalog zur Ausstellung*, Hamburg 1979.

Hayn, H. and Gotendorf, A., *Bibliotheca Germanorum Erotica & Curiosa*, vol. III, Munich 1913, 171–258, *s.v.* 'Hexenwesen'.

Heckel, G., 'Hexenverfolgungen in Schwabach', *Die Heimat. Beilage zum*

Schwabacher Tagblatt, (1932), nos. 6–8.

Hegel, K. (ed.), *Die Chroniken der deutschen Städte vom 14. bis ins 16. Jahrhundert*, vols. X–XI, Leipzig 1872–4.

Heikkinen, A., Allies of the Devil. Notions of witchcraft and demonic magic in late 17th century Finland (approx. 1640–172), in: Ders., Paholaisen Liittolaiset. Noita- ja magiakäsityksia ja -oikeudenkäyntejä Suomessa 1600-luvun jälkipuoliskolla. Helsinki 1969, 374–394.

Henker, M., 'Zur Prosopographie der Pfalz- Neuburgischen Zentralbehörden im 17. Jahrhundert', Ph.D. thesis, Munich 1984.

Henningsen, G., 'Hexenverfolgung und Hexenprozesse in Dänemark', in Degn *et al., Hexenprozesse*, 143–50.

Hentrich SJ, W., *Gregor von Valentia und der Molinismus. Ein Beitrag zur Geschichte des Prämolinismus*, Innsbruck 1928.

Her, B., 'Ein Hexenprozess zu Schongau vom Jahr 1587. Nach den Originalacten geschichtlich dargestellt', *Oberbayer. Archiv*, 11 (1850), 128–44.

'Grosser Hexenprozess zu Schongau von 1589 bis 1592', *Oberbayer. Archiv*, 11 (1850), 356– 80.

Herre, F., *Das Augsburger Bürgertum im Zeitalter der Aufklärung*, Augsburg 1952.

Herzog, K.-P., 'Das Strafsystem der Stadt Rothenburg ob der Tauber im Spätmittelalter', Dr. jur. thesis, Würzburg 1971.

Hesse, D., 'Der Strafvollzug der freien Reichsstadt Schweinfurt', Dr. jur. thesis, Würzburg 1975.

Heydenreuter, R., *Der landesherrliche Hofrat. Studien zum Behördenaufbau und zur Behördenreform unter Herzog bzw. Kurfürst Maximilian*, Munich 1980.

Heyl, G., 'Der geistliche Rat in Bayern unter Kurfürst Maximilian I. (1598–1651)', PhD thesis, Munich 1956.

'Die Protokolle der kurbayrischen Zentralbehörden', *Mitteilungen f. d. Archivpflege in Bayern*, 4 (1958), 54–6.

Hibler, I.J., *Geschichte des oberen Loisachtales und der Grafschaft Werdenfels*, Garmisch 1908.

Hinckeldey, C. (ed.), *Strafjustiz in alter Zeit*, Rothenburg o.T. 1980.

Hipper, R., *Sonthofen im Wandel der Geschichte*, Kempten 1978.

Hirn, J., *Erzherzog Maximilian der Deutschmeister, Regent von Tirol (1595–1618)*, 2 vols., Innsbruck 1915/36.

Hirschmann, A., 'Johann Reichard. Ein Sittenbild aus der Zeit der Hexenverfolgungen', *Hist. Pol. Blätter*, 161 (1918), 679–81.

Hobmair, K., *Hachinger Heimatbuch*, Oberhaching 1979.

Hobsbawm, E.J., 'The Crisis of Seventeenth Century Europe', in Aston, *Crisis*, 5–58.

Hofmann, C., 'Des Mathias von Kemnat Chronik Friedrichs I. des Siegreichen', in *Quellen und Erörterungen zur Bayrischen und Deutschen Geschichte*, vol. II, Munich 1862.

Hofmann, K., *Oberstdorfer Hexen auf dem Scheiterhaufen*, Oberstdorf 1931.

Hofmann, S., 'Protokoll eines Verhörs eines Hexenprozesses von 1629 aus Reichertshofen', *Sammelblatt d. Hist. Ver. Ingolstadt*, 89 (1980), 153–229.

Honegger, C. (ed.), M. Bloch, F. Braudel, L. Febvre *et al., Schrift und Materie der Geschichte. Vorschläge zur systematischen Aneignung historischer Prozesse*, Frankfurt am Main 1977.

(ed.), *Die Hexen der Neuzeit. Studien zur Sozialgeschichte eines kulturellen Deutungsmusters*, Frankfurt am Main 1978.

Hopkins, C.E., *The Share of Thomas Aquinas in the Growth of the Witchcraft Delusion*, Philadelphia 1940.

Hoppstetter, H., 'Die Hexenverfolgungen im Saarländischen Raum', *Zs. f. d. Gesch. d. Saargegend*, 9 (1959), 210–67.

Hörger, H., 'Wirtschaftlich-soziale und gesellschaftlich-ideologische Aspekte des Hexenwahns. Der Prozess gegen Simon Altseer aus Rottenbuch 1665', *ZBLG*, 38 (1975), 945–66.

Horsley, R., 'Who were the Witches? The Social Roles of the Accused in the European Witch Trials', *Journal of Interdisciplinary History*, 9 (1978/9), 689–715.

Horst, C.G., *Zauber-Bibliothek, oder, von Zauberei, Theurgie und Mantik, Zauberern, Hexen und Hexenprozessen, Dämonen, Gespenstern und Geistererscheinungen (...)*, 6 vols., Mainz 1821–6.

Hubensteiner, B., Die Geistliche Stadt. Welt und Leben des Johann Franz Eckher von Kapfing und Lichteneck, Fürstbischofs von Freising (1695–1727), München 1954.

–, Vom Geist des Barock, Kultur und Frömmigkeit im alten Bayern, München 1978².

Huber, A., *Hexenwahn und Hexenprozesse in Straubing und Umgebung*, Straubing 1975.

Hunecke, V., 'Überlegungen zur Geschichte der Armut im vorindustriellen Europa', *Geschichte und Gesellschaft*, 9 (1983), 480–512.

Hüttl, L., *Caspar von Schmid (1622–1693), ein kurbayrischer Staatsmann aus dem Zeitalter Ludwigs XIV.*, München 1971.

Jäger, 'Geschichte des Hexenbrennens in Franken im siebzehnten Jahrhundert aus den Original Process-Acten', *Archiv d. Hist. Ver. Unterfranken*, 2 (1834), 1072.

Jahn, J., 'Augsburgs Einwohnerzahl im 16. Jahrhundert – ein statistischer Versuch', *ZBLG*, 39 (1976), 379–96.

Schwabmünchen – Geschichte einer Stadt, Schwabmünchen 1984.

Janssen, J. and Pastor, L., *Culturzustände des deutschen Volkes seit dem Ausgang des Mittelalters bis zum Beginn des Dreissigjährigen Krieges*, 8 vols., Freiburg im Breisgau 1885–94.

Jöcher, C.G., *Allgemeines Gelehrten-Lexikon*, 4 vols. and 7 suppl. vols., Leipzig 1750–87, repr. Hildesheim 1961.

Jordan, G., 'Kulturbilder aus früheren Zeiten. Kleine Hexengeschichten' (Lindau), *Bodensee Heimatschau*, 12 (1932), 20, 24.

Junginger, F., *Geschichte der Reichsstadt Kaufbeuren im 17. und 18. Jahrhundert*, Neustadt/Aisch 1965.

Jungkunz, W., 'Die Sterblichkeit in Nürnberg', *Mitteilungen f. d. Gesch. der Stadt Nürnberg*, 42 (1951), 289–352.

Kamen, H., *The Iron Century. Social Change in Europe 1550–1650*, London 1971.

The Spanish Inquisition, London 1965.

Keenan, M.E., 'The Terminology of Witchcraft in the Works of Augustine', *Classical Philology*, 35 (1940), 294–7.

Kellenbenz, H., *Deutsche Wirtschaftsgeschichte*, vol. I, Munich 1977.

Kerler, 'Unter Fürstbischof Julius. Kalendereinträge des Tuchscherers Jacob Röder', *Archiv d. Hist. Ver. Unterfranken*, 41 (1899), 60ff.

Keyser, E. and Stoob, H., *Bayerisches Städtebuch*, 2 vols., Stuttgart 1971.

Kieckhefer, R., *European Witch Trials: Their Foundations in Popular and Learned Culture 1300–1500*, London 1976.

Kiessling, E., 'Zauberei in den germanischen Volksrechten', Dr. jur. thesis, Frankfurt 1940.

Kinsmann, R.S. (ed.), *The Darker Vision of the Renaissance*, Berkeley 1974.

Kippenberg, H.G. and Luchesi, B. (eds.), *Magie. Die sozialwissenschaftliche Kontroverse über das Verstehen fremden Denkens*, Frankfurt am Main 1978.

Kirchner, J., 'Aus Alt-München. Die letzte Münchner Hexen', *Münchener Rundschau*, 9 July 1905, 4–5.

Kisskalt, K., 'Epidemiologisch-statistische Untersuchungen über die Sterblichkeit von 1600–1800', *Archiv für Hygiene und Bakteriologie*, 137 (1953), 26–42.

Klarwill, V. (ed.), *Fugger-Zeitungen. Ungedruckte Briefe an das Haus Fugger aus den Jahren 1568–1605*, Vienna 1923.

Klein, H., 'Die älteren Hexenprozesse im Lande Salzburg', *Mitteilungen der Gesellschaft für Salzb. Landeskunde*, 97 (1957), 17–50.

Knapp, H., *Alt-Regensburgs Gerichtsverfassung, Strafverfahren und Strafrecht bis zur Carolina. Nach urkundlichen Quellen dargestellt*, Berlin 1914.

Kneubühler, H.P., 'Die Überwindung von Hexenwahn und Hexenprozess', Dr. jur. thesis, Zürich 1977.

Kobolt, A. M., Baierisches Gelehrten-Lexikon, 2 Bde., Landshut 1795/1824.

Koch,. J., *Jesuitenlexikon. Die Gesellschaft Jesu einst und jetzt*, Paderborn 1934.

Kocka, J., 'Zurück zur Erzählung? Plädoyer für eine historische Argumentation', *Geschichte und Gesellschaft*, 10 (1978), 395–408.

(ed.), *Sozialgeschichte und Kulturanthropologie* (= *Geschichte und Gesellschaft*, 10 (1984), Heft 3), Göttingen 1984.

König, H., 'Jacob Gretser SJ (1562–1625). Ein Charakterbild', *Freiburger Diözesanarchiv*, 77 (1957), 136–70.

Koeniger, A.M., 'Zum Kapitel Hexenprozesse', *Zs. d. Hist. Ver. Schwaben und Neuburg*, 33 (1907), 73–83.

Kipitzsch, F., Die Sozialgeschichte der deutschen Aufklärung als Forschungsaufgabe, in: Ders., Aufklärung, Absolutismus und Bürgertum in Deutschland, München 1976, 11–173.

Kors, A.C. and Peters, W., *Witchcraft in Europe 1100–1700. A Documentary History*, Philadelphia 1972.

Köstler, J., 'Oberpfälzische Hexenprozesse', *Die Oberpfalz*, 8 (1914), 56–9.

Krahn, G., *Chronik von Reichertshofen*, Ingolstadt 1963.

Kramer, K.-S., 'Volksglauben in Nördlinger Urfehdebüchern', *Bayer. Jb. f. Volkskunde*, (1957), 43–50.

Volksleben im Fürstentum Ansbach und seinen Nachbargebieten (1500–1800), Würzburg 1961.

Volksleben im Hochstift Bamberg und im Fürstentum Coburg (1500–1800), Würzburg 1967.

'Schaden- und Gegenzauber im Alltagsleben des 16.–18. Jahrhunderts nach archivalischen Quellen aus Holstein', in Degn *et al., Hexenprozesse*, 222–40.

Krämer, W., *Geschichte der Gemeinde Gauting*, Gauting 1949.

Kurtrierische Hexenprozesse vornehmlich an der unteren Mosel, Munich 1959.

Krauss, W., 'Schwarze Magie. Hexerei zur Zeit des Dreissigjährigen Krieges', *Oberpfälzer Heimat*, (1978), 145–51.

Krebs, E., 'Verfassung und Verwaltung der Stadt Dillingen unter der Regierung des Hochstifts Augsburg 1258–1802', Dr. jur. thesis, Munich 1949.

Kretz, H.-J., 'Der Schöppenstuhl zu Coburg', Dr. jur. thesis, Würzburg 1972.

Krick, F., 'Ein Hexenprozess gegen eine Ulmerin – Aus dem Ilmer Winkel',

Mitteilungen des Hist. Ver. Neu Ulm (1913), 5–14 (series).

Kuczynksi, J.J., *Geschichte des Alltags des deutschen Volkes*, vols. I and II, Cologne 1981–2.

Kuhn, T.S., *Die Entstehung des Neuen. Studien zur Struktur der Wissenschaftsgeschichte*, Frankfurt am Main 1978.

Kuisl, F., *Die Hexen von Werdenfels*, Garmisch- Partenkirchen n.d.

Kunstmann, H.H., *Zauberwahn und Hexenprozess in der Reichsstadt Nürnberg*, Nuremberg 1970.

Kunze, M., 'Johann Simon Wagnereckh. Ein Jurist in der Zeit der Hexenprozesse', *Journal für Geschichte* (1983), no.9, 4–11.

'Zum Kompetenzkonflikt zwischen städtischer und herzoglicher Strafgerichtsbarkeit in Münchner Hexenprozessen', *Zeitschrift der Savigny- Stiftung für Rechtsgeschichte. Germanistische Abteilung*, 87 (1970), 305–14.

'Der Prozess Pappenheimer', Dr. jur. thesis, Munich 1980.

Der Prozess Pappenheimer, Ebelsbach 1981.

Die Strasse ins Feuer, Munich 1982.

Küther, C., Räuber und Gauner in Deutschland. Das organisierte Bandenwesen im 18. und 19. Jahrhundert, Göttingen 1976.

Labouvie, E., 'Die 'soziale Logik' der Hexenprozesse. Herrschaften im Saarraum als Beispiel' (dissertation), Saarbrücken 1983.

Lamb, H.H., *Climate*, 2 vols., New York 1977–8.

Lamberg, M.G., Count, *Criminalverfahren vorzüglich bei Hexenprozessen im ehemaligen Bistum Bamberg während der Jahre 1624–1630*, Nuremberg 1835.

Lammert, G., *Volksmedizin und medizinischer Aberglaube in Bayern und den angrenzenden Bezirken*, Würzburg 1869 (reprint 1981).

Geschichte der Seuchen-, Hungers- und Kriegsnoth zur Zeit des Dreissigjährigen Krieges, Berlin 1890 (reprint 1971).

Lampe, H.-S., 'Die Darstellung des Teufels in den geistlichen Spielen Deutschlands. Von den Anfängen bis zum Ende des 16. Jahrhunderts', Ph.D thesis, Munich 1963.

Lang, K.H., *Neuere Geschichte des Fürstentums Baireuth*, vol. III (1557–1603), Nuremberg 1811.

Längin, G., *Religion und Hexenprozess*, Leipzig 1888.

Lanzinner, M., *Fürst, Räte und Landstände in Bayern 1511–1598*, Göttingen 1979.

Larner, C., *Enemies of God. The Witch-Hunt in Scotland*, Baltimore 1981.

Lea, H.C., *Materials Towards a History of Witchcraft*, London/New York 1957.

Lehmann, H., 'Hexenverfolgung und Hexenprozesse im Alten Reich zwischen Reformation und Aufklärung', *Jb. des Instituts f. deutsche Geschichte (Tel Aviv)*, 7 (1978), 13–70.

'Hexenprozesse in Nordwestdeutschland und Skandinavien im 16., 17. und 18. Jahrhundert. Bemerkungen zum Forschungsstand', in Degn *et al., Hexenprozesse*, 9– 13.

'Hexenglaube und Hexenprozesse in Europa um 1600', in Degn *et al., Hexenprozesse*, 14–27.

Leiser, W., *Strafgerichtsbarkeit in Süddeutschland. Formen und Entwicklungen*, Cologne/Vienna 1970.

Lenk, L., *Augsburger Bürgertum in Späthumanismus und Frühbarock (1580–1700)*, Augsburg 1968.

Le Roy Ladurie, E., *Montaillou. Ein Dorf vor dem Inquisitor*, Frankfurt am Main 1980.

'Die Geschichte von Sonnenschein und Regenwetter', in Honegger, *Schrift*, 220–46.

Karneval in Romans, Stuttgart 1982.

Die Bauern in Languedoc, Darmstadt 1985.

Leuchtman,H., 'Zeitgeschichtliche Aufzeichnungen des Bayerischen Hofkapell-altisten Johannes Hellgemayr aus den Jahren 1595–1633', *Oberbayer. Archiv*, 100 (1975), 142–221.

Leutenbauer, S., *Hexerei- und Zaubereidelikt in der Literatur von 1450–1550. Mit Hinweisung auf die Praxis im Herzogtum Bayern*, Berlin 1972.

Leventhal, H., *In the Shadow of Enlightenment: Occultism and Renaissance Science in Eighteenth Century America*, New York 1976.

Liebelt, K., 'Geschichte der Hexenprozesse in Hessen-Kassel, *Zs. d. Ver. f. hess. Gesch. und Landeskunde*, 58 (1932), 1–44.

Lieberich, H., 'Rechtsgeschichte Baierns und des baierischen Schwaben', in Roth, H. and Schlaich, H.W., (eds.), *Bayerische Heimatkunde. Ein Wegweiser*, Munich 1974, 195–212.

Lieberwirth, R., *Christian Thomasius. Sein wissenschaftliches Lebenswerk. Eine Bibliographie*, Weimar 1955.

Liedke, V., 'Scharfrichter in Bayern', *Blätter des Bayer. Landesvereins für Familien-kunde*, 26 (1963), 316–27.

Lindner, A., *Die Schriftsteller (. . .) des Benediktinerordens*, 2 vols., Regensburg/ Schrobenhausen 1880–4.

Lorenz, S., *Aktenversendung und Hexenprozess. Dargestellt am Beispiel der Juris-tenfakultäten Rostock und Greifswald, (1570/82–1630)*, Frankfurt am Main 1982.

Lory, K., 'Hexenprozesse im Gebiet des ehemaligen Markgrafenlandes', in *Fest-gabe Karl Theodor von Heigel*, Munich 1903, 290–304.

Lüers, F., 'Hexen', *Bayerische Wochenschrift für Pflege von Heimat und Volkstum*, 10 (1932), 17– 391 (series).

Lurz, W., *Adam Tanner und die Gnadenstreitigkeiten des 17. Jahrhunderts. Ein Beitrag zur Geschichte des Molinismus*, Breslau 1932.

Macfarlane, A., *Witchcraft in Tudor and Stuart England*, London 1970.

The Origins of English Individualism, Oxford 1978.

Mack, F., 'Das religiös-kirchliche Brauchtum im Schrifttum Jacob Gretsers', PhD thesis, Freiburg im Breisgau 1949.

Mahal, G., *Faust. Die Spuren eines geheimnisvollen Lebens*, Zürich 1982.

Malinowski, B., 'Gedanken zum Problem des Zauberwesens', in *Die Dynamik des Kulturwandels*, Vienna 1951, 185–96.

Mandrou, R., *Magistrats et sorciers en France au XVIIème siècle*, Paris 1968.

'Das europäische Barock: pathetische Mentalität und soziale Umwalzung', in Honegger, *Schrift*, 368–92 (1st publ. in *Annales E.S.C.*, 15 (1960), 898–914).

'Die französischen Richter und die Hexenprozesse im 17. Jahrhundert', in Honegger, *Die Hexen*, 309–36.

Markmiller, F., 'Die Beschwörungen des Martinsbucher Pfarrers Johann Weiss gegen Ende des 16. Jahrhunderts', *Der Storchenturm* (1970), no. 9, 55–66.

'Verhandlungen über Hexen- und Zauberwesen im Pfleggericht Dingolfing. Nach Unterlagen des 16. bis 18. Jahrhunderts', *Der Storchenturm* (1970), no. 9, 67–71.

Mauss, M., *Soziologie und Anthropologie*, vol. I, *Theorie der Magie. Soziale Mor-phologie*, Munich 1974.

Mayer, B., *Geschichte der Stadt Lauingen*, Dillingen 1866.

Mayer, F. and Wagner, R., *Der Altlandkreis Aichach*, Aichach 1979.

Medick, H., '"Missionare im Ruderboot"? Ethnologische Erkenntnisweisen als Herausforderung an die Sozialgeschichte', *Geschichte und Gesellschaft*, 10 (1984), 295–320.

Mehrle, P.-D., *Die Strafrechtspflege in der Herrschaft Kisslegg von den Anfängen bis zum Jahre 1633*, Pfullingen 1961.

Meili, D., Hexen in Wasterkingen. Magie und Lebensform in einem Dorf des frühen 18. Jahrhunderts, Basel 1980.

Memminger, A., *Das verhexte Kloster. Nach den Akten dargestellt*, Würzburg 1904.

Merkle, S., Die kirchliche Aufklärung im katholischen Deutschland, Berlin 1910.

Merzbacher, F., 'Geschichte der Hexenprozesse im Hochstift Würzburg', *Mainfränkisches Jahrbuch für Gesch. u. Kunst*, 2 (1950), 162–85.

'Ein Kinderhexenprozess in der Reichsstadt Schweinfurth', *Schweinfurter Heimatblatt*, (1950), no. 15.

'Das "alte Halsgerichtsbuch" des Hochstifts Eichstätt. Eine archivalische Quelle zur Geschichte des Strafvollzuges im 15. und 16. Jahrhundert und zur rechtlichen Volkskunde', *Zs. der Savigny-Stiftung für Rechtsgesch. Germanistische Abteilung*, 73 (1956), 375–96.

Die Hexenprozesse in Franken, 2nd edn Munich 1970.

Messerer, R., Briefe an den Geheimen Rat Johann Caspar Lippert (1758–1800). Ein Beitrag zur Geistes- und Kulturgeschichte Bayerns in der 2. Hälfte des 18. Jahrhunderts, in: Oberbayern. Archiv 96 (1972), 1–803; 101 (1976), 129–282; 104 (1979), 259–426.

Metz, J., 'Ein Moosburger Hexenprozess', *Der Isargau*, 1 (1927), 64–8.

Meusel, J. G., Lexikon der vom Jahre 1750–1800 verstorbenen Teutschen Schriftseller, Bde., Leipzig 1802–1816.

Meyer, C., *Chronik der Stadt Weissenburg in Bayern*, Munich 1904.

Michelet, J., *Die Hexe*, Munich 1974.

Midelfort, H.C.E., 'Recent Witch Hunting Research or Where Do We Go from Here?', *The Papers of the Bibliographical Society of America*, 62 (1968), 373–420.

'Witchcraft and Religion in Sixteenth Century Germany: The Formation and Consequences of an Orthodoxy', *Archiv für Reformationsgeschichte*, 62 (1971), 266–78.

Witch Hunting in Southwestern Germany 1562– 1684. The Social and Intellectual Foundations, Stanford 1972.

'The Renaissance of Witchcraft Research', *Journal of the History of the Behavioral Sciences*, 13 (1977), 294–7.

'Witch Hunting and the Domino Theory', in Obelkevich, *Religion*, 277–89.

Minder, R., *Der Hexenglaube bei den Iatrochemikern des 17. Jahrhunderts*, Zürich 1963.

Monter, E.W. (ed.), *European Witchcraft*, New York 1969.

'Inflation and Witchcraft: The Case of Jean Bodin', in Rabb and Seigel, *Action*, 371–89.

'The Historiography of European Witchcraft: Progress and Prospects', *Journal of Interdisciplinary History*, 2 (1972), 435–51.

Witchcraft in France and Switzerland: The Borderlands during the Reformation, Ithaca/London 1976.

Moser, H., *Chronik von Kiefersfelden*, Rosenheim 1959.

Muchembled, R., 'Sorcellerie, culture populaire et christianisme au XVIème siècle principalement en Flandre et en Artois', *Annales E. S. C.*, 25 (1970), 264–84. 'The Witches of the Cambrésis. The Acculturation of the Rural World in the Sixteenth and Seventeenth Centuries', in Obelkevich, *Religion*, 221–77.

Kultur des Volkes – Kultur der Eliten. Die Geschichte einer erfolgreichen Verdrängung, Stuttgart 1982.

Muck, G., *Geschichte des Klosters Heilsbronn von der Urzeit bis zur Neuzeit*, 3 vols., Nördlingen 1879.

Müller,I., 'Arzneien für den "gemeinen Mann". Zur Vorstellung materieller und immaterieller Wirkungen stofflicher Substrate in der Medizin des 16. und 17. Jahrhunderts', in Telle, *Pharmazie*, 27–35.

Müller, M., *Das Weitnauer Tal. Geschichte, Wirtschaft, Kultur*, Kempten 1980.

Münch, Th., Der Hofrat unter Kurfürst Max Emanuel von Bayern (1679–1726), München 1979.

Murray, M.A., *The Witch Cult in Western Europe*, 2nd edn Oxford 1962.

Naess, H.E., 'Die Hexenprozesse in Norwegen', in Degn *et al., Hexenprozesse*, 167–72.

Nagl, H., 'Der Zauberer-Jackl Prozess. Hexenprozesse im Erzstift Salzburg (1675–1690)', *Mitteilungen der Gesellschaft für Salzburger Landeskunde*, 112/113 (1972–3), 385–541; 114 (1974), 79–243.

Nauert, C.G., 'Magic and Scepticism in Agrippa's Thought', *Journal of the History of Ideas*, 18 (1957), 161–82.

Nemec, H., *Zauberzeichen. Magie im volkstümlichen Bereich*, Vienna/Munich 1976.

Neue Deutsche Biographie, (NDB) (ed. by the Historical Commission of the Bavarian Academy of Sciences), Berlin 1953– .

Neumeyer, A.F., *Der Mühldorfer Hexenprozess der 16jährigen Dienstmagd Marie Pauer von der Katharinenvorstadt Anno 1749/50*, Mühldorf 1980 (1st edn 1926).

Nikl, P., 'Barbara Kleusl von Hemau. Eine Hexengeschichte aus dem 17. Jahrhundert', *Neuburger Kollektaneenblatt*, 47 (1883), 1–13.

Nugent, D., 'Witchcraft Studies 1959–1971: A Bibliographical Survey', *Journal of Popular Culture*, 5 (1971), 711–25.

Obelkevich, H.J. (ed.), *Religion and the People 800– 1700*, Chapel Hill 1979.

Obrist, J., 'Der Kitzbüheler Hexenbrand vom Jahr 1594', *Tiroler Bote* (1892), 1860–7 (series).

Oestreich, G., *Geist und Gestalt des frühmodernen Staates. Ausgewählte Aufsätze*, Berlin 1969.

Osterreich, T.K., *Die Besessenheit*, Langensalza 1921.

Oswald, J., 'Die tridentinische Reform in Altbaiern (Salzburg, Freising, Regensburg, Passau), in Schreiber, *Das Weltkonzil*, II, 1–37.

Ott, G. M., Das Bürgertum der geistlichen Residenzstadt Passau in der Zeit des Barock und der Aufklärung, Passau 1961.

Parker, G. and Smith, L.M. (eds.), *The General Crisis of the Seventeenth Century*, London 1978.

Paulus, J., 'Mittelalterliche Justiz in Rötz', *Die Oberpfalz*, 60 (1972), 22–4.

Paulus, N., *Hexenwahn und Hexenprozess, vornehmlich im 16. Jahrhundert*, Freiburg im Breisgau 1910.

Peinkofer, M., '"Die Hex"' von Wittersitt. Ein Hexenprozess aus dem Bayrischen Wald aus dem Jahr 1703', in *Werke*, I, *Der Brunnkorb*, Passau 1977, 86–92.

Peitzsch, W., Kriminalpolitik in Bayern unter der Geltung des Codex Juris Bavarici von 1751, München 1967.

Peuckert, W.E., *Deutscher Volksglauben des Spätmittelalters*, Stuttgart 1942.

Pansophie. *Versuch zur Geschichte der weissen und schwarzen Magie*, 2nd edn Berlin 1956.

Die grosse Wende. *Das apokalyptische Saeculum und Luther*, 2 vols., 2nd edn Darmstadt 1966.

Quellen und Untersuchungen zur Geschichte des Hexenglaubens im 16. und. 17. Jahrhundert, Hildesheim 1968.

Pfaundler, I., 'Über die Hexenprozesse des Mittelalters, mit spezieller Beziehung auf Tirol', *Zs. des Ferdinandeums für Tirol und Vorarlberg*, 9 (1843), 81–143.

Pfeiffer, W.M., *Transkulturelle Psychiatrie*, Stuttgart 1971.

Pfeilschifter, G., Des Exorziaten Gassner Tätigkeit in der Konstanzer Diözese im Jahre 1774, in: Hist. Jb. d. Görres-Gesellschaft 52 (1932), 401–441

Pfister, K., *Kurfürst Maximilian und seine Jahrhundert*, Munich 1948.

Pfister, O., *Das Christentum und die Angst*, Frankfurt am Main 1985.

Pfeilschifter-Baumeister, G., Der Salzburger Kongreß und seine Auswirkungen 1770–1777. Der Kampf des bayrischen Episkopats gegen die staatskirchenrechtliche Aufklärung unter Kurfürst Max III. Joseph, Paderborn 1929.

Pitzer, E., 'Weltliche Regierung und Landeshoheit im Hochstift Freising', *Sammelblatt d. Hist. Ver. Freising*, 22 (1953), 1–40.

Phayer, F. M., Religion und das gewöhnliche Volk in Bayern in der Zeit von 1750–1850, München 1970.

Pietsch, F., Der Kulmbacher Hexenprozeß von 1666, in: Fränkische Heimat Kulmbach (1961), Nr. 7.

Pleyer, R. Der HexenprozeßSchuster (1728–34). Ein Beitrag zum Historischen Volks-leben in Bayrisch Schwaben MA München 1983.

Pölnitz, G. Freiherr von, 'Johann Philipp von Gebsattel und die deutsche Gegenreformation', *Hist. Jb. der Görres-Gesellschaft*, 50 (1950), 47–69.

Julius Echter von Mespelbrunn, Fürstbischof von Würzburg und Herzog von Franken, (1573–1617), Munich 1934.

'Petrus Canisius und das Bistum Augsburg', *ZBLG*, 18 (1955), 352–94.

Prantl, C. von, *Geschichte der Ludwig-Maximilians Universität in Ingolstadt, Landshut, München*, 2 vols., Munich 1872.

Prechtl, J.B., *Chronik der ehemals bischöflichen freisingischen Grafschaft Werdenfels*, Augsburg 1850.

Pultz, H., 'Die Tortur im bayerischen Strafverfahren von Kreittmayr bis Feuerbach', Dr. jur. thesis, Erlangen 1946.

Raab, M. 'Grosser Hexenprozess in Geisling', *Verhandlungen des Hist. Ver. Niederbayern*, 65 (1915), 73–99.

Rabb, T. K., *The Struggle for Stability in Early Modern Europe*, New York 1975.

Rabb, T.K. and Seigel, J. (eds.), *Action and Conviction in Early Modern Europe*, Princeton 1969.

Radbruch, G. (ed.), *Die peinliche Gerichtsordnung Kaiser Karls V von 1532 (Carolina)*, 2nd edn Stuttgart 1975.

Radlkofer, M., 'Die Theuerung zu Augsburg in den Jahren 1570 und 71', in *Zeitschrift des Historischen Vereins für Schwaben und Neuburg*, 19 (1892), 45–87.

Rapp, L., *Die Hexenprozesse und ihre Gegner in Tirol. Ein Beitrag zur Kulturgeschichte*, Innsbruck, 1874 (2nd edn Brixen 1891).

Rappel, J., 'Historische Heimatnachrichten', *Die Oberpfalz*, 58 (1970), 141.

Redlich, V., *Tegernsee und die deutsche Geistesgeschichte im 15. Jahrhundert*, Munich 1931.

Reger, A., 'Die letzte Hexe Regensburgs', *Die Oberpfalz*, 58 (1970), 239–40.

Aus der Geschichte der Stadt Kemnath, Kallmünz 1981.

Regnet, C.A., 'Von Zauberapparaten und Hexenakten im Reichsarchiv zu München', *Archivalische Zeitschrift*, 6 (1881), 244–51.

Reiter, E., *Martin von Schaumburg, Fürstbischof von Eichstätt (1560–1590) und die Trienter Reform*, Munich 1965.

Ried, K., *Neumarkt in der Oberpfalz*, Neumarkt 1960.

Riegler, F., *Hexenprozesse mit besonderer Berücksichtigung des Landes Steiermark*, Graz 1926.

Riezler, S., *Geschichte der Hexenprozesse in Bayern. Im Lichte der allgemeinen Entwickelung dargestellt*, Stuttgart 1896 (reprint Aalen 1968 with numerous errors, an inadequate afterword and a catastrophic map).

Geschichte Baierns, vols. 4–6, Gotha 1899–1903.

'Paul Laymann und die Hexenprozesse. Zur Abwehr', *Historische Zeitschrift*, 84 (1900), 244–56.

Rinck, G., Hexenprozeß anno 1679 in Cham, in: Die Oberpfalz 68 (1989), 93.

–, „Du bist ein Narr und bleibst närrisch'. Chamer Gerichtsakten von 1670, in: Die Oberpfalz 72 (1984), 92.

Robbins, R.H., *The Encyclopedia of Witchcraft and Demonology*, London 1959.

Romano, R. and Tenenti, A., *Die Grundlegung der modernen Welt. Spätmittelalter, Renaissance, Reformation*, Frankfurt am Main 1967.

Rösel, R., Die letzte Hexe von Schweinfurth anno 1728, in: Schweinfurter Heimatblätter 12 (1932), 33–34.

Rosenthal, E., *Geschichte des Gerichtswesens und der Verwaltungsorganisation Baierns*, 2 vols., Würzburg 1889/1906.

Roskoff, G., *Geschichte des Teufels*, 2 vols., Leipzig 1869.

Roth, F., 'Der Augsburger Jurist Dr Hieronymus Fröschl und seine Hauschronik 1528–1600', *Zs. d. Hist. Ver. Schwaben und Neuburg*, 38 (1912), 1–81.

Rottenkolber, J., 'Der Kemptener Fürstabt Heinrich von Ulm (1607–1616)', *Allgäuer Geschichtsfreund*, new series, 15 (1918), 1–132.

'Geschichte des hochfürstlichen Stiftes Kempten', *Allgäuer Geschichtsfreund*, new series, 34 (1932), 5–128; 35 (1933), 129–283.

Rückert, G., 'Der Hexenwahn. Ein Kulturbild aus Lauingens Vergangenheit', *Alt-Lauingen. Organ des Altertums-Vereins*, 2 (1907), 25–77 (series).

Russell, J.B., *Witchcraft in the Middle Ages*, Ithaca/London 1971.

Saalfeld, D., 'Die Wandlungen der Preis- und Lohnstruktur während des 16. Jahrhunderts in Deutschland', in Fischer, W. (ed.), *Beiträge zu Wirtschaftswachstum und Wirtschaftsstruktur im 16. und 19. Jahrhundert*, Berlin 1971, 9–28.

Sattler, P.M., *Chronik von Andechs*, Donauwörth, 1977.

Sauter, J.G., *Zur Hexenbulle 1484. Die Hexerei mit besonderer Berücksichtigung Oberschwabens. Eine culturhistorische Studie*, Ulm 1884.

Scharold, 'Zur Geschichte des Hexenwesens im ehemaligen Fürstenthume Würzburg', *Archiv d. Hist. Ver. Unterfranken*, 5 (1839), 165–73; 6 (1840), 128–34.

Schattenhofer, M., *Beiträge zur Geschichte der Stadt München*, Munich 1984 (=*Oberbayerisches Archiv*, 109/I (1984), 1–223).

'Henker, Hexen und Huren', *Oberbayer. Archiv*, 109 (1984), 119–43.

450   *Sources and Literature*

Scheidl, J., 'Die Bevölkerungsgeschichte des altbayrischen Landgerichts Dachau im Laufe früherer Jahrhunderte. Ein kritischer Versuch', *ZBLG*, 3 (1930), 357–86.

Schellhass, K., *Der Dominikaner Felician Ninguardia und die Gegenreformation in Süddeutschland und Österreich 1560–1583*, 2 vols., Rome 1930/1939.

Schenda, R., 'Der "gemeine Mann" und sein medikales Verhalten im 16. und 17. Jahrhunderte', in Telle, *Pharmazie*, 9–20.

Scherr, J., *Deutsche Kultur- und Sittengeschichte*, eleventh edn Leipzig 1902.

Schieder, T. (ed.), *Handbuch der europäischen Geschichte*, vols. 3 and 4, Stuttgart 1971/1968.

Schilling, A. 'Drei Hexenverbrennungen zu Ulm', *Württembergisches Vierteljahreshefte für Landesgeschichte* (1883), 137–41.

Schilling, H., 'The European Crisis of the 1590s: The Situation in German Towns', in *European Crisis* Clark, 135–56.

Schindler, N., 'Spuren in die Geschichte der "anderen" Zivilisation. Probleme und Perspektiven einer historischen Volkskulturforschung', in Dülmen and Schindler, *Volkskultur*, 13–78.

'Karneval, Kirche und die verkehrte Welt. Zur Funktion der Lachkultur im 16. Jahrhundert', *Jahrbuch für Volkskunde* (1984), 9–57.

Schlögl, R., 'Bauern, Krieg und Staat. Oberbayerische Bauernwirtschaft und Territorialstaat im 17. Jahrhundert', PhD thesis, Erlangen-Nuremberg 1985.

Schmeller, J.A. and Fromann, G.U., *Bayerisches Wörterbuch*, 2 vols., 2nd edn Munich 1872/1877 (reprint 1983).

Schmid, F., 'Die Zauberei und die Bibel', *Zs. für katholische Theologie*, 26 (1902), 107–30.

Schmid, U., 'Von Zauberern und Hexen in Burghausen', *Heimatland*, 5 (1954), 42–4.

Schmid, W.M., *Altertümer des bürgerlichen und Strafrechts, insbesondere Folter- und Strafwerkzeuge des Bayerischen Nationalmuseums*, Munich 1908.

Schmidlin, J., *Die kirchlichen Zustände in Deutschland vor dem Dreissigjährigen Krieg und nach den bischöflichen Diözesanberichten an den Heiligen Stuhl*, 3 vols., Freiburg im Breisgau 1908–10.

Kirchliche Zustände und Schicksale des deutschen Katholizismus während des Dreissigjährigen Krieges nach den bischöflichen Romberichten, Freiburg im Breisgau 1940.

Schmidt, H., 'Vordringender Hexenwahn (Rothenburg)', *Fränkischer Feierabend*, 2 (1954), 77–95.

Schmidt, O., brauchtum und Aberglauben in der Oberpfalz 1809, in: Verhandlungen des Hist. Ver. Oberpfalz und Regensburg 121 (1981), 489–502.

Schmidt, J.W.R. (ed.), J. Sprenger and H. Institoris, *Der Hexenhammer zum ersten Male ins Deutsche übertragen und eingeleitet von J.W.R. Schmidt*, Berlin 1906 (reprint Darmstadt 1974).

Schmitz, H.J., *Die Bussbücher und die Bussdisziplin der Kirche. Nach handschriftlichen Quellen dargestellt*, Mainz 1883.

Die Bussbücher und das kanonische Bussverfahren. Nach handschriftlichen Quellen dargestellt, Düsseldorf 1898.

Schmölz, F. and Schmölz, T., 'Die Sterblichkeit in Landsberg am Lech von 1585–1785', *Archiv für Hygiene und Bakteriologie*, 136 (1952), 504–40.

Schneid, J., 'Das Rechtsverfahren wider die Hexen zu Wemding im ersten Drittel des 17. Jahrhunderts', *Oberbayer. Archiv*, 57 (1913), 118–95.

Schnepf, C., 'Magdalena Scherer. Eine Hexengeschichte aus dem Jahre 1617', *Neuburger Kollektaneenblatt*, 44 (1880), 59–78.

Schöck, I., *Hexenglaube in der Gegenwart. Empirische Untersuchungen in Südwestdeutschland*, Tübingen 1978.

Schoenemann, T.J., 'The Witch-Hunt as a culture change phenomenon', *Ethos*, 3 (1975), 529–54.

'The Role of Mental Illness in the European Witch-Hunts of the Sixteenth and Seventeenth Centuries: An Assessment', *Journal of the History of the Behavioral Sciences*, 13 (1977), 337–51.

Schöll, W., 'Der Codex Juris Bavarici Judiciarii von 1753 im Vergleich mit der prozessrechtlichen Gesetzgebung von 1616', Dr. jur. thesis, Munich 1965.

Schormann, G., *Hexenprozesse in Nordwestdeutschland*, Hildesheim 1977.

Hexenprozesse in Deutschland, Göttingen 1981.

Schott, C., *Rat und Spruch der Juristenfakultät Freiburg im Breisgau*, Freiburg im Breisgau 1965.

Schreiber, G., *Das Weltkonzil von Trient. Sein Werden und Wirken*, 2 vols., Freiburg im Breisgau 1951.

Schremmer, E., *Die Wirtschaft Bayerns. Vom hohen Mittelalter bis zum Beginn der Industrialisierung. Bergbau, Gewerbe, Handel*, Munich 1970.

Schrenck-Notzing, N. Freiherr von, 'Das Hochstift Freising und seine Beamten. Zur Genealogie der freisingischen Pfleger in den österreichischen Herrschaften 1550–1800', *ZBLG*, 28 (1965), 190–258.

Schrittenloher, J., 'Aus der Gutachten- und Urteiltätigkeit der Ingolstadter Juristenfakultät im Zeitalter der Hexenverfolgungen', *Jb. f. fränk. Landesforschung*, 23 (163), 315–53.

Schrott, L. (ed.), *Bayerische Kirchenfürsten*, Munich 1964.

Schubert, E., *Arme Leute, Bettler und Gauner im Franken des 18. Jahrhunderts*, Neustadt/Aisch 1983.

Schuegraf, R., 'Zum Hexenprozess', *Zs. d. deutsche Kulturgeschichte*, 3 (1858), 764–73.

Schuhmann, H., *Der Scharfrichter. Seine Gestalt – seine Funktion*, Kempten 1964.

Schultze, J., 'Richtlinien für die äussere Textgestaltung bei Herausgabe von Quellen zur neueren deutschen Geschichte', *Blätter für deutsche Landesgeschichte*, 98 (1962), 1–11.

Schulze, W., *Reich und Türkengefahr im späten 16. Jahrhundert. Studien zu den politischen und gesellschaftlichen Auswirkungen einer äusseren Bedrohung*, Munich 1978.

Schwaiger, G., *Kardinal Franz Wilhelm von Wartenburg als Bishof von Regensburg*, Munich 1954.

Schwarzenfeld, G., *Rudolf II. Der saturnische Kaiser*, Munich 1961.

Seger, O., Der letzte Akt im Drama der Hexenprozesse in der Grafschaft Vaduz und Herrschaft Schellenberg, in: Jb. d. Hist. Ver. des Fürstentums Liechtenstein 57 (1957), 137–227; 59 (1959), 331–349.

Seifriz, K., 'Ein Hexenprozess und der Scharfrichter Meister Christoph Hiert von Biberach', *Anzeiger vom Oberland* (1933) no. 160.

Seils, E.-A., *Die Staatslehre des Jesuiten Adam Contzen, Beichtvater Kurfürst Maximilian I. von Bayern*, Lübeck 1968.

Seufert, A., 'Hexenprozess in Reichertshofen im Jahre 1629', *Ingolstädter Heimatgeschichte*, 2 (1930), nos. 2–3.

Siebel, F.W., 'Die Hexenverfolgung in Köln', Dr. jur. thesis, Bonn 1959.

Simmel, R. 'Ein schwesterlicher Hexenprozess', *Tiroler Heimatblätter*, 9 (1930), 234–6.

Simon, M., *Evangelische Kirchengeschichte Bayerns*, 2 vols., Nuremberg 1940/1952 (2nd edn).

Snell, O., *Hexenprozesse und Geistesstörungen. Psychiatrische Untersuchungen*, Munich 1891.

Soldan, G.W., Heppe, H. and Bauer, H., *Geschichte der Hexenprozesse*, 2 vols., 3rd edn Hanau 1912 (reprint n.d.).

Solleder, F., *München im Mittelalter*, Munich 1938 (reprint 1962).

Soman, A., 'The Parlement of Paris and the Great Witch Hunt (1565–1640)', *Sixteenth Century Journal*, 9 (1978), 31–44.

Souden, D., 'Demographic Crisis and Europe in the 1590s', in Clark, *European Crisis*, 231–43.

Specht, T., *Geschichte der ehemaligen Universität Dillingen*, Freiburg im Breisgau 1902.

Specker, H.E., 'Nachtridentinische Visitationen im Bistum Würzburg als Quelle für die katholischen Reform', in Zeeden and Molitor, *Die Visitation*, 37–49.

Spielmann, H.K., *Die Hexenprozesse in Kurhessen nach den Quellen dargestellt*, 2nd edn Marburg 1932.

Spindler, J., 'Heinrich V von Knöringen, Fürstbischof von Augsburg (1598–1646), *Jb. d. Hist. Ver. Dillingen*, 24 (1911), 1–139; 25 (1915), 1–255.

Spindler, M. (ed.), *Handbuch der Bayerischen Geschichte*, vol. 2, *Das alte Bayern. Der Territorialstaat vom Ausgang des 12. Jahrhunderts bis zum Ausgang des 18. Jahrhunderts*, 2nd edn Munich 1977; vols. III/1–2, *Franken, Schwaben, Oberpfalz bis zum Ausgang des 18. Jahrhunderts*, 2nd edn Munich 1979 (the name of the relevant author is given in parentheses).

Spindler, M. and Diepolder, G. (eds.), *Bayerischer Geschichtsatlas*, Munich 1969.

Spirkner,B., 'Ein Beitrag zu den religiös-sittlichen Zuständen Altbayerns vor und nach dem Dreissigjährigen Krieg', *Verhandlungen d. Hist. Verein Niederbayern*, 62 (1929), 217–44.

Staber, J. 'Die Predigt des Tegernseer Priors Augustin Holzapfler als Quelle für das spätmittelalterliche Volksleben Altbayerns', *Bayer.Jb. f. Volkskunde*, 1960, 125–35.

'Ein altbayerischer Beichtspiegel des 15. Jahrhunderts' (Cgm. 632), *Bayer. Jb. f. Volkskunde*, (1963), 7–24.

Kirchengeschichte des Bistums Regensburg, Regensburg 1966.

'Die Domprediger im 15. und 16. Jahrhundert', in Fischer, J., *Der Freisinger Dom. Beiträge zu seiner Geschichte*, Freising 1967, 119–40.

Stadelmann, J., 'Hexenprozesse', in Zeller, J., *Wertacher Geschichtsbuch. Eine Heimatchronik. Beilage des Wertacher Landboten* (1938) 53–5.

Stebel, H.-J., 'Die Osnabrücker Hexenprozesse', Dr. jur. thesis, Bonn 1968.

Stegmüller, F., *Geschichte des Molinismus*, Münster 1935.

Steichele, A. v., Schröder, A. and Ziepfl, F., *Das Bistum Augsburg historisch und statistisch beschrieben*, 10 vols., Augsburg 1861–1940.

Steinhuber SJ, A., *Geschichte des Kollegium Germanikum Hungarikum in Rom*, 2 vols., 2nd edn Freiburg im Breisgau 1906.

Steinruck, J., *Johann Babtist Fickler. Ein Laie im Dienst der Gegenreformation*, Münster 1965.

Stieve, F., *Briefe und Akten zur Geschichte des Dreissigjährigen Krieges*, vols. 4–6, Munich 1876.

Das kirchliche Polizeiregiment in Baiern unter Maximilian I. 1595–1651, Munich 1876.

'Der Hexenwahn', in *Abhandlungen, Vorträge, Reden*, Leipzig 1900, 300–18.

Stintzing, R. von, *Geschichte der deutschen Rechtswissenschaft*, 3 vols., Munich 1880/1910 (reprint 1957).

Stockinger, L., 'Invidia, curiositas und Hexerei. Hexen- und Teufelsglaube in literarischen Texten des 17. Jahrhunderts', in Degn *et al., Hexenprozesse*, 14–27.

Stone, L., 'The Disenchantment of the World', *New York Review of Books*, 2 December 1971, 17–25.

Stötter, 'Walburga Weyenmayerin', *Schwäbische Heimat. Beilage zum Günz- und Mindelboten* (1926), no. 14.

Streidl, H., *Heimatbuch Pfaffenhofen/Ilm*, Pfaffenhofen 1979.

Striedinger, I., *Der Goldmacher Marco Brogadino*, Munich 1928.

Strüber, S., P. Jordan Simon aus dem Orden der Augustiner-Eremiten. Ein Lebensbild aus der Aufklärungszeit, Würzburg 1930.

Sturm, A., Ein verspäteter Hexenprozeß, in: Die Oberpfalz 18 (1924), 148–50.

Sugenheim, S., *Bayerns Kirchen- und Volkszustände, im 16. Jahrhundert*, Giessen 1842.

Svátek, J., 'Hexenprozesse in Böhmen', in *Culturhistorische Bilder aus Böhmen*, Vienna 1879, 3–40.

Tazbir, J., 'Hexenprozesse in Polen', *Archiv für Reformationsgeschichte*, 71 (1980), 280–307.

Telle, J., *Pharmazie und der gemeine Mann. Hausarznei und Apotheke in deutschen Schriften der frühen Neuzeit*, Wolfenbüttel 1982.

Thieser, B., 'Die Oberpfalz im Zusammenhang des Hexenprozessgeschehens im süddeutschen Raum während des 16. und 17. Jahrhunderts,' PhD thesis, Bayreuth 1987.

Thomas, K., 'History and Anthropology', *Past and Present*, 24 (1963), 3–24.

Religion and the Decline of Magic. Studies in Popular Beliefs in Sixteenth and Seventeenth Century England, Harmondsworth 1980 (1st edn London 1971).

Thorndyke, L., *A History of Magic and Experimental Science*, 8 vols., New York 1923–58.

Tilly, C. (ed.), *The Formation of National States in Western Europe*, Princeton 1975.

Tischer, F., 'Ein Hexenprozess des Jahres 1536', *Altnürnberger Landschaft*, 3 (1954), Heft 2, 9–14.

Tramer, M., 'Kinder im Hexenglauben und Hexenprozess des Mittelalters', *Acta Paedo-psychiatrica, Zs. f. Kinderpsychiatrie*, 11 (1945), 140–9, 180–7.

Trevor-Roper, H.R., 'Der europäische Hexenwahn des 16. und 17. Jahrhunderts', in *Religion, Reformation und Sozialer Umbruch. Die Krisis des 17. Jahrhunderts*, Frankfurt am Main 1970, 95–180 ('The European Witch Craze of the Sixteenth and Seventeenth Centuries', in *Religion, the Reformation and Social Change*, London 1967, 90–192).

'The General Crisis of the Seventeenth Century', in Aston, *Crisis*, 59–96.

Unold, J.F., *Geschichte der Stadt Memmingen. Von Anfang der Stadt bis zum Tod Maximilians Joseph I. König von Bayern*, Memmingen 1826.

Unverhau, D., 'Akkusationsprozess – Inquisitionsprozess. Indikatoren für die Intensität der Hexenverfolgung in Schleswig- Holstein', in Degn *et al., Hexenprozesse*, 59–142.

'"Meisterinnen" und deren "Kunstfruwen" in Schleswig und Angeln um die

454   *Sources and Literature*

Mitte des 16. Jahrhunderts. Von magischen Frauengemeinschaften und Hexensekten', *Jb. d. Heimatvereins Schleswigsche Geest* (1984), 60– 80.

Vierhaus, R., *Deutschland im Zeitalter des Absolutismus*, Göttingen 1978.

Vierling, A., 'Unvertilgbarer Volksglaube und Aberglaube nach ältestem bayrischen Volksrecht', *Oberbayer. Archiv*, 52 (1904/7) 147–172.

'Die Handschriften der Kgl. Hof- und Staatsbibliothek in München mit kirchlichen Bussbüchern', *Oberbayer. Archiv*, 54 (1909), 249–82.

Voitel, F., *Scheiterhaufen in Wemding 1609–1631*, Wemding 1958.

Völk, J., 'Ein Günzburger Hexenprozess', *Schwäbische Heimat. Beilage zum Günz- und Mindelboten* (1928), nos. 8–9.

Wachter, G. F. v., Der letzte Hexenprozeß des Stifts Kempten, in: Allgäuer Geschichtsfreund, NF, 5 (1892), 8–63 (in Fortsetzungen).

Wagner, E., 'Hexenglaube in Franken heute', *Jb. f. fränk. Landesforschung*, 30 (1970), 343–56.

Wagner, H., Aberglaube und Hexenprozesse im Bezirk Grafenau im 17. und 18. Jahrhundert, in: Passauer Jahrbuch Ostbayrische Grenzmarken 1 (1957), 91–95.

Waibel, G., 'Dokumente über 'Falschmiethe' in Unterthingau', *Der Hochvogel* (1927), no. 14.

Walker, D.P., *The Decline of Hell. Seventeenth Century Discussion of Eternal Torment*, London 1964.

Spiritual and Demonic Magic from Ficino to Campanella, Notre Dame 1976.

Wanderer, K.P., 'Gedruckter Aberglaube. Studien zur volkstümlichen Beschwörungsliteratur', PhD thesis, Frankfurt 1975.

Warmbrunn, P., *Zwei Konfessionen in einer Stadt. Das Zusammenleben von Katholiken und Protestanten in den paritätischen Reichsstädten Augsburg, Biberach, Ravensburg und Dinkelsbühl von 1548 bis 1648*, Wiesbaden 1983.

Weber, H., *Johann Gottfried von Aschhausen, Fürstbischof von Würzburg und Bamberg, Herzog zu Franken*, Würzburg 1889.

Weber, L., *Veit Adam Gepeckh, Fürstbischof von Freising 1618–1651*, Munich 1972.

Weber, M., *Wirtschaft und Gesellschaft*, 5th edn Tübingen 1976.

Webster, C., *The Great Instauration. Science, Medicine and Reform, 1626–1660*, New York 1976.

Wehn, C., Der Kampf des, , Journals von und für Deutschland' gegen den Aberglauben seiner Zeit, Diss. phil. Köln 1937.

Weigel, M., 'Zur Geschichte des Aberglaubens in der Oberpfalz', *Die Oberpfalz*, 28 (1934), 192–3.

Weiland, L., 'Ein Hexenprozess im elften Jahrhundert', *Zeitschrift für Kirchengeschichte*, 9 (1888), 592f.

Weis, W., *Chronik der Stadt Dillingen*, 2nd edn Dillingen 1888.

Weitnauer, A., 'Allgäuer Hexen', *Unser Allgau* (1948), no. 2.

Allgäuer Chronik, 3 vols., Kempten 1969–72.

Wendehorst, A., 'Johann Gottfried von Aschhausen, (1575–1622)', in G. Pfeiffer (ed.), *Fränkische Lebensbilder*, 9 (1980), 167–86.

Wesche, H., *Der althochdeutsche Wortschatz im Gebiete des Zaubers und der Weissagung*, Halle 1940.

Westermayer, G., *Chronik der Burg und des Marktes Tölz*, 2nd edn Tölz 1893.

Wiedemann, M., 'Hexenprozesse zu Wasserburg', *Bodensee Heimatschau*, 8 (1929), nos. 2–3.

'Über die niederen Gerichte des westlichen Allgäus im 17. und 18. Jahrhundert',

Sources and Literature 455

in Müller, *Das Weitnauer Tal*, 313–45.

Wieser, M., *Schloss Staufeneck. Ein Heimatbuch aus dem Rupertiwinkel*, n.p. 1979.

Wilbertz, G., 'Die Hexenprozesse in Stadt und Stift Osnabrück', in Degn, *et al.*, *Hexenprozesse* 218–22.

Wilczek, G., 'Jahresbericht des Jesuitenkollegs zu Ingolstadt von 1598', *Ingolstädter Heimatblätter*, 31 (1967), 42; 32 (1968), 1.

'Die Universität zu Ingolstadt', *Ingolstädter Heimatblätter*, 35 (1972) (series).

Winteler, J., *Der Prozeß gegen Anna Göldi im Urteil der Zeitgenossen*, Glarus 1951.

Winter, E., *Frühaufklärung*. Der Kampf gegen den Konfessionalismus in Mittel- und Osteuropa und die deutsch-slawische Gegegnung, Berlin (Ost) 1966.

Wittmann, P., 'Friedrich Förner, Weihbischof zu Bamberg', *Hist. Pol. Blätter*, 36 (1880), 565ff., 656ff.

'Die Bamberger Hexenjustiz 1595–1631', *Archiv für das katholische Kirchenrecht*, 50 (1883), 177–223.

'Das Bamberger Trudenhaus', *Zeitschrift des Alterthumsvereins*, new series, 5 (1892), 21–6.

Wolf, H.-J., *Hexenwahn und Exorzismus. Ein Beitrag zur Kulturgeschichte*, Kriftel/ Taunus 1980.

Wolf, P.P. and Breyer, C.W.F., *Geschichte Maximilians I. und seine Zeit*, 4 vols., Munich 1807–11.

Wolfart, H., *Geschichte der Stadt Lindau in Bodensee*, vol. I, Lindau 1909.

Wolff, A., *Gerichtsverfassung und Prozess im Hochstift Augsburg in der Rezeptionszeit*, Dillingen 1913.

Wolff, H., *Geschichte der Ingolstädter Juristenfakultät, 1472–1625*, Berlin 1973.

Wulz, G., 'Der Prozess der Hexe Rebekka Lemp', *Der Rieser Heimatbote* (1937), no. 131.

'Nördlinger Hexenprozesse', *Rieser Heimatverein* (Jahrbuch), 20 (1937), 42–72; (1938), 95–121.

'Nördlinger Hexenprozesse vor 1589', *Der Rieser Heimatbote* (1938), no. 140.

'Die Nördlinger Hexen und ihre Richter. Eine familiengeschichtliche Studie', *Der Rieser Heimatbote* (1939), nos. 142–7.

'Wilhelm Friedrich Lutz', in G. Freiherr von Pölnitz (ed.), *Lebensbilder aus dem Bayerischen Schwaben*, 5 (1956), 198–220.

Wunder, H., 'Hexenprozesse im Herzogtum Preussenwährend des 16. Jahrhunderts', in Degn *et al.*, *Hxenprozesse*, 179–204.

Zallinger, O. von, *Das Verfahren gegen dielandschädlichen Leute in Süddeutschland*, Innsbruck 1895.

Zeeden, E.W., *Deutsche Kultur in der frühen Neuzeit*,Frankfurt am Main 1960.

Die Entstehung der Konfessionen, Munich/Vienna 1965.

and Molitor, H.G., *Die Visitation im Dienste der kirchlichen Reform*, Münster 1977.

Zelzer, M., *Geschichte der Stadt Donauwörth von denAnfängen bis 1618*, Donauwörth 1958.

Zenz, E., 'Dietrich Flade, ein Opfer desHexenwahns', *Kurtrierisches Jb.*, 2 (1962), 41–69.

'Cornelius Loos – ein Vorläufer Friedrich Spees im Kampf gegen den Hexenwahn', *Kurtrierisches Jb.*, 21 (1981), 147–53.

Zguta, R., 'Witchcraft Trials in 17th CenturyRussia', *American Historical Review*, 82 (1977), 1187–1207.

Ziegeler, W., *Möglichkeiten der Kritik am Hexen- undZauberwahn im ausgehenden Mittelalter*, Cologne/Vienna, 1973.

Zilboorg, G., *The Medical Man and the Witch During the Renaissance*, Baltimore 1935.

Zillhardt, G., *Der Dreissigjährige Krieg in zeitgenössischer Darstellung. Hans Heberles 'Zeytregister' (1618–1672). Aufzeichnungen aus dem Ulmer Territorium. Ein Beitrag zur Geschichtsschreibung und Geschichtsverständnis der Unterschichten*, Ulm 1975.

Zingerle, I.V., *Ein Beitrag zu den Hexenprozessen in Tirol im 17. Jahrhundert*, Innsbruck 1882.

Zirkel, H.B., *Geschichte des Marktes Oberstdorf*, 4 vols., Oberstdorf 1974.

Zoepfl, F., *Deutsche Kulturgeschichte*, 2 vols., Freiburg im Breisgau 1928/30.

Geschichte der Stadt Mindelheim, Munich 1948.

'Heinrich von Knöringen, Bischof von Augsburg', in Schrott, *Bayerische Kirchenfürsten*, 168–79.

'Hexenwahn und Hexenverfolgungen in Dillingen', *ZBLG*, 27 (1964), 235–45.

Das Bistum Augsburg und seine Bischöfe im Reformationsjahrhundert, Munich/Augsburg 1969.

Zorn, W., *Augsburg. Geschichte einer deutschen Stadt*, 2nd edn Augsburg 1972.

Handels- und Industriegeschichte Bayerisch-Schwabens 1648–1870, Augsburg 1961.

(ed.), *Historischer Atlas von Bayerisch-Schwaben*, Augsburg 1955.

Zwetsloot, SJ, H., *Friedrich Spee und die Hexenprozesse. Die Stellung und Bedeutung der Cautio Criminalis in der Geschichte der Hexenverfolgung*, Trier 1954.

Index

Aachen, Hans von, 105
Abegg, Johann Christoph, Chancellor of
    Court Council, 244, 296, 306, 316
Abel, W., 92–93, 101, 333, 407
Abenberg, 94, 153
Abensberg, witch trials in, 53, 73, 95, 137,
    196, 230, 232, 243, 251, 254, 296, 339
Aberholl, Barthlemess, executioner, 127
Abriel, Jörg, executioner of Schongau,
    127, 136, 138, 142, 143, 144, 157, 195,
    201
absolutism, in Duchy of Bavaria, 18, 404
Academy of Sciences, Bavarian, 360, 363,
    369, 368, 371, 375, 376, 377
accusations of witchcraft, see witchcraft,
    accusations of
Ackher, Dr Paulus zum, Court Councillor,
    133, 227, 298–9, 320
Agnes, bath–house keeper of Mindelheim,
    witch, 77
Agobard, Archbishop of Lyons, 66
Agrippa von Nettesheim, magician, 45,
    411
Aibling, 26, 53, 57, 138, 296
Aichach, 53, 55
Airimschmalz, Konrad, Abbot of
    Tegernsee, 74
Albertinus, Aegidius, 221, 222, 238, 298,
    414
Albertus Magnus, Bishop of Regensburg,
    Saint, 411
Albrecht V, Duke of Bavaria, 18, 105, 410
Albrecht VI, brother of Elector
    Maximilian I, 224,
Albrecht, Bernhard, priest of Augsburg, 32
Albrecht, D., 105
alchemists, 21
Allgäu, 21, 92, 93, 94
Alps, the, 9
Alsace, 13, 25, 77
Altdorf, University of, 155, 312

Altmühl valley, 307
Altötting, 106–7, 362, 410
Altseer, Simon, witch of Rottenbuch, 332,
    plate 13
Alzenau, *Freigericht* of, 95, 224
Amberg, 18, 48, 307, 340
Amerin, Maria Anna, witch of Landshut,
    347
Amorbach, 157
anabaptists, 19, 21
Andechs, 92
Andreae, Jacob, Tübingen theologian, 198
Anna of Mindelheim, witch, 77
Ansbach, Margravate of
    arrest of C. von Pappenheim, 193
    decline of witch hunting in, 216,
    eschatological obsessions of ruling
        house, 414
    executioner of Oettingen active in, 185,
        204–5
    influence of *Malleus* in, 214
    influenced by Nuremberg, 207
    rejects persecution as Catholic, 312, 403
    witch trials in (1590) 154–5, 392 (1660s)
        333,
Ansbach-Bayreuth, Principality of, 138,
    153, 391
anthropology, social, 6, 7–8
anti–persecution party in Bavaria, 239–46
Antonius, Suffragan Bishop of Eichstätt,
    46
Aquaviva, Claudius, SJ, General of Jesuit
    order, 259
Aschaffenburg, 38, 156, 157, 224, 225, 227,
    310
Aschhausen, Johann Gottfried von, Bishop
    of Bamberg, 225–9, 414
Aston, T., 407
astrology, 94, 110–111
Attel, monastic estate, 59
Auerberg, the, 26, 136

Auerburg, 57
Auersperg, J.F., Count, Imperial Court
  Councillor, 384
Augsburg, diocese, 45
Augsburg, Imperial Free City
  accusations of witchcraft increase in,
    122
  advice sought by Kempten 1665, 330
  archives of, 31, 43
  Canisius in, 104–5
  chroniclers of 390
  conflicts with Prince–Bishopric, 46
  economy of, 21, 92–96, 100–1, 144, 333
  executions in, 43–4, 102, 165
  soothsayers in, 171–2, 176,
  sorcerer punished in, 41
  trials for witchcraft in, 42, 63, 64, 98,
    99, 157, 162–3, 180, 199, 311, 328, 333
Augsburg, Prince-Bishopric of
  'backwardness' theory inapplicable in,
    402
  Court Council of, 30–31, 158, 312
  extent of, 123
  suppressed in 1806, 387
  witch trials in 1590s, 45–7, 64, 128, 138,
    139, 140, 162, 182, 209; in 17th
    century, 224–5, 230, 296, 312, 403
Augustine, St 360, 377
Aurbach, Hieronymus, Court Councillor
  and Chancellor of Freising, 275
Austria, 10, 12, 25, 27, 122, 400–1, 403
Autun, 70
Aventinus, Johannes Turmair, humanist,
    83, 103

Bacon, Francis, 415
Baden, Margravate of, 80, 118, 135, 266,
    268, 394
Baden-Württemberg, *Land* of Federal
  Republic of Germany, see Germany,
  southwest
Bader, G., 10
Baldus, Italian jurist, 266
Bamberg, Imperial Free City, 80, 96, 167
Bamberg, Prince–Bishopric of
  great persecutions in 24, 38, 97, 156,
    224–9, 310–11, 316, 322
  mandate against treasure seeking, 340
  suppressed in 1806, 387
  banishment, penalty for sorcery, 41, 54,
    55, 79
Bärnstein, 26, 57, 343
Barth, Bernhard, *Rentmeister* and
    Hofoberrichter
  and trial of K. Hell, 253

opponent of witch hunting in Court
  Council, 272, 274–6, 278. 279–80,
  opposed witch hunt in Wemding, 280–281,
    293–4, 296
Barthel, J.C. ,347
Baschwitz, K. 27
Basque country, 13
Bavaria, *Land* of Federal Republic of
  Germany, 13, 17, 37–9
Bavaria, Principality (Duchy to 1623,
  Electorate 1623–1806)
  absolutism, 18,404
  alleged 'heartland' of witch hunting,
    23–5, 38, 403, 406, 407
  authors on witchcraft concentrated in,
    219
  church and state, 289, 378–9
  Court Council, see Court Council,
    Bavaria
  Estates of, 102
  influence on Franconian witch hunts,
    314–16
  justice, system of, 30, 31, 47–50, 389
  kingdom 1806, 387
  laws on witchcraft, 80, 118
  nobles' power broken, 102–3
  population 21
  witch trials in, 47–60, 63; (1590s)
    134–42,   389
Bayreuth, Margravate of 154–5, 216,312
beggars and vagrants, 100–1, 102
Beilngries, 94
Bekker, Balthasar, Dutch Cartesian, 331,
    357, 364
Bemelburg, Konrad von, the elder, 280
Bemelburg, Konrad von, the younger, 280,
    293, 294
Benandanti, 177, 179
Benediktbeuern, 152
Berchtesgaden,336
Berg, Adam, printer of Munich, 115
Berg, Marquard vom, Bishop of
  Augsburg, 122–3, 128, 391, 414
Bergin, Anna, widow and printer, 285
Berlin, 349
Bernauerin, Agnes, murdered lover of
  Duke of Bavaria, 68
Berne, 70
Bernhard of Como, Italian inquisitor, 68
Beyrin of Winden, witch, 275, 277–8, 279
Biberach, 94, 330
Biberach, the Master of, executioner, see
  Vollmair, Hans and Vollmair,
  Christoph
Bible, 116, 365, 366, 368, 377

Bihlerin, Maria, 329 plate 12
Binsfeld, Peter, suffragan Bishop of Trier,
  cited by G. von Valentia, 220; Stengel,
  322; Witweiler, 223; Wagnereckh, 240,
  260
  contacts with Bavaria, 24
  criticised by Haslang, 258; by Tanner
  266
  died 1598, 262
  influence in University of Ingolstadt 137,
  140, 173, 207, 218, 251, 256
  translated into German, 141 plate 7, 201
  zeal discredited, 206, 267, 403
Bireley, R., S.J. 238,314
Bittelmayr, Margarethe, wife of town clerk
  and witch of Eichstätt, 244
Bittelmayr, Matthias, Chancellor of
  Landshut, 316
Blarer, Johann Erhart, von Wartensee,
  Prince-Abbot of Kempten, 414
Blocksberg, the, 403
Blocksberger, F.N. (pseud.), see Mayer,
  Andreas Ulrich
Blumenscheinin, Maria, sorceress of
  Augsburg, 86
Bobingen, 99, 126, 128, 164–5,187–8
Bodin, Jean, jurist and demonologist
  believed in witches' sabbath, 14
  cited by Carpzow, 331; by Wagnereckh,
  240, 255
  influence in University of Ingolstadt 137,
  218; on James VI, 13
  on proverbial ugliness of witches, 160
  reformulated assumptions of the *Malleus*,
  214
  similarities with Rémy, 262
  translated by Fischart, 125
  zeal discredited, 206, 207
Bodmann, Rupert, Prince-Abbot of
  Kempten, 336
Bogen, 343
Bohemia, 17, 21, 25, 27, 122
Bologna, University of, opinion on
  witchcraft 1602, 261–2, 263, 266, 268,
  325, 394
Bonelli, OFM, Inquisitor, 358
Bonet, Niclas, Court Councillor and
  Chancellor of Brixen, 296
Bonschab, Lorenz, Burgomaster of
  Eichstätt, 244
Bonschab, Maria, witch of Eichstätt, 244
Bossius, Italian jurist, 266
boy-sorcerers, see children
Bozen, 190
Brackert, W. 27

Brandenburg, 404
Braudel, F., 100
Braun, Heinrich, OSB, Munich school
  reformer, 374, 380, 399
Braunau, 78
Braunin, Maria, witch of Augsburg, 168
Breitenfeld, battle of, 310
Bremen, 72
Brenz, Johann, Tübingen reformer, 198,
  214, 217, 405
Brixen, 72, 296, 400
Brugglacher, Johann Georg, Court
  Councillor, 244, 296, 304
Brunner, O., 15
Brunswick-Wolfenbüttel, 13
Buchloe, 164
Buecher, Hans, Burgomaster of
  Donauwörth, 211
Buecher, Katharina, witch, 211
Bullinger, H., Swiss reformer, 213
Burgau, Margravate of, 19, 79, 94, 133,
  163, 202, 172
Burghausen,
  executions in, 343, 347, 348, 349
  plague in, 94
  seat of *Regierung,* 48–9
  sorceress of, 290
  witch trials in, 18, 26, 53, 57, 77–8
Burgrain, 142
Buslidius, Johannes, SJ, Court Confessor,
  238, 261, 263, 265
Byloff, F. 10

Cadolzburg, 155
Calvin, Jean, 307
Calvinism, 213
Calw, 342
Canisius, Petrus, SJ, Counter-reformer
  counter-reformation activity in Augsburg,
  104–5, 123–4
  on increase of witchcraft, 108–9
  supporter of witch hunting 24, 390, 393,
  395
Canon Episcopi, 65–6, 68, 213, 217
capitalism theory of witchcraft, 8, 13,
  402
Carinthia, 337, 343
Carolina, Constitutio Criminalis,
  criteria of sorcery, 162, 168, 170, 172,
  285
  invoked by Haslang, 258; by Ingolstadt
  opinion of 1601, 252, 253
  penalties for sorcery, 80, 115, 118, 345,
  354
  referred to in 1612 Mandate, 286

invoked by Haslang (*cont.*)
    replaced in Bavaria, 1751, 348
    torture, 184
Carpzow, Benedikt, Saxon jurist, 331, 344,
    350, 354, 357
Cartesianism, 5
Carus, Julino, 266
Cäsarius von Heisterbach, Cistercian, 361
Castiglione, Baldassare, Italian courtier,
    103
cathedral chapters, 102, 404
Catholic League, 106, 235, 282, 310
Catholics,
    and Enlightenment, 334
attitudes to witchcraft, harden in sixteenth
    cent. 11, 216–8, 312–12; divided in
    seventeenth cent. 322–8; influenced by
    Tanner, 355–7; onset of debate 357–9;
    public debate and victory of
    enlightenment 359–81; summary
    392–4, 402–4
causa domini, 31, 50
Charles V, Emperor, 5
Chaunu, P. 89
Chiemsee, diocese, 72, 289
children,
    accusations made by, 126, 164–5, 167, 180,
        183, 308, 341, 398
    bands of 336–7, 342–3, 398
    tried as witches 336–8, 342–4
Chlingensberg, Christoph and Hermann
    Anton von, Ingolstadt jurists, 220,
    331, 357
Christian-August von Pfalz-Sulzbach,
    Prince and theosophist, 356
Cities, Imperial Free
    compared with Prince-Bishoprics, 45
    contrasts between, 20
    different reactions to 1590 persecution,
        121, 144–7, 151, 201–6, 311–14
    executions in, 327–8
    patriciates of, 103
    witch trials in, 39–43
clergy, 81, 363, 370, 381–4
climate, 99
Coburg, 154–5, 312, 338, 391
Codex Juris Bavarici Criminalis, 348, 350
Codex Maximileaneus of 1616, 295
Colbert, J.B., 344, 346
Colmberg, 154
Cologne, 18, 266, 268,
confessional opinion, see Catholics,
    Protestants
confessions, 151, 184, 212, 397
conservatism, 384

Constance, diocese of, 45, 70, 72, 77
Constitutio Criminalis Carolina, see
    Carolina
Contzen, Adam, SJ 24, 222, 237–9, 314,
    318, 320, 393
Corbinian, Bishop of Freising, 66–7
Council of Basle, 76
Council of Trent, 103
Counter-Reformation, 5, 18, 111, 217,
    393
counterspells, 87–8
Court Council, of Duchy of Bavaria
    archives of, as source, 30, 31, 52, 53, 55,
        59–60, 138, 291, 301, 308, 327, 338
    composition fluid in 1620s, 310
    debates on witchcraft in, 139, 217, 272–7
    Mandate of 1612, 283, 287–8
    pro- and anti-persecution parties in, 235,
        238, 240–1, 244, 268, 270–2, 279–80,
        281–2, 295–7
    role in witch trials, 48–50, 233–4, 247–8,
        291–5, 394, 395
    visitations of (1608), 275, 276, 279; (1617),
        289
    Wagnereckh's chancellorship of, 270–2
Court Council, of Prince-Bishopric of
    Augsburg,
    archives of, 46–7, 180
    caution on denunciations, 209
    discussion of witchcraft in 1589–92, 158
    role in witch trials, 126, 162, 179
courts, of law, see justice, system of
courts, princely, 103, 105
Crailsheim, 155
Creusen, 154
crime, patterns of, 53 table 4, 55, 56–7
crimen exceptum, 215, 231, 312
crises, agrarian
    correlation with witch hunts, 91–99, 100–1,
        309, 388–9, 407–8, 411–12
    of 1562–92, 144
    of 1586–7, 122
    of 1597–1601, 230
    of 1607–8, 276, 291
    of 1610–11, 282, 291
    of 1614–15, 291, 296, 298
    of 1620s, 301
    signs of God's wrath, 110, 111
'crisis of the late sixteenth century', 89–114
'crisis of the seventeenth century', 90, 411
crops, damage to, by witches, 77, 85, 89,
    98, 107, 131, 135, 136
cursing, see Threats
Cusan, Nicolaus, SJ, Ingolstadt
    theologian, 323

Dachau, witch trials in 53, 55, 56, 57, 276, 296, 307, 344
Danaeus (Daneau), Lambertus, Calvinist theologian, 406
Dandorf, H. A. von, Court Councillor, 296
Däubler, executioner of Augsburg, 124, 149
Deggelin, Ulrich, Chancellor of Kempten, 414
Deggendorf, 53, 344
Deism, 345, 364
Dell'Osa, Ardoino Ubbidiente (pseud.) see Simon, Jordan
Delrio, Martin, SJ demonologist and polymath
  approved by Buslidius, 261–2
  cited by Carpzow, 331; by Wagnereckh, 240, 259, 300
  contacts with Bavaria, 24
  Disquisitiones Magicae of, 247, 264 plate 9
  importance of, 223
  Malleus and, 13
  'mountain' theory of, 9
  opposed by Dillingen in 1601 opinion, 256; by Haslang, 257; by Spee, 324
  reputation in eighteenth century, 322, 344, 350
demonologists, 1, 13, 262–3, 358, 405–6
Denich, Joachim, Ingolstadt jurist, 242–3, 254, 305
Denich, Kaspar, Ingolstadt jurist, 243, 300, 305–6, 395
Denich, Sebastian, S.J., 323
Denmark, 12, 122, 213
denunciations
  Catholic authorities to consider in principle, 249, 254, 255
  credibility of, 83–4, 183, 187, 188–9, 203, 248, 325–6, 327, 328
  decree of 1601 on, 272
  Delrio on, 263
  expansion of witch trials by 134, 157, 189–93, 204, 205–6
  grounds for torture, 266–7, 299
  reliance on, criticised by opponents of witch hunting, 233–4, 258, 270
Descartes, René, 375
Devil, the
  fear of his power, 116, 117
  'five works of', 173–4
  hallucinations caused by, 259, 260, 315
  lies of, 255, 326
  pact with, 11, 14–15, 67, 73, 107, 109, 118, 160, 164, 173, 183, 218, 286, 297, 308,
  338, 346, 348, 351, 353, 354, 357, 360, 365, 377, 410
  Protestant views of, 112–13, 213, 215–16
  sexual relations with, 14, 15, 107, 164, 183, 341, 343, 346, 351
3, Dickhell, Hieronymus, witch specialist and Chancellor, 304, 313
Diemantstein, Hieronymus von, bewitched judge, 130, 159
Diessen, 307
Diessenstein, 26, 57, 343
Dietterin, Lucia, witch of Schongau, 195
Dillingen, city
  capital of Prince–Bishopric of Augsburg, 19, 46
  conflicts between city and government, 202
  plague in, 92
  witch-trials in, 22, 93, 95, 107, 123–6, 129, 130, 135, 164, 168, 182, 190, 252, 230, 347, 389
Dillingen, University of, 123–4, 218, 255, 256, 330, 385, 394
Dingolfing, witch trials at, 26, 53, 57, 78, 79, 232, 276, 343
Dinkelsbühl, 42, 147, 216, 328
Dinkelscherben, 129, 167, 230
Donaumünster, 133
Donauwörth
  annexed by Bavaria, 18
  executioner of, 131
  recatholicised, 64
  witch trials in, 42, 43, 46–7, 53, 60, 95, 190, 210–11, 276, 280–1, 292, 307, 391–3
Donnersberger, Joachim, Chancellor
  committee under him investigates suicide of 'Beyrin of Winden', 277–8, 286
  censures Dr Vagh, 279
  intervenes in Sattler case, 294
  moderate on witch hunting, 239, 265, 270, 288, 316, 393, 394
  objects to 1612 mandate, 288
Drach, J.J., *Ordinarius* of the *Schöppenstühl* of Coburg, 312
Drechsel, Walter, Chancellor of Neuburg, 131
Drexel, Jeremias, SJ court preacher, 24, 222–3, 238, 393
Duhr, B., SJ, 167
Dulac, J.C. von, Court Councillor, 348
Dürer, Albrecht, 82
Durich, Fortunat, O.F.M., 366

Eberlerin, Anna, witch of Augsburg, 335 plate 14

Echter von Mespelbrunn, Julius, Bishop of
  Würzburg, 156, 225–9, 414
Eggenfelden, 137, 152
Ehinger, Christoph, Augsburg theologian,
  334
Ehrenberg, Philip Adolf von, Bishop of
  Würzburg, 223, 226–9, 320–1, 414
Eibsee, 170
Eichstätt, city, 127, 157, 185, 186, 204–5,
  313
Eichstätt, Prince-Bishopric of
  great persecutions in, 13, 24, 38, 45, 96,
  97, 138, 140, 153–4, 224–9, 301, 314,
  315, 316
  mandate against treasure seeking, 340
  suppressed 1806, 387
Eiselin, Ingolstadt Jesuit, 253
Eisenheimer, *Rentmeister*, 280
Elchingen, 20
Elias, N., 103, 410
Ellingen, witch trials at (1575) 93; (1590)
  134, 145, 155, 158, 169–70, 180, 391
Ellwangen, 95, 165, 221, 225, 229, 296,
  299, 312, 382, 384
Els of Ettringen, famous soothsayer, 171,
  172
Elsas, M.J., 34, 92
Elsenheimer, Christoph, *Rentmeister*, 244
Elymas the Sorcerer, 365
England, 11, 12, 359, 405
Enlightenment
  apologetic function of history in, 2, 4
  breakthrough in Bavaria in 1760s, 352,
  359–81, 399
  Catholic areas lagged in, 334, 344–6
Enzensbergerin, Anna, witch of
  Oberstdorf, 178
epidemics,
  correlation with witch hunts, 92, 94, 95,
  96, 301, 407–8
  signs of God's wrath, 110,
Epple, Burgomaster of Wemding, 303
Epstein, 384
Erastus, Thomas, physician, 406
Erding, 56, 57, 138, 343, 344
Erfurt, University of 359
Ernst, Dr J., Chancellor, 244
Ernst of Bavaria, Bishop of Cologne and
  Freising, 142, 223
Erolzheim, 133
eschatology, 113, 116
Eschenlohe, 143
Essex, 11, 84, 90
Essing, 137
Esslingen, 342

estates
  of Bavaria, 18, 80, 102, 241, 242, 246,
    281
  of Tyrol, 72
Ettal, Abbey of, 143, 152
Evans-Pritchard, E.E., 7, 11, 14, 413
Eve, 196
Everhard, Nikolaus, Ingolstadt jurist, 220
executioners
  criticism of, 204–5
  role in witch trials, 78, 79, 124–5, 126–8,
    129, 131, 143, 157, 161, 184–6, 389
executions,
  chiefly for crimes against property, 57
  concentrated in great witch hunts, 35,
    52, 55, 61–2, 392
  confessions read out at, 212
  declined for decades after 1500, 5
  distribution of, 36, 41, 42–3, 43–4, 48,
    61–2, 63, 64, 132–3, 147–52, 327–8
  executions for witchcraft ended by
    Maria Theresa in Habsburg lands,
    373
  last executions for witchcraft, 344–54
  protests at, 195–6, 197
  recantations at, 314
  spectacular scale of, 102
exorcism, 109, 166
Eyb, Gabriel von, Bishop of Eichstätt, 46

Faber, Albrecht, Chancellor of Bishopric
  of Augsburg, 129
Faber, Hieronymus, Cort Councillor, 274
Fachineus, Andreas, Ingolstadt jurist, 220
Falkenturm, the, 49, 50, 55, 233, 252, 253,
  275, 347
family trials, 338, 340–1
Farinacius, Italian jurist, 266
Fasold, Dr G., ducal councillor in
  Ingolstadt, 304, 305
Faust, Jörg, magician, 70, 411, 414
Ferchl, G., 48
Ferdinand, Duke of Bavaria, 135, 298
Ferdinand II, Holy Roman Emperor, 136,
  316, 318, 319, 323, 325
Ferdinand III, Holy Roman Emperor, 223
Ferdinand Maria, Elector of Bavaria,
  106–7, 224, 323, 356
feudalism, transition to capitalism, 8, 13
Feuerbach, J.P.A., Bavarian penal law
  reformer, 387
Fichard, Johann, Frankfurt jurist, 252, 357
Fickler, Johan Baptist, tutor of Bavarian
  princes, 219, 237–8, 414
Fickler, Johann Christoph, 219–220

Finauer, P.P., Munich publisher, 371, 380
fines, 54, 79, 152
Fischart, Johan, author, 14, 125, 160
Flade, Dietrich, Burgomaster of Trier, executed for witchcraft, 126, 247, 252, 260
Flick, Johann SJ, 225
flight, witches', see witches' flight
Flöckh, Dorothea, née Hofmann, witch of Bamberg, 316, 317, 318
Flöckh, Dr G.H., councillor of Bamberg, 316, 318
'fools', role in trials for witchcraft, 164, 166–8, 183
Förner, Friedrich, Suffragan Bishop of Bamberg,
   contact with Bavaria, 24
   death 1630, 320–1
   denounced, 318
   persecutor of witches, 219, 225–9, 324, 414
France, 12, 68, 69, 110, 358, 405
Francisci, Adam, Lutheran, 116
Franconia
   comparison with SE Germany, 36–8, 309, 401, 405, 409
   great witch hunts (16th cent.) 64, 92, 95, 132, 133, 153–6; (C17th) 33, 42–3, 96–7, 224–9, 290, 301, 413
Frankfurt am Main, 361
Frauenchiemsee, 91
Freiburg im Breisgau, University of, 218, 255, 256–7, 394
Freising, city
   city law code of 1328, 69
   sorcerer lynched, 66
   witch trials, 168, 180, 190, 192, 350–1
Freising, diocese, 45
Freising, Prince-Bishopric of
   archives of, 38
   suppressed 1806, 387
   surrounded by Bavaria, 19
   witch trials in (C16th) 113, 138, 142–4, 159, 161, 168–9, 203, 209; (C17th) 311, 326; (1720–22) 333, 337, 344
Frey, Bernhard, SJ, court confessor, 323, 356
Friedberg, 26, 53, 57, 296, 307
Friedrich Wilhelm I, Elector of Brandenburg-Prussia, 344, 346
Frölich, G.L., Chancellor of Neuburg, 131
Frölich von Frölichsburg, Tyrolean jurist, 331, 336, 344, 350, 355, 357
Fuchs von Dornheim, Johann Georg II,

Bishop of Bamberg, 226–9, 316–7, 318, 319, 320, 321, 414
Fugger, Alexius von, 216
Fugger, counts 19, 20, 109
Fugger, Ignaz Anton von, Bishop of Regensburg, 352, 382
Fugger, Jacob von, 409
Fugger lordships, 36, 133
Fugger newsletters, 32, 125–6
Fugger, Markus ('Marx'), 35–6, 131
Fugger, Octavian, 126
Fulda, 95, 224, 295
Fürstenberg, Count, President of Imperial Court Council, 317, 318
Füssen, 129

Gaar, Georg, SJ, 358–9
Gailkircher, Johann, Chancellor of Court Council, 237, 241, 248, 271, 295
Galilei, Galileo, scientist, 415
Ganzer, Benno, OSB, 366, 371, 379
Garmisch, witch trials at, 94, 98, 142, 143, 158, 160, 171, 180, 182, 185, 190, 197–8
Gassner, J.J., exorcist and faith healer, 352–3, 382–5
Gebsattel, Johann Philipp, Bishop of Bamberg, 413–4
Geiler von Keisersberg, preacher, 74
Geisenfeld, 276
'Geistnandl', witch of Vilsbiburg, 349–50
Geneva, 213
Gemmingen, Johann Otto von, Bishop of Augsburg, 313
Georg Friedrich, Margrave of Ansbach, 116, 154–5
Gepeckh, Veit Adam, Bishop of Freising, 414
Germany,
   northwest, 90, 345, 405
southeast
   compared with other regions, 37, 400–5
   decline in C17th, 33
   heterogeneity of, 27
   witch trials (C16th), 29–30, 33, 37, 60–65, 90, 12, 158, 189, 390–3; (after 1660) 331–2, 342–3
southwest
   compared with SE Germany, 400–5
   fragmentation of 17
   Midelfort's findings on, 11, 13
   Riezler took examples from, 25
   witch trials in 64, 122, 165
Gerolfing, 53, 307
Gerolzhofen, 156

Gewold, Christoph, Privy Secretary
  Catholic convert, 395
  intercedes for Munich witch, 273
  investigates leak from Court Council,
    253
  persecutor, 237, 414,
  protégé of A. Hunger, 221, 237
  relations with Wagnereckh, 237, 271
Geyern, Lordship of, 133, 134, 391
Gilg, Aurelio, Court Councillor, 395
Glarus, 353, 385
Gobat, Georg, SJ, 323
God, witches as agents of his punishment,
    104, 106, 107, 108, 109, 110, 111,
    117–19
Goedelmann, Johann Georg, Rostock
  jurist, 212, 251, 252, 256, 258, 313,
    357, 392
Goehausen, Hermann, jurist and
  demonologist, 246
Göggingen, 128, 163
Göglerin, Maria Elisabeth ('Gusterer
  Liesl'), witch of Neumarkt, 349
Golser, Georg, sceptical Bishop of Brixen,
    72
Goubert, P., 333, 408
Graser, Johann Baptist, luminary, 359
Gregor von Valentia, S.J., Ingolstadt
  theologian
  influence of, 218
  supporter of persecution, 24, 223, 266,
    393, 414
  taught at Universityof Dillingen, 124,
    256
  taught Gretser, 21, 237, 238
  taught Tanner, 245
  tutor of Bavarian princes, 136
Greiffenklau, J.H.P., Bishop of Würzburg,
    347
Gretser, Jacob, SJ ideologist of witch
  hunting
  supporter of persecution, 24, 223, 238,
    252, 255, 294
  University of Dilingen and, 256
  University of Ingolstadt and, 247, 250
  relied on by Wagnereckh, 252, 265
Grien, Hans Baldung, painter, 82
Griepen, Paris von, Capuchin, 316
Griesbach, witch trials in, 26, 53, 57, 59,
    98, 122, 137, 138, 152, 159, 182
Grimoald, Agilolfing Duke of Bavaria, 66
Grossaitingen, 129, 167
Gruber, witch family of Haidau, 341
Gsellin, Anna, witch of Augsburg, 161,
    200

Guarinoni, Hippolytus, physician of Hall
  in Tyrol, 409
Gufer, Abraham, councillor of Kempten,
  treasure seeker, 340
Gufer, Tobias, councillor of Kempten,
  treasure seeker, 340
Gumpelzheimer, 43
Gumppenberg, Benigna, bewitched
  noblewoman, 190
Gundelfingen, 79
Gundelfingerin, Dorothea, wife of
  Burgomaster of Nördlingen, 192
Günzburg, 79, 202, 353
Gurjewitsch, A., 67
Gustavus Adolphus, King of Sweden, 310,
    311
'Gusterer Liesl', see Göglerin, Maria
  Elisabeth
  gypsies, 19, 21

Haag, 343
Habsburg lands, 17
Haidau, 340–1
Haidenbucher, Magdalena, abbess and
  diarist, 91
Haiderin, Ursula, witch of Nördlingen,
    166–7, 187, 188
Hall in Tyrol, 72, 143, 409
Halle, University of, 334
Haller, Leonhard, Suffragan Bishop of
  Eichstätt, 46
Hallstadt, 226
'Hammer of Witches', see *Malleus
  (Maleficarum)*
Hammermayer, L., 378
Hanau, County of, 224
Hanover, 13
Hansen, J., 3
Harsee, Court Councillor of Bamberg,
    318
Hartlieb, Johann, physician and occultist,
    71, 77, 390
harvests, failure of, see crises, agrarian
Haslang, Heinrich II, President of Court
  Council
  cites Delrio, 263
  criticises procedure in witch trials, 233–4
  Deductio negativa of, 255
  leads anti-persecution party, 265, 268,
    394
  opposes University of Freiburg opinion,
    257–9
  President of Court Council, 1601–8,
    240–1
  relations with Kaspar Hell, 243

Haslang, Rudolf von, Privy Councillor, 240

Hauber, E.D., luminary, 358

Haunold, Christoph, Ingolstadt jurist, 350

Haussmännin, Walburga, midwife and witch of Dillingen, 123

Heerbrand, Jacob, Tübingen theologian, 198

Heidelberg, 71,

Heidenhein, 154

Heilbrunner, Jacob, Lutheran theologian, 130, 215

Heilbrunner, Philipp, Lutheran theologian, 130

Heilsbronn, 154, 155

Hell, Kaspar, sr, Ingolstadt jurist, 242–3, 251, 252–3, 260, 315, 394, 395

Hell, Kaspar, SJ, 243, 269, 315

Hellgemayr, Johann, musician and diarist, 95

Hellmitzhofen, 156

Helmishofen, 128

Hemau, 216

Hengersberg, 26, 57

Hepstein, Johann, Nuremberg jurist, 82

heresy, combined with sorcery in eleborated concept of witchcraft, 13, 68–9

Herrieden, 153, 228

Herwarth, Hans Friedrich, judge of Schongau, 139, 181

Herwarth, Hans Paul von Hohenfels, 181–2,

Herwarth, Johann Georg, scholar and Chancellor of the Estates
accused of sorcery by Wagnereckh, 242,
efforts to restrain persecution, 270, 393
independent of princely favour, 404,
moderate on witchcraft, 240–1, 316, 394
scientific interests, 415
serves on Donnersberger committee, 277
supports Haslang, 265

Hesse, 10, 13

Heuberg, the, 125, 180

Heydenreuter, R., 295

Hiert, Christoph, executioner of Biberach, 125

Hildebrandt, Conrad, Imperial Court Councillor, 318

Hildesheim, Bishopric of, 18

Himmler, Heinrich, 37

Hindelang, 88, 169

Höchstadt, 76, 126, 130, 131, 175, 196, 201

Hohenegg, Albrecht von, Prince-Abbot of Kempten, 414

Hohenems, Ferdinand Carl Franz von, deposed tyrant, 336

Hohenschwangau, 53, 296

Hohentrüdingen, 154, 155

Holl, Maria, tavernkeeper, witch of Nördlingen, 146

Holland, 13

Holy Cross, Abbey of (Donauwörth), 131, 134

Holzapfler, Augustin, OSB, Prior of Tegernsee, 73

Holzheim, executioner of, 131

Holzmann, Barnabas, painter of Augsburg, 101

Horn, Dr, son of Chancellor of Bamberg, 229

hospitals, 167–8

H-Sonderkommando, researches of, 37–9, 43, 58, 226, 227, 327

Hugo, Nikolaus, Lutheran Superintendent of Coburg, 263

Hundt, Georg, *Hofoberrichter*, 281–2, 295–6

Hundt, Wiguläus, Court Councillor, 219

Hungary, 373

hunger, see crises, agrarian

Hunger, Albrecht, Ingolstadt theologian, 218, 220, 221, 247, 250, 414

Hunger, Wolfgang, jurist and Chancellor of Freising, 81

Ickstatt, Johann Adam von, 381

Illereichen, 62, 92, 112

Immenstadt, 77

Imperial Chamber Court (*Reichskammergericht*), 320

Imperial Court Council (*Reichshofrat*), 317, 318

Imperial Free Cities, see Cities, Imperial Free

inflation
correlation with witch hunts, 91–99, 100, 406–7
of 1589–90, 145
of 1594, 230
of 1607–8, 276
in 1660–1762, 333

Ingolstadt, city
criminal justice system, 137
executions, 136
Faust in, 70
government suspicious of, 202,
hospital inmates accused of witchcraft, 168
patriciate of, 242

466   *Index*

Ingolstadt, city (*cont.*)
population, 21
witch trials in, 53, 232, 296, 300, 303–6, 307,
Ingolstadt, University of
Bavarian princes educated at, 136–7
denies knowledge of 1611 mandate, 289
Enlightenment at, 381
importance for SE Germany, 218, 219
influence of Tanner at, 268–9
opinion of 1590, 139–40, 168, 173–4, 183, 195, 205, 207–8, 269
opinion of 1601, 241, 243, 249–53, 254, 256
opinion sought in 1649, 330
opponents of persecution at, 393, 397
supporters of persecution at, 123, 247
Inquisition, 45
Innsbruck, 362, 400
Institoris, H., papal inquisitor,
witch-hunting activities of, 13, 42, 45, 71–4, 77, 78, 79, 81, 107, 240, 351
'iron century' (1550–1650), 5, 112, 407
Irsee, monastery, 20, 152, 391
Isenburg-Büdingen, County of, 326
Ismaning, County of, 142, 143
Isny, 70
Italy, 12, 25, 68, 69, 358–9

James VI and I, King of Scotland and England, 13, 405
Janssen, J., 89
Jena, Univesity of, 312
Jesuits, 18–19, 24, 394–5
Jews, 19, 112
Joachim, Elector of Brandenburg, 74
Joan of Arc, 70
Job, Book of, 112, 117–8
Jocher, Wilhelm, Privy Councillor, 239, 242, 270, 271, 277, 293, 314, 316, 394
Johann Casimir, Prince of Coburg, 312
Joseph II, Holy Roman Emperor, 385
Junius, Johann, Burgomaster of Bamberg, witch, 314
Jura, 12, 24,
justice, system of
brutalisation of, 102
in Duchy of Bavaria, 30, 31, 47–50, 389
in noble territories, 58–9, 132
in Prince-Bishopric of Augsburg, 46

Kallmünz, 133
Kaltenthal, Lordship of, 146, 391
Kaltern, 190
Kamen, H. 15, 112, 407

Kant, Immanuel, 375
Karl Albrecht, Elector of Bavaria and Holy Roman Emperor, 378
Kätzlerin, Brigitha, witch of Garmisch, 190
Kaufbeuren, Imperial City
archives of, 43
Bavarian military intervention in, 18
economic crisis, 20, 402,
witch trials in, 134–5, 144–6, 210, 215, 392,
Kautz, J.F. von, Imperial Councillor, 366, 372
Kelheim, 57, 136, 137–8, 232, 233, 250, 251
Kellerin, Margarethe, wife of Dillingen councillor, witch, 126
Kemnath, 71
Kempten, Imperial City
absence of witch hunt in 1590, 98
archives of 43
economic crisis, 20 145, 402
sought advice of Augsburg 1665, 330
treasure seeking trials, 340
Kempten, Prince-Abbacy of,
accusations of witchcraft (1549) 79, 87, 113
Court Council of, 30,
population, 21
reluctance to persecute, 403
suppressed in 1806, 387
witch trials in, 330, 336, 352–4, 381, 399
Kepler, Johannes, 177, 241, 415
Kerblin, Else, wife of judge of Schwabsoien, 136
Khepserin, witch of Munich, 279
Khlesl, Melchior, Cardinal of Vienna, 317
Kieckhefer, R., 14
Kipper- und Wipper crisis, 301
Kleinaitingen, 14, 128, 188
Kling, 53, 296
Klöck, Ursula, witch of Obergrainau, 170–1
Klopstock, Friedrich Gottlieb, poet, 361
Knapp, H. 43
Knöring, Heinrich V von, Bishop of Augsburg, 230, 414
Knöringen, Johann Egolf von, Bishop of Augsburg, 124, 409
Knox, John, Scottish reformer, 409
Koberger, printer of Nuremberg, 73
Kohlbrenner, J.S., luminary, 380
Kolb, Wolfgang, witch commissioner, 226, 227, 229, 300, 303, 305, 306, 320
Koller, Jakob, see Zauber–Jackl

Kollmann, J.A., school reformer, 366, 380
Kösching, 53
Kötzting, 26, 53, 57, 296, 307
Kracker, Jakob, Guardian of
 Reichertshofen, 309
Kraiburg, 57, 138
Kramer, K.-S., 43
Krazberg, 53, 161, 276, 307, 344
Kreittmayr, W.X.A., Privy Councillor,
 348, 350, 381

Lagus, Kaspar, Ingolstadt jurist, 115, 203,
 220, 243
Lagus, Maria, mother of Kaspar Hell,
 243
Lamormaini, W., SJ, confessor of
 Emperor Ferdinand II, 318
Landau on Isar, 343
Landsberg on Lech, 18, 26, 53, 55, 57, 78,
 79, 276, 290, 296
Landshut
 archives of, 26, 38
 executions at, last for witchcraft in
 Bavaria, 347, 348, 349, 350, 389
 population, 21
 seat of *Regierung*, 48–9
 sorcerer punished in 1417, 70
 witch trials at, 155, 232, 276, 296, 339
Langenegg, 353
Langenzenn, 127, 154, 158
Larner, Christina, 402
Laufen, 336
Lauingen, 22, 127, 131, 157, 184, 330
Lavater, J.K., Zurich theologian, 382
law, codes of, 68–9; see also *Carolina,
 Codex Maximileaneus, Codex Juris
 Bavarici Criminalis, Lex Baiuvariorum
 Layenspiegel,* 76, 81
Laymann, Paul, SJ, 269, 323, 355, 357, 395
Laynez, Diego, SJ General of Jesuit order,
 108
Leib, Kilian, Prior of Rebdorf, 46
Leibniz, G.W., philosopher, 32, 326
Lempin, Rebecca, witch of Nördlingen,
 146
Lerchenfeld, F.X., Rentmeister of
 Straubing, 362
Lermoos, 143
Le Roy Ladurie, E., 94, 99
Leuker, Esaias, Court Councillor, 292,
 293, 294
Leutenbauer, S., 26,81
Leuter, Hans, carpenter of Soyen, 88
Leutkirch, Imperial City, 94
Lex Baiuvariorum, 66

Liebelt, K. 10
Liège, 18, 142
Limpurg, County of, 133, 156
Lindau, Imperial City, 20, 41, 42, 43, 70,
 77, 330
Lipsius, Justus, scholar, 263
'Little Ice Age', 99
Locher, Georg, Town Clerk of Munich,
 243, 252, 295, 300, 394
'Lochstein, Veremund von' (pseud.), see
 Osterwald, P.
Lodron, Count, treasure seeker, 339
Löher, Hermann, 269
Loos, Cornelius, 212, 247
Lori, Johann Georg, luminary, 369, 381
Lorichius, Jodocus, Freiburg theologian,
 217
Lorraine, 13, 262, 266, 268
Lory, K., 312
Loschert, Oswald, Premonstratensian
 Abbot of Oberzell, 346–7, 366, 372
Löwenstein-Wertheim, County of, 13, 133,
 156, 311, 330
Lucerne, 70
Ludwig the Bavarian, Duke of Bavaria
 and Holy Roman Emperor, 69
Luther, Martin, 307
Lutherans, 76,
Lutz, Wilhelm Friedrich, Superintendent
 of Nördlingen, 198–9

Macfarlane, A., 11, 12, 13, 14, 17, 27, 81,
 84, 90, 402, 406
Mack, Magdalena, witch of Wemding, 244
Maffei, Scipio, Italian enlightened thinker,
 358–9, 360, 363, 364, 373, 377
Magdeburg, 72
magic
 context of belief in witchcraft, 15, 83–9,
 398–9, 402, 411
 'disappearance' after Reformation, 8
 indicator of witchcraft, 172–6, 270, 276,
 278, 299, 399
 magicians not witches in sense of
 elaborated concept of witchcraft, 17
 Mandate of 1612 on, 286
 popular magical culture, 6, 7, 79–80, 81,
 83–9, 149, 176–80
Mainbernheim, 156
Mainburg, Lower Bavaria, 276, 307, 339,
 369
Mainz, 13, 38, 157, 266,
Mair, Michael, innkeeper of Abensberg,
 232, 243,
Mairhofer, Matthias, 220

Mairin of Abensberg, witch, 232, 243, 252
Malefizkommissionen, 227
Malinowski, B., 7
Malleus Maleficarum, 13, 71–4, 76, 77,
   106, 116, 125, 141, 206, 213, 218, 331
Mandate against superstition and
   witchcraft, of 1612,
   background to issue of, 283–91
   reprinted 1665, 331, 333
   reprinted 1677, 339
   Wagnereckh attempts to have it widely
   published, 299
Mandrou, R., 413
Manzin, Leopold, S.J., Ingolstadt
   theologian, 323
Manzius, Caspar, Ingolstadt jurist, 220,
   331, 350
Marburg, University of, 312, 330
Maria Theresia, Holy Roman Empress,
   345, 346, 358, 373, 374
Marian Congregation, 106, 107
Markmiller, F., 343
Marktbreit, 156
Marquartin, Maria, Augsburg soothsayer,
   174
Marquartstein, 53, 297, 307
Marsilius, Italian jurist, 266
Martini, Friedrich, 218, 219, 255
Marwick, M.G. 14
Mary, the Virgin, 106–7, 353
März, Angelus, OSB, 366, 368–71, 379
Massachusetts, 165, 342
Maximilian I, Duke of Bavaria (Elector,
   1623)
   appoints Kolb, 229, 303
   appoints von Nottenstein, 307
   audience with P. zum Ackher, 298
   Contzen and, 314
   cult of Mary, 106–7
   decrees of 163, 324
   favourites of, 221
   fear of bewitchment, 409
   policy on witch trials, 202, 235–6, 237–8,
      248, 254, 257, 267, 279, 285, 293–4,
      304, 405,
   promotes Wagnereckh, 270
   studies at Ingolstadt, 136, 243
   zeal for Counter-Reformation, 230, 414
Maximilian I, Holy Roman Emperor, 74,
   219
Maximilian II Emanuel, Elector of
   Bavaria, 378
Maximilian III Joseph, Elector of Bavaria,
   370–1, 375, 381
Maximilian IV Joseph, Elector, later King

of Bavaria, 386
Mayer, Andreas Ulrich ('F.N.
   Blocksberger') 366, 369–71, 376, 380
Mayr, Beda, O.S.B., 375
Mayr, J. chronicler of Freising, 110
Meggelin, Joachim, S.J,. 192
Mellrichstadt, 156
Memmingen, Imperial City
   accusations of witchcraft (1790), 345
   archives of, 43
   economic crisis, 92, 98
   population, 21
   Protestant clergy of, 199
   reluctance to persecute after 1590, 311
   treasure seekers, 339
   witch trials, 42, 78, 88, 328, 340, 397
Memminger, A., 346
men, role of, 337–8, 398, 401
mental ilness, see 'fools'
mentalities, shifts in, 8, 104–14, 321, 09–12
Mergentheim, 256
Merz, Agnellus, OSA, Munich reactionary,
   363–5, 367–8, 370, 371, 373, 379
Merz, Alois, S.J., Augsburg reactionary,
   384
Merzbacher, F. 10, 22, 320
methodology, of this study, 28, 29–33
Meyfahrt, J.M., Lutheran theologian, 269,
   324, 356, 395
Midelfort, H.C.E.,
   compared with Macfarlane, 27
   confessional interpretation of, 117, 213,
      219, 393, 402, 404–5
   definition of witch hunt, 16
   on F. Spee, 356,
   underestimated burnings at Ellwangen, 225

Miltenberg, 227
Mindelheim, 307, 308
'Mirrors of Justice,' 68
misogyny, see women, role of
Mittenfels, 307
Mittenwald, 142, 143, 185
Model, J.M., Munich jurist, 366
Modestin, Anna, witch of Augsburg, 150
Molitor, Ulrich, jurist of Constance, 217
Mora, Sweden, 342
morality, crimes against, 53, 55
morality, legislation on, 107–8
Montaigne, Michel de, 66, 91, 94, 212
Monter, E.W., 12, 14, 16
Montgelas, Max von, Bavarian Minister,
   386, 387
Moosburg, 56, 343, 344
Moravia, 122

Moser, Baltahsar von Filseck, 197
Mossau, 346
'mountain theory of witchcraft', 9
Muchembled, R., 67, 398, 406
Mühldorf, 343, 348–9, 350, 351
Müller, Anna, witch of Bamberg, 192
Mumprecht, Christoph, jurist of
    Pfalz-Neuburg, 130, 214
Munich, city
    archives of, 57
    government suspects city magistrates,
        202, 282
    legal position of, 49
    patriciate of, 103, 242
    population, 21
    price series for, 95, 333
    witch trials, 59, 102, 147, 182, 190, 210,
        232, 297, 300, 307, 344, 347
Munich, *Rentamt* of, 10, 48–53
Münster, 18
Muratori, Lodovico, Italian luminary, 358,
    363
Murnau, 53, 297

Napoleon Bonaparte, 387
Nennslingen, 134
Nesselwang, 128
Netherlands, 110
Neuburg on Danube, 19, 397
Neudecker, Georg, Burgomaster of
    Bamberg, 221
Neudecker, Johannes, doctoral candidate
    in Ingolstadt, 221
Neuessing, 137
Neumarkt, 348–50
Neuötting, 349, 361
Neustadt on Danube, 137, 338,339
Neustadt on Saale, 359
Nibelungenlied, 163
Nickhlin, Catharina, witch of Ingolstadt,
    305–6, 308
Nicolai, Friedrich, luminary, 361
Nider, Johannes, OP, preacher, 70–71, 77,
    390
Nidermayr, Lorenz, judge and sorcerer,
    294
nobles,
Niederaltaich, 363, 372
    judicial powers of, 58
    political power broken in Bavaria, 102–3
Nordendorf, 133
Nördlingen, Imperial City
    economy, 402
    extradition to Oettingen, 33
    Lutz as superintendent of, 198–9

soothsayer of, 85–6
sorcerey trial, 77, 78, 79
witch trials, 20, 22, 98, 145–7, 155, 162,
    163, 166–7, 175, 180, 182, 196–7, 215,
    230, 392
Nottenstein, Hans Martin Staphylo,
    witchcraft commissioner, 307
nunneries, possession of, 167
Nuremberg, Imperial Free City
    archives, 41
    attitude to witchcraft, 117, 119, 145,
        147–8, 215
    debates on witchcraft, 82
    decline of persecution in 216, 311–12
    economy, 144, 327–8, 345
    executes Stigler, 172, 392
    influence on Franconian persecutions,
        314–16
    Protestant clergy of, 199
    relations with Ansbach, 155, 197, 207
    sorcerers, 41, 68

Oberaltaich, 362
Oberdorf, Markt-Oberdorf, in persecution
    of 1590s, 122, 124, 126, 127, 128–9,
    134, 152, 209, 210
Obergrainau, 170
Oberhausen, 163
Obermarchtal, 124
Oberndorf, 36,
Oberottmarshausen, 188
Oberstdorf, witch trials at, 86, 124, 125,
    127, 177–81, 182, 186, 190
Oberzell, 362
Ochsenhausen, Abbey, 127
Odenwald, 157
Oettingen, Count Friedrich, 172, 190, 197
Oettingen, Count Wilhelm, 131
Oettingen, county of,
    executioner of, 184–5
    population, 21
    religious division, 20
    witch trials, 132–3, 146, 230,
Oettingen-Oettingen, county of, 20, 21,
    132, 215, 312
Oettingen im Ries, county of, 19
Oettingen-Wallerstein, County of, 13,20,
    127, 132, 155, 190, 211, 227, 301, 311
Ortenburg, Joachim von, Protestant
    'frondeur', 242
Osnabrück, Bishopric of, 18
Ossuna, Francesco de, demonologist, 32
Osterwald, Peter von, luminary, 369, 374,
    376–80, 382, 399
Osterzell, Lordship of, 128, 133, 134, 210

Ottobeuren, monastery, 20, 152

Paderborn, 13, 18
Padua, University of, 261, 394
Palatinate, 118
Pappenheim, von, 133, 147, 391
Pappenheim, Cäcilie von, *Erbmarschällin*, 155, 191, 193
Pappenheimer, witch family, 232
Paracelsians, 21
Paris, 344
Partenkirchen, 142, 143, 185
Passau, 17, 60, 73, 82, 296, 387
pauperisation, 100, 101
Paur, Marie, witch of Mühldorf, 232, 251, 348–9
Paur, Simon, Burgomaster of Kellheim, 232
Peissenberg, the, 136, 175
Peiting, 175
penance, for sorcery, 70
people and authorities, 181–3
Peringer, Johann, Privy Councillor, 239, 318
Perneder, Andreas, Munich jurist, 81, 269, 391
persecution,
  Bavaria said to be heartland of, 23–5
  chronology and distribution of, 4–5
  definition of, 16
  fantasy to believe in wide or long–lasting persecution, 57
  few apologists for before Reformation, 79, 80
  no concerted plan for in 1590, 115
  pent-up demand for, 142–3, 157–8
  routine of, 129
  unsatisfactory results of, 139
  see also witch hunts, trials for witchcraft

persecution party, in Bavarian Court Council, 230–3, 235–9
Peuter, Chancellor of Prince-Bishopric of Augsburg 126
Pezzl, J., luminary, 381
Pfaffenhofen, 55, 276, 292, 297, 307, 339
Pfalz-Neuburg, Principality of
  accusations of witchcraft in, 79
  belief in magic, 119
  Catholic clergy of, 312–13
  conflict between cities and government, 202
  executioners, 184, 185
  influence of Dillingen, 126
  Protestant authorities willing to

persecute, 214, 215, 216, 217, 396
  recatholicised in 1614, 64
  witch trials, 129–31, 138, 391
Pfeffel, C.F,. 369, 374, 379, 380
Philipp-Ludwig, Count Palatine of Neuburg, 116, 129–30
Pius VI, Pope, 385
Planch, A. ,OSB, 371
Plantsch, Martin, Tübingen theologian, 74
Pless, 78
poaching, 15, 55
poisoning, 189, 345
Poissl von Atzenzell, Kaspar, Guardian of Werdenfels, 182, 190
politici, 314
Polling, 369
Pölnitz, G. von, 105
Pomerania, 13
Popp, Anton von, Imperial Court Councillor, 316, 319
population, 21, 96–97, 100, 103, 112, 144
possession, demonic, 109, 166–7
Prague, 241
Premb, parish priest, 366, 372
Pretzelerin, Catharina, witch of Augsburg, 150
Preysing, Johann Christoph, Court Councillor, 238
Price Revolution, see inflation
prices, see inflation
property, crimes against, 53, 55, 57
Protestantism, and witch hunting, 12, 213–16, 327, 392–3, 402–3
Prussia, 12, 344, 359
public opinion, 197–8
Pyrenees, 9

Rain on Lech, 138, 307, 310, 340
Randeckh, Lordship of, 133, 137, 216, 391
Rauhenlechsberg, 138
Ravensburg, 72, 79, 97
Rebdorf, 228
Rechberg, county of, 20, 391
Rechberg, Wolf Konrad von, Supreme Chancellor,
  independent of princely favour, 404,
  investigated corruption charge against Gailkircher, 241,
  mandate of 1612, 288
  opposed Wagnereckh, 242, 393
  Sattler case, 293–4
Regen, 26, 53, 57, 138, 297, 343
Regensburg, Colloquy of, 259
Regensburg, Diet of, 1630, 317–20
Regensburg, diocese, 45, 81

Regensburg, Imperial Free City,
  accusations of witchraft, 145
  pragmatic policy in 1590, 147, 150–1,
    311, 391
  sorcerers, 40, 41, 68
  witch trials, 77, 79
Regensburg, Prince-Bishopric of
  absence of witch hunting in 1590, 152;
    after 1630, 326
  archives of, 38
  Gassner affair and, 383, 385
  suppressed 1806, 387
  surrounded by Bavaria, 19
  regional variations, 9–13, 400–405
Rehlinger, Augsburg patrician, 172
Reichard, Johannes, parish priest and
  witch of Eichstätt, 228, 313
Reichenhall, 26, 57, 276, 292, 336
Reichertshofen, 98, 303, 307, 311, 340, 397
Reinboldt, sorcerer, 290
Reisacher, Wilhelm, Court Councillor, 296
Rémy, Nicolas, demonologist, 262, 266,
    267
Renata of Lorraine, Duchess of Bavaria,
    105
Rentämter, 47–51
Resenberger, Manz, witchfinder of
  Garmisch, 170–1
Rettenberg, witch trials at 88, 124, 126,
    129, 135, 158, 177, 178, 179, 180, 182,
    186
Reutlingen, 342
Revelation, Book of, 113, 117, 365, 366,
    372, 412
Rhineland, 13, 18
Richel, Bartholomaeus, Chancellor of
  Eichstätt, 228, 239, 244, 316
Richel, Maria, née Bonschab, witch of
  Eichstätt, 228, 244
Riedenburg, 53, 232, 233, 272, 273–4
Riedmüller, soothsayer of Riedenburg, 273
Rieger, Court Councillor, 296
Riezler, S., historian, 10, 23, 24–25, 27, 64,
    81, 101, 137–8
Röder, clothshearer and chronicler of
  Würzburg, 96
Roggenburg, monastery, 20, 152
Rohr, 73
Rome, 316
Rosenheim, 26, 57, 79, 276, 297, 307, 308
Ross, Balthasar, judge of Fulda, 295
Roth, Honorius zu Schreckenstein,
  Prince-Abbot of Kempten, 352
Rothenburg ob der Tauber, 147, 216, 311,
    328

Rothenfels, County of, 19, 77
Rottenbuch, Provost of, 143
Rottenburg, Lower Bavaria, 307
Rovereto, 359
Rudolf II, Holy Roman Emperor, 111,
    159, 409
Rumpfinger, judge of Freising, 357

Saalfeld, D., 100
Sachs, Hans, Meistersinger of Nuremberg,
    82–3
Sachsen-Coburg, Principality of, 38
Sachsenspiegel, 68
Salem, Mass., 342
Salzburg, city, 18, 81, 349
Salzburg, Prince-Bishopric, 17, 333, 336,
    342–3, 345, 362
Salzburg, University of, 336
Satan, see Devil, the
Sattler, Gottfried, executed judge of
  Wemding, 292–5
Saulgau, 78
Saxony, 66, 109, 118, 404
scapegoating, 412
Schaden, F.M., Oettingen councillor
Schalhammer, Beda., OSB, 372
Schaumburg, Martin von, Bishop of
  Eichstätt, 153, 414
Scheiner, Christoph, SJ, 415
Scheurl, Christoph, Nuremberg jurist,
    82
Scheyern, Abbey of, 362, 368–8, 399
Schiltenbeger, J.P., Ingolstadt jurist, 220
Schlampin, Els, witch of Garmisch, 188
Schlehdorf, Abbot of, 143
Schleiss von Löwenfeld, B.J., Rosicrucian,
    384 Schlettstadt, see Sélestat
Schmeller, J.A., 138
Schmid, C. Burgomaster of Dillingen,
    313
Schmid, U., 303, 343
Schneeberg-Treffelstein, 152
Schnepf, Erhard, Tübingen theologian,
    198
Schober, Vitus, 220
Schobinger, Ottheinrich, Court Councillor,
    280, 292
Schönauerin, Maria, witch of Augsburg,
    172
Schönborn, Johann Philipp von, Bishop of
  Würzburg, 326, 356
Schongau
  accusations of witchcraft, 98, 122
  archives of 56,57
  executioner of, 157

Schongau (*cont.*)
   witch trials (1590), 119, 135–6, 139, 158,
      160, 167, 169, 174, 175, 180, 182, 191,
      195
Schorer, Christoph, chronicler of
   Memmingen, 110
Schormann, G., 14, 17, 25, 37, 90, 121,
   404
Schrenck, Octavian, jurist and Chancellor
   of Regensburg, 81
Schrobenhausen, 307
Schubart, C.F.D., luminary, 385
Schusterin, Brigitha, witch of
   Donauwörth, 280
Schusterin, Maria, witch of
   Schwabmünchen, 341
Schwabach, 154–5
Schwabeck, 171
Schwaben, Marktschwaben, 26, 57, 78,
   274–5
Schwabenspiegel, 68, 69, 80
Schwäbisch Hall, 215
Schwabmünchen,
   executioner of, 124, 126, 127, 129, 143
   prison , 188
   witch trials (1590), 135, 165, 167, 180,
      189, 209; (1721–34), 341; (1731), 356
Schwabsoien, 191
Schwägelin, Maria Anna, witch of
   Kempten, 353–4
Schwalbach, Walbrecht von, 134, 169–70
Schwarzkonz, Dr, witch commissioner,
   227, 318
Schweinfurt, 39, 327
Schwendi, Alexander von, *Landamman*,
   178
Scot, Reginald, English nobleman, 406
Scotland, 11, 12, 109, 213, 405–6, 409
Seckendorff, Caspar von, Bishop of
   Eichstätt, 153–4
Secta Gazariorum, 68, 71
Secta Vaudensium, 68
Seefeld in Tyrol, 143
Seinsheim, County of 133, 156
Seld, Thomas, Chancellor of Augsburg,
   125
Sélestat, 77, 78
Semler, J.S., luminary, 384
Senckenberg, Imperial Court Councillor,
   361
Seyfert, J. preacher of Ulm, 356
Simon, Jordan, OSA, 14, 359, 360, 366,
   373–4, 399
Simon Magus, 365
Singer, Maria Renata, nun and witch of

Würzburg, 346, 357
slander, as witch, 59
Soldan, G.W., 14
Sonnenfels, A. von, Vienna hebraist, 367,
   373
Sonthofen, see Rettenberg-Sonthofen
soothsayers, corroborate charges of
   witchcraft, 85–6, 142, 170–2, 183,
   207
sorcery,
   associated with heresy, 41, 67–70
   legislation against, 65–6, 72, 80–1; see
      also *Carolina*
   Lutherans stigmatise Catholic practices
      as, 76
   penalties for, abolished 1818, 387
   popular magical culture and, 83–9,
      173
   relationship with witchcraft, 3, 15–16,
      76, 117–9, 168, 274
   trials for, 45, 53, 66, 69–70, 79, 115, 118,
      162
Spain, 358
Spalt, 92, 153
Spee, Friedrich, SJ
   admitted existence of witches, 218
   attacked motives of judges in witch
      trials, 389
   follower of Tanner, 245, 269, 295, 395
   influence in C17th and C18th, 323–4,
      325, 326, 350, 354–7
spells, 'turning' of, 87–9
Spener, Philipp Jacob, pietist, 32
Speyer, 147, 316
Spielmann, H.K., 10
Spitzel, Gottlieb, theologian 334
Sprenger, J., Inquisitor, 13, 42, 45, 71–4,
   77, 78, 79, 81, 107, 240, 391
Stachelin, Margaretha, witch of
   Nördlingen, 197
Stadtamhof, 53, 297, 347
Stadtmann, Chancellor of Ansbach, 155
Starnberg, 53, 57, 152, 297
Statler, Benedikt, S.J., Ingolstadt
   theologian, 385
Stauderin, Anna, witch of Augsburg, 149
Stauffenberg, bewitched Bishop's
   Governor, 126
Stauffenberg, Wilhelm Schenck von, Court
   Councillor in Dillingen, 129
Steigenberger, Gerhoh, 369
Stein, Erhard vom, Prince-Abbot of
   Kempten, 414 Steingaden, Abbot of,
   171
Stengel, Georg, SJ, 223, 322

Sterzinger, Ferdinand, O.Theat., luminary,
  address to Bavarian Academy, 360–3,
  condemns monastic education, 376
  death, 386,
  followers of, in Bavaria, 374–5, 377,
    379–80, 399
  polemic with Merz, 364–73
  role in Gassner affair, 382, 384, 385
Sterzinger, Josef, O.Theat., 14, 371
Steten, von, Augsburg patrician, 172
Stevartius, Petrus, SJ, 220, 250
Stigler, Friedrich, executed witchfinder,
  148, 172
Stigma diaboli, 161, 169, 185, 204, 205, 328
Stöckhlin, Konrad, horse herdsman and
  member of the night band, 124–5,
  171, 177–80, 186
Stone, L. 89, 170
Strasbourg, diocese of, 72
Straubing,
  archives of, 26, 53, 58, 137, 138
  seat of *Regierung*, 18, 48–9, 288
  Sterzinger and, 362
  witch trials, 307, 343, 347, 348–9, 351
Strauss, Barbara, wife of Chancellor of
  Ellingen, witch, 134
Strewbin, Ursula, witch of Pless, 88
Stricker, the, C13th S. German poet, 65,
  66
Stuttgart, 92,
Styria, 73, 357, 343
Sulzbach, 356
superstition, 15–16, 325, 381–7
Swabia,
  Catholic preponderance, 20
  economy, 19, 100, 145, 402,
  fragmentation, 27, 32
  influence of Protestant authorities in,
    207
  literature on witch trials, 22
  population, 21
  witch hunt of 1590, 119, 122, 157
Sweden, 165
'Swedish solution', 310–11, 320
Switzerland, 10, 12, 25, 70

Tannberg, Gundaker von, Court
  Councillor, 242, 277, 280
Tanner, Adam SJ
  admits reality of witches' flight, 415
  cites Sattler case, 295
  first Catholic theologian to criticise
    persecution, 195, 245–6, 268–9, 395
  influence of, 322–3, 324, 325, 328,
    354–7, 363

recommends procedure for witch trials,
  320
Theologia scholastica, title page of, 396
  plate 17
Tanner, Hans Christoph, 244, 296, 297
Tapfheim, 131
Tartarotti, Hieronymus, Abbot of
  Rovereto, 358–9, 360, 363, 374
Tegernsee, 73
Teisbach, 343
Teisendorf, 336
Tengler, Christoph, Ingolstadt theologian,
  74, 76
Tengler, Ulrich, Höchstadt jurist, 75, plate
  3, 76, 79, 391
Territorial Ordinance of 1766, 373, 374
Tettnang, county of, 124, 179
Theresa of Avila, St, 17
Thirty Years War, 5, 20, 21
Thomas Aquinas, St 67, 360, 364, 377
Thomas, K., 7, 12, 67, 89, 121
Thomasius, Christian, 14 218, 331, 334,
  354, 356, 357, 364
threats, 101, 168–70
Tilly, Count, Governor of Ingolstadt,
  305
Tilly, Tserclaes, military commander, 310
Tittmöning, 336
Tölz, Bad Tölz, 135, 297
Töpsl, Franz, Provost of Polling, 369
torture,
  abolished 1808, 387
  Catholic universities' opinion of, 208,
    249, 261
  confessions obtained under, 397
  criteria for infliction of, 184, 254–5, 266,
    267, 299
  Court Council and, 234
  mandate of 1612 and, 285
  misgivings about, 204–6
  new tortures devised, 228
  offset against sentence, 297
  public opposition to, 200–1
  purpose of, 297
  role in witch trials, 14, 15, 57, 78, 85,
    148–9, 183–6, 194–5, 277, 278, 279,
    397
Tradel, Georg, Augsburg jurist, 146, 150
Tramin, 190
Transylvania, 12, 213, 373
Traunstein, 26, 57, 79, 152, 297, 307, 336
treasure seeking, 338–40
Treichlinger, Court Councillor of
  Kempten, 354
Trevor-Roper, H.R., 9, 23–4, 27

trials for witchcraft
criticism of, 233–5
definition of, 15–16
difficulties of, 151–2
distribution of, 4, 5, 307–10, 388–92; in
Duchy of Bavaria 47–60; in Imperial
Cities, 39–44; in Prince-Bishopric of
Augsburg 45–7; in SE Germany, 60–5
exceptional nature of, 35, 344, 412–13,
historical research on, in Bavaria,
23–7; in Franconia, 21–3
popular pressure for, 182–3
procedure, 389–90
resistance to, 194–202
sources for, 29–32, 35, 36, 37–9, 41,
55–6
transformation into witch hunts, 12
for trials in particular places/ of
particular persons, see entries for
those places/ persons; see also
persecution, witch hunts.
Trier, 13, 24, 122, 165, 232, 249, 260,
266–7
Trithemius, Johannes, OSB, Abbot,
humanist and demonologist, 74, 79,
219, 411
Trostberg, 336
Tübingen, University of 198, 207, 214,
312, 330, 334, 405
Turner, V., 14
Tyrol, 72, 336, 337, 343, 354, 400

Überlingen, 94
Ulm
accusations of witchcraft, 145
economy, 144
intercedes with Nördlingen, 196
legal opinion sought, 330
Protestant clergy of, 199
reluctance to persecute witches, 147, 311
Unterföhring, 144
Unterthingau, 77, 152
Upper Palatinate
abstained from persecution in 1590, 152,
216, 403
annexed to Bavaria 1623, 48
Calvinist ruling house, 20
executioner of Eichstätt active in, 185
H-Sonderkommando indexes on, 37
recatholicised after 1623, 65
Urban VIII, Pope, 325
Ursberg, 20, 152

Vaduz, County of, 334–6
Vagh, Cosmas, Court Councillor

abject apology of, 280
Catholic convert, 395
prepared mandate of 1612, 242, 281, 288
protégé of Wagnereckh, 237, 271–2
rebuked by Maximilian I, 279
role in trial of K. Hell, 252–3, 260; in
Munich witch trial, 273
'sideways promotion' of, 295
vagrants, see beggars and vagrants
Valais, Canton, 70
Venice, Inquisition of, 177
Viechtach, 307, 361
Vienna, 316
Vilsbiburg, 349
Vilshofen, 343
violence, crimes of, 53, 55
Vischer, Veit, executioner of
Schwabmünchen, 127, 143
Vitelleschi, Mutius, SJ, General of Jesuit
order, 315
Vohburg, 55, 137, 196, 232, 233, 276, 307,
338
Vollmair, Caspar, executioner of
Nördlingen, 147, 184
Vollmair, Christoph, executioner of
Biberach, 126–7, 143, 162–3,
Vollmair, Hans, executioner of Biberach,
94, 124, 126–7, 128, 134, 136, 157,
165, 184, 185, 186, 201
Vorarlberg, 125, 179

wages, and prices, 100
Wagner, H., 343
Wagnereckh, Heinrich, Chancellor of
University of Dillingen, 221
Wagnereckh, Johann Sigismund,
Chancellor of Court Council
attacks Haslang, 259
attacks Ingolstadt jurists, 252–3
cites Binsfeld, 260
Codex Maximileaneus and, 295
confers with P. zum Ackher, 298–9
counter-opinion of 1601, 251
death, 1617, 296
Deductio affirmativa, 257
defends need for persecution, 247–9
dominates Court Council, 239–42,
270–9, 281–3
identifies 'objects of sorcery', 298
leads Munich trial of 1600, 232
mandate of 1612 and, 283, 287
one of few native Bavarian champions
of persecution, 395
opponents in Court Council, 265
responds to Delrio's opinion, 263

rise to power, 236–9
role in Sattler case, 293–4
seeks opinion of Catholic territories, 266
Wagnerin, Sabina, sorceress of Augsburg, 86
Wahrlieb, G., 2
Waizenegger, Ferdinand, Ingolstadt jurist, 220
Walch, Jacob, ox-herdsman, 177, 179
Waldburg, county, 13
Waldburg, Otto Truchsess von, 123
Waldburg–Wolfegg, County of, 125
Waldsee, 94
Wallerstein, 306, 389
Wangen, 94
Wann, Paul, preacher in Passau cathedral, 73–4
Wanner, Matthäus, Chancellor of Prince-Bishopric of Augsburg, 313
Wars of Religion, 5
Wartenberg, F.W., Bishop of Regensburg,
Wasserburg, Lake Constance, 36, 297, 328, 330, 397
Wasserburg on Inn, 53, 343
weather magic, 84, 159, 160, 168–9, 369
Weber, Josef, Dillingen professor, 385
Wegmann, Hektor, Ingolstadt theologian, 217
Wegmann, Marcus, deacon of Höchstadt, 130
Wehringen, 128, 188
Weihenstephan, 66
Weilheim, 55, 93–4, 135, 297, 307
Weiss, Johann, parish priest and sorcerer, 84
Weissenburg, Imperial City, 39, 42, 82, 125, 134, 145, 147, 158
Weissenhorn, 79
Welf principalities, 404
Wemding
  Kolb as persecutor at, 229
  Sattler case at, 242, 291–5, 398
  witch trials (1609–11), 280–2, 294, 397; (1614–16) 297; (1629), 303–8
Wensin, Lorenz von, Master of the Hunt, 280–1, 296
Werdenfels, county of
  hail shower blamed on witches, 94
  witch trials in 1590, 142–4, 170, 171, 174, 180, 182, 185, 187, 188, 197, 201, 203–4
Werdenstein, Veit von, 87
Wertingen, 131
Wesenbeck, Petrus, Coburg jurist, 110, 312
Westenrieder, Lorenz von, 379, 386

Westerstetten, Johnan Christoph von, Bishop of Eichstätt, 154, 221, 225, 226, 242, 304, 321, 414
Westphalia, 13
Wettenhausen, 20, 152
Weyer, Johann,
  blamed the Devil for deluding witches, 166
  confessions a problem for, 164
  criticism of witch hunts, 212–14
  followed by Goedelmann, 392
  followers among Catholics, 217
  in Bavarian debate, 255
  insisted on need to execute allies of the Devil, 357
  rejected by Lutherans, 109–10
  Rémy attempts to refute, 262
Widmann, Matthias, 71, 77
Wiesensteig, Lordship of, 92,
Wilhelm V 'the Pious', Duke of Bavaria,
  abdication of, 241
  'bewitched', 298
  'conversion' experience, 105
  cult of Mary 106
  death 1626, 320
  decree of 113,
  demands opinion from Court Council, 39
  portrait of, 105
  supporter of persecution, 224
  zealous Counter-Reformer, 414
Windsbach, 155
Windsheim, Imperial City, 39, 42, 94, 156
Winter, Anton, Coburg jurist, 312, 319, 320, 323
witch-hunts,
  analogy with epidemics, 121
  chronology and distribution, 4, 36, 61–4,

  correlation with agrarian crises, 91–9,
  difficulties of quantification, 36
  exceptional events, 83
  social expansion of, 188–93, 228
  see also persecution, trials for witchcraft; and for witch hunts in particular places see entries for those places.
witch towers, 49
witchcraft,
  concept of, hardens into a virtual Catholic dogma, 217–18; reception in SE Germany, 35, 65–83, 390–1
  debate on, key to understanding trials in Bavaria, 28
  definition of, 13–15,
  fear of, 115–121

witchcraft (*cont.*)
  historical research on, 1–17, 390
  increasing belief in, later C16th, 158–68
  legislation on, 65, 66, 80–81, 115, 118
  Protestants begin to question, 212–16
  term falls from grace in C18th, 345,
    360–1
'Witchcraft War', Bavarian, 362–81
witches, belief in existence of, 17, 139, 211,
  322, 345
witches' flight, 14, 15, 65, 67 203, 218, 328,
  346
witches' mark see *stigma diaboli*
witches' sabbath, 14, 15, 81, 136, 160, 164,
  218, 260, 328, 346
witches' shot (lumbago), 172
witchfinders, 148, 172
Wittelsbachs, 20, 223–4
Wittenberg, 213
Wittislingen, 126
Wittmann, P., 10
Witweiler, G., S.J., 223
Wolf, Burgomaster of Ingolstadt, 307
Wolff, Christian, enlightened philosopher,
  367
Wolfgang Wilhelm, Count Palatine of
  Neuburg, 409
Wolfratshausen, 26, 53, 57, 297
Wolkenstein, P.A. von, Privy Councillor,
  239, 318
Wolter, J.A. von, court physician, 384
women, role of, 160–2
Wulz, G., 43
Württemberg, Duchy of, 92, 129–130, 213,
  392, 405

Wurzach, 94
Würzburg, Imperial Free City
  bewitched nunnery in (1749), 346–7
  enlightenment in, 345
  witch trials in 1590, 156; in 1610–12, 95
  sorcerer executed 45,68
Würzburg, Prince-Bishopric,
  contacts with Bavaria, 24
  first executions for witchcraft, 156
  great persecutions in C17th, 38, 97,
    224–9, 320–1, 322, 326
  suppressed 1806, 387
  Swedish occupation of, 310–11
Würzburg, University of, 218, 326

Zapf, G.W., notary of Augsburg, 384
Zauber-Jackl (Koller, Jakob), 336–7,
  342–3, 344, 371, 375
Zedler, J.J., encyclopaedist, 322, 336, 344
Zeil, 226
Zerritschin, Veronica, witch of Landshut,
  350–1
Zeschlin, Johann, Chancellor of
  Pfalz-Neuburg, 304, 342
Ziegler, Hieronymus, Ingolstadt jurist,
  219
Zindecker, Leonhard, 220
Zöthin, Maria, witch of Neumarkt, 349
Zugspitze, the, 170
Zusmarshausen, 129, 149, 150, 162–3,
  209
Zwaifelin, Anna, witch of Nördlingen,
  197
Zwiesel, 53
Zwingli, Ulrich, 307

Past and Present Publications

General Editor: JOANNA INNES, *Somerville College, Oxford*

Family and Inheritance: Rural Society in Western Europe 1200–1800, edited by Jack Goody, Joan Thirsk and E. P. Thompson*

French Society and the Revolution, edited by Douglas Johnson

Peasants, Knights and Heretics: Studies in Medieval English Social History, edited by R. H. Hilton*

Town in Societies: Essays in Economic History and Historical Sociology, edited by Philip Abrams and E. A. Wrigley*

Desolation of a City: Coventry and the Urban Crisis of the Late Middle Ages, Charles Phythian-Adams

Puritanism and Theatre: Thomas Middleton and Opposition Drama under the Early Stuarts, Margot Heinemann*

Lords and Peasants in a Changing Society: The Estates of the Bishopric of Worcester 680–1450, Christopher Dyer

Life, Marriage and Death in a Medieval Parish: Economy, Society and Demography in Halesowen 1270–1400, Ziv Razi

Biology, Medicine and Society 1740–1940, edited by Charles Webster

The Invention of Tradition, edited by Eric Hobsbawm and Terence Ranger*

Industrialization before Industrialization: Rural Industry and the Genesis of Capitalism, Peter Kriedte, Hans Medick and Jürgen schlumbohm*

The Republic in the Village: The People of the Var from the French Revolution to the Second Republic, Maurice Agulhon†

Social Relations and Ideas: Essays in Honour of R. H. Hilton, edited by T. H. Aston, P. R. Coss, Christopher Dyer and Joan Thirsk

A Medieval Society: The West Midlands at the End of the Thirteenth Century, R. H. Hilton

Winstanley: 'The Law of Freedom' and Other Writings, edited by Christopher Hill

Crime in Seventeenth-Century England: A County Study, J. A. Sharpe†

The Crisis of Feudalism: Economy and Society in Eastern Normandy c. 1300–1500, Guy Bois†

The Development of the Family and Marriage in Europe, Jack Goody*

Disputes and Settlements: Law and Human Relations in the West, edited by John Bossy

Rebellion, Popular Protest and the Social Order in Early Modern England, edited by Paul Slack

Studies on Byzantine Literature of the Eleventh and Twelfth Centuries, Alexander Kazhdan in collaboration with Simon Franklin†

The English Rising of 1381, edited by R. H. Hilton and T. H. Aston*

Praise and Paradox: Merchants and Craftsmen in Elizabethan Popular Literature, Laura Caroline Stevenson

The Brenner Debate: Agrarian Class Structure and Economic Development in Pre-Industrial Europe, edited by T. H. Aston and C. H. E. Philpin*

Eternal Victory: Triumphant Rulership in Late Antiquity, Byzantium, and the Early Medieval West, Michael McCormick†*

East-Central Europe in Transition: From the Fourteenth to the Seventeenth Century, edited by Antoni Mączak, Henryk Samsonowicz and Peter Burke*

Small Books and Pleasant Histories: Popular Fiction and its Readership in Seventeenth-Century England, Margaret Spufford*

Society, Politics and Culture: Studies in Early Modern England, Mervyn James*

Horses, Oxen and Technological Innovation: The use of Draught Animals in English Farming 1066–1500, John Langdon

Nationalism and Popular Protest in Ireland, edited by C. H. E. Philpin

Rituals of Royalty: Power and Ceremonial in Traditional Societies, edited by David Cannadine and Simon Price*

The Margins of Society in Late Medieval Paris, Bronislaw Geremek†

Landlords, Peasants and Politics in Medieval England, edited by T. H. Aston

Geography, Technology, and War: Studies in the Maritime History of the Mediterranean, 649–1571, John H. Pryor*

Church Courts, Sex and Marriage in England, 1570–1640, Martin Ingram*

Searches for an Imaginary Kingdom: The Legend of the Kingdom of Prester John, L. N. Gumilev

Crowds and History: Mass Phenomena in English Towns, 1780–1835, Mark Harrison

Concepts of Cleanliness: Changing Attitudes in France since the Middle Ages, Georges Vigarello†

The First Modern Society: Essays in English History in Honour of Lawrence Stone, edited by A. L. Beier, David Cannadine and James M. Rosenheim

The Europe of the Devout: The Catholic Reformation and the Formation of a New Society, Louis Châtellier†

English Rural Society, 1500–1800: Essays in Honour of Joan Thrisk, edited by John Chartres and David Hey

From Slavery to Feudalism in South-Western Europe, Pierre Bonnassie†

Lordship, Knighthood and Locality: a Study in English Society c. 1180–c. 1280, P. R. Coss

English and French Towns in Feudal Society: A Comparative Study, R. H. Hilton*

An island for Itself: Economic Development and Social Change in Late Medieval Sicily, Stephan R. Epstein

Epidemics and Ideas: Essays on the Historical Perception of Pestilence, edited by Terence Ranger and Paul Slack*

The Political Economy of Shopkeeping in Milan, 1886–1922, Jonathan Morris

After Chartism: Class and Nation in English Radical Politics, 1848–1874, Margot C. Finn

Commoners: Common Right, Enclosure and Social Change in England, 1700–1820, J. M. Neeson*

Land and Popular Politics in Ireland: County Mayo from the Plantation to the

Land War, Donald E. Jordan Jr.*

The Castilian Crisis of the Seventeenth Century: New Perspectives on the Economic and Social History of Seventeenth Century Spain, I. A. A. Thompson and Bartolomé Yun Casalilla

The Culture of Clothing: Dress and Fashion in the Ancien Régime, Daniel Roche*

The Sense of the People: Politics, Culture and Imperialism in England, 1715–1785, Kathleen Wilson

Witchcraft in Early Modern Europe: Studies in Culture and Belief, edited by Jonathan Barry, Marianne Hester and Gareth Roberts

God Speed the Plough: The Representation of Agrarian England, 1500–1660, Andrew McRae

The Wild and the Sown: Botany and Agriculture in Western Europe, 1350–1850, Mauro Ambrosoli

Witchcraft Persecutions in Bavaria: Popular Magic, Religious Zealotry and Reason of State in Early Modern Europe, Wolfgang Behringer

* Also published in paperback
† Co-published with the Maison des Sciences de l'Homme, Paris